VIETNAM

VIETNAM

REAPING THE WHIRLWIND

VYNETTE HOLLIDAY

First Edition: 14 June 2026
ISBN 978-0-646-73785-0

A catalogue record for this book is available from the National Library of Australia

Permissions

All quoted material has been attributed to sources or is in the Public Domain.

Publishing
Vynette Holliday
vynetteholliday@gmail.com

Cover Art and Design
Naomi McKenzie

for

Edward Patrick (Ted) Wixted
1927-2001

for

Deborah
1963-2003

and for

Geoff Hornibrook and James McKenzie who supported me from the beginning, made valuable content suggestions, and encouraged me to persevere through the hard times.

Table of Contents

Part I: The Petrov Affair

Part II: Staging

Part III: The Dogs of War

Part IV: The Road of No Return

Part V: In the Shadow of the Cross

Part VI: Appendices

Introduction

Of all the defining moments in 20th-Century American history, none left deeper wounds than Vietnam. It shattered the foreign policy consensus that had guided the United States since World War II, fractured a nation's identity, and spread dissension into every corner of American political and cultural life.

But what truly drove the United States and its allies into that catastrophic conflict in Vietnam?

Written from a uniquely Australian perspective, this work will attempt to answer that question by furnishing evidence supporting the following claims:

> That there were two principal operating forces which prevailed upon the United States to wage war in Vietnam. Those forces were: the Capitalist 'free world' and its political, economic, and military systems marshalled for the purpose of preventing the peoples of Indo-China and their resource-rich lands from falling into the hands of 'Communists'; and the network of militant brethren, political stooges, military cabals, and press outlets of the Catholic Church all sharing common cause to prevent Catholic populations in Vietnam from falling into the hands of the 'Godless'.
>
> That a covert intelligence mission code-named *Operation Petrov* was a fraud resulting in the eventual introduction of Australian ground troops into Vietnam and it will argue that this Australian commitment endorsed and escalated American involvement since the United States now had the support of a Western ally to cloak the War in international legitimacy.
>
> And, finally, that two enabling factors kept the United States and Australia in Vietnam long after victory was possible: the neutralization at crucial turning points of four men who all possessed the power or potential power to either stop or significantly shorten the duration of the Vietnam War; and the systematic and ongoing lies told to the American people by Presidents and their closest advisors about the progress of the War, constantly reassuring them that victory was just around the corner despite knowing that the War was a failed proposition almost from its beginning.

The End was Contained in the Beginning
— ORWELL

Catholic Church Glossary

- The term "Catholic Church", properly known as the "Holy Roman Catholic and Apostolic Church", refers to the Latin Church of the Catholic communion headquartered in Rome, in contradistinction to the 21 other particular Churches of the Catholic communion, including the Byzantine, Alexandrian, Armenian, Antiochian and Chaldean Catholic Churches.
- The term "Pope" refers to the Bishop of Rome who is also known as the Supreme Pontiff (*Pontifex Maxiumus*). The Pope exercises world-wide dominion over the congregations of the Catholic Church.

The terms "Papacy", "Holy See", "Apostolic See", and "Vatican", are often used interchangeably but all refer the central administration comprising the Pope and his Curial Government which is headquartered in the independent Vatican City State enclave in Rome.

PART I

The Petrov Affair

It was the multitude, by its vote, that sent Christ to be crucified.

CHAPTER ONE

Australian Governance

The Constitutional Monarchy

Australia is a constitutional monarchy, which means that it has a queen or king as its head of state whose powers are limited by a Constitution. Australia's current head of state is King Charles III. In practice, the monarch plays no role within the Australian political system and is merely a figurehead. He or she is formally represented by a Governor General who is appointed on the recommendation of Australia's Prime Minister. The Governor-General chairs the Executive Council, gives formal assent to legislation, makes appointments on the advice of the government, and performs a host of other executive and ceremonial functions.

The Constitution

The Commonwealth of Australia was created on 1st January 1901 when six former British colonies—now the six States of Australia—agreed to form a Federation. The Australian Constitution, which took effect on the same day, is the founding document of Australia and the pre-eminent source of law in the country.

The Constitution can be amended only with the approval of Australian electors. Any proposed amendment must be put to the vote of all electors at a referendum.

At the referendum, the proposed amendment must be approved by a 'double majority'. That is, a national majority of electors in the states and territories, and a majority of electors in a majority of the states (i.e. at least four out of six states).

Since Federation, only eight out of 44 proposals to amend the Constitution have been approved. Voting in referenda is compulsory for enrolled electors. (The importance of the Australian Constitutional system will become evident.)

The Constitution sets out the powers of each of the three branches of governance—Legislative, Executive, and Judicial.

The Branches

The Federal Legislative branch consists of a bicameral Parliament having two chambers: the House of Representatives (Lower House) and the Senate (Upper House). Legislation has to be approved by both houses before it can become law.

The political party or coalition of parties gaining the most seats in a Federal election for the House of Representatives forms the Government. The Parliamentary leader who has the support of a majority of members in the House of Representatives becomes the Prime Minister and is formally appointed to the role by the Governor-General.

The Senate is known as the 'house of review'. Voters elect 12 Senators from each of the six States and two from each of its two Territories.

The Federal Executive branch consists of the Prime Minister, the members of Parliament chosen by him to form the Ministry, with the most senior Ministers, including the Prime Minister, forming the Cabinet. The Executive carries out the day-to-day government and administration of the country. It proposes laws to the parliament and executes the laws passed by the Parliament.

The Federal Judicial branch allows for the establishment of the country's courts of law and the appointment and removal of it judges. The purpose of the courts is to interpret all laws, including the Constitution, making the rule of law supreme. The High Court of Australia is the ultimate authority on the constitutionality of laws.

The Parties

Since the Australian Federation was formed, politics has generally been a contest between the Australian Labor Party, established in 1901, and a number of anti-Labor parties. Notable among these are the Liberal Party of Australia (founded in 1944 by Robert Menzies), and the National Party, both of which have generally conservative policies. These two conservative parties, in coalition, formed the federal government for the years from 1949-1972. The social-democratic ALP, linked closely with the country's trade unions, normally has retained the support of the working class. Although it has always had a left wing that espouses various brands of socialism, it has generally favoured practical reforms to socialist theories.

Notes

- Voting for eligible adults over the age of 18 is compulsory in Australia;
- Besides being tiresome for readers, it is not necessary for our purposes to describe State, Territory, or local tiers of governance within Australia.

CHAPTER TWO

The Fatal Plague

Within a few months of the Bolshevik October Revolution of 1917, the Russian Government had declared the separation of Church and State and seized all church lands. Although the initial target of the Bolsheviks was the Russian Orthodox Church, and although that Church was not in communion with the Holy See, the authorities in Rome could clearly see that the writing was on the wall for them also if Communism were allowed to spread into Western Europe. From the Holy See's point of view, the fact that an ex-seminarian of the Russian Orthodox Church, Josef Stalin, had been appointed General Secretary of the Communist Party of the Soviet Union's Central Committee on 3rd April 1922 was all the proof one needed that the menace of atheistic Communism had infected even those who had once given their allegiance to Christianity.

In 1922, Count John de Salis, the British minister to the Holy See, confirmed the fear and hysteria gripping the Vatican and Pope Pius XI when he reported to the Foreign Office in London that: "Everything in the Vatican is dominated by the Pope's fear of Russian Communism, that the Soviets may reach Western Europe".[1]

Catholic Action

While the forces of European Fascism were busy countering Communism by consolidating political power in Germany, Italy, Spain and Portugal, Pope Pius XI was also busy countering Communism with the publication of his 23rd December 1922 Encyclical *Ubi Arcano Dei Consilio* in which he outlined a strategy to counter the current evils.

This strategy, to be known as 'Catholic Action', would encourage, promote, and hand-pick Catholic men and women who would devote themselves to pursuing the best interests of the Church in their respective societies without the necessity of becoming priests or nuns. The effect of the policies, plans and edicts of this Pope were to transform the immense Catholic apparatus throughout the world into one gigantic political party, one which could easily defeat any candidate, president, or prime minister, one which could also elect its own leaders with absolute allegiance to Rome. Coincidentally, or not, this Encyclical was published only seven days before

1 Rhodes, Anthony. *The Vatican in the Age of Dictators 1922-1945*. Hodder & Stoughton: London, 1973, p. 18.

the formation of the Union of Soviet Socialist Republics (USSR) on 30th December 1922.

A later Encylical of this Pope deserves special mention in this context.[2] As far as timing is concerned, the publishing of *Divini Redemptoris: On Atheistic Communism* (19th March 1937) is disturbing…and revealing.

Divini Redemptoris: On Atheistic Communism

In this Encyclical, Pope Pius XI makes the following selection of statements:

> …Entire peoples find themselves in danger of falling back into a barbarism worse than that which oppressed the greater part of the world at the coming of the Redeemer.
>
> This all too imminent danger, Venerable Brethren, as you have already surmised, is **bolshevistic and atheistic Communism**, which aims at upsetting the social order and at undermining the very foundations of Christian civilization. (paras 2 and 3)
>
> …With reference to Communism, Our Venerable Predecessor, Pius IX, of holy memory, as early as 1846 pronounced a solemn condemnation, which he confirmed in the words of the Syllabus directed against "that infamous doctrine of so-called Communism which is absolutely contrary to the natural law itself, and if once adopted would utterly destroy the rights, property and possessions of all men, and even society itself." Later on, another of Our predecessors, the immortal Leo XIII, in his Encyclical *Quod Apostolici Muneris*, defined Communism as **"the fatal plague** which insinuates itself into the very marrow of human society only to bring about its ruin." (para 4)
>
> …**The militant leaders of Catholic Action** thus properly prepared and armed, will be **the first and immediate apostles of their fellow workmen.** They will be an invaluable aid to the priest in carrying the torch of truth, and in relieving grave spiritual and material suffering, in many sectors where inveterate anti-clerical prejudice or deplorable religious indifference has proved a constant obstacle to the pastoral activity of God's ministers. In this way they will collaborate, under the direction of **especially qualified priests**, in that work of spiritual aid to the laboring classes on which We set so much store, because it is

2 'Pius XI Encyclicals'. *Vatican* <https://www.vatican.va/content/pius-xi/en/encyclicals.index.html#encyclicals> Accessed 27 March 2022.

the means best calculated to **save these, Our beloved children, from the snares of Communism.**[3] (para 66)

In this Encyclical, the Pope portrayed Catholics and Communists as locked in a Manichean battle that would not end until one or the other was defeated. It therefore represented a call to arms which was answered by Catholic Action groups, Catholic press outlets, and Catholic political organisations worldwide, all of which swung into action to further its implementation and, in the words of the Pope: "to save these, Our beloved children, from the snares of Communism".

3 'Pius XI Encyclicals'. *Vatican* <https://www.vatican.va/content/pius-xi/en/encyclicals/documents/hf_p-xi_enc_19370319_divini-redemptoris.html> Accessed 27 March 2022.

CHAPTER THREE

Enemies Within

Section 1: Bartholomew Augustine Santamaria

The Totalitarian

The Pope's call to the "militant leaders of Catholic Action" in his 1937 Encyclical, *Divini Redemptoris: Against Atheistic Communism,* travelled far across land and sea to lodge in the imagination of a young Melbourne lawyer and office-bearer of Catholic Action in Australia, Bartholomew Augustine Santamaria.

Santamaria was an ideologue, a man holding in his heart the seeds of intransigence, zealotry and conspiracy, a man thus eminently suitable for the battle envisaged by Pope Pius XI. His admiration of totalitarian policies and of leaders such as Italy's Mussolini was expressed in writings and speeches:

> He proclaimed that parliamentary liberal democracy, which had caused both the Great War and the Great Depression, was undeniably a failure as a political system. The genius of fascism, he argued, was that it sought to heavily regulate and moderate–and thereby avoid the extreme excesses of both free economic competition and restrictive state power. Mussolini had brought "under his control the industrial and scientific forces" of Italy and constrained "business magnates and financial mountebanks." [4] "Thus the fascist way out of the present economic crisis was a combination of private enterprise and state control". [5]

And again:

> Mussolini has declared that the salvation of the world lies in the totalitarian state...He was wrong. It lies in totalitarian Catholicism. That means integral

4 Henderson (2015), as cited in Bell, 'The Kingdom of God versus the Kingdom of Man: BA Santamaria and the origins of the Movement'. *Links International Journal of Socialist Renewal* <http://links.org.au/kingdom-god-versus-kingdom-man-ba-santamaria-origins-the-movement> Accessed 4 July 2022.

5 Duncan, Bruce. *Crusade or Conspiracy: Catholics and the Anti-Communist Struggle in Australia.* UNSW Press, 2001, p. 19.

> Catholicism. It means that your whole life and personality must be developed in a Catholic way.[6]

Section 2: The Movement

Santamaria and Daniel Mannix

In 1941, Santamaria, together with Archbishop Daniel Mannix of Melbourne, formed the political wing of the Australian Catholic Church known as the 'Movement', formally titled the 'Catholic Social Studies Movement'.

The press organ of the Movement was the rabidly anti-communist *News Weekly*, regularly distributed at Catholic Churches.

In an article appearing in the *Journal of the Australian Catholic Historical Society* and entitled 'Father Con Reis and the Movement's attempted takeover of Catholic Immigration', Gerard Henderson spoke of Santamaria's aims:

> On 11 December 1952, he (Santamaria) wrote to Archbishop Mannix that within a few years his Movement would have taken over the labour movement and there would be Movement members in state and federal parliaments.
>
> Thus, wrote Santamaria, for the first time in the Anglo-Saxon world since the Reformation, Australian governments would soon be implementing Catholic social programmes....[7]

The Movement had embarked immediately after the Second World War on a campaign targeting trade unions affiliated with the Labor Party which, until relatively recent times, was considered to be the party of the working class. In comparison to the non-Catholic majority of the Australian population at that time, the Labor Party membership comprised relatively large numbers of working class Catholics. As such, it was the party most vulnerable to infiltration by the Movement.

At first, its activities were presented as a counterweight to Communist Party members within the trade unions who, it was claimed, exercised undue influence on Labor Party policy. Behind the mask of dislodging 'communists' from their positions, the Movement began a campaign to gain control of the formulation of Labor Party policy

---

6 Ibid, p. 17.

7 Henderson, Gerard. (2015) 'Mr Santamaria and the Bishops' in *Journal of the Australian Catholic Historical Society* vol. 36 p. 143.

by setting up predominantly Catholic Action groups of dissidents (the Industrial Groupers), whose real allegiance was to Santamaria and Mannix.

In his review of Ross Fitzgerald's book *The Pope's Battalions: Santamaria, Catholicism and the Labor Split,* Michael Sexton, the New South Wales Solicitor General, wrote:

> Two figures dominate the story: Daniel Mannix, who left Ireland in 1913 to become Melbourne's Catholic Archbishop, and B.A. Santamaria, born two years later in the same city. Together they were to trigger events that changed the course of Australian political history...They were unlikely characters to be involved in an attempt to take over a political party in a parliamentary democracy. Both rejected the legacies of the Reformation and the Enlightenment—the notion of a pluralist and secular society. There was, of course, no separation of church and state in Mannix's Ireland, nor in Santamaria's models of Franco's Spain and Salazar's Portugal.
>
> ...Immediately after the war, industrial groups were established in the ALP to combat communists in the trade unions. Much of the support for these groups was provided by the Catholic Social Studies Movement, which came to be known simply as the Movement. Under Santamaria, the enormous financial resources of the Church were available to it, together with large reserves of manpower in almost every local parish. Santamaria made no bones about his long-term goal, writing to Mannix that the "Social Studies Movement should within a period of five or six years be able to completely transform the leadership of the labour movement...They should be able to implement a Christian social program in both the state and the federal spheres."[8]

From the outset, the Movement's activities were clandestine. In September 1954, a newspaper article mentioned the name of B.A. Santamaria for the first time. This ended a long period of press silence. It was not until 1962, twenty-one years after the Movement was formed, that the collaboration between Santamaria and Mannix became public through the following interview conducted by the Australian public broadcaster:

> Interviewer: "Now there's a Catholic organisation which was set up, in 1941 I understand, to fight Communism in the Australian Labor Party, in the trade unions, which I'll call the Movement. Now was the idea of the Movement originally yours?"

8 Fitzgerald (2003), as cited in Sexton, 'The Pope's Battalions: Santamaria, Catholicism and the Labor Split'. *Sydney Morning Herald*, 14 June 2003.

Archbishop Mannix: "I don't claim that it was originally mine, but however it originated I was in favour of it anyway."[9]

Despite the Archbishop's rather evasive reply, a letter Santamaria addressed to his 'lifelong friend and mentor' in 1948 demonstrates their long-term private alliance and all-encompassing aims:

> Unless Catholic Action genuinely aims at the creation of a Christian social order by means of a large scale action in the social, economic, political and cultural spheres, we are wasting our time. [10]

An extract from Archbishop Mannix's entry in the *Australian Dictionary of Biography* reads:

> Controversies in the Church following the 1954 (sic) Labor split elicited from the Vatican a condemnation of 'the Movement' as impolitic and theologically unsound...'Rome has blundered again', he said; 'Santamaria is the saviour of Australia'. He intervened in subsequent elections, allowing his auxiliary bishop to pronounce that no Catholic could vote in conscience for Labor, although in 1960 three of the four Federal Labor leaders including Calwell, a future papal knight, were Catholics.[11] (See Note)

Apart from, and more important than, the implementation of Catholic social programmes, it had become imperative for the Movement and its co-conspirators that the Labor Party never come to power and that their stated policy of non-intrusion and non-interference in the domestic affairs of foreign nations not be realised because it had been taking steps since the early 1950's to ensure that Australia, together with the projected involvement of the United States, would intervene in Indo-China in the likely event that France would lose control of its colonies of Vietnam, Cambodia and Laos.

When the French-held garrison at Dien Bien Phu in Vietnam did eventually fall on 7th May 1954 after a four month siege led by Vietnamese nationalist Ho Chi Minh, the reason behind the Movement's determination to prevent the Labor Party from gaining office was made abundantly clear—Catholic populations must not fall into the hands of 'communists'.

9 Australian Broadcasting Commission interview with Archbishop Daniel Mannix, January, 1962.

10 Henderson (1982), as cited in Mathews, 'Collateral Damage: B. A. Santamaria and the Marginalising of Social Catholicism'. *Labour History*, vol. 92. Liverpool University Press, May 2007, p. 100.

11 Mannix, Daniel, by James Griffin. *Australian Dictionary of Biography*, vol. 10, 1986. <https://adb.anu.edu.au/biography/mannix-daniel-7478> Accessed 14 May 2022.

For example, on 8th July 1954, readers of Catholic newspapers and periodicals worldwide were confronted by alarmist articles similar to the following which appeared in the Australian press:

> Million Catholics face crisis in Indo-China… [12]

Michael Costigan, former Executive Secretary to the Bishops' Committee for Justice, Development, Ecology and Peace wrote of Santamaria's personal involvement in the Catholic struggle against Vietnam's communists. In September 1957, Santamaria sponsored South Vietnam President Ngo Dinh Diem's official visit to Australia. In April 1963, Santamaria also sponsored a visit to Australia by Diem's brother, Bishop Ngo Dinh Thuc. Costigan writes:

> …Santamaria and I met occasionally at functions, one memorable occasion being a closed gathering of Catholic editors, organised by Santamaria in April 1963 at the Essendon headquarters of the Columban Fathers, to hear and question the visiting Archbishop Ngo Dinh Thuc of Hue, Vietnam. The historian Val Noone reports on this clandestine meeting in *Disturbing the War* (Spectrum Publications, 1993, page 80). The visitor's upbeat description of the struggle with the communists in his country was also covered in the *Advocate* (18th April 1963).
>
> The claim in the headline, probably composed by me, that the Church was flourishing in spite of the communist threat, makes odd reading when it is recalled that, on 2nd November 1963, barely six months after Thuc's visit to Australia, his brother, Presiden Ngo Dinh Diem, himself a previous Santamaria-sponsored Australian visitor, was assassinated in Saigon. [13]

These two men, Santamaria and Mannix, aided and abetted by their political and press allies, and heavily financed from 1945 by the Catholic Bishops, engaged in subversive activities which undermined the democratic process and ultimately led to Australia's involvement in the Vietnam War with all its incalculable consequences.

The one man who stood as a bulwark against the Movement and almost succeeded in thwarting its ambitions was Dr. Herbert Vere Evatt who became leader of the Labor Party in 1951. Tragically for all involved, Dr. Evatt was successfully targeted for destruction by the Movement. However, as will be seen in the following Chapters, he

12 *Advocate* (Melbourne, Victoria), 8 July 1954, p. 3.

13 Costigan. M. (2015) 'B.A. Santamaria: Remembered by one who knew him a little' in *Journal of the Australian Catholic Historical Society* vol. 36 p.p. 163-64.

left for posterity all the evidence necessary to expose the most consequential political fraud ever foisted on an unsuspecting Australian public.

Section 3: The Triumvirate

Strange Bedfellows

Robert Gordon (later Sir Robert) Menzies was born on 20th December 1894 at Jeparit in the State of Victoria. He studied law at the University of Melbourne, graduated with first class honours in law in 1916, was admitted to the Victorian bar in 1918, and became a King's Counsel in 1929.

In 1928, Menzies entered the Victorian parliament and, in 1935, Federal Parliament. He was Attorney-General in the Lyons government and won the United Australia Party leadership after Lyons' death in 1939. He became Prime Minister for the first time on 26th April 1939.

Menzies held office through the early years of World War II until 1941 when he lost the confidence of members of his party and was forced to resign. As an Opposition backbencher during the war years, he helped create the Liberal Party of Australia in 1944 and became Leader of the Opposition in 1946. At the 1949 Federal Election, he defeated Ben Chifley's Labor Party and once again became Australia's Prime Minister.

Just like Santamaria and Mannix, Menzies was a fervent anti-communist and vowed to outlaw the Communist Party a month before he won the December 1949 Federal Election:

> The Communists are the most unscrupulous opponents of religion, of civilised government, of law and order, of national security. Abroad, but for the threat of aggressive Russian Imperialism, there would be real peace today.
>
> Communism in Australia is an alien and destructive pest. If elected, we shall outlaw it. The Communist Party will be declared subversive and unlawful, and dissolved. A receiver will be appointed to deal with its assets. Subject to appeal, the Attorney-General will be em-powered to declare other bodies substantially Communist; to follow the party into any new form and attach illegality to that new association.
>
> No person now a member of the Communist Party all be employed or paid a fee by the Commonwealth; nor shall any such person be eligible for any office in a registered industrial organisation. The laws with respect to sedition or other subversive activities will be reviewed and strengthened. Conviction under such

> laws will disqualify from employment under the Crown or from office in a registered organisation.
>
> These are far-reaching proposals. But half-measures are no good if, in the bitter conflict between the Communists and our decent, peaceful people, the people are to win.[14]

Whilst a Catholic of Italian origin like Santamaria and a Catholic of Irish origin like Mannix would appear to have nothing in common in terms of religion or descent with a Protestant of Scots origin like Menzies, their shared fear and loathing of atheistic communism led them to forge an alliance not unlike the First Roman Triumvirate of Julius Caesar, Marcus Crassus and Pompey the Great, an alliance which the Roman historian Livy[15] described as a "conspiracy against the state by its three leading citizens" and as a "private agreement". Although Prime Minister Menzies was the only one who could be described as a "leading citizen", the virtual anonymity of his co-conspirators rendered their "private agreement" to target and tarnish the reputations of those who expressed opposition to their policies all the more effective.

Following his success in the December 1949 Federal Election, Prime Minister Menzies—with the overt support of his press allies and the covert support of Santamaria and Mannix—was able to entrench the Liberal Party in power, a situation which lasted from 1949 to 1972. By ensuring the continued re-election of the Liberal Party Government, the Movement and its political allies succeeded in involving and then enmeshing Australia in a war in Vietnam.

Note

Arthur Calwell was leader of the Australian Labor Party from 1960-1967. He was an opponent of Australia's involvement in the Vietnam War and condemned conscription as 'immoral'.

---

14 Robert Gordon Menzies on behalf of the Liberal /Country Party Coalition, Melbourne, Victoria, November 10, 1949. *Australian Federal Election Speeches.* <https://electionspeeches.moadoph.gov.au/speeches/1949-robert-menzies> Accessed 5 May 2022.

15 'First Triumvirate'. *Livius* <https://www.livius.org/articles/concept/triumvir/first-triumvirate/> Accessed 5 May 2022

CHAPTER FOUR

Herbert Vere Evatt

Section 1: The Backstory

Doctor Herbert Vere Evatt, or the 'Doc' as he was sometimes referred to, was born on 30th April 1894 at East Maitland in the State of New South Wales. He was educated at Fort Street High School, Sydney, and the University of Sydney. A brilliant scholar, he won prizes and scholarships in the fields of Mathematics, Philosophy, English literature and Law. He attained the degrees of B.A. (triple first-class honours and University Medal), M.A., LL.B. (first class honours and University Medal), LL.D and D. Litt. Evatt's LL.D thesis examining aspects of constitutional monarchy was later published as *The King and his Dominion Governors* in 1936.

Evatt edited Australia's oldest literary journal, *Hermes*, which showcased the work of Sydney university students, tutored at his college, and presided over the University Union from 1916-1917.

He also contributed significantly to Australian cultural life, especially in the 1930's, supporting the Contemporary Art Society and serving as president of the trustees of the Public Library of New South Wales. No Australian leading a life of the mind in those years was more brilliant, ambitious and ubiquitous. He argued unpopular causes; he was in the forefront of those who believed that Australia could be more than just an outpost of empire noted for just its sporting prowess and borrowed culture; and he walked confidently in the world beyond its borders.

Section 2: Standing Down

Evatt joined the Australia Labor Party in 1925 and was elected to serve as a Member of the New South Wales Legislative Assembly for the Sydney seat of Balmain.

Following his rejection for service in World War I because of astigmatism, Evatt had also pursued a legal career and was appointed a King's Counsel in 1929.

He quit State politics in 1930 when, just a year after being appointed a King's Counsel, he was elevated to serve as a justice of the High Court of Australia, the youngest person to be appointed to such a position.

Evatt quickly distinguished himself as a brilliant and liberal judge and a respected author in the fields of law and history (as noted previously, Evatt's LL.D thesis examining aspects of constitutional monarchy was later published as *The King and his Dominion Governors* in 1936).

In 1940, Evatt stepped down from the High Court, arguably the most exalted position in the land, to stand as a federal Labor Party candidate. He won the Sydney seat of Barton at the elections of the same year. When Labor gained power under John Curtin in 1941, Evatt was appointed Attorney-General and Minister for External Affairs. (From 1946 to 1949 he was Deputy Prime Minister to Ben Chifley).

Section 3: The Statesman

During the Second World War years, Evatt led many significant overseas missions for the Australian government. He was instrumental in bringing home Australian troops from the Middle East and in securing military aircraft to support Australia's war effort in the Pacific. During his years as Minister for External Affairs, Evatt completely reorganized the department and laid the foundations for an active and independent Australian foreign policy. He championed the cause of the smaller nations having a voice alongside the great powers on questions of international and global significance.[16]

Evatt attended the United Nations originating conference in San Francisco and spoke to the great powers on behalf of the other nations of the world with a voice that commanded universal respect. After three months of diplomatic struggle, the Charter of the United Nations was adopted; a Charter that had become more humane and larger in scope, now containing provisions for the poor, the weak and the oppressed, provisions that had never been envisaged by the great powers:

> Herbert Vere 'Doc' Evatt – our External Affairs Minister in the 1940's – was a leader at the originating conference in San Francisco in 1945, where he helped craft the UN Charter. [17]

Evatt was Chairman of the Far Eastern Commission, USA, 1945; President of the South Pacific Regional Conference, Canberra, 1947; and Chairman of the British Commonwealth Conference on the Japanese Peace Treaty, 1947.

16 'Evatt Collection', *Flinders University Library* <https://library.flinders.edu.au/accessing-collections/special/evatt-collection> Accessed 13 April 2022.

17 '75 years of support for the United Nations', *Australian Government Department of Prime Minister and Cabinet* <https://www.pmc.gov.au/news-centre/international-policy/75-years-support-united-nations> Accessed 11 April 2022

He led the Australian delegations to the United Nations in 1946, 1947 and 1948 and was elected President of the General Assembly at its Third Session from 1948-49. He was the first chairman of the UN Atomic Energy Commission and chairman of the Palestine Commission.

Evatt presided over the December 1948 adoption and proclamation of the Universal Declaration of Human Rights, the cornerstone of human rights protection throughout the modern world. He took an uncompromising stand for just principles in public life and was widely recognised around the world as a supporter of the right of small nations to peaceful development and equality. Also during his presidency, Australia was second only to the United States in its contribution to the UN's International Children's Emergency Fund, where Evatt protected its Appeal for Children from premature closure on the grounds that children's needs were one of the forces that bind nations together.

Faith Bandler, the leader of the 1967 referendum that formally recognised indigenous Australians, and one of Evatt's greatest admirers, paid him tribute in a speech to the inaugural meeting of the Evatt Foundation in 1979:

> Dr Evatt fought for the oppressed, he fought for our political rights and civil liberties, our freedom of thought and action. We would not find it possible to be as outspoken today as we are if Dr. Evatt had not fought for us as a judge, as a politician and as an Australian.[18]

Section 4: The Midwife

To mark the 62nd anniversary of the United Nations General Assembly's adoption of the partition resolution that led to the creation of the Jewish homeland, the Executive Council of Australian Jewry (ECAJ), the National Council of Jewish Women of Australia (NCJWA), and the Zionist Federation of Australia held a 'Tribute to Doc Evatt' dinner on 29th November 2009 to acknowledge the pivotal role played by Australia, in particular by Dr. Evatt, in the establishment of the State of Israel. The Tribute reads:

> Chairman of the Ad-Hoc Committee on Palestine, Dr. H. V. Evatt, was responsible for steering the proposal through. As president of the assembly in May 1949, he also presided over the historic vote that saw Israel admitted to the UN.

18 'Doc Evatt-A Brilliant and Controversial Character', *Evatt Foundation* <https://www.evatt.org.au/about> Accessed 13 April 2022.

The dinner, held at Moriah College, was attended by more than 160 communal leaders, as well as Israeli Ambassador Yuval Rotem, Attorney-General Robert McClelland and Evatt's daughter, Rosalind Carrodus.

Hailing Evatt as "a shining example of the power of the human spirit, the strength of the will and a commitment to justice that all people should aspire to", Ambassador Rotem quoted the Doc's private secretary, who wrote: "The tiny republic, which embodies the age-old dreams of world Jewry and Zionism, was **born in 1948 with this man as midwife.**"[19]

On 20th February 2019, Milton Dick, the Speaker of the Australian House of Representatives, addressed Parliament on the occasion of the 70th anniversary of Australia's formal diplomatic relationship with the state of Israel:

Today we recognise the 70th anniversary of the formal beginning of Australia's friendship with Israel. It was not long after David Ben-Gurion, the first Prime Minister of Israel, publicly read the declaration of independence of Israel on 14 May 1948 that Australia and Israel formalised our partnership together.

When officially announcing in 1949 that Australia would recognise Israel as a state, Prime Minister Ben Chifley said Israel would be 'a force of special value in the world'. Since that time, it has proved to be so. In the 70 years since then, the friendship and mateship between our two countries have only grown closer.

Our support for Israel has been long and unwavering. It was only two years earlier, prior to our formal partnership, that Australia was the first country to vote yes to the 1947 United Nations partition plan that called for the establishment of a Jewish state. Of course, it was Australia's Minister for External Affairs from 1941 to 1949, the great Doc Evatt, who presided over the Universal Declaration of Human Rights as President of the General Assembly of the United Nations, and who also chaired the committee that recommended to the UN that Israel be welcomed into the international community of nations.

A few short months later, on 18th May 1949, Israel's UN representative, Abba Eban, wrote to Evatt thanking him for Australia's steadfast support of Israel:

"We are deeply indebted to the Australian Delegation for its consistent and effective support of our cause in the Assembly and its organs through all the stages of the consideration of our problem by the United Nations.

19 'Community Leaders acknowledge Doc Evatt' (3 December 2009) *The Australian Jewish News.* <https://www.australianjewishnews.com/community-leaders-honour-doc-evatt/> Accessed 27 January 2025.

> "We are grateful to you for the decisive part you played in the proceedings. It was under your chairmanship and thanks in so large measure to your determined lead that Israel was admitted to the United Nations when barely a year old.
>
> "The manner in which you steered to a vote the second historic Resolution, representing as it does the culmination of the process initiated by the first, the warmth and eloquence with which you welcomed Israel into the family of nations, have earned for you the undying gratitude of our people. This shows the depth of our two great countries' bonds with each other from the very start". [20]

Evatt would later write in his memoirs:

> I regard the establishment of Israel as a great victory of the United Nations.

Section 5: The Nominee

In 1950, Dr. Evatt was nominated for the Nobel Peace Prize:

> Mr. Churchill, President Truman, and Australia's Dr. Evatt are among candidates who have been proposed for this year's Nobel Peace Prize.
>
> The list submitted last night by the Norwegian Nobel Prize Institute also includes India's Prime Minister (Mr. Nehru) ; former Palestine peace mediator, Dr. Ralph Bunche; New Zealand writer, Francis Carlisle; and King Paul, of Greece. [21]

He was again nominated in 1953 for his work in the United Nations. (Shamefully, the Australian Dictionary of Biography entry for Dr. Evatt fails to mention either of his nominations for the Nobel Peace Prize.)

On the occasion of his death on 2nd November 1965, members of the General Assembly of the United Nations stood to honour his memory and his contribution.

---

20 ' 70th Anniversary of Australia's Formal Diplomatic Relationship with the State of Israel' (20 February 2019) *Milton Dick MP.* < https://www.miltondick.com.au/news/speeches-transcripts/70th-anniversary-of-australia-s-formal-diplomatic-relationship-with-the-state-of-israel/> Accessed 27 January 2005.

21 'Dr. Evatt on Nobel Peace Prize List'. *The Sydney Morning Herald* (NSW), 1 March 1950, p. 3.

Section 6: The Sacrificial Victim

Dr. Evatt was well aware that his opposition to the Communist Party Dissolution Bill, his virtually single-handed defeat of the subsequent Referendum, his challenges to the non-judicial behaviour of the judges at the *Royal Commission on Espionage*, his exposure of the lies told by the Petrovs and others at the Royal Commission, and his description of the Petrov Affair as a fraud engineered by ASIO, would earn him a host of powerful enemies. Yet, no matter the cost to himself, he would not be deterred.

Despite the breadth of Dr. Evatt's achievements, which have not been surpassed by any other Australian, this host of powerful and implacable enemies pursued him to the grave and beyond, described by them as paranoid, as mentally unbalanced, as insatiably ambitious, as a flawed hero, as a disloyal communist sympathiser, ad infinitum, ad nauseam.

Given the way he was depicted during the Petrov Fraud and is still being depicted by those who have a stake in blackening his name and reputation, it is hardly surprising that he is now largely unheralded in his own land.

Yet, this is the man who:

- stepped down from the most exalted office in the land to enter the political fray in the hope of improving the lot of his fellow Australians;
- stood as a bulwark against the Triumvirate and almost succeeded in thwarting its ambition to eventually enmesh Australia in a war in Vietnam;
- stood virtually alone between the civil liberties of the Australian citizen and the establishment of a police state;
- supported of the right of small nations to peaceful development and equality.
- helped craft the United Nations Charter;
- was President of the UN General Assembly at its Third Session from 1948-49;
- presided over the adoption and proclamation of the Universal Declaration of Human Rights;
- played a pivotal role in the establishment of the State of Israel;
- and was twice nominated for a Nobel Peace Prize.

Nevertheless, the day will come when Doctor Evatt will be shown to be the great Australian that he was—and never greater than during his defence of Australia against the perpetrators of the Petrov Affair.

Australians can never repay the debt owed to Dr. Evatt, as shall presently be seen.

CHAPTER FIVE

The Communist Party Dissolution Bill

Section 1: The Background

The Second World War had been won at enormous cost by an anti-Fascist alliance that had also created the United Nations. Yet, just a few short years after that hard-won victory, the Australian Prime Minister, Robert Menzies, introduced into the Federal Parliament a Bill which, behind all the legal jargon, would have endowed him with wartime emergency powers, elevated him to the position of legal dictator of his country, a position held by other notables such as Mussolini and Hitler, and given him the power to establish a Tribunal based on the United States McCarthy model.

The Australian political scene in this era reflected that of the United States of America where anti-communist hysteria, incited by press, priest and politician, manifested itself in McCarthyism. The strategies, the techniques of deception, the pose of moral righteousness, the theme of patriotism masking calculated intent, the repetitive drumming of single words to produce conditioned-reflex responses—much had been learned from Nazi-era Germany.

Section 2: The Bill

The Bill was introduced into Federal Parliament on 27th April 1950. The intention of the *Communist Party Dissolution Bill* of 1950 was to stifle all legitimate opposition to the policies of the Menzies anti-communist government in the guise of controlling 'communists'.

The Bill was temporarily shelved, then reintroduced by Menzies on 28th September 1950. It passed through the House of Representatives on 3rd October and the Senate on 19th October 1950. *The Communist Party Dissolution Act 1950* commenced upon the Bill receiving royal assent the next day. The *Act* was, according to its description:

> An Act to provide for the Dissolution of the Australian Communist Party and of other Communist Organizations, to disqualify Communists from holding certain Offices, and for purposes connected therewith.

The preamble declared that the Communist Party was engaged in subversion and involved in activities to overthrow the system of government in Australia.

As well as dissolving the Party and confiscating its property without compensation, the *Act* also empowered the Government to declare persons and organisations as 'communist'. Declared persons could not work for the Government or in specified industries. If a person was declared to be a 'communist', and they wished to challenge the declaration, they had to prove that they were not a 'communist'. Thus, the burden of proof was reversed.

Ben Chifley, the leader of the Labor Party, had issued his own sober reflection on the proposed *Communist Party Dissolution Act* on 23rd May 1950:

> This measure [the Dissolution Act] will to some degree be administered in an atmosphere of national hysteria, worked up by politicians and other persons, and by the press...There is great danger that the hysteria and fear complex that has been aroused may result in grave injustices being done to individuals. The multitude can make grave mistakes. **It was the multitude, by its vote, that sent Christ to be crucified.**[22]

Section 3: The Challenge

Just hours after the *Communist Party Dissolution Act* received royal assent on 29th October 1950, the Australian Communist Party, certain of its members, a number of trade unions, and certain union officials commenced proceedings in the original jurisdiction of the High Court. They challenged the validity of the *Act* on grounds that:

- it was outside the scope of Commonwealth legislative power and it was not brought within legislative power by the statements in the preamble because those statements, or some of them, were not in accordance with fact;
- it was contrary to Ch III (by usurping the judicial power of the Commonwealth and conferring judicial power upon the Parliament);
- it was an acquisition of property without just terms contrary to s 51(xxxi);
- it contravened the freedom of inter-State intercourse, trade and commerce guaranteed by s 92; and

22 'What would Evatt do?' (December 2011) *Evatt Journal*, Vol. 10, No. 1. <https://www.evatt.org.au/post/what-would-evatt-do> Accessed 28 May 2022.

- it was inconsistent with the maintenance of the constitutional integrity of the States.[23]

On 25th October 1950, Dr. Evatt, Deputy Leader of the Opposition Labor Party and the immediate past-President of the Third Session of the United Nations General Assembly, accepted a brief from the Waterside Workers' Federation and the Federated Ironworkers' Association to appear on their behalf when the case was heard before the Full Court of the High Court.

From that day forward, Dr. Evatt was a man marked for destruction by the Movement, by Menzies, and by their press and radio allies. An example of the type of atmosphere being created around Dr. Evatt is illustrated by the headline 'Evatt's Red Brief arouses M's H.R' on the next day's front page of Brisbane's *The Courier Mail* when Harold Holt, a future Prime Minister of Australia, whined in Federal Parliament that:

> the people of Australia would read great significance into Dr. Evatt's appearance. [24]

Section 4: The High Court Ruling

On 9th March 1951, by a 6-1 majority, the High Court of Australia ruled the *Communist Party Dissolution Act* to be invalid. The extreme, totalitarian nature of the legislation was made clear in the judgement delivered by Mr. Justice Williams:

> The outstanding character of the Act is that, in the words of Knox C.J. in Ex parte Walsh and Johnson (1925) 37 CLR, at p 69, the enactment in its main provisions "prohibits no act, enjoins no duty, creates no offence, imposes no sanction for disobedience to any command, prescribes no standard or rule of conduct". It operates to dissolve the Australian Communist Party and to forfeit its property to the Commonwealth, and to make other bodies of persons who were in the prescribed period or **are likely to be tainted with communism,** corporate or unincorporate, liable to be dissolved and their property forfeited to the Commonwealth, and to make persons who were in the prescribed period or are communists liable to be deprived of important contractual rights without

23 Hon. Justice Michelle Gordon AC (23 July 2021) 'Communist Party Case: Core Themes and Legacy' (p. 11). *Centre for Comparative Constitutional Studies* <https://cdn.hcourt.gov.au/assets/publications/speeches/current-justices/gordonj/Gordon_J_-_Communist_Party_Case_paper.pdf>. Accessed 21 May 2022.

24 'Evatt's Red Brief arouses M's H.R.' *The Courier Mail* (Brisbane, QLD), 26 October 1950, p. 1.

> creating any offence the commission of which will entail such consequences, and indeed without proof that they have committed any offence against any law of the Commonwealth, without a trial in any court, and without such bodies or persons having any right to prove that they have not done anything prejudicial to the security and defence of the Commonwealth or to the execution or maintenance of the Constitution or of the laws of the Commonwealth.[25]

On 13th March 1951, four days after the High Court handed down its decision, Prime Minister Menzies made a statement to the House of Representatives. He said that:

> While he had "no legal criticisms to make" of the Court's decision, "it would be foolish to pretend that the decision had not given grave concern to the Government, and to millions of the Australian people". He said that the Government was considering "whether any new and adequate constitutional power to deal directly with the Communist wreckers could be obtained either by referred powers from the States or by direct constitutional amendment approved by the people at a referendum. [26]

Within 10 days of the High Court decision, Menzies convinced the Governor General that the Australian Labor Party-dominated Senate made Parliament unworkable. A double dissolution of both Houses of Parliament followed and an election date of 28th April 1951 was set.

Anti-communist hysteria whipped up by politicians, by mainstream press and radio, and by Catholic newspapers and periodicals, dominated the entire election campaign. Not surprisingly, the Menzies Liberal-Country Party Coalition Government was returned to office, albeit with a slim majority in both Houses of Parliament.

---

25 Mr. Justice Williams (para 19). 'Australian Communist Party v. The Commonwealth [1951] HCA 5; (1951) 83 CLR 1'. *High Court of Australia* <http://www8.austlii.edu.au/cgi-bin/viewdoc/au/cases/cth/HCA/1951/5.html> Accessed 18 May 2022.

26 'Prime Minister Menzies Statement' (13 March 1951). House of Representatives, 19th Parliament, 1st Session. *Historic Hansard* < https://historichansard.net/hofreps/1951/19510313_reps_19_212/#subdebate-31-0> Accessed 27 November 2022.

In 1973, the Sydney *Tribune* newspaper published a series of articles reflecting on the *Communist Party Dissolution Bill.* The article of 26th June revealed the Triumvirate's behind-the-scenes machinations to take over the Labor Party:

> In Victoria, B. A. Santamaria had, over some years and with the help of Catholic forces, built up an organisation, the Industrial Groups, in the trade unions and the Labor Party...The Industrial Groups supported Menzies' Bill. Indeed, they were poised and ready for the time when, as they hoped, the Government's Bill became law and the authorities forcibly removed the communists and militant trade union leaders, and allowed them to move in and take over the unions.[27]

In 2021, seventy years after the High Court Ruling, the Hon. Justice Michelle Gordon AC reflected on the crucial nature of the judgement:

> It is the clearest example in our constitutional history of the Court positively asserting its constitutional function, a function which is critical for the protection of the rule of law. However the rule of law is to be defined, there is no doubt about its "irreducible minimum" – "that Government should be under law, that the law should apply to and be observed by Government and its agencies, those given power in the community, just as it applies to the ordinary citizen".[28]

27 *Tribune* (Sydney, NSW), 26 June 1973, p. 5.

28 Hon. Justice Michelle Gordon AC (23 July 2021) 'Communist Party Case: Core Themes and Legacy' (p. 45). *Centre for Comparative Constitutional Studies* <https://cdn.hcourt.gov.au/assets/publications/speeches/current-justices/gordonj/Gordon_J_-_Communist_Party_Case_paper.pdf>. Accessed 21 May 2022.

CHAPTER SIX

The Pilgrim's Progress

Following the Federal Election of December 1949, won by Menzies largely on a relentless anti-communist campaign, and the April 1950 introduction of the *Communist Party Dissolution Bill*, another powerful player arrived on the Australian scene to support the Triumvirate and its allies in spreading the anti-communist message throughout the country. The beginning of her pilgrimage from Lisbon was announced on 30th October 1950 by Brisbane's *The Courier Mail:*

> The statue of Our Lady of Fátima (Portugal's Lourdes) has left Lisbon on a Far Eastern pilgrimage. It will travel by way of Rome, Athens, Cairo, and Bombay to Singapore, Australia, Timor, Portugese Macao, and Japan. [29]

The "Pilgrim Statue" of Our Lady of Fátima departed Singapore on 30th December 1950 on board the ship *Gorgon*, a most interesting name considering the symbolism. After disembarking at Perth, she boarded an aircraft to fly to Melbourne. The Catholic newspaper, the *Advocate*, announced her scheduled arrival in Melbourne on 20 January under the banner head 'World Pilgrimage of Our Lady of Fátima':

> The "Pilgrim Statue" of Our Lady of Fátima, which has now visited thirty three countries in Europe, Africa, India and Asia, will arrive at Essendon airport on Saturday, January 20, at 9.30 a.m. After a reception at the aerodrome it will be carried in a procession of cars from Essendon to St. Patrick's Cathedral, where it may be seen throughout the day. In the evening, at the Cathedral, there will be Rosary and Benediction at 7.30, and at Midnight, Solemn High Mass, at which his Grace the Archbishop (Mannix) will preside... It arrived from Singapore in Perth on the ship *Gorgon* on Saturday last.[30]

Both Catholic and non-Catholic newspapers and periodicals reported extensively on her journey to Australia, her six-month progress throughout the country, then on her departure from Darwin on 5th July 1951.

Our Lady of Fátima had been associated with anti-communism even before the 1941 publication of the second part of the 'secret' of Fatima in which she issued grave warnings about Russia (see Notes):

29 *The Courier Mail* (Brisbane QLD), 30 October 1950, p. 4.

30 *Advocate* (Melbourne, Victoria), 11 January 1951, p. 7.

> If my requests are heeded, Russia will be converted, and there will be peace; if not, she will spread her errors throughout the world, causing wars and persecutions of the Church. The good will be martyred; the Holy Father will have much to suffer; various nations will be annihilated. In the end, my Immaculate Heart will triumph. The Holy Father will consecrate Russia to me, and she will be converted, and a period of peace will be granted to the world.[31]

From October 1942, Cardinal Schuster, Archbishop of Milan, had publicly interpreted the Fátima second 'secret' text in an anti-communist sense:

> "When the promise of the Blessed Virgin is fulfilled", he said, "it will be the most beautiful and total victory of the Church over Bolshevism." [32]

On 25th January 1951, the Very Reverend Father Daniel Daly delivered an impassioned sermon in the presence of the statue of Our Lady of Fátima enshrined in Melbourne's St. Patrick's Cathedral. Part of his sermon included the following:

> The children at Fátima had been shown a vision of the Immaculate Heart of Mary wounded by the sins of the world; they had been shown a brief but terrible vision of hell. To save poor sinners Our Lord wished that devotion to the Immaculate Heart of Mary be established in the world. "If people will do what I ask," said Our Lady, "many souls will be saved and there will be peace in the world." If the Blessed Virgin's requests were granted, she said, Russia would be converted and there would be peace; if they were not Russia would spread its errors throughout the world, provoking wars and persecution against the Church, many good people would be martyred, the Holy Father would have much to suffer, many nations would be annihilated. The outlook was gloomy, but there was a ray of hope. Mary's Immaculate Heart would triumph.[33]

Thus, during the crucial period from January 1951 to July 1951 when anti-communist hysteria gripped the nation, Our Lady of Fátima joined her considerable voice to the chorus.

---

31 'Fátima in Lucia's Own Words: Sister Lucia's Memoirs'.(16th Edition 2007). Translated from Portuguese by the Dominican Nuns of the Perpetual Rosary of the Monastery Pius XII, Fátima. Ed. Fr. Louis Kondor SVD. *Secretariado Dos Pastorinhos, Fátima, Portugal.* Third Memoir p.124. Imprimatur: António Augusto dos Santos Marto, Bishop of Leiria-Fátima, July 2007. <https://www.piercedhearts.org/hearts_jesus_mary/apparitions/fatima/MemoriasI_en.pdf>.

32 Excerpt From: Frere Michel de la Sainte Trinite. *The Whole Truth about Fatima - Vol I.* p. 675. Apple Books.

33 *Advocate* (Melbourne, Victoria), 25 January 1951, p. 7.

Notes

During her journeying through Australia, Pope Pius XII said in a 13th May radio broadcast to pilgrims at Fátima that Our Lady of Fátima was travelling the world claiming her dominion.

See Appendix C: *The Cult of Fátima* for an explanation of its development and how the 'Great Secret' of Fatima was deployed in the 20th Century by a Church determined to eradicate atheistic communism.

CHAPTER SEVEN

The Referendum

After his 13th March 1951 speech to the House of Representatives, Prime Minister Menzies initiated the Referendum. In accordance with s 128 of the Constitution, the Referendum sought to add a new s 51A into the Constitution that would give the Commonwealth Parliament the constitutional power to ban the Communist Party and permit the Parliament to re-enact the law held invalid by the High Court on 9th March.

The question to be put to Australian voters on 22nd September 1951 was:

> Do you approve of the proposed law for the alteration of the Constitution entitled 'Constitution Alteration (Powers to deal with Communists and Communism) 1951'?

In the lead-up to the Referendum, the Australian press combined selective reporting with a systematically biased pattern of emphasis. The following representative reports appearing in just two newspapers indicate the course which the mainstream press was following and the intellectual climate being deliberately created.

On 10th September, *The Courier Mail,* Brisbane's morning daily, reported the views of Dr. James Duhig, the Roman Catholic Archbishop of Brisbane:

> "The aim of Communism was to wipe out the Christian faith in every country where it could get control," Archbishop Duhig said in St. Stephen's Roman Catholic Cathedral yesterday. "Yet we are asked to be gentle towards Communists here in Australia and to give Communism a trial," he said. "If we did so, persecution of Christianity would come to this country as it did to others."[34]

Three days later, after a few preliminary remarks, *The Courier Mail* declared its trust in Prime Minister Menzies:

> All electors who are convinced that more drastic measures must be taken to defend Australia against international Communism and its agents in this country have one good reason for trusting Mr. Menzies rather than Dr. Evatt on this issue. Mr. Menzies is the head of a government that has been trying

34 'Red Aim-Erase Christianity'. *The Courier Mail* (Brisbane, Qld), 10 September 1951, p. 3.

> since the end of 1949 to carry out its undertaking to the people to outlaw the Communist Party...Mr. Menzies says that it must have more power under the Constitution to achieve this task...The Commonwealth Parliament will be able to use the power a 'YES' vote will give it only for such purposes and in such ways as a majority of Federal electors may sanction.[35]

By 19th September, just three days before voting, Archbishop Duhig's views had crystallised and he made his position clear:

> "I believe that in voting for 'NO' in the referendum I would be voting against the best interests of Australia," said the Roman Catholic Archbishop of Brisbane, Dr. J. Duhig. Archbishop Duhig said last night he would not cast "any vote that would favour Communism." He said: "By voting against the government I would vote for a continuance of a false liberty..."
>
> Archbishop Duhig said he had determined to say nothing on the Communist referendum until he had seen a statement in which 10 clergymen had opposed a 'YES' vote...
>
> "I do not agree with the statements of those clergymen," he said. He said he could not imagine Russia holding a referendum... "I do not think anyone who stands for Communist principles can be loyal to Australia," Dr. Duhig added. "...If it is a matter of loyalty to some foreign power or to Australia, I will always put Australia first."[36]

(Note that the Vatican State is a foreign power. Archbishop Duhig's first loyalty, according to the Sacred Canons, is to the Bishop of Rome.)

The same newspaper article added:

> The Roman Catholic Archbishop of Sydney (Cardinal Gilroy) has advised people to vote in the referendum on Communism according to their consciences, and not according to party politics. He said that whatever the referendum result, the government should take quick and effective action to deal with Communism.

The day before voting, the *Townsville Daily Bulletin* acknowledged that Dr. Duhig's call to vote 'Yes' could influence the outcome:

35 'A question of trust'. *The Courier Mail* (Brisbane, Qld), 13 September, p. 2.

36 'Dr. Duhig on Referendum: 'No' vote will favour Reds'. *The Courier Mail* (Brisbane, Qld), 19 September 1951, p. 3..

> Whatever may be the result in other States, indications are that the Referendum will be carried in Queensland on Saturday. One powerful factor is the announcement of Archbishop Duhig in recent days that he intended to vote 'Yes.' This is certain to influence not only a large section of the Catholic vote, but also many others who might have been wavering.[37]

The newspaper's confidence was misplaced. By polling eve, Dr. Evatt had turned the situation around. A million voters were thought to have switched sides in just six weeks.

On the morning of voting day, 22nd September, *The Courier Mail* editorial urged all "sensible" Australians to vote 'YES'. [38]

Later that same day, the Australian public voted on the proposed constitutional amendment.

"Sensible" Australians voted 'NO'.

Given its vigorous 'YES' vote campaign, *The Courier Mail* could hardly hide its spleen and knew just who to blame for the Referendum's defeat:

> Dr. Evatt flew up and down the country sowing doubts about 'justice for all'. His professional propagandists played up those fears with a cunning unequalled in Australian campaigning.[39]

At the opening of the Referendum campaign, opinion polls had indicated that 80% of the Australian public supported the Menzies proposal. Despite all the mainstream media bias and other factors which told him that his cause was hopeless and doomed to failure, Dr. Evatt had criss-crossed the country warning Australians to resist this draconian legislation and not to take any risks with the Constitution. As Frank Bongiorno of the *Australian National University* observes.

> Evatt's triumph was to turn the rhetoric of cold war anti-communism back on his opponents. His technique was to associate the government's proposed methods with "the revolutionary procedures of totalitarianism and Fascism" and argue against attacking "communism by the methods of the jackboot, the spy system and the concentration camp." [40]

---

37 'Queensland indicates a 'Yes' vote'. *Townsville Daily Bulletin* (Qld), 21 September 1951, p.1.

38 'Big 'Yes' vote likely in Queensland'. *The Courier Mail* (Brisbane, Qld), 22 September 1951, p.1.

39 'Why did nation say 'No?' *The Courier Mail* (Brisbane, Qld), 24 September 1951, p. 1.

40 Frank Bongiorno, 'Amid the panic, a sense of purpose', *Inside Story.* < https://insidestory.org.au/amid-the-panic-a-sense-of-purpose/> Accessed 28 May 2022.

In a life already studded with remarkable achievements, this was Dr. Evatt's finest hour. Had the government succeeded in having the Constitution changed in the way it wished, and in banning the Communist Party, modern Australian history may have turned out very differently.

In a speech marking the fiftieth anniversary of its defeat, former High Court Judge, Michael Kirby, spoke of its significance for Australia's democracy and history. He referred to:

> The wisdom of the Australian people, half-way through the first century of their federal Constitution, in defeating a referendum that would have left a permanent blot on our freedoms. Truly the referendum vote of 22 September 1951 was a critical moment for freedom in Australia. It should not be forgotten.[41]

Yet, despite the breadth of Dr. Evatt's achievements which have not been surpassed by any other Australian, despite being the one who stood virtually alone between the civil liberties of the Australian citizen and the establishment of a police state, he is now largely forgotten in his own country and his reputation has been permanently sullied by implacable enemies who pursued him to the grave and beyond. (See Chapter Four: *Herbert Vere Evatt*).

41 Michael Kirby (13 August 2001). 'A Forgotten Constitutional Jubilee: The Fiftieth Anniversary of the Defeat of the Referendum on Communists and Communism in September 1951'. *University of Adelaide Law School.* <http://www.michaelkirby.com.au/images/stories/speeches/2000s/vol48/2001/1736-FORGOTTEN_CONSTITUTION_JUBILEE.doc> Accessed 28 May 2022.

CHAPTER EIGHT

The Gouzenko Affair

Section 1: A Genuine Defector

In Ottawa on 5th September 1949, a Russian cipher clerk, Igor Gouzenko, defected from the Russian Service and sought asylum in Canada. According to Canada's Human Rights History site:

> On the evening of 5 September 1945, a young, frightened Russian cipher clerk who worked in the Soviet embassy in Ottawa left his office with several top-secret documents hidden under his coat. Igor Gouzenko carried a terrible secret, one that he hoped would buy him asylum: evidence that a Soviet-led spy ring was operating in Canada. [42]

Gouzenko's defection and the contents of his documents caused enormous concern for the security of Canada and its American and British allies.

News of the discovery of the Soviet spy operation was withheld from the public until 3rd February 1946 when American journalist Drew Pearson broke the story. The next day, Canadian Prime Minister William King informed his Cabinet of the Gouzenko Affair for the first time. On 15th February 1946, the Canadian Government announced the establishment of a Royal Commission.

Investigations by the Royal Commission confirmed the existence of a spy ring which was aimed most particularly at obtaining atomic secrets:

> Gouzenko's stolen documents identified approximately twenty Canadians and Americans as Soviet assets with varying levels of placement and access in government, the military and academia. The Soviets' American assets included Alger Hiss and other highly placed officials. Also betrayed by Gouzenko's documents were the British nuclear scientists Alan Nunn May and Klaus Fuchs, and Canadian Member of Parliament Fred Rose. One of Fuchs' contacts, Harry Gold, also confessed and named as a fellow Soviet asset David Greenglass, Ethel Rosenberg's brother who in turn implicated the Americans

42 'Gouzenko Affair'. *Canada's Human Rights History* <https://historyofrights.ca/history/gouzenko/2/> Accessed 18 June 2022.

> Julius and Ethel Rosenberg in Soviet atomic espionage. [43] (Julius and Ethel Rosenberg were executed for treason in 1953.)

Gouzenko's defection is often cited as marking the commencement of the Cold War.

Section 2: The Resurrection

The sequence of events recorded below tells its own story. Note the use made of the press by the U.S. State Department.

The Canadian Government had given Gouzenko a new identity and had protected him since his defection in 1946. Without warning, in March 1953, the entire front cover of the U.S. magazine *Coronet* featured the sensational headline: 'Startling! Exclusive! Stalin sent me to spy school' by Igor Gouzenko. The article, as told by Gouzenko to Ann Fromer, appeared on pages 85-92. [44]

It begins with an editorial introduction:

> Late one night in the code room of Soviet spy headquarters for North America, Igor Gouzenko put a carefully prepared plan into action. He slipped 109 secret documents into the lining of his coat. Then he walked out of the building—the Soviet Embassy in Ottawa—for the last time.
>
> Why did Gouzenko voluntarily change his allegiance to democracy? What single incident convinced him that the Soviet cause he was serving was false?
>
> In this article are the answers. Here, for the first time, Igor Gouzenko tells the story of one of the most sinister adventures of our time. —The Editors.

The article then continues with Gouzenko's account:

> My name is Igor Gouzenko. My two children have never heard that name. Nor have our neighbors in the community where we now live quietly as Canadian citizens.
>
> Fewer than a dozen people—my wife, myself, and a tight-lipped handful of Royal Canadian Mounted Police and FBI officials—share the secret. Only they know that the man I now am was the Russian intelligence officer who made a decision which was to change the course of today's history—and tomorrow's.

43 Jens, Erik D. (2015) 'The 'Great Gouzenko: Political, Intelligence, and Psychological Factors in the Defection That Triggered the Cold War'. *American Intelligence Journal,* vol. 32, no. 1, p. 191. JSTOR, <http://www.jstor.org/stable/26202119> Accessed 27 Jun. 2022.

44 Igor Gouzenko as told to Ann Fromer. (March 1953). 'Stalin sent me to spy school'. *Coronet Magazine*, David. A. Smart: Chicago, pp. 85-92.

> …I brought with me 109 highly incriminatory documents. These, and my personal testimony of activities I participated in both in Moscow and Ottawa, added up to an incredible blueprint of Soviet espionage, reaching into the heart of every nation.

Consider the following excerpt, supposedly in Gouzenko's own words, which betrays an in-depth knowledge of U.S. foreign policy and values which reflect those which the U.S. government wished to portray on the international stage:

> However, to understand why espionage continues unabated, an American must understand: First, that the violation of another country's private affairs is as much an instrument of Soviet policy as is the Monroe Doctrine an instrument of American policy. Second, that in the Soviet system, Americans are dealing with a people whose training, whose thinking, whose very conception of right and wrong, of international morality, are utterly contrary to their own.

Gouzenko also tells of his assassination fears:

> Today my wife Anna (Svetlana) and I are under sentence of death, pronounced in absentia by the Military Tribunal in Moscow.

The story was picked up and referenced for months by many other press outlets. The first question that should have been raised is this: why did some "tight-lipped" official leak Gouzenko's identity to the publishers of *Coronet* and sensationalise his story seven years after his defection?

Section 3: Cloak and Dagger

A long series of events which strained U.S.-Canadian relations commenced on 26th October 1953 with the *Chicago Tribune*'s publication of a front page article titled 'Reds Still Spying in US, Exposer warns'.

The article stated that Gouzenko gave an 'exclusive interview' from a 'Town in Canada' to *Tribune* reporter Eugene Griffin and that the interview had been conducted in 'circumstances of cloak and dagger secrecy'. The article is headed 'Sen. McCarthy talk sought by Gouzenko':

> "Senator McCarthy is doing important patriotic work," Gouzenko said. "If he or Sen. Jenner (R. Ind.) or their committees feel that I may be of assistance in their anti-communist investigations, I would be glad to help. I think a talk with them would be worthwhile".

Gouzenko again spoke of his fear of discovery:

> "We are more fearful for our children than for ourselves," Gouzenko said. "The most important thing is secrecy, to keep our friends from knowing who we really are because their talk would spread." [45]

The question must also be asked: what inducements was Gouzenko offered by the editors of *Coronet* magazine and the *Chicago Tribune* to place himself and his wife in jeopardy if they indeed feared for their lives?

Another article by Eugene Griffin headlined 'Gouzenko Suggests Sen. McCarthy Meet Him Privately' appeared in the *Chicago Tribune* edition of 28th October. This article, datelined Ottawa, Oct. 27, states that neither the Canadian Government nor the Royal Canadian Mounted Police were aware of Gouzenko's dealings with representatives of the U.S. media until it was reported in the Canadian press:

> While Gouzenko and his wife and children are protected by the mounties, he is not at all times in their presence. The interview was arranged thru one of his new friends who are aware of his identity.
>
> Canadian papers today reported Justice Minister Stuart Garson as saying that he and **the mounties had no knowledge of Gouzenko's meeting** with the reporter until they read the story.[46]

Therefore the 26th October *Tribune* story, two days before, had made the following incorrect assertion:

> When she and Gouzenko came to meet this reporter, they left their children at home in **care of mounties**, who pose as something else in the Gouzenko neighbourhood.

Section 4: Nothing to see here

On 17th November 1953, the Hon. Lester Pearson, Canadian Secretary of State for External Affairs, addressed the Canadian House of Commons. His statement included the following:

45 'Reds still spying in US, Exposer Warns'. (26 October 1953). *Chicago Tribune*, Robert. R. McCormick: Chicago, Illinois, pp.1-2.

46 'Gouzenko suggests Sen. McCarthy Meet Him Privately'. (28 October 1953). *Chicago Tribune*, Robert. R. McCormick: Chicago, Illinois, p. 6.

As honorable members may know, the government on October 29 received a request from the United States government transmitting a request from Mr. Robert Morris, counsel for the United States Senate internal security subcommittee, to interview Igor Gouzenko in this country. These requests arose out of a statement which Mr. Gouzenko was reported to have made to the reporter of the *Chicago Tribune* to the effect that he had some further information, and that he would be glad to appear before the United States Senate subcommittee. When this report appeared in the press the Royal Canadian Mounted Police immediately interviewed Mr. Gouzenko to ascertain whether he had such additional information since, if he did, this information should have been passed on to the Canadian authorities and that part of it, if any, of interest to the appropriate United States authorities would have been forwarded to them.

... When interviewed, Mr. Gouzenko informed the R.C.M.P. that **he had no further information to offer** other than that which had already been reported by the royal commission some years ago. He further stated to the R.C.M.P. that he had been **misquoted** by the *Chicago Tribune*, and he denied that he had criticized the manner in which his evidence had been used. In the circumstances the Canadian government, Mr. Speaker, considered that the reasons for Mr. Morris' request to interview Mr. Gouzenko had disappeared, having been based on a misunderstanding of the position.

I might add, Mr. Speaker, that any information from Mr. Gouzenko which could have been of value to the United States authorities had originally been forwarded to them as soon as it became available...[47]

Section 5: The Refusal

The Canadian Government declined to make Gouzenko available on the grounds that the *Chicago Tribune* article had misrepresented Gouzenko's position.

On 19th November, Canadian Member of Parliament Mr. J. Diefenbaker asked Pearson if the government was likely to change its decision given pressure from news reports that the U.S. government was renewing its application?

To which Pearson responded:

47 The Hon. Lester Pearson (17 November 1953). *Canadian Hansard.* The Linked Parliamentary Data Project (LiPaD), University of Toronto. <https://www.lipad.ca/full/1953/11/17/3/#1739185> Accessed 3 September 2022.

> I can only say in reply to the question that **notwithstanding press reports to the contrary,** no such second request has yet been made to the Canadian government. If such a request were made I should think that, **unless it included new information and new factors bearing on the case there would be no reason to change the decision already made.**[48]

Section 6: The McCarthyite Circus

In a speech to the Canadian Parliament on 23rd November, Mr. David Croll delivered a damning indictment of McCarthyism and those McCarthyites who were attempting to use Gouzenko in furtherance of their own agendas. Mr. Croll's speech deserves to be read in full but space dictates just the following extracts:

> The spectacle of what McCarthyism has done to our good neighbours to the south has been a source of sadness and concern to thinking people everywhere. No one will disagree that subversives in government are despicable and should be cleared out, as they have been in this country; but to do this in an atmosphere of popular hysteria and to make it a combination of witch hunt and a three-ringed circus is to debase the functions of democracy and prevent the carrying out of the true processes of law.
>
> So long as McCarthyism stayed at home we remained silent on the principle that the domestic affairs of a country were that country's problem. But the situation has changed. The McCarthyites are no longer content to pour their malice on their fellow citizens; they want to throw mud across the border at Canada. They have singled out as their first candidate the Secretary of State for External Affairs (Mr. Pearson).

During his speech, Mr. Croll referenced several Canadian newspaper reports which were critical of attempts to smear Mr. Pearson using the usual McCarthyite tactics. He then continued:

> Now, by trying to smear the minister they hope to blackmail this government into handing over for their purposes and for their use Igor Gouzenko, who is a ward of the government, in order that he may provide for them another act in their variety show. As things stand now they have pretty well used up all their ammunition but they figure that Gouzenko will keep them on the front page for

48 Ibid. 19 November 1953. < https://www.lipad.ca/full/1953/11/19/1/> Accessed 3 September 2022.

at least another month. To accomplish that, they have not hesitated to smear a distinguished member of this house and of the Canadian government.

I find it rather amusing that suddenly a great clamour has come from the various cat's-paws of McCarthyism for the production of Gouzenko in order that he may be used as new exhibit No. 1. I am quite sure that until a few days ago not one of them had ever heard his name or known of his existence. Now, all of a sudden, they have become authorities on the subject. They know all about Gouzenko and the valuable information they suggest he is so eager to give. What they are trying to do is to use a little blackmail on the government.

Before we lose sight of Gouzenko—and we should lose sight of him for everybody's good, including his own—let us remember one or two important things. On November 17, 1953, the Secretary of State for External Affairs (Mr. Pearson), speaking on the orders of the day, made two things abundantly clear. **The first thing was that Gouzenko himself said he had no information other than that reported in the royal commission on June 27, 1946, which is available to everyone for one dollar**, and I am sure that the congressional committee can afford it. The second thing was that any information which could have been of value to the United States authorities or to any of our allies had originally been forwarded to them as soon as it became available.

It is important to note that the whole transcript of his evidence, not what appeared in the report of the royal commission but a full transcript of his evidence, was sent to the United States government and other governments if they were concerned. I think that this house should recall that for the last seven years Mr. Gouzenko has not been in contact with spies. His bosom friends have been the R.C.M.P., and they have been good friends.

The McCarthyites now want Igor Gouzenko to join the circus and do some one-night stands on television...Gouzenko is manna from Heaven to them.

...What is important is that now for the first time we have a deliberate attempt to export McCarthyism to Canada. I am glad to say that up until now that vicious ideology has not been able to gain a foothold in this country. The big lie and the big smear have never had a place in Canadian politics; and, as the saying goes, we aim to keep it that way. But these purveyors of fear and hate overlooked the fact that a boundary line divides North America into two sovereign countries, and I repeat the expression "sovereign countries". When the United States state department—and I am sure with considerable reluctance—asked that the congressional committee be permitted to question Gouzenko, the request was turned down for a good reason. The last thing we in this country

> want is to get ourselves involved in an American political hassle, for that is what it essentially is.
>
> The rejection filled the McCarthyites with uncontrollable rage. How dare anyone have the temerity to say no to them? *The New York Times*, a very reliable paper, says that pressure is being exerted by the state department on the Canadian government to give ground. In order to attain their purpose, they have turned their guns on the minister, secure in the knowledge that he could not reply.
>
> ... A second request for Igor Gouzenko has been made by Washington. This reveals the **power of McCarthyism** in the American political life, for a request is usually not renewed once it has been declined.[49]

On 21st November 1953, despite all evidence to the contrary, the *Chicago Tribune* upheld the veracity of its article of 26th October.[50]

On 25th November, Lester Pearson, the Canadian Secretary of State for External Affairs, traced the steps by which the situation had developed. He reiterated that:

> The Canadian government of course fully appreciate the importance of the closest possible co-operation between the Canadian and United States governments in exchanging information important to the national security of both countries. It has therefore long been our practice, and remains our practice, that security information should be exchanged on a confidential basis, which should be respected on both sides, between the competent authorities responsible for the internal security of our two neighbouring countries.
>
> In accordance with this principle all information which Mr. Gouzenko has at any time presented to the Canadian government has been placed at the disposal of the responsible United States authorities as it became available. Moreover, facilities are and always have been extended to these competent United States government authorities to clarify any point arising out of any of Mr. Gouzenko's evidence or information at any time they may wish to do so.
>
> The federal bureau of investigation in Washington therefore has always had access to Mr. Gouzenko's special knowledge as and when requested. We have

49 Ibid. 23 November 1953. < https://www.lipad.ca/full/1953/11/23/3/> Accessed 4 September 2022.

50 'Big Story Is Just Beginning, He Tells Tribune'. (21 November 1953). *Chicago Tribune*: Chicago, Illinois, p. 1.

been glad to have for years a liaison officer of the F.B.I. in Ottawa, just as there has been an R.C.M.P. officer in the same capacity in Washington.[51]

Section 7: The Backdown

On 26th November 1953, the Canadian Government finally yielded to the **"power of McCarthyism"** and granted Washington's renewed application to interview Gouzenko with the following stipulations:

> "...The Canadian Government is willing, if Mr. Gouzenko agrees, to make arrangements for a confidential meeting, *under Canadian auspices*, at which any person designated by the United States Government could be present, it being understood...that the evidence or information thus secured would not be made public without the approval of the Canadian Government.[52]

In January 1954, six years after publication of his book, *The Iron Curtain*, and nine years after his defection, the U.S. Ambassador to Canada, Douglas Stuart, and two senators, William Jenner and Pat McCarran journeyed to Canada to question Gouzenko, ostensibly on matters of importance to the U.S. Senate Sub-Committee on Internal Security of the Judiciary Committee. (See Note on McCarran)

On 4th January 1954, Mr. J.G. Sourwine, counsel for the United States representatives, questioned Gouzenko at a meeting chaired by Chief Justice J. C. McRuer of the Supreme Court of Ontario.

As is clear from the meeting transcript, the Chairman repeatedly objected to the line of questioning from counsel for the United States representatives, saying that the information they were seeking was already known to the relevant authorities in the United States:

> ...the government of Canada appointed a royal commission to examine Mr. Gouzenko very exhaustively with reference to all matters within his knowledge and the results of that examination were passed to the relevant authorities in the United States.[53]

51 The Hon. Lester Pearson (25 November 1953). *Canadian Hansard.* The Linked Parliamentary Data Project (LiPaD), University of Toronto. < https://www.lipad.ca/full/permalink/1739884/ > Accessed 6 September 2022.

52 *The Ottawa Journal,* The Journal Publishing Company: Ottawa. 26 November 1953, p.6.

53 'Testimony of Former Russian Code Clerk Relating to the Internal Security of the United States'. U.S. Government Printing Office: Washington, 1955. Original: *The Ohio State University* (Moritz Law Library), p. 11.

It was a prior stipulation of the meeting that if any information were discovered, then it would not be divulged to any person except with the express consent of the Government of Canada. [54]

Since Gouzenko had already been "exhaustively" questioned at the Canadian Royal Commission and the Soviet assets exposed and dealt with years before, it is not surprising that nothing of any value whatever remained to be disclosed.

Note

Senator Pat McCarran was the principal sponsor of the US *Internal Security Act* of 1950. This legislation, also known as the *Subversive Activities Control Act* or the *Concentration Camp Law* required Communist organisations to register with the federal government.

Section 8: The Delay

Although the Canadian Government had offered in late January to release the 4th January meeting transcript to U.S. authorities, Mr. Roch Pinard, Parliamentary Assistant to the Canadian Secretary of State for External Affairs, said no response had been forthcoming by 16th February:

> ...After the meeting the Canadian authorities examined the transcript of the proceedings in order to determine whether there was any reference either in the questions or in the answers, publication of which in this context might jeopardize Canadian security investigations or might prejudice unfairly the reputation of individuals or organizations in Canada or might be open to question on grounds of international propriety, as relating primarily to the interests of a friendly third country.
>
> With the exception of a few words in the transcript-in fact, there were about two or three sentences comprising about 30 or 35 words-which fell within one or other of these categories, the Canadian government saw no objection from its point of view to making the transcript public if the United States government so wished. The Canadian government did not, however, consider that it would be appropriate to make the transcript public unless the United States government requested that this action be taken, since the inquiry related directly to names of persons in the United States or to the internal security of the United States.

54 Ibid. p. 6.

> The Canadian government therefore informed the United States government in the latter part of January that it was prepared to make public the transcript with or without any further deletions, if the United States government wished this done. Up to the present time no further word has been received from the United States government on this question.[55]

In late January 1954, the American journalist Drew Pearson had conducted a televised interview with Gouzenko who wore a pillowcase over his head so he could not be identified. The interview made world headlines. Despite Australian press statements to the contrary, the Canadian Government was not approached nor consulted in any way about the interview. On 1st April 1954, the following question was asked in the Canadian Parliament:

> Did the Canadian government, or anyone on behalf of Canada, concur in arrangements for Igor Gouzenko to appear on a TV program with Mr. Drew Pearson on an American network? [56]

To which question, the Hon. Stuart Garson, Minister of Justice and Attorney General of Canada replied—No.

Although the Canadian Government had made the offer in late January, it was not until the 13th April that Justice Minister Garson announced that the Canadian Parliament had "this month" received a note from the U.S. Government requesting release of the 4th January interview transcript. The request was granted. Minister Garson went on to say:

> ...it will not be surprising to members of the house that the transcript of Mr. Gouzenko's evidence at this January 4 meeting discloses very little-if indeed there is any information not already available to the public.[57]

---

55 Mr. Roch Pinard (16 February 1954). *Canadian Hansard.* The Linked Parliamentary Data Project (LiPaD), University of Toronto. < https://www.lipad.ca/full/1954/02/16/4/#1750013 > Accessed 8 September 2022.

56 Hon. Stuart Garson (1 April 1954). *Canadian Hansard.* The Linked Parliamentary Data Project (LiPaD), University of Toronto. < https://www.lipad.ca/full/1954/04/01/2/#1759620 > Accessed 12 September 2022.

57 Ibid. 13 April 1954.

Section 9: Serendipity

On 13th April 1954, the very same day as Stuart Garson announced to the Canadian Parliament that the Gouzenko transcript was now publicly available, Menzies announced to the Australian Parliament that Vladimir Petrov had defected.

The timing of both Menzies' announcement and the 4th January 1954 questioning of Gouzenko indicates a foreknowledge in the United States of coming events in Australia. The intent was to reinforce and authenticate the Petrov defection by apparent similarities with the Igor Gouzenko case and to provide a recent precedent for the establishment of the Australian *Royal Commission on Espionage.*

Several pointers serve to index the real nature of what was attempted by the U.S. State Department:

- The issue was opened up by a newspaper article which was then used as a lever by the U.S. State Department in its initial approach to Canada;
- The 4 January 1954 interview with Gouzenko added no new information whatsoever to what had been common knowledge for years. At least a third of the interview was taken up with suggestions, prompted from Gouzenko, as to how to induce further defections, the offering of money to achieve this purpose, and the treatment which should be accorded any such defectors. His suggestions are striking in light of subsequent developments in Australia;
- The long delay throughout February and March and the sudden request in April for the release of the January 4 interview transcript;
- This delay served to bring public attention to both Gouzenko and Petrov at the same time, facilitating case comparisons by a compliant media.

Section 10: Playing the Game

Australian newspapers such as Brisbane's *The Courier Mail* were more than willing to play the game for Menzies:

> When in 1945 a member of the Russian Soviet Embassy staff in Canada, Igor Gouzenko, sought political asylum in Canada and offered to disclose all he knew concerning the organisation and activities of an espionage system directed from the Soviet Embassy, the Canadian Government appointed a Royal Commission to examine him and investigate his evidence. Australia's Federal

> Government is confronted with a similar situation, and Mr. Menzies' instant decision to follow the Canadian precedent will have national approval…[58]

On the same day, *The Sydney Morning Herald* Editorial drew readers' attention to:

> …a distressing similarity to the initial disclosures of Igor Gouzenko in Canada…[59]

Unlike the gullibility or otherwise of *The Sydney Morning Herald* Editor, the dissimilarity between the defections of Petrov and Gouzenko was pointedly explained by Dr. Evatt on 28th October 1954 in an address to Federal Parliament:

> …The truth has not come out, but it is coming out. Instead of it being a Gouzenko case, it is the very reverse. Instead of Petrov seeking asylum and being in danger, he was under Security observation; he was under cultivation for two years before April this year. He never had any real intention of going back to Russia from before two years ago. Dr. Evatt said it is "just absurd" to say that Petrov's life was in danger in Australia. Petrov was nothing like Gouzenko, but was a man determined under the appropriate circumstances to stay in Australia.[60]

At the Royal Commission, the references to Gouzenko began immediately:

1. The activities in Australia which Petrov has discovered to us are a quite remarkable counterpart of what happened in Canada... (Windeyer T:8, 17th May 1954);
2. The similarity of the system operating in Canada and that operating in Australia is quite striking as one gets to know the whole story (Windeyer T:11, 17th May 1954);
3. To Mr. Justice Owen, George Ronald Richards of ASIO said the organisation had closely studied Igor Gouzenko's defection in Canada;[61]

58 'Inquiry on Russians'. *The Courier Mail* (Brisbane, QLD), 14 April 1954, p. 2.

59 'Communist Espionage in Australia'. *The Sydney Morning Herald* (NSW), 14 April 1954, p. 2.

60 'Dr. Evatt Address' (28 October 1954). *Historic Hansard.* House of Representatives, 21st Parliament, 1st Session. <https://historichansard.net/hofreps/1954/19541028_reps_21_hor5/#subdebate-28-0> Accessed 14 October 2024.

61 'Doctors Helped Study Petrov: Inquiry Evidence'. *The Sydney Morning Herald* (NSW), 8 September 1954, p. 4

4. The phrase "in the net" expressed a key idea in both Gouzenko and Petrov (T:951pa166, 17th September 1954);

5. I submit that the Gouzenko proceedings should not be invoked as any corroboration of Petrov's story, but on the contrary, my submission is that they constitute one of the bases on which his story has been erected (T:1122pa622, E.F. Hill);

6. Then I submit that the whole process of code names, of secret meeting places, of this belief that the MVD did this particular work, the process of studying people, of getting them into the net, was well known to Bialoguski from the Australian Security Service and from the Gouzenko Report (T:1116pa444, E.F. Hill).

In making submissions 5 and 6, Mr. Hill (counsel for Rupert Lockwood), was asserting that conspirators had brought the *Petrov Papers* into being. Petrov and Dr. Michael Bialoguski of the Australian Security Intelligence Organisation were the prime suspects.

The Gouzenko case echoed and re-echoed on countless occasions through the Royal Commission proceedings, ultimately to find its way into the final Report (R:7pa17, R:4pa64).

Note

(See Chapter Nine: *Operation Petrov* for list of abbreviations.)

CHAPTER NINE

Operation Petrov

Australians are entitled to reach the conclusion that Australian newspaper editors know no history, know no philosophy, know nothing of public administration, know no ethics and know no bounds.

Operation Petrov is the name given to the 1951-1954 Australian Security Intelligence Organisation operation which was launched with military precision upon an unsuspecting Australian public in April 1954, some weeks before the May 1954 Federal election. It should go down in historical annals as the embodiment of viciousness, vindictiveness, extent and cunning.

The Operation, conceived by ASIO in July 1951, was launched on 19th March 1954. On that day, George Ronald Richards, the Deputy Head of ASIO, met with a staff member of the Russian Embassy in Canberra, Vladimir Mikhailovich Petrov. At that meeting, one of twelve such meetings between the pair, Richards enticed Petrov to defect by showing him the sum of £5,000 pounds.

On 2nd April 1954, Petrov signed a statement seeking asylum in Australia. The next day, 3rd April, he was paid the agreed sum of £5,000 pounds. On 4th April 1954, officers of ASIO visited the Prime Minister with documents allegedly delivered to them by Petrov.

Of all this three-year activity, the Australian people remained blissfully unaware.

Note

Although it has been claimed by various sources that ASIO's plan for Petrov's defection was named 'Cabin-12', evidence given at the Royal Commission reveals that it was named *Operation Petrov* (T:823).

Section 1: Abbreviations and Major Characters

- R: *Report of the Royal Commission on Espionage*, 1955.
- T: *Transcript of Daily Proceedings of the Royal Commission on Espionage*, (1954-1955).
- ASIO: Australian Security Intelligence Organisation.

- Bialoguski, Dr. Michael: Petrov's Security Service contact from July 1951 to April 1954.
- Dalziel, Alan: a member of Dr. Evatt's staff.
- Evatt, Dr. Herbert Vere: Leader of the Australian Labor Party and of the Federal Opposition.
- Grundeman, Albert: a member of Dr. Evatt's staff.
- Ligertwood, George Coutts: Royal Commissioner.
- Lockwood, Rupert: Journalist.
- Owen, William Francis Langer: Chair of the Royal Commission.
- Ollier, Madame Rose M. Second Secretary of the French Embassy in Canberra.
- O'Sullivan, Fergan: Press Secretary to Evatt from 1st April 1953 to 4th June 1954.
- Petrov, E.A. and V.M.: Members of the Russian Embassy staff, Canberra 1951-54.
- Philp, Roslyn Foster Bowie: Royal Commissioner.
- Richards, George Ronald: Deputy Head of ASIO in charge of *Operation Petrov*.
- Spry, Colonel Charles Chambers Fowell: Director of ASIO.
- Windeyer, William John Victor: Commonwealth Counsel assisting the Royal Commission.

Section 2: Operational Objectives

The prime objectives of *Operation Petrov* were:

- To destroy opposition to Prime Minister Menzies agenda and ensure his victory in the May 1954 election;
- To execute a plan conceived at least fifteen months previously to destabilise Dr. Evatt and impugn his reputation thereby ensuring his early removal from office in the event he became Prime minister after the May 1954 election;

- To hand the policy-making apparatus of the Labor Party to the Santamaria forces within that party so that the current policy of non-interference in the domestic affairs of foreign nations would never be implemented;
- To open the way for Australia to collaborate with the United States and intervene in Indo-China when France lost control of its colonies of Vietnam, Cambodia and Laos;
- To set up a McCarthy-style Tribunal disguised as a Royal Commission which would operate in a similar fashion to that in the United States.

Section 3: Operational Timeline

The following timeline is based primarily on the *Transcript of Daily Proceedings of the Royal Commission on Espionage* and the *Report of the Royal Commission on Espionage.*

February 1951

5th February: The Petrovs arrive in Australia from London aboard the *Orcades* (T:326). A Security watch was instituted immediately. The idea of remaining in Australia first occurred to Petrov in 1952 (T:260).

July 1951

7th July: Security Officer, Dr. Michael Bialoguski, makes contact with Petrov (T:902, T:968).

January 1953

28th January: Santamaria's publication, *News Weekly*, predicts developments connected with Petrov (T:958, T:1014).

February 1953

Journalist Fergan O'Sullivan applies for a position on Dr. Evatt's staff.

April 1953

1st April: Fergan O'Sullivan begins work with Dr. Evatt as an employee of the Prime Minister's Department.

May 1953

May 1953: Mrs. Petrov is photographed sitting next to Fergan O'Sullivan during a film evening at the Russian Embassy (evidence given at Commission on 31st August 1954). [62]

5th May: Petrov notified that he is to return to Russia on 17th July (T:135). This information became known to Security in the same month (T:999).

19th May: Petrov treated for an eye condition by Dr. Halley Charles Beckett, an opthalmic surgeon with offices in MacQuarie St. Sydney (T:736, T:763).

21st May: Russian Embassy film evening for Embassy staff.

22nd May: Petrov admitted to Canberra Hospital (R:420).

22nd May: At 3:45 p.m., Rupert Lockwood arrives in Canberra.

22nd May: Drinking rendezvous between O'Sullivan, Grundeman and Lockwood.[63]

22nd May: Russian Embassy film evening for the press. (See Note)

23rd May: O'Sullivan invites himself and Lockwood to a meal at a residence where Albert Grundeman was staying.

24th May: Grundeman leaves Canberra at 7 p.m. and arrives in Sydney at 9 p.m.

25th May: O'Sullivan living in Evatt's house while Evatt is in England attending coronation of Queen Elizabeth II. Lockwood leaves Canberra.

29th May: O'Sullivan still in Canberra.

30th May: Petrov discharged from hospital.

June 1953

19th June: Bialoguski searches Petrov's wallet.

July 1953

July 1953: Petrov picked up from Sydney's Mascot aerodrome by Fergan O'Sullivan who is driving a Federal Government vehicle.

17th July: Petrov fails to return to Russia.

---

62 'Petrov was "Almost Mad'. *The Sydney Morning Herald* (NSW), 1 September 1954, p. 4.

63 'Lockwood on Information in "J"'. *The Sydney Morning Herald* (NSW), 25 August 1954, p. 8.

17th July: Security approach Dr. Beckett. Dr. Beckett, with whom Dr. Bialoguski shared rooms in Sydney's MacQuarie Street, sounds out Petrov as to his intentions (T:763, T:737, T:763).

22nd July: Evatt returns from England.

23rd July: Petrov visits Security agent Beckett again.

September 1953

1st-12th September: Bialoguski is interviewed by Geoffrey Yeend, Menzies' private secretary, about reimbursement for his Petrov activities (TPS138-40) [64]

November 1953

20th November: Mrs. Evdokia Petrov sacked from her Embassy employment (T:737).

December 1953

1st December: Security Conference in Canberra to discuss Petrov's impending defection (T:737).

Bialoguski takes Petrov to inspect a poultry farm near Sydney and pays a deposit for which he is reimbursed by the Security Service.

January 1954

23rd January: Meeting between Petrov, Bialoguski and Beckett.

February 1954

17th February: Security circulates instructions to Commonwealth Department heads to receive Petrov if he approaches their offices (T:963).

20th February: Petrov fails to attend scheduled meeting with George Ronald Richards, the Security Officer in charge of *Operation Petrov* (T:740). Later, he is said to have been preparing documents for handing to Security.

27th February: Through the agency of Security agent Beckett, Petrov meets George Ronald Richards of ASIO for the first time (T:740). Twelve such meetings were held between Richards and Petrov (T:736-T762).

64 Bialoguski, Michael. *The Petrov Story*. Heinemann: Melbourne, 1955, p. 122. 140.

March 1954

19th March: Richards shows Petrov the sum of £5,000 at Bialoguski's flat in Sydney.

20th March: First mention of documents. First meeting between Petrov and Richards with no third party present.

April 1954

2nd April: Petrov signs application for asylum.

3rd April: Petrov defects from the Russian Service in Sydney (T:752) and is paid £5,000. At the time of his defection, Petrov had been scheduled to leave Australia by sea on 8th May.

4th April: Colonel Charles Spry (Head of ASIO), George Ronald Richards (Deputy Head of ASIO) and an interpreter visit Prime Minister Menzies with Petrov's documents in hand (T:760, T:923,T:1104). Menzies "handles" document 'J'.[65]

19th April: Mrs. Petrov flies from Sydney's Mascot airport bound for Darwin. (See Chapter Eleven: *Incident at Mascot.*)

20th April: Mrs. Petrov defects from the Russian service. As a result of events which take place in Darwin, the Soviet Union breaks off diplomatic relations with Australia.

Notes

At the Commission hearings of 14th July 1954, Mr. Petrov admitted that he had met Fergan O'Sullivan several times and in July 1953 had been picked up from Sydney's Mascot aerodrome and driven to "town" in O'Sullivan's Federal Government vehicle.[66]

Section 4: Zero Hour

Zero Hour for *Operation Petrov* was 8.00 p.m. on 13th April 1954, less than 24 hours prior to the termination of the 20th Federal Parliament. To a surprised Opposition, and an equally surprised Australia, Prime Minister Menzies announced Petrov's defection. In the same statement, he announced his intention to appoint a Royal Commission to investigate espionage.

65 'Petrov Wanted Job on Land'. *The Courier Mail* (Brisbane, QLD), 9 September 1954, p. 6.

66 'Journalist says he was author of Document J'. T*he Sydney Morning Herald* (NSW), 15 July 1954, p. 4.

The significant points in Menzies' announcement were:

1. Vladimir Petrov—a member of the staff of the Russian Embassy—had defected;
2. Documents had been delivered by Petrov to the Security Service;
3. These documents revealed the "outlines of systematic espionage";
4. Australians named in the *Petrov Papers* were referred to under the cover of code names;
5. A Royal Commission was to be appointed to investigate the Soviet espionage revealed in the documents. This course been decided on by Cabinet Ministers to whom Menzies had revealed Petrov's defection on the same day.

Viewed in retrospect, the one remarkable omission from the announcement is the fact that Petrov had been paid £5,000 on 3rd April 1954. No mention was made of this payment by Menzies. The omission was all the more remarkable in that Petrov included a pointed request for assistance in the statement which Menzies read to Parliament:

> "I wish to become an Australian citizen as soon as possible and I ask for protection for myself and assistance to establish myself comfortably in this country".

The leader of the Opposition Labor Party, Dr. Evatt, was not in Parliament at the time of the announcement—he had left at 5:30 p.m. for a gathering at Fort Street High School in Sydney. It was his 60th birthday. Menzies' timing of the launch of *Operation Petrov* was impeccable.

Parliament terminated within 24 hours of Menzies' shock announcement. In that time, approval had been given for the setting up of a Royal Commission. In giving this approval, Parliament was entirely dependent upon the integrity of Menzies—he alone had sighted Petrov's documents.

During the 111 days from Parliament's termination on 14th April until its next sitting on 4th August, the Australian public was delivered into the hands of the press. There was no opportunity for parliamentary oversight of any of Menzies' actions, including the terms of reference of the *Royal Commission on Espionage,* the appointment of Commissioners on 3rd May, or of his interactions with the Australian Security Intelligence Organisation and other involved parties. Dr. Evatt was deprived of the platform that Parliament could otherwise have afforded him.

Section 5: No Bounds

When Prime Minister Menzies announced Petrov's defection and the setting up of a Royal Commission on 13th April 1954, a blitzkreig propaganda campaign orchestrated by Menzies and his press allies swung into action with a barrage of reports which did not specify their sources of information but gave vague attributions such as: hints by Cabinet Ministers; speculations by Canberra officials; legal opinion in Canberra, and so forth.

The arrogance of the press is perhaps best illustrated by *The Sydney Morning Herald* editorial of 19th April. The editorial writer saw fit to give Dr. Evatt, a jurist of international reputation, a lesson in jurisprudence. [67]

Periods of crisis demand detached and objective reporting. In the artificially created crisis of the Petrov era, this is exactly what Australia did not receive. The Australian press enjoyed the rights of a free society but declined to accept its obligations. The immediate interests of the press—destruction of the Australian Labor Party as a political force and removal from politics of Dr. Evatt—overrode other considerations. Evatt's altruism was misrepresented as egotism and his fight to preserve a free society as a fight to preserve himself politically. The press professed itself unaware of any threat to the free society—except from communism.

Australians are entitled to reach the conclusion that Australian newspaper editors know no history, know no philosophy, know nothing of public administration, know no ethics and know no bounds.

Section 6: Hoisting the Flag

Both inside and outside Parliament, the Santamaria group within the Labor Party revealed its first public move in a long-range strategy aimed at having Australia assist the U.S. in preserving the interests of the Catholic Church in Vietnam.

When Parliament resumed on 4th August after the 1954 May election, John Mullens, a member of the Santamaria group, posed a question:

> Is the Prime Minister aware that there is an almost complete unawareness in this country of the full implications of the position in Indo-China, including the facts that the frontier of the Red Empire is now nearer to Australia, and

67 'Bringing the Petrov Case into Party Politics'. *The Sydney Morning Herald* (NSW), 19 April 1954, p. 2.

that 1,000,000 Christians in Indo-China have been delivered into terror and tyranny?...[68]

Outside Parliament, Catholic newspapers and periodicals such as the Melbourne Catholic *Advocate* and Santamaria's *News Weekly* were similarly alarmed. For example:

> Million Catholics face crisis in Indo-China: The greatest sell-out of Christian people since Poland may now threaten the Catholics of North Vietnam, writes Father Patrick O'Connor, National Catholic Welfare Council Correspondent at Hanoi, on the current armistice negotiations between the French and the Communist Viet Minh forces.
>
> Last week's withdrawal in the Red River delta—the biggest of the Indo-China war—left a million Catholics in Communist hands and drew a strong protest from the new Catholic Vietnam Premier, Ngo Dinh Diem. (A.A.P., 3 July.) [69]

Michael Costigan, former Executive Secretary to the Bishops' Committee for Justice, Development, Ecology and Peace wrote of Santamaria's personal involvement in the Catholic struggle against Vietnam's communists. In September 1957, Santamaria sponsored South Vietnam President Ngo Dinh Diem's official visit to Australia. In April 1963, Santamaria also sponsored a visit to Australia by Diem's brother, Bishop Ngo Dinh Thuc. Costigan writes:

> ...Santamaria and I met occasionally at functions, one memorable occasion being a closed gathering of Catholic editors, organised by Santamaria in April 1963 at the Essendon headquarters of the Columban Fathers, to hear and question the visiting Archbishop Ngo Dinh Thuc of Hue, Vietnam. The historian Val Noone reports on this clandestine meeting in *Disturbing the War* (Spectrum Publications, 1993, page 80). The visitor's upbeat description of the struggle with the communists in his country was also covered in the *Advocate* (18th April 1963).
>
> The claim in the headline, probably composed by me, that the Church was flourishing in spite of the communist threat, makes odd reading when it is recalled that, on 2nd November 1963, barely six months after Thuc's visit

68 John Mullens (4 August 1954). *Historic Hansard.* House of Representatives, 21st Parliament, 1st Session. <https://historichansard.net/hofreps/1954/19540804_reps_21_hor4/#debate-11> Accessed 28 May 2024.

69 *Advocate* (Melbourne, Victoria), 8 July 1954, p. 3.

to Australia, his brother, President Ngo Dinh Diem, himself a previous Santamaria-sponsored Australian visitor, was assassinated in Saigon. [70]

Section 7: Evidentiary Summary

As already noted in Chapter Eight: *The Gouzenko Affair*, the U.S. State Department had begun its preparations for Petrov's defection in October 1953 when it applied pressure on the Canadian Government to resurrect the former Russian spy, Igor Gouzenko, from his oblivion of the previous 8 years. This disinterment of Gouzenko was necessary to provide an authenticating principle in advance for the material that Petrov was to 'deliver' to Australian Security representatives. The evidence yet to be presented will demonstrate that:

1. The Australian Security Service had been busy throughout 1953 preparing the *Petrov Papers* and adapting them into Russian. They were then delivered to Petrov on the eve of his long awaited defection. For £5,000 pounds and promises of more, Petrov agreed to say that he brought these documents from the Russian Embassy.
2. The persons who were named in the *Petrov Papers* were those who would have been summoned to appear before a McCarthy-style tribunal if its establishment had not been thwarted by the failure of Menzies' 1951 Communist Party Dissolution Bill and the subsequent Referendum. The Petrov defection and subsequent Royal Commission enabled the government to circumvent the rejection of the Referendum proposals.
3. The three Inquisitors—Justices Owen, Ligertwood and Philp—were aware at all times that the documents 'delivered' by Petrov, the documents which constituted the sole basis for the Royal Commission coming into existence, were forgeries. A possible alternative, that all three judges were completely incompetent, is untenable.

Note

It is beyond the scope or intent of this work to examine the minutiae of all the varied and conflicting strands of evidence contained in the *Transcript of Daily Proceedings of the Royal Commission on Espionage*. Therefore, only the evidence which best demonstrates the manifest absurdity of the claim that Petrov brought the *Petrov Papers* from the Russian Embassy will be addressed.

70 Costigan. M. (2015). 'B.A. Santamaria: Remembered by one who knew him a little'. *Journal of the Australian Catholic Historical Society* vol. 36 pp. 163-64.

CHAPTER TEN

A Couple of Rabbits

On 6th April 1954, just seven days before Menzies announced Petrov's defection, the Government's chances of being returned at the May 1954 election were slim according to *The Sydney Morning Herald*:

> The Liberal Party is hoping that the Prime Minister, Mr. Menzies, will pull a couple of rabbits out of the top hat which he wore with such assurance during the Royal tour. It looks as if he will have to do so if his Government is to survive the election in May. [71]

Section 1: The first rabbit

The first rabbit Menzies pulled from his top hat was the Petrov defection and the resulting establishment of the *Royal Commission on Espionage.*

Throughout the election campaign, Menzies' political supporters continually linked Dr. Evatt and the Australian Labor Party with Petrov and communism while his media supporters blanketed the country in an avalanche of conjecture and hysteria about the existence of 'fifth columns' and the breadth of Soviet hostility towards Australia. For example, on 18th May 1954, the second day of sittings of the Royal Commission, *The Courier Mail*'s banner headline read: 'Russian Secret Service had Five Aims in Australia: Plans included fifth column'.[72]

Section 2: The second rabbit

Although most political analysts of the period claim that because the Petrov defection wasn't highlighted by Menzies during the election period and therefore had little impact on voters, they fail to take into account the deep-seated fear of communism already inculcated into the minds of Australians.

71 'Pre-Election Session: A Test Of Party Leaders' Form'. *Sydney Morning Herald* (NSW) 6 April 1954, p 2.

72 'Russian Secret Service had Five Aims in Australia: Plans included fifth column'. *The Courier Mail* (Brisbane, Qld), 18 May 1954, p. 1.

They also fail to recognise that Menzies' deliberate policy of appearing to stand above the fray of petty party politics was to foster a carefully calculated public image acceptable to the majority of Australians and to the governments of the United States, Canada, and the United Kingdom.

What political analysts of the period have also failed to understand or take account of is that Menzies could afford to project a statesmanlike image to the world precisely because, whatever the election outcome, he had another rabbit ready to pull out of his top hat. That rabbit was foreknowledge of the contents of Document J which, according to Security Agent Richards, Menzies had "handled" on 4th April, nine days before Petrov's defection. [73] (See Chapter Twenty: *Document J.*)

If, therefore, Menzies lost the election and the Labor Party under Dr. Evatt were to take the reins in May, Evatt's reputation would be so shredded by Document J disclosures to come from the Royal Commission that there would be a crisis of confidence in the Government. Menzies would then call for a double dissolution of both Houses of Parliament and would certainly regain office once a compliant press heralded his return as a saviour from the 'communist' menace. (See Chapter Fourteen: *Nailing the Coffin.*)

Section 3: The Breeders

The character assassination of Dr. Evatt was channelled through his former press secretary Fergan O'Sullivan. (See Chapter Nineteen: *Document H.*)

Journalist O'Sullivan was a member of *The Sydney Morning Herald* staff at the time the 6th April article was published.

At the *Royal Commission on Espionage,* it was revealed that Dr. Michael Bialoguski (Petrov's main security contact) had approached *The Sydney Morning Herald* in the closing months of 1953, mentioned the name "Petrov", and offered to write articles outlining his experiences (T:998pa1147).

Thus, seven days before Petrov defected, two leading figures in the Petrov Fraud were, or had been, associated with *The Sydney Morning Herald* in some capacity.

O'Sullivan certainly knew of the pending defection as he had placed himself close to Evatt in preparation (see *Document H*). Bialoguski certainly knew of the pending defection as he had been grooming Petrov since 7th July 1951 and, as Mr. E.F. Hill, counsel for Rupert Lockwood said of the 6th April article at the *Royal Commission on Espionage*:

73 'Petrov Wanted Job on Land'. *The Courier Mail* (Brisbane, QLD), 9 September 1954, p. 6.

> I submit that the rabbit was bred by Dr. Bialoguski as part of a conspiracy. Dr. Bialoguski is a very good judge of the market.[74]

It was also revealed by Bialoguski himself that on 8th May 1953, eleven months before Petrov defected, he had approached Harry Mullin, the U.S. Vice Consul in Sydney, and offered his services to the U.S. on a matter of international importance. [75]

We need hardly be told what the matter was. His services were declined as events were proceeding according to a defection timeline and had almost a year yet to run. (See Chapter Nine: *Operation Petrov.*)

Section 4: The Election Campaign

On 24th May, *The Courier Mail* left no doubt in readers' minds as to its loyalties by featuring a large election campaign advertisement, the wording and emphasis of which is reproduced below:

> During eight years of Labour Government in Canberra – the Communist Conspiracy was the greatest threat to Progress and Security. **Don't give the Reds a second chance.** Remember that Labour's history of appeasement of the Reds fermented class warfare, promoted strikes, arrested Australia's development. The Menzies Government defeated the Communist Conspiracy. **What happened in 1949 could happen again if Dr. Evatt were Prime Minister.**
>
> Dr. Evatt was the Red's advocate in the Arbitration Court. Dr. Evatt was a bitter opponent of the Secret Ballot Legislation that has destroyed Red Power in the unions. Dr. Evatt was Attorney General when Red sabotage was undermining the Australian economy. **Communism is a world menace. It could become a menace in Australia again if Dr. Evatt runs true to form. Return the Menzies Government on May 29th.**[76]

The picture was completed by a photo of Menzies as opposed to a hammer and sickle.

By ceaseless repetition, a compliant press conditioned the minds of Australians to react in a given way whenever the term 'Communism' was mentioned. 'Communism' came to signify everything that was odious, impious, undemocratic and unpatriotic. Australians were conditioned to respond accordingly.

---

74 'Petrov's Evidence on Documents True, says Judge'. *The Sydney Morning Herald* (NSW), 30 September 1954, p. 7.

75 Bialoguski, Michael. *The Petrov Story*. Heinemann: Melbourne, 1955, p. 122.

76 *The Courier Mail* (Brisbane, Qld), 25 May 1954, p.7.

The May 1954 election campaign was fought by allies of Menzies on three principles—doubt, fear and confusion. Doubt of Evatt, fear of communism, and confusion of the issues. In this assault on the people's minds, priest, press, politician, and certain members of the judiciary, all played key roles. Modelling the Reichstag fire principles resulted in Menzies' final victory, but only by a slender majority.

CHAPTER ELEVEN

Incident at Mascot

Section 1: Kidnapped

The day following Menzies' announcement on 13th April that Petrov had defected, his wife Evdokia gave an press interview at the Soviet Embassy in Canberra with the consent of the Soviet Ambassador, Mr. N.I. Generalov:

> Before consenting, Mr. Generalov consulted his Press Attache. Then he went to a telephone and a few minutes later Mrs. Petrov entered the Ambassador's room. Asked if she had elected to stay with the Soviet Embassy, Mrs. Petrov said: "Yes".
>
> "It is difficult to speak now", she said. "I don't believe my husband would go to your country like this. I don't think he would do this himself. I think he has been kidnapped.
>
> "He had to come to Canberra on April 6. He did not come. I am sure he is kidnapped and what the papers write today is only a lie".
>
> Mr. Generalov and his Press Attache, who were seated at a table with Mrs. Petrov, nodded their heads when she said, "I am sure he is kidnapped".
>
> Mrs. Petrov continued: "1 think it is a lie because if it wasn't a lie he would be given permission to meet an official of the Embassy. I am sure he wants to speak to officials of the Embassy. I think he will try and get in touch with me. He wouldn't leave me because we married each other. He never did what has happened now". [77]

Following this press conference, speculation mounted as to when Mrs. Petrov might return to Moscow, speculation which was further fuelled by the transmission of a letter from Mr. Petrov to the Soviet Embassy asking to see his wife alone at a place and time to be determined by Australian authorities. Fearing a trap, Mrs. Petrov refused.

77 '"He is kidnapped", says Petrov's Wife'. *The Sydney Morning Herald* (NSW), 15 April, 1954, p. 1.

Section 2: The Press Legend

Meanwhile, the press had discovered that flight bookings for the 19th April had been made for Mrs. Petrov and three other Soviet officials to leave for Moscow via Sydney, Darwin and Singapore. The press and Australian government officials insisted that Mrs. Petrov was being taken from Australia against her will and even hinted at her receiving severe punishment.[78]

Therefore, by the time the Soviet party reached Sydney's Mascot airport on the evening of the 19th April, the public hysteria whipped up by the press resulted in the presence of a large anti-communist crowd of eastern Europeans and so-called 'white Russians' readied for a fight. The tactics of the Australian press are highlighted by *The Sydney Morning Herald's* dramatic account of the scene accompanied by an equally dramatic photo of two Russian men holding between them a weeping Mrs. Petrov:

> **"I Do Not Want To Go"**
>
> One thousand struggling, fighting and screaming people at Kingsford Smith Airport (sic) last night attempted to stop Mrs. Evdokina Petrov from returning to Russia.
>
> ...Police, security officers, and airport officials fought for eight minutes to get Mrs. Petrov on to the plane's gangway. Hundreds of screaming, struggling people booed a Russian courier, Mr. V. Karpinsky, and an Embassy official, who were with Mrs. Petrov. New Australians in the crowd shouted that Mrs. Petrov was screaming in Russian: "I do not want to go".
>
> ...Mr. Karpinsky and the Russian Embassy official dragged Mrs. Petrov, who was weeping and dazed, for 200 yards along the tarmac and pushed her up the gangway. About 20 people clung to the side of the gangway and punched at Mr. Karpinsky and the Embassy official and two uniformed airport officers who were helping to drag Mrs. Petrov aboard the plane.
>
> When Mrs. Petrov reached the top of the gangway the crowd pulled it away from the side of the plane. Mrs. Petrov, the two Russian men, and the two airport officers balanced for a minute on the narrow, swaying platform 15 feet above the ground before police could push the gangway back.
>
> As Mrs. Petrov was dragged through the plane's doorway about 20 people began swarming after her up the steps.

78 'Mrs. Petrov's "Crime" In Eyes of Soviet Law'. *The Sydney Morning Herald* (NSW), 19 April 1954, p. 2.s

> The Russian courier, Mr. Karpinsky, one of Mrs. Petrov's escorts, was punched and kicked frequently in the melee and the Russian commercial attache, N. Kovalev, another escort and a small man, received a continuous battering.[79]

The melee at the airport also frustrated ASIO since they had hoped to confront Mrs. Petrov with her husband who had been brought to Mascot concealed in the back of a utility van (Evidence of Security Officer G.R. Richards at T:774,775).

The Soviet Ambassador, Mr. N.I. Generalov arrived at Parliament House the next day to lodge a protest note upon receiving reports from Darwin:

> He (Generalov) was immediately taken to the office of Sir Philip McBride, who is acting as Minister for External Affairs…
>
> …Mr. Generalov told Sir Philip that his Embassy had received reports from Darwin that there had been an armed assault on the Russian diplomats and the two couriers.
>
> He said, "I present now the most energetic protest against the armed assault on the Russian diplomatic courier and on the compulsory detention of the Soviet official, Mrs. Petrov".
>
> Sir Philip McBride told Mr. Generalov that the Embassy would be given a formal reply when the Government had received all information.
>
> He said, as a preliminary reply, that he had received a report that Mrs. Petrov had voluntarily sought the protection of the Australian Government.
>
> Sir Philip added: "It is reported to me, that when Mrs. Petrov, Mr. Kislitsin and the two couriers alighted from the plane, certain Australian officials offered to engage the party in conversation. The Deputy Administrator of the Northern Territory was present. While the conversation was proceeding, Australian officials observed a menacing movement by one of the couriers, who possessed a loaded pistol. The second courier was found to be similarly armed. The weapons were removed by the officials of the Northern Territory responsible for keeping peace. After the removal of the weapons the couriers were allowed to move at will".[80]

Only after Mrs. Petrov had spoken to her husband from Darwin did she refuse to continue her journey to Russia and only after she had seen and talked to him face to face in Sydney did she sign her own formal application for asylum.

---

79 'Officials Drag Mrs. Petrov Into Aircraft: "Help Me" Appeal to Crowd Reported'. *The Sydney Morning Herald* (NSW), 20 April, 1954, p. 1.

80 'Russians Quick to Lodge Protest'. *The Sydney Morning Herald* (NSW), 21 April, 1954, p. 1.

Section 3: The Evidentiary Reality

The demonstrable facts are as follows:

- Mrs. Petrov left Sydney's Mascot aerodrome bound for Darwin in the evening of 19th April 1954;
- Demonstrators were allowed onto the tarmac area and even pulled the passenger steps from the side of the aircraft (T:658pa1061);
- A press photographer travelled on the aircraft and the press carried a moment by moment description of events (T:658pa1032-1065);
- Mrs. Petrov boarded the aircraft with two couriers who had arrived from Russia. These couriers left Russia before Petrov defected and were on normal Embassy business (T:186pa340);
- Newspapers carried headlines that Mrs. Petrov called for help in Russian, yet Mrs. Petrov spoke fluent English. It was demonstrated conclusively that she did not call for assistance (T:646pa471, T:658pa1065);
- On 12th July 1954, when testifying at the *Royal Commission on Espionage*, Mrs. Petrov admitted that her sole concern was to board the aircraft at Mascot airport and get back to the Soviet Union. She had been frightened of the crowds and believed that the Russian couriers were protecting her and helping her to safely board the aircraft; [81]
- At Darwin, as part of a pre-arranged plan, Mrs. Petrov was deliberately separated from the Russian couriers; [82]
- The couriers, who enjoyed diplomatic immunity, were manhandled and disarmed by Australian police; [83]
- The Russian Embassy Second Secretary, F. Kislitsin, protested vehemently at their treatment saying that "Couriers have the right to carry guns. You are willing to break international diplomatic immunity. Couriers have diplomatic personal immunity". [84]

81 'Lockwood Refuses to Answer Questions'. *The Sydney Morning Herald* (NSW), 13 July 1954, p. 4.

82 'Mrs. Petrov Chooses Australia'. *The Sydney Morning Herald* (NSW), 21 April 1954, p. 1.

83 'Mrs. Petrov's Terror Ends'. *The Courier Mail* (Brisbane, QLD), 21 April 1954, p.1.

84 Ibid.

At the Royal Commission, Mrs. Petrov told a harrowing story of events at the Russian Embassy between the time of Petrov's defection and the Mascot flight. Dr. Evatt's circular cross-examination subsequently manoeuvred her into revealing that the harrowing details were imaginary. Subsequent to Dr. Evatt's appearance at the Commission, there is no support whatsoever in the Transcript for the press legend of the Mascot flight.

Section 4: The CIA and the Flight of Fancy

The part played in the Petrov Affair by the Central Intelligence Agency and the United States State Department is evidenced by the blackmail of Canada over the Gouzenko Affair. (See Chapter Eight: *The Gouzenko Affair.*)

According to CIA director, Allan Dulles, Petrov's defection was of surpassing importance:

> The Soviets had suffered an enormous setback in Australia in 1954 when the KGB resident Vladimir Petrov, defected ... [85]

George Ronald Richards, the Security officer in charge of *Operation Petrov,* claimed that ASIO was in constant liaison with the Security services of friendly countries (T:757pa367). These security services obviously included the CIA.

On 8th May 1953, eleven months before Petrov defected, Dr. Michael Bialoguski, the main Security contact with Petrov, approached Harry Mullin, the U.S. Vice Consul in Sydney, and offered his services to the U.S.A. on a matter of international importance.[86] We need hardly be told what the matter was. His services were declined as events were proceeding according to a defection timeline and had almost a year yet to run. (See Chapter Nine: *Operation Petrov.*)

Allan Dulles also commented on the flight of Mrs. Petrov from Mascot to Darwin on the night of 19th April 1954:

> The reader may recall the sensational news photos in 1954 which showed Soviet thugs strong-arming the wife of defector Vladimir Petrov, KGB chief in Australia, in an attempt to get her on a plane and take her back to Russia against her will. Only the quick intervention of the Australian police stayed Mrs. Petrov from being abducted.[87]

85 Dulles, Allen. W. *The Craft of Intelligence.* Harper and Row: New York, 1963, p. 166.

86 Bialoguski, Michael. *The Petrov Story.* Heinemann: Melbourne, 1955, p. 122.

87 Dulles, Allen. W. *The Craft of Intelligence.* Harper and Row: New York, 1963, p. 139.

Section 5: The Consequences

On 23rd April 1954, Russia demanded the recall of all Australian diplomats from Moscow as a result of the Petrov Affair and announced that the Russian Ambassador and all other diplomatic staff in Australia had been ordered back to the Soviet Union. The main reasons were:

- the refusal by the Australian Government to hand over the self-confessed spies and traitors, Vladimir and Evdokia Petrov;
- the Australian Government's unquestioning acceptance of the claim that documents were taken from the Russian Embassy in Canberra;
- the flagrant violation of international diplomatic immunity by the Australian authorities;
- the assault on the Russian courier and the Russian commercial attache at Mascot airport and the forcible detention and disarming of the Russian couriers when they and Mrs. Petrov disembarked in Darwin.

This severing of diplomatic ties made international front page news. [88]

Section 6: The Best Man

The potential consequences of the severing of diplomatic ties with Russia during the crucial years of the Cold War, and other events connected with the Petrov Affair, were beyond the capacity of Prime Minster Menzies to manage without support. From beginning to end, he was assured of the backing of the CIA and the U.S. State Department.

In 1965, when the decision was made to send Australian combat troops to Vietnam, Menzies had made himself so dependable in U.S. eyes that, even before receiving a response from Australia to a request for ground troops, the U.S. Special Assistant for National Security, McGeorge Bundy, sent President Johnson a Memo on 8th April 1965 specifically asking Johnson to send Menzies a letter of appreciation. The Memo read:

> "Sir Robert Menzies has been **the best man of all on Vietnam** in recent weeks. A good sample is his performance with some Australian Bishops attached at

88 'Soviet Break with Australia'. *The Guardian* (London), 24 April 1954, p. 1.

Tab A in a note from the Australian Ambassador. But you will have seen other statements in the Press.

"I thought you might want to send him something short and sweet like the letter at Tab B. I have changed the his title to "Dear Sir Robert" to make it a little more informal, and which I thought you might like, but it can be done the other way if you prefer and there is also a "Dear Prime Minister" letter attached". [89]

89 Folder, 'McGeorge Bundy, Vol. 9, March-April 14, 1965 [1 of 2]', Memos to the President, NSF, Box 3, *LBJ Presidential Library* <https://discoverlbj.org/item/nsf-memos-b03-f01> Accessed 2 February 2026.

CHAPTER TWELVE

The Royal Commission

Section 1: The Structure

The Australian Royal Commission is very much like the British Tribunal described in 1967 by Lord Salmon, a Lord Justice of Appeal:

> The Tribunal's Inquiry is inescapably inquisitorial...there are no pleadings defining the issues to be decided, no charges, no indictments or depositions. It is therefore difficult for persons to know in advance of the hearings what allegations may be made against them...The inquisitorial powers necessarily conferred upon Tribunals expose the ordinary citizen to the risk of having his private life uncovered which would otherwise remain private and to the risk of having baseless accusations made against him in public thereby causing him much distress and pain.[90]

The Royal Commissioners took full advantage of the latitude provided by this structure as evidenced by their declaration during the proceedings that their judicial offices and oaths imposed upon them no particular obligations (T:379-381).

Section 2: First Strike

A flurry of intentionally confusing press and radio reporting opened the way for allies of Menzies to suggest that the Royal Commission should commence before the May election just to "clear the air". Hence, the first sittings which opened in Canberra's Albert Hall on 17th May, presented the media with another platform from which to bombard the electorate. The intemperance of media attacks on Dr. Evatt is infamous.

Counsel for the Commonwealth, William John Victor Windeyer QC, was appointed counsel for the Commission and K.H. Herde, an official seconded from the Prime Minister's Department, was appointed Secretary.

90 Salmon, 1967, as cited in Dunne, M.G.L. 'The Royal Commission on Espionage, 1954-1955' (December 1979), p. 78. *University of Adelaide* < https://hdl.handle.net/2440/22500> Accessed 8 June 2023.

On 17th May, the first day of sittings, Windeyer gave a carefully crafted opening address intended to make the most of what would be placed before the Commission. In the politically-charged atmosphere of the upcoming election, Windeyer announced to a primed media that the Commission would deal with "**treasonable activities, espionage**, and **other grave matters**".[91]

However, and clarified only with hindsight, there were certain nuanced remarks which placed the emphasis on attempts at Soviet espionage rather than their actual success and played down the significance of the *Petrov Papers* as actual espionage documents.

Windeyer also made a few procedural remarks and officially handed over the so-called 'Moscow Letters' to the Commissioners (T:3-21). He proposed that the services of a Major Arthur Herbert Birse from England be retained as official translator of both the documents and the testimony to be given by the Petrovs. Major Birse had been appointed supposedly because he was not involved in Australian politics. However, he was hardly an apolitical functionary having been recommended by ASIO and, once in Australia, had been wined and dined by Prime Minister Menzies. In December 1954, for example, he had addressed the Royal Empire Society on the threat to capitalism posed by the Soviet Union despite its talk of peaceful co-existence.[92]

On 18th May, more documents were handed over to the Commissioners including the English language Documents H and J and the G series. (See Chapter Thirteen: *The Petrov Papers*). Windeyer stated that from the evidence contained in the documents, together with that to be provided by the Petrovs, a clear distinction between ordinary Soviet diplomatic activity and Soviet espionage in Australia would emerge.

George Ronald Richards, the Deputy Head of ASIO, who had enticed Petrov on 19th March by showing him the sum of £5,000, and paying him his reward money on 3rd April for claiming he brought the *Petrov Papers* from the Russian Embassy, gave evidence at the Commission on 18th May but neglected to mention that money had changed hands.

Most notably, Windeyer asserted that the evidence would reveal the existence of a spy-ring which had operated some years before in the Department of External Affairs. A willing press sensationalised Windeyer's remarks about a "spy-ring"and created the impression that he had revealed a Soviet espionage operation in Australia

91 'Russian Secret Service Had Five Aims In Australia'. *The Courier Mail* (Brisbane, QLD), 18 May 1954, pp. 1, 3.

92 "Red Policy Has Never Changed" *The Sun News-Pictorial*, Melbourne (VIC), 7 December 1954, p. 2.

in which communists were involved. It was a short step to link Communists with treason.

The Commission sat for only 20 minutes on 19th May and then adjourned until June. This brief period dealt mainly with the correspondence which had passed between the Australian Department of Foreign Affairs and the Russian Embassy concerning the Petrovs.

Throughout the first sittings from 17-19 May, the Petrovs were presented by Windeyer to be innocent people who had fled the persecution of Soviet Communism. They must, therefore, be credible witnesses. An illusion was maintained that Petrov's defection had been sudden and shattering. The truth concerning ASIO's dealings with him over a period of three years was yet to be revealed.

The dominant impression given at the first sittings was that Australia had been gravely menaced by Soviet espionage. The public were led to believe that startling revelations were to come at the June sittings after the 29th May election.

Section 3: The Inquisitors

Prime Minister Menzies was personally responsible for the selection of Commissioners William Francis Langer Owen (Chairman), Roslyn Foster Bowie Philp and George Coutts Ligertwood, judges of the New South Wales, Queensland and South Australian Supreme Courts respectively.

Victoria rightly declined to make a judge available on the basis that former Victorian Chief Justice, Sir William Irvine, had established the proper function of the Judiciary, which was not to be drawn into the region of political controversy lest it lose the confidence of the people:

> The duty of his Majesty's Judges is to hear and determine issues of fact and of law arising between the King and a subject, or between subject and subject, presented in a form enabling judgment to be passed upon them and when passed to be enforced by process of law. There begins and ends the function of the judiciary.
>
> It is mainly due to the fact that, in modern times at least, the Judges in all British communities have, except in rare cases, confined themselves to this function, that they have attained and still retain the confidence of the people.[93]

93 Winterton, G. 'Judges as Royal Commissioners'. *University of New South Wales Law Journal*, Vol. 10, 1987, p. 109 < https://www.unsw.edu.au/content/dam/pdfs/law/unsw-law-journal/1980-1989/Vol-No-10-1-11.pdf> Accessed 22 May 2026.

Section 4: Refining the Methods

In modern western democracies, it is no longer acceptable to use methods favoured by the Spanish Inquisition and Hitler's Gestapo. However, it is still possible to destroy lives using more subtle, and in some ways more effective, methods such as those that were on display during the *Royal Commission on Espionage*.

The Charade

The *Royal Commission on Espionage* was a charade designed to create a respectable *façade*. It was founded on the logical fallacy that if the Commissioners proved Petrov's documents to be factually accurate, they also proved them to be authentic. Accuracy is not a guarantee of authenticity. A document can be accurate in every respect and still be forged. This operational fallacy prevented the authenticity of Petrov's documents from ever being tested.

The Pattern

The pattern of Inquisition conveys a very clear impression of what Menzies and his instrument, the Australian Security Service, would have attempted had Menzies received the totalitarian powers he sought in the 1951 referendum. The Inquisitors received their list of heretics, not direct from the Security Service as would have occurred in 1951, but in the form of the *Petrov Papers.*

The Obstructionism

Evidence was produced piecemeal: no clear picture was allowed to emerge. Each counsel was restricted to the area of his own client's interests. The Commissioners asserted the sufficiency of security records available to them which counsel could never see or test. Most counsel entered the Commission during its progress as and when their clients were named. These counsel were to a large extent in the hands of the Commissioners.

The Burden of Proof

Dr. Evatt, labouring under all these disadvantages, challenged the authenticity of the documents. The Commissioners placed Evatt in the position of being required to demonstrate that the documents were forged, thereby reversing the burden of proof.

The Shields

The Commissioners had three shields: the alleged need for secrecy where Security was concerned; the need to retain documents relating to persons not yet named; and the superior status they enjoyed as Royal Commissioners. They used whatever shield was appropriate for the occasion.

The Double Standards

Double standards were employed on many occasions. For example, in the case of Madame Rose Ollier (see Chapter Sixteen: *Madame Ollier*), hotel bookings which proved her innocence were ignored whereas in the case of Rupert Lockwood, alleged author of the Commission's Document J, the Commissioners were pleased to use hotel bookings as evidence against him.

The Nomenclature

Misleading nomenclature was used throughout. Photographs produced by Petrov were called the 'Moscow Letters'. The Commissioners referred to these photographs as 'originals' (R:44). Besides being nothing more than photographs, the question of whether they had in fact originated in Moscow was never asked or investigated.

The Game Players

The Australian press created a respectable *façade* for the Commission and played along with the charade from beginning to end, denigrating any who questioned its methods but reserving its most venomous commentary for Dr. Evatt.

The tactics and techniques of the press throughout the crucial period following Menzies' shock announcement of Petrov's defection would well repay a detailed study. Assertions, imputations, innuendos, anonymous sources, pseudo-authoritative sources, irrelevancies, over-emphasis, the conveying of judgements instead of facts by means of careful choice of language, selective reporting...the list goes on and on.

Consider just one sentence from Brisbane's *The Courier Mail* of 14th April 1954, the day after Petrov's defection:

> But Cabinet yesterday morning was alarmed at the *prima facie* evidence of a spy ring centred in the national capital, operated by a foreign Power, and allegedly using Australians as agents.[94]

The Royal Commission failed miserably to live up to the startling revelations hinted at in the article. It failed miserably to uncover any "*prima facie*" evidence of the "spy ring" operated by a "foreign power" and no Australians were charged or convicted of being foreign "agents".

As noted elsewhere, periods of crisis demand detached and objective reporting. In the artificially created crisis of the Petrov era, this is exactly what Australia did not receive. The Australian press enjoyed the rights of a free society but declined to accept its obligations. The immediate interests of the press—destruction of the Australian Labor Party as a political force and removal from politics of Dr. Evatt—overrode other considerations. Evatt's altruism was misrepresented as egotism and his fight to preserve a free society as a fight to preserve himself politically. The press professed itself unaware of any threat to the free society—except from communism.

Australians are entitled to reach the conclusion that Australian newspaper editors know no history, know no philosophy, know nothing of public administration, know no ethics and know no bounds.

Note

Over a period of 10 months, the Commission sat on 126 days in 3 venues, examined 119 witnesses, and received over 500 exhibits, including the documents that Petrov allegedly handed Australian authorities following his defection (the *Petrov Papers*). It published almost 3,000 pages of transcript.

An interim report dealing with the authenticity of exhibits H and J, two of the *Petrov Papers*, was presented to the Governor-General on 21st October 1954. (See Chapter Twenty-Three: *The Interim Report.)*

94 'Prime Minister Orders Royal Commission: Russian Spies Here'. *The Courier Mail* (Brisbane, QLD), 14 April 1954, p. 1.

CHAPTER THIRTEEN

The Petrov Papers

Section 1: The Origin

An analysis of the physical form and scope of the documents reveals that the documents could have originated from sources possessing the following:

- Access to a Russian typewriter and to photographic facilities;
- The services of a typist skilled in Russian;
- The services of a person who could write Russian;
- Access to information of a security nature relating to Australian citizens who had had dealings with Russia, or who were connected with the Australian Department of External Affairs, or with the Australian Communist Party between 1945 and 1954.

The conditions are satisfied equally by only two sources—the Australian Security Service (ASIO) and the Soviet Union's Ministry of Internal Affairs (MVD).

Section 2: The Physical Form

The documents consisted of:

a. 101 photographs of Russian typewriting;

b. 17 supplementary pages handwritten in Russian by the Petrovs;

c. 9 lists of names handwritten in Russian by others;

d. 9 lists of names handwritten in Russian by the Petrovs;

e. 37 carbon copy pages of typewriting in English;

f. 3 typewritten pages in English.

The English-language material was said to have originated in Australia and will be discussed later (See Documents H and J). The possibility of forging the rest of the material is immediately obvious—there was not one single original Russian Embassy document.

Section 3: Principle of Interpretation

The information contained in the documents related to persons in Australia. No communication from Canberra to Moscow was produced: all the information on Australians purportedly came from Moscow.

This situation is so obviously the reverse of the natural and normal order of affairs that it suggests as a very first principle of interpretation that all the references in the documents be reversed to restore normalcy. When this is done it becomes clear that the documents are actually Australian Security Service documents adapted into Russian.

Section 4: Commission Terminology

The documents were described at the Commission in terms which concealed their real nature:

a. The 101 photographs of Russian typewriting became the 'Moscow Letters';
b. The 17 supplementary pages handwritten in Russian by the Petrovs became the 'deciphered list of insertions' in the Letters;
c. The 9 lists of names handwritten in Russian by others became part of the 'G series of documents';
d. The 9 lists of names handwritten in Russian by the Petrovs became the other part of the 'G series of documents';
e. The 37 carbon copy pages of typewriting in English became 'Document J';
f. The 3 typewritten pages in English became 'Document H'.

Section 5: Scope and Contents

The Russian language documents (a—d above), allegedly were, or arose from, instructions received from Moscow by the Russian Embassy in Canberra. These documents dovetailed to provide a list of the names of people who—strangely enough—had aroused the interest of the Australian Security Service between 1945 and 1954.

Insurmountable difficulties would arise from the fact that Petrov produced documents relating to events which occurred prior to his arrival in Australia in 1951.

Section 6: The Pre-emptive Strike

Three days after Menzies' shock announcement of Petrov's defection came the pre-emptive strike designed to blunt opposition to any claims that the Petrov documents were forgeries.

A *Sydney Morning Herald* front page article of 16th April titled 'No bid by Russians to see Petrov: May claim files are forgeries' included the following:

> The Soviet Press Attache, Mr. G.I. Kharikovetz, today denied any files were missing. He laughed over the telephone and said, "There is not a thing missing. All the Embassy documents are here."
>
> It is believed that Mr. Kharikovetz's statement indicates that **the Russians will claim that the documents are forgeries** when they are produced at the Royal Commission.

The article then continues:

> Australian officials said tonight that the claim that no Russian Embassy documents are missing might literally be true. As the chief Russian Secret Police official in Australia, Petrov was in a class apart from other diplomatic representatives, they said.

These unidentified 'Australian officials' go on to make a ludicrous claim about a man who was not a 'Russian Secret Police official', as he claimed, but a simple Third Secretary:

> He probably had his own files, which not even the Russian Ambassador saw.[95]

Even more ludicrous was the suggestion that the files that even the Russian Ambassador knew nothing about were in a "really secret safe":

> It was reported early this morning that Petrov had given the Australian Government a "safe-full of files-the really secret safe from the Russian Embassy."[96]

95 'No bid by Russians to see Petrov: May claim files are forgeries'. *The Sydney Morning Herald* (NSW), 16 April 1954, p. 1.

96 "The Really Secret Safe". *The Sydney Morning Herald* (NSW), 14 April 1954, p. 1.

CHAPTER FOURTEEN

Nailing the Coffin

Section 1: The Focus

On 11th June 1954, after the May election, the *Royal Commission on Espionage* reconvened in Sydney. It soon became clear that the Commission's investigations had undergone a change in direction. Espionage was no longer the point of concern. Much time was occupied in establishing the authorship of, and generally discussing, documents 'H' and 'J'. (See Chapter Thirteen: *The Petrov Papers.*)

Before the June Sydney sittings adjourned to Melbourne, a statement was issued by counsel assisting the Commission:

> Mr. Windeyer said that the first two matters dealt with by the Petrovs in their evidence would be (1) their personal history and their activities and duties as MVD agents and (2) **the discovery of the authors of the documents known as 'H' and 'J'.**
>
> Mr. Windeyer said these two documents were in English and evidence would indicate that they were written by two Australians and that they supplied them to the MVD man at the Russian Embassy.[97]

As will be seen, the author of Document 'H' and the alleged author of Document 'J', the only document that really mattered, were not waiting to be discovered but were already known to the Commissioners, to ASIO, and to Menzies.

Section 2: The Cloak and Dagger Men

The Melbourne sittings of the Royal Commission opened on 30th June 1954 in the High Court Building.

On 6th July, Vladimir Petrov began testifying about his relationship with George Ronald Richards, the Deputy Director of ASIO. The following compilation of the

97 'Q.C. Tells of Spy Plan Pattern: Sydney Hearing Opens'. *The Sydney Morning Herald* (NSW), 12 June 1954, p. 1.

most crucial 1954 interactions between the two men is taken from Petrov's testimony of 6th July [98] and from Richards' testimony of 8th September: [99]

- Petrov met George Ronald Richards 12 times in Sydney and Canberra before he finally defected. In Canberra, they usually met by night in a car, the first time near the home of Kislitsin (Second Secretary at the Russian Embassy);
- On 19th February, Richards met Petrov at Dr. Michael Bialoguski's flat in Sydney and told him about a proposed gift of £5,000;
- On 19th March, Richards again met Petrov at Bialoguski's flat where he showed Petrov the sum of £5,000 pounds;
- On 20th March, Richards met Petrov in a park near Sydney's King's Cross before taking him to a flat at King's Cross;
- On 25th March, Richards *accidentally* met Petrov drinking in a bar at the Kingston Hotel in Canberra. They had a brief meeting and, later that day, Richards arranged a meeting with Petrov which took place in Richards' car;
- On 31st March, Richards and Petrov talked about a party meeting at the Russian Embassy at which he and Mrs. Petrov had been criticised. Petrov told Richards then that he had decided definitely that he would not go back to the Embassy after 3rd April;
- On 1st April, Richards met Petrov at night in a Canberra street. Petrov said his decision to stay in Australia was firm and he would not go back to the Embassy again. Petrov handed over a bag containing personal belongings to Richards;
- Throughout the night of 1st April, Richards and other Security officers patrolled the Russian Embassy and the homes of Embassy officials;
- At 8:30 a.m. on 2nd April, Richards saw Petrov leave his home for Canberra airport carrying a satchel. Petrov and Richards travelled on the same plane to Sydney. They did not sit next to each other, and did not indicate that they recognised each other. When their plane landed at Mascot, they met for a few minutes and arranged a meeting at the Kings Cross (Sydney) Security flat that afternoon;

98 'Petrov Given £5,000 On Day He Left Reds'. *The Sydney Morning Herald* (NSW), 7 July 1954, p. 4.

99 'Petrov Wanted Job on Land'. *The Courier Mail* (Brisbane, QLD), 9 September 1954, p. 6.

- At the Security flat meeting on the afternoon of 2nd April, Richards said that Petrov opened his satchel and took from it documents in two white envelopes. Richards suggested that Petrov should sign his application for political asylum. Petrov said he was very tired and wished to sleep. Richards left him in the flat which was under the observation of Security officers;

- At 6 p.m. on 2nd April, Richards said that Petrov signed the asylum document and at 8 p.m., Colonel Charles Spry (Director of ASIO) arrived at the flat. Two Security officers were within earshot to take shorthand notes of the conversation in case the recording arrangements broke down (microphones had previously been installed in the flat);

- Richards said that Petrov handed the documents which he had previously shown to him to Colonel Spry, who examined them. **The first document Petrov showed them was what was now called Document J**. It interested them because it was in English. Richards said Document J was a group of documents of foolscap size, folded together. They were stapled in sections;

- At 9 p.m. on 2nd April, Richards said that Colonel Spry left the flat. Petrov said he had an appointment to see Bialoguski. Later that same night, Richards received a call from Bialoguski to say that Petrov was with him. Richards then went to see Petrov at Bialoguski's flat and they talked generally about Petrov's decision to stay in Australia;

- On 3rd April, Petrov officially defected from the Russian service. He met Richards at Mascot airport where he was given the promised £5,000.

Note

Petrov claimed to have worked for Russian Military Intelligence (the KI) and gave evidence about its internal workings and structure as proof. However, ASIO was already in possession of this information and one of their officers had prepared a handy reference chart of its structure for the Commissioners (T:83, Exhibit 55). Petrov provided no information on this matter that was not already known to western intelligence agencies.

Section 3: A "highly-paid and important person"

At 12:30 p.m. on 6th July, Mrs. Petrov stepped into the witness box:

> She was wearing a royal blue tailored suit, a white blouse and a close-fitting white hat which accentuated her fair complexion, relieved only by the red line of

> her lips. She seemed very nervous and unsure as she took the oath, repeating the words after the Chairman of the Commission, Mr. Justice Owen, with a slight quiver in her voice.
>
> She quickly regained her composure and showed the sophistication and training which had taken her to the rank of captain in the Russian intelligence service and now, at 40 years of age, to an international celebrity.[100]

The many assertions made in the article about this "international celebrity", particularly that she was a "captain in the Russian intelligence service", rely on no evidence whatever besides that of the Petrovs themselves.

The article continues:

> She spoke fluent English in a barely audible voice with a soft, musical accent, and used the services of the official interpreter, Major A. H. Birse, only when the questions were involved, or for long answers.
>
> She smiled frequently, and laughed gaily as her assurance increased.
>
> Several of Mrs. Petrov's answers showed a keen sense of humour. Questioned as to the cost of a "nice handbag" in Moscow, in an attempt to assess the relative value of her salary as an MVD (Ministry of Internal Affairs) officer, she laughed, and replied: "It is very difficult for me to estimate the cost of a nice handbag in Moscow, because I never had one".

Similarly trivial and gushing press reports at first glamorised her personal appearance:

> The swearing-in was done with deference. Petrova took the Christian oath. That business done, she turned her profile to the body of the court again, and the examination began. As the questions piled up, she continued to stand stiffly upright, the fine small figure precisely tailored in junior navy, a lace blouse buttoned at the throat, a little white cap pressed down on golden curls which escaped around the neck.
>
> To the spectators, she continued to appear in profile, which is her best aspect. High, smooth forehead, Patrician nose, full lips firmly pressed together to give them a neatly curving pout, clean-cut chin and clear neck-line— these are as finely modelled as a face on a Greek medallion.

Before reigning in the enthusiasm a little:

100 'Mrs. Petrov's Search for Agents'. *The Sydney Morning Herald* (NSW), 7 July 1954, p. 1.

> Full-face, the effect is a little further from perfection. The face has a Slavic breadth, though not too much for beauty. The jawline is blurring a little and the downward droop to the mouth suggests bitterness and frustration. She is not unmarked by life. None of which spoils the smile.[101]

The fawning and frivolous reporting of the press successfully drew attention away from any questionable testimony she gave about her life, her family, her claims about working for Russian intelligence, her salary and etc. Since any assertion that she worked for Russian intelligence at the Canberra Embassy could probably be challenged, she claimed not to know her official posting but said that she was the secretary to the Ambassador and bookkeeper to the Embassy.

After hearing from Mrs. Petrov, Mr. Justice Owen and Windeyer joined the press chorus of adulation:

> Mr. Windeyer: Mrs. Petrov was obviously a highly-paid and important person.
>
> Mr. Justice Owen: Obviously.[102]

Section 4: Surprise Attack

The Second Rabbit

(See Chapter Ten: *A Couple of Rabbits*)

On 15th July 1954, a surprise attack, conceived with cunning and duplicity, was executed with ruthlessness by Royal Commission Chair Mr. Justice Owen when he announced that three members of Dr. Evatt's staff had been named on page 35 of Document J as sources of information by the author. Owen went on to say that:

> "... it is very disturbing to find a document of this sort in which the writer claims to have got information from two persons who are in the secretariat of a man who holds a very high position in political life... What disturbs us is that the document quotes as sources on various matters, some of which are of a confidential nature, three members of the secretariat of the Leader of the Opposition..." (T:297-8)

These "three members of the Secretariat of the Leader of the Opposition" were Fergan O'Sullivan, Albert Grundeman and Alan Dalziel. Evatt's connection with

101 'Blonde Petrova, Captain of Spies'. *The Age* (Melbourne, VIC), 7 July 1954, p. 2.

102 'Evidence Given By Mrs. Petrov'. *The Sydney Morning Herald* (NSW), 7 July 1954, p. 5.

Document J through these men was trumpeted by press outlets such as *The Sydney Morning Herald* whose front page blared: 'Three of Evatt's Staff Listed: Alleged Sources in Document J'.[103]

Whether the contents of Document J reflected badly on Evatt or not was besides the point. The intention was to leave the public wondering what kind of man would employ, at one time or another, three informants for the Soviet Union. Dr. Evatt was shocked when he heard of Owen's statement. He questioned his staff who protested their innocence.

Evatt immediately sent a telegram to the Commission expressing his anger that the names of members of his Secretariat had been introduced into the enquiry without warning. He protested that basic procedures of justice were not being observed:

> ...The course taken in naming persons... is quite opposed to the basic procedures of justice which were outlined at certain stages of the Commission. No notice having been given, injury to individuals is immediate and may be irreparable...(T:309).

Regardless of Evatt's protest telegram, the Commissioners announced that Albert Grundeman and Alan Dalziel would be required to give evidence when the Commission reconvened in Sydney.

On 12th August 1954, Dr. Evatt made the following public statement:

> "The Petrov letters" case will rank in Australian history as an equivalent of the notorious Zinovieff letter used to defeat a British Labor Government.
>
> This statement, headed "The Petrov Deal", was made outside Parliament tonight by the Federal Opposition Leader (Dr. Evatt). In the statement, Dr. Evatt accuses the Prime Minister of "making a deal"with Vladimir Petrov "for the purpose of improperly influencing the Australian people at the election".
>
> Dr. Evatt states:—
>
> "One of the keys to the Petrov matter is the payment to Petrov of £5,000 by the Commonwealth Government through the agency of the Security Service.
>
> Four questions arise:—
>
> "Why did not Mr. Menzies inform the people of Australia on April 13—nine days after the payment of the £5,000— that Petrov, who only sought democratic freedom, was paid £5,000 in addition to being granted political asylum?

103 'Three of Evatt's Staff Listed: Alleged Sources in Document J'. *The Sydney Morning Herald* (NSW), 16 July 1954, p. 1.

"Why was this vital fact kept back from the knowledge of the people of Australia from April 4, when the payment was made, until after the general election?

"Why did the Security Service employ an intermediary or intermediaries to bargain with Petrov during 1953, and has any sum of money been paid or promised to this intermediary or intermediaries?

"What financial arrangements have been made for the maintenance of the Petrovs, and what money, property or consideration have they received from the Government or the Security Service, or from persons or corporations outside the Government itself?

"I believe that when the tangled skein of this matter is finally unravelled, the Petrov-Menzies letters case will rank in Australian history as an equivalent of the notorious Zinovieff letter which was used to defeat a Labor Government in the British election of 1924, or the burning of the Reichstag, which ushered in the Hitler regime in 1933".[104]

Evatt's public statement not only targeted Menzies' credibility but also that of the Commissioners and ASIO.

On the same day, Menzies responded in Parliament to Evatt's public statement. *The Courier Mail*'s banner headline read: 'PM, Evatt Clash on Petrov: "£5,000 Deal" charge from Opposition':

> "From 3 days before I made the statement to this house, (13th April 1954) I knew all the names of the people who had been or were associated with the Right Honourable gentleman (Evatt) and whose names were mentioned in the *Petrov Papers* and I remained silent. I remained silent from beginning to end of the election campaign. I thought that was playing the game fairly. The Honourable gentleman does not ask me why I did not in this house on April 13th tell the people the contents of the *Petrov Papers*, because if I did **he would not be here tonight"**. [105]

The inflammatory statements by Justice Owen on 15th July and Menzies on 12th August received corresponding treatment from the press. Sensational headlines dramatised Evatt's link with Petrov through his staff.

104 '"Petrov Deal" Alleged by Dr. Evatt.' *The Advertiser* (Adelaide, SA), 13 August 1954, p. 1.

105 'PM, Evatt Clash on Petrov: "£5000 Deal" charge from Opposition'. *The Courier Mail* (Brisbane, QLD), 13 August 1954, p. 1.

Also on 12th August, Prime Minister Menzies stated to Parliament that the name of Petrov only became known to him on Sunday 11th April or Saturday evening 10th April:

> "Therefore, I say to the House and to the country that the name of Petrov became known to me for the first time on Sunday night, the 11th April, or the preceding Saturday night. It was one of those nights, when the head of the Australian Security Service came to see me at the Lodge in Canberra with the first two or three literally translated documents that Petrov had handed over".[106]

This statement was contradicted at the Royal Commission by both George Ronald Richards (Deputy Director of ASIO) and Colonel Charles Spry (Director of ASIO). Both men insisted that they had flown to Canberra with some of the *Petrov Papers* on 4th April and had a forty-five minute discussion with Menzies during which an outline of the contents of all the documents had been presented (Spry T:1104, Richards T:760, 1031). Spry also stated he had told Menzies of a possible defection as early as 10th February. In a belated response, Menzies stated in Parliament on 25th October 1955:

> "Early in February, 1954, I now learn that the Solicitor General and the Secretary of the Department of External Affairs, as individuals, were warned of the possibility of a defection. This warning was given orally by the Director-General, and was given to no other people except the Attorney General and the Minister for External Affairs. I was myself told that there was the possibility of a defection, but the identity of the subject was not disclosed, nor did I ask for it. The head of my department was not informed at any stage prior to the actual defection. I repeat that I had not heard of Petrov before his actual defection in 1954".[107]

106 'Prime Minister Menzies Statement' (12 August 1954). *Historic Hansard.* House of Representatives, 21st Parliament, 1st Session. <https://historichansard.net/hofreps/1954/19540812_reps_21_hor4/#debate-18> Accessed 8 May 2024.

107 'Prime Minister Menzies Statement' (25 October 1955). *Historic Hansard.* House of Representatives, 21st Parliament, 1st Session. <http://historichansard.net/hofreps/1955/19551025_reps_21_hor8/#debate-42> Accessed 27 June 2023.

Despite Menzies' denial, Spry continued to insist that he named Petrov to Menzies on 10th February. [108] In addition, Menzies had specifically instructed Spry not to brief Dr. Evatt on security matters some time before the election.[109] Thus, according to the Director of ASIO, Menzies had known all about the possible defection of Petrov since 10th February 1954 and his actual defection since 4th April. The timing of the announcement was deliberately delayed until 13th April, the night before Parliament was due to rise for the upcoming election.

It is a demonstrable fact that Prime Minister Menzies lied to the Australian Parliament, thus holding that body in contempt.

108 Spry, 1973, as cited in Dunne, M.G.L. (December 1979), p. 95. 'The Royal Commission on Espionage, 1954-1955'. *University of Adelaide.* < https://hdl.handle.net/2440/22500> Accessed 8 June 2023.

109 Ibid.

CHAPTER FIFTEEN

Interlude

Amended Royal Commission Act

To resolve any lingering problems which had been expressed about the legal status of the Royal Commission, and to thwart the rising pamphleteering and public speaking campaign critical of the Commission, Prime Minister Menzies introduced into the Federal Parliament on 11th August 1954 amendments to the *Royal Commission on Espionage Act 1954* which had authorised and regulated the conduct of the Commission.

These new amendments invested the Commission with the status of a judicial proceeding under Section III of the Crimes Act (1914-1950). Under the previous legislation, it had been an offence to give false testimony but Section III made it an offence regardless of whether the Commission was properly held, whether or not the testimony was admissable or inadmissable, whether or not a witness was at all competent to give evidence, and that a witness could be compelled to make self-incriminating statements or statements incriminating a spouse.

As an additional benefit, the amendments also included **making it an offence either by speech or writing to bring the Royal Commission into disrepute or contempt.**

The new Act covered all bases and bestowed upon the Commissioners almost limitless powers.

The Act was passed unamended by Parliament on 12th August and the new *Royal Commission on Espionage Act 1954* came into force when it received Royal Assent on 14th August 1954, just in time for the August sittings to begin.

CHAPTER SIXTEEN

Madame Ollier

The *Royal Commission into Espionage* produced no spies. But it did produce one arrest—Mme. Rose M. Ollier of the French Embassy staff.

Section 1: Dr. Evatt's Protest

The Australian Minister for External Affairs had advised the French Ambassador in Canberra on 11th May 1954 that Madame Ollier, a Second Secretary in the French Embassy, appeared to be involved in the Petrov Affair. She had been ordered to New Caledonia by the French Government and had left Australia on 21st May 1954 aboard the vessel *Quebec.* Following evidence given by the Petrovs at secret sittings of the commission in Melbourne on 20th July 1954, Madame Ollier was arrested on 22nd August 1954 and then transferred to France to await trial.

On 5th September 1954, Dr. Evatt protested at the Royal Commission against Madame Ollier's treatment and at her summary removal from Australia:

> "Mme. Ollier, second secretary of the French Embassy in Canberra, was deprived of the ordinary safeguards of justice", the Leader of the Federal Opposition (Dr. H. V. Evatt) said last evening. Dr. Evatt appealed to the French Government to intervene in Australia on Mme. Ollier's behalf.
>
> **Mme. Ollier was named before the Royal Commission on Espionage as an informer. She was alleged to have given information to the Petrovs on the shipment of arms to Indo-China.**
>
> Mme. Ollier was reported to be returning to France under arrest, and would be tried in Paris on a charge of endangering French security. An announcement of the arrest was made by the French Ambassador (M. Louis Roché) in a statement to the Commission, and released through the Commission on Friday.
>
> Dr. Evatt said the announcement was injurious to Mme. Ollier and demanded immediate action by the French Government.
>
> He added: "Despite the recent public statements by Colonel Spry (Director of ASIO) and Mr. Richards of the Australian Security Service, to vindicate and glamorise the Petrovs, it is quite possible, and I believe likely, that Madame Ollier is completely innocent of wrong doing.

"It was the two Petrovs, in the secrecy of an in-camera hearing, who made allegations against her after she had been whisked out of the country by M. Louis Roché. She was thus prevented from defending her honor and patriotism. Today she will find herself defamed throughout the world. Surely this is worse than McCarthyism. Indeed it resembles the arbitrary methods of *lettre-de-cachet* which the French eliminated early in the history of the French Republic".[110]

Section 2: The French Ambassador's Rejoinder

The French Ambassador to Australia, M. Louis Roché, to-day made a strong official protest against Dr. Evatt's statement that the French Government acted improperly in the Madame Ollier case.

M. Roche said that the French Government had acted against Madame Ollier after making its own independent inquiries. He delivered the protest verbally to the Secretary of the Department of External Affairs, Mr. A. H. Tange.

...The Embassy would like the Government to make public the sequence of events leading to Madame Ollier's arrest. These are:

- The Minister for External Affairs, Mr. R. G. Casey, on May 11 informed M. Roche that Madame Ollier appeared to be involved in the Petrov case;
- French authorities made their own independent inquiries;
- On May 21 the French Government ordered Madame Ollier to be transferred to New Caledonia, pending further inquiries;
- She was not arrested until August 22.

The French Embassy believes that these facts refute charges made by Dr. Evatt.

French officials in Australia are also upset at Dr. Evatt's statement that some French Foreign Office officials continue to associate themselves with the "pro-Hitler Vichy Government of war-time France".

110 'Madame Ollier Deprived' of Justice'. *Advocate* (Burnie, TAS), 6 September 1954, p.3.

> French sources have taken this as a reflection on M. Roché which they say is completely unwarranted. M. Roché was a Free French Government official throughout the war, working for the B.B.C. for a considerable period.[111]

Section 3: The Alleged Evidence

The principal allegation levelled against Mme. Ollier was that she had given information to the Petrovs about a French shipment of arms to Indo-China.

The evidence produced against Mme. Ollier hinged on 5 events:

1. A note allegedly delivered to Ollier by Petrov (April - May 1953);
2. Dr. Bialoguski's discovery of a different note in Petrov's wallet (June 1953);
3. Petrov's hospitalisation in Canberra (May 1953);
4. Alleged meetings between Ollier and Petrov (June 1953 onwards);
5. A car accident involving Petrov on 24th December 1953.

An attempt to reconstruct the chronology of these events reveals the contradictions. Petrov's meetings with Mme. Ollier allegedly began after he passed a note to her at a screening of films at the Soviet Embassy in April 1953 (T: pF-G, 20th July 1954). He never wrote to Ollier again (T:F). The note appointed a meeting for one month's time. Petrov's reason for the distant appointment was that he was entering Canberra Hospital for treatment to his eyes (T:G).

The date of the note, April 1953, was confirmed by Mrs. Petrov. Subsequently this date was changed to 21st May 1953 (T:1005pa1472). It was changed back to April by the commissioners in their Final Report (R:175pa620).

Unfortunately for the commissioners, the note could not have been sent in either April or May 1953.

In their Report, the commissioners stated that Petrov met Mme. Ollier on 11th June 1953 as a result of the note. The note itself, and Petrov's subsequent explanation, clearly stated that more than a month was to elapse before the meeting. Therefore the note could not have been delivered to Mme. Ollier on 21st May 1953. But the note could not have been delivered in April either for it makes reference to Petrov's impending hospitalisation and Petrov was not in possession of that information

111 'French Ambassador's Strong Protest on Evatt's Statement'. *The Sydney Morning Herald* (NSW), 7 September 1954, p. 3.

until 19th May 1953 at the very earliest. (Petrov was in hospital from the 22-30 May 1953).The speed with which he was hospitalised was cause for comment (T:1025pa772, T:991pa779-884).

Petrov's note to Mme. Ollier never existed. The story was part of a frame-up.

A further absurdity arose when the Security agent Dr. Bialoguski, a drinking partner of Petrov's, claimed to have found a previous note when he searched Petrov's wallet. Petrov was allegedly carrying this note hoping to deliver it to Mme. Ollier for the purpose of arranging meetings. Yet the date on which Bialoguski searched Petrov's wallet was 19th June 1953, a date by which not only was Petrov supposed to have delivered a note, but also by which he was supposed to have already had a clandestine meeting with Mme. Ollier. Bialoguski avoided giving this date when pressed at the Commission but he gave the date in connection with another matter (T:1005pa1474, T:1310pa690).

Section 4: A Proven Liar

Petrov claimed to have had two further meetings with Mme. Ollier: on 17th December 1953 at Queanbeyan (NSW) and on 24th December 1953 at Cooma (NSW).

Queanbeyan—17 December 1953

Evidence before the Commission showed that Petrov was in Sydney on 17th December 1953 arranging with Dr. Beckett and Dr. Bialoguski for his eventual defection. No explanation was offered as to how he was able to meet Madame Ollier on the same date in Queanbeyan. The collision of purpose between the two meetings—the Sydney 'defection' meeting and the Queanbeyan 'espionage' meeting —is most marked.

Cooma—24 December 1953

On 3rd September 1954, a signed statement by Petrov dated 28th June 1954 was incorporated into the Transcript and labelled Exhibit 86. In this statement, Petrov claimed to have met with Mme. Ollier in Cooma on 24th December 1953.

On that date, an accident near Canberra completely destroyed his Embassy vehicle and put him out of social circulation for a week (T:738pa329-33). The incident also drew police suspicions (T:261pa411-422).

Extract from Petrov's signed statement (Exhibit 86)

> "At about 7 a.m. on the 24th December. 1953, I was driving my car from Canberra to Cooma for the purpose of keeping an appointment with Madame Ollier at 8 a.m. on that day. When I was about 17 miles from Canberra, I was involved in an accident and my car overturned and caught fire. The car was a total wreck and I hailed a passing motorist who gave me and my dog, Jack, a lift as far as Cooma.
>
> "When I arrived at Cooma I proceeded to the railway station and ascertained that there was no train to Canberra on that date, but there was one leaving for Queanbeyan at 4 o'clock that afternoon. I then walked around the shopping centre in Cooma and at 12 noon I noticed Madame Ollier sitting in her car outside a cafe there. I spoke to her and we then went into the cafe and had coffee. She informed me that she had noticed my car burnt out whilst driving to Cooma.
>
> "She also informed me that she was unable to obtain information as to the nature of the armament which was being forwarded from Australia to French Indo-China. Her reason being that this information was contained in the safe of the Ambassador.
>
> "This particular meeting had been arranged between us for 8 a.m. on that date as Madame Ollier was passing through that town on her way to Melbourne.
>
> "After leaving Madame Ollier, I later caught the 4 o'clock train to Queanbeyan from where I caught a taxi to the Soviet Embassy".[112]

However, Dr. Evatt and others conclusively proved that Mme. Ollier was in Twofold Bay, five hours driving time distant from Cooma, on the date given by Petrov.

The wife of the proprietor of the Hotel Eden at Twofold Bay where Mme. Ollier stayed made the following declaration:

> Hotel Eden (Vincent T. Welsh, proprietor), Eden, Sept. 26, 1954.
>
> *To whom it may concern*
>
> Madame Ollier, of Canberra, booked in at this hotel at 12.30 p.m. in time for lunch on Xmas Eve, December 24th, 1953, and remained till Jan. 2nd, 1954. At no time during this period was she absent from any meal.
>
> (Sgd.) Eileen M. Welsh. J.P. , (Wife of Vincent T. Welsh).[113]

---

112 'French Official Arrested'. T*he Sydney Morning Herald* (NSW), 4 September 1954, pp. 1, 4, 5.

113 'Evatt Claims New Facts On Petrov'. *The Sydney Morning Herald* (NSW), 2 October 1954, p. 1.

Section 5: A "self-confessed spy and traitor"

On 7th September, the Royal Commissioners withdrew Dr. Evatt's right to appear at the Commission, ostensibly over his public statement protesting the treatment of Madame Ollier. However, on 16th September, Evatt applied for readmission to represent as senior counsel his clients Alan Dalziel and Albert Grundeman.

Dr. Evatt's application for fresh leave to appear was, unsurprisingly, rejected. (See Chapter Twenty: *Gulliver among the Lilliputians.*)

The day before Dr. Evatt's fresh leave to appear before the Commission was rejected, Australian Senator Dorothy Tangney joined her voice to the chorus of protest against the treatment of Madame Ollier:

> Senator Dorothy Tangney said in Sydney to-night she could say from personal knowledge that some of the statements made about Madame Ollier were incorrect. Senator Tangney, a West Australian, was supporting Dr. Evatt's protest on the arrest of Madame Ollier, following allegations by Mr. and Mrs. Petrov at a secret hearing of the Royal Commission on Espionage.
>
> She said "I consider it imperative that Madame Ollier be given the opportunity to face her accusers, some of whose statements in regard to her were definitely untrue…I know this of my own knowledge and I won't mind being called to substantiate what I say.
>
> "…She was always a welcome guest among diplomats and Parliamentarians for her friendliness and charm. The mental agony she has undergone and will undergo could have been obviated if she had been given an opportunity to face her accusers here in Australia".
>
> Senator Tangney said this was vastly different from the treatment given Mrs. Petrov, **a self-confessed spy and traitor** to her own country and for whom no a money, effort, or publicity was spared to save her from being brought to justice in her own land.[114]

As for the secret information allegedly given to Petrov by Madame Ollier, and which he testified to in the 20th July secret sittings, it had been reported in the press weeks previously:

114 'Senator Tangney Joins Defence of Madame Ollier'. *The Canberra Times* (ACT), 6 September 1954, p. 1.

> The *Radnor* is the second ship to load equipment under an agreement reached last year by which Australia gave surplus obsolete equipment to the French for use in Indo-China.[115]

Section 6: Madame Ollier Acquitted

On 5th January 1955, Madame Ollier was granted provisional liberty and freed from a Paris prison by a French Military Tribunal:

> Madame Rose-Marie Ollier, former French diplomat brought back from New Caledonia last year to answer treason charges,was granted provisional liberty yesterday from the Paris prison. Madame Ollier has been awaiting trial for almost three months on charges of "intelligence with the enemy and with failing to disclose espionage activities." Military magistrate, M. Jean Giraud, ordered the attractive 46-year-old widow to be set free yesterday.
>
> The charges arose from the Petrov espionage inquiry in Australia, during which it was alleged that Madame Ollier had passed information about French military cargoes bound for Indo-china to members of the Russian Embassy in Canberra.[116]

After being granted provisional liberty on 5th January 1955, Madame Ollier was finally acquitted on 20th October 1955. Dr. Evatt expressed his satisfaction:

> The Leader of the Opposition (Dr. Evatt) said today he felt a special satisfaction at the acquittal of Madame Ollier by the French tribunal of allegations made against her by the Petrovs. He said he had protested publicly at the complete denial of justice in the proceedings of the Royal Commission without Madame Ollier being heard.
>
> Dr. Evatt said be had communicated with the French Government and with the French Tribunal, to whose sense of responsibility and fairness he paid tribute.[117]

115 'Troops ready to load arms cargo'. *The Courier Mail* (Brisbane, QLD), 9 April 1954, p.1.

116 'Madame Ollier Released'. *The Canberra Times* (ACT), 6 January 1955, p. 4.

117 'Mme. Ollier Acquitted on Espionage Count'. *The Canberra Times* (ACT), 22 October 1955, p. 1.

CHAPTER SEVENTEEN

The Moscow Letters

The 101 photographs of Russian typewriting labelled by the Commission as the 'Moscow Letters'.

Persons who were named in the *Petrov Papers*, especially in the Moscow Letters, and summoned to appear before the Royal Commission, were those who would have been summoned to appear before a McCarthy-style tribunal if its establishment had not been thwarted by the failure of Menzies' 1951 Communist Party Dissolution Bill and the subsequent Referendum. The Petrov defection and subsequent Royal Commission enabled the government to circumvent the rejection of the Referendum proposals.

Section 1: Duplicity

When the final *Report of the Royal Commission on Espionage* containing translations of all the Russian language documents was published, already existing suspicions as to the authenticity of the Moscow Letters were further heightened since, in some cases, information would have been difficult for Moscow to learn but readily available to ASIO.

For example, two witnesses, Norman Herbert Russell and Neville Isaksen, visited the Soviet Union as part of a delegation and were brought before the Commission because their names appeared in the Moscow Letters in connection with the trip.

Letter Number 1 dated 2nd January 1952 concerning Norman Herbert Russell said that:

> While he was in Moscow, Russell, together with Neville Isaksen, another member of the delegation, secretly and without telling anyone visited the British Embassy where he spent several hours. The following day, they explained their absence by saying that, having gone out for a walk, they allegedly met a young Russian who spoke English, who invited them to a restaurant where they sat for several hours (R:317).

Both men had visited the Embassy but they denied they were ever asked about their absence or that they had offered the excuse stated in the Letter. They believed that their visit to the Embassy had remained a secret to the Soviet authorities but that it had been made known to ASIO in 1952 when Isaksen's diary in which he recorded the incident had been seized by Customs officials and passed on to ASIO (T:1800-1, 1810).

There were a number of other cases where information would have been readily available to ASIO but either difficult to learn or of no interest to Moscow.

For example, several people whose addresses were listed in the Letters denied having any affiliation with the Communist Party or ever being in contact or corresponding with the Soviet Union. Being recent immigrants, these addresses would have been readily available to Australian authorities but the Commissioners had no explanation as to how or why these people would have been of any interest to the Soviets.

Also problematic was the case of Dr. K.K. Barris who had emigrated from Greece and had worked for the Australian wartime security service. The only connection Dr. Barris had with communists or the Communist Party is that he had once sponsored an old school friend member as a suitable immigrant to Australia. This friend happened to be a member of the Greek Communist Party. Dr. Barris had in this fashion come to the attention of the Australian authorities. The Commissioners were unable to explain who had provided Moscow with the information that Dr. Barris was "regarded as a leftist" by "members of the security service" (R:240, T:1648-50).

Section 2: Post-facto Concoctions

The Petrovs insisted that the Moscow Letters came from Moscow on film and that Mr. Petrov had made photographic prints from the film. These were the prints in the Commission's possession. As each letter was allegedly being prepared in Moscow, the date was marked on it. Therefore, the date of the letter was as much a part of it as the information it contained (R:41).

A major problem for the Commissioners was prochronism in that some of the dated Moscow Letters described situations which could not have existed at that time, having occurred after the date on which the Letter allegedly came into existence.

The previously noted Letter Number 1 dated 2nd January 1952 concerning Mr. Norman Herbert Russell said that:

> Whilst refraining from taking any active part in the fight for peace, he does not, it is true, decline to carry out individual assignments to that end (T:1783-6, 1812).

In mid-1951, Mr. Russell had gone abroad as a delegate of the Clerks' Union to attend a Peace Movement conference in Berlin. He also visited the Soviet Union on his travels, staying overseas until 21st January 1952. It was not until March 1952, some two months after the date on the Moscow Letter, did the question of Russell doing any assignments in the Peace Movement arise. [118]

Again in Letter Number 1 of 2nd January 1952, Mr. Charles Bresland was mentioned in the following terms:

> At the present time, Bresland is...Secretary of the executive branch of the Eureka Youth League (R:316).

Bresland testified that while he was certainly on the executive of the League in January 1952, he did not become Secretary until April 1952 (T:2429).

There was also the case of Mr. G.R. Anderson, mentioned in the Letter dated 6th June 1952. In that Letter, Moscow allegedly writes to Mr. Petrov stating that:

> We cannot agree with your opinion that the study and cultivation of Anderson should be terminated merely because he was not elected in the trade union and was left without work (R:341).

Anderson had been State Deputy President of the Clerks' Union and had not lost this office in the Union until July 1952, a month after the date of the Letter.

There is also the case of Max Falstein who was an elected member of the Australian House of Representatives. Falstein was mentioned in G9, one of Petrov's notes allegedly written by Sadovnikov and represented to be an extract from a Moscow Letter dated 10th November 1949. Falstein was referred to as a "former" member of Parliament in this document which is dated a month before he lost his seat at the 1949 election. **Moreover, his stated age in the document was correct for 1954, not 1949.**

Moscow's uncanny knack for clairvoyance was not addressed at the Commission. The failure of dates to match events in some of the Moscow Letters constitutes a *prima facie* case that those letters could not have existed on the dates stipulated in the Letters themselves. These facts cannot be reconciled with the way in which the Petrovs claimed that the Letters were prepared and sent from Moscow.

118 Dunne, M.G.L. 'The Royal Commission on Espionage, 1954-1955' (December 1979), p. 253. *University of Adelaide* < https://hdl.handle.net/2440/22500> Accessed 31 May 2024.

CHAPTER EIGHTEEN

The 'G' Series of Notes

The nine lists of names handwritten in Russian by the Petrovs and the nine lists of names handwritten in Russian by others.

Section 1: Authentic ASIO

Although complex, a thorough understanding of the stories told by the Petrovs about the 'G' series is essential.

Among the documents allegedly brought by Petrov from the Russian Embassy and handed to ASIO were 18 handwritten Notes.

These Notes were labelled by the Royal Commission as the 'G' Series. They referred either to persons by their real names, some with biographical information, or to persons by code names which were readily identifiable by cross-reference to other Notes in the G Series. The information in these Notes is clearly of ASIO origin as the persons named were those who had come to the attention first of the Commonwealth Investigation Service (CIS) and then the Australian Security Intelligence Organisation (ASIO) between 1945 and 1954. (See Chapter Seventeen: *The Moscow Letters.*)

According to evidence given by the Petrovs during the course of the Commission, these eighteen Notes comprised:

- Nine allegedly handwritten between the years 1945 and 1949 by Sadovnikov, a former MVD Chief Resident in Australia. These notes had been left by Petrov's predecessors for his guidance. They were labelled by the Commission as G1-G3, G5-G10 .
- Eight handwritten by Petrov between 1952 and 1954. These Notes were labelled by the Commission as G11-G18.
- One handwritten by Petrov copied from two notes allegedly left behind by Sadovnikov. This Note was labelled by the Commission as G4.

In summary, Petrov allegedly delivered to ASIO nine Notes in handwriting not his own (allegedly Sadovnikov's), and nine Notes in his own handwriting, one of which (G4) was a copy of the two Sadovnikov Notes left behind.

The incriminating evidence concerning Max Falstein, previously mentioned in Chapter Seventeen: *The Moscow Letters*, was contained in one of the alleged Sadovnikov notes so we are able to bypass all the arguments about whether the handwriting was Sadovnikov's or not. (Dr. Evatt produced a handwriting expert whose findings pointed to forgery.)

It is demonstrable that not only did Petrov collaborate with ASIO in the actual fabrication of the G Series but also that the three judges who sat as Royal Commissioners incriminated themselves by avoiding at every turn the very first question that should have been asked—what is the provenance of these documents?

Section 2: Scribal Errors

Petrov's notes G12 and G13 provide clear evidence of his direct participation with ASIO in their fabrication because he made the type of errors which could only have occurred while copying English handwriting into Russian, not Russian handwriting into Russian.

Two Examples

Daginian instead of **Daghian** and **Veler** instead of **Peter**.

Firstly, Petrov substituted "in" for the "h" in Daghian. Every typist will recognise the cause of this simple error. It was an English "h", written with the initial downstroke separated from the rest of the letter, reading as "in".

Likewise, had the other word "Peter" been in Russian, Petrov could not possibly have mistaken it because it was virtually his own name. It takes little to visualise how the English word is written. There was a split stem on the "P" making it appear as a "V", the "t" was looped to look like "l" with the crossbar of the "t" disconnected and placed over some other letter, both common features in English handwriting.

There can be no doubt that Petrov was copying English handwriting into Russian handwriting. There was certainly enough time for Petrov and ASIO to fabricate the documents because Petrov had been in Australian hands since at least July 1951 when contact was established between himself and Dr. Michael Bialoguski, an ASIO Officer (T:902, T:968).

Note

See Chapter Twenty-One: *The Chain of Transmission—G Series* for the major changes and an infinity of minor contradictions in Petrov's account about how he allegedly removed the documents from the Russian Embassy.

CHAPTER NINETEEN

Document H

The three pages of typewriting in English labelled by the Commission as Document 'H' was a series of pen picture of Canberra Press Gallery journalists allegedly written by journalist Fergan O'Sullivan (T:293pa753).

As noted elsewhere, the Triumvirate could not allow Dr. Evatt to become Prime Minister in May 1954 as he would have implemented Labor Party policy in respect of Indo-China.

Therefore, a 'legitimate' reason had to be found to remove him from office if or when he did become Prime Minister. This 'legitimate' reason would be the revelations to emerge about Evatt at the Royal Commission, revelations which Menzies and his co-conspirators had engineered beforehand.

Section 1: Fergan O'Sullivan

The revelations to emerge would hinge on Fergan O'Sullivan. O'Sullivan had been planted on Dr. Evatt's staff in the full knowledge that he would eventually admit in the Royal Commission to being the author of Document H (the three typewritten pages in English).

Just by 'chance'

The demonstrable facts concerning O'Sullivan are as follows:

- In early 1953, Evatt had employed a Miss Bell as his press secretary. Miss Bell was not a professional journalist;
- The Australian Journalists' Association represented to Evatt that he should place a professional journalist in the position of press secretary. Evatt acquiesced. O'Sullivan was at this time secretary of the Parliamentary Press Gallery in Canberra;
- O'Sullivan made two approaches to obtain the position on Evatt's staff (T:308pa301). O'Sullivan finally obtained the position and began duties with Evatt on 1st April 1953;

- O'Sullivan allegedly wrote the series of pen pictures of Canberra Press Gallery journalists known as Document H between September and November 1951. He acknowledged authorship to the Commission after first making the appearance of declining to answer;
- At the time of writing Document H, O'Sullivan was not Evatt's press secretary: he was a reporter with the *Sydney Morning Herald* (See Chapter Ten: *A Couple of Rabbits*);
- In May 1953, O'Sullivan caused Albert Grundeman, one of Dr. Evatt's staff, to be in Canberra by specifically requesting his assistance while Dr. Evatt was attending the Coronation of Queen Elizabeth II. He then introduced Grundeman to Lockwood in a Canberra hotel bar by which means the Commission was able to associate Grundeman with Lockwood, the alleged author of Document J (R:41pa126);
- O'Sullivan adventitiously introduced Grundeman's name at the Commission in connection with this Canberra meeting although making the appearance of not remembering it took place in May 1953 (R:423-4pa28, T:1044pa173, T:440pa586, T:512pa139);
- Santamaria's publication, *News Weekly,* predicted developments connected with Petrov as early as 28th January 1953 (T:958pa551, T:1014pa247);
- O'Sullivan's connection with the Document H was known to Menzies by 10th April at the latest, long before Windeyer announced on 11th June that the Commission would concentrate on the authorship of documents H and J;
- O'Sullivan remained on Evatt's staff until after the May 1954 election. He informed Dr. Evatt on 4th June 1954 of his connection with Document H and was dismissed immediately.

The facts demonstrate that O'Sullivan became linked with Evatt on the initiative of the AJA and O'Sullivan himself. Moreover, as the *News Weekly* article demonstrates, Petrov's defection was already being planned before O'Sullivan began working for Dr. Evatt on 1st April 1953.

The Commissioners stated in their Report: "It was only **chance** that O'Sullivan happened to become later a member of Dr. Evatt's secretariat..." (R:37pa107(2).

Thus, with the stroke of a pen, the Commissioners dismissed what must have been glaringly obvious to even the most casual observer—the role played by O'Sullivan in the political destruction of Dr. Evatt.

On 14th July 1954, Fergan O'Sullivan entered the witness box at the Royal Commission and was handed exhibit H:

> To Mr. Windeyer, O'Sullivan said he was a journalist and had been employed by *The Sydney Morning Herald.* On April 1, 1953, he was appointed Press secretary to the Leader of the Opposition, Dr. H. V. Evatt. His services as Press secretary were terminated on June 4, 1954.
>
> O'Sullivan said he was treated as being a member of the Prime Minister's Department. The dismissal notice had been sent from the Prime Minister's Department, and he had received a letter from Dr. Evatt as well.
>
> Mr. Windeyer asked O'Sullivan if he was the author of exhibit 'H'.
>
> O'Sullivan: Yes.
>
> O'Sullivan said he thought it was about the second half of 1951 when he typed it. He had then been employed by *The Sydney Morning Herald* as a Parliamentary reporter at Canberra.
>
> Mr. Windeyer: Can you tell me when you typed it and whom you gave it to?
>
> O'Sullivan: To Pakhomov (TASS* representative before Viktor Antonov. Also temporary successor to Valentin Sadovnikov, MVD Chief Resident in Australia until 1951).
>
> Mr. Justice Owen: You said you typed it in the second half of 1951. Did you hand it over immediately after then?
>
> O'Sullivan: Within a day or so.[119]

On that same day, Mr. Petrov re-entered the witness box and was questioned about his relationship with O'Sullivan by Mr. Justice Owen and Windeyer:

> Petrov, handed exhibit 'H', said the first time he saw the document was when Pakhomov brought it to the Embassy early in 1952. Pakhomov said he had received it from O'Sullivan. A telegram was sent to Moscow stating that Pakhomov had received the document and that the film of it would be sent in the diplomatic bag.
>
> Petrov said Pakhomov first introduced him to O'Sullivan in the Press gallery. He met O'Sullivan later at an Embassy reception and at the Capitol Theatre in

119 'Journalist says he was author of Document H'. *The Sydney Morning Herald* (NSW), 15 July 1954, p. 4.

Canberra. He had also met him in Sydney twice. They went in the plane from Canberra to Sydney together in July 1953 and, at Mascot aerodrome, they had a cup of coffee together.

O'Sullivan had a Commonwealth car at the airport to meet him and they went to town together.

First, they went to O'Sullivan's house, where O'Sullivan left some books Afterwards, they went to the railway station where, he (Petrov) left the car and went to the Russian Social Club alone. Petrov said he met O'Sullivan the next day and they had lunch together at the *Adria* restaurant. They were together for an hour and had just a social talk. They separated after lunch and he did not meet him again.

Petrov said O'Sullivan gave him his Canberra telephone number but he (Petrov) did not ring up.[120]

On 16 August, Fergan O'Sullivan was recalled to the witness box:

> Fergan O'Sullivan, former Press-secretary to Dr. Evatt, was recalled to the witness box yesterday morning. He admitted that when he informed Dr. Evatt on June 3 1954, that he had written document 'H', Dr. Evatt had been "amazed and disgusted".
>
> He had received a letter of dismissal the next day.[121]

While Dr. Evatt had been "amazed and disgusted" to discover that O'Sullivan was the author of Document H, he would have been immeasurably more so to discover that O'Sullivan and Petrov had had several meetings and that Petrov, an employee of the Russian Embassy, had been chauffeured around in a vehicle owned by the Federal Government and funded by the Australian taxpayer.

At the Commission hearings of 31st August 1954, Dr. Evatt cross-examined Mrs. Petrov about her relationship with Fergan O'Sullivan:

> When the hearing resumed yesterday Dr. Evatt, who is appearing for two members of his staff, Alan Dalziel and Albert Grundeman, cross-examined Mrs. Petrov.
>
> She said she had met Fergan O'Sullivan only once.

120 'Journalist says he was author of Document H'. *The Sydney Morning Herald* (NSW), 15 July 1954, p. 4.

121 'Party May Reserve Its Judgement'. *The Sydney Morning Herald* (NSW), 17 August 1954, p. 1.

> When Dr. Evatt referred to a photograph of her sitting next to O'Sullivan, Mrs. Petrov said: "When this picture was taken I did not know him at all. We just happened to be together at a film night at the Soviet Embassy."[122]

Undoubtedly, these meetings between Petrov and O'Sullivan, as well as the film night at the Soviet Embassy where O'Sullivan and Mrs. Petrov "just happened to sit together" led to Dr. Evatt's charge that all three had conspired to produce Document J, the only document that really mattered for the Commissioners. (See Chapter Twenty: *Document J.*)

* The official Soviet news agency

Section 3: The Deafening Silence

Although Fergan O'Sullivan worked for Dr. Evatt, he came under the jurisdiction of the Prime Minister's Department for administrative purposes (T:267pa671). Menzies knew of O'Sullivan's authorship of Document H by 10th April at the latest but failed to notify Evatt. He took no administrative action to bring about O'Sullivan's dismissal. Instead, he remained silent.

O'Sullivan claimed that he did not realise until about 25th May, a few short days before the election, that one of the documents being investigated by the Commission was Document H, the three page summary he had written about Canberra Press Gallery journalists (T:293).

The day after his initial questioning at the Royal Commission on 14th July, O'Sullivan was questioned further about Document H:

> He denied he had known the document was among the papers Petrov had given to Australian security officials…He first realised he was involved when he read a Newcastle newspaper report of proceedings of the Commission.[123]

By claiming ignorance, O'Sullivan was able to justify his continuing silence until after the election when it was no longer necessary to keep Dr. Evatt uninformed.

Yet, while O'Sullivan claimed not to know that Document H was among the *Petrov Papers* and was being investigated by the Commission, a fellow journalist wrote about it less than 24 hours after Menzies' 13th April announcement of Petrov's defection and the establishment of the Royal Commission:

122 'Petrov was "Almost Mad"'. *The Sydney Morning Herald* (NSW), 1 September 1954, p. 4.

123 'Witness tells why he wrote Document H'. *The Sydney Morning Herald* (NSW), 16 July 1954, p. 4.

> Among the papers Petrov brought out from the legation is an elaborate series of dossiers on Australians, including members of the Canberra Parliamentary Press Gallery. It was stated authoritatively that no pressmen were involved in anything of a suspicious nature, but the pen pictures that the Russians had compiled of the individual pressmen were colourfully accurate in some cases.[124]

Apart from O'Sullivan's activities, Evatt had no connection whatsoever with the *Petrov Papers*. Note particularly that O'Sullivan, in whom all the odium of Evatt's connection with Petrov was embodied, author of a document which was used against Evatt, remained on Evatt's staff until after the election, which very nearly returned Evatt as Prime Minister. Had Evatt become Prime Minister in May 1954, the use to which O'Sullivan would be have been put for anyone intent on Evatt's destruction will be evident to all.

Note

Mrs. Petrov claimed never to have heard of Document H until the Commission began (T:654pa868, T:1013pa404-416).

124 'I talked with Petrov a month ago: he showed no sign of grave step he planned'. Leo McDonnell, *Brisbane Telegraph* (QLD), 14 April 1954, p. 15.

CHAPTER TWENTY

Document J

The thirty-seven carbon copies of typewriting in English labelled by the Commission as Document 'J' and allegedly authored by Rupert Lockwood.

The main phase of the Commission dealing with Document J lasted from 16th August to 8th October 1954.

Section 1: Overview

The Document J in the possession of the Commission was divided into sections: American; Japanese; a loose sheet J 35 headed 'Dr Evatt'; and 'Sources'. In the margin of the main text were hand-written block capital letters referring the reader to the appropriate place in the 'Sources' section. Fergan O'Sullivan was cited as the 'source' for J 35, the loose sheet headed 'Dr. Evatt' and Grundeman and Dalziel were cited in the 'Sources' as being informants on other matters (T:296-97).

The evidence heard explored the range of circumstances in which it was claimed that Document J was produced.

Windeyer and his juniors had to contend with three other counsel and their juniors during the main Document J phase. Appearing for Rupert Lockwood was Mr. E.F. Hill, a Melbourne barrister and Victorian State Secretary of the Communist Party. Appearing for Fergan O'Sullivan, Dr. Evatt's former Press Secretary and author of Document H, was Mr. J. Meagher while Dr. Evatt had sought and obtained leave to appear on behalf of Alan Dalziel and Albert Grundeman, the members of his staff who were named in Document J.

Section 2: The One that Mattered

As noted in Chapter Ten: *A Couple of Rabbits*, Prime Minister Menzies could afford to project a statesmanlike image to the world precisely because, whatever the May 1954 election outcome, he had another rabbit ready to pull out of his top hat. That rabbit was foreknowledge of the contents of Document J which, according to George

Ronald Richards (Deputy Director of ASIO), Menzies had "handled" on 4th April, nine days before Petrov's defection.[125]

If, therefore, Menzies lost the election and the Labor Party under Dr. Evatt were to take the reins in May, Evatt's reputation would be so shredded by Document J disclosures to come from the Royal Commission that there would be a crisis of confidence in the Government. Menzies would then call for a double dissolution of both Houses of Parliament and would certainly regain office once a compliant press heralded his return as saviour from the 'communist' menace.

When George Ronald Richards (Deputy Director of ASIO) testified at the Royal Commission on 8th September 1954, he stated the following:

> Richards said that at 8.30 a.m. on 2nd April, he saw Petrov leave his home carrying a satchel. Petrov was on his way to Canberra airport. When their plane landed at Mascot (Sydney), they met for a few minutes and arranged a meeting at the Kings Cross (Sydney) Security flat that afternoon.
>
> ...At the security flat meeting on the afternoon of 2nd April, Richards said that Petrov opened his satchel and took from it documents in two white envelopes.
>
> ...Richards said that Petrov handed the documents which he had previously shown to him to Colonel Spry (Director of ASIO) who examined them.*
>
> **...The first document Petrov showed them was what was now called Document J.** It interested them because it was in English. Richards said Document J was a group of documents of foolscap size, folded together. They were stapled in sections.[126]

As also noted previously, because of its non-interventionist policy on Indo-China, the major reason for the establishment of the *Royal Commission on Espionage* was to prevent the Labor Party under Dr. Evatt from assuming power at the May 1954 election. To realise this aim, the shredding of Dr. Evatt's reputation was crucial. Document J was crucial. It was the only document that really mattered at the Commission. For Richards to admit that J was the first document allegedly shown to them by Petrov is incriminating of itself.

125 'Petrov Wanted Job on Land'. *The Courier Mail* (Brisbane, QLD), 9 September 1954, p. 6.

126 'Security Officer Slept in Room'. *The Sydney Morning Herald* (NSW), 9 September 1954, p. 4.

Mrs. Petrov was the main witness concerning Document J. On 8th July, despite the objections of Mr. E.F. Hill, counsel for Rupert Lockwood, that neither he nor his client had seen Document J, Mrs. Petrov entered the witness box and identified Rupert Lockwood as its author. [127]

She testified that, at some point, Viktor Antonov, a Sydney correspondent for the official Russian news agency TASS, had told Mr. Petrov that Rupert Lockwood was willing to provide information to the Soviet Union. Lockwood agreed to prepare a document but wished to do so in the safety of the Soviet Embassy. According to Mrs. Petrov, she reported the proposal to the Moscow Centre of the MVD which approved the scheme but asked that Lockwood should not confine himself to general information but provide precise details of sources for that information.

Mrs. Petrov testified that she herself had allowed Lockwood to enter the Embassy and observed him typing over a period of three days. She herself had even brought lunch for Lockwood and given him some typing paper. Two copies of the document were made: an original which had been sent to Moscow and a carbon copy—Document J—which Mr. Petrov had brought from the Soviet Embassy and which, it was alleged, was now the document before the Commission. At the end of each day, she alleged, she had collated the document and prepared the original for despatch to Moscow (T:188-190).When asked if Lockwood had received any money for his work, Mrs. Petrov replied that he had received £30 when he finished the work and several bottles of what she thought was brandy. [128]

The next day, 9th July, Mrs. Petrov continued her testimony about Lockwood. She alleged that, as the work on the typing of the document was completed each day, she took it upstairs and put the pages in the MVD safe. She thought she gave them back to Lockwood each morning. After the typing was finished, she never met Lockwood again and never heard from him.[129]

Elsewhere in her 9th July testimony, Mrs. Petrov said:

> There were occasions when I accompanied him. He always came in through the back door and **never through the main entrance.**[130]

127 'Mrs. Petrov Identifies Lockwood'. *The Sydney Morning Herald* (NSW), 9 July 1954, p. 4,5.

128 Ibid.

129 'Certain I Have Been Named a Traitor'. *The Sydney Morning Herald* (NSW), 10 July 1954, p. 4.

130 'Mrs. Petrov Identifies Lockwood'. *The Sydney Morning Herald* (NSW), 9 July 1954, p. 4,5.

Continuing her evidence on Document J, Mrs. Petrov alleged that the TASS representative, Antonov, had given a statement to Mr. Petrov in which Lockwood allegedly said that he would provide information but that he was afraid of writing anything at home or anywhere in Australia. Mrs. Petrov said the statement added that Lockwood suggested that he should write the information "somewhere in one of the countries of the Peoples' Democracies, or in New China, or in the Soviet Embassy in Canberra". [131]

Mrs. Petrov was then cross-examined by Mr. E.F.Hill (counsel for Rupert Lockwood):

> Mrs. Petrov said that when letters were sent to MVD headquarters in Moscow, secret parts were ciphered before the document was photographed and sent. Couriers carried the sealed packets, stamped by the cipher department, in their inside pockets.
>
> **All MVD documents were kept in the department's safe, to which only she and her husband had access.** (See Chapter Twenty-One: *The Chain of Transmission* for lies told by the Petrovs about access to keys and safes.)
>
> Mrs. Petrov said that document J was in the safe from 1953 until it was taken by Mr. Petrov...Mrs. Petrov said she sent the original of document J to Moscow.
>
> However, she also admitted under cross-examination by Dr. Evatt on 31st August that she had not read Document J in its entirety but had just glanced through it (T:223).[132]

On 12th July, Mrs. Petrov was again asked about Document J:

> To Mr. Justice Philp, Mrs. Petrov said document J was written in April 1953 (It was actually in May). She had not seen Lockwood from April 1953 until last Friday when she identified him in court.[133]

On 24th August 1954, Rupert Lockwood again testified before the Royal Commission.

He admitted typing material for Viktor Antonov in the Russian Embassy in Canberra over a period of three days beginning on 23rd May and ending on the 25th May 1953. Lockwood said he had paid for his own rail fares from Sydney to Canberra on the 22nd May and for the return journey on 25th May. He denied he

131 'Lockwood' ordered out of Box'. *The Sydney Morning Herald* (NSW), 10 July 1954, p. 1.

132 Ibid, p. 4.

133 'Lockwood Refuses to Answer Questions'. *The Sydney Morning Herald* (NSW), 13 July 1954, p. 4.

had received either money or a present of three bottles of brandy from Antonov for writing the material and he strenuously denied ever having met Mrs. Petrov.

He described Mrs. Petrov's story that he had received £30 as "pure invention". He added:

> "If I had thought that the material I supplied to Antonov was going to be sent to the Soviet Government or to the Security Police, I would have fainted with horror.
>
> "I did not know that there could be a Petrov in this world. I was completely confident that the material was merely for Antonov's personal guidance.
>
> "I did not dream that it would later be used to blackmail the entire Australian Labour movement. I think something funny has been going on".
>
> ...Lockwood said evidence given by Mrs. Petrov that it had been suggested that he should write document J in one of the peoples' democracies or in China was "absolute nonsense".[134]

To Mr. Justice Philp, Lockwood said that page 35 of document J was false (the page headed 'Dr. Evatt'). There was material in document J which was not supplied by him and he did not know whether it was true or false. Lockwood said document J was false when it made Albert Grundeman and Alan Dalziel sources of information.

On the same day, Dr. Evatt addressed the Commission:

> Dr. Evatt said there were portions of document J which could only "derive from O'Sullivan". This was evident by the style and method of presentation, and the ignorance of Australian history which were foreign to the Lockwood documents produced to the Commission. It was submitted that the authorship of document J extended much further than Lockwood.
>
> "The evidence before the Commission is that document J is the work solely of Lockwood", Dr. Evatt said. "We will submit that this is not so, and that the Petrovs must have been aware of it. My submission will be that the typing in document J is intended to confuse and deceive".[135]

On 26th August, Lockwood continued his testimony, reiterating that he had received no payments whatever for the material and that he had never met Mrs. Petrov or accompanied her anywhere:

---

134 'Lockwood on Information in "J"'. *The Sydney Morning Herald* (NSW), 25 August 1954, p. 8.

135 Ibid.

> Lockwood said he received no payments whatever for the material.
>
> Mr. Hill (counsel for Lockwood) said Mrs. Petrov had said she had met Lockwood several times and had accompanied him on other occasions.
>
> Lockwood said he had never met Mrs. Petrov and she had never accompanied him anywhere.
>
> Lockwood denied that Mrs. Petrov had brought him documents from a safe each day he worked at the Embassy. He went to the Embassy because there was nowhere else in Canberra where he could type and have these discussions with Antonov. There was nothing sinister in going there. **He always went through the front gate** and assumed that the Embassy would be under surveillance by the Security police.[136]

Compare Lockwood's statement with the 9th July evidence given by Mrs. Petrov:

> "There were occasions when I accompanied him. He always came in through the back door and **never through the main entrance**". [137]

Section 4: A Carbon Footprint

Before Dr. Evatt was ejected from the Commission, he questioned George Ronald Richards (Deputy Head of ASIO) at the hearings of 26th August:

> In reply to Dr. Evatt, Richards said he looked on document 'J' as one document separated into parts. Richards agreed that page 35 of the document (the page headed 'Dr. Evatt') had staple marks. He said that when he had examined the document originally he knew from its appearance that **page 35 had been attached at one period to some other material.**
>
> He received certain documents which were in separate parts and one of these was now document 'J'. Richards said page 35 was not pinned to the other sections of document 'J'.
>
> He had received documents from Vladimir Petrov, former third secretary of the Russian Embassy, in the afternoon of April 3. They were in an envelope. The documents were folded together and page 35 was in the same bundle of documents which were now known as document 'J'. All the documents received from Petrov were photographed about 11 p.m. on the night of April 3.

136 'Unusual Features in "J"' . *The Sydney Morning Herald* (NSW), 27 August 1954, p. 7.

137 'Certain I Have Been Named a Traitor'. *The Sydney Morning Herald* (NSW), 10 July 1954, p. 4.

> ...Dr. Evatt said it was important that page 35 had not been stapled to other sections of document 'J' when it was handed over.
>
> Richards said that he did not know when **document 'J' was stapled together by Mr. B. B. Riley,** one of the Junior counsel assisting the Commission. It was some weeks after he had received the documents from Petrov.
>
> Dr. Evatt said that page 35 was unrelated to document 'J' and was put into the document to make it appear that it was part of the original.
>
> To Dr. Evatt, Richards said that he had sought the permission of the **Commissioner of Police, Mr. C. J. Delaney,** for photographs to be taken of the pages of document 'J'. The **original** of document 'J' was in the custody of N.S.W. police experts while the photographs were taken.

At this point in Richards' testimony, Windeyer intervened to clarify any misunderstandings which Richards may have introduced:

> Mr. Windeyer: My instructions are that the only photostats of 'J'were taken on the night of April 3 by the Australian Security Intelligence Organisation. The **originals** were handed to the **N.S.W. police experts,** who photographed them, after unfastening any staples. The prints which have been made available to counsel are taken from the police negatives.[138]

The Document J allegedly handed over by Petrov to Richards was a carbon copy of an original which had, again allegedly, been sent to Moscow. This carbon copy had passed through the hands of, in order, Vladimir Petrov, George Ronald Richards, Colonel Spry [139] and Prime Minister Menzies.[140]

Then this carbon copy had been photographed by New South Wales Police. Copies made from photographic negatives of the carbon copy had then been presented to the Commission and stapled together by Mr. B.B. Riley, junior counsel assisting the Commission.

There was never an 'original' of Document J despite the deceptive use of the word by both Windeyer and Richards.

---

138 'No Slur on Journalists, Judge Says'. *The Sydney Morning Herald* (NSW), 27 August 1954, p. 7.

139 'Security Officer Slept in Room'. *The Sydney Morning Herald* (NSW), 9 September 1954, p. 4.

140 'Petrov Wanted Job on Land'. *The Courier Mail* (Brisbane, QLD), 9 September 1954, p. 6.

Section 5: A Fabrication and a Forgery

On 27th August, Dr. Evatt again addressed the Commission on the subject of Document J:

> The Leader of the Federal Opposition, Dr. H. V. Evatt, Q.C., alleged at the Royal Commission on Espionage yesterday that document 'J' was "a fabrication and a forgery" and that Fergan O'Sullivan had typed at least part of it.
>
> Dr. Evatt said the document had been "concocted" as a conspiracy to harm the political party which he and his two clients (members of his staff) represented.
>
> Dr. Evatt, speaking heatedly, said he alleged that document 'J' had been compiled for a local political purpose. "I will say that 'J' is a fabricated document, a concoction that was brought together at the time it was handed to Mr. G. R. Richards (Deputy Director of Security)", he said.[141]

Throughout the Document J phase, there were repeated attempts by the Commissioners and Windeyer (counsel assisting the Commission) to link Rupert Lockwood with the Document J alleged to have been given by Petrov to George Ronald Richards and now in the possession of the Commission. At the same time, the Commissioners and Windeyer employed every possible means at their disposal to avoid investigating the Document's provenance and to prevent Fergan O'Sullivan's crucial role in the charade from ever being investigated.

Note

A copy of the page headed 'Dr. Evatt' (Document J 35) can be viewed by accessing the National Archives of Australia website and searching for the papers of Professor K.H. Bailey related to the *Royal Commission on Espionage.* [142]

141 Document Forgery, Dr. Evatt Claims'. *The Sydney Morning Herald* (NSW), 28 August 1954, p. 1.

142 'Papers of Professor K.H. Bailey related to *Royal Commission on Espionage'. National Archives of Australia* < https://recordsearch.naa.gov.au/ >

CHAPTER TWENTY-ONE

The Chain of Transmission

It should have been a simple matter for Petrov to give a coherent account of how he acquired and removed the documents from the Russian Embassy. Instead we find a complicated series of documents and a veritable complex of stories. Petrov changed his story every time he told it. Every change was necessary at the point in the proceedings where it was introduced. Every change won the approbation of the Commissioners.

Section 1: Petrov's Original Account

To simplify this account, the term 'Safe 1' is substituted for the MVD 'Secret Safe' and the term 'Safe 2' for the MVD Money Safe. Another safe, the Embassy safe, is not relevant and is disregarded:

- All the documents were removed from Safe 1 on 20th February 1954 at 10.00 p.m. (T:1009, T:1149). All of the documents produced at the Commission were placed in two envelopes and then transferred to Safe 2 (T:1027, T:1023. T:1010, T:1026). A certificate, or "act" was placed in Safe 1 indicating that the 101 photographs (the 'Moscow Letters') had been destroyed in accordance with instructions (T:237, T:713, T:717, T:1092-3, T253);
- The two envelopes in which the transferred documents had been placed were wrapped inside a copy of the *Pravda* newspaper and concealed in a drawer in Safe 2 under other papers (T:1004,T:1009);
- On 1st April 1954, the documents were removed from Safe 2, taken to Petrov's private residence in Canberra, and hidden under a mattress (T:1004);
- On 2nd April 1954, Petrov took the documents to Sydney where he showed them to Richards of the Security Service;
- The documents were finally handed to Richards on 3rd April 1954, still in two white envelopes and still wrapped in a copy of *Pravda*;

- The documents delivered to Richards were in exactly the same condition as they were when transferred from Safe 1 to Safe 2 on 20th February 1954 (T:754).

The following elements of the account require thorough investigation:

1. The layout of the Russian Embassy in Canberra and the location of Safes 1 and 2;
2. The keys to Safe 1 (the MVD 'Secret Safe');
3. The alleged transfer of documents from Safe 1 to Safe 2 on 20th February 1954.

When all these elements are subjected to such an investigation, it will become apparent that Petrov's original account of how he acquired and removed the documents from the Russian Embassy was a total fabrication.

Section 2: Location of Safes

The Russian Embassy in Canberra was a "plain rectangular two story building of light coloured brick with a blue-grey roof".[143]

Safe 1, from which Petrov allegedly took the documents on 20th February 1954, was in the room of the head of the cipher department (T:208pa747), in the MVD section on the second floor (T:101pa834). According to Petrov's descriptions, Safe 2 must also have been located in the same section on the same floor. But Petrov also said Safe 2 was on the floor above Safe 1. It was "upstairs" in relation to Safe 1; Safe 1 was "downstairs" in relation to Safe 2 (T:1004, T:1009pa38-40, 55).

Petrov's descriptions of the location of Safe 1 in relation to Safe 2 require the addition of a third story to the Embassy building.

Section 3: The Keys to Safe 1

Access to Safe 1, the MVD 'secret safe', is crucial. Was Mrs. Petrov, not Petrov himself, responsible for its contents? Did Petrov have open access? If Petrov had open access, could he have forged documents and placed them in the safe? At all times, the Petrovs insisted that there were only 2 keys—a 'working' key and a 'spare' key. Who controlled the working key? Who held the spare key and was it under seal? Were

143 'Prime Minister Orders Royal Commission: Russian Spies Here'. *The Courier Mail* (Brisbane, QLD). 14 April 1954, p.1.

there more than two keys? A multitude of questions hinge on the facts concerning the keys to Safe 1, the MVD 'secret safe'.

Note carefully the differences in specifications in the following stories. A minimum of 6 keys, and very probably more, would be necessary to satisfy all specifications.

The Petrovs, while retaining their basic story about there being 2 keys, simply changed the specifications to meet all the demands made on their story under cross-examinations. In the following list of specifications, the 'working key' will be referred to as 'a' and the 'spare' key as 'b'. One alone was needed to open the safe:

- **a.** **1 key:** This key was kept in a sealed envelope in the table of the chief cipher clerk, Prudnikov (T:99). To open the safe, Mrs. Petrov had to obtain this key from Prudnikov. After use, the key was as resealed in an envelope and returned. Prudnikov would not hand this key to Mr. Petrov (T:665). Prudnikov could not break the seal (T:209). At lunch or after work it was handed over by register to a duty commandant (T:665).
- **b.** **1 key:** This key was the spare key 'b' kept by Prudnikov the chief cipher clerk. He could not use it (T:209). (Key 'b' was the spare key, key 'a' the one in use.)
- **c.** **1 key:** This key was kept by the cipher clerk in a table drawer in a sealed packet. Petrov could open the safe with this key at any time. He did not have to ask Mrs. Petrov. (This could not be key 'a' because Prudnikov would not give him that key. It could not be key 'b' because that key was kept sealed.)
- **d.** **1 key:** The working key 'a' was kept in the table of the chief cipher clerk. It was sealed. Petrov obtained the seal from Mrs. Petrov before taking the key. After use he resealed the key and replaced it. The seal was then returned to Mrs. Petrov (T:100). (This could not be key 'c'. With 'd' Petrov had to ask Mrs. Petrov because she controlled the seal, but with key 'c' he did not have to ask Mrs. Petrov.)
- **e.** **1 key:** This was not the usual working key 'a' but the spare key 'b'. This key was kept in a specially made bag sealed by Mrs. Petrov. Mr. Petrov could take this key but he would have to wait for Mrs. Petrov to unseal it (T:665). She alone had access to the safe (T:665).
- **f.** **1 key:** This key was kept in the safe of the head of the code section of the Embassy (T:99-100) who was not the chief cipher clerk (T:100). (This could not be any of the keys supposedly held by Prudnikov.)
- **g.** **1 key:** This was the usual working key. 'a'. It was always kept by Mrs. Petrov (T:642, T:99). (Mrs. Petrov withdrew the existence of this key after reading portion of her previous evidence.)

The Petrovs were allegedly highly trained MVD operators, opening and shutting their 'secret safe' as part of their daily routine. Possession of the keys meant control of the safe yet they could not give a coherent account of the procedure required to obtain possession of the keys. The force of the disparities in the various statements is striking.

Section 4: The Transfer of Documents

In his original account, Petrov claimed that all of the documents produced at the Commission were transferred within the Embassy from Safe 1 to Safe 2 on 20th February 1954. The date for the removal of the documents from Safe 1 was clearly specified with the greatest of precision on dozens of occasions.

These documents included those referred to as the 'Moscow Letters' (the 101 photographs of Russian typewriting), the 17 supplementary pages handwritten in Russian by the Petrovs, the 18 notes handwritten in Russian and labelled by the Commission as G1-G18 (the 'G' Series), the 37 carbon copy pages of typewriting in English (Document J) and the 3 pages of typewriting in English (Document H).

All these documents were placed in two white envelopes and wrapped in a copy of *Pravda*.(T1017pa405, T1005pa1455-63-64, T1026-7, T1128pa800-809, T1023pa649, Transcript for 20th, 21st and 29th September 1954.)

According to his original account, Petrov spent that day, 20th February 1954, at the Kirketon Hotel in Sydney. He left Sydney by ANA aircraft at 6.10 p.m. (T1012pa174-6, T1016). At 10.00 p.m. the same night, he and his wife were in the 'secret' section of the Russian Embassy in Canberra with Safe 1 (the 'secret safe') wide open and all the secret documents lying on a table (T713pa812, T717pa991).

Petrov pretended to destroy by fire the 'Moscow Letters' (the 101 photographs of Russian typewriting) in accordance with a set procedure. He and his wife then signed a certificate that these photographs had been destroyed. The certificate, or 'act', was inserted in Safe 1. The date was particularly insisted upon and received the imprimatur of the commissioners (T1004pa1438, T1092pa744, T1093pa760, T1009pa23, T237pa179, T642pa283, T253pa33-5, T747pa87-90.)

No change in condition of documents

As noted, in his original account, Petrov claimed that **all** of the documents produced at the Commission were transferred within the Embassy from Safe 1 to Safe 2 on 20th February 1954. That date for the removal of the documents from Safe 1 was clearly specified with the greatest of precision on dozens of occasions.

When **all** of these documents were finally delivered to Security by Petrov, they were contained in 2 white envelopes and wrapped in a copy of *Pravda*. The documents were thus claimed to be in exactly the same state as when transferred from Safe 1 to Safe 2 on 20th February 1954.

Section 4: The 'G' Series

Although complex, a thorough understanding of the varied accounts told by the Petrovs about the 'G' series is essential.

Among the documents allegedly brought by Petrov from the Russian Embassy and handed to ASIO were 18 handwritten Notes.

These Notes were labelled by the Royal Commission as the 'G' Series. They referred either to persons by their real names, some with biographical information, or to persons by code names which were readily identifiable by cross-reference to other Notes in the 'G' Series. The information in these Notes is clearly of ASIO origin. (See Chapter 18: *The 'G' Series of Notes.)*

According to evidence given by the Petrovs during the course of the Commission, these eighteen Notes comprised:

- Nine allegedly handwritten between the years 1945 and 1949 by Valentin Sadovnikov, a former MVD Chief Resident in Australia. These notes had been left by Petrov's predecessors for his guidance. They were labelled by the Commission as G1-G3, G5-G10 .
- Eight handwritten by Petrov between 1952 and 1954. These Notes were labelled by the Commission as G11-G18.
- One handwritten by Petrov copied from two notes allegedly left behind by Sadovnikov. This Note was labelled by the Commission as G4.

In summary, Petrov allegedly delivered to ASIO nine Notes in handwriting not his own (allegedly Sadovnikov's), and nine Notes in his own handwriting, one of which (G4) was a copy of the two Sadovnikov Notes left behind.

Section 5: The Sadovnikov Notes

Note

The Sadovnikov Notes is a term given by the Commission to the nine Notes allegedly handwritten by Valentin Sadovnikov. These Notes either referred to persons by their real names, some including biographical information, or to persons by code names which were readily identifiable by cross-reference to other Notes in the G Series.

The incriminating evidence concerning Max Falstein, previously mentioned in Chapter Seventeen: *The Moscow Letters*, was contained in G9, one of the alleged Sadovnikov notes so we are able to bypass all the arguments about whether the handwriting was Sadovnikov's or not. In addition, Dr. Charles Monticone, a handwriting expert with over twenty years courtroom experience in testing disputed documents, was of the opinion that the Sadovnikov Notes in the possession of the Commission were forged.

The 'N' Envelope

In addition to the nine Sadovnikov Notes produced at the Commission, there were the two Notes left behind by Sadovnikov, making a total of eleven Notes allegedly left in the MVD 'secret' safe (Safe 1) by Petrov's predecessors at the Embassy.

Until 20th October 1954, these eleven Notes were referred to at the Commission as loose sheets of paper.

On that date, Windeyer announced out of nowhere that the nine Sadovnikov Notes delivered by Petrov to ASIO had actually reposed in Safe 1 in a sealed envelope marked 'N' throughout the entire period from 1951-54. The two remaining Sadovnikov Notes left behind in Safe 1 had been sealed in a similar envelope.

As Windeyer's authority, he cited a statement labelled Exhibit 52 which was submitted by Petrov to the Commission on 30th June 1954.

There are three peculiar features connected with this Exhibit 52 :

- its details were never recorded in the Transcript;
- it referred to only two of the nine Sadovnikov Notes;
- for some time subsequent to the introduction of Exhibit 52, no mention was made of an 'N' envelope but only of loose sheets of paper.

The contradictions and variations concerning the eleven Sadovnikov Notes and the 'N' envelope allegedly containing nine of these Notes are of such magnitude that a selection of them is simply recorded. In reading these entries, bear in mind the full significance of the word 'sealed'.

Evidence given by Mrs. Petrov

T:2809—Mrs. Petrov had seen the nine Sadovnikov Notes in detail at least as early as February 1952. The Notes appeared to be kept as loose papers together in the MVD safe (Safe 1). (Transcript dates: 1st July, 20th July, 21st July 1954).

T:1760pa434 —Mrs. Petrov said there were two loose sheets of paper left in Safe 1 after Petrov defected. (Nine of the eleven Notes had allegedly been taken by Petrov). Petrov's successor destroyed these two loose sheets of paper. There was no suggestion that these were contained in an envelope (T:2809pa118-9, 21 July 1954).

T:2098pa568—Mrs. Petrov handed over the contents of Safe 1 to Petrov's successor on 8th April 1954.

T:222—Mrs. Petrov handed over the contents of Safe 1 to Petrov's successor on 15th April 1954.

T:1775pa23—The 'N' envelope containing the nine Sadovnikov Notes was sealed when Mrs. Petrov first received it from Sadovnikov. It remained sealed until she opened it for Petrov's successor, Kovalenok, in April 1954.

T:2004pa174— Mrs. Petrov did not see the contents of the 'N' envelope until the Royal Commission. She had only been given a quick glance at the contents when Sadovnikov was sealing up the packet before passing it on to his successor Ivan Pakhamov through her. (See also T:2006pa217).

T:2801-03—Mrs. Petrov could identify every document taken from the 'N' envelope.

T:1299pa269—Mrs. Petrov herself actually put the material in the 'N' envelope.

T1298-1300 —Mrs. Petrov was even able to identify the Note known as 'G13' as coming from the 'N' envelope. (Unfortunately for both her and the Commissioners, this was a totally different Note which had nothing to do with the alleged 'N' envelope).

T:2005pa185, 193— Mrs. Petrov may not have seen the 'N' envelope containing the nine Notes while it was in Safe 1—Petrov had his shelf (1952-54) and she had hers.

T:2005pa184— The original 'N' envelope containing the nine Sadovnikov Notes was in Safe 1 until a week before Petrov defected.

Evidence given by Mr. Petrov

T:99, T: 2799—Mr. Petrov had seen the nine Sadovnikov Notes in detail at least as early as February 1952. The Notes appeared to be kept as loose papers together in the MVD safe (Safe 1). (Transcript dates: 1st July, 20th July, 21st July 1954).

T:352pa59 —Mr. Petrov first saw the eleven Sadovnikov Notes in February 1952. (See also T:124pa159).

T:1753pa158— Mr. Petrov first saw the eleven Sadovnikov Notes in March 1954.

T:1753pa166—Mr. Petrov first saw the sealed 'N' envelope allegedly containing the nine Sadovnikov Notes in February 1952 when Sadovnikov's temporary successor Ivan Pakhamov handed it over to him.

T:1525pa28– Mr. Petrov copied the 2 Sadovnikov Notes (G4) and extracted the remaining eight (G1-G3, G5-G10) the first time he opened the 'N' envelope.

T:1758pa375—The documents removed from the 'N' envelope were transferred immediately to Safe 2 by Petrov.

T:1758pa358— Mr. Petrov never saw any of the 'N' documents until the end of March 1954. (See alsoT:1617pa49, T:2245pa292, T:1344pa836, T:1478pa46).

T:2009pa335 —The 'N' envelope could be opened only with the permission of Moscow. (See also T:2014pa584).

T:2004pa146 —Mr. Petrov could open the 'N' envelope any time he chose.

Section 6: The Travesty

The conflicting evidence told by the Petrovs about the acquisition and removal of the *Petrov Papers* is more than adequate to demonstrate that the documents were forged and that the entire proceedings of the Royal Commission was a travesty:

The finger of accusation points at the Australian Security Intelligence Organisation. The test of *Cui-bono* points also in the same direction.

It is untenable that three judges should be so hopelessly incompetent as not to notice the many irreconcilable statements made by the Petrovs. Their imprimatur was placed so readily upon Petrov's infinity of stories that it becomes just as readily evident that Petrov's evidence was tailored to keep the Commission in progress in accordance with demands made upon Petrov by the Commissioners themselves.

The documents were delivered to Petrov by the Australian Security Intelligence Organisation in order that they might constitute the basis for a legal inquisition into the affairs of persons in whom Security was interested.

At the same time an attempt was made by means of the English-language documents to frame and destroy Dr. Evatt.

Section 7: The Reasoning

There were three main reasons for all the foregoing changes and contradictions in Petrov's account:

1. Petrov had to justify his inaction with regard to persons concerning whom he had allegedly received instructions. His dilemma was that he had to claim to have received instructions yet acknowledge that he did not act upon them.
2. Protection for Mrs. Petrov whose relatives still resided in the USSR. Mrs. Petrov as "an MVD operator", had both to be aware of a change in the condition of documents in the Embassy prior to Petrov's departure in order to support Petrov's story, and at the same time not be aware in order to maintain her own claim that she did not know he intended to defect. In other cases, she had both to know and not to know of the references to particular persons in the documents.
3. To deny fraud, forgery, and conspiracy allegations made by Dr. Evatt and others, Petrov had to deny opportunity and this involved him in denying he had access to the documents. At other times he had to claim he had open access.

The reasons for the changes and contradictions in Mrs. Petrov's account were:

1. She had both to know that the **original** 'N' envelope (the one containing the nine Sadovnikov Notes had changed to an envelope containing the two remaining Sadovnikov Notes (Exhibit 52) — thus confirming that the documents were actually taken from it—and not to know the same thing because it incriminated her in Petrov's preparations for defection. (She insisted strenuously at all times that she knew nothing of his plans.)
2. She had both to know what was in the 'N' envelope (to confirm authenticity of the documents) and not to know because of action, or inaction connecting her with persons named in the Sadovnikov Notes. And so on, and so forth…

Notes

The date chosen for the removal of the documents from Safe 1 (the 'secret safe')— 20th February 1954— was 7 days before Petrov had his first contact with the Deputy Head of ASIO, George Ronald Richards. Clearly, the purpose of choosing that date was to have 'evidence' on record that the documents existed before ASIO came into the picture directly.

Despite his thirty-three month association with Petrov, Security agent Bialoguski not once heard Petrov mention documents. The Commissioners, Petrov, counsel for the Security Service and Bialoguski himself all took pains to emphasise that point (T:973; R:29).

This denial was necessitated by allegations that Bialoguski conspired with Petrov for the purpose of obtaining a large sum of money from Security. Note also that Bialoguski colluded with Petrov to purchase Scotch Whisky from those Sydney wholesalers with an embassy discount and sell it for profit to night clubs[144]

144 Cain, Frank: 'The Petrov Affair and fake documents: another look'. *Honest History.* <https://honesthistory.net.au/wp/cain-frank-the-petrov-affair-and-fake-documents-another-look-2/> Accessed 21 August 2024.

CHAPTER TWENTY-TWO

Gulliver among the Lilliputians

See also Chapter 20: *Document J*

Section 1: The one that mattered

From 16th August 1954, the day when Dr. Evatt first appeared before the *Royal Commission on Espionage* as senior counsel for members of his staff, Alan Dalziel and Albert Grundeman, the accounts told by the Petrovs about how the *Petrov Papers* came into existence and how they were removed from the Russian Embassy began to fall apart piece by piece, especially as it concerned Document J.

Authorship of J was of critical importance. Not only was the credibility of the Petrovs and Richards of ASIO at stake but also the entire basis on which the Royal Commission was established, namely the allegation that Petrov took the documents from the MVD safe at the Russian Embassy and handed them to ASIO.

From the many persons named in Document J, the Commissioners had chosen to focus on Dr. Evatt's staff members. Evatt was right to be suspicious of their motives. His course of action in the Commission was to attempt to demonstrate that the documents had nothing to do with espionage but were brought into existence for the sole purpose of undermining himself and the Australian Labor Party through his staff. This of course meant that he had to challenge the credibility of the Petrovs and Richards of ASIO.

To prove that Document J was a forgery, Evatt had first to examine it. This was no simple matter as the Commissioners had already refused Rupert Lockwood's counsel permission for Lockwood (the alleged author) to see it. Although Evatt had already argued long and hard for access (T:381), he had been supplied only with typed extracts relevant to his clients until 20th August when both he and Mr. Hill, counsel for Lockwood, were finally granted access to Document J (T:505).

After Lockwood and his counsel had examined Document J, Lockwood stated that while the document was based on the material he had supplied to Antonov, (a TASS representative) he denied being its author since completely new sections had been added of which he had no knowledge. In particular, he denied authorship of J 35, the loose sheet headed 'Dr. Evatt' (T:477, 495-501, 536).

When Doctor Evatt was finally granted permission to see Document J, he compared photographs of the document allegedly taken on the night of Petrov's defection with the document now in possession of the Commission. Evatt noticed that J 35, the page headed 'Dr. Evatt', did not have the same tiny pinholes as did the other pages in J. Evatt argued that J 35 was an insertion; that Lockwood may not have done the lettering on J; and that the tattered condition of J indicated that it had passed through many hands rather than resting securely in the MVD safe as alleged.

He further suggested that the Petrovs had been paid £5000 pounds by ASIO in return for claiming that fabricated documents had come from the Russian Embassy. Evatt named Fergan O'Sullivan as co-conspirator with the Petrovs and charged that it was he who had written Document J and not Lockwood. He also charged that ASIO had been negligent in not checking the authenticity of the documents or the credibility of the Petrovs before going to the Prime Minister with their 'revelations' (T:683).

From all of the above, Evatt concluded that J 35 had been a loose sheet added to the rest of J in order to incriminate him (T: 461, 573, 590). When testifying at the Royal Commission on 26th August 1954, George Ronald Richards of ASIO admitted that when he received J it was in four separate parts and that J 35 was indeed a loose sheet of paper which had at one time been attached to a missing document or documents.[145]

Section 2: The 'ring-in'

At the Royal Commission hearings of 28th August 1954, Windeyer argued that the material written in the Soviet Embassy by Rupert Lockwood was the Document J now in the possession of the Commission. His case relied on the evidence given by Inspector James Rogers of the New South Wales Police who had been called in by the Commissioners as their handwriting and document expert. Rogers had claimed that the block capital lettering on J was identical with the lettering on Lockwood's passport application which the Commission had obtained for the purposes of comparison. He further claimed that the typing styles of J and other material Lockwood had written were identical and that the typewriter used for J was the same as that used for official letters from the Soviet Embassy.

However, when Rogers was cross-examined by Dr. Evatt on 28th August, he admitted that J 35 (the page headed 'Dr. Evatt') was typed on a different typewriter and that it may have been a "ring-in":

145 'No Slur on Journalists, Judge Says'. *The Sydney Morning Herald* (NSW), 27 August 1954, p. 7.

Evatt: Did you notice anything about Page 35 from a physical point of view?

Rogers: Essentially, it does not belong there.

Evatt: You mean because of its context and meaning?

Rogers: No. Because of its mechanical construction. I would say it is put there because of its meaning.

Evatt: What do you mean by its mechanical construction?

Rogers: The fact that it is apparently typed at a different stage by a different machine to Pages 36 and 37. It is my opinion that it was put in that place because it relates closely to the material on the previous page. The marks on the top of Page 35 appeared to have been made by a pin and not a staple.

Evatt: It might have been a document which could be characterised as a "ring in" to this Document J?

Rogers: It could be. [146]

Rogers' testimony was the only evidence independent of hearsay by the Petrovs that Lockwood was the author of the Document J in the possession of the Commission and that this document was identical to the one he had typed in the Soviet Embassy and which had then been sent to Moscow. (Evidence of Passport Officer R.W. Edwards at T:234-5 and of Inspector J.H. Rogers at T:239-247).

Section 3: The one that didn't matter

Dr. Evatt requested that the Commissioners call to give evidence Dr. Charles Monticone, an expert with over twenty years courtroom experience in testing disputed documents. At first the Commissioners seemed to agree but the very next day they changed their minds arguing that experts may give conflicting evidence and, since the decision about which expert opinion to accept was theirs alone, they would accept the evidence of Inspector Rogers that Lockwood was the author of the Document J in possession of the Commission.

Evatt argued that if the Commissioners refused to hear evidence because it may disagree with that already presented, it was tantamount to saying that only one side of a case should be heard since it was known in advance that the opposing side would disagree.

146 'Evatt claims on Document J: Says Lockwood not the author'. *The Courier Mail* (Brisbane, QLD) 28 August 1954, p. 1.

In order to minimise the significance of authorship, the Commissioners said they now believed that the issue of the lettering on the Document was only **of minor significance** (T:717-8, 721-4).

Only later, after Evatt had been ejected from the Commission, did his junior counsel succeed in reading into the Transcript Monticone's opinion on the documents. Monticone regarded Rogers' examination of the documents as totally inadequate in that he had failed to take into account all the dissimilarities between Lockwood's block lettering and those in the margins of Document J. In his view, they were not all written by the same person (T:1060).

After a short examination of Monticone's opinion, Mr. Justice Owen declared that "it was not a document that carried any weight to my mind" (T:1033).

Now that the true authorship of Document J was perilously close to being revealed, Mr. Justice Owen attempted to downplay the significance of the following statement he gave on 15th July when he effectively delivered Dr. Evatt into the hands of the Triumvirate and their press henchmen:

> "... it is very disturbing to find a document of this sort (J) in which the writer claims to have got information from two persons who are in the secretariat of a man who holds a very high position in political life...What disturbs us is that the document quotes as sources on various matters, some of which are of a confidential nature, three members of the secretariat of the Leader of the Opposition..." (T:297-8)

Section 4: A "foul and most serious conspiracy"

At the Royal Commission hearings of 1st September 1954, Dr. Evatt alleged that four persons were connected with the "conspiracy" involving Document J:

> Dr. H. V. Evatt yesterday accused the Australian Security Service deputy director (Mr. G. R. Richards) concerning a "conspiracy for a local political purpose". Crowded public galleries at the Espionage Royal Commission listened in stunned silence to the Federal Opposition Leader.
>
> He named four people whom he alleged were connected with the "conspiracy" involving Document J.
>
> Dr. Evatt said the four were: Former Soviet spy chief in Australia, Vladimir Petrov; his wife, Evdokia Petrov, also a former Russian spy; Dr. Evatt's former Press secretary, Fergan O'Sullivan; and Mr. Richards.

> Chairman of the Commission (Mr. Justice Owen) said Mr. Richards should have the opportunity to consider whether he and the Australian Security Service should be legally represented at the Commission to defend the charges of "criminal conspiracy".
>
> ...Dr. Evatt had been told he must name the persons he alleged were involved in a conspiracy over Document J. Document J was one of the secret papers handed over to the Security Service by Petrov, when he sought political asylum in Australia.
>
> Document J named Dr. Evatt's private secretary Mr. A. Dalziel and assistant secretary Mr. A. Grundeman as sources of information for the Russians.
>
> Dr. Evatt is appearing before the Commission for Dalziel and Grundeman. Fergan O'Sullivan has admitted that he wrote Document H—a dossier on members of the Canberra Press Gallery. The three Judges frequently interrupted Dr. Evatt with demands that he answer their questions specifically as he replied to the ultimatum.
>
> Dr. Evatt said he would call evidence to substantiate charges that Document J had been used in a "foul and most serious conspiracy" to injure himself and members of his staff.
>
> He said Mr. Richards had failed in his duty to his country by accepting a "fabricated document" without making proper investigations.
>
> He told the commission: "The sensational way in which the documents were handed over by Petrov indicates an intention in his mind to make the documents of assistance to the Federal Government on the eve of an approaching election".[147]

Also on 1st September, Evatt made a formal application to inspect the records of the Security Service relating to interviews and other matters between Security officials and the Petrovs. Mr. Justice Owen refused his application:

> Mr. Windeyer said that diaries, reports, tape recordings and other secret security material would be made available to the Commission, and the Commission only. He had made inquiries and had received notification from the Attorney-General that this security material would be made available only on condition that only the Commission was allowed to inspect it.
>
> Mr. Justice Owen said the Commission did not propose to make available to anyone, including Dr. Evatt, reports by Security officers to their superiors in the

147 'Doctor Evatt Accuses Security Service: Names 4 people in "conspiracy" over Document J'. *The Courier Mail* (Brisbane, QLD), 2 September 1954, p. 1.

service. "We think that to take that course would be utterly improper and would tend to prejudice the security of our country and we do not propose to take it", he said.

Dr. Evatt said that he (and other counsel) should be able to inspect the reports and files of documents.[148]

Section 5: Desperate Measures

On 7th September, the Royal Commissioners withdrew Dr. Evatt's right to appear at the Commission, ostensibly over his public statement protesting the treatment of Madame Ollier. (See Chapter Sixteen: *Madame Ollier.*)

In addition to the treatment of Madame Ollier, the ostensible reason given by the Commissioners for withdrawing Dr. Evatt's leave to appear, Evatt had foreshadowed several courses of action he was going to take in future. These were:

- He would prove that Lockwood was not the author of Document J;[149]
- He would question Dr. Michael Biologuski about evidence given in Melbourne by Petrov;[150]
- He would question George Ronald Richards further about Document J;[151]
- He would bring further evidence that Document J was a forgery;[152]
- He would further question Inspector Rogers about Document J and refute certain of his evidence;[153]
- He would prove that it was an open secret that Petrov was planning defection from as early as January 28, 1953;[154]

---

148 'Conspiracy Claim: Three Names'. *The Sydney Morning Herald* (NSW), 2 September 1954, p. 1.

149 'Document Forgery, Dr. Evatt Claims'. *The Sydney Morning Herald* (NSW), 28 August 1954, p. 1.

150 'No Indication of Forgery in Document J'. *The Sydney Morning Herald* (NSW), 31 August 1954, p. 6.

151 'Conspiracy Claim: Three Names'. *The Sydney Morning Herald* (NSW), 2 September 1954, pp. 1,4.

152 Ibid.

153 Ibid.

154 Ibid.

- He would closely examine certain aspects of the Moscow Letters to ascertain their authenticity.[155]

On 16th September, Evatt applied for readmission to again represent as senior counsel his clients Grundeman and Dalziel. His application for fresh leave to appear included the following statement which illuminates just how far the Commissioners were willing to go to ensure that Evatt did not have the opportunity to cross-examine Richards any further:

> My exclusion from the Commission was directed on September 7th, the very day appointed for the cross-examination of Mr. G.R. Richards (Deputy Director of Security). It was also the day that Sir Garfield Barwick, QC, (council for Mr. Richards and the Security Service) came into the case...[156]

Dr. Evatt's application for fresh leave to appear was, unsurprisingly, rejected. Evatt's persistent and penetrating questioning of witnesses thus far had edged ever closer to exposing the charade that was the Royal Commission. The courses of action Evatt had foreshadowed as well the further cross-examination of Richards, the Petrovs, Inspector Rogers, and Michael Bialoguski would have been viewed by the Commissioners with mounting desperation.

Section 6: Statement of Concern

On 10th September 1954, three days after his leave to appear was withdrawn, Dr. Evatt issued a statement which dealt with the misconceived functions of the Royal Commission, the way in which it had been conducted, and his ejection on the very day scheduled for the cross-examination George Ronald Richards. The most relevant parts of his statement were reported in the press and are listed below:

Judicial Procedures

> "The members of the present Commission have at times departed from the safeguard of established judicial procedure. There is no appeal whatever from any of their many decisions already given. Some of these decisions are manifestly wrong, notably the refusal to hear the evidence of the handwriting expert Dr. Monticone.

155 'Shot if she went back to Russia says Mrs. Petrov'. *The Sydney Morning Herald* (NSW), 3 September 1954, p. 6.

156 'Claim of Conspiracy Fantastic'. *The Courier Mail* (Brisbane, QLD), 17 September 1954, p. 9.

“Even with Judges acting judicially, the right and duty of public criticism do not disappear. As one great English Judge has rightly said: ‘Justice is not a cloistered virtue—she must be allowed to suffer the scrutiny and respectful, even though outspoken, comment of ordinary men’. [157]

“And the same Judge added: ‘Whether the authority and position of an individual Judge, or the due administration of justice, is concerned, no wrong is committed by any member of the public who exercises the ordinary right of criticising, in good faith, in private or public, the public act done in the seat of justice’”.[158]

Concealed Payment

“…There has been a radical change in the picture of Petrov as presented by Mr. Menzies on April 13th before the elections and the true facts which are coming out in small installments.

“The Commission commenced its sittings on May 17th. It was then known to the Government that a large sum of money had been paid to Petrov before he handed over the documents to the Security Service. Yet the case was presented to the people at Canberra without any disclosure of this very large grant of money out of the public purse to an informer. Even now the full sum is not yet ascertained.

“The Australian public should have been given the truth of the matter by demand of the Royal Commission at the very opening of the sittings on May 17th last”.

Fabricated Documents

“…At the express direction of the Commission, I formulated specific charges in relation to exhibit J. It was, I submit, quite wrong to force me to specify them at that time. But I did so and have consistently adhered to them.

“They were based on the allegation of a conspiracy of which the two Petrovs were the centre. It was a conspiracy to fabricate exhibit J and a charge against Security Officer Richards that he had paid a large sum of money to Petrov and accepted the documents without taking proper care to test their genuineness when proper testing at the time would immediately have revealed the exhibit as faked and fraudulent in vital respects.

157 ‘Evatt Asks For Wider Basis in Petrov Inquiry’. *The Sydney Morning Herald* (NSW), 11 September 1954, pp. 1, 3.

158 Lewis, G. *Lord Atkin*. Hart Publishing: Oxford, 1996, p. 96.

"Subsequently my exclusion as counsel prevented my cross-examination of Richards for the purpose of making good additional parts of our case.

"...In exhibit J there are no less than 50 persons named as informants. In addition to O'Sullivan, ex-employee of the 'S.M. Herald,' only two persons of this very large number have been named before the Commission. Why should the names of these other informants be kept out of the case while the present staff of the Labor leader are alone named and injured? [Fergan O'Sullivan, who was Press secretary to Dr. Evatt, has admitted to the Commission that he wrote document 'H' for the Russian Embassy.]

"The defence raised by my two clients was first that they were completely innocent of disclosing any confidential matter. But second I submitted—as counsel was entitled to do—that the inclusion of their names in exhibit J was a fraud and a fake. That was only another way of saying that two persons or more were involved in the concoction that necessarily involved a conspiracy to fabricate the document which would be ultimately revealed to Security Service for the fraudulent purpose of assisting in the sale of such documents to the Government of Australia.

"It is beyond dispute that Document J has been physically manipulated in such a way that one vital page was never physically attached to any other portion of the same group of documents. Moreover, that self-same page had clearly been attached to one or more separate documents which were not produced by Petrov to Security Officer Richards. In other words the vital page was "rung in" before Security Service received the documents, while at the same time Petrov seems to have "rung out" one or more other documents which were not produced.

"...in our view the fabrication has extended to the even more important documents called the 1952 Moscow Letters; these must have been concocted long after 1952 for the very purpose of implicating persons named therein as possible agents or informants and for deceiving and defrauding the Security Service and Australian taxpayer.

"...I demanded the right to question Dr. Bialoguski who is now admitted to have been a 'go between' for Security Service with Petrov. His evidence should and could have been called months ago. It shows that Petrov was preparing himself for defection over a very long period and had ample time to fabricate documents. Through Bialoguski, Petrov received further money from the Commonwealth.

"...The research and preparation involved in relation to the case of fabrication of Document J and of the Moscow Documents made the exclusion of myself as senior counsel a grave interference with the case of my clients especially as

Richards, Bialoguski and the Petrovs were coming up as witnesses. The decision to exclude counsel should have been reviewed and set aside.

"...Clearly the Petrov case has changed from an ordinary espionage case to a conspiracy to fabricate documents and to see them defraud the people of Australia".

Madame Ollier

"...the present Commissioners have mentioned or allowed to be mentioned, the names of some persons as being involved in misconduct not only without prior notice, causing almost irreparable injury, but (in the case of Mme. Ollier), without affording her the slightest opportunity of defending herself against her accusers (the two Petrovs).

"...Because as Leader of the Opposition I made a public criticism of the French Ambassador, which was completely justified, I was excluded as counsel. That is, I was excluded as counsel because as Labor leader I expressed an opinion on a matter of extreme public concern".

The Petrovs

"From time to time the Commission has strongly rebuked those who dared to criticise the two Petrovs. At the same time the Commission has in effect sanctioned by ignoring streams of newspaper articles and propaganda as well as broadcasting commentaries defending and even glamorising the two Petrovs. Some of the newspapers concerned were included amongst those who were anxious to purchase the right of the Petrov story explaining why 'They Chose Freedom'.

"There are instances in the transcript where members of the Royal Commission have interfered with the examination of witness in a way which resulted in the assistance of the Petrovs and the hindering of cross examination. This fact added to the avoidable secrecy gravely impaired the effectiveness of the inquiry and hindered an effective cross-examination which is essential to the British system of justice".

The Judges

"Unfortunately, each of the three Judges of the Commission was personally selected by the Prime Minister. In the case of Queensland, this caused a public criticism by the Premier who pointed out that, although the Chief

Justice of that State had nominated a distinguished Judge to act, his name was immediately rejected by the Prime Minister".

Summary

"Summarising the position, I submit that the general proceedings of the commission show that it has misconceived its functions, that it proceeded on the assumption that the Petrov story must be substantially true, that its procedures were not in accord with the established practice of Courts of Justice and resulted in in-justice, that there was a partial and discriminating selection of names mentioned in Exhibit J, that evidence obviously admissible has been rejected out of hand, that comments favourable to the Petrovs have been condoned by the commissioners who from the first have taken up a fallacious attitude too favourable to the Petrovs notwithstanding that their credibility is one of the essential elements in the case.

"The Commissioners by their conduct of the inquiry have, it is submitted, failed to discharge their statutory duty and acted erroneously in point of law".[159]

Section 7: Security 'Concerns'

Throughout the period of Dr. Evatt's appearance at the Commission, his persistent and penetrating questioning of witnesses edged ever closer to exposing the Petrovs and others as liars. Time and again, the Commissioners assured counsels appearing for witnesses that they alone had access to a vast cache of material supplied to them by ASIO which had convinced them of the credibility of the Petrovs and ASIO. This material could not be made available to Evatt or any other counsel because it fell under the umbrella of 'security concerns'.

Section 8: A 'frame-up'

After Menzies' 12th August 1954 speech in Parliament (See Chapter Fourteen: *Nailing the Coffin*), Alan John Dalziel sent Menzies a telegram to protest his use of Parliamentary privilege to attack him:

"You are reported as mentioning my name under cover of Parliamentary privilege. This would seem to conform to the pattern followed by your duly

159 'Evatt Asks For Wider Basis in Petrov Inquiry'. *The Sydney Morning Herald* (NSW), 11 September 1954, pp. 1, 3.

appointed instrument, which publicly named me without warning, on the basis of the infamous Document J. It would now seem you are following the same methods which allow some persons mentioned in J to be cited while other names, which are said to include your own and other anti-Labour politicians, are suppressed". [160]

On 13th September 1954, Dalziel gave evidence at the Royal Commission without the benefit of his senior counsel, Dr. Evatt. Questioned by Sir Garfield Barwick, QC, Dalziel said that a telegram he sent to the Prime Minister Mr. Menzies on August 14th last had been composed by himself without any consultation with other persons:

> Dalziel added: "The telegram's contents came from the heart as I felt at the time. The telegram added: 'As a fellow Presbyterian, I suggest that we both appear before the Courts of our Church where I may be happy to have my moral integrity and loyalty to my country tested with yours'".
>
> Sir Garfield: Did you have any information on August 16th or 17th that document 'J' had been written by more than one person?
>
> Dalziel: I knew nothing about document 'J' except a document circulated among Federal members which was supposed to be an abridgement of 'J'. I heard certain members say that Mr. Menzies was in the document. They alleged that this was the reason why they wanted to keep document J 'smothered', because Mr. Menzies and other anti-Labour members were in the document.
>
> Sir Garfield: Do you say that document 'J' as a whole was fabricated to hurt you?
>
> Dalziel: The references to me in document 'J' are demonstrably false and were put in the document to frame me.
>
> Dalziel said he was not accusing Petrov or Richards of putting this material into document 'J' or having any part in making it up. He did not know who had made up document 'J'.

Mr. Justice Owen ordered that the reference concerning Dalziel in Document J should be read out. This stated that Dalziel had given information to the author of Document J that a Professor Kluckhohn had visited Australia to investigate alleged pro-Russian sympathies in Australian schools. Dalziel said he had never met Kluckhohn in his life. He said that Lockwood was just a nodding acquaintance, and the last time he had met Lockwood was about four years ago:

160 '2 of staff subpoenaed: Evatt silent on spy probe appearance'. *The Courier Mail* (Brisbane, QLD), 14 August, p.1.

> He (Dalziel) said that he accused Richards of being negligent in not testing the document fully before accepting it. The Australian Embassy in Washington could easily have contacted Professor Kluckhohn, who would have told them that he had never met Dalziel. [161]

Sir Garfield Barwick then followed with a question which may have caused his ASIO client a little unease:

> Barwick: Do you say Petrov made the document up?
>
> Dalziel: I don't know who wrote it.

Dalziel went on to say that he did not claim Richards (ASIO) had any part in making it up but that he was "grossly negligent for not testing it".

Dalziel was given permission to study Document J in an anteroom while Albert Grundeman gave evidence.

Grundeman agreed with Dalziel about ASIO's supposed "negligence":

> "...I think Mr. Richards was negligent in not testing the truth of the documents". Grundeman added that he thought the portion of Document J, referring to him, should have been shown to him by a Security officer so that he could deny it, even before it was shown to the Prime Minister.

Dalziel then re-entered the courtroom and told Mr. Justice Owen that he had read through document J. Dalziel declared that he thought some of the references contained in the last three pages of J appeared to have been manufactured:

> Mr. Meagher (counsel for O'Sullivan): What do you think now about the alleged authorship of document 'J' by O'Sullivan?
>
> Dalziel: I think that parts of pages 35, 36 and 37 appear to be manufactured. The parts where members of Dr. Evatt's staff are said to be sources of information, particularly Grundeman, were not within their knowledge. The information about the visa belonging to Dr. Evatt was demonstrably false.
>
> Mr. Meagher: Are you suggesting that O'Sullivan is the author of the part relating to Dr. Evatt?
>
> Dalziel: He could have been the source of information.
>
> Mr. Meagher: Having read the whole of document 'J', would it ever come to your mind that the document was written by O'Sullivan?

161 'Attempt to frame him in Document J'. *The Sydney Morning Herald* (NSW), 14 September 1954, p. 4.

Dalziel: Not all of it.

Mr. Meagher: You suggest that some of it could have been written by O'Sullivan?

Dalziel: **The last three pages could have been written by him.** [162]

The Commission's *Transcript of Daily Proceedings* and the *Report of the Royal Commission on Espionage* reveal that, before he was ejected from the Commission, Dr. Evatt's persistent and penetrating questioning of witnesses had edged ever closer to demonstrating that the *Petrov Papers* were forgeries and that his proposed courses of action at the Commission were likely to remove any remaining doubts as to the identity of the forgers.

162 'Document J Reference to him untrue says Dalziel'. *Brisbane Telegraph* (QLD), 13 September 1954, p. 2.

CHAPTER TWENTY -THREE

The Interim Report

In the face of mounting criticism by counsel appearing for witnesses, especially surrounding the provenance of Document J, the Royal Commissioners decided to issue an Interim Report which was tabled in Federal Parliament on 26th October 1954.

The Commissioners main conclusions concerned the English language documents H and J.

They found that Document H was an authentic document and that the Petrovs' statements regarding the document were proven to be true (R:420). Although their claim that O'Sullivan wrote the document was correct, the Commissioners accepted the word of the Petrovs alone that Document H had been used for espionage purposes.

Document J was the main focus of the Interim Report. The Commissioners found that Rupert Lockwood was the sole author based on the testimony of the Petrovs (R:420, 427). Inspector James Rogers' testimony was the only other evidence independent of hearsay by the Petrovs that Lockwood was the author of the Document J in the possession of the Commission and that this document was identical to the one he had typed in the Soviet Embassy and which had then been sent to Moscow (Evidence of Passport Officer R.W. Edwards at T:234-5 and of Inspector J.H. Rogers at T:239-247).

The Commissioners refused to hear or take account of any evidence to the contrary.

Just as with Document H, the Commissioners did not attempt to explain Document J's significance in relation to espionage. Rather, they spoke of the "charges of infamy" made by Doctor Evatt and his junior counsel:

> "All we heard was constant re-iteration of vague charges of infamy" (R:425).

According to the Report, charges against ASIO were "entirely disproved" and were "calculated to not only arouse disquiet in Australia but also to shake the confidence of other friendly nations in the integrity of that service" (R:428-9).

The Report sought to establish that the Commissioners, after examining all the issues patiently and judiciously, had come to the correct conclusion that Documents H and J were authentic and that the integrity of ASIO was beyond question.

On 28th October 1954, Dr. Evatt addressed Parliament on the subject of the Interim Report. The most relevant points of his address were:

1. That if he had been warned, he would never have left the House just hours prior to Menzies' shock announcement of Petrov's defection on 13th April;
2. That there was an absolute contradiction between the facts as stated by the Prime Minister on the 13th April and the facts as proved in evidence before the Royal Commission;
3. That the 13th April claim by Menzies that Petrov had only come to the attention of ASIO a few days previously was untrue;
4. That when the Royal Commission opened in Canberra, not a word was said in the opening address that Petrov had been paid £5,000;
5. That the Leader of the Opposition (Evatt) receives the confidence of the Director-General of Security and, as such, is as much entitled to information about Petrov as is the Prime Minister;
6. That within an hour of discovering on 4th June that his press officer Fergan O'Sullivan was the author of Document H, Evatt had dismissed him;
7. That the government had known months before about O'Sullivan but allowed him to remain on Evatt's staff;
8. That Menzies knew by 4th April at the latest that names of persons on his staff were mentioned in Document J and that page 35 of the document was a special page headed with his (Evatt's) name. Yet he said nothing although, as Leader of the Opposition, it was Menzies' duty to warn him;
9. That the physical evidence showed that page 35 of Document J was not attached to the other pages but had been inserted separately;
10. That when Evatt saw page 35 of Document J, he concluded immediately from its style and language that O'Sullivan was the author (The Interim Report concluded that Lockwood was the sole author of Document J);
11. That if Lockwood was not the sole author as the Petrovs claimed, then they and the actual authors had entered into an agreement for the purpose of producing Document J.

For Dr. Evatt's complete address,which contains elements crucial to a more thorough understanding of the forces at work in *Operation Petrov*, see *Hansard* [163]

163 'Dr. Evatt Address' (28 October 1954). *Historic Hansard.* House of Representatives, 21st Parliament, 1st Session. < https://historichansard.net/hofreps/1954/19541028_reps_21_hor5/> Accessed 27 November 2022.

CHAPTER TWENTY -FOUR

Enemies Unmasked

Section 1: The Movement

(See also Chapter Three: *Enemies of the People* and Chapter Eight: *The Gouzenko Affair.*)

On 9th October 1954, Dr. Evatt publicly stated that the Australian Security Intelligence Organisation and the Triumvirate had at least 15 months foreknowledge of Petrov's defection. More disturbingly, all the interconnected events leading up to the defection pointed to collusion between the Australian Intelligence Network, the Australian and United States Governments, and the Movement led by B.A. Santamaria:

> A close link existed between the Security Service and the Santamaria group controlling the Melbourne paper *News Weekly*, Dr. Evatt said last night.
>
> ...Dr. Evatt said *News Weekly* had "prior knowledge" that the former Third Secretary at the Russian Embassy (Vladimir Petrov) would defect...Dr. Evatt added: "The significant fact is that 15 months before the supposedly spontaneous coming across of Petrov, this newspaper and the anti-Labor group which control it forecast disclosures soon to be made on the activities of Petrov. That they knew at the very least of the Security Service's special knowledge of Petrov is proved beyond doubt by their unguarded boast, 'We tipped you off 15 months ago'".
>
> 1 repeat that Petrov's defection was not a sudden and immediate desire for asylum and freedom, nor a spontaneous wish to embrace the democratic way of life. It was the culminating point in a very prolonged process of the nursing of Petrov by the Security Service for a period of more than two years until the time was ripe to make the melodramatic announcement of political asylum.
>
> Dr. Evatt said the link between the Santamaria group and the Security Service would have to be exposed in the public interest. An article in *News Weekly* on April 28th last conclusively proved his assertion that the newspaper had forecast Petrov's defection in January 1953. Dr. Evatt said.

He added that, on April 28th, after Petrov's defection, but before the opening session of the Royal Commission, the *News Weekly* in a specially panelled paragraph on its front page boasted of its "tip-off" 15 months before. The paper (*News Weekly*) then quoted its own article of January, 1953.

Dr. Evatt said: "It stated that startling repercussions were expected to follow disclosures soon to be made on the activities of certain members of the Soviet Diplomatic Service in Australia. It then stated that the case of the Third Secretary of the Russian Legation was a sample of what would be revealed in the anticipated disclosures. The Third Secretary was Petrov".

"The point is that those controlling the anti-Labor newspaper, *News Weekly*, must have been in the closest touch with the Security Service. The closeness of the link between this anti-Labor group I have mentioned and the Security Service will be cleaned up. The link was forged in a manner calculated to discredit the Labor movement on the eve of an election". [164]

Section 2: The Spectre of Vietnam

Dr. Evatt's assertions were met at the time with pious accusations of 'sectarianism' by Santamaria. For example, in *The Sydney Morning Herald* article of 21st October 1954, he denied that he was the mastermind of the ALP Industrial Groups and spoke of the "flames of sectarian bitterness" and the "frightening spectre of religious intolerance". Santamaria went on to warn Australians of a coming war, a war which had long been in the planning by the Movement:

> "Because of the rapid unification of part of South-East Asia under Chinese Communism, this country will face a **fundamental military challenge to its very existence within 25 years.**
>
> "If all Australians were united, our backs would still be to the wall. But if the trade-unions are to fall again to Communism, and if the nation is to engage in fratricidal strife, because of the calculated use of the weapon of sectarianism, we can roll up the map of Australia. It will not be needed again".[165]

164 'Evatt attack on Catholic Paper: Security Service Link Claimed'. *The Daily Telegraph* (Sydney, NSW), 10 October 1954, p. 6.

165 'Mr. Santamaria answers critics'. *The Sydney Morning Herald* (NSW), 21 October 1954, p. 5.

Section 3: "Cold and malevolent treachery"

On 27th October 1954, Dr. Evatt addressed the Federal Executive of the Australian Labor Party and repeated in detail his assertions of 10th October. The essential elements of his address are reproduced below.

Concerning the Santamaria group's infiltration of the Labor Party

> "Meetings of the parliamentary Labor party were being used systematically in 1954 as a forum for attacks on Evatt by an organised group within the ALP which was motivated by "cold and malevolent treachery". False reports of events at the meetings were a deliberate attempt to subvert the leadership of the party by systematic defamation.
>
> "The attitude of the group was expressed from week to week in the Melbourne paper *News Weekly*. The leader of the group of which *News Weekly* was the organ was B.A. Santamaria".

Concerning the Petrov conspiracy

> "The defection of Vladimir Petrov from the Russian Embassy in April 1954 was carefully organised and timed to coincide with the May 1954 federal election.
>
> "Menzies withheld vital information and misled parliament and the Australian people in his original statement announcing Petrov's defection.
>
> "Evatt's activities in establishing evidence at the Royal Commission which completely destroyed Menzies' original statements about Petrov, were bitterly attacked by a member of the Santamaria group within the ALP.
>
> "*News Weekly*, the organ of Santamaria's Movement, had shown an awareness of Petrov's impending defection 15 months before it took place.
>
> "When the facts of the Petrov Affair were finally known, it would rank in history as an equivalent of the notorious Zinovieff letter of 1924, and of the use made by the Hitler regime of the Reichstag fire of 1933".

Concerning Fascism

In his concluding remarks, Dr. Evatt warned of the dangers of Fascist control of the Labor Party.

> "The greatness of the Labor Movement is that it continues after our death for the noble purposes of still carrying on and carrying out its great objectives. Any secret organisation, the object of which is to gain control of the Party in order

> to concentrate on a policy of sheer anti-Communism must in the long run assist Communism just as McCarthyism has done in the USA.
>
> "The Movement and its members have a right to be as anti-Communist as much as they wish. They have no right to subvert the Labor Party in order to dedicate it solely or primarily to anti-Communist activities. They have a complete right to their own opinion. But they have no right to infiltrate into and seize control of the Labor Movement or the trade union movement. Labor cannot survive on the basis of a party within the party.
>
> "Once it was the danger from Communism. Today it is a danger perilously akin to Fascism".[166]

More than two years after Dr. Evatt's assertion that Santamaria was the leader of the group which had infiltrated the Labor Party, at a time when it was evident to all and no longer possible to deny, Santamaria himself finally admitted the truth of the assertion:

> B.A. Santamaria, big-shot back room boy of the Industrial Groups, has brazenly admitted the truth of Dr. Evatt's charge that an "outside influence" has long been working to white-ant the labor movement.
>
> Writing in the *Bombay* (India) *Examiner*, Santamaria defends the right of the Movement to penetrate working class organisations and subvert their policies. Although Santamaria openly admits the influence of a section of the Roman Catholic hierarchy in the Movement, he makes it clear that the Industrial Groups are a reactionary political organisation and not a religious one.
>
> He praises the "reliability" of some non-Catholics who play a leading role in the Industrial Groups, and bitterly attacks those many Catholics who defend Labor policy.
>
> Santamaria's latest manifesto of disruption has roused widespread anger in the Catholic Church as well as the labor movement.
>
> Mrs. Jean Daly, a prominent Catholic lay woman, was one of the first to attack his article. Mrs. Daly—who has been Australian representative to the Status of Women Commission of the United Nations, president of the UN Association in Australia, vice-president of the NSW Division of the St. Joan's International Alliance and a prominent CUSA worker— wrote in the English paper *Tablet* that Santamaria's ideas did not accord with the teaching of the Church and that his activities had been harmful.

166 'The Movement is a danger to Labour Party akin to Fascism'. *Queensland Times* (Ipswich, QLD), 1 December 1954, p. 1.

> "This is the major reason," she wrote, "why many important lay Catholics (and it is common knowledge that the disagreement does not end with the laity) have declined to be associated with or approve of the Movement and the activities of Santamaria".
>
> That only a minority of Catholics support the Industrial Groups' disruptive activities has been bitterly lamented by Santamaria for a long time. Yet he continues to try to deceive Catholic workers by clothing his disruption in a religious garb.[167]

As for Dr. Evatt's October 1954 assertions concerning the Petrov Affair, it proved to be all that he had claimed. Although successfully targeted for destruction by the Triumvirate (see Chapter Three: *Enemies of the People*), he left for posterity all the evidence necessary to expose their treachery, evidence gleaned from his penetrating questioning of the Petrovs and other witnesses at the *Royal Commission on Espionage* and which only became apparent by a painstaking analysis of the evidence contained within the *Transcript of Daily Proceedings of the Royal Commission on Espionage* and the *Report of the Royal Commission on Espionage.*

167 'Santamaria Exposes Himself'. *Tribune* (Sydney: NSW), 26 September 1956, p. 2.

CHAPTER TWENTY-FIVE

The Final Report

Section 1: 'Witnesses of truth'

The final *Report of the Royal Commission on Espionage* was presented to the Governor-General on 22nd August 1955 and to Federal Parliament on 14th September 1955.

It concluded that the *Petrov Papers* were genuine and that the Petrovs were 'witnesses of truth'.

ASIO's briefings and strongly-held anti-communist views were the lens through which the Commissioners interpreted all the evidence. The *Report of the Royal Commission on Espionage* is a case study in prejudice, obfuscation and deception.

As is evident by systematic analysis of the *Transcript of Daily Proceedings of the Royal Commission on Espionage*, the three judges appointed by Menzies to play the role of Inquisitors avoided implementing proper judicial procedures at every turn thereby preventing the provenance of the *Petrov Papers* from ever being tested.

Section 2: Bought for a price

Unfortunately for Menzies and ASIO, when they chose Vladimir Petrov to be their defector, they did not choose wisely. They suborned Petrov, an inept and drunken oaf, by providing him with a succession of parties and prostitutes, by bribing him with the promise of a poultry farm, and by eventually paying him £5,000 pounds to say he brought the fabricated *Petrov Papers* from the Russian Embassy in Canberra.

Another poor choice was Petrov's groomer, security agent Dr. Michael Bialoguski. On 8th May 1953, eleven months before Petrov defected, Bialoguski had approached Harry Mullin, the U.S. Vice Consul in Sydney, and offered his services to the U.S.A. on a matter of international importance. [168]

We need hardly be told what the matter was. His services were declined as events were proceeding according to a defection timeline and had almost a year yet to unfold. (See also Chapter Nine: *Operation Petrov.*)

168 Bialoguski, Michael. *The Petrov Story*. Heinemann: Melbourne, 1955, p. 122.

Bialoguski had also colluded with Petrov to purchase Scotch Whisky from those Sydney wholesalers with an embassy discount and sell it for a profit to night clubs.[169]

Both men could be bought for the right price, and they were.

During the course of the Royal Commission, the Petrovs were unable to provide consistent evidence about any aspect of their accounts. If they were indeed 'witnesses of truth', as the Commissioners described them, describing the accounts should have been a relatively simple matter. However, the evidence contained in the Transcript demonstrates that there were three major switches of direction in the narrative, each necessary to cover up the vulnerability of the previous version. It all fell apart piece by piece and their contradictory evidence mounted up correspondingly.

Analysis of the *Transcript of Daily Proceedings of the Royal Commission on Espionage* and the *Report of the Royal Commission on Espionage* reveals that every single aspect of the Petrovs' accounts were total fabrications.

Perhaps it was expected that no one would ever subject the Transcript and the Report to a painstaking analysis and catalogue all the discrepancies and contradictions contained within them. Unfortunately for the perpetrators, however, it has been done, more than once.

---

169 Cain, Frank: '*The Petrov Affair and fake documents: another look.*' *Honest History.* <https://honesthistory.net.au/wp/cain-frank-the-petrov-affair-and-fake-documents-another-look-2/> Accessed 21 August 2024.

CHAPTER TWENTY-SIX

Ignorance is Bliss

Despite the involvement of ASIO in the three-year successful suborning of Vladimir Petrov, and the knowledge in certain government departments that a defection was pending, Prime Minister Menzies claimed that he never once heard the name 'Petrov' until 10th April 1954, three days before the defection. That is his story.

The evidence tells a different story

- The B.A. Santamaria publication *News Weekly* forecast on 28th January 1953 that disclosures concerning the work of a Third Secretary of the Russian Embassy would have startling repercussions (T:958pa551);
- The U.S. Vice Consul in Sydney, Harry Mullin, knew of the "international importance" of Security contact Michael Bialoguski's work in May 1953 (TPS140, TPS122); [170]
- Prior to 12th September 1953, the day on which the Russian Ambassador Lifanov officially bid farewell to Menzies, Bialoguski was interviewed by Geoffrey Yeend, Menzies' private secretary, over a dispute between Security as to the manner of reimbursement (TPS138-40) [171] for his services in connection with an 'enormous setback' about to be received by the U.S.S.R;[172]
- A conference of Australian Security representatives was held on 1st December 1953 in preparation for Petrov's defection (T:737pa298-300);
- In the closing months of 1953, Bialoguski visited *The Sydney Morning Herald*, mentioned the name 'Petrov', and offered to write articles outlining his experiences (T:998pa1147);
- To ensure that Petrov received asylum immediately he defected, the heads of Federal government departments were notified on 17th February 1954 of the action which was to be taken if such would eventuate (T:963pa787);

170 Bialoguski, Michael. *The Petrov Story*. Heinemann: Melbourne, 1955, p. 122. 140.

171 Ibid.

172 Dulles, Allen. W. *The Craft of Intelligence*. Harper and Row: New York, 1963, p. 117.

- On 4th April 1954, George Ronald Richards, Colonel C.C.F. Spry and a translator went to Canberra with the *Petrov Papers* and laid them before Menzies (T:923pa303 of 16th September 1954, T:1104pa45-49 of 29th September 54).

- Months after this evidence had been established absolutely, Menzies was still insisting that he first heard the name 'Petrov' on 10th April 1954, three days before Petrov's defection. By insisting on this date as the first on which he heard the name 'Petrov', he was able to distract attention from the more than coincidental timing of Igor Gouzenko's resurrection in Canada on 13th April 1954, thus protecting his secret association with those in the U.S. who had engineered the resurrection;

- A similar position existed with regard to Menzies' knowledge of the payment of £5,000 pounds to Petrov on 3rd April 1954. Menzies said he first heard of this payment on 9th May 1954.[173] His reason for choosing this date was that Mrs. Petrov came on the Australian payroll on 10th May 1954.[174] As he could not deny knowledge of the payment to Mrs. Petrov, and this implied knowledge of the previous payment to Vladimir Petrov, Menzies chose the last date available to him, 9th May 1954;

- When George Ronald Richards, the Deputy Head of ASIO who made the payment, gave his evidence on 18th May 1954, he suppressed all reference to the £5,000 pounds. The Australian public did not learn of this reimbursement to Petrov 'for services rendered' until long after the May 1954 election. Windeyer knew, Richards knew, Menzies knew. But not the Australian people.

Despite all of the above, the Prime Minister of Australia, Robert Gordon Menzies, remained blissfully ignorant of Petrov's impending defection until 10 April 1954.

As a result of the Petrov Affair, Menzies was able to consolidate his grip on power until his retirement in January 1966 by which time he had committed Australian combat troops to Vietnam.

173 'Petrov Payment Leads to Bitter Exchanges'. *The Age* (Melbourne, VIC), 13 August 1954, p.1.

174 ''Embassy was told'. *The Age* (Melbourne, VIC), 18 September 1954, p.5.

A Final Word

As noted in previous Chapters, it had become imperative for the Movement and its co-conspirators that the Labor Party never come to power and that their stated policy of non-intrusion and non-interference in the domestic affairs of foreign nations not be realised because it had been taking steps since the early 1950's to ensure that Australia, together with the projected involvement of the United States, would intervene in Indo-China in the likely event that France would lose control of its colonies of Vietnam, Cambodia and Laos.

When it became clear that French defeat was inevitable, *Operation Petrov* was launched with the 13th April 1954 announcement of Petrov's defection just three weeks before the final defeat of the French Union Forces at Dien Bien Phu on 7th May 1954.

CHAPTER TWENTY-SEVEN

Revisionism

In the 1990's, a succession of press reports and articles suggested that the legitimacy of Petrov's status as a spy was proven by documents from the 1940's emerging from Russian and U.S. Archives. Nothing could be further from the truth. The archival material proves only that more and more of the information supposedly revealed in the *Petrov Papers* was already in ASIO's possession by 1954.

There could be no better example of an attempt to transform Petrov's status than an *Australian Dictionary of Biography* article by Phillip Deery.[175]

From being an inept and bumbling oaf who colluded with Dr. Michael Bialoguski to purchase Scotch Whisky from those Sydney wholesalers with an embassy discount and sell it to night clubs, [176] Petrov is transformed into a person of who had much to offer to Western intelligence.

Manifest errors in the article are as follows.

Access to Embassy Safes

> *Evdokia's expertise in 'sigint' (signals intelligence) was as important as the information Vladimir had gleaned from his unrestricted access to embassy safes.*

A Demonstrable Lie

Petrov did not have unrestricted access to embassy safes. (See Chapter Twenty-One: *The Chain of Transmission*).

An Unverified Claim

There is no evidence whatever that Evdokia Petrov had "*expertise in 'sigint' (signals intelligence)*". On the contrary, at the Royal Commission she claimed not to know her official posting but said that she was the secretary to the Ambassador and bookkeeper to the Embassy.

175 Deery, P. 'Vladimir Mikhailovich Petrov'. *Australian Dictionary of Biography*, <https://adb.anu.edu.au/biography/petrov-vladimir-mikhailovich-18740> Accessed 14 August 2024.

176 Cain, Frank: 'The Petrov Affair and fake documents: another look.' *Honest History*. <https://honesthistory.net.au/wp/cain-frank-the-petrov-affair-and-fake-documents-another-look-2/> Accessed 21 August 2024.

Burgess and Maclean

During an early debriefing with ASIO on 6 April 1954, Petrov had revealed the whereabouts of the two missing British diplomats, Guy Burgess and Donald Maclean. His revelation that they had defected to the Soviet Union caused great consternation in Britain.

A Demonstrable Lie

The whereabouts of Burgess and Maclean were unknown and their defection not confirmed until 1956 when the pair called a press conference and revealed that they were in Moscow. [177]

Highly Prized Intelligence

The intelligence that the Petrovs supplied to ASIO and, by default, the Western intelligence community, was highly prized. They identified six hundred Soviet intelligence officers; gave detailed information on espionage activity in Britain, Sweden, and the United States; provided new insights into Soviet methods of disinformation and crypto-analysis; contributed to the further decrypting of the Venona cables of Soviet intelligence messages; and were debriefed by overseas spy agencies about the organisation, structure, and modus operandi of Soviet espionage.

A Demonstrable Lie

These bold claims stand in stark contrast to the T*ranscript of Daily Proceedings of the Royal Commission on Espionage* and the *Report of the Royal Commission on Espionage* which reveal Petrov's true worth to Western Intelligence. Consider also the view of Dr. John Burton, the head of the Australian Department of External Affairs (1947-1951) who said that **Petrov was "too stupid" to be of value** and was unlikely to have had access to any significant information; his defection, therefore, was of little concern to the Russians.[178]

The Venona Decrypts

The defections resulted in the Royal Commission on Espionage, which commenced on 17 May 1954. It sat for 126 days, examined 119 witnesses and received over five hundred exhibits. The latter included the controversial 'Petrov Papers,' a substantial number of documents he had removed from the Soviet embassy over several months and handed over to ASIO at the time of defection. Although many communist

177 'Burgess and Maclean tell why they fled'. *The Argus* (Melbourne, VIC), 13 February 1956, p. 2.

178 Burton, P. Edwards, M. *Persons of Interest: An Intimate Account of Cecily and John Burton,* Canberra: ANU Press, 2022, p. 214.

supporters alleged the Petrov Papers to be forgeries, the Venona decrypts confirmed their authenticity when they were published in 1996.

A Demonstrable Lie

Petrov did not remove documents piecemeal from the Soviet Embassy over a period of several months. Petrov's evidence at the Royal Commission was as follows:

> He removed **all** the documents from a Russian Embassy Safe on the evening of 20th February 1954, placed them in two white envelopes, wrapped the envelopes in a copy of *Pravda*, and then transferred them to another Embassy safe.
>
> On 1st April 1954, Petrov removed the documents from the second safe, took them to his private residence and hid them under a mattress. On 2nd April, Petrov took the documents to Sydney where he showed them to George Ronald Richards (Deputy Head of ASIO). The documents were finally handed to Richards on 3rd April, still in two white envelopes and still wrapped in a copy of *Pravda*.

Petrov's entire account of how he obtained and removed the *Petrov Papers* from the Russian Embassy is demonstrably false. (See Chapter Twenty-One: *The Chain of Transmission*.)

The Venona Decrypts did not confirm the authenticity of the *Petrov Papers*. What they did confirm was that the information contained in the material allegedly taken from the Russian Embassy by Petrov was already in the possession of ASIO.

The manifest errors in the *Petrov Papers* also confirm that they were concocted by ASIO from this material. (See, for example, Chapter Eighteen: *The 'G' Series of Notes* and Chapter Twenty-One: *The Chain of Transmission*).

This demonstrable fact was also noted by Dr. Gregory Pemberton, an expert in International relations and military history, who maintained that the documents in the *Petrov Papers* did not emanate from Moscow but were written and planted by ASIO.[179]

179 Pemberton, Gregory. 'Petrov: History Rewritten', *Weekend Australian*, 6–7 November 1993, p. 19.

PART II

Staging

Every war when it comes, or before it comes,
is represented not as a war but as an act of self-defense
against a homicidal maniac.

— ORWELL

CHAPTER TWENTY-EIGHT

The Chinese Revolution

Note

On 29th August 1949, the Soviet Union detonated its first atomic device, marking the beginning of the nuclear arms race between the United States and the Soviet Union.

Section 1: The Struggle

In 1923, the Chinese Communist Party (CCP) joined with the Nationalist Government of Chiang Kai-shek (ROC) in the 'First United Front' to rid the nation of the warlords that prevented the formation of a strong central government. This collaboration lasted until the 'White Terror' of 1927 when the Nationalists turned on the Communists, killing them or purging them from the party.

After the Japanese invaded Manchuria in 1931, the Nationalist Government faced the triple threat of Japanese invasion, Communist uprising, and warlord insurrections. As with the first effort at cooperation between the Nationalist Government and the Chinese Communist Party, this 'Second United Front' was short-lived. The Nationalists expended needed resources on containing the Communists rather than focusing entirely on Japan while the Communists worked to strengthen their influence in rural society.

During World War II, popular support for the Communists increased. United States officials in China reported a dictatorial suppression of dissent in Nationalist-controlled areas. These polices, combined with wartime corruption, made the government vulnerable to the Communist threat. The CCP, for its part, experienced success in its early efforts at land reform and was lauded by peasants for its unflagging efforts to fight against the Japanese invaders.

The Japanese surrender set the stage for the resurgence of civil war in China. Though only nominally democratic, the Nationalist Government continued to receive U.S. support both as its former wartime ally and as the sole option for preventing Communist control of China. U.S. forces flew tens of thousands of Nationalist Chinese troops into Japanese-controlled territory and allowed them to accept the Japanese surrender.

Meanwhile, the Soviet Union occupied Manchuria and only retreated when Chinese Communist forces were in place to claim that territory.

In 1945, Chiang Kai-shek, the leader of the Nationalist Party (Kuomintang), and Mao Zedong, the leader of the Communist Party, met for a series of talks on the formation of a post-war government. Both agreed on the importance of democracy, a unified military, and equality for all Chinese political parties. The truce was tenuous, however, and in spite of repeated efforts by U.S. General George Marshall to broker an agreement, by 1946 the two sides were fighting an all-out civil war.

As the civil war gained strength from 1947 to 1949, eventual Communist victory seemed more and more likely. Although the Communists did not hold any major cities after World War II, they had strong grass-roots support, superior military organisation and morale, and large stocks of weapons seized from Japanese supplies in Manchuria.

Section 2: 'Losing' China

Years of corruption and mismanagement had eroded popular support for the Nationalist Government. Early in 1947, the ROC was already looking to the island province of Taiwan, off the coast of Fujian Province, as a potential point of retreat. Although officials in the Truman Administration were not convinced of the strategic importance to the United States of maintaining relations with Nationalist China, the U.S. Administration did not want to be charged with facilitating the 'loss' of China to communism. Military and financial aid to the floundering Nationalists continued, though not at the level that Chiang Kai-shek wanted.

On 1st October 1949, after a string of military victories, Mao Zedong proclaimed the establishment of the People's Republic of China (PRC). Chiang Kai-shek and his forces fled to Taiwan to regroup and plan for their efforts to retake the mainland.

The ability of the PRC and the United States to find common ground in the wake of the establishment of the new Chinese state was hampered by both domestic politics and global tensions. In August of 1949, the Truman administration published the 'China White Paper', which explained past U.S. policy toward China based upon the principle that only Chinese forces could determine the outcome of their civil war. Unfortunately for Truman, this step failed to protect his Administration from charges of having 'lost' China.

The unfinished nature of the revolution, leaving a broken and exiled but still vocal Nationalist Government and Army on Taiwan, only heightened the sense among U.S. anti-communists that the outcome of the struggle could be reversed. [1]

For these anti-communists, the establishment of the Peoples Republic of China was new proof of evil Communist intentions. Press, priest and politician repeatedly told the American people that they should be fearful of subversive communist influence in their lives. Communists could be lurking anywhere, using their positions in various professions to aid the program of world communist domination.

This paranoia about the internal communist threat—known as the Red Scare—reached a fever pitch in the early 1950's when Senator Joe McCarthy of Wisconsin launched a series of highly publicised probes into alleged communist penetration of the State Department, the White House, the Treasury, and even the U.S. Army. McCarthy's denunciations created a climate of fear and suspicion across the country, leading eventually to the American public's acceptance of involvement in the Vietnam War.

1 'Milestones in the History of U.S. Foreign Relations: The Chinese Revolution of 1949'. *Office of the Historian, Foreign Relations Institute, United States Department of State* <https://history.state.gov/milestones/1945-1952/chinese-rev> Accessed 21 March 2025.

CHAPTER TWENTY-NINE

The Korean War

Section 1: Policy Path

The collapse of the Chinese Nationalist Government of Chiang Kai-shek in 1949 sharpened American apprehensions over communist expansion in the Far East and hastened U.S. measures to counter the threat posed by Mao's China.

The U.S. sought to create and employ policy instruments in Asia similar to those it was bringing into play against the Soviets in Europe: economic aid, military assistance, and collective security.

Thus, in the closing months of 1949, the course of U.S. policy was set to block further communist expansion in Asia. On that policy course lay the Korean War of 1950-1953, the forming of the Southeast Asia Treaty Organization of 1954, and the progressively deepening U.S. involvement in Vietnam.[2]

Note

See Chapter Forty: *The Pentagon Papers* for an introduction to the Pentagon Papers and the enduring impact of their publication on the American body politic. The Pentagon Papers can be accessed at the *National Archives and Records Administration* https://www.archives.gov/research/pentagon-papers

Section 2: Red Lines

Japan had occupied the Korean Peninsula from 22nd August 1910 until 15th August 1945. Following defeat in World War II, the Japanese rulers of Korea left the country on 2nd September 1945.

The peninsula was then divided into zones of occupation by the victorious U.S. and Soviet Union armies. Various Korean groups from far right nationalists to communists claimed to speak for an independent government but none could reach an agreement with the Soviet and U.S. occupying forces. By 1948, separate governments had formed, each claiming control of the entire peninsula. A border

2 Pentagon Paper [Part I] Vietnam and the U.S. 1940-1950. p. A-6. *National Archives and Records Administration.* < https://www.archives.gov/research/pentagon-papers> Accessed 25 August 2025.

was established along the 38th parallel to separate the communist government in the north from the republican government in the south. The following brief summary is reproduced in part from the United States National Archives:

> After five years of simmering tensions on the Korean peninsula, the Korean War began on 25 June 1950 when the Northern Korean People's Army invaded South Korea in a coordinated general attack at several strategic points along the 38th parallel, the line dividing communist North Korea from the non-communist Republic of Korea in the south. North Korea aimed to militarily conquer South Korea and therefore unify Korea under the communist North Korean regime. Concerned that the Soviet Union and Communist China might have encouraged this invasion, President Harry S. Truman committed United States air, ground, and naval forces to the combined United Nations forces assisting the Republic of Korea in its defense. President Truman designated General Douglas MacArthur as Commanding General of the United Nations Command (UNC).
>
> ...In October, the United Nations, urged by the United States Government, approved the movement of UN forces across the 38th parallel into North Korea in an effort to unify the country under a non-communist government. In spite of warnings issued by the Chinese Government, the United Nations forces moved toward the Yalu River, marking the North Korean border with Manchuria. Discounting the significance of initial Chinese attacks in late October, MacArthur ordered the UNC to launch an offensive, taking the forces to the Yalu. In late November the Chinese attacked in full strength, pushing the UNC in disarray south of the 38th parallel with the communist forces seizing the South Korean capital, Seoul.
>
> In early 1951 the Chinese offensive lost its momentum and the UNC, bolstered by the revitalized 8th U.S. Army led by General Matthew B. Ridgway, retook Seoul and advanced back to the 38th parallel. From July 1951, until the end of hostilities, the battle lines remained relatively stable and the conflict became a stalemate. The Truman Administration abandoned plans to reunite North and South Korea and instead decided to pursue limited goals in order to avoid the possible escalation of the conflict into a third world war involving China and the Soviet Union.[3]

On 27th July 1953, an armistice was signed, ending organized combat operations and leaving the Korean Peninsula divided at the 38th parallel, much as it had been

---

3 ' Korean War'. *National Archives: Dwight D. Eisenhower Presidential Library.* < https://www.eisenhowerlibrary.gov/research/online-documents/korean-war> Accessed 10 February 2025.

since the close of World War II. Note that U.S. Secretary of State, John Foster Dulles, objected to proposals by China and the Soviet Union for a diplomatic reunification of Korea, thus leaving the Korean conflict unresolved. [4]

Dulles was also the person most responsible for thwarting the establishment of a unified Vietnamese State. (See Chapter Thirty-Four: *The Geneva Accords*)

Section 3: The Footnotes

The numberless dead sacrificed on the altar of humanity's interminable wars are rarely afforded more than just a footnote in history. So it was, and so it always will be.

During the Korean War and the reconstruction period following the signing of the Armistice Agreement, twenty-two countries, including Australia and New Zealand, contributed either combat forces or medical assistance to support South Korea under the United Nations flag.

The total casualties of those twenty-two countries were approximately 40,730 dead, 103,460 wounded, with around 5, 800 taken prisoners of war.

From the Australian contingent, 340 were killed and 1,216 wounded. A further 30 became prisoners of war. Out of the 6,000 strong New Zealand contingent who served in Korea, 45 were killed and 79 were wounded.

An estimated two million North and South Korean civilians died.

4 Bailey, Sydney D. (July 13, 1992). *The Korean Armistice*. Springer, ISBN 978-1-349-22104-2.

CHAPTER THIRTY

The Anzus Treaty

On 1st September 1951, the Australian Government signed the ANZUS Treaty, forming a defensive pact with the United States of America and New Zealand.

The treaty stated that 'each party recognises that an armed attack in the Pacific area on any of the Parties would be dangerous to its own peace and safety and declares that it would act to meet the common danger in accordance with its constitutional processes'.

The following summary of the reasoning behind the establishment of the ANZUS Treaty is reproduced from the United States Office of the Historian:

> As the other Allied powers turned their attention to the reconstruction of postwar Europe and Japan in the post World War II era, the governments of Australia and New Zealand remained concerned about the possibility of future Japanese expansionism and grew apprehensive about the rise of communism, particularly in East Asia.
>
> ...The outbreak of the Korean War led Australia and New Zealand to commit troops through the United Nations and alongside the NATO allies, demonstrating both their concern over the threat of communism and their commitment to doing their part to help contain it in the region.
>
> Most importantly, the U.S. decision to end the occupation of Japan and seek a peace treaty was met with great suspicion and disapproval from officials in the South Pacific, and that made the United States more willing to develop a security treaty to gain Antipodean support for the final peace agreement.
>
> In April of 1951, U.S. President Harry Truman announced that negotiations on a tripartite security treaty between the United States, Australia and New Zealand would occur concurrently with the negotiations for a final peace treaty with Japan. Both treaties were concluded in mid-1951, and the ANZUS Treaty was ratified by the United States and entered into force in 1952. [5]

The former Secretary of the Australian External Affairs Department, Dr. John Wear Burton, observed in his book *The Alternative* that:

5 'The Australia, New Zealand and United States Security Treaty (ANZUS Treaty) 1951', *Office of the Historian, Foreign Relations Institute, United States State Department.* <https://history.state.gov/milestones/1945-1952/anzus.> Accessed 10 February 2025.

Australia has left itself no more freedom of action than if it were a state of the American Union.[6]

The ANZAC Backstory

Anzac Day is a national day of remembrance in Australia and New Zealand. Observed on 25th April each year, Anzac Day was originally established to honour the members of the Australian and New Zealand Army Corps (ANZAC) who served in the Gallipoli campaign.

In 1915, Australian and New Zealand soldiers formed part of an Allied expedition that set out to capture the Gallipoli Peninsula to open the way to the Black Sea for the Allied navies. The ANZAC force landed at Gallipoli on 25th April and met fierce resistance from the Ottoman Army commanded by Mustafa Kemal (later known as Atatürk). What had been planned as a bold strike to knock the Ottomans out of the war quickly became a stalemate and the campaign dragged on for eight months.

At the end of 1915, the Allied forces were evacuated after both sides had suffered heavy casualties and endured great hardships. The Allied deaths totalled over 56,000, including 8,709 from Australia and 2,721 from New Zealand.

Since fighting side by side as ANZACs in the Gallipoli campaign, Australia and New Zealand have had a long-standing defence and security relationship. The ANZUS Treaty continues to underpin the strategic relationship between the two countries and formalises the commitments that they have to each other as allies.

Note

United States Secretary of State, John Foster Dulles, was the initiator of the ANZUS Treaty, the architect of the SEATO Treaty, and the person most responsible for thwarting the establishment of a unified Vietnamese State. (See Chapter Thirty-Four: *The Geneva Accords*)

6 Burton, J.W. *The Alternative*, Morgans Publications: Sydney, 1954, p. 75.

CHAPTER THIRTY-ONE

French Indo-China

Section 1: 'Civilising'

The rise of French capitalism in the 1850's fuelled a need for overseas markets and access to raw materials. Like other European powers, France sought to expand its colonial empire and establish its dominance in Southeast Asia, competing with British influence in the region.

In 1857, France used the execution of two Spanish Catholic missionaries by Vietnamese Emperor Tu Duc as a pretext for military action.

A French naval expedition landed at Tourane (Da Nang) in 1858 and captured the town, marking the beginning of a series of military expeditions that pitted the Second French Empire, later the French Third Republic, against the Vietnamese Empire. France emerged victorious, defeating the Vietnamese and their Chinese allies in 1885, incorporating modern-day Vietnam, Laos, and Cambodia into the French colonial Empire, and establishing the territory of French Indo-China in 1887.

The champions of French colonialism justified it as an ongoing responsibility to 'civilise' the peoples of Southeast Asia. In reality, French colonialism in Vietnam had primarily economic motives. Not only did it produce rice, rubber, tea and coffee, coal and zinc, but the colony demonstrated France's great power status. Whatever the causes, the outcomes for the people of Vietnam were dispossession, control, exploitation and brutality.

France installed a series of puppet Nguyen-dynasty emperors and employed a network of French-speaking Vietnamese officials, known as Mandarins, who put the Vietnamese people to work, building roads and canals, railroads, and bridges.

However, just as they had fought against earlier invasions by the Chinese, the Vietnamese began to resist French occupation and, by the early 20th Century, nationalism was on the rise.

Section 2: Ho Chi Minh

Ho Chi Minh (originally Nguyen Sinh Cung) was born on 19th May 1890 in Hoang Tru in central Vietnam. The youngest of three children, he and his siblings grew up in a strongly nationalistic household. He left Vietnam in 1911 for Europe where he worked in London and Paris.

In 1919, he appealed to the Versailles Peace Conference on the basis of Woodrow Wilson's principle of self determination for all nations but had been disappointed by the lack of support given native peoples struggling for independence from colonial rule.

In 1920, Ho became a member of the group that founded the Communist Party of France. He then travelled to Moscow in 1923 where he studied Marxist doctrine before returning to Asia in 1924. Ho then moved to Canton in China where he began to organise a communist movement made up largely of Vietnamese exiles but, three years later, was forced to leave China after the Government launched an anti-communist crackdown.

During the 1930's, Ho returned to China and spent three years in a Hong Kong prison before being released.

Japanese Occupation

In June 1940, Nazi Germany defeated the French Third Republic and the colonial administration of French Indo-China passed to the pro-German Vichy French State.

Taking advantage of the German victory over France, Japan stationed troops in northern Indo-China in September 1940 to secure a base for the resolution of the Second Sino-Japanese War (1937–1945).

To some Vietnamese, the coming of the Japanese seemed to signal a welcome end to white colonial rule but Ho Chi Minh, still in exile in China, saw the Japanese as alien invaders who were no more welcome than the French, being only interested in exploiting his country and seizing Vietnamese crops to fill their own rice bowls. The time had come, he said, to rally patriots of all ages and all types: peasants; workers; merchants; and soldiers to defeat the Japanese and the collaborationist French.

In February of 1941, after three decades away from his homeland, Ho Chi Minh slipped back across the Chinese border into Vietnam and set up headquarters in a limestone cave near the remote village of Pac Bo in Cao Binh Province.

In May of 1941, Ho Chi Minh, Vo Nguyen Giap and Pham Van Dong formed the Viet Minh (League for the Independence of Vietnam), a nationalist coalition dedicated to achieving liberation from French colonial rule and fighting Japanese occupation. Giap's liberation army began to wage guerrilla warfare against the Japanese, who had completely overrun Indo-China.

In July of 1941, the Japanese Army advanced to the southern part of Indo-China to procure a vital jumping-off point for the invasion of Southeast Asia. A treaty for mutual defense between the French Vichy government and Japan was concluded prior to the outbreak of the Pacific War in December 1941.

Due to France's occupation by Germany and weak colonial forces in Indo-China, France was forced to accept the stationing of the Japanese Army on its territory. Indo-China found itself in the unique situation of being occupied by Japan while remaining a French colony.

With the liberation of Paris in August 1944 and an Allied victory on the horizon, the Japanese became concerned about an uprising by French colonial forces. By this time, the Vichy regime had ceased to exist but its colonial administration in Indo-China was still in place.

On 9th March 1945, despite France having anticipated the move, Japan launched a *coup d'état*. French garrisons all over the colony were attacked and overrun. The Japanese replaced French officials and effectively dismantled their control of Indo-China.

During the *coup*, Japan urged the traditional rulers of different regions to declare independence. Bao Dai, Emperor of the Vietnamese Nguyen Dynasty, announced Vietnamese 'independence' and the puppet State of Vietnam came into existence on 11th March 1945 with Bao Dai as nominal leader. The Nguyen dynasty ended with the abdication of Bao Dai following the surrender of Japan to the Allies on 2nd September 1945.

Note that Ho and Giap's Viet Minh worked closely with United States military representatives when both parties shared the common aim of defeating the Japanese.

Independence

On 2nd September 1945, the same day as the surrender of Japan to the Allies, Ho Chi Minh and his Viet Minh forces seized the opportunity. Before a half million people in Hanoi's Ba Dinh Square, Ho Chi Minh proclaimed the establishment of the Provisional Government of the Democratic Republic of Vietnam (DRV).

The first lines of his speech repeated verbatim the famous second paragraph of America's 1776 Declaration of Independence, thus framing Vietnam's struggle for independence in universal terms appealing to Americans:

> All men are created equal. They are endowed by their Creator with certain inalienable Rights; among these are Life, Liberty and the pursuit of Happiness.

Ho Chi Minh missed the opportunity to highlight French hypocrisy and quote the national motto—Liberté, Égalité, Fraternité—which symbolised the fundamental principles of the French Republic, stemming from the era of the French Revolution.

The Democratic Republic of Vietnam was recognised as the legal government of Vietnam by the Chinese Government on 18th January 1950 and, twelve days later, by the Soviet Government.

Communist or Nationalist?

There has been much debate about Ho Chi Minh's ultimate motivation. Did he regard himself as a communist or as a nationalist? William vanden Heuvel, a former Representative of the United States to the European Office of the United Nations, was in Saigon when the French Union Forces were finally defeated on 7th May 1954. He said:

> I was executive assistant to William J. Donovan, Wild Bill Donovan, and spent the last six years of his life with him. And in the context of that, I had a very clear understanding of his attitude, certainly, and of the OSS attitude (Office of Strategic Services). And they certainly saw Ho Chi Minh differently as how he was seen in Washington. They saw him, yes, as a Communist, but dominantly as a nationalist. [7]

Among the 20th Century revolutionaries, Ho Chi Minh waged the longest—and the costliest in terms of human lives sacrificed—battle against colonial power. The forces he led fought and defeated the Japanese, the French and finally the Americans in his fight for Vietnamese independence.

Note

The Nguyen Dynasty's origins are deeply entwined with Vietnam's centuries-long narrative of division, conflict, and aspiration for unity. Following an extended period of civil unrest, Nguyen Phuc Anh united Vietnam, celebrated his coronation at Huế on 1 June 1802 and proclaimed himself Emperor with the title Gia Long. His ascension heralded the commencement of the Nguyen Dynasty.

---

7 vanden Heuvel, William (10 March 2006). 'Vietnam and the Presidency—How we got in: The United States, Asia and Vietnam'. *JFK Presidential Library and Museum* < https://www.jfklibrary.org/events-and-awards/kennedy-library-forums/past-forums/transcripts/vietnam-and-the-presidency-how-we-got-in-the-united-states-asia-and-vietnam> Accessed 14 March 2025.

Section 3: Vo Nguyen Giap

Born around 1911 in Quang Binh Province, Vo Nguyen Giap grew up in a politically active family that instilled in him anti-colonial sentiments.

As previously noted, in May 1941, Ho Chi Minh, Vo Nguyen Giap and Pham Van Dong formed the Viet Minh (League for the Independence of Vietnam), a nationalist coalition dedicated to achieving liberation from French colonial rule and fighting Japanese occupation.

By December 1944, Giap had already begun to develop a distinctive theory of warfare that relied on guerilla tactics until a full scale, conventional attack could be mounted. His army, Giap said, would be "everywhere and nowhere".

Inspired by Napoleon, Lawrence of Arabia, and Mao Zedong, Giap's military leadership was characterized by a blend of strategic brilliance and a ruthless commitment to his cause, garnering both admiration and criticism.

His most notable military achievement was the decisive victory at Dien Bien Phu on 7th May 1954, which marked the end of French colonial rule in Vietnam and established him as a national hero.

Giap's strategies emphasized guerrilla tactics, surprise attacks, and the importance of peasant support, which became fundamental elements in his campaigns against the United States during the Vietnam War. He orchestrated the Tet Offensive in 1968, a campaign that, despite heavy losses, demonstrated the Viet Cong's capability to strike throughout South Vietnam.

Upon his death in 2013, *The New York Times* published an obituary which read, in part:

> Vo Nguyen Giap, the relentless and charismatic North Vietnamese general whose campaigns drove both France and the United States out of Vietnam, died on Friday in Hanoi. He was believed to be 102.
>
> ...General Giap was among the last survivors of a generation of Communist revolutionaries who in the decades after World War II freed Vietnam of colonial rule and fought a superpower to a stalemate.
>
> ...To his American adversaries, however, from the early 1960's to the mid-1970 s, he was perhaps second only to his mentor, Ho Chi Minh, as the face of a tenacious, implacable enemy. And to historians, his willingness to sustain staggering losses against superior American firepower was a large reason the war dragged on as long as it did, costing more than 2.5 million lives—more then 58,000 of them American—sapping the United States Treasury and

> Washington's political will to fight, and bitterly dividing the country in an argument about America's role in the world that still echoes today.
>
> ...His admirers put him in the company of MacArthur, Rommel and other great military leaders of the 20th century. But his critics said that his victories had been rooted in a profligate disregard for the lives of his soldiers.
>
> ...General Giap understood something that his adversaries did not, however. Early on, he learned that the loyalty of Vietnam's peasants was more crucial than controlling the land on which they lived. Like Ho Chi Minh, he believed devoutly that the Vietnamese would be willing to bear any burden to free their land from foreign armies.[8]

Following Vietnam's reunification in 1975, Giap served in various political roles until his retirement, leaving a complex legacy as one of the key figures in Vietnam's fight for sovereignty and a symbol of national resilience.

8 Gregory, Joseph R. 'Gen. Vo Nguyen Giap, Who Ousted U.S. From Vietnam, Is Dead' (4 October 2013). *The New York Times* < https://www.nytimes.com/2013/10/05/world/asia/gen-vo-nguyen-giap-dies.html> Accessed 7 November 2025.

CHAPTER THIRTY-TWO

The First Indo-China War

The following content is reproduced, paraphrased, or adapted from the Pentagon Paper [Part I] Vietnam and the U.S., 1940-1950 and 'The First American Commitment in Indo-China: The Acceptance of the "Bao Dai Solution": 1950' by Gary R. Hess.

See also Chapter Forty: *The Pentagon Papers* for an introduction to the Pentagon Papers and the enduring impact of their publication on the American body politic.

Section 1: The Prelude

Shortly following President Truman's entry into office on 12th April 1945, the U. S. assured France that it had never questioned, even by implication, French sovereignty over Indo-China. The U.S. policy was to press France for progressive measures in Indo-China, but to expect France to decide when its peoples would be ready for independence; such decisions would preclude the establishment of a trusteeship in Indochina except with the consent of the French Government. These guidelines, established by June 1945 before the end of the World War II, remained fundamental to U.S. policy.

With British cooperation, French military forces were re-established in South Vietnam in September 1945. The U.S. expressed dismay at the outbreak of guerrilla warfare which followed and pointed out that while it had no intention of opposing the re-establishment of French control:

> ...it is not the policy of this government to assist the French to re-establish their control over Indo-China by force, and the willingness of the U.S. to see French control re-established assumes that the French claim to have the support of the population in Indo-China is borne out by future events.

On 6th March 1946, France and Ho Chi Minh signed an Accord in which Ho acceded to French re-entry into North Vietnam in return for recognition of the Democratic Republic of Vietnam (DRV) as a "Free State" part of the French Union.

As of April 1946, allied occupation of Indo-China was officially terminated, and the U.S. acknowledged to France that all of Indo-China had reverted to French control.

Thereafter, the problems of U.S. policy toward Vietnam were dealt with in the context of the U. S. relationship with France.[9]

Note

In July 1945 at Potsdam, Germany, the Allied leaders had made the decision to divide Indo-China in half—at the 16th parallel—to allow Chiang Kai-shek to receive the Japanese surrender in the North, while Lord Louis Mountbatten would receive the surrender in the South. The Allies agreed that France was the rightful owner of French Indo-China, but because France was critically weakened as a result of the German occupation, a British-Indian force was installed in order to help the French Provisional Government in re-establishing control over their former colonial possession.

Section 2: The Flash-Point

Despite Ho Chi Minh's declaration of independence and the Viet Minh's cooperation with U.S. forces against Japan during World War II, the U. S. began to ferry French troops to Vietnam in late 1945 to re-establish French colonialism. Armed with American weapons and supported by British troops, the French re-conquest of Vietnam began with an attack on Saigon on 22nd September 1945, marking the beginning of the First Indo-China War.

When the new French Premier Leon Blum took office in mid-December 1946, Ho Chi Minh sent him a telegram with proposals for easing tensions in Vietnam, but the message did not reach Paris until 26th December.

By that time, a flash-point had been passed. On 19th December 1946, after several days of mounting animosity punctuated with violence, Vietnamese troops had cut off Hanoi's water and electricity supplies and attacked French posts using small arms, mortar and artillery.

...The fighting flared across North Vietnam and, two days later, the guerrilla war in South Vietnam quickened pace. The French responded to the initial attacks with an occasional savagery which rendered increasingly remote any hope of restoration of the status quo. [10]

And so began the eight-year long First Indo-China War.

---

9 Pentagon Paper [Part I] Vietnam and the U.S. 1940-1950. p. A-3. *National Archives and Records Administration.* < https://www.archives.gov/research/pentagon-papers> Accessed 25 August 2025.

10 Ibid. p. A-32.

Section 3: The Anomaly

In the latter months of 1948, the Office of Intelligence Research in the U.S. Department of State surveyed communist influence in Southeast Asia. Evidence of Kremlin-directed conspiracy was found in almost all countries except Vietnam:

> Since 19th December 1946, there have been continuous conflicts between French forces and the nationalist government of Vietnam. This government is a coalition with avowed communists in influential positions. The French admit its influence but refuse to deal with its leader, Ho Chi Minh, due to his communist status.
>
> The Vietnam press and radio haven't adopted an anti-American position. The French colonial press has been strongly anti-American and accused the U.S. of imperialism in Indo-China, similar to Moscow's official stance. The Vietnam radio has been watched for a new position toward the U.S., but no change has appeared. There's also no sign of a split within the coalition government of Vietnam.
>
> **Evaluation.** If there's a Moscow-directed conspiracy in Southeast Asia, Indochina is an anomaly. Possible explanations are:
>
> 1. Moscow hasn't issued rigid directives;
> 2. The Vietnam government doesn't feel it needs to purge its rightist elements;
> 3. The Vietnam Communists aren't subservient to Moscow's foreign policies;
> 4. Moscow has made a special dispensation for the Vietnam government.
>
> Of these, the first and fourth seem most likely.[11]

Section 4: The 'Bao Dai' Solution

In 1949, former Emperor Bao Dai was installed by France to head the anti-communist State of (South) Vietnam, a puppet government that served as a counter to the communist Viet Minh.

During January 1950, France took the first concrete steps toward transferring public administration to Bao Dai's State of Vietnam. Ho Chi Minh denied the legitimacy of the latter, proclaiming the DRV as the "only legal government of the Vietnam people".

11 Ibid. p. A-6.

On 29th January 1950, the French National Assembly approved legislation granting autonomy to Bao Dai's State of Vietnam.

The acceptance of what became known as the 'Bao Dai Solution' led the United States to provide increasing financial and military support to France, bringing American prestige and resources into the conflict.

On 1st February 1950, U.S. Secretary of State (Dean) Acheson made the following public statement:

> The recognition by the Kremlin of Ho Chi Minh's communist movement in Indochina comes as a surprise. The Soviet acknowledgement of this movement should remove any illusions as to the 'nationalist' nature of Ho Chi Minh's aims and reveals Ho in his true colors as the mortal enemy of native independence in Indochina.

Formal French ratification of Vietnamese independence was announced on 2nd February 1950. On the same day, President Truman approved U.S. recognition for Bao Dai's State of Vietnam. French requests for aid in Indo-China followed within a few weeks. On 8th May 1950, the Secretary of State (Dean Acheson) announced that:

> The United States Government, convinced that neither national independence nor democratic evolution exist in any area dominated by Soviet imperialism, considers the situation to be such as to warrant its according economic aid and military equipment to the Associated States of Indochina (Vietnam, Laos, Cambodia) and to France in order to assist them in restoring stability and permitting these states to pursue their peaceful and democratic development.

The U. S. thereafter was deeply involved in the developing war (the First Indo-China War). But it cannot be said that the extension of aid was a *volte-face* of U.S. policy precipitated solely by the events of 1950. It appears rather as the *denouement* of a cohesive progression of U.S. policy decisions stemming from the 1945 determination that France should decide the political future of Vietnamese nationalism. Neither the modest O.S.S. (Office of Strategic Services) aid to the Viet Minh in 1945, nor the U.S. refusal to abet French recourse to arms the same year, signaled U.S. backing of Ho Chi Minh. To the contrary, the U.S. was wary of Ho, apprehensive lest Paris' imperialism be succeeded by control from Moscow.

Both the apparent fruition of the Bao Dai Solution, and the patent alignment of the DRV with the USSR and Communist China, impelled the U.S. to more direct intervention in Vietnam.[12]

Truman's commitment of 2nd February 1950 had come after five years of agonizing reflection over the Indo-China situation. Throughout that period, American policy-makers deliberated fundamental issues: the relationship of the Viet Minh to the Soviet Union; the influence of the Chinese civil war on Indo-China and the remainder of Southeast Asia; the viability of the Bao Dai solution; and whether France should be pressed to adopt a liberal colonial policy.[13]

Section 5: Allied Chasms

Note

Between 26th April and 21st July 1954, a conference was due to be convened at Geneva to settle outstanding issues arising from arising from the Korean War and the First Indo-China War. (See Chapter Thirty-Three: *The Geneva Accords.*)

Massive Retaliation

On 12th January 1954, U.S. Secretary of State, John Foster Dulles, described the doctrine of Massive Retaliation in a speech to the Council on Foreign Relations in New York. He argued that rather that adopt a costly and dangerous response to localised communist threats around the world, America would acquire "massive retaliatory power" as a deterrent to communist aggression:

> What the Eisenhower administration seeks is a similar international security system. We want, for ourselves and the other free nations, a maximum deterrent at a bearable cost... Local defences must be reinforced by the further deterrent of massive retaliatory power. A potential aggressor must know that he cannot always prescribe battle conditions that suit him...
>
> The President and his advisers, as represented by the National Security Council, had to make some basic policy decisions. This has been done. The basic decision was to depend primarily upon a great capacity to retaliate, instantly, by means and at places of our choosing. Now the Department of Defence and the Joint

12 Ibid. pp. A-7-8.

13 Hess, G. 'The First American Commitment in Indo-China: The Acceptance of the "Bao Dai Solution" 1950' in *Diplomatic History,* Vol. 2, No. 4 (FALL 1978), p. 331..

> Chiefs of Staff can shape our military establishment to fit our policy, instead of having to try to be ready to meet the enemy's many choices...[14]

Dulles' speech sent a shock wave through allied capitals, especially when, just a few weeks later on 1st March 1954, the United States detonated the first high-yield thermonuclear device at the Bikini Island atolls in the Pacific. His doctrine of massive retaliation implied that he was unafraid to use nuclear weapons and the allies feared the consequences of such brinkmanship.

Less than two months after Bikini, while at the Geneva Conference, the British Foreign Secretary and Conference co-chair, Anthony Eden, expressed such a fear when he said:

> It is the two countries likely to suffer most from bombing—ourselves and Russia—that are most anxious to obtain a settlement.[15]

On 3rd February 1954, the Eisenhower administration warned that Chinese aggression in Indo-China would have "grave consequences that might not be confined to China" and followed up by increasing the military commitment in Vietnam. As Robert Randle observed:

> The administration noted in a 3rd February news conference that the U.S. Military Assistance Advisory Group in Indo-China would be increased by 200 men. In addition, about forty medium bombers (B-26's) would be supplied to the French, which were added to the C-119 troop transports given earlier.[16]

United Action

On 29th March 1954, Secretary of State Dulles delivered an address on 'The Threat of Red Asia' to the Overseas Press Club of America in New York. In that speech, the Secretary outlined the position of the administration with regard to Indo-China and also Communist China. He reaffirmed the support of the United States for the struggle being waged by French Union forces in Indo-China and described the independence movement, the Viet Minh, as a component part of the communist imperialist movement headed by the Soviet Union and Communist China.

---

14 'Evolution of Foreign Policy' (12 January 1954). Council on Foreign Relations, John Foster Dulles Papers, MC016, Public Policy Papers, Department of Special Collections, *Princeton University Library*. < https://findingaids.princeton.edu/catalog/MC016_c9804> Accessed 29 January 2026.

15 Carlton, D. *Anthony Eden*. Great Britain: Penguin Press, 1981, p. 349.

16 Randle, R. *Geneva: 1954*. Princeton University Press: New Jersey, 1969, p. 29.

Dulles described the importance of resisting communist aggression in Indo-China in these words:

> If the Communist forces were to win uncontested control over Indo-China or any substantial part thereof, they would surely resume the same pattern of aggression against the other free peoples in that area.
>
> The propagandists of Red China and of Soviet Russia make it perfectly apparent that the purpose is to dominate all of Southeast Asia. Now Southeast Asia is an important part of the world. It is the so-called 'rice bowl'. It is an area that is rich in many raw materials...And in addition to these tremendous economic values, the area has great strategic value...Communist control of Southeast Asia would carry a grave threat to the Philippines, Australia and New Zealand...The entire western Pacific area, including the so-called 'offshore island chain', would be strategically endangered.

He then went on call for United Action and, after noting Chinese assistance to the Viet Minh, prophesied that aggression would lead to action in places of the free world's choosing, so that the aggression would surely cost more than it would gain.[17]

With the French Union forces facing defeat, Dulles proposed that the United States, Britain, France, Australia, and New Zealand issue a joint declaration warning Communist China against intervention in Indo-China. The Leader of the British Labour Party's left wing made his view of the matter clear:

> Mr. Aneurin Bevan, leader of the British Labour Party's left wing said at Dudley (Worcestershire) last night that Britain should tell the United States she 'was not going to join in a sort of **holy war** against the extension of Communism in South-East Asia or any where else'. [18]

United Action did the opposite of what it was originally intended to do: instead of creating an allied unity to negotiate from a position of strength, it exposed deep chasms within the infrastructure of the allied relationship. Thus, the U.S. and its allies approached the Geneva Conference holding vastly different viewpoints.

---

17 Pentagon Paper [Part II: U.S. Involvement in the Franco-Viet Minh War, 1950-1954]. pp. B-20, 21. <https://www.archives.gov/research/pentagon-papers> Accessed 25 August 2025.

18 'Request for six-nation warning'. *The Courier Mail* (Brisbane, QLD), 10 April 1954, p. 5.

CHAPTER THIRTY-THREE

The Geneva Accords

The Geneva Accords were the outcome of the Conference held in Geneva, Switzerland, between 26th April and 21st July 1954. The Conference was convened to settle outstanding issues arising from the Korean War and the First Indo-China War.

The participating governments were France, the Union of Soviet Socialist Republics, the Peoples Republic of China, the United States, the United Kingdom, delegates from Cambodia and Laos, and representatives of the State of (South)Vietnam and the Democratic Republic of (North) Vietnam.

Section 1: Dien Bien Phu

While fought years before American combat troops would be involved in Vietnam in any significant way, the Battle of Dien Bien Phu would have a profound effect on American decision-making.

When General Henri Navarre took command of the Indo-China War in May 1953, he began preparing a strategy whereby the French would establish a fortified airfield near the village of Dien Bien Phu along the Laotian border with the hope of impeding Viet Minh supply routes and luring the communist forces into attacking the well-defended French position.

In November 1953, the French occupied the airfield area while the Viet Minh forces under Vo Nguyen Giap built up their strength in the surrounding hills amassing large quantities of supplies including heavy artillery and anti-aircraft weapons. Many artillery pieces were secretly dragged up the hills surrounding the base until they could fire down on the French from concealed positions.

In March 1954, in response to French appeals for more aid, U.S. Secretary of State, John Foster Dulles, helped plan and promote *Operation Vulture*, a proposed B-29 bombing assault on the Viet Minh positions to relieve the beleaguered French forces.

The Joint Chiefs of Staff drew up plans to deploy tactical atomic weapons, U.S. aircraft carriers sailed to the Gulf of Tonkin, and reconnaissance aircraft flew over Dien Bien Phu during the siege. [19]

19 Maclear, M. *The ten thousand day war: Vietnam, 1945-1975*. St. Martin's Press: New York, 1981, p. 57.

Unwilling to make a unilateral move, President Eisenhower requested British support but Foreign Secretary, Anthony Eden, was opposed to the action, partly from fear of Chinese intervention and, ultimately, a third world war.[20] Dulles and Eden had heated exchanges [21] before *Operation Vulture* was cancelled despite Dulles' objections.[22]

French Foreign Minister, Georges Bidault, later claimed that Dulles had offered him the use of nuclear weapons to end the siege.[23]

On 13th March, a massive bombardment signalled the beginning of the end for the French who were unable to maintain counter-battery fire on the Viet Minh positions and the airfield was quickly rendered unusable. Air re-supply was impeded by the powerful air defenses the Viet Minh had amassed and the French were gradually diminished within their fortress.

On 7th May 1954, during the Geneva Conference, the garrison at Dien Bien Phu finally fell to Ho Chi Minh and the Viet Minh forces, marking the end of the First Indo-China War.

Some 2,200 French troops were killed at Dien Bien Phu and another 6,500 were taken prisoner, some of whom died in captivity. Dien Bien Phu would loom large in coming years, especially during the 1968 Battle of Khe Sanh. [24]

Note

After securing an armistice in Korea on 27th July 1953, President Eisenhower was determined to ensure that there would be no repeat performance in Vietnam. His compromise solution was to give France more money and weapons to fight the Communists, resulting in the United States paying around 80% of the cost of the French war against the Viet Minh.

20 Fall, Bernard B. *Street Without Joy The French Debacle in Indo-China.* Stackpole Books: Pennsylvania,1961, p. 323.

21 Sherwood, Elizabeth D. *Allies in Crisis: Meeting Global Challenges to Western Security.* Yale University Press: New Haven CT, 1990, pp. 52-53.

22 Tucker, S. *Vietnam* (illustrated ed.), Routledge, 1999, p. 76.

23 Duiker, W. U. *S. Containment Policy and the Conflict in Indochina.* Stanford University Press, 1994, p. 166.

24 Key Battles. *Pritzker Military Museum and Library* < https://www.pritzkermilitary.org/explore/vietnam-war/key-battles> Accessed 31 March 2025.

Section 2: Partition

The second phase of the Geneva Conference concerning Indo-China resumed on 11th July. The Accords established a cease-fire demarcation line at the 17th parallel (latitude 17° N) to separate the Viet Minh forces in the North from French and Vietnamese allied forces in the South with a Demilitarized Zone (DMZ) 10 kilometers (6 miles) wide separating the two.

North of the line was the Democratic Republic of Vietnam led by Ho Chi Minh with its capital at Hanoi while South of the line was the State of Vietnam which had its capital at Saigon and was nominally under the authority of the former Vietnamese Emperor Bao Dai.

Anthony Eden noted in his memoirs how John Foster Dulles pushed for United Action once more after Dien Bien Phu. Said Eden:

> I found it hard to see how pretending we were going to help the French would really help anybody.[25]

Townsend Hoopes argued that bringing up this issue again made Eden fear that efforts to reach a settlement could be jeopardised. He noted also that the British were despairing about Dulles' discussions with Australia and New Zealand about a collective pact for Indo-China (the SEATO Treaty) and separate French-U.S. talks about increased aid.[26]

Within the councils of the U.S. Government, the concession of half of Vietnam to the Communists was considered another retreat before communist expansion.

Secretary of State Dulles publicly drew two lessons from Geneva:

1. That popular support was essential to combat communist subversion; and
2. Collective defense against aggression could not be devised after the aggression was in progress.

He went on to assert that a collective security system in Southeast Asia could in the future check both outright aggression and subversion. The U.S. moved promptly to convene an international conference at Manila in late summer 1954 to devise such a security system.[27] (See also Chapter Thirty-Six: *The SEATO Treaty.*)

25 Carlton, D. *Anthony Eden*. Penguin Press: Great Britain, 1981, p. 125.

26 Hoopes, Townsend. *The Devil and John Foster Dulles*. Boston: Atlantic Monthly Press, 1973, p. 231.

27 Pentagon Paper [Part IV. A. 1.] Evolution of the War. NATO and SEATO: A Comparison. pp. A-12,13. <https://www.archives.gov/research/pentagon-papers> Accessed 25 August 2025.

Section 3: Ngo Dinh Diem

Ngo Dinh Diem was born in 1901 to a prominent family whose ancestors had been among the earliest Catholic converts in Vietnam. In his younger years, Diem had held important positions as a promising member of the mandarinate, a corps of high-end civil servants who ran the machinery of Vietnam on behalf of the French.

In 1933, he served as the Emperor Bao Dai's minister of the interior but resigned and withdrew from public life that same year in frustration at French unwillingness to countenance his legislative reforms. Relinquishing his titles and decorations, Diem spent the next 12 years living quietly in Huế .

In 1945 he was captured by the forces of Ho Chi Minh who invited Diem to join Ho's independent government in the newly declared Democratic Republic of Vietnam in the hope that Diem's presence would translate into Catholic support. Diem rejected the proposal, however, and went into self-imposed exile.

The Travelling Salesman

In 1951, Diem found his way to the United States where he worked for the next three years establishing contacts and offering his perspectives on the situation in Vietnam and the policies that should be adopted in South-East Asia.

American assessments of Diem were varied. He had attributes that appealed to some U.S. leaders in that he was a fanatically religious and vehemently anti-Communist. Yet there was concern about his lack of experience and his capacity to govern.

Diem managed, however, to gain favor with some high-ranking officials, along with numerous journalists, academics, and the former director of the Office of Strategic Services,William J. Donovan. Though few people knew it at the time, New York's Cardinal Spellman had played a prominent role in creating and mentoring Diem's political career. (See Chapter Fifty-Nine: *The Militia of Christ.*)

Diem returned to Vietnam as the 1954 Geneva Conference was drawing to a conclusion. The Geneva Accords confirmed Bao Dai as South Vietnam's 'chief of state' but the former emperor was little more than a figurehead who spent more time in France than in his native country. The United States pushed Diem into the spotlight as a potential leader despite the fact that he was scarcely known in the South, considered by the French to be unstable, and despised by the Viet Minh.

Bao Dai considered that the newly formed State of (South) Vietnam would need American support and that Diem's Catholic and anti-Communist background would be an appealing advantage. Following a meeting between Bao Dai and Diem in

France on 16th June 1954, Diem was officially appointed Prime Minister on 24th June 1954.

In an October 1955 referendum, Bao Dai was overthrown and Diem designated as President of the State of Vietnam.

Section 4: The Phantom Elections

On 21st July 1954, a Conference Final Declaration issued by the British co-chair, Anthony Eden, stipulated that internationally supervised general elections must be held by July 1956 to create a unified Vietnamese State. Despite being parties to the drafting of the Accords, they were not directly signed nor accepted by delegates of either the State of (South)Vietnam or the United States.

Secretary of State Dulles rejected the partitioning of Vietnam and the holding of elections to unify the country, insisting that the anti-communist State of Vietnam should be the legitimate Vietnamese government. He refused to shake hands with, or speak directly to, Chinese or Viet Minh delegates and subsequently left the Conference to avoid direct association with the negotiations.

For the Viet Minh, the Geneva Accords represented an opportunity to win over the whole country through an election and finally secure Vietnam's independence. The Viet Minh's hopes were raised because a definite date for the election had been set forth in both a bilateral armistice agreement with France as well as in the Final Declaration, and also because of the publicly positive stance taken by the United States at the time.

Following the Geneva Accords, there was to be a 300-day period in which people could freely move between the two regions of Vietnam. During that 300 days, the United States and the Catholic Church mounted a campaign to convince Catholics in the North to move to the South. (See Chapter Thirty-Five: *The New Exodus.)* Between 800,000 and one million Vietnamese moved South during this period, some of whom would go on to form Diem's power base.

CHAPTER THIRTY-FOUR

The New Exodus

During the two-year period of grace before the general elections mandated by the Geneva Accords were due to be held on 20th July 1956, hundreds of thousands of Catholics moved from Northern Vietnam to Southern Vietnam. The intent of the exodus was to establish a bloc in the south on which to base opposition to the implementation of the Accords. It was feared that if elections were held, as many as 80% of the Vietnamese people would vote for Ho Chi Minh as the popular hero of their liberation.[28]

This large-scale Exodus was organised by parish priests and partly enabled by the United States Navy:

> After the 1954 Geneva Accords divided Vietnam into two zones at the 17th parallel, the U.S. Navy relocated refugees, military forces, and equipment from North to South Vietnam in a humanitarian operation known as Passage to Freedom (August 1954–May 1955). Sailors built shelters and latrines, rationed food and water, controlled the spread of disease, improved sanitation, and provided medical care at ports of embarkation and on transport ships. The nearly 311,000 people who moved south formed the core of non-Communist resistance in Vietnam.[29]

In his book, *The Two Viet-nams: A political and military analysis*, war correspondent Bernard B. Fall describes the exodus in the following terms:

> Although there is no doubt that hundreds of thousands of Vietnamese would have fled Communist domination in any case, the mass flight was admittedly the result of an extremely intensive, well conducted, and in terms of its objective, very successful American psychological warfare operation. Propaganda slogans and leaflets appealed to the devout Catholics with such themes as **'Christ has gone to the South' and 'The Virgin Mary has departed from the North'**; and

28 Eisenhower, Dwight D. *Mandate for Change, 1953-1956: The White House Years*. Doubleday & Company Inc: New York, NY. 1963, p. 372.

29 'Passage to Freedom'. *Hampton Roads Naval Museum*. < https://www.history.navy.mil/content/history/museums/hrnm/explore/VietnamExhibitPage/BeginningsReloadV1/PassagetoFreedomReloadV2.html> Accessed 11 September 2025.

> whole bishoprics—Bui-Chu and Phat-Diem,for example—packed up, lock stock and barrel, from the bishops to almost the last village priest and faithful.
>
> Of the 860,000 who fled South at this time, 600,000 were Catholics. Although 65 percent of the total Catholic population left North Vietnam, more than 99.5 percent of the non-Catholics stayed put. The Tongkinese Catholics fled because they had a long experience of persecution at the hands of their non-Catholic fellow citizens–not because of the psychological warfare campaign ...[30]

Bernard Fall lost his life in Vietnam on 21st February 1967. He took pride in the fact that his books and articles, some of which were published on Vietnam and guerilla warfare in general, were based not on conventional scholarly research in libraries, or even in the capital cities of South-East Asia, but on first hand combat involvements.

Despite the first-hand knowledge of those on the ground like Bernard Fall, the Exodus was consistently misrepresented to the world as a flight of Catholic refugees from communist terror:

> Yesterday, the French Delegate-General in Hanoi, M. Jacques Copain, said he expected several hundred thousand Vietnamese to abandon their homes before the Viet Minh regime took over.
>
> The Mayor of Hanoi. Mr. Do Quang Giais, said he expected two to three million Vietnamese to leave the Red River delta area alone for South Vietnam.
>
> ...M. Copain said he has prepared a scheme which will enable one million people to be evacuated through Haiphong in the next 300 days. He said that a propaganda war has already broken out in Hanoi to win over the sympathies of the residents.
>
> Vietminh agents are trying to persuade the people to stay, while the Vietnamese Government is preparing to send out teams to persuade people to leave.
>
> This is a difficult choice for those Vietnamese who have invested their life savings in small shops or restaurants in Hanoi, and for the peasants in the delta who work ancestral rice paddies.
>
> Between two and three million of them are Roman Catholics who are torn between the love of their homes and their hatred of Communism.
>
> ... In Saigon yesterday, the Vietnamese Government ordered all flags flown at half-mast for the next three days because of the Geneva partition decision.[31]

30 Fall, Bernard B. *The Two Viet-nams: A political and military analysis*. Frederick A. Praeger: New York, 1966, pp. 153-154.

31 'Exodus from Red Vietnam'. *The Sydney Morning Herald* (NSW), 24 July, 1954, p. 1.

Even before the Geneva Accords Final Declaration of 21st July 1954, readers of Catholic newspapers and periodicals worldwide were confronted by alarmist articles similar to those which appeared in the Australian press. For example:

> Million Catholics face crisis in Indo-China: The greatest sell-out of Christian people since Poland may now threaten the Catholics of North Vietnam, writes Father Patrick O'Connor, National Catholic Welfare Council Correspondent at Hanoi, on the current armistice negotiations between the French and the Communist Viet Minh forces.
>
> Last week's withdrawal in the Red River delta—the biggest of the Indo-China war—left a million Catholics in Communist hands and drew a strong protest from the new Catholic Vietnam Premier, Ngo Dinh Diem. (A.A.P., 3 July.) [32]

Robert Shaplen's work *The Lost Revolution*, as cited in the Pentagon Papers, also references the Exodus and argues that it led to the Buddhist Crisis of 1963 which, in turn, resulted in the assassination of Ngo Dinh Diem and his brother on 2nd November 1963:

> An estimated one million Catholics fled the North and resettled in the South. Diem, animated, no doubt, by religious as well as humanitarian sympathy, and with an eye to recruiting political support from his coreligionists, accorded these Catholic refugees preferential treatment in land redistribution, relief and assistance, commercial and export-import licenses, government employment, and other government largess.
>
> Because Diem could rely on their loyalty, they came to fill almost all important civilian and military positions. As an institution, the Catholic Church enjoyed a special legal status. The Catholic primate, Ngo Dinh Thuc, was Diem's brother and advisor. But prior to 1962, there had been no outright discrimination against Buddhists. However, among South Vietnam's 3-4 million practicing Buddhists and the 80% of the population who were nominal Buddhists, the regime's favoritism, authoritarianism, and discrimination created a smoldering resentment. [33]

(See also Chapter Thirty-Nine: *Allied Crossroads.*)

---

32 *Advocate* (Melbourne, Victoria), 8 July 1954, p. 3.

33 Shaplen, 1966, as cited in the Pentagon Papers [Part IV: B-5]. Evolution of the War. Counterinsurgency: The Overthrow of Ngo Dinh Diem, May-Nov 1963. p. 4. <https://www.archives.gov/research/pentagon-papers> Accessed 31 January 2026.

CHAPTER THIRTY-FIVE

The SEATO Treaty

A September 1954 conference in Manila eventuated in a security agreement termed 'The Southeast Asia Collective Defense Treaty and Protocol Thereto, September 8 1954'. The agreement, ratified by the U.S. Senate and enacted on 19th February 1955, created the *Southeast Asia Treaty Organization*. The following is reproduced from a Robert Menzies Institute article entitled 'SEATO Established':

> The Treaty complemented the ANZUS security pact to form the basis of the Menzies Government's Cold War defensive strategy. It was primarily concerned with halting the spread of communism in South East Asia, a fundamental concern for Australia due to the prevailing domino theory which held that one state falling to communism greatly increased the likelihood that its neighbours would experience the same fate.
>
> SEATO was directly modelled on NATO, however its scope was far more limited in that it did not provide for standing forces under a joint command, but merely prescribed collective action to meet a common danger in a similar manner to ANZUS itself.
>
> Treaty signatories included Australia, New Zealand, the United States, the United Kingdom, France, Pakistan, the Philippines, and Thailand. The provisions of the treaty also covered South Vietnam, Cambodia, and Laos, even though they were not signatories as they were prevented from signing military alliances by the 1954 Geneva Agreements that had brought to a close the First Indo-China War.
>
> Perhaps the greatest and certainly the most controversial impact of SEATO was that the treaty was used to justify the collective international effort to defend South Vietnam from both North Vietnamese aggression and internal insurgents, and was thus part of the reason why Australia joined the Vietnam War via a commitment of ground troops in the final year of Menzies's time in office. The primary rationale for Australia's commitment was not SEATO itself, even though it was cited, but the domino theory which underpinned it. Australia also felt a strategic need to keep the United States interested in South East Asia and to prove itself a loyal ally deserving of the goodwill implied by ANZUS.

> Notably not all the members of SEATO became involved in the Vietnam War, even though the United States did try unsuccessfully to invoke the treaty. [34]

As Jeffrey Record, Professor Emeritus at the U.S. Air Force's Air War College, writes in his book *The Wrong War: why we lost in Vietnam*:

> No other member of SEATO felt obliged by the treaty to fight in South Vietnam, notwithstanding official U.S. portrayal of the war from its inception as a case of international aggression as clear cut as North Korea's invasion of South Korea and even as a would-be Soviet attack on Western Europe.
>
> **Alone among SEATO members other than the United States, Australia contributed forces in a size proportionally significant to its total armed forces. New Zealand, Thailand, and the Philippines all sent token contingents, the latter two countries in exchange for substantial U.S. military assistance.**
>
> South Korea, not a SEATO member, provided substantial forces—two army divisions and a marine brigade—but only in exchange for hefty U.S. military assistance to Seoul and a pledge by the United States not to redeploy to Vietnam either of the two U.S. divisions stationed in Korea. "The Asian [allies] were ready to fight to the last American", complained Clark Clifford, (Robert) McNamara's successor as Secretary of Defense. [35]

Although it is claimed that SEATO was a defensive strategy, its architect, U.S. Secretary of State, John Foster Dulles, stated that SEATO's principle purpose was to give the U.S. President the legal authority to intervene in Indo-China. [36]

34 'SEATO Established'. *Robert Menzies Institute* < https://www.robertmenziesinstitute.org.au/on-this-day/seato-established/ >Accessed 12 February 2025.

35 Record, J. *The Wrong War: why we lost in Vietnam*. Naval Institute Press: Maryland, 1998. < https://archive.nytimes.com/www.nytimes.com/books/first/r/record-war.html> Accessed 14 February 2025.

36 'United States Senate Congressional Record' (3 June 1964). *Central Intelligence Agency* < https://www.cia.gov/readingroom/docs/CIA-RDP66B00403R000200150045-3.pdf> Accessed 12 February 2025.

PART III

The Dogs of War

"Cry Havoc!"—and let slip the dogs of war...

— JULIUS CAESAR

CHAPTER THIRTY-SIX

Theoreticals

Section 1: The Domino Theory

At a news conference on 7th April 1954, U.S. President Dwight D Eisenhower was asked to comment on the strategic importance of Indo-China to the free world. Eisenhower spoke of the considerations that must be kept in mind. His essential points were:

- The specific value of a locality in its production of materials that the world needs—tin, tungsten, rubber etc;
- The possibility that more people may come under a dictatorship that is inimical to the free world such as happened in Asia where some 450 million have been lost to the communist dictatorship in China;
- The 'falling domino' principle where the last one is certain to fall quickly. The possible 'domino' sequence of events are the loss of Indochina, Burma, Thailand, the Peninsula, and Indonesia. The possible consequences of these losses are incalculable to the free world;
- If these are lost, the geographical situation threatens the so-called island defensive chain of Japan, Formosa, and the Philippines and to the south, it threatens Australia and New Zealand.

In response to other questions, the President said that he had not yet received any positive responses to a request for united action. While he was not sure that the Indo-China situation should be brought before the United Nations, he was sure that the situation should not be handled by one nation acting alone. He also said the chances of achieving a satisfactory negotiated settlement at the forthcoming Geneva Conference were not good and, finally, he refused to comment on whether the United States was prepared, as a last resort, to "go it alone" in Indo-China.[1]

1 'Foreign Relations of the United States, 1952-1954, Indochina, Volume XIII, Part 1'. *Office of the Historian, U.S. Department of State* < https://history.state.gov/historicaldocuments/frus1952-54v13p1/d716> Accessed 1 March 2025.

The Fallacy

According to the Pentagon Papers, the 'domino theory' and the assumptions behind it were never questioned. The homogeneity of the nations of Southeast Asia was taken as a given, as was the linkage in their ability to remain democratic, or at an acceptable minimum, non-communist nations. Undoubtedly, in the first decade of the cold war there existed an unfortunate stereotype of a monolithic communist expansionary bloc. It was reinforced by a somewhat emotional approach on the part of many Americans to communism in China and Asia. This 'syndrome' was, in part, the result of the 'fall' of China, which some felt could have been averted, and a few hoped would still be reversed.

Accordingly, not sufficient cognizance was taken of the individuality of the states of Southeast Asia and the separateness of their societies. Probably there was some lack of knowledge in depth on the part of Washington policy-makers about the area. No one before World War II had expected that the United States would be called upon to take a leadership role in these remote colonial territories of our European allies.

In hindsight, these shortcomings may have led to the fallacious belief that a neutralist or communist Indo-China would inevitably draw the other states of Asia into the communist bloc or into neutralism. But the 'fallacy' was neither evident then, nor is it demonstrable now in retrospect.[2]

Section 2: The Personification Theory

John Foster Dulles and the Devil

In 'Apostle of Brinkmanship', a review of *The Devil and John Foster Dulles* by Townsend Hoopes, Felix Morley writes:

> "The Devil," of course, is international communism and the major emphasis of the book is on the efforts of Mr. Dulles, as Secretary of State from 1953 to 1959, to cramp, cabin and confine this sinister force, so ironically built into world power by the diplomacy of Franklin D. Roosevelt. As a West German ambassador (Albrecht von Kessel) said of Dulles, he believed that "Bolshevism

2 Pentagon Papers[Part II] U.S. Involvement in the Franco-Viet Minh War, 1950-1953. p. A-52. *National Archives and Records Administration.* < https://www.archives.gov/research/pentagon-papers> Accessed 25 August 2025.

was a product of the Devil and that God would wear out the Bolsheviks in the long run".[3]

Billy Graham and the Disciples of Lucifer

Billy Graham (1918-2018) was an American Baptist minister and probably the best-known evangelist preacher of the 20th Century. In the following extract from the August 1954 edition of *The American Mercury*, Graham describes communism as "Satan's religion" and communist leaders as "disciples of Lucifer":

> The Communist revolution that was born in the hearts of Marx and Engels in the middle of the 19th century is not going to give up or retreat. No amount of words at the United Nations, or peace conferences in the Far East, is going to change the mind of Communism. It is here to stay. It is a battle to the death: either Communism must die, or Christianity must die...
>
> Has it ever occurred to you that the Devil is a religious leader and millions are worshipping at his shrine today? ... The name of this present-day religion is Communism... The Devil is their god, Marx their prophet, Lenin their saint and Malenkov their high priest. Denying their faith in all ideologies, except their religion of revolution, these diabolically-inspired men seek in devious and various ways to convert a peaceful world to their doctrine of death and destruction.
>
> So fanatical and ruthless are these disciples of Lucifer that in thirty years they have slaughtered millions of innocent persons and stand prepared with poised weapons to kill millions more in an all-out effort to spread their doctrines to the ends of the earth...[4]

Section 3: The Exceptionalist Theory

We Are The World

American exceptionalism is the idea that for historical, ideological, or religious reasons, the United States of America is a unique and even morally superior country, destined to play a distinct and positive role on the world stage.

3 Morley, F. (1974). 'Apostle of Brinkmanship'. [Review of the book *The Devil and John Foster Dulles* by Townsend Hoopes] *Modern Age*, Summer 1974, pp. 332-334.

4 'Billy Graham on Communism: "Satan's Religion"' (1954). *Alpha History* < https://alphahistory.com/coldwar/billy-graham-communism-satans-religion-1954/> Accessed 2 March 2025.

Critics of the concept claim that the idea of American exceptionalism suggests that the U.S. is better than other countries, has a superior culture, or has a unique mission to transform the planet and its inhabitants.

On 10th March 2006, the *JFK Presidential Library and Museum* hosted a symposium entitled 'Vietnam and the Presidency—How we got in: The United States, Asia and Vietnam'. The following is reproduced or adapted from an address made during the symposium by Marilyn Young, Professor of History at New York University:

> The U.S. in pursuit of its policies in the world does not negotiate over interests because it insists, "We are the world".
>
> In Vietnam, the only troops described as foreign are from North Vietnam itself. American troops seemed never to be termed foreign, as if Americans were everywhere indigenous. It is thus possible for policy-makers, historians, journalists and the public to imagine that the U.S. acts always and everywhere on behalf of others as it would on its own behalf for the freedom and well being of whatever country to which it has brought a war.
>
> The conviction of its own good intentions, of its overall beneficence in the world, shields American politicians from taking responsibility for the disasters they create and persuades the electorate that the wars into which they have been led are all, at least at the start, just. The central mechanism of the U.S. policy in the 1940's, as today, the pivot around which all the rest rotates, is the conviction that the particular national interests of the United States are identical with the transcendent, universal interests of humanity.
>
> The increasingly evident falsehood of this claim produces what Che Guevara once hoped for, "two, three, many Vietnams'. Thank you.[5]

Above all, there is the conviction so basic to Americans as a people that they can succeed because they are Americans. The purity of their motives and the skill of their methods will bring success even though the odds against them may seem high.

The Gunman

In his book, *The Brothers,* a joint biography of John Foster Dulles and his brother Allen Dulles, award-winning foreign correspondent Stephen Kinzer writes:

5 Marilyn Young. (10 March 2006) 'Vietnam and the Presidency—How we got in: The United States, Asia and Vietnam'. *JFK Presidential Library and Museum* < https://www.jfklibrary.org/events-and-awards/kennedy-library-forums/past-forums/transcripts/vietnam-and-the-presidency-how-we-got-in-the-united-states-asia-and-vietnam> Accessed 14 March 2025.

> During the 1950's, when the Cold War was at its peak, two immensely powerful brothers led the United States into a series of foreign adventures whose effects are still shaking the world.
>
> John Foster Dulles was secretary of state while his brother, Allen Dulles, was director of the Central Intelligence Agency. In this book, I place their extraordinary lives against the background of American culture and history. I use the framework of biography to ask: Why does the United States behave as it does in the world?
>
> The Brothers explores hidden forces that shape the national psyche, from religious piety to **Western movies—many of which are about a noble gunman who cleans up a lawless town by killing bad guys.** This is how the Dulles brothers saw themselves, and how many Americans still see their country's role in the world.
>
> Propelled by a quintessentially American set of fears and delusions, the Dulles brothers launched violent campaigns against foreign leaders they saw as threats to the United States. These campaigns helped push countries from Guatemala to the Congo into long spirals of violence, led the United States into the Vietnam War, and laid the foundation for decades of hostility between the United States and countries from Cuba to Iran.
>
> The story of the Dulles brothers is the story of America. It illuminates and helps explain the modern history of the United States and the world.[6]

Of John Foster Dulles, he writes that:

> He was more responsible for the U. S. involvement in Vietnam than any single individual…we could have avoided the entire American involvement in Vietnam absent Foster's decisions at the Geneva conference in 1954.

6 Kinzer, Stephen. *The Brothers*. StephenKinzer.com <https://stephenkinzer.com/2013/10/the-brothers/> 8 October 2013. Accessed 14 May 2025.

CHAPTER THIRTY-SEVEN

The Orchestra

Section 1: Pavlov's Dogs

Beginning in the early 1950's, the peoples of Australia and the United States were subjected to an orchestrated campaign to ensure that they would react in a given way whenever the term 'Communism' was used. 'Communism' came to signify everything that was odious, impious, undemocratic and unpatriotic.

For example, press hysteria during the Petrov era in Australia and the McCarthy era in the United States produced the same predictable responses and laid the groundwork of public support for involvement in the Vietnam War.

When ground combat troops were eventually sent to Vietnam, the war was presented to the public as a war against 'Communism'. Press, priest and politician repeatedly claimed that only a direct confrontation with the enemy in Vietnam itself would stop 'Communism' from spreading. If Vietnam were to fall, they said, 'Communism' would be at the very gates.

The terms North Vietnam, Ho Chi Minh, Viet Minh and Viet Cong became synonyms for 'Communism' which stimulated predictable responses. Support for intervention in the domestic affairs of Vietnam was translated by this technique into a justifiable war against aggression—Communist aggression.

Section 2: All the way with Diem

Australia

In September 1957, Ngo Dinh Diem, President of South Vietnam, paid an official visit to Australia sponsored by Bartholomew Augustine Santamaria. (See also Chapter Three: *Enemies Within.*)

Diem addressed Federal Parliament and was made an honorary Knight Grand Cross of the Order of St. Michael and St. George, one of the highest imperial honours that can be bestowed on a non-British subject. (At that time, Australians were British subjects.)

Diem was universally lionised by Australian politicians and the Australian press, praising him for what they perceived to be his successful, democratic and righteous rule in South Vietnam. At the same time, they turned a blind eye to his repressive regime and corrupt practices.

The Australian Catholisc leadership and press were particularly glowing towards the South Vietnamese head of state. In Robert Shaplen's work *The Lost Revolution*, as cited in the Pentagon Papers, we read of Diem's largesse towards his co-religionists:

> Because Diem could rely on their loyalty, they came to fill almost all important civilian and military positions. As an institution, the Catholic Church enjoyed a special legal status. The Catholic primate, Ngo Dinh Thuc, was Diem's brother and advisor. But prior to 1962, there had been no outright discrimination against Buddhists. However, among South Vietnam's 3-4 million practicing Buddhists and the 80% of the population who were nominal Buddhists, the regime's favoritism, authoritarianism, and discrimination created a smoldering resentment. [7]

This "smoldering resentment" led eventually to the Buddhist Crisis of 1963 which, in turn, led to the assassination of Diem and his brother on 2nd November 1963. (See also Chapter Forty-Four: *Backfire.*)

The United States

In June 1954, Bao Dai had appointed Ngo Dinh Diem as Prime Minister of the new State of Vietnam established according to the Geneva Accords.

Diem's many failings were common knowledge:

> 20th June 1954—The Premier of France, Pierre Mendès-France, said that he "expected to have considerable difficulty with the new (South) Vietnam government". Diem, he said, was a "fanatic". His thoughts were echoed by other French officials: "Diem is too narrow, too rigid, too unworldly", said one. [8]

Despite being aware of Diem's failings, the United States then took a number of steps in direct violation of the Geneva Accords:

7 Shaplen, 1966, as cited in the Pentagon Paper [Part IV: B-5]. Evolution of the War. Counterinsurgency: The Overthrow of Ngo Dinh Diem, May-Nov 1963. p. 4. <https://www.archives.gov/research/pentagon-papers> Accessed 31 January 2026.

8 Jacobs, Seth. *Cold War Mandarin: Ngo Dinh Diem and the Origins of America's War in Vietnam 1950-1963.* Rowman and Littlefield Publishers: Maryland, 2006, pp. 39-40.

29th September 1954—The United States and France concluded an agreement that henceforth all U.S. aid to Vietnam would go directly to the (South) Vietnamese government rather than through the French government; [9]

22nd October 1954—The U.S. Department of State instructed the Military Assistance Advisory Group (MAAG) in Saigon to begin a "program of training the number of (South) Vietnamese armed forces necessary to carry out internal security missions";[10]

24th October 1954—President Eisenhower sent a letter to Prime Minister Diem promising U.S. assistance if Diem met "standards of performance". Diem agreed. This letter was later cited as the initial commitment by the U.S. to support South Vietnam;[11]

8th November 1954—General Lawton Collins arrived in Saigon as special representative of the United States. He affirmed President Eisenhower's earlier expression of support for Ngo Dinh Diem. Collins promised $100 million in U.S. aid and stated that the Diem government "is the legal government in Vietnam". He warned the South Vietnamese army that it would receive American assistance only if it supported Diem. [12]

President Eisenhower had rejected various proposals for direct U.S. military intervention in Vietnam at that time, including that of Joint Chiefs of Staff Chairman, Admiral Arthur W. Radford, who advocated an expeditionary force for the Hanoi-Haiphong region.

Earlier, during the siege of Dien Bien Phu, Radford, a determined anti-Communist and interventionist, had even suggested threatening the Viet Minh with a tactical nuclear attack.

However, Eisenhower had reached a compromise—set up a "stable, independent government" in South Vietnam. This came to be known as the Diem Solution. The decision to consolidate Diem in power in Saigon would eventually result in the Vietnam War.[13]

---

9 Fall, Bernard. 'South Viet-Nam's Internal Problems' (September 1958) *Pacific Affairs,* Vol. 31, No. 3 p. 244.

10 Logevall, Fredrik. *Embers of War: the Fall of an Empire and the Making of America's Vietnam.* Random House: New York, 2012, p. 630.

11 Bowman, John. *The World Almanac of the Vietnam War.* Bison Books: Winnipeg, 1985, p. 39.

12 Ibid, pp. 39-40.

13 Ngo Vinh Long. 'After the Fall of Saigon'. *Cairo Review of Global Affairs* <https://www.thecairoreview.com/essays/after-the-fall-of-saigon/> Accessed 14 March 2025.

During his two terms in office, Eisenhower invested so much American prestige and effort into the success of South Vietnam under Diem that, by the end of the 1950's, America had become deeply involved in its fate. Eisenhower created a Vietnam which his successors would wage a bitter—and failed—war to keep.[14]

Section 3: The Quasi-Police State

As revealed in the Pentagon Papers, successive U.S. administrations were aware at all times of the brutal nature of the Diem regime. The following is reproduced from the Pentagon Paper [Part IV: A-5]. Evolution of the War, Origins of the Insurgency.

> Ngo Dinh Diem presided over a state which, for all the lip service it paid to individual freedom and American style government, remained a one party, highly centralized familial oligarchy in which neither operating democracy, nor the prerequisites for such existed. On 11 January 1956, in Government of the Republic of Vietnam (GVN) Ordinance Number 6, President Diem decreed broad governmental measures providing for "the defense of the state and public order", including authority to detain "individuals considered a danger to the state" or to "national defense and common security" at re-education centers. One month after the date of the scheduled Geneva plebescite, on 21 August 1956, the Government of Vietnam proclaimed Ordinance Number 47 which defined as a breach of law punishable by death any deed performed in or for any organization designated as "Communist".
>
> ...In July 1956, the month the Geneva elections were scheduled to have been held, the U.S. Army attache in Saigon noted in his monthly report that: "Orders have reportedly been issued to all Viet Minh cadres in Free Viet Nam to increase their efforts to reorganize and revitalize the military units in their zones of responsibility. These cadres have, however, encountered considerable difficulty in motivating their adherents to work for the Communist cause. The military and political cadres are making little progress due to the Communist Denunciation Campaigns promoted by the Government of the Republic of Vietnam (GVN)..."[15]

14 'The Age of Eisenhower: America's Vietnam'. *The Miller Centre*, University of Virginia < https://millercenter.org/the-presidency/educational-resources/age-of-eisenhower/americas-vietnam> Accessed 12 April 2025.

15 Pentagon Paper [Part IV A-5] Evolution of the War. Origins of the Insurgency, p. 45. *National Archives and Records Administration* <https://www.archives.gov/research/pentagon-papers> Accessed 31 January 2026.

As American foreign policy analyst William Henderson wrote in the January 1957 issue of *Foreign Affairs*: "South Vietnam is today a quasi-police state characterised by arbitrary arrests and imprisonment, strict censorship of the press, and the absence of an effective political opposition. All techniques of political and psychological warfare, as well as pacification campaigns involving extensive military operations, have been brought to bear against the underground".[16]

(See also Chapter Thirty-Nine: *Allied Crossroads.*)

Notes

See Chapter Forty for an introduction to the Pentagon Papers and the enduring impact of their publication on the American body politic. The Pentagon Papers can be accessed at the National Archives https://www.archives.gov/research/pentagon-papers

While New Zealand also experienced anti-communist paranoia during this period, the level of its intensity was far less than in Australia and the United States so it is not referenced in this Chapter

16 Ibid.

CHAPTER THIRTY-EIGHT

Threat Reduction

Section 1: Herbert Vere Evatt

See Part I for an exhaustive analysis of *Operation Petrov.*

As explained in Part I, certain anti-communist groups in Australia had been taking steps since the early 1950's to ensure that Australia, together with the projected involvement of the United States, would intervene in Indo-China in the likely event that France would lose control of its colonial empire. (See Part I-3: *Enemies Within.*)

When it became clear that the French Union Forces were facing final defeat in Vietnam, *Operation Petrov* was launched on 13th April 1954 with the announcement of the defection of an alleged Soviet spy, Vladimir Petrov. Just three weeks later, on 7th May, Dien Bien Phu fell to the Viet Minh, marking the end of the French colonial empire in Indo-China.

The prime objective of *Operation Petrov* was to destroy the reputation of the Leader of the Australian Labor Party, Doctor Herbert Vere Evatt, thereby ensuring his Party's defeat in the May 1954 Australian elections. The Labor Party's policy of non-interference in the domestic affairs of foreign nations, specifically Vietnam, would therefore never be implemented.

As a result of the political assassination of Dr. Evatt, the leader of the communist-baiting Liberal Party, Robert Menzies, retained his position as Australian Prime Minister. Through orchestrated campaigns of 'red-scare' mongering, Menzies was able to consolidate his grip on power until he committed Australian ground troops to Vietnam in April 1965.

This Australian commitment, in turn, endorsed and escalated American involvement since the United States now had the support of a Western ally to cloak the War in international legitimacy.

Section 2: John Fitzgerald Kennedy

Idealism

President John F. Kennedy assumed the office of President on 20th January 1961, following an eight-year career in the Senate. The first Catholic president, Kennedy was also the second youngest to ever serve in the office. In his inaugural address, Kennedy proclaimed:

> Let every nation know, whether it wishes us well or ill, that we shall pay any price, bear any burden, meet any hardship, support any friend, oppose any foe, in order to assure the survival and the success of liberty.

Kennedy came into the presidency determined to reenergize the foreign policy establishment. To that end, he assembled a team of young White House and National Security Council advisers—the so-called "best and the brightest"—which included Walt Rostow, Ted Sorensen and Arthur Schlesinger, Jr.

Kennedy appointed Dean Rusk as his Secretary of State, Robert S. McNamara, the president of Ford Motor Company, as his Secretary of Defense, and Harvard Dean McGeorge Bundy as his National Security Adviser. The Director of the Central Intelligence Agency, Allen W. Dulles, continued in the position he had held since 1953.

The Kennedy administration inherited the containment doctrine of the 1940's and 1950's which maintained the belief that Communism was a threat to the United States. However, the brinkmanship of the Eisenhower era seemed archaic to the Kennedy idealists in their new international vision. Kennedy implemented the 'flexible response' defense strategy, one that relied on multiple options for responding to the Soviet Union, discouraged massive retaliation, and encouraged mutual deterrence.

The Bay of Pigs

In April 1961, a short few months into his administration, Kennedy authorized a clandestine invasion of Cuba by a brigade of Cuban exiles. The CIA covert operation had been formulated and approved under President Eisenhower. Relying on faulty intelligence, the operation collapsed in two days with the defeat and capture of anti-Castro forces at the Bay of Pigs. The spectacular failure of this Cold War confrontation was a setback for Kennedy, and one he became determined to overcome. Though he took full responsibility for the failed operation, the CIA's reputation was tarnished and Kennedy soon replaced Director Allen W. Dulles with John A. McCone. Similarly, the Bay of Pigs fiasco affected Kennedy's respect for the advice of the Joint Chiefs of Staff, placing a strain on the civil-military relationship that would remain under stress throughout the administration. McNamara's management reforms in the Pentagon, the administration's focus on counterinsurgency warfare, and finally the policy toward the war in Vietnam all found the uniformed military leadership in disagreement with the administration.

The Cuban Missile Crisis

The Cold War reached a frightening apex when in late 1962 the Soviet Union gave the Cuban Government medium-range ballistic missiles to defend against another U.S. invasion. American intelligence photographed Cuban missile sites, leading to a naval blockade and quarantine of Cuba. The tense thirteen days of the Cuban Missile Crisis tested the mettle of the Kennedy administration and his team of trusted advisers. The crisis was resolved, partly through a secret deal where the U.S. agreed to remove Jupiter nuclear missiles from Turkey in exchange for the Soviet Union removing missiles from Cuba.

Staring into the Abyss

On the morning of 10th June 1963, President Kennedy arrived on the campus of American University in Washington D.C. to deliver a speech calling for an end to the Cold War. The speech, composed without input from the Joint Chiefs of Staff, the CIA, or the State Department, was one of the most extraordinary Presidential speeches of the 20th Century. His 'Strategy of Peace' was a rallying cry for an end to the nuclear arms race with the Soviet Union and the beginning of a new era of peace with all nations:

> What kind of peace do I mean? What kind of peace do we seek? Not a Pax Americana enforced on the world by American weapons of war. Not the peace of the grave or the security of the slave. I am talking about genuine peace, the kind of peace that makes life on earth worth living, the kind that enables men and nations to grow and to hope and to build a better life for their children--not merely peace for Americans but peace for all men and women--not merely peace in our time but peace for all time.
>
> ...No government or social system is so evil that its people must be considered as lacking in virtue. As Americans, we find communism profoundly repugnant as a negation of personal freedom and dignity. But we can still hail the Russian people for their many achievements--in science and space, in economic and industrial growth, in culture and in acts of courage.

> Among the many traits the peoples of our two countries have in common, none is stronger than our mutual abhorrence of war. Almost unique among the major world powers, we have never been at war with each other. And no nation in the history of battle ever suffered more than the Soviet Union suffered in the course of the Second World War. At least 20 million lost their lives. Countless millions of homes and farms were burned or sacked. A third of the nation's territory, including nearly two thirds of its industrial base, was turned into a wasteland--a loss equivalent to the devastation of this country east of Chicago.
>
> ...So, let us not be blind to our differences--but let us also direct attention to our common interests and to the means by which those differences can be resolved. And if we cannot end now our differences, at least we can help make the world safe for diversity. For, in the final analysis, our most basic common link is that we all inhabit this small planet. We all breathe the same air. We all cherish our children's future. And we are all mortal.
>
> ...The United States, as the world knows, will never start a war. We do not want a war. We do not now expect a war. This generation of Americans has already had enough--more than enough--of war and hate and oppression. We shall be prepared if others wish it. We shall be alert to try to stop it. But we shall also do our part to build a world of peace where the weak are safe and the strong are just. We are not helpless before that task or hopeless of its success. Confident and unafraid, we labor on--not toward a strategy of annihilation but toward a strategy of peace.[17]

More than 60 years later, this inspiring speech has lost none of its power to move us towards a desire for peace and an unequivocal condemnation of war. And, like President Kennedy, **if we stare into the abyss, we will recoil from what we see.**

Banning the Bomb

On 26th July 1963, Kennedy delivered a radio and television address to the American people urging support for a Limited Nuclear Test Ban Treaty:

> Yesterday a shaft of light cut into the darkness. Negotiations were concluded in Moscow on a treaty to ban all nuclear tests in the atmosphere, in outer space, and under water. For the first time, an agreement has been reached on bringing the forces of nuclear destruction under international control--a goal first sought

17 'Commencement Address at American University' 10 June 1963). *John F. Kennedy Presidential Library and Museum.* <https://www.jfklibrary.org/archives/other-resources/john-f-kennedy-speeches/american-university-19630610> Accessed 12 June 2024.

> in 1946 when Bernard Baruch presented a comprehensive control plan to the United Nations.
>
> ...Since the beginning of history, war has been mankind's constant companion. It has been the rule, not the exception. Even a nation as young and as peace-loving as our own has fought through eight wars. And three times in the last two years and a half I have been required to report to you as President that this Nation and the Soviet Union stood on the verge of direct military confrontation--in Laos, in Berlin, and in Cuba.
>
> ...This limited test ban, in our most careful judgment, is safer by far for the United States than an unlimited nuclear arms race. For all these reasons, I am hopeful that this Nation will promptly approve the limited test ban treaty. There will, of course, be debate in the country and in the Senate. The Constitution wisely requires the advice and consent of the Senate to all treaties, and that consultation has already begun. All this is as it should be. A document which may mark an historic and constructive opportunity for the world deserves an historic and constructive debate.
>
> It is my hope that all of you will take part in that debate, for this treaty is for all of us. It is particularly for our children and our grandchildren, and they have no lobby here in Washington.
>
> ...But now, for the first time in many years, the path of peace may be open. No one can be certain what the future will bring. No one can say whether the time has come for an easing of the struggle. But history and our own conscience will judge us harsher if we do not now make every effort to test our hopes by action, and this is the place to begin. According to the ancient Chinese proverb, "A journey of a thousand miles must begin with a single step."
>
> My fellow Americans, let us take that first step. Let us, if we can, step back from the shadows of war and seek out the way of peace. And if that journey is a thousand miles, or even more, let history record that we, in this land, at this time, took the first step.[18]

Over the next two months, President Kennedy convinced a fearful public and a divided Senate to support the Treaty, which it finally did on 23rd September 1963 by an 80-19 margin. Kennedy signed the ratified Treaty on 7th October 1963.

18 'John F. Kennedy: Radio and Television Address to the American People on the Nuclear Test Ban Treaty'(26 July 1963). *The American Presidency Project* < https://www.presidency.ucsb.edu/documents/radio-and-television-address-the-american-people-the-nuclear-test-ban-treaty> Accessed 12 June 2024.

Presidential speech writer, Ted Sorenson, believed that no other accomplishment resulting from Kennedy's time in the White House gave him greater satisfaction than the ratification of the Limited Nuclear Test Ban Treaty.

Disengaging

On 20th September 1963, during the Buddhist Crisis (see also Chapter Forty-Four: *Backfire)*, President Kennedy addressed the United Nations and expressed his concern over the repressive activities of Diem's Saigon regime.

At that time, there were around 17,000 U.S. military advisors in Vietnam. Also in that month of September, Kennedy ordered U.S. Secretary of Defense, Robert McNamara, and Chair of the Joint Chiefs of Staff, General Maxwell Taylor, to go to Vietnam on a 10 day fact-finding mission.

John M. Newman claims in his book *JFK and Vietnam: Deception, Intrigue and the Struggle for Power* that Kennedy had decided to begin a phased withdrawal from Vietnam and that he had ordered this withdrawal to begin:

> On October 2, 1963, Kennedy received the report of a mission to Saigon by McNamara and Maxwell Taylor, chairman of the Joint Chiefs of Staff (JCS). The main recommendations, which appear in Section I(B) of the McNamara-Taylor report, were that a phased withdrawal be completed by the end of 1965 and that the "Defense Department should announce in the very near future presently prepared plans to withdraw 1,000 out of 17,000 U.S. military personnel stationed in Vietnam by the end of 1963".
>
> On October 5, Kennedy made his formal decision. Newman quotes the minutes of the meeting of that day:
>
> The President also said that our decision to remove 1,000 U.S. advisors by December of this year should not be raised formally with Diem. Instead the action should be carried out routinely as part of our general posture of withdrawing people when they are no longer needed. [19]

In their 1972 book, *Johnny, We Hardly Knew Ye*, his close friends and advisors, Kenneth P. O'Donnell and David F. Powers, describe the aftermath of an Oval Office meeting that Kennedy had with Senator Mike Mansfield on Vietnam:

> After Mansfield left the office, the president said to me, "In 1965, I'll become one of the most unpopular presidents in history. I'll be damned everywhere as

19 Galbraith, James K. 'Exit Strategy' (October/November 2003) *Boston Review*, October/November 2003. < https://www.bostonreview.net/articles/galbraith-exit-strategy-vietnam/> Accessed 24 August 2025.

> a communist appeaser. But I don't care. If I tried to pull out completely now from Vietnam, we would have another Joe McCarthy scare on our hands, but I can do it after I'm re-elected. So we had better make damned sure that I am reelected". [20]

On 11th October 1963, Kennedy signed National Security Action Memorandum No. 263 which called for the removal of 1,000 U.S. personnel from Vietnam by December.

In 1973, *Rolling Stone* magazine interviewed Daniel Ellsberg (The Pentagon Papers). In that interview, Ellsberg quotes Robert Kennedy who said that his brother was "absolutely determined not to send combat troops". [21]

Driving in Dallas

A few short weeks after approving National Security Action Memorandum No. 263 and vowing to pull all personnel out of Vietnam if he were re-elected in 1964, President John F. Kennedy drove into downtown Dallas on 22nd November 1963 to begin his re-election campaign.

By this time, he had made a host of powerful enemies in the upper echelons of the intelligence, military and business communities, not to mention the Mafia, southern segregationists, and both pro and anti Castro Cubans. In their minds, he was guilty of not following through on the Bay of Pigs, dis-empowering the CIA and firing its leaders, concluding the Test Ban Treaty, resisting involvement in Laos, planning to dis-engage from Vietnam, encouraging third-world nationalism, flirting with ending the Cold War, and accepting a negotiated settlement in the Cuban missile crisis. In some quarters, the expressions of rage were visceral.

In addition, a number of his policies had aroused the ire of arguably the most influential churchman in America, New York's Cardinal Spellman. Spellman was a friend of J.Edgar Hoover (an avowed enemy of the Kennedy brothers) and a foe of Martin Luther King Jnr. and the civil rights movement. Notably, the Cardinal was also the one of the prime instigators of the Vietnam War.

Wanted for Treason

On that day in Dallas, a poster similar to those to be found in police stations papered the city. It featured front and side photos of Kennedy which mimicked police 'mug

---

20 O'Donnell, K, and Powers, D. *Johnny, We Hardly Knew Ye: Memories of John Fitzgerald Kennedy*. Litttle, Brown and Company: Boston. 1972, p. 16.

21 Jann Wenner (6 December 1973) 'Daniel Ellsberg: The Rollling Stone Interview Part II'. *Rolling Stone* < https://www.sscnet.ucla.edu/polisci/faculty/trachtenberg/vietnam/ellsberg%20rolling%20stone%20%28final%29.pdf> Accessed 24 August 2025.

shots'. The poster was emblazoned with the headings: **Wanted for Treason:** ***This man is wanted for treasonous activities against the United States.***

Then followed a list of crimes of which the President had been adjudged guilty. The main points were:

- Betraying the Constitution (which he swore to uphold);
- Turning the sovereignty of the United States over to the communist controlled United Nations;
- Betraying our friends (Cuba, Katanga, Portugal) and befriending our enemies (Russia, Yugoslavia, Poland);
- Being wrong on innumerable issues affecting the security of the United States (United Nations, Berlin Wall, Missile removal, Cuba, Test Ban Treaty etc);
- Being lax in enforcing Communist Registration laws;
- Supporting and encouraging Communist-inspired racial riots;
- Consistently appointing Anti-Christians to Federal office and upholding the Supreme Court in its Anti-Christian rulings.

As the poster so obligingly reminds us, the President was in mortal danger by going to Dallas that day. Just how much danger, however, was lost on the innumerable people worldwide who were profoundly shocked and saddened by the news coming out of Dallas that afternoon of the 22nd November. It is surely one of the great tragedies of the 20th Century that John F. Kennedy was cut down in his prime before he could finish what he had so hopefully begun.

The Warren Commission, strongly influenced by ex-CIA Director, Alan Dulles, later concluded that Lee Harvey Oswald was the lone assassin although, unlike most lone assassins with a cause, Oswald vehemently denied his guilt. The case against him was made mostly by the national media. The public found the Warren Commission Report unconvincing. A selection of United States historians are of the view that the Kennedy assassination initiated the distrust that the American people now have in their government.

Such was the fog of misinformation and disinformation streaming out of Dallas and Washington at that time that the party or parties responsible for his assassination will now never be known for certain. The alleged lone assassin, Lee Harvey Oswald, was himself silenced by a bullet in the basement of Dallas Police Headquarters two days after the assassination of Kennedy.

However, the reader could ask themselves the classical Latin question: *cui bono*—who has most to gain? The answer will then naturally follow by evaluating the evidence. (See also A Cable Mystery).

War Drums

There would be important changes to many of Kennedy's policies, particularly on the Soviet Union and Vietnam, during Lyndon Baines Johnson's Presidency.

In his inaugural address of January 1961, Kennedy had told the world that the torch had been passed to a new generation of Americans but, with his murder, the torch passed into the hands of Johnson, Richard Nixon, Gerald Ford and Ronald Reagan, leaders who would systematically destroy the promise of Kennedy's final year as they returned the country to war and repression.

Two days after taking office, and one day before John Kennedy's burial, Johnson met with his military advisers and told them that he was not going to lose Vietnam. He had not agreed with Kennedy's decision to withdraw from Vietnam so on 26th November 1963, he issued National Security Action Memorandum No. 273 signalling his intention to take a more hands-on approach. Full-scale United States involvement in Vietnam would soon follow.

The war was a nightmarish bloodbath of America's own making, eating Vietnamese and Americans alike for a decade. More horrifying events would take place before the end of the 1960's, a litany of body blows such as the drug-fuelled Manson murders, widespread anti-war and race riots, and the assassinations of Doctor Martin Luther King Jnr. and Robert F. Kennedy.

As Oliver Stone reminds us so forcefully:

> In hindsight, on that afternoon in Dallas when President Kennedy's head was blown off in broad daylight, it was as if a giant, hideous Greek Medusa had unearthed its face to the American people, freezing us with an oracle of things yet to come.[22]

A Cable Mystery

On 26th November 1963, four days after the assassination of Kennedy, a Memorandum from the CIA Deputy Director of Plans (Frank Wisner) was sent to the FBI Director (J. Edgar Hoover). The Memorandum advised the FBI that a cable

22 Chapter Six of Oliver Stone's documentary series *The Untold History of the United States* (available in print, as an audio book, and on some streaming platforms).

had been received from the CIA station in London. The subject was: 'Assassination of President Kennedy—Reported Anonymous telephone message'.

The cable relayed information which had been received from the British Security Service MI-5. MI-5 considered the information credible and of sufficient importance to inform the CIA station in London. The cable containing the information from MI-5 reads as follows:

> The British Security Service (MI-5) has reported that at 18:05 GMT on 22 November, an anonymous telephone call was made in Cambridge, England, to the senior reporter of the Cambridge News. The caller said only that the Cambridge News Reporter should call the American embassy in London for some big news and then hung up.
>
> After word of the President' death was received, the reporter informed the Cambridge police of the anonymous call and the police informed MI-5. The important point is that the call was made, according to MI-5 calculations, about 25 minutes before the President was shot. The Cambridge reporter has never received a call of this nature before and MI-5 state that he is known to them as a sound and loyal person with no security record.
>
> MI-5 noted that similar anonymous phone calls of a strangely coincidental nature have been received by persons in the UK over this past year, particularly in connection with the case of Dr. Ward. The British Security Service stated its desire to assist in every possible way on any follow-up investigations required within the UK.[23]

Points to Consider

- According to MI-5, some unnamed person in the UK was in a position to know of assassination plans;
- The FBI did not take up MI-5's offer to assist in follow-up investigations;
- The intriguing inclusion of the case of "Dr. Ward" in information concerning the assassination of President Kennedy.

Dr. Stephen Ward was known to have worked with MI-5 and was arguably the key figure in the Profumo Affair, a political and intelligence scandal of the early 1960's which helped to topple Harold Macmillan's conservative government. An article in

---

23 'Assassination of President Kennedy- Reported Anonymous Telephone Message' (23 November 1963). JFK Assassination Records. Document No. 104-10400-10016. *National Archives and Records Administration* < https://www.archives.gov/research/jfk/release-2017-2018?page=376&sort=asc&order=Pages%20Released> Accessed 25 August 2025.

The Guardian: 'How MI5 chiefs abandoned Stephen Ward to take the blame in the Profumo scandal' makes for fascinating reading and may explain a possible connection between Ward and Kennedy. [24]

Section 3: Robert Francis Kennedy

As early as 6th September 1963, the thoughts of incumbent Attorney General Robert Kennedy were turning to disengagement in Vietnam:

> Robert Kennedy speculates that if the war can be won neither with Diem nor in the event of a disruptive coup, we should perhaps be considering a U.S. disengagement. [25]

A Malaise of Spirit

On 10th February 1968, Kennedy penned an editorial for *The New York Times*. It read, in part:

> As 1967 came to an end, E. B. White observed in a Topics column on this page that all Americans seemed to be asking the same questions: "What happened? What went sour? What did I do wrong? Who's to blame?"
>
> President Johnson speaks of a mood of "restlessness". Cabinet officers and commentators, poets and protesters tell us that America is deep in a malaise of the spirit, discouraging initiative, paralyzing will and action, dividing Americans from one another by their age, their views and the color of their skin.
>
> Demonstrators shout down Government officials and the Government drafts protesters. Anarchists threaten to burn the country down, and some have begun to try, while tanks have patrolled American streets and machine guns have fired at American children. Our young people, the best educated and comforted in our history, turn from the Peace Corps and public commitment of a few years ago to lives of disengagement and despair, turned on with drugs and turned off America. Indeed, we seem to fulfill the vision of Yeats: "Things fall apart; the center cannot hold; Mere anarchy is loosed upon the world".

---

24 Doward, Jamie (26 January 2020) 'How MI5 chiefs abandoned Stephen Ward to take the blame in the Profumo scandal'. *The Guardian*. <https://www.theguardian.com/uk-news/2020/jan/26/mi5-abandoned-stephen-ward-profumo-scandal> Accessed 16 January 2025.

25 Pentagon Paper [Part IV: B-5]. Evolution of the War. Counterinsurgency: The Overthrow of Ngo Dinh Diem, May-Nov. 1963 p. xviii. *National Archives and Records Administration* <https://www.archives.gov/research/pentagon-papers> Accessed 12 November 2025.

...So half a million of our finest young men struggle, and many die, in a war halfway around the world; while millions more of our best youth neither understand the war nor respect its purposes, and some repudiate the very institutions of a Government they do not believe.

...Our power is enormous, the greatest the world has ever seen. Yet, as we see old allies pulling back to their shores, and old alliances dissolving in quarrels, we sense that even America cannot act as if no other nation existed, flaunting our power and wealth against the judgment and desires of neutrals and allies alike. We wonder if we still hold "a decent respect to the opinions of mankind" or whether, like Athens of old, we will forfeit sympathy and support alike, and ultimately our own security, in the single-minded pursuit of our own goals and objectives.[26]

Choices

On 18th March 1968 at the University of Kansas, Kennedy spoke further of the grave issues which occupied his mind during the Battle of Khe San:

...We have three choices: We can either pull out of South Vietnam unilaterally and raise the white flag—I think that's unacceptable.

Second, we can continue to escalate and send more men there until we have millions and millions more men and we can continue to bomb North Vietnam. In my judgment, we will be no nearer victory than we are now.

And the third step that we can take is to go to the negotiating table...that is the course of action I would like to see. I would like to see the United States government make it clear to the government of Saigon that we are not going to tolerate their corruption and the dishonesty. I think that we should make it clear to the government of Saigon that if we're going to draft 18 and 19 year-old here in the United States, and we're going to send them to fight and die in Khe Sanh, that we want the government of South Vietnam to draft their 18 and 19-year-olds.

And I want to make it clear that if the government of Saigon feels Khe Sanh or Que Son and the area in the demilitarized zone are so important, I want to see those American marines out of there and South Vietnamese troops in there.

I want to have an explanation as to why American boys killed two weeks ago in South Vietnam, were more than three times as many as the soldiers of South

26 Robert F. Kennedy (10 February 1968) Topics: 'Things Fall Apart; the Center Cannot Hold...' *The New York Times*, p. 3. < https://www.nytimes.com/1968/02/10/archives/topics-things-fall-apart-the-center-cannot-hold-.html> Accessed 12 November 2025.

Vietnam. I want to understand why the casualties and the deaths over the period of the last two weeks, at the height of the fighting, should be so heavily American casualties, as compared to the South Vietnamese. This is their war. I think we have to make the effort to help them, I think that we have to make the effort to fight, but I don't think that we should have to carry the whole burden of that war, I think the South Vietnamese should. [27] (The Battle of Khe San lasted from 21st January to 9th July 1968.)

End the War

Just two weeks later, in a speech delivered at Pennsylvania State University on 2nd April 1968, Kennedy again called for an end to the Vietnam War through a negotiated settlement. His speech included the following:

> Everywhere the American people seek not revenge but reconciliation. They seek both at home and abroad solutions of friendship, not force. They seek an end to the war in Vietnam, not through withdrawal or escalation, but through a negotiated settlement in which both sides put away the tools of violence and killing, and labor instead at the conference table for an honorable settlement. [28]

Two days later, prominent anti-Vietnam war activist Martin Luther King Jnr. was assassinated in Memphis, Tennessee. A year before his death, King had observed that:

> If America's soul becomes totally poisoned, part of the autopsy must read Vietnam...[29]

On 5th June 1968, just one month after Dr. King's assassination, Kennedy was himself shot at the Ambassador Hotel in Los Angeles following a victory speech upon winning the California primaries. Just 26 hours later, he was pronounced dead.

On 29th March 1973, the last United States combat troops left South Vietnam, ending direct United States military involvement in the Vietnam War. There can be little doubt that, had Kennedy gone on to win the Presidency in November 1968, he

---

27 Robert F. Kennedy. 'Remarks at the University of Kansas, March 18, 1968'. *John F. Kennedy Presidential Library and Museum* < https://www.jfklibrary.org/learn/about-jfk/the-kennedy-family/robert-f-kennedy/robert-f-kennedy-speeches/remarks-at-the-university-of-kansas-march-18-1968> Accessed 12 November 2025.

28 'Fifty years ago, RFK's speech at The Palestra on Vietnam' (5 June 2018). *Penn Today* <https://penntoday.upenn.edu/news/fifty-years-ago-rfks-speech-palestra-vietnam> Accessed 27 December 2025.

29 Extract from Martin Luther King Junior Speech, Riverside Church, New York City, NY. 4 April 1967.

would have sought a negotiated settlement and the slaughterhouse of Vietnam would have been considerably shortened.

Section 4: Harold Edward Holt

In June of 1966, the Australian Prime Minister, Harold Holt, had visited President Lyndon Johnson at the White House and declared that Australia was 'a staunch friend that will be all the way with LBJ'.

Just 18 months later, on 17th December 1967, Harold Holt disappeared while swimming at Cheviot Beach near Portsea, Victoria, a beach which is notorious for its dangerous conditions marked by powerful rip currents and hidden submerged rocks.

Despite a massive search in and around Cheviot Beach, no body or other evidence was recovered. Holt was presumed to have accidentally drowned and his memorial service five days later was attended by many world leaders.

Nature abhors a vacuum so, in the absence of his body, there emerged a number of allegations, rumours and conspiracy theories which continue to this day. The most outrageous of these was the assertion that he had been a Chinese spy and that he had been picked up from Cheviot Beach by a Chinese submarine.

Nevertheless, to have a Head of State disappear without trace was an event unparalleled in the history of western democracy so there was a general air of disbelief, not only in Australia but worldwide.

While sources cannot be named, there is a strong possibility that Holt did not drown accidentally but entered the water with a reckless disregard for his life owing to an increasing remorse and despair over his role in escalating the Vietnam War. His state of mind was observed by those close to him who saw him reading certain material highly critical of Australian involvement in the Vietnam War and laying out reasons for that involvement, an involvement which did not correspond with the usual narrative but laid the lion's share of the blame at the feet of a Triumvirate consisting of the then Prime Minister, Robert Menzies, and his close allies Bartholomew Augustine Santamaria and Archbishop Daniel Mannix. The material provided all the evidence necessary to convince even a hardened skeptic. (See Part I-3: *Enemies Within* and Part II-34: *The New Exodus.*)

Holt was also heard to speak despairingly of "our boys in Vietnam".

While his state of mind on the day he entered the boiling surf of Cheviot Beach cannot now be known, there are unimpeachable sources which testify to his intentions regarding the Vietnam War.

In a 1985 televised interview addressing the theory that the CIA had assassinated Harold Holt, William McMahon, a former Australian Prime Minister, and Don Chipp, the leader of the Australian Democrats Party, spoke of Holt's concerns over Vietnam. The interview begins with an introduction and is followed by remarks from McMahon and Chipp:

> **Introduction:** Although Australia and the world never knew it, there is evidence that Harold Holt was about to pull his troops out of the agonising war five years earlier.
>
> **McMahon:** He was the one who, over time, was realising that we'd gone too far. He was not going to give any more troops. When Clark Clifford and General Maxwell Taylor came out here, we had several meetings with them together with Ed Clark, the Ambassador. You knew then from what Harold had said that this was the end of the Australian contribution and probably our withdrawal from Vietnam.
>
> **Chipp:** He was realising that there were real human beings getting their guts shot out, real young Aussie boys. And I had a feeling that he was ready to start pulling boys out of Vietnam, not putting more in.

This televised interview can be accessed at the National Film and Sound Archive.[30] Footage of the first news reports of Holt's disappearance can also be accessed at the National Film and Sound Archive.

Section 5: Neutralising

Doctor Evatt was cut down by a political assassination, John F. Kennedy and Robert F. Kennedy by assassins's bullets, and Harold Holt disappeared in circumstances unparalleled in western democracies. These four men, two Australians and two Americans, all had the power or potential power to either stop or significantly shorten the Vietnam War. The possibility that all four would be neutralised at crucial turning points just by random chance is vanishingly small.

Note

See Chapter Forty: *The Pentagon Papers* for an introduction to the Pentagon Papers and the enduring impact of their publication on the American body politic. The Pentagon Papers can be accessed at the National Archives https://www.archives.gov/research/pentagon-papers

30 *National Film and Sound Archive.* <https://www.nfsa.gov.au/collection/curated/asset/98247-cia-assassination> accessed 30 December 2024.

PART IV

The Road of No Return

The past was erased, the erasure was forgotten
the lie became the truth.

— ORWELL

CHAPTER THIRTY-NINE

Allied Crossroads

Section 1: Australia

Casting Lots

On 10th November 1964, the Australian Government introduced a compulsory selective National Service Scheme. In announcing this decision to Parliament, Prime Minister Robert Menzies referred to 'aggressive Communist' developments in Asia, such as 'recent Indonesian policies and actions' and a 'deterioration in our strategic position', as being influential in the decision being reached.

This *National Service Act* of 1964 required all 20 year old males to register for compulsory national service. From these, a number would be conscripted into the Army to perform two years' continuous full-time service in the Regular Army Supplement, followed by three years part-time service in the Regular Army Reserve. National servicemen on full-time duty were liable for what was called 'special overseas service', which included combat duties in Vietnam.

The process for choosing who would be conscripted was similar to a lottery. Numbered marbles, each representing a day of the year, were placed in a barrel. A predetermined number were then drawn individually and randomly by hand. If the number picked corresponded to the day of the year on which a person was born, they were conscripted into the Army.

The Best Man

According to the following article in *The New York Times*:

> President Johnson decided on 1st April 1965 to use American ground troops for offensive action in South Vietnam because the Administration quickly found that sustained bombing of North Vietnam— begun on 2nd March—was not going to stave off collapse in South Vietnam.
>
> ...National Security Action Memorandum 328, dated 6th April 1965, reported that the President had "approved an 18-20,000 man increase in U. S. military support forces to fill out existing units and supply needed logistic personnel". Further, he approved sending ashore two Marine battalions that Gen. William

> C. Westmoreland, the commander in Vietnam, had asked for on 17th March, adding to two Marine battalions with 3,500 men that had landed on 8th March as defenders of Da Nang airfield.
>
> President Johnson also approved deployment of a Marine air squadron and "a change of mission for all Marine battalions .... to permit their more active use..." He approved "urgent efforts" to get South Korean, Australian and New Zealand troops.[1]

Australia learned almost immediately of these "urgent efforts" and of the likelihood that it would be asked to provide a battalion.

During the Petrov era and the resulting *Royal Commission on Espionage,* Menzies had made himself so dependable in U.S. eyes that, even before receiving a response from Australia to a request for ground troops, the U.S. Special Assistant for National Security, McGeorge Bundy, sent President Johnson a Memo on 8th April 1965 specifically asking Johnson to send Menzies a letter of appreciation. The Memo read:

> Sir Robert Menzies has· been **the best man of all on Vietnam** in recent weeks. A good sample is his performance with some Australian Bishops attached at Tab A in a note from the Australian Ambassador. But you will have seen other statements in the Press.
>
> I thought you might want to send him something short and sweet like the letter at Tab B. I have changed the his title to "Dear Sir Robert" to make it a little more informal, and which I thought you might like, but it can be done the other way if you prefer and there is also a "Dear Prime Minister" letter attached. [2]

Perfidious

As noted, Prime Minister Menzies had introduced the National Service Scheme in November 1964 which allowed for young men to be conscripted for service in Vietnam.

Late in the evening of 29th April 1965, Menzies stood in the half-empty House of Representatives and announced that Australia would soon send an infantry battalion to Vietnam:

---

1 'Use of U.S. Troops decided in April '65'. (1 July 1971) *The New York Times* <https://www.nytimes.com/1971/07/01/archives/use-of-us-troops-decided-in-april-65.html> Accessed 11 April 2025.

2 Folder, 'McGeorge Bundy, Vol. 9, March - April 14, 1965 [1 of 2]', Memos to the President, NSF, Box 3, *LBJ Presidential Library* <https://discoverlbj.org/item/nsf-memos-b03-f01> Accessed 2 February 2026.

> The Australian Government is now **in receipt of a request from the Government of South Vietnam for further military assistance.** We have decided—and this has been after close consultation with the Government of the United States —to provide an infantry battalion for service in South Vietnam. In case there is any misunderstanding, 1 think I should say, Sir, that we decided in principle some time ago - weeks and weeks ago - that we would be willing to do this if we received the necessary request from the Government of South Vietnam and the necessary collaboration with the United States. This is not to be regarded as something that has suddenly arisen out of more recent events.[3]

Menzies then read out the text of a message he had received that day from President Johnson:

> Dear Mr. Prime Minister: I am delighted at the decision of your Government to provide an infantry battalion for service in South Vietnam **at the request of the Government of South Vietnam.**

Menzies lied to Parliament by claiming that he was sending the battalion in response to a request from the government of South Vietnam. As diplomatic cables at the time demonstrate, it was a cunning manoeuvre engineered by Menzies to imbue the deployment with some type of international legitimacy:

> As evidenced in several diplomatic cables, Australia's ambassador to South Vietnam was instructed to pressure Quat (then Prime Minister of South Vietnam). Three hours before Menzies was due to make the announcement in parliament, the Prime Minister received word from his ambassador that Quat had finally given a verbal agreement for the despatch of Australia troops. **He had also agreed that this be framed as a request from Saigon.** [4]

Unlike the Australian public who remained unaware of Menzies' theatrical duplicity and largely supported the decision to send an infantry battalion to Vietnam, it would have come as no surprise to President Johnson who was already the architect of the faked Tonkin Gulf Incident which formed the legal basis for the American war effort in Vietnam.

The deployment of combat troops signalled to the world that Australia was effectively at war.

---

3 'Prime Minister Menzies Speech' (29 April 1965). House of Representatives, 25th Parliament, 1st Session. *Historic Hansard* < https://historichansard.net/hofreps/1965/19650429_reps_25_hor45/#debate-0> Accessed 16 Feb. 2025.

4 'Australian Troops committed to Vietnam'. *National Museum of Australia.* <https://www.nma.gov.au/defining-moments/resources/australian-troops-committed-to-vietnam> Accessed 15 Feb 2025.

'All the way with LBJ'

On 26th January 1966, Harold Holt was sworn in as Australian Prime Minister following the retirement of Robert Menzies six days earlier.

On 6th March, just weeks after becoming Prime Minister, Holt announced that the Australian commitment in South Vietnam would be increased to 4,350 defence force personnel and would include conscripts.

In June of 1966, Harold Holt visited President Lyndon Johnson at the White House. At a press conference, Holt declared that Australia was 'a staunch friend that will be all the way with LBJ'. On 18th October 1966, Holt committed a further 1,700 defence force personnel to Vietnam.

Just a few days later, between 20-23 October, Johnson was an official prime ministerial guest in Australia, marking the first official visit by a U.S. President. During this historic trip, Johnson called on U.S. allies to increase support in Vietnam. Johnson's visit, together with the campaign for the upcoming federal election, were the focus for large anti-Vietnam War demonstrations.

The Death Knell

On 26th November 1966, an election was due to be held for the Australian Federal House of Representatives. Prime Minister Holt's Liberal Party campaigned on the issue of support for Australian and United States involvement in the Vietnam War. The leader of the opposition Australian Labor Party campaigned on the issues of conscription and extracting Australian troops from the 'civil war' in Vietnam.

On 10th November 1966, 16 days prior to the election, Arthur Calwell, leader of the Opposition Labor Party, delivered the following impassioned campaign speech:

> The most important issue in this campaign is Conscription, the conscription of a section of our twenty year old youths, against their wishes and their wills, to kill or be killed in the undeclared, civil war in Vietnam... Conscription is immoral, it is unjust and it is a violation of human rights...There are 600,000 Australian mothers with sons between 15 and 20 years of age and many of these boys could be sent away to die or be wounded in the long, cruel dirty war that is raging in Vietnam.
>
> **... The Labor views on Vietnam are supported by opinions expressed by the late President J. F. Kennedy, and by other distinguished Americans like his two famous brothers, Senators Robert and Edward Kennedy and by Senators Fulbright and Mike Mansfield and twenty four other outstanding Senators.**

> ...Our first act as a Government will be to abolish conscription and give orders that all conscripts in camp in Australia shall be discharged forthwith. The remainder of our troops will be brought home at the earliest practicable moment after consultation with our Allies and so as not to endanger the lives of any Australian or allied troops.[5]

Given the media's orchestrated campaign presenting Australian involvement in Vietnam as a war against 'communist aggression', together with the sensational reporting of Holt's declaration in July that Australia was 'all the way with LBJ' and of Johnson's visit to Australia calling for increased support from U.S. allies just one month before the election, it was hardly surprising that the Liberal Party won the election and that Harold Holt remained Australian Prime Minister, a result which sounded the death knell for many.

Section 2: New Zealand

Core Beliefs

New Zealand's military involvement in South Vietnam had its roots in two beliefs held as articles of faith by the decision-makers after the 1950's. The first, and the most important, was that New Zealand depended for its security upon the United States.

The second belief was that communist governments in Southeast Asia would pose a strategic threat to New Zealand's security. Thus, when the United States became involved in preventing the rise to power of a communist government in South Vietnam, the two imperatives to New Zealand involvement reinforced one another.

In addition, New Zealand had developed the habit of co-operation with its other ally, Australia, in regional security matters, and Australia's enthusiasm for involvement became a third factor in New Zealand's policy.

Countdown to Commitment

On 4th December 1964, the U.S. Assistant Secretary of State, William Bundy, jointly briefed the New Zealand and Australian ambassadors about U.S. plans in Vietnam. Bundy stated that President Johnson would shortly contact their respective prime ministers to urge "a considerable augmentation" of both nations' efforts in South Vietnam. Ominously, he added that further U.S. actions could involve air strikes

5 'Arthur Calwell Speech' (10 November 1966). Australian Federal Election Speeches, *Museum of Australian Democracy* < https://electionspeeches.moadoph.gov.au/speeches/1966-arthur-calwell> Accessed 4 February 2025.

against North Vietnam and even the deployment of ground forces. Bundy implied that, in the latter eventuality, Australia and New Zealand might contribute forces.[6]

New Zealand Prime Minister, Keith Holyoake, wrote to President Johnson on 24th February 1965 to explain that his government had considered sending more engineers (deployed in June 1964), but that it was "just not possible politically to step up our military aid where coup succeeds coup and the whole situation in Vietnam remains so chaotic".[7]

A Fateful Decision

On 9th April 1965, news reached Wellington that the Australian Government had decided in principle to send a battalion if requested. New Zealand was initially more reluctant than Australia to commit combat forces to and it took Wellington over a month longer than Canberra to respond to the very clear U.S. desire for a combat contribution.

On 24th May 1965, Cabinet approved the dispatch of an artillery battery of approximately 120 men, a decision which was announced publicly at the opening of Parliament on 27th May 1965.[8]

When New Zealand policy-makers agreed to send combat forces, it was not because of a firm conviction that their small contingent could help hold Vietnam, which was not strategically vital to New Zealand, but because they were unwilling to risk an alliance which was. As would be the case thereafter, New Zealand policy toward the Vietnam War in May 1965 was more a response to U.S. policy toward that conflict than a response to the conflict itself.

What role then, if any, did Australia's actions play in leading New Zealand to its reluctant decision to enter the Vietnam War? Clearly New Zealand's stance did not affect Australian decision-making in the least. In a direct sense, the converse was also true. Though New Zealand's decision to commit was made for alliance reasons, it was to maintain close relations with Washington, not Canberra. Staying in line with Australia was merely a welcome bonus.

Yet there is an important sense in which Australian actions helped tip the balance in leading the Holyoake Government to override its qualms about combat involvement

6 'New Zealand Ambassador, Washington, to Minister of External Affairs' (4 December 1964), 478/4/6, *Records of the Ministry of Foreign Affairs and Trade* (MFAT), Wellington.

7 'Minister for External Affairs to New Zealand Ambassador, Washington' (24 February 1965), 478/4/6, *Records of the Ministry of Foreign Affairs and Trade* (MFAT), Wellington.

8 'Memorandum by I. Stewart to A. McIntosh' (14 May 1965). Cabinet Minute, 65/18/53, 31 May 1965, 478/4/6, *Records of the Ministry of Foreign Affairs and Trade (*MFAT) New Zealand Parliamentary Debates, Vol. 342, pp. 1-2.

in Vietnam. In effect, Canberra's robust stance set limits on New Zealand's freedom of manoeuvre in dealing with the U.S. on Vietnam and undermined its arguments for not supporting the introduction of ground forces. Even if only implicitly, Australia did become a yardstick by which the U.S. could judge New Zealand's responses.

Exasperated policy-makers in Wellington were thereby left with few palatable options. As Alister McIntosh (N.Z. Secretary of External Affairs) bemoaned privately only days after recommending to the Prime Minister that New Zealand send combat troops to Vietnam: "We can't afford to be left too far behind Australia and we can't afford not to support the Americans—though I have the gravest doubts about their coming out of this with any degree of success".[9]

In retrospect, those doubts were well justified. Although scholars continue to debate many aspects of the Vietnam War, there is widespread agreement that it proved a disaster for Washington: "the single greatest error the U.S. made in fighting the Cold War", as John Lewis Gaddis has described it. [10]

What If?

That error would probably not have been avoided, even if Australia had emulated New Zealand in questioning the course on which the U.S. was bound in 1965.

Dr. Roberto Rabel posed the following hypothesis:

> But if Australia and New Zealand had **both** questioned from the outset the wisdom of an open-ended combat commitment in Vietnam, they might have helped the US to attempt a more measured and less costly approach to the problem of Vietnam. Instead, the "robust" Australians only encouraged U.S. combat intervention, while the "reluctant" New Zealanders were rendered powerless to refuse involvement. It was but one of many missed opportunities of the Vietnam War.[11]

9 'Alister McIntosh to Frank Corner' (5 May 1965). McIntosh Papers, *Records of the Ministry of Foreign Affairs and Trade* (MFAT), Wellington.

10 Gaddis, John Lewis. *We now know: rethinking Cold War history*. Clarendon Press: Oxford, 1997, p. 189.

11 Rabel, Dr. Robert. 'We cannot afford to be left too far behind Australia: New Zealand's entry into the Vietnam War in May 1965'. *Journal of the Australian War Memorial*. Issue 32, April 1999. <https://www.awm.gov.au/articles/journal/j32> Accessed 11 April 2025.

CHAPTER FORTY

The Pentagon Papers

The lies revealed in the papers were of a generational scale, and, for much of the American public, this grand deception seeded a suspicion of government that is even more widespread today.

All the Pentagon Papers can be accessed through the *National Archives and Records Administration* Website at https://www.archives.gov/research/pentagon-papers

To grasp the entire context of material referenced, it is advised that the relevant paper be accessed and consulted in depth.

Section 1: A Pivotal Moment

On 13th June 1971, a story by journalist Neil Sheehan appeared on the front page of *The New York Times*. It was titled: 'Vietnam Archive: Pentagon Study Traces 3 Decades of Rising U.S. Involvement' and begins:

> A massive study of how the United States went to war in Indochina, conducted by the Pentagon three years ago, demonstrates that four administrations progressively developed a sense of commitment to a non-Communist Vietnam, a readiness to fight the North to protect the South, and an ultimate frustration with this effort—to a much greater extent than their public statements acknowledged at the time.[12]

On the same front page of *The New York Times*, an article titled 'Vast Review Took More Than a Year' by journalist Heidrick Smith included the following:

> As some top policy makers came to question the effectiveness of the American effort in mid-1967, the report shows, their policy papers began not only to seek to limit the military strategies on the ground and in the air but also to worry about the impact of the war on American society.
>
> "A feeling is widely and strongly held that 'the Establishment' is out of its mind", wrote John T. McNaughton, Assistant Secretary of Defense, in a note

12 Sheehan, Neil. 'Vietnam Archive: Pentagon Study Traces 3 Decades of Rising U.S. Involvement' (13 June 1971). *The New York Times*, p. 1.

to Secretary McNamara in early May, 1967. Mr. McNaughton, who three years earlier had been one of the principal planners of the air war against North Vietnam, went on to say:

> "The feeling is that we are trying to impose some U.S. image on distant peoples we cannot understand (any more than we can the younger generation here at home), and that we are carrying the thing to absurd lengths. Related to this feeling is the increased polarization that is taking place in the United States with seeds of the worst split in our people in more than century".
>
> At the end of June, 1967, Mr. McNamara—deeply disillusioned with the war —decided to commission the Pentagon study of Vietnam policy that Mr. McNaughton and other high officials had encouraged him to undertake. [13]

On 23rd June 1996, to mark the twenty-fifth anniversary of the leaking of excerpts from the Pentagon Papers, *The New York Times* published an article titled 'Twenty-Five Years Later: Lessons from the Pentagon Papers'. The article included the following extracts:

> Twenty-Five years ago this month, *The New York Times* began publishing the Pentagon Papers, a documentary history tracing the ultimately doomed involvement of the United States in a grinding war in the jungles and rice paddies of Southeast Asia.
>
> They demonstrated, among other things, that the Johnson Administration had systematically lied, not only to the public but also to Congress, about a subject of transcendent national interest and significance.
>
> The Government sought and won a court order restraining further publication after three articles had appeared. Other newspapers then began publishing. They, too, were restrained, until finally, on June 30, 1971, the United States Supreme Court ruled, by a vote of 9 to 0 (corrected to 6 to 3), that publication could resume.
>
> Then as now, the fight over the top-secret papers, whose compilation had been ordered by Robert S. McNamara when he was Defense Secretary, stood as a pivotal moment in the ages-old struggle between the Government and the press. But few would have guessed how much it would change the news media, how much it would change the public view of the news media and the Government and how little it would change the way the Government conducts its business.

13 Smith, Heidrick. 'Vast Review Took More Than a Year' (13 June 1971). *The New York Times*, p. 1.

> Opponents of the Vietnam war, including Daniel Ellsberg, the onetime hawk turned dove who played a key role in making the papers public, hoped that doing so might persuade President Richard M. Nixon to change his policy on Vietnam. It did not. Less than a year after publication, Haiphong Harbor was mined, and the war dragged on.
>
> ... Victory emboldened the news media, and the contents of the Pentagon Papers themselves guaranteed, at least for the generation of journalists directly involved, that every Government utterance would be subject to skeptical (and too often cynical) scrutiny. The Nixon Administration responded by creating the Plumbers unit (so called because they were to deal with leaks like that of the papers). That step in turn led to the Watergate scandal and ultimately to Nixon's resignation.[14]

Section 2: View from the CIA

A few weeks after *The New York Times* began publishing excerpts from the Pentagon Papers, a Central Intelligence Agency (CIA) Memorandum dated 8th July 1971 with the subject line 'The Pentagon Papers' described what was included in the Papers and what impact public knowledge of their contents would have on the workings of government.

Background

The set of documents that has become informally termed the 'Pentagon Papers' is in fact a study entitled 'United States-Vietnam Relations 1945-1967' produced by a group labelled 'Vietnam Task Force' in the Office of the Secretary of Defense. The study consists of 46 volumes of text plus a four-page '47th volume' that includes the two-page transmittal memorandum by which Leslie H. Gelb (Chairman of the Task Force) formally forwarded the whole study to the Secretary of Defense plus a two-page 'outline' (i.e., table of contents).[15]

As a quick examination of the outline will illustrate, the study is an amalgam of narrative text by members of the Task Force who wrote it plus compendia of official documents grouped by period or subject or both. In virtually every volume, the narrative text quotes extensively (and usually quite selectively) from a variety of

14 Apple, R.W. 'Twenty-Five Years Later: Lessons from the Pentagon Papers' (23 June 1996). *The New York Times,* 23 June 1996, p. 5.

15 'The Pentagon Papers' (8 July 1971). CIA Memorandum: Approved for release 12 May 2004. *Central Intelligence Agency* <https://www.cia.gov/readingroom/docs/CIA-RDP80R01720R000200160016-2.pdf> Acccessed 20 Sept. 2025.

official documents. Not all of these are reproduced separately in the documentary annexes, but in many cases the quotations are collectively so extensive that most of the document in question is reproduced at some point or other in the study. In addition, every volume (and, usually, every section) of narrative text has a fairly elaborate set of footnotes which cite by full title, identifying number (e.g., SNIE 10-4-54) and issue date virtually every document discussed, alluded to or quoted from in the text itself. The documents cited, quoted from or discussed span the entire classification gamut from overt published material (e.g., books and articles) to Top Secret documents carrying a variety of additional restrictive indicators.

The study was commissioned in June 1967 by then Secretary McNamara who levied the requirement on the Office of International Security Affairs, at that time headed by John McNaughton. Morton. H. Halperin, McNaughton's Deputy for Policy Planning and Arms Control, was apparently given command oversight of the project and the Task Force which did the actual work was chaired by one of Halperin's subordinates, Leslie H. Gelb. (Both Gelb and Halperin are now with the Brookings Institute.)

Some 35 people—officers from the military services, Defense Department civilian employees (including Daniel Ellsberg) and a variety of outside consultants, many but not all from the RAND Corporation—seemed to have worked on various parts of the study at various times. Despite the dates given in its title (1945-1967), from the standpoint of substance, the study effectively cuts off with President Johnson's 31 March 1968 speech. When the various parts of the study were actually written cannot be determined with certainty, though its various portions were clearly written by different people at different times and the end result is much more a collection of separate monographs than a unified whole. It would appear that all portions of the study were completed by the summer or early fall of 1968.

As a glance at Gelb's transmittal memorandum will demonstrate, however, the study was not formally dispatched through channels to the Secretary of Defense (Mr. Clifford) until 15th January 1969. President Nixon's inauguration was, of course, on Monday, 20th January 1969. Thus the study was in fact dispatched with only two working days left before the change of administration in the Defense Department.

Damage Assessment

There are repeated references to the (CIA) Agency, its activities, its officers (some identified by name) and its alleged positions throughout most of the narrative portion of the study. Also the narrative is replete with allusions to, discussions of and quotations from (augmented by specific footnote citations) a wide range of Agency documents: operational cables, raw field reports, Headquarters disseminations,

National Intelligence Estimates and Special National Intelligence Estimates, formal memoranda and studies from the Office of Current Intelligence and special task groups, informal and in some cases internal memoranda, and memoranda from the Director (Mr. McCone) to the President.

In assessing the damage done in having the study pass in its entirety into the public domain and/or unfriendly hands (e.g., the Soviet Government), it must of course be recognized that all of the material in the Pentagon study is now at least three years old and some of it is over twenty years old. Nonetheless, we are concerned about the following areas of actual or potential damage: (Although the document was approved for release on 12th May 2004, some of the next sections are redacted.)

- Given the fact that—whatever be its legal status or name—a struggle is going on in which the U.S. is involved on one side and North Vietnam on the other, in which armed force is being used, Americans are being killed, and which the U.S. Government is trying to end through negotiations currently in progress. It is hard to escape the fact that the leak of the Pentagon papers provides propaganda and political action ammunition of inordinate value to those presently engaged in armed conflict with the United States;
- Finally, the leak of the study raises the whole range of issues associated with the right -or even ability-of the U.S. Government to conduct private business privately. It also raises a range of basic issues concerning the right or ability of officials in any administration to engage in frank debates or discussions associated with their official responsibilities without having their views and actions subject to hostile, out-of-context criticism at some later date and in some changed and later climate but within a time span whereby such retrospective review can adversely affect such officials' public or private careers without their having any effective means of seeking recourse or redress. In short, the leak of the Pentagon papers raises the basic issue of the U.S. Government's right or ability to have or protect secrets of any nature.

Unauthorized Hands

One of the major questions obviously raised by the matter of the Pentagon papers is that of precisely what is now floating about in unauthorized hands outside of government control. The answer is that we do not really know. Ellsberg, for one, clearly had access to the whole study and is presumed to have copied all of it. He is believed to have turned over a complete version to the Senate Foreign Relations Committee in 1970. Apparently he did not give a complete version to *The New York*

Times since that paper, by the inventory it furnished the court, does not have the four negotiations volumes that constitute section VI-C. Whether these volumes are floating around elsewhere is a matter of conjecture, though there are grounds for believing that the Soviet Embassy (at least) was given a complete set by someone. [16]

Section 3: Publish and be Damned

Ellsberg, Russo and Sheehan

Daniel Ellsberg (1931-2023) completed a PhD in economics from Harvard in 1962, joined the RAND Corporation and began studying game theory as applied to crisis situations and nuclear warfare.

In August 1964, Ellsberg was appointed special assistant to Assistant Secretary of Defense for International Security Affairs John McNaughton. As American involvement in Vietnam deepened, he went to Saigon in 1965 to evaluate civilian pacification programs. Ellsberg then joined Major General Edward Lansdale, and for 18 months accompanied combat patrols into the jungles and villages.

In 1967, Ellsberg, along with 34 other analysts, contributed to the top-secret 47-volume study of classified documents on the conduct of the Vietnam War. He returned to the RAND Corporation in 1968.

In 2021, *The New York Times* published a Special Report marking the 50th anniversary since its leaking of excerpts of the Pentagon Papers. Included in the Special Report are articles titled 'We're going to publish: An Oral History of the Pentagon Papers' and 'The Secrets and Lies of the Vietnam War, Exposed in One Epic Document', both of which are reproduced in part below:

> On Oct. 1, 1969, Daniel Ellsberg walked out of the RAND Corporation offices, where he worked as a Defense Department consultant, into the temperate evening air of Santa Monica, Calif. In his briefcase was part of a classified government study that chronicled 22 years of failed United States involvement in Vietnam. By then, the war had killed about 45,000 Americans and hundreds of thousands of Vietnamese. He had been posted in Vietnam, and even worked on the study he now carried. Having become convinced that the war was not only unwinnable but also a crime, he was now determined to stop it…

16 'The Pentagon Papers' (8 July 1971). CIA Memorandum: Approved for release 12 May 2004. *Central Intelligence Agency* <https://www.cia.gov/readingroom/docs/CIA-RDP80R01720R000200160016-2.pdf> Acccessed 20 Sept. 2025.

> He quit RAND, moved east for a fellowship at M.I.T. and for the next year tried to persuade members of Congress to help him expose the study—later known as the Pentagon Papers—to the world. It was not working. On the night of March 2, 1971, he was in Washington, D.C., and looked up Neil Sheehan, a *New York Times* reporter he had first met in Vietnam. [17]
>
> … After *The New York Times* began publishing the Pentagon Papers on Sunday, June 13, 1971, the nation was stunned. The response ranged from horror to anger to disbelief. There was furor over the betrayal of national secrets. Opponents of the war felt vindicated. Veterans, especially those who had served multiple tours in Vietnam, were pained to discover that Americans officials knew the war had been a failed proposition nearly from the beginning.
>
> The revelations in the Pentagon Papers infuriated a country sick of the war, the body bags of young Americans, the photographs of Vietnamese civilians fleeing U.S. air attacks and the endless protests and counter-protests that were dividing the country as nothing had since the Civil War. The lies revealed in the papers were of a generational scale, and, for much of the American public, this grand deception seeded a suspicion of government that is even more widespread today.[18]

The Handover

On 16th June 2023, *The New York Times* published an Obituary on the death of Daniel Ellsberg. The Obituary provides information about the relationships between Ellsberg, Russo and Sheehan and how excerpts from the Pentagon Papers passed into the hands of *The New York Times*:

> With Anthony J. Russo Jr., a RAND colleague he had met in Vietnam, Mr. Ellsberg, who had a top-secret security clearance, photocopied the 47-volume Pentagon study. Still believing he could work within the system, Mr. Ellsberg in 1970 gave partial copies to Senator J. William Fulbright, the chairman of the Foreign Relations Committee, and others in Congress. All refused to act.
>
> Frustrated, disillusioned and aware that he might be committing a crime and could be sent to prison, Mr. Ellsberg approached Neil Sheehan, a veteran *New York Times* correspondent he had met in Vietnam, with the documents. The

17 Harlan, J. and Gallagher, B. 'We're going to publish: An Oral History of the Pentagon Papers' (July 2021). *The New York Times*. < https://www.nytimes.com/interactive/2021/06/09/us/pentagon-papers-oral-history.html> Accessed 23 September 2025.

18 Becker, Elizabeth. 'The Secrets and Lies of the Vietnam War, Exposed in One Epic Document' (9 June 2021). *The New York Times* <https://www.nytimes.com/2021/06/09/us/pentagon-papers-vietnam-war.html?smid=nytcore-ios-share&referringSource=articleShare> Acessed 23 September 2025.

transfer was a delicate matter. In an account that was withheld at his request until after his death in 2021, Mr. Sheehan told a *Times* colleague, Janny Scott, a dramatic story of how he had obtained the 7,000-page scoop of a lifetime.

Mr. Ellsberg, he said, first agreed to turn over the papers if *The Times* would publish them and do its best to protect the identity of its source. But when Mr. Sheehan arrived at an apartment in Cambridge, Mass., where the papers were stashed, Mr. Ellsberg changed the terms, saying Mr. Sheehan could study the papers and take notes, but not photocopy them. He gave Mr. Sheehan a key to the apartment and left town.

Mr. Sheehan, believing the papers were "the property of the people" and had been paid for with "the blood of their sons," as he said, broke the deal, had copies made and took a set to New York, where teams of *Times* reporters and editors worked in a hotel suite around the clock for weeks to prepare the trove of national secrets for publication. Mr. Ellsberg did not learn of Mr. Sheehan's duplicity until June 13, 1971, when *The Times* published the first of nine installments of excerpts and analytical articles on the Pentagon Papers.

The Reaction

Attorney General John N. Mitchell, citing espionage and conspiracy statutes, warned *The Times* that it had jeopardized national security and said the newspaper faced ruinous legal action. Editors, lawyers and *The Times'* publisher, Arthur O. Sulzberger, conferred, and publication resumed. After the third installment, however, the Justice Department obtained an injunction, halting publication.

Mr. Ellsberg, meantime, leaked the papers to other publications, including *The Washington Post*. The government sued. *The Times* and *The Post* carried their cases to the Supreme Court, which lifted the injunction on June 30, allowing publication to resume.

The Pentagon Papers revealed not only that successive presidents had widened the war, but also that they had been aware that it was not likely to be won. The documents also disclosed rife cynicism among high officials toward the public and disregard for the enormous casualties of the war.

The Watergate "Plumbers"

The White House soon began to pursue Mr. Ellsberg, who had gone into hiding. Under President Nixon's domestic affairs adviser, John D. Ehrlichman, a unit called the "plumbers" was formed to plug leaks and carry out covert operations, including a burglary at the office of Mr. Ellsberg's psychiatrist (no damaging files were found). The burglary in 1972 at the Democratic Party headquarters at the Watergate complex in Washington was organized by two former members of the plumbers, E. Howard Hunt and G. Gordon Liddy. The arrest of the Watergate burglars began an unraveling that led to Nixon's resignation in 1974.

The Trials

Mr. Ellsberg, who surrendered, and Mr. Russo, his colleague, were charged with espionage, conspiracy and other crimes carrying a total of 115 years in prison. After a procedural mistrial in 1972, they were tried in 1973 before Judge William M. Byrne Jr. in federal court in Los Angeles. Before the case went to the jury, however, the judge dismissed all the charges on the grounds of government misconduct.

Judge Byrne said that G. Gordon Liddy and E. Howard Hunt, who engineered the Watergate burglary, had broken into the office of Lewis J. Fielding, Mr. Ellsberg's former psychiatrist, in a failed attempt to find damaging evidence against him; that the F.B.I. had illegally wiretapped Mr. Ellsberg's conversations; and that during the trial Mr. Ehrlichman had offered the judge the directorship of the F.B.I.[19]

A War of Aggression

In a 2002 memoir, Ellsberg wrote about the Vietnam War, stating that:

> It was no more a "civil war" after 1955 or 1960 than it had been during the U.S.–supported French attempt at colonial reconquest. A war in which one side was entirely equipped and paid by a foreign power—which dictated the nature of the local regime in its own interest—was not a civil war. To say that we had "interfered" in what is "really a civil war," as most American academic writers and even liberal critics of the war do to this day, simply screened a more painful reality and was as much a myth as the earlier official one of "aggression from the North". In terms of the UN Charter and of our own avowed ideals, it was a war of foreign aggression, American aggression. [20]

19 McFadden, Robert D. 'Daniel Ellsberg, Who Leaked the Pentagon Papers, Is Dead at 92' (16 June 2023). *The New York Times*. < https://www.nytimes.com/2023/06/16/us/daniel-ellsberg-dead.html?smid=nytcore-ios-share&referringSource=articleShare> Accessed 22 September 2025.

20 Ellsberg, Daniel. *Secrets: A Memoir of Vietnam and the Pentagon Papers*. New York: Viking Press: New York, 2002, pp. 258–260.

The following Acronyms are found mainly in Chapters dealing with the Pentagon Papers.

South Vietnam

ARVN: Army of the Republic of Vietnam.

GVN: Government of Vietnam.

RVN: Republic of Vietnam.

RVNAF: Republic of Vietnam Armed Forces.

SVN: South Vietnam.

North Vietnam

DRV: Democratic Republic of Vietnam.

PAVN: Peoples Army of Vietnam

NLF: National Liberation Front

LASV: Liberation Army of South Vietnam (Viet Cong)

United States

CIA: Central Intelligence Agency.

CINCPAC: Commander in Chief, U.S. Pacific Command.(Admiral Ulysses S. Grant Sharp Jr. from 1964-1968.)

COMUSMACV: Commander, U.S. Military Assistance Command, Vietnam (General Paul D. Harkins from January 1962-June 1964 and General William Westmorland from June 1964-June 1968)

DIA: Defence Intelligence Agency

JCS: Joint Chiefs of Staff.

MACV: Military Assistance Command, Vietnam.

MAAG: Military Assistance Advisory Group.

NCS: National Security Council.

NIB: National Intelligence Board.

NSAM: National Security Action Memorandum.

TAOR: Marines Tactical Area of Responsibility.

CHAPTER FORTY-ONE

Retrospect

United States involvement in Vietnam began in secrecy. It ended in humiliation thirty years later, witnessed by the entire world.

Before the war was over, almost 59,000 Americans, Australians and New Zealanders would be dead, at least 250,000 South Vietnamese troops, and over a million North Vietnamese soldiers and Viet Cong guerillas. Two million civilians North and South are thought to have perished, as well as tens of thousands more in the neighbouring states of Laos and Cambodia.

For many Vietnamese, it was a brutal civil war. For others, the bloody climactic chapter in a century-old struggle for independence. For the soldiers who fought in it, and for those who fought against it back in their home country, as well as for those who merely glimpsed it on the nightly news, the Vietnam War was a decade of agony.

Vietnam seemed to call everything into question, the value of honour and gallantry, the qualities of cruelty and mercy, the candour of governments, and what it means to be a patriot.[21]

The Pentagon Papers

The Pentagon Papers demonstrate conclusively that American Presidents and their closest advisors had steered the United States into deeper and deeper involvement in Vietnam despite knowing that the war had been a failed proposition almost from the beginning.

For example, they had known in 1966 that the Saigon Government was weak, incompetent and corrupt:

- The GVN (Government of South Vietnam is riddled with corruption… there is corruption high and low.

They had known that the enemy was disciplined and resilient:

- Hanoi's determination [despite our bombing] to continue its policy of supporting the insurgency in the South appears as firm as ever;

21 Burns & Novick (2017). S1E1 - Déjà Vu (1858-1961) *The Vietnam War.* Television Documentary narrated by Peter Coyote.

- The indirect effects of the bombing on the will of the North Vietnamese to continue fighting...have not shown themselves in any tangible way.

Despite constantly reassuring the American people that victory was just around the corner, they admitted that:

- The solution lies in girding, openly for a longer war;
- The prognosis is bad...Success is a mere possibility;
- The odds are less than even;
- We have failed consistently since 1961 to make a dent in the problem.

Yet they had routinely lied about all these issues to Congress and the American people. [22]

One of the most striking revelations to emerge from the Pentagon Papers is found in a joint Memorandum to President Kennedy from Dean Rusk (Secretary of State) and Robert McNamara (Secretary of Defense) dated 11th November 1961. The Memo said in part:

> The United States should commit itself to the clear objective of preventing the fall of South Vietnam to Communism...We should be prepared to introduce United States combat forces if that should become necessary for success. Dependent upon the circumstances, it may also be necessary for United States forces to strike at the source of the aggression in North Vietnam.

Thus, to ensure South Vietnam would not fall into the hands of 'Communists', the introduction of U.S. combat forces and possible operations against North Vietnam were being deliberated over two years before the landing of the first Marines at Da Nang and the commencement of the *Rolling Thunder* bombing campaign against North Vietnam, and almost four years before Congress and the American people became aware that their country was already involved in a ground war in Vietnam. [23] (See also Chapter Forty-Seven: *The Die is Cast.*)

---

22 Pentagon Paper [Part IV: C.6.a] Evolution of the War. U.S. Ground Strategy and Force Deployments: 1965 - 1967. Volume I: Phase II, Program 3, Program 4. pp. 85, 86, 89, 90, 91. *National Archives and Records Administration* <https://www.archives.gov/research/pentagon-papers> Accessed 12 November 2025.

23 Pentagon Paper [Part IV: B-1] Evolution of the War. The Kennedy Commitments and Programs: 1961, p. 125. *National Archives and Records Administration* <https://www.archives.gov/research/pentagon-papers> Accessed 12 November 2025.

The Five O'Clock Follies

U.S. military officers and their civilian counterparts regularly stood before the Saigon press corps in the Rex Hotel reciting statistics and telling tales that bore no resemblance to the reality of war that the journalists had seen for themselves. The exercise was so ludicrous that journalists began calling the daily sessions the 'Five O'Clock Follies'.

In March 2017, Hugh Greenaway penned an article for *The New York Times* titled 'What I Saw in Vietnam'. Fifty years after his arrival in Saigon in March 1967, he wrote in part:

> …50 years ago this month, the mood of American officials was all upbeat, get-on-the team optimism. We were winning. Secretary of Defense Robert McNamara famously said that "every quantitative measurement we have shows we are winning the war".
>
> …In Saigon I went to the famous "five o'clock follies" in which American officials briefed the press on the progress of the war—so many enemy weapons captured, so many enemies killed: "the body count". The briefings bore less and less resemblance to what my colleagues and I were seeing in the field, the burned out villages, the civilians caught in cross fires, the napalm strikes, and how impossible it was going to be to win the proverbial "hearts and minds" with the blundering, damaging colossus of military action, always the bluntest of tools. I saw how the body count got inflated as it was passed up the chain of command. I saw how corruption was eating at the entrails of the successive South Vietnamese governments we were installing.
>
> It wasn't that the American briefers were actually lying to us. They were, as the journalist Sebastian Junger wrote about American optimism in Afghanistan, simply inviting you to join a conspiracy of wishful thinking.
>
> …There were battles for nameless, numbered hills, 881, 875, numbered for their height in meters. The North Vietnamese tactic was to move onto a hill, fortify it to withstand heavy booming and shelling, and then draw us up the hills in pointless battles in which Americans would be killed in ever greater numbers. The Vietnamese would always lose more men than we did, but they knew we were fighting on their home turf, and they knew that we would be the ones to tire first and go home, just as had the French…[24]

24 Greenaway, H.D.S. (15 March 2017). 'What I Saw in Vietnam'. *The New York Times* <https://www.nytimes.com/2017/03/15/opinion/what-i-saw-in-vietnam.html> Accessed 18 January 2026.

The Eternal Optimists

On 10th November 1966, Defense Secretary Robert McNamara and General Wheeler, Chairman of the Joint Chiefs, participated in a news conference. General Wheeler read a short prepared statement explaining that, after his recent trip to Saigon, he was able to report to the President that:

> The war in my judgment continues in a very favorable fashion. General Westmoreland retains the initiative and in every operation to date has managed to defeat the enemy.[25]

With enough force to seize the initiative from the Viet Cong sometime in 1966, General Westmoreland expected to take the offensive and, with appropriate additional reinforcements, to have defeated the enemy by the end of 1967. [26]

With the enemy still not "defeated", Westmoreland addressed the National Press Club in Washington on 21st November 1967. He gave his audience an optimistic assessment of the war in Vietnam, going so far as to say:

> I am absolutely certain that whereas in 1965 the enemy was winning, today he is certainly losing. [27]

Despite the public show of optimism by McNamara, Wheeler and Westmorland, at no point during the course of the Vietnam War was the enemy "losing". At no point during the course of the Vietnam War was the United States "winning".

What Went Wrong?

On 10th February 1968, Robert Kennedy, the brother of the slain President, wrote an editorial for *The New York Times* in which he spoke of the Vietnam War and the malaise of spirit then gripping his country. It read, in part:

25 Pentagon Paper [Part IV: C.6.a] Evolution of the War. U.S. Ground Strategy and Force Deployments: 1965 - 1967. Volume I: Phase II, Program 3, Program 4. p. 103. *National Archives and Records Administration* < https://nara-media-001.s3.amazonaws.com/arcmedia/research/pentagon-papers/Pentagon-Papers-Part-IV-C-6-a.pdf> Accessed 6 February 2026.

26 Pentagon Paper [Part IV: C-5] Evolution of the War. Phase I in the Build-up of U.S. Forces: March-July 1965 p. 8. *National Archives and Records Administration* < https://nara-media-001.s3.amazonaws.com/arcmedia/research/pentagon-papers/Pentagon-Papers-Part-IV-C-5.pdf> Accessed 6 February 2026.

27 'General Westmorland's Address to the National Press Club' (21 November 1967) *DocsTeach, National Archives and Records Administration.* < https://www.docsteach.org/documents/document/westmoreland-press-club> Accessed 8 April 2025.

> As 1967 came to an end, E. B. White observed in a Topics column on this page that all Americans seemed to be asking the same questions: "What happened? What went sour? What did I do wrong? Who's to blame…?"[28]

We owe it to the living and the dead to attempt to answer these questions and hold up to the gaze of history those parties who bear the brunt of the responsibility. We will therefore retrace the steps by which the United States, Australia and New Zealand, made the fateful decision to send so many to their deaths along the road of no return from the slaughterhouse of Vietnam.

Notes

Space in this work is reserved for those Pentagon Papers which demonstrate the depths of government betrayal of Congress and the American people. Hence, for other Papers referenced, only brief extracts will be provided. As always, context is king so readers are advised to consult the Paper from which an extract is reproduced at the *National Archives and Records Administration* <https://www.archives.gov/research/pentagon-papers>

The Pentagon Papers are mainly arranged according to topic. Since there is a considerable overlapping of their contents in terms of time, Chapters are arranged chronologically rather than topically where at all possible.

---

28 Robert F. Kennedy, 'Topics: 'Things Fall Apart; the Center Cannot Hold…' (10 February 1968) *The New York Times* < https://www.nytimes.com/1968/02/10/archives/topics-things-fall-apart-the-center-cannot-hold-.html> Accessed 12 November 2025.

CHAPTER FORTY-TWO

The Gamble

"It seemed for a while that the gamble against long odds had succeeded".

Notes

The Pentagon Papers reproduced or paraphrased in forthcoming Chapters are those which most adequately represent the state of knowledge and the mind-set of the decision-makers; which demonstrate the depths of betrayal of Congress and the American people by those decision-makers; and which prove that American Presidents and their closest advisors had steered the United States into deeper and deeper involvement in Vietnam despite knowing that the war was a failed proposition almost from the beginning.

In this Chapter, brief, edited-for-clarity extracts with explanatory notes are reproduced or paraphrased from the Pentagon Paper [Part IV: B-3] Evolution of the War. Counterinsurgency: The Advisory Build-up, 1961-67. For the reasons given in the introductory *Retrospect* Chapter, we will focus here only on the early 1960's. As always, readers are urged to consult an extract's entire context at the *National Archives and Records Administration* <https://www.archives.gov/research/pentagon-papers>

Section 1: The Pessimists

The United States decided, shortly after the Geneva Accords (1954) and during the period of French withdrawal from Indo-China, to give military assistance and advice to the newly proclaimed Republic of (South)Vietnam.

The Joint Chiefs of Staff were pessimistic. The creation of a Vietnamese Army, they said, might not even lead to internal political stability, much less assure the capability to protect South Vietnam from external aggression. The JCS also believed that the limitations imposed by the Geneva agreements on the number of U.S. military personnel would make it impractical to attempt to train a new Army--particularly given the paucity of experienced leaders, which was the legacy of French colonialism. The President's military advisors did not wish to assume the responsibility for failure without the resources and influence which would offer a better chance for success.

The available record does not indicate any rebuttal of the JCS's pessimistic appraisal of the situation. What it does indicate is that the U.S. decided to gamble with very limited resources because the potential gains seemed well worth a limited risk. "I cannot guarantee that Vietnam will remain free, even with our aid", General J. Lawton Collins reported to the National Security Council, "But I know that without our aid Vietnam will surely be lost to Communism".

Secretary of State John Foster Dulles was instrumental in deciding for political reasons to undertake a modest program of military advice aimed at producing political stability. Once launched, however, the program of advice and assistance came to be dominated by conventional military conceptions. Insuring internal stability is a "lesser included capability" of armed force, the reasoning went; the principal purpose of such a force is to protect the territorial integrity of the nation.

It was such a conventional force that the small United States Military Assistance Advisory Group (USMAAG) attempted to produce from 1955 until about 1960. The Army of the Republic of Vietnam (ARVN) was made to "mirror image" the U.S. Army to the extent permitted by differences in equipment and locale. The number of U.S. advisors (approximately doubled by "The Equipment Recovery Mission"--a thinly veiled device to increase the number of Americans in Vietnam) remained stable throughout this period. The ARVN developed into a multi-divisional force oriented primarily toward conventional defense. The later transition to a force designed for counter insurgent warfare was thereby made more difficult.

It seemed for a while that the gamble against long odds had succeeded. The Viet Minh were quiescent; the Republic of Vietnam Armed Forces (RVNAF) were markedly better armed and trained than they were when the U. S. effort began (at which time they were unarmed and untrained), and President Ngo Dinh Diem showed a remarkable ability to put down factions threatening the Government of South Vietnam's (GVN) stability and to maintain himself in office.

Disintegration

However, this period of apparent stability disappeared by mid-1961 as the Viet Minh (relabelled Viet Cong-- a contraction for Vietnamese Communist) stepped up terrorism, sabotage, and military action by increasingly large units. Now, the prospect for South Vietnam's independence was at least as dark as it had been six years earlier.

But the U.S. military advisors in Vietnam had learned--or at least thought they had learned during this period of gradual disintegration-- the true nature of the battle in which they were engaged by proxy. This was an unconventional, internal war of counter insurgency rather than a conventional struggle against an external foe.

It was a battle for the "hearts and minds" of the indigenous (and especially the rural) population rather than a contest to win and hold key terrain features. It was an inter-meshed political-economic-military war rather than one in which political and economic issues were settled by military victory.

Foredoomed Plan

U.S. advisors in Vietnam--and U.S. military and civilian theorists in other places as well--formulated during this period a rudimentary doctrine of counter insurgent warfare. In response to (Soviet) Premier Khrushchev's endorsement of "wars of national liberation", they proposed to help free world nations save themselves from communism by a series of sequential actions that dealt with the symptoms of social revolution (the insurgency) as well as its causes (the frustration of expectations of social justice).

Thus, at almost the same time that the U.S. began its advisory buildup in South Vietnam in late 1961, military and civilian practitioners found themselves in possession of a simple, apparently logical, outline sketch of a method by which to counter the communist-captured insurgency. Physical security from the acts of the insurgents was a necessary but not a sufficient condition for success. In addition to security, the Vietnamese government had to establish the services which would link it in classic terms of legitimacy to its subjects. We would fight fire with fire and we would fight it with water, too.

The decisions made by the Kennedy Administration from mid-1961 onward, culminating in the expansion of the U.S. advisory effort following General Maxwell D. Taylor's mission to Saigon in October 1961, did not simply set out to explain this newly-articulated counter-insurgency theory and doctrine to the GVN. They attempted to induce the GVN to reform itself so that identification with its populace would be possible. Beyond this, they chose to attempt to help the Vietnamese, in Taylor's words, "as friends and partners--not as arms-length advisors and show them how the job might be done--not to tell them or do it for them..."

The expectation among U.S. policy-makers--recorded in National Security Action Memorandum (NSAM) 111--was that the GVN and the U.S. would mutually agree upon necessary steps to end the insurgency. The U. S., for its part, would underwrite an increase in the Armed Forces of South Vietnam (RVNAF) and provide advisors throughout the military structure down to battalion level and in each provincial capital. The GVN would rationalise its lines of authority and begin reform measures to bring it closer to the Vietnamese people. This was, of course, a U.S. expectation, not an agreed *quid pro quo*.

Diem was unwilling to permit the U.S. to share in his formulation of plans. He was even afraid to discuss the U.S. expectations candidly with his own cabinet ministers. It is a matter of record that he did not reform his government. ("He will not reform because he cannot", J. Kenneth Galbraith cabled President Kennedy. See Note)

What remains in issue is whether he could have done so. If he could not, the U.S. plan to end the insurgency was foredoomed from its inception, for it depended on Vietnamese initiatives to solve a Vietnamese problem.

Gamble Turns to Commitment

Thus the U.S. overall plan to end the insurgency was on shaky ground on the GVN side. Diem needed the U.S. and the U.S. needed a reformed Diem. As U.S. advisors began deploying to Vietnam for service with tactical units in the field, the gamble of the mid-50's was transferred into a broad commitment.

President Kennedy and his advisors were determined to save Vietnam from communism by helping the Vietnamese to save themselves. One side of the dual U.S. thrust (GVN reform) was already in trouble. What of the "friends and partners" who were to share the dangers and tasks of the RVNAF in the field? What was expected of them? What advantages would accrue from their presence in Vietnam?

The available record is almost totally devoid of any explication (much less any debate) on these questions. General Taylor's report of his mission to Saigon implies an unambiguous convergence of interests between the advisors and the advised. All that was needed was greater competence. More U.S. advisors at more places working on problems of Vietnamese training and operations could not but have an overall beneficial effect.

Great Expectations

It is necessary to surmise the expectations in the policy-makers minds of just how this would come about. First, they seem to have expected the increased U.S. advisory presence to lead directly to increased RVNAF competence in technical and tactical areas. Basic military skills--how to move, shoot, and communicate --could be improved and the improvements sustained by a continuing U.S. presence at many operational levels.

Second, the U.S. policy-makers could receive reports from an omnipresent U.S. "network" which would permit them to become better informed about what was really taking place in Vietnam, not only with respect to VC activity but with reference to Army of the Republic of Vietnam (ARVN) plans, operations, and problems as well.

Finally, the U.S. expected to realize increased influence within the RVNAF from the presence of advisors. (And it expected, as NSAM 111 made clear, to realize increased influence with the GVN in exchange for increasing its visible commitment to South Vietnamese independence.)

The Ostrich

Increased influence can, of course, be gained in many ways. U.S. advisors could, by example, promote more aggressive Vietnamese leadership and improved standards of conduct. A well-coordinated advisory network could exert persuasive pressure throughout the RVNAF to adopt certain policies or practices. And the U.S. providers of the material resources could, if they wished, keep a tight hand on the spigot and control the flow. They could exert influence negatively. The U.S. was anxious to avoid this last-mentioned approach to increased influence. "Leverage", as it is now commonly known, was a subject rarely discussed, much less practiced. **The "Limited Partnership" finessed the whole issue of sanctions by assuming (or hoping or pretending, one cannot know which) that no problem existed.**

The process of countering insurgency, most commonly called pacification, received a great amount of attention and publicity at the same time the U.S. was increasing its field advisors with the ARVN from a handful to over 3,000. Earlier, in 1960, the United States Military Assistance Advisory Group (USMAAG) had pressed upon the GVN a national Counter Insurgency Plan for Vietnam (CIP) which was really an organizational blueprint for reordering the GVN-RVNAF lines of command to permit effective action. The nub of the problem was that the political leaders in rural areas (Province and District Chiefs--almost a all military officers) were responsible to Saigon directly while RVNAF had a separate chain of command.

In 1961, the MAAG presented its complementary Geographically Phased Plan which specified the relative priority for clearing out the VC, holding, then building GVN at the "rice roots". The object, as the U.S. advisors saw it, was to have a workable national plan upon which to base the entire US/GVN effort.

The Strategic Hamlet Program soon became the unifying vehicle to express the pacification process. The theory was that of physical security first, then government programs to develop popular allegiance but the facts were over expansion, counter-productive coercion in some areas, widespread mismanagement, and dishonesty. **U.S. policy-makers were not, however, aware of how badly things were going until they became much worse.** Optimism dominated official thinking. No need was perceived for new departures… (See also Chapter Fifty-Five: *Programmed to Fail.*)

One cannot judge accurately the reasons why U.S. leaders in Vietnam and Washington thought the counter-insurgent effort was making headway, but the fact that it was not is crystal clear in retrospect. The expectation that GVN and U.S. interests were sufficiently parallel to permit greater U.S. influence solely as a result of a larger U.S. presence foundered on the personalities and the felt necessities of the Ngo brothers. The extent to which RVNAF technical-tactical competence was increased during this period remains a subject of disagreement but it was not increased sufficiently to "turn the tide" of the war. That much is indisputable.[29]

Note

Harvard economist John Kenneth Galbraith was a prominent critic of U.S. involvement in Vietnam. He served as President Kennedy's ambassador to India from 1961-1963. Galbraith feared that escalating the war would derail President Kennedy's domestic agenda, particularly his plans for full employment, education, and the "War on Poverty". He also worried it could tear the Democratic Party and the nation apart.

29 Pentagon Paper [Part IV: B-3] Evolution of the War. Counterinsurgency: The Advisory Build-up, 1961-67. pp. i-v. *National Archives and Records Administration* <https://www.archives.gov/research/pentagon-papers> Accessed 15 December 2025.

CHAPTER FORTY-THREE

Enterprise Vietnam

"We should be prepared to introduce United States combat forces if that should become necessary for success".

The Pentagon Paper [Part IV: B-1] Evolution of the War. The Kennedy Commitments and Programs: 1961 focuses on appraisals of the situation in Vietnam and suggested courses of action by United States decision-makers. Edited-for-clarity extracts with explanatory notes are reproduced in this Chapter. Readers are urged to consult an extract's entire context at the *National Archives and Records Administration* <https://www.archives.gov/research/pentagon-papers>

Laos

For a necessary background to this Paper, see details of President Kennedy's first foreign policy crisis in 'Milestones in the History of U.S. Foreign Relations: The Laos Crisis 1960–1963' at the *Office of the Historian, U.S. Department of State* <https://history.state.gov/milestones/1961-1968/laos-crisis>

Section 1: Crisis Situations

The Diem Crisis

When President Kennedy took office in January 1961, the prospect of an eventual crisis in Vietnam had been widely recognized in the government, although nothing much had yet been done about it. Our Ambassador in Saigon had been sending worried cables for a year and twice in recent months (in September 1960 and again in December). He had ended an appraisal of the situation by cautiously raising the question of whether the U. S. would not sooner or later have to move to replace Ngo Dinh Diem, President of South Vietnam.

Barely a week after taking office, Kennedy received and approved a Counter-Insurgency Plan (CIP) which had been going through drafting and staffing for the previous eight months. The CIP was a most modest program by the standard we have become accustomed to in Vietnam. It offered Diem financial support for a 20,000 man increase in his army, which then stood at 150,000, plus support for about half of the counter-guerrilla auxiliary force known as the Civil Guard. In return, it asked Diem for a number of reforms which appeared to the American side as merely common sense.

The CIP was superseded by an enlarged version of the same program, and the only longer term significance the original program held was that it presumably offered the Administration a lesson in dealing with Diem (and perhaps, although it was not foreseen then, a lesson in dealing with Vietnamese governments generally.) The negotiations dragged on and on; the U. S. military and eventually most of the civilians both in Saigon and Washington grew impatient for getting on with the war. Diem promised action on some of the American points, and finally even issued some decrees, none of which were really followed up...

Negotiations with Diem came to an end in May 1961, not because the issues had been resolved, but because the U. S. decided to forget trying to pressure Diem for a while and instead try to coax him into reforming by winning his confidence. Partly, no doubt, this reflected the view that pressure was getting nowhere and the alternative approach might do better. Mainly, however, the changed policy, and the somewhat enlarged aid program that accompanied it, reflected the pressures created by the situation in neighboring Laos.

The Enterprise Crisis

A preliminary step came on 20th April 1961. Immediately following the Bay of Pigs disaster, and with the prospect of a disaster in Laos on the very near horizon, President Kennedy asked Deputy Secretary of Defense (Roswell) Gilpatric to work up a program for saving Vietnam...

The program was delivered, as requested, a week later. It was a somewhat enlarged version of the CIP, with the implication, not spelled out in the paper, that the new effort would be put into effect without making any demands on Diem...

There is nothing to suggest that anything more was expected of Gilpatric's program, and indeed all the evidence suggests that the main point of the exercise was to work General (Edward) Lansdale into the role of government-wide coordinator and manager of the country's first major test in the new art of counter-insurgency. **Lansdale served as Executive Officer of the Task Force which Gilpatric organized and which he proposed should be given a continuing, dominant role in managing the Vietnamese enterprise.**

By the time the report was submitted on 27th April, when the Laos crisis was reaching its peak, a new Geneva conference had been agreed upon. But there were serious doubts that the pro-western side in Laos would be left with anything to negotiate about by the time the conference opened. Even the U.S.-favored settlement (a coalition government) represented a major, if prudent, retreat from the previous U.S. position taken during the closing months of the Eisenhower Administration.

So the situation in Laos was bad, if unavoidable; and it followed right on the heels of the Bay of Pigs, and at a time when the Soviets were threatening to move against Berlin. The emphasis of the Gilpatric Task Force shifted from shaping up the counterinsurgency aid program for Vietnam, to finding ways to demonstrate to the South Vietnamese (and others) that a further retreat in Laos would not foreshadow an imminent retreat in Vietnam.

The Vietcong Crisis

Establish Training Centres

On 28th April, an annex to the Task Force report proposed to counter the impact of Laos with U.S. support for an increase in South Vietnamese forces (the original report had proposed only more generous financial support for forces already planned under the ClP) and, further, a modest commitment of U.S. ground combat units in South Vietnam, with the nominal mission of establishing two training centers.

Intervene if Necessary

On 29th April, Kennedy endorsed the proposals of the original draft, but took no action on the far more significant proposals in the annex. On 1st May, a revised Task Force draft came out, incorporating the Laos Annex proposals, and adding a recommendation that **the U. S. make clear an intent to intervene in Vietnam to the extent needed to prevent a Viet Cong victory.**

Station American Forces

At this point, practical control of the Task Force appears to have shifted out of the hands of the Department of Defense to the Department of State. A State redraft of the report came out on 3rd May which eliminated the special role laid out for General Lansdale, shifted the chairmanship of the continuing Task Force to State, and blurred, without wholly eliminating, the Defense-drafted recommendations for sending U. S. combat units to Vietnam and for public U.S. commitments to save South Vietnam from Communism.

But even the State re-draft recommended consideration of stationing American troops in Vietnam, for missions not involving combat with the Viet Cong, and a bilateral U. S.-South Vietnam security treaty. On 4th and 5th May, still acting under the pressures of the Laos crisis, **the Administration implied that it was considering stationing American forces in Vietnam…**

On 8th May, Kennedy signed a letter to Diem, to be delivered by Vice President Johnson the next week, which promised Diem strong U. S. support, but did not go beyond the program outlined in the original Task Force report; it offered neither to finance expanded South Vietnamese forces, nor to station American troops in Vietnam...

The Crisis of Morale

A new, and much more serious sense of crisis developed in September 1961. This time, the problem was not directly Laos, but strong indications of moderate deterioration of Diem's military position and very substantial deterioration of morale in Saigon. There was a sharp upswing in Viet Cong attacks in September, including a spectacular raid on a province capital 55 miles from Saigon during which the province chief was publicly beheaded by the insurgents.

At the end of September, Diem surprised Ambassador (Frederick) Nolting by asking for a U. S./Government of South Vietnam defense treaty. By Diem's account, the loss of morale in Saigon was due to worries about U. S. policy growing out of the Laos situation. Both U.S. officials in Washington and South Vietnamese other than those closest to Diem, though, put most of the blame on deterioration within South Vietnam, although the demoralizing effect of Viet Cong successes was unquestionably magnified by uncertainties about the U.S. commitment to Vietnam.

The Crisis of Confidence

In response, President Kennedy sent General Maxwell Taylor and Walt Rostow, then both on the White House staff, to Vietnam, accompanied by some less prominent officials from State and Defense. What Taylor and Rostow reported was that Saigon faced a dual crisis of confidence, compounded out of doubts arising from Laos that the U. S. would stick by South Vietnam, and doubts, arising from the Viet Cong successes, that Diem' s unpopular and inefficient regime could beat the Viet Cong anyway.

The report said that a U.S. military commitment in Vietnam was needed to meet the first difficulty; and that the second could best be met by supplying a generous infusion of American personnel to all levels of the Vietnamese government and army, who could, it was hoped, instill the Vietnamese with the right kind of winning spirit, and reform the regime"from the bottom up" despite Diem's weaknesses. The report recommended the dispatch of helicopter companies and other forms of combat support, but without great emphasis on these units. Probably, although the record does not specifically say so, there was a general understanding that such units would be sent even before the report was submitted, and that is why there is relatively little emphasis on the need for them.

The crucial issue was what form the American military commitment had to take to be effective. Taylor, in an 'eyes only' cable to the President, argued strongly for a task force in the Delta, consisting mainly of army engineers to work where there had been a major flood. The Delta was also where the VC were strongest, and Taylor warned the President that the force would have to conduct some combat operations and expect to take casualties.

But Taylor argued that the balance of the program, less this task force, would be insufficient, for we had to **"convince Diem that we are willing to join him in a showdown with the Viet Cong..."**

Showdown with Diem

We do not know what advice President Kennedy received from State: (Ted) Sorenson claims all the President's advisors on Vietnam favored sending the ground force; but George Ball, at least, who may not have been part of the formal decision group, is widely reported to have opposed such a move; so did (John Kenneth) Galbraith, then Ambassador to India, who happened to be in Washington, and perhaps some others (See Note).

From Defense, the President received a memo from McNamara for himself, Gilpatric, and the Joint Chiefs of Staff, stating that they were "inclined to recommend" the Taylor program, but only on the understanding that it would be followed up with more troops as needed, and with a willingness to attack North Vietnam.

(The JCS estimated that 40,000 American troops would be needed to "clean up" the Viet Cong.) The Taylor Mission Report, and Taylor's own cables, had also stressed a probable need to attack, or at least threaten to attack, North Vietnam.

The McNamara memo was sent on 8th November. But on the 11th November, Secretary of State (Dean) Rusk and McNamara signed a joint memo that reversed McNamara's earlier position: it recommended deferring, at least for the time being, the dispatch of combat units. This obviously suited Kennedy perfectly, and the National Security Action Memorandum embodying the decisions was taken essentially verbatim from the recommendations of the Rusk/McNamara paper, except that a recommendation that the U.S. was committing itself to prevent the loss of Vietnam was deleted.

But where the Taylor Report had implied a continuation of the May policy of trying to coax Diem into cooperating with the U.S., the new program was made contingent on Diem's acceptance of a list of reforms; further Diem was to be informed that if he accepted the program the U. S. would expect to "share in decision-making"... rather than “advise only”.

Thus, the effect of the decision was to give Diem less than he was expecting (no symbolic commitment of ground forces) but to accompany this limited offer with demands for which Diem was obviously both unprepared and unwilling to accede to.

On top of this, there was the enormous (and not always recognized) extent to which U.S. policy was driven by the unthinkability of avoidably risking another defeat in Southeast Asia hard on the heels of the Laos retreat.

Consequently, the U. S. bargaining position was feeble. Further, Galbraith at least, and probably others, advised Kennedy that there was not much point to bargaining with Diem anyway, since he would never follow through on any promises he made. (Galbraith favored promoting an anti-Diem military coup at the earliest convenient moment.) Kennedy ended up settling for a set of promises that fell well short of any serious effort to make the aid program really contingent on reforms by Diem. Since the war soon thereafter began to look better, Kennedy never had occasion to reconsider his decision on combat troops; and no urgent reason to consider Galbraith's advice on getting rid of Diem until late 1963. [30]

Section 2: The Deteriorating Situation

In a joint Memorandum to the President dated 11th November 1961, Dean Rusk (Secretary of State) and Robert McNamara (Secretary of Defense) addressed the deteriorating situation in South Vietnam with President Kennedy. The Memorandum identified U.S. interests and objectives, a selection of which are reproduced below:

U.S. National Interests

The deteriorating situation in South Vietnam requires attention...the loss of South Vietnam to Communism would involve the transfer of a nation of 20 million people from the free world to the Communist bloc. The loss of South Vietnam would make pointless any further discussion about the importance of Southeast Asia to the free world; we would have to face the near certainty that the remainder of Southeast Asia and Indonesia would move to a complete accommodation with Communism...

The United States, as a member of SEATO, has commitments with respect to South Vietnam under the Protocol to the SEATO Treaty. Additionally, in a formal

30 Pentagon Paper [Part IV: B-1] Evolution of the War. The Kennedy Commitments and Programs: 1961. pp. i-vi. *National Archives and Records Administration* <https://www.archives.gov/research/pentagon-papers> Accessed 15 December 2025.

statement at the conclusion session of the 1954 Geneva Conference, the United States representative stated that the United States "would view any renewal of the aggression...with grave concern and seriously threatening international peace and security". The loss of South Vietnam to Communism would not only destroy SEATO but would undermine the credibility of American commitments elsewhere. Further, loss of South Vietnam would stimulate bitter domestic controversies in the United States and would be seized upon by extreme elements to divide the country and harass the Administration.

It seems, on the face of it, absurd to think that a nation of 20 million people can be subverted by 15-20 thousand active guerillas if the Government and people of· that country do not wish to be subverted.

South Vietnam is not, however, a highly organized society with an effective governing apparatus and a population accustomed to carrying civic responsibility. Public apathy is encouraged by the inability of most citizens to act directly as well as by the tactics of terror employed by the guerrillas throughout the countryside.

Inept administration and the absence of a strong non-Communist political coalition have made it difficult to bring available resources to bear upon the guerrilla problem and to make the most effective use of available external aid. Under the best of conditions, the threat posed by the presence of 15-20 thousand well-disciplined guerrillas would be difficult to meet.

U.S. Objectives

The United States should commit itself to the clear objective of preventing the fall of South Vietnam to Communism The basic means for accomplishing this objective must be to put the Government of South Vietnam (GVN) into a position to win its own war against the guerrillas. We must insist that the Government of South Vietnam itself take the measures necessary for that purpose in exchange for large-scale United States assistance in the military, economic and political fields.

At the same time we must recognize that it will probably not be possible for the GVN to win this war as long as the flow of men and supplies from North Vietnam continues unchecked and the guerrillas enjoy a safe sanctuary in neighboring territory.

We should be prepared to introduce United States combat forces if that should become necessary for success. Dependent upon the circumstances, it may also be necessary for United States forces to strike at the source of the aggression in North Vietnam.

U.S. Force Suggestions

The commitment of United States forces to· South Vietnam involves two different categories: (A) Units of modest size required for the direct support of South Vietnamese military effort, such as communications, helicopter and other forms of airlift, reconnaissance aircraft, naval patrols, intelligence units, etc., and (B) larger organized units with actual or potential direct military missions.

Category (A) should be introduced as speedily as possible. Category (B) units pose a more serious problem in that they are much more significant from the point of view of domestic and international political factors and greatly increase the probabilities of Communist bloc escalation. Further, the employment of United States combat forces (in the absence of Communist bloc escalation) involves a certain dilemma: if there is a strong South-Vietnamese effort, they may not be needed; if there is not such an effort, United States forces could not accomplish their mission in the midst of an apathetic or hostile population. Under present circumstances, therefore, the question of injecting United States and SEATO combat forces should in large part be considered as a contribution to the morale of the South Vietnamese in their own effort to do the principal job themselves.

If we commit Category (B) forces to South Vietnam, the ultimate possible extent of our military commitment in Southeast Asia must be faced. The struggle may be prolonged, and Hanoi and Peiping (Beijing) may overtly intervene. It is the view of the Secretary of Defense and the Joint Chiefs of Staff that, in the light of the logistic difficulties faced by the other side, we can assume that the maximum United States forces required on the ground in Southeast Asia would not exceed six divisions, or about 205,000 men. This would be in addition to local forces and such SEATO forces as may be engaged. It is also the view of the Secretary of Defense and the Joint Chiefs of Staff that our military posture is, or with the addition· of more National Guard or regular Army divisions adequate to furnish these forces and support them in action can be made without serious interference with our present Berlin plans.[31]

Section 3: Crisis Management

Following their Memorandum addressing the deteriorating situation in South Vietnam, Rusk and McNamara provided the President with a recommended program of actions, some of which were:

31 Pentagon Paper[Part IV: B-1] Evolution of the War. The Kennedy Commitments and Programs: 1961, pp. 125-128. *National Archives and Records Administration* <https://www.archives.gov/research/pentagon-papers> Accessed 15 December 2025.

- Commit the United States to preventing the fall of South Vietnam to Communism and to introduce such US and other SEATO forces as may be necessary to achieve this objective;
- Plan for the use of a "significant" number of United States forces to signify determination to defend South Vietnam and assist in suppressing the Viet Cong insurgency short of engaging in detailed counter-guerilla operations but including relevant operations in North Vietnam;
- Provide the Government of South Vietnam (GVN) with helicopters, light aviation, and transport aircraft, manned to the extent necessary by United States uniformed personnel and under United States operational control;
- Provide additional equipment and United States uniformed personnel as may be necessary for air reconnaissance, photography, instruction in and execution of air-ground support techniques, and for special intelligence;
- Provide small craft, including such United States uniformed advisers and operating personnel as may be necessary for quick and effective operations in effecting surveillance and control over coastal waters and inland waterways;
- Provide such increased economic aid as may be required to permit the GVN to pursue a vigorous flood relief and rehabilitation program, to supply material in support of the security effort, and to give priority to projects in support of this expanded counter-insurgency program. (This could include increases in military pay, a full supply of a wide range of materials such as food, medical supplies, transportation equipment, communications equipment, and any other items where material help could assist the GVN in winning the war against the Viet Cong.)

It is most striking that to ensure South Vietnam would not fall into the hands of communists, the introduction of "substantial" U.S. ground combat forces to assist in suppressing the Viet Cong insurgency and possible operations against North Vietnam were being deliberated more than two years before the landing of the first Marines at Da Nang and the commencement of the *Rolling Thunder* bombing campaign against North Vietnam, and almost four years before Congress and the American people became aware that their country was already involved in a ground war in Vietnam. (See also Chapter Forty-Seven: *The Die is Cast*)

Note

Space in this work is reserved for forthcoming Papers which reveal the extent to which Congress and the American people were deceived about the war in Vietnam.

Readers are, however, urged to consult this entire Paper for a detailed chronology of events; mounting problems with President Diem; as well as for the numerous ambiguities, contradictory reports, opposing views of decision-makers, and the conflicting advice to the President from his advisors. (For the remainder of the Rusk/ McNamara recommended program of action see pages 129-133 of this Paper.)

Personalities

Theodore Chaikin (Ted) Sorensen was President Kennedy's special counsel, adviser, and primary speechwriter.

Under Secretary of State, George Wildman Ball was a major dissenter against the escalation of the Vietnam War. Ball advised against deploying U.S. combat forces, as he believed it would lead the United States into an unwinnable war and result in a prolonged conflict.

Harvard economist John Kenneth Galbraith was a prominent critic of U.S. involvement in Vietnam. He served as President Kennedy's ambassador to India from 1961-1963. Galbraith feared that escalating the war would derail President Kennedy's domestic agenda, particularly his plans for full employment, education, and the "War on Poverty". He also worried it could tear the Democratic Party and the nation apart.

CHAPTER FORTY-FOUR

Backfire

"...as the nine-year rule of Diem came to a bloody end, our complicity in his overthrow heightened our responsibilities and our commitment in an essentially leaderless Vietnam".

During his two terms in office, President Eisenhower's administration had chosen to spend billions of American dollars supporting the increasingly brutal South Vietnamese regime of President Ngo Dinh Diem. It was envisaged that all this effort would help create a pro-American bastion in Southeast Asia and halt the spread of Communism. Eisenhower had invested so much American prestige and effort into the success of South Vietnam under Diem that, by the end of the 1950's, the United States had become deeply involved in its fate.

By 1960, there was a growing public awareness of Diem's quasi-police state, his favoritism towards Catholics, and his persecution of Buddhists. The U.S. Ambassador in Saigon had been sending worried cables for a year--twice in September and December 1960. He had appraised the situation and raised the question of whether the U. S. would not sooner or later have to move to replace Ngo Dinh Diem. [32]

When President Kennedy took office on 20th January 1961, his administration found it increasingly difficult to justify U.S. support for Diem's regime to the American people and to Congress. The situation had reached crisis point by May 1963. (Note that, as evidenced in the Pentagon Papers, successive White House administrations and top echelons of their respective Departments of Defense, State, National Security Councils and the CIA were aware at all times of the brutality of Diem's regime.)

The following edited-for-clarity extracts with explanatory notes are reproduced or paraphrased from a detailed chronology of the *Coup d'état* against the Saigon government found in the Pentagon Paper [Part IV: B-5]. Evolution of the War. Counterinsurgency: The Overthrow of Ngo Dinh Diem, May-Nov. 1963. It is referenced at length because it was at this point that the United States made the crucial decision about Vietnam—to stay? or to go? The choices were there. (See Summary and Analysis.)

32 The Pentagon Paper [Part IV: B-1] Evolution of the War. The Kennedy Commitments and Programs: 1961, p. i. *National Archives and Records Administration* <https://www.archives.gov/research/pentagon-papers> Accessed 15 December 2025.

Incidentally, the entire chronology reveals the Defense Department's minute-by-minute intelligence on the developing situation and its concern about the plausible deniability of its CIA agents and other covert sources.

The Buddhist Crisis

Robert Shaplen's work *The Lost Revolution*, as cited in the Pentagon Papers, analyses the religious origins of the Buddhist Crisis:

> The religious origins of the Buddhist Crisis are traceable to the massive flight of Catholic refugees from North Vietnam after the French defeat in 1954. An estimated one million Catholics fled the North and resettled in the South. Diem, animated, no doubt, by religious as well as humanitarian sympathy, and with an eye to recruiting political support from his co-religionists, accorded these Catholic refugees preferential treatment in land redistribution, relief and assistance, commercial and export-import licenses, government employment, and other government largess.
>
> Because Diem could rely on their loyalty, they came to fill almost all important civilian and military positions. As an institution, the Catholic Church enjoyed a special legal status. The Catholic primate, Ngo Dinh Thuc, was Diem's brother and advisor. But prior to 1962, there had been no outright discrimination against Buddhists. However, among South Vietnam's 3-4 million practicing Buddhists and the 80% of the population who were nominal Buddhists, the regime's favoritism, authoritarianism, and discrimination created a smoldering resentment. [33]

The beginning of the end for Diem can be traced through events to the regime's violent suppression of a Buddhist protest demonstration in Huế on 8th May 1963.

On that day, Government troops fired on demonstrators, killing nine and wounding fourteen. The incident triggered a nationwide Buddhist protest and a crisis of popular confidence in the Diem regime. The Saigon government maintained that the incident was an act of Viet Cong terrorism.

Madame Nu, wife of Diem's powerful brother, Ngo Dinh Nhu, publicly accused the Buddhists of being infiltrated with communist agents.

At noon on 11th June 1963, in the middle of a downtown Saigon intersection, a Buddhist monk, Thich Quang Duc, immersed himself in gasoline and set himself

---

33 Shaplen, 1966, as cited in the Pentagon Paper [Part IV: B-5] Evolution of the War. Counterinsurgency: The Overthrow of Ngo Dinh Diem, May-Nov. 1963 p. 4. *National Archives and Records Administration* <https://www.archives.gov/research/pentagon-papers> Accessed 15 December 2025.

afire. His protest suicide was photographed and was front page material in the world's newspapers. Shock and indignation were universal. Mme. Nhu subsequently referred to it as a "barbecue".

On 5th August, a second Buddhist monk committed suicide by burning himself to death in the continuing protest against the Diem regime. Two more monks followed him on 15th and 18th August.

Ten senior army generals met on 20th August and decided that, in view of the deteriorating political situation, they would ask Diem for a declaration of martial law. The generals met first with Ngo Dinh Nhu and then with Diem to propose that martial law be decreed forthwith. Diem approved the proposal and the decree took effect at midnight.

Shortly after midnight on 21st August, under the cover of the military martial law, forces loyal to Nhu and under his orders attacked pagodas throughout Vietnam, arresting monks and sacking buildings. Over 30 Buddhists were injured and more than 1400 arrested. At 9:30 a.m. a strongly worded statement was released by the U.S. State Department deploring the raids as a direct violation of Diem's assurances to the U.S.

The Ultimatum

On 24th August, the U.S. Department of State sent a message by cable to Henry Cabot Lodge Jr., the American Ambassador to South Vietnam. (See Cable 243)

The cable acknowledged Nhu's responsibility for the raids and said that the U.S. could no longer tolerate his continuation in power. If Diem was unable or unwilling to remove him, the South Vietnamese generals were to be told that the U. S. would be prepared to discontinue economic and military support, would accept the obvious implication (a *coup*) and would promise assistance to them in any period of interim breakdown of the Government of South Vietnam (GVN).

In a 2nd September television interview with CBS News' Walter Cronkite, President Kennedy expressed his disappointment with Diem's handling of the Buddhist crisis and his concern that a greater effort was needed by the GVN to win popular support. This could be done, he felt, "with change in policy and perhaps with personnel..."

Four days later, the National Security Council decided to instruct Ambassador Lodge to reopen "tough" negotiations with Diem and to start by clarifying to him the U.S. position. Attorney General Robert Kennedy (JFK's brother) speculated that if the war could not be won with Diem, or by the event of a disruptive *coup*, the U.S. should perhaps be considering a disengagement. (See Chapter Thirty-Eight: *Threat Reduction: Robert Francis Kennedy.*)

On 12th September, with White House approval, Senator Frank Church introduced a resolution in the Senate condemning the South Vietnamese Government for its repressive handling of the Buddhist problem and calling for an end to U.S. aid unless the repressions were abandoned.

Following a meeting of the National Security Council on 2nd October, the White House issued a press statement that reiterated the U.S. commitment to the struggle against the Viet Cong, announced a 1,000 man troop withdrawal, and dissociated the U.S. from Diem's repressive policies.

The Countdown

In message 63560 of 6th October, Washington clarified its views on a *coup* by stating that the U. S. would not thwart such a move if it offered prospects of a more effective fight against the Viet Cong. If a *coup* did eventuate, the security and deniability of all contacts must be paramount.

On 22nd October, the State Department published a controversial research memorandum which took issue with the Pentagon's optimism on the progress of the war. **The memo stated that certain definitely negative and ominous trends could be identified.**

In an exchange of messages between Washington, Ambassador Lodge, and General Harkins (MACV-Military Assistance Command Vietnam) on 30th October, Lodge told Washington that he was powerless to stop the *coup* and that the matter was entirely in Vietnamese hands. Harkins disagreed.

The *coup d'état*

At 1:45 p.m. on 1st November, the U.S. was informed that a *coup* was underway. Around this time, *coup* forces seized key installations in Saigon, including the post office, police headquarters, radio stations, airport, and naval headquarters. They also deployed for attacks on the Gia Long palace, the palace guard barracks, and to block any counter-attack from outside the city.

Around 4:00 p.m. the first skirmish took place at the palace and guard barracks. Diem and Nhu realized the *coup* was serious. Shortly after, the generals contacted the two brothers and told them to surrender. They refused.

At 4:30 p.m. the generals announced the *coup* on radio and demanded the resignations of Diem and Nhu. At the same time, Diem called Ambassador Lodge and asked for the U.S. position. Lodge told Diem that the U.S. could not yet have a view on the matter but expressed concern for his safety.

Around 8:00 p.m. Diem and Nhu escaped from the palace through one of the secret underground passages constructed for just such emergencies. They were met by a Chinese friend who took them to a previously prepared hideaway in Cholon. (The "Chinatown" of Saigon.)

A tank and artillery assault on the palace began around 9:00 p.m. and continued throughout the night until the palace fell to the attackers around 6:30 a.m. on 2nd November. Colonel Thao, the commander of the attacking force, learned of Diem's whereabouts and went to arrest him after receiving permission from the JGS. (The Joint General Staff was a body of senior uniformed leaders in the South Vietnamese military.)

At 6:45 a.m. Thao arrived at the Cholon house but was overheard by Diem and Nhu as he was speaking to the JGS on the telephone. The brothers escaped to a nearby Roman Catholic Church.

At 6:50 a.m. Diem phoned Army General Don and surrendered unconditionally. He and his brother were taken prisoner and executed shortly after in the back of an armored personnel carrier en route to JGS headquarters.[34]

Summary and Analysis

The Diem *coup* was one of those critical events in the history of U.S. policy that could have altered our commitment. The choices were there:

1. Continue to plod along in a limited fashion with Diem despite his and Nhu's growing unpopularity;
2. Encourage or tacitly support the overthrow of Diem, taking the risk that the GVN might crumble and/or accommodate to the VC; and
3. Grasp the opportunity—with the obvious risks—of the political instability in South Vietnam to disengage.

The first option was rejected because of the belief that we could not win with Diem-Nhu. The third was never seriously considered a policy alternative because of the assumption that an independent, non-communist South Vietnam was too important a strategic interest to abandon and because the situation was not sufficiently drastic to call into question so basic an assumption. The second course was chosen mainly for the reasons the first was rejected—Vietnam was thought too important: we wanted to win and the rebellious generals seemed to offer that prospect.

34 Pentagon Paper [Part IV: B-5]. Evolution of the War. Counterinsurgency: The Overthrow of Ngo Dinh Diem, May-Nov. 1963 pp. i-xxxi. *National Archives and Records Administration* <https://www.archives.gov/research/pentagon-papers> Accessed 15 December 2025.

In making the choice to do nothing to prevent the *coup* and to tacitly support it, the U.S. inadvertently deepened its involvement...

For the military *coup d'état* against Ngo Dinh Diem, the U. S. must accept its full share of responsibility. Beginning in August of 1963, we variously authorized, sanctioned and encouraged the *coup* efforts of the Vietnamese generals and offered full support for a successor government.

In October, we cut off aid to Diem in a direct rebuff, giving a green light to the generals. We maintained clandestine contact with them throughout the planning and execution of the coup and sought to review their operational plans and proposed new government. Thus, as the nine-year rule of Diem came to a bloody end, our complicity in his overthrow heightened our responsibilities and our commitment in an essentially leaderless Vietnam. [35]

Cable 243

Cable 243 was sent when President Kennedy and three of his top officials were absent from Washington. Kennedy's recorded conversations reveal his reservations about U.S. support for a military *coup* and document the meetings the President held with State Department, White House, military, and intelligence advisors during the week after Cable 243 was sent. Cable 243 has been described by historian John W. Newman as the "single most controversial cable of the Vietnam War".[36]

Note

The Vietnam Task Force, Office of the Secretary of Defense, obligingly provided the Summary and Analysis of the choices facing the U.S. Administration.

35 Ibid. p. viii.

36 Jacobs, Seth. *Cold War Mandarin: Ngo Dinh Diem and the Origins of America's War in Vietnam,* 1950–1963. Rowman & Littlefield: Maryland, 2006, p. 161.

CHAPTER FORTY-FIVE

"Everywhere and Nowhere"

Giap's most notable military achievement was the decisive victory at Dien Bien Phu in 1954...

Vo Nguyen Giap

As previously noted, Ho Chi Minh, Vo Nguyen Giap and Pham Van Dong created the League for the Independence of Vietnam in May 1941. Better known as the Viet Minh, Giap's army began in December 1944 to wage guerrilla warfare against the Japanese, who had completely overrun Indo-China.

By this time, Giap had already begun to develop a distinctive theory of warfare that relied on guerilla tactics until a full scale, conventional attack could be mounted. His army, Giap said, would be "everywhere and nowhere".

Inspired by Napoleon, Lawrence of Arabia, and Mao Zedong, Giap's military leadership was characterized by a blend of strategic brilliance and a ruthless commitment to his cause, garnering admiration and also criticism for his disregard of human life.

Giap's most notable military achievement was the decisive victory at Dien Bien Phu in 1954, which marked the end of French colonial rule in Vietnam and established him as a national hero. His strategies emphasized guerrilla tactics, surprise attacks, and the importance of peasant support, which became fundamental elements in his campaigns against the United States during the Vietnam War.

The Viet Cong

General elections for the unification of North and South Vietnam were mandated by the Geneva Accords to be held by July 1956. The formation of the Viet Cong can be traced to the announcement by Ngo Dinh Diem on 20th July 1955 that South Vietnam would not participate in re-unification talks.

Under the terms of the Accords, military personnel had been ordered to return to their place of origin, either North or South Vietnam. However, many Viet Minh soldiers who had participated in the eight-year struggle against France remained in South Vietnam, mostly in rural or remote areas.

When it became evident that the re-unification elections would never be held, an insurgency began throughout the South conducted mainly by the Viet Minh cadres who had remained behind.

Beginning in 1959, they were rejoined by soldiers who had gone to the North and were now being re-infiltrated into the South. Together, these Viet Minh veterans constituted the expanding insurgent organization in the South, now known as the Viet Cong.

On 20th December 1960, Hanoi sanctioned the formal establishment of the National Liberation Front (NLF) modelled on the Viet Minh movement that had fought French colonialism.

The front's program called for the overthrow of Diem's regime in South Vietnam, liquidation of all foreign interference, human rights and democratic freedoms, a "land to the tiller" policy, an independent economy, the establishment of a national coalition government, a foreign policy of peace and neutrality, and peaceful reunification of the country.

The Viet Cong armed movement in the South was now formally organised and led by the National Liberation Front and conducted military operations under the name of the Liberation Army of South Vietnam (LASV). The organisation had both guerrilla and regular army units, as well as a network of cadres who organized and mobilised peasants in the territory the Viet Cong controlled.

The Viet Cong's widespread, coordinated attacks against government positions throughout South Vietnam, marked the beginning of the Vietnam War.

The Viet Cong's first major victory of the Vietnam War was the Battle of Ap Bac which began on 2nd January 1963 in a village in Dinh Tuong province located 50 miles southwest of Saigon. Three hundred and fifty Viet Cong defeated the 2500-man 7th Infantry Division of the Army of South Vietnam (ARVN), even though South Vietnam had American assistance in weapons, equipment and planning.

The Ho Chi Minh Trail

To facilitate the movement of men and materiel to the insurgents in the South, construction had begun on a logistical network of roads and trails running from North Vietnam to South Vietnam through the Kingdoms of Laos and Cambodia. This network became famously known as the Ho Chi Minh Trail. The following will focus on the Laotian Trail since it alone remained open throughout the war.

Laos

The end of World War II had left Laos in political chaos. France, displaced from their protectorate by the Japanese, moved to reassert control in January 1946. The Kingdom of Laos was officially proclaimed as part of the colonial French Union when a new Constitution was promulgated in 1947.

The Laotian nationalist movement, the Pathet Lao, was an ally of the Viet Minh in its eight-year long war with France which finally came to an end with the French defeat at Dien Bien Phu in 1954. The Geneva Accords of 1954 established the sovereignty of Laos but civil war soon broke out as the Royal Lao government fought Pathet Lao insurgents.

On 28th July 1959, the People's Army of Vietnam (PAVN) in collaboration with the Pathet Lao invaded Laos and occupied the east of the country. In September 1959, the PAVN established the 559th Transportation Group, a unit charged with the logistics of moving the necessities of war from North Vietnam to the South. Its foremost feat was building and maintaining the Ho Chi Minh Trail which ran down the eastern spine of Laos along its border with Vietnam.

In his work, *The War Against Trucks: Aerial Interdiction in Southern Laos, 1968–1972*, Bernard Nalty describes the features of the Trail:

> The trail developed into an intricate maze of 5.5-metre-wide dirt roads (paved with gravel in some areas), foot and bicycle paths and truck parks. There were numerous supply bunkers, storage areas, barracks, hospitals, and command and control facilities, all concealed from aerial observation by an intricate system of natural and man-made camouflage that was constantly improved. By 1973, trucks could drive the entire length of the trail without emerging from the canopy except to ford streams or cross them on crude bridges built beneath the water's surface.[37]

The following is reproduced from an essay entitled *Laos* on the *JFK Presidential Library and Museum* website:

> After the surrender of the Japanese in World War II, the French attempted to reassert dominion over Laos and the rest of French Indochina, which included Vietnam and Cambodia. The Communist Laotian nationalist movement, the Pathet Lao, was an ally of the Vietnamese in the struggle with France. After the French were defeated by the Vietnamese, the Geneva Accords of 1954

37 Nalty, Bernard. *The War Against Trucks: Aerial Interdiction in Southern Laos, 1968–1972*. Air Force History and Museums Program. 2005 (PDF). < https://media.defense.gov/2010/Oct/06/2001329752/-1/-1/0/AFD-101006-027.pdf> Accessed 26 March 2025.

> established the sovereignty of Laos. Civil war soon broke out, however, as the Royal Lao government, supported by the United States, fought Pathet Lao insurgents, supported by the Communists in neighboring North Vietnam.
>
> The Eisenhower government committed millions of dollars in aid and teams of military advisers to prevent the takeover of Laos by the Pathet Lao. Shortly before John F. Kennedy's inauguration, President Eisenhower warned his successor that the effort was on the verge of failure and the U.S. military might need to intervene. Kennedy moved cautiously. He rejected a variety of proposals to send American forces and concluded that a negotiated settlement with the Soviet Union and other interested parties was the best he could achieve. A 1962 peace conference in Geneva produced a Declaration on the Neutrality of Laos and a three-part coalition government divided between pro-American, pro-Communist and neutral factions.
>
> Soon after the accord was reached, civil war resumed. As American military involvement in Vietnam grew, Laos became another battlefield in that region. Running through eastern Laos, the Ho Chi Minh trail was a crucial North Vietnamese supply route for Communist forces in South Vietnam. To disrupt the flow of supplies, the United States bombed parts of Laos for nearly a decade, until a cease-fire agreement was reached in 1973. In 1975, the Pathet Lao took control of the country. [38]

North Vietnamese support for the Pathet Lao in the Laotian civil war enabled the construction of the Ho Chi Minh Trail which survived a relentless air campaign comparable to any interdiction bombing in World War II.

38 'Laos' (November 2024). *JFK Presidential Library and Museum.* < https://www.jfklibrary.org/learn/about-jfk/jfk-in-history/laos> Accessed 27 March 2025.

CHAPTER FORTY-SIX

The Tonkin Gulf Incident

'The Secrets and Lies of the Vietnam War...'

On 9th June 2021, *The New York Times* published an article by Elizabeth Becker titled 'The Secrets and Lies of the Vietnam War, Exposed in One Epic Document'. This article formed part of a special report to mark the 50th anniversary of its publication of the Pentagon Papers. The following is an edited extract from Becker's article:

> After President Kennedy was assassinated on 22nd November 1963, the Vietnam issue fell to President Lyndon Johnson. Johnson ordered officials to draft a resolution for Congress to grant him the authority to fight in Vietnam without officially declaring war.
>
> Missing was a pretext, a small-bore "Pearl Harbor" moment. That came on August 4, 1964, when the White House announced that the North Vietnamese had attacked the U.S.S. Maddox in international waters in the Gulf of Tonkin. This "attack", though, was anything but unprovoked aggression. Gen. William C. Westmoreland, the head of U.S. forces in Vietnam, had commanded the South Vietnamese military while they staged clandestine raids on North Vietnamese islands. North Vietnamese PT boats fought back and had "mistaken Maddox for a South Vietnamese escort vessel" according to a report. (Later investigations showed the attack never happened.)
>
> Testifying before the Senate, (Defense Secretary) McNamara lied, denying any American involvement in the Tonkin Gulf attacks: "Our Navy played absolutely no part in, was not associated with, was not aware of any South Vietnamese actions, if there were any".
>
> Three days after the announcement of the "incident", the administration persuaded Congress to pass the Tonkin Gulf Resolution to approve and support "the determination of the president, as commander in chief, to take all necessary measures to repel any armed attack against the forces of the United States and to prevent further aggression" — an expansion of the presidential power to wage war that is still used regularly. Johnson won the 1964 election in a landslide.[39]

39 Becker, E. 'The Secrets and Lies of the Vietnam War, Exposed in One Epic Document' (9 June 2021). *The New York Times*. < https://www.nytimes.com/2021/06/09/us/pentagon-papers-vietnam-war.html?smid=nytcore-ios-share&referringSource=articleShare> Accessed 21 September 2025.

CHAPTER FORTY-SEVEN

The Die is Cast

"In the history of the Vietnam War, the Year 1965 is notable for momentous and fateful U.S. decisions..."

The Pentagon Paper [Part IV: C-5] Evolution of the War. Phase I in the Build-up of U.S. Forces: March-July 1965 focuses on the U.S. Government's decision to intervene in South Vietnam. Edited-for-clarity extracts with explanatory notes are reproduced in this Chapter. Readers are urged to consult an extract's entire context at the *National Archives and Records Administration* <https://www.archives.gov/research/pentagon-papers>

Section 1: Fateful Choices

First Ground Troops

In the history of the Vietnam War, the Year 1965 is notable for momentous and fateful U.S. decisions, most notably the acceptance by the President of the United States of the concept that U.S. troops would engage in offensive ground operations against Vietnamese insurgents.

In February, after a dramatic increase in activity initiated by the Viet Cong, the United States responded by increasing its own level of commitment to the Republic of (South) Vietnam (RVN). For the first time, U.S. jet aircraft were authorized to support the Armed Forces of South Vietnam (RVNAF) in ground operations in the South without restriction.

In immediate retaliation for guerrilla raids on U.S. installations in the South, U.S. aircraft also began bombing targets in the southern reaches of North Vietnam. In early March, the latter program evolved into *Rolling Thunder*, the sustained bombing of the North. Also, during March, two U.S. Marine battalions were landed at Da Nang on the coast of Central Vietnam. The airbase at Da Nang was a major supporter of the *Rolling Thunder* bombing, and the mission of the Marines was to strengthen its defenses. **Those troops represented the first U.S. ground combat commitment to the Asian mainland since Korea.**

Mixed Views

While the pace of military activity in 1965 was on the rise, the political situation in South Vietnam remained as unpredictable as it had been throughout the previous year. A very confusing series of events in the middle of February culminated in the departure of the volatile General Nguyen Khanh. Left in his stead were two civilians, Prime Minister Phan Huy Quat and Chief of State Phan Khac Suu.

The rate of ground combat activity dropped off in March and remained low for the next month and a half. The Viet Cong eased the pressure on the Government of South Vietnam (GVN) considerably and yielded the initiative to the government armed forces. The performance of the Armed Forces of South Vietnam (RVNAF), whose effectiveness was called into question with the deployment of U.S. troops to look after major bases, began to improve according to the statistical indicators used to measure the progress of the war. Whenever the RVNAF succeeded in locating and fixing the Viet Cong, the government troops and their officers seemed to demonstrate more offensive spirit and willingness to engage.

The reaction of the U.S. community to the period of quiescence in the spring of 1965 was mixed. Pessimistic predictions in March as to the capability of the RVNAF to withstand the next wave of Viet Cong offensive activity were offset by convictions that ongoing U. S. aid programs were adequate to meet the situation provided the GVN resolved its internal contradictions and devoted its energies to the war.

Trying Times

The drop in activity during the spring of 1965 was not unprecedented. The Viet Cong had traditionally yielded the initiative to the more highly mobile RVNAF during the dry season, and they were expected to reappear with the advent of the summer season, or rainy season, in May and June. The official estimates of the Viet Cong Order of Battle, including in April the confirmed presence in the South of at least one battalion of the North Vietnamese Army, provided little cause for comfort. Coupled with reports that the Viet Cong were concentrating their forces in a few critical areas, the estimates of enemy capability were a sure indication that the coming summer monsoon in 1965 would provide a sore test of the RVNAF's ability.

The test began in earnest in May as the Viet Cong mounted a regiment-sized attack on the capital of Phuoc Long Province (South East Vietnam). The enemy scored again with the successful ambush of an Army of the Republic of (South) Vietnam (ARVN) infantry battalion and its rescue force near Quang Ngai in I Corps (see Note) later that month. The Quang Ngai action left two ARVN battalions decimated, and American officers who had witnessed the battle went away with the distinct impression that the RVNAF were close to collapse.

The impression was confirmed during the battle of Dong Xoai in mid June. In a textbook display of tactical ineptitude, battalions of ARVN's finest reserves were frittered away piecemeal during the fighting. The violence of the action at Dong Xoai and the level of RVNAF casualties during the second week of June 1965 were both unprecedented.

As the summer wore on, the focus of the enemy campaign shifted to the highlands of the II Corps (see Note). By early July, Viet Cong successes in taking remote District Headquarters heralded the expected loss of the entire highlands area and the possible establishment there of a National Liberation Front government.

General Westmoreland responded immediately to the marked upsurge in Viet Cong activity by requesting U.S. and Third Country reinforcements in June to spell the RVNAF during their time of trial and to blunt the Viet Cong offensive by conducting operations throughout the country against them. The collapse of the Quat government in mid-June and its succession by an untested military regime further increased the urgency associated with Westmoreland's request.

The debate in U.S. official circles over the extent of American involvement in the war, a debate which had followed a devious course all through the spring of 1965, moved onto a higher plane at this juncture. [40]

Section 2: Ground Strategy Debates

All through early 1965, officials in the U.S. Government debated the level of effort required of the United States in order to achieve its objectives in South Vietnam. Generally stated, those objectives were to insure that the Communist insurgents were defeated in their efforts to take over the government of South Vietnam and that a stable and friendly government was maintained in its place.

The debate over ground strategy was characterized by an almost complete lack of consensus throughout the first half of 1965. Proposals for levels of commitment ranging from a couple of battalions to several divisions were under consideration simultaneously. For each identifiable strategy—security, enclave, and search and destroy—there were many proponents, some of them quite vociferous. The announcements of decisions regarding the ground buildup were invariably couched

40 Pentagon Paper [Part IV: C-5] Evolution of the War. Phase I in the Build-up of U.S. Forces: March-July 1965 pp. 2-3. *National Archives and Records Administration* <https://www.archives.gov/research/pentagon-papers> Accessed 17 December 2025.

in terms which gave clear indication to more aggressive proponents that their turn might yet come. [41]

Security Strategy

The strategy of security arose with the beginning of the bombing programs and was designed simply to increase security of U.S. bases and installations supporting those programs. It was conceived at a time when enthusiasm for the bombing programs was high and its proponents were at pains to insure that U.S. troops did not get involved in the ground war. All 9 of the U.S. Battalions deployed to Vietnam by June 1965 had base security as their primary mission, and 21 of the 44 U.S. and Third Country Battalions deployed by the end of 1965 were so oriented.

In part, however, most of those units were deployed for far more ambitious reasons. At a maximum, four Marine and possibly two Army Battalions were recommended for deployment solely under the provisions of the security strategy, and the strategy was a dead letter by the time most of those deployments had been approved.

The strategy of security expired along with the early hopes that *Rolling Thunder* could succeed by itself. The non-involvement of the "security troops" in the ground war was designed to keep U.S. casualties to a minimum and to facilitate withdrawal. By deploying its own troops to secure bases, the U.S. showed lack of confidence in the RVNAF, but by keeping U.S. troops out of the fighting, it demonstrated at the same time belief that the RVNAF would be able to hold on until the other side decided it had had enough.

Because of the well-known shibboleth about U.S. involvement in an Asian ground war and because of the ponderous nature of ground force deployments, it was inevitable that some observers would see in the strategy of security the crossing of a threshold. [42]

A Brief Tenure

The rationale that got two Marine Battalions into Da Nang in March 1965 was plausibly advanced on several subsequent occasions as additional troops were deployed to various locations in Vietnam. Whether or not it was publicly offered as a rationale, the strategy of deploying troops for the security of bases was short-lived. The Marines hardly had their feet dry when several proposals were brought forward to get U.S. troops actively engaged in the ground war. These proposals, the first of which followed close on General Johnson's return from his Vietnam inspection trip

41 Ibid. p. 4.

42 Ibid. p. 5.

between the 5th and 12th March, were the center of much private debate in the spring and early summer of 1965. That debate went on largely behind the scene while the American public was in ignorance of the proceedings. The strategy of security effectively became a dead letter on the 1st of April, but the change in strategy was not revealed publicly until the 8th June. [43] (See Section 10: *The Bombshell.*)

Enclave Strategy

The President decided during National Security Council meetings on 1st and 2nd April 1965 to involve U.S. ground combat units in the war against the insurgents.

He did this in the sober awareness that *Rolling Thunder* was unlikely to produce immediate results, but also with the caveat that U.S. troops might not do too well in an Asian insurgency environment. The enclave strategy, which had been presented by the Ambassador to South Vietnam, Maxwell Taylor, as a way to get U.S. troops engaged at relatively low risk, was implicitly endorsed by the President.

The strategy proposed that U.S. troops occupy coastal enclaves, accept full responsibility for enclave security, and be prepared to go to the rescue of the RVNAF as far as 50 miles outside the enclave. Initially, the U.S. was to experiment with four Marine battalions in two coastal enclaves to see if the concept and the rules for operating with the RVNAF were feasible.

Without the benefit of any experimentation, the number of battalions was increased at the Honolulu Conference in mid-April to 17 and the number of enclaves to 5. The enclave strategy as formalized at Honolulu was designed to frustrate the Viet Cong in the South while *Rolling Thunder* continued to hammer the North. The intent was not to take the war to the enemy but rather to deny to him certain critical areas while simultaneously providing assistance to the RVNAF if they should run into difficulty. The RVNAF were expected to continue aggressively prosecuting the war against the enemy's main forces, thereby bearing the brunt of the casualties.

The enclave strategy was controversial and expectations for it ran the gamut from extreme optimism to deep pessimism. Ambassador Taylor expected it to buy some time for the Vietnamese to eventually save themselves. General Westmoreland and other military men expected it to guarantee defeat for the U.S. and the RVNAF, who were already demonstrating that they were incapable of defeating the enemy.

Masterpiece of Ambiguity

A masterpiece of ambiguity, the enclave strategy implied a greater commitment to the war on the part of the U.S., but simultaneously demonstrated in the placing

43 Ibid. p.55.

of the troops with their backs to the sea a desire for rapid and early exit. While purporting to provide the basis for experimentation with U.S. soldiers in an unfamiliar environment, it mitigated against the success of the experiments by placing those troops in close proximity to the Vietnamese people, where the greatest difficulty would be encountered. In order to prove the viability of its reserve reaction foundation, it required testing but the rules for commitment were not worked out until the strategy was already overtaken by events.

As a consequence of this delay, several opportunities were passed up when the RVNAF really needed help and U.S. troops were available. The whole enclave concept implied that the RVNAF would ultimately prevail, but in any case the Viet Cong could never win as long as certain areas were denied to them. The enclave strategy tacitly yielded the initiative to the enemy, but the initiative was not seen as the vital factor. The key was to be able to outlast the enemy at lowest cost to the United States.

Search and Destroy Strategy

Almost in reaction to the dearth of proposals to seize the initiative from the enemy, General Westmoreland exerted consistent pressure for a free hand to maneuver U.S. and Third Country forces in South Vietnam. His search and destroy strategy, which was given Presidential sanction during the summer of 1965, was articulated by both Westmoreland and the Joint Chiefs of Staff (JCS) in keeping with sound military principles garnered by men accustomed to winning. The basic idea behind the strategy was the desire to take the war to the enemy, denying him freedom of movement anywhere in the country and taking advantage of the superior firepower and maneuverability of U.S. and Third Country forces to deal him the heaviest possible blows. In the meantime, the RVNAF, with superior knowledge of the population and the role of the Viet Cong, would be free to concentrate their efforts in populated areas.

Defeat the Enemy in the South

Search and destroy was given approval at a time when there was very little hope for results from the *Rolling Thunder* program. The bombing became, therefore, an adjunct to the ground strategy as the war in the South assumed first priority. Accompanying the strategy was a subtle change of emphasis-instead of simply denying the enemy victory and convincing him that he could not win, the thrust became defeating the enemy in the South. This was sanctioned implicitly as the only way to achieve the U.S. objective of a non-communist South Vietnam. It was conceivable, of course, that sometime before total defeat, the North Vietnamese and the Viet Cong might decide that they had had enough. In this event, the U.S. could halt its efforts short of complete defeat of the insurgents and negotiate a settlement to the conflict from a much stronger position than that offered by all of the alternate strategies.

The strategy described above with all its implications evolved in piecemeal fashion during June and July 1965. Westmoreland was first given authority in June to commit U.S. ground forces anywhere in the country when, in his judgment, they were needed to strengthen the relative position of the RVNAF. His first major operation with U.S. troops under the new aegis was on 27th June, and that force made a deep penetration into the Viet Cong base area of War Zone 'D' Northwest of Saigon. Once the forces had been liberated from the restrictions of the coastal enclaves, the next step was to decide how much reinforcement was needed in order to insure that the Viet Cong and their North Vietnamese allies could not win.

The "Win" Phase

The force decided upon to insure that the Viet Cong and their North Vietnamese allies could not win was 44 U.S. and Third Country battalions. The President approved that number in mid-July. Finally, the amount of additional force required to seize the initiative from the enemy and to commence the "win" phase of the strategy was the next topic of discussion after the 44 battalions had been approved.

Defense Secretary Robert McNamara received Westmoreland's first estimate during talks in Saigon between 16th and 20th July 1965. Based on what he knew then of Viet Cong and DRV intentions and capabilities, Westmoreland asked for 24 additional maneuver battalions and a healthy support package. The figure was revised upward several times later in the year as increased intelligence revealed the extent of Democratic Republic of (North) Vietnam (DRV) infiltration and Viet Cong build-up.

Force levels for the search and destroy strategy had no empirical limits. The amount of force required to defeat the enemy depended entirely on his response to the build-up and his willingness to continue the fight. The 44 battalions seen in mid-summer 1965 as the amount required to deny victory to the Viet Cong exceeded the amount forecast by the enclavists to achieve that end for two reasons. First, the enemy had by the end of June revealed that he was much stronger than had originally been surmised. Second, the 44 battalions had a dual mission: they were not only to hold the fort, but were also to lay the groundwork for the subsequent input of forces to implement the next phase of the strategy.

No Assurances

Ambassador Taylor expected the search and destroy strategy and the force associated with it to accomplish little more than would have been accomplished by the enclave strategy at less cost. He was convinced that only the Vietnamese could save their own country, and too-aggressive use of foreign troops might even work against them in that regard. George Ball of the State Department wrote that there was no assurance no matter what the U.S. did that it could defeat the enemy on the battlefield or drive him to the conference table. The larger force associated with the search and destroy strategy signified to Ball no more than acceptance by the U.S. of a higher cost to ultimately be incurred. The 44 battalion force seemed to William Bundy, Assistant Secretary of State, to be an ultimatum presented to the DRV which would in all probability trigger some sort of dire response.

Ground War Now a Reality

Westmoreland expected the 44 battalions and the search and destroy strategy to hold things together long enough to prepare the way for later input of greater force. With enough force to seize the initiative from the Viet Cong sometime in 1966, Westmoreland expected to take the offensive and, with appropriate additional reinforcements, to have defeated the enemy by the end of 1967. Exactly what the President and his Secretary of Defense expected is not clear, but there are manifold indications that they were prepared for a long war.

The acceptance of the search and destroy strategy and the eclipse of the denial of victory idea associated with the enclave strategy left the U.S. commitment to Vietnam open-ended. The implications in terms of manpower and money are inescapable. Written all over the search and destroy strategy was total loss of confidence in the RVNAF and a concomitant willingness on the part of the U.S. to take over the war effort. U.S. involvement in an Asian ground war was now a reality. [44]

Strategies Round-Up

In conclusion, it seems clear that the debate over ground commitments and accompanying strategy followed closely the course of expectations about the *Rolling Thunder* bombing program and the development of the situation in South Vietnam itself. The strategy of security was eclipsed because *Rolling Thunder* was taking too long. The enclave strategy was never unanimously endorsed and it never got off the ground. It was based on the assumption that victory could be denied to the enemy in the South while *Rolling Thunder* punished him in the North.

It was hoped that the U.S. would achieve its objectives because the enemy in frustration would eventually give up. The whole enclave idea was conceived in a period of relative quiet, and certainly the experimentation aspect of it pre-supposed a relatively stable situation. In the heat of the summer monsoon offensive, it became a moot question whether or not a negative approach like the enclave strategy could

44 Ibid. pp. 5-8.

deny victory, and more important, whether or not there would be an RVNAF left to shore up.

In June, *Rolling Thunder* and the ground strategy switched places in the order of priorities as far as achieving U.S. objectives was concerned: First, a positive strategy for the employment of the forces, the search and destroy strategy, was approved. Secondly, a force of 44 battalions was recognized as sufficient to prevent collapse while the stage was being set for further deployments. 44 battalions was probably about the maximum the traffic would have borne at that juncture in any case. Final acceptance of the desirability of inflicting defeat on the enemy rather than merely denying him victory opened the door to an indeterminate amount of additional force.

The 44 battalions, or Phase I as they were later called, were supposed to stem the tide of the Viet Cong insurgency and enable the friendly forces to assume the offensive.

Monumental Implications

No further proof of the monumental implications of the endorsement in the summer of 1965 of the search and destroy strategy, the 44 battalions, and the "win" concept is required beyond the present state of the war in Vietnam. At this writing, the U.S. has reached the end of the time frame estimated by General Westmoreland in 1965 to be required to defeat the enemy. It has committed 107 battalions of its own forces and a grand total of 525,000 men. The strategy remains search and destroy, but victory is not yet in sight. [45]

(Note that General Westmorland had stated that the enemy would be defeated by the end of 1967 and that the last date referred to in the Pentagon Papers is March 1968.)

Caveats

The bulk of this paper is taken up in describing the various proposals put forward by exponents of the strategies. The numerous decision points are identified and the expectations of decision-making principals involved are analyzed. Ancillary reasons for advancing proposals are identified as such and discussed. The position of each of the principals is described only as clearly as it emerges from the files of the Secretary of Defense. Thus, the JCS are treated as a monolith, although it is common knowledge that there is always considerable dissension and debate amongst the Chiefs themselves. While they might have been unanimous in their recognition that U.S. bases needed securing, the Chiefs did not see eye to eye during ensuing debates over the enclave or search and destroy strategies.

45 Ibid. pp. 9-10.

The Chief of Staff of the Air Force and the Commandant of the Marine Corps were known proponents of the enclave concept, but the Chairman of the JCS and the Chief of Staff of the Army were equally determined to see the deployment of several divisions of troops for unlimited combat operations.

Through all of the strategy debate in early 1965 ran a common thread—the concern with possible intervention in the conflict by elements of the North Vietnamese Army or the Communist Chinese Army or a combination of both. A variety of CINCPAC contingency plans were in existence at the time which addressed the problem and called for various deployments, some of them pre-emptive, to deal with it. The JCS consistently mentioned the problem as an additional justification for deployments they were advocating, but the National Intelligence Board just as consistently discounted the possibility of such intervention. Covert infiltration of elements of the North Vietnamese Army, however, was another matter. It was recognized early in the debate as something to be reckoned with even though the real extent of the infiltration was not confirmed for some time. In any case, contingency deployments were not intended to deal with the latter type of provocation. [46]

Section 3: Situation Reports

Political

Despite its rather inauspicious beginning in February 1965, the Saigon government had by early April convinced the CIA that for the first time the progressive deterioration in the South Vietnamese political situation had come to a halt. All the disruptive elements in the Vietnamese body politic remained, but Prime Minister Quat displayed considerable talent in placating dissidents and was setting about in his own quiet manner to tidy up the chaotic Saigon government.

By mid-May, to the dismay of the U.S. Mission, Quat's government began to manifest considerable strain. The Buddhists, a not always consistent pressure group, felt that Quat was too busy trying to please everyone instead of initiating a strong action program. The Catholics, on the other hand, were fearful of a Buddhist-dominated government and Saigon was full of rumors of the formation of Catholic paramilitary units. Colonel Pham Ngoc Thao, a familiar plotter, was said to have unsuccessfully attempted a coup on behalf of the Catholics around the 20th of May.

46 Ibid. pp. 8-9.

An apparently routine cabinet shuffle proposed by Premier Quat at the end of May precipitated a crisis which led to the fall of his government. Quat was forced to resign and senior generals of the RVNAF took over the government.

Following the military takeover, a National Leadership Committee was formed. On 21st June, Major General Nguyen Van Thieu was installed as Chief of State with Air Vice Marshall Nguyen Cao Ky as the new Prime Minister. The accession of Thieu-Ky ended for the moment any hopes for the establishment of effective civilian government in Vietnam.

The sole bright spot in an otherwise very gloomy situation was the total absence of any violence associated with the military takeover. The new leaders came to office with an announced determination to maintain stability and to vigorously prosecute the war. Given the military situation at that time, little credence could be lent to their pronouncements. [47]

Military

The Viet Cong were unusually inactive throughout March and April 1965. There had been no major defeat of the enemy's forces and no signs of any major shift in strategy on his part. Hence it was assumed that he was merely pausing to regroup and to assess the effect of the changed American participation in the war embodied in the *Rolling Thunder* air strikes and in the deployment of the Marines on the 8th March.

...Incremental gains all over the country contributed to an air of euphoria manifested in the occasional expression of cautious optimism which crept into weekly or monthly situation reports, such as Ambassador Taylor's lengthy NODIS (Not for Distribution) cable to the President on the 13th April, and the following excerpts from the March and April evaluation reports from COMUSMACV:

> **March 1965** : Events in March were encouraging...RVNAF ground operations were highlighted by renewed operational effort. Viet Cong activity was considerably below the norm of the preceding six months and indications were that the enemy was engaged in the re-supply and re-positioning of units possibly in preparation for a new offensive, probably in the II Corps area. In summary, March has given rise to some cautious optimism. The current government appears to be taking control of the situation and, if the present state of popular morale can be sustained and strengthened, the GVN, with continued U.S. support, should be able to counter future VC offenses successfully.
>
> **April 1965**: Friendly forces retained the initiative during April and a review of events reinforces the feeling of optimism generated last month. In summary,

47 Ibid. pp. 41-42.

> current trends are highly encouraging and the GVN may have actually turned the tide at long last. However, there are some disquieting factors which indicate a need to avoid overconfidence. A test of these trends should be forthcoming in the next few months if the VC launch their expected counter-offensive and the period may well be one of the most important of the war.

In view of the fact that nothing had basically changed in the South, it seems inconceivable that anyone was really fooled by the dramatic drop in enemy-initiated activity. Most official observers were hardheaded and realistic following the landing of the two Marine Battalions in March. COMUSMACV certainly was in the long and detailed "Commander's Estimate of the Situation" which he completed on 26th March. (For the Commander's Estimate in detail, see pages 84-89 of this Paper.)

In summary, General Westmoreland said in the Estimate that while the program of air activity against the North might ultimately succeed in causing the DRV to cease its support of the war, it would not in the short run have any major effect on the situation in the South. The RVNAF, although at the moment performing fairly well, would not be able in the face of a VC summer offensive to hold in the South long enough for the bombing to become effective.

Situation Well in Hand

Realistic assessments of the situation in March notwithstanding, some of the parlance in cables and messages between Washington and Saigon expressed conviction that **the situation in Vietnam was well in hand**, and resisted radical changes or even urgent revision of ongoing U.S. programs.

For example, the Ambassador to South Vietnam, Maxwell Taylor, reacted strongly to proposals that U.S. military-civil affairs personnel be introduced into the aid effort. He told McGeorge Bundy (U.S. Special Assistant for National Security Affairs) that the GVN was winning the war without such help. Taylor said:

> I am greatly troubled by DOD 152339Z April 15th (a cable from McNaughton to Saigon containing a seven point program with 'highest authority' sanction). First, it shows no consideration for the fact that, as a result of decisions taken in Washington during my visit, this mission is charged with securing implementation by the two month old Quat government of a 21 point military program, a 41 point non-military program, a 16 point Rowan USIS (United States Information Program) and a 12 point CIA program. Now this new cable opens up new vistas of further points as if we can win here somehow on a point score. We are going to stall the machine of government if we do not declare a moratorium on new programs for at least six months.

> Next, it shows a far greater willingness to get into the ground war than I had discerned in Washington during my recent trip...

After expressing further concerns about the proposals, Taylor concluded by saying:

> Mac, can't we be better protected from our friends? I know that everyone wants to help, but there's such a thing as killing with kindness. In particular we want to stay alive here because we think we're winning--and will continue to win unless helped to death. [48]

Section 4: A Pivotal NSAM

On the 17th March 1965, Westmoreland had sought Ambassador Taylor's concurrence in a proposal to deploy an additional Marine Battalion to Phu Bai near Hue on the northern coast in I Corps (see Note). Westmoreland wanted to reduce some of the density of aircraft at Da Nang by moving helicopters to the strip at Phu Bai and the Marine battalion was needed to protect that strip. Taylor cabled Washington a lengthy analysis of the pros and cons of Westmorland's proposal.

CINCPAC (Admiral Sharp) forwarded Westmoreland's Phu Bai proposal to the Joint Chiefs of Staff on the 19th March and further recommended that the remainder of the 9th Marine Expeditionary Brigade, one Battalion plus headquarters elements, be landed at Da Nang within a month in order to consolidate command and control and build up the defense of that base.

The JCS recommended both measures to the Secretary of Defense on the 25th March, and they were discussed by the National Security Council and Ambassador Taylor during the latter's visit to the United States in late March-early April 1965. [49]

NSAM 328

The President accepted both measures recommended by the JCS. In National Security Action Memorandum 328, he approved the deployment of the two additional Marine battalions and the same time, by changing the Marines' mission to include offensive operations, he ended the strategy of security.

NSAM 328 is a pivotal document. It marks the acceptance by the President of the United States of the concept that U.S. troops would engage in offensive ground operations against Asian insurgents. It indicates as well the anxiety of the President-

48 Ibid. pp. 42-46.

49 Ibid. 56-58.

-his decision to proceed very slowly and carefully so that U.S. policy should appear to be wholly consistent. Thus the President only approved the deployment of two additional Marine Battalions, although he was doubtless aware of Joint Chiefs of Staff proposal favored by the Secretary of Defense and forwarded by the Chiefs on the 20th March, which called for the deployment of a three division force--two U.S. and one Korean.

Need for Secrecy

At the President's request, all National Security Council members were admonished in NSAM 328 not to allow the release of any premature publicity for the actions dealing with the Marines and their mission. As a result, the change of mission was not publicized until it crept out almost by accident in a State Department release on the 8th June. (See Section 10: *The Bombshell.*)

Nor was the change of mission clearly defined in NSAM 328. The Marine Battalions were to be permitted more active use "under conditions to be established and approved by the Secretary of Defense in consultation with the Secretary of State" and, of course, their new mission was subject to the approval of the GVN.

...It is pretty clear, then, that the President intended, after the early April National Security Council meetings, to cautiously and carefully experiment with U.S. forces in offensive roles. There was sober awareness that the North Vietnamese were not going to quit and that the U.S. was well on its way to being committed on the ground. *The Rolling Thunder* program, if it was going to bear any fruit at all, certainly was not going to do so in the next few months. [50]

The Horns of a "Trilemma"

The U.S. decision-makers really were on what Assistant Secretary of Defense McNaughton described as "the horns of a trilemma". McNaughton had jotted down some notes on the 24th March which accurately described the predicament facing the U.S. Government. The question, according to McNaughton, was: "Can the situation inside South Vietnam be bottomed out (a) without extreme measures against the DRV and (b) without deployment of large numbers of U. S. (and 3rd Country) combat troops inside South Vietnam?"

McNaughton's answer was "perhaps, but probably no". Because that was the case, he went on, the U.S. was faced with the "trilemma". Policy appeared to be drifting even though there was consensus that present action probably would not prevent collapse

50 Ibid. pp. 59-60..

of the GVN. All three choices for remedial action so far presented had been rejected. These choices were:

1. Will-breaking strikes against the DRV which risked escalation flash and were thus too risky;
2. Large U.S. troop input which raised the old spectre of an Asian land war and recalled memories of the French defeat;
3. Exit from the scene through negotiation which insured, because of the current situation, humiliation of the U.S.

The alternatives, as described above by Mr. McNaughton, went into the National Security Council discussions which took place during the Ambassador's visit. What came out of those discussions was NSAM 328 and the decision to proceed ahead very slowly with ground force involvement.

The Spectre of Dien Bien Phu

Missing from NSAM 328 was the elucidation of a unified, coherent strategy. Ambassador Taylor, among others, had raised the question as to whether or not Western troops could fight effectively in Vietnam. No one could forget the French failure, and the Ambassador's reservations received due attention. Before devising a strategy for the use of U.S. ground forces, however, it was deemed necessary to experiment with small numbers of them to see how they would do. There was time to indulge the luxury of a leisurely build-up. The situation was bad, but currently the GVN was doing a bit better, and nothing pointed to immediate collapse.

The early April NSC meetings had signalled the beginning of the enclave strategy. U.S. forces would operate within strictly limited boundaries (originally not to exceed 50 miles from base) and would have their backs to the sea. No Dien Bien Phu's would be presented for the enemy to exploit as supplies and reinforcements could be brought in with ease over sea Lines of Communication controlled entirely by the U.S. Navy. As a corollary, the U. S. forces could be withdrawn with equal ease should the situation so dictate. [51]

Primary Focus

In the air

NSAM 328 had its primary focus on air action against the DRV and Laos. The text of the NSAM said that, subject to continuing review, the President approved the following general framework of continuing action against North Vietnam and Laos:

51 Ibid. p. 60.

- We should continue roughly the present slowly ascending tempo of *Rolling Thunder* operations, being prepared to add strikes in response to a higher rate of Viet Cong operations, or conceivably to slow the pace in the unlikely event VC slacked off sharply for what appeared to be more than a temporary operational lull;
- The target systems should continue to avoid the effective range of MIGs. We should continue to vary the types of targets, stepping up attacks on lines of communication in the near future, and possibly moving in a few weeks to attacks on the rail lines north and northeast of Hanoi;
- Air operation in Laos, particularly route blocking operations in the Panhandle area, should be stepped up to the maximum remunerative rate.

On the ground

In regard to action on the ground, NSAM 328 said in relation to force level increases:

- The President approved an 18-20,000 man increase in U.S. military support forces to fill out existing units and supply needed logistic personnel;
- The President approved the deployment of two additional Marine Battalions and one Marine Air Squadron and associated headquarters and support elements;
- The President also approved the urgent exploration with the Korean, Australian, and New Zealand Governments, of the possibility of rapid deployment of significant combat elements from their armed forces in parallel with the additional Marine deployment approved.

Mission Change

NSAM 328 sanctioned a change in mission for U.S. ground forces in Vietnam, but it did so in very cautious language:

> The President approved a change of mission for all Marine battalions deployed to Vietnam to permit their more active use under conditions to be established and approved by the Secretary of Defense in consultation with the Secretary of State.

This language may indicate that the President wanted to experiment very carefully with a small amount of force before deciding whether or not to accept any kind of ground war commitment. Implicit in the size of that force and in its location was the option to quickly evacuate it should the U.S. so desire.[52]

(For the full text of NSAM 328, see page 124 of this Paper.)

Security Justification

From the 11th through the 14th of April, the two additional Marine battalions approved by the President in NSAM 328 had been deployed to Hue/Phu Bai and Da Nang. Their landing brought the total number of U.S. maneuver battalions in South Vietnam to four, all Marines. Although security was no longer the only authorized mission for these units, it certainly was their primary mission. The Marines set about consolidating and developing their two coastal base areas, and, although they pushed their patrol perimeters out beyond their tactical wire and thereby conducted active rather than passive defense, they did not engage in any offensive operations in support of ARVN for the next few months. [53]

The security of U.S. bases was consistently offered, along with other reasons, to justify the further deployment of ground combat units. In fact, looking back on the force deployments, the JCS in November 1965 stated that 21 of the original 44 "Phase I" U.S./3rd Country battalions, whose deployment to Vietnam was accomplished in the latter half of 1965, were committed to base and installation security. [54]

Section 5: Unfortunate Oversight

Commander's Estimate

The "Commander's Estimate of the Situation" (referenced previously), which was prepared by General Westmoreland and his staff during the early weeks of March 1965 and completed on the 26th, was a classic Leavenworth-style analysis, detailed and thorough in its consideration of possible U.S. courses of action.

Copies of the Estimate, which in bulk amounted to a full half inch of foolscap paper, were delivered to Washington by Brigadier General De Puy, Westmoreland's Assistant Chief of Staff J-3 (Operations), who was traveling with Ambassador Taylor to the NSC meetings of 1st and 2nd April. If the awesome bulk of the Estimate deterred anyone from giving it the careful study it merited, that is **most unfortunate**. As Westmoreland himself said:

52 Ibid. pp. 67-69.

53 Ibid. p. 62.

54 Ibid. p. 65.

Recognizing recent marked changes in situation in SVN, we considered it appropriate to undertake a classical Commander's Estimate of the Situation to think through in a logical and precise manner strategy, objectives, enemy capabilities and our own possible courses of action before making what may prove to be in the light of history a momentous recommendation. In addition, by reducing the Estimate to writing we expose our thoughts to others, thus making possible careful review by higher authority and perhaps introduction of new considerations that were not apparent here.

Objective Choices

In order to achieve its objectives, the U.S. was presented, as Westmoreland saw it, essentially with three possible Courses of Action, there being several variations on one of the choices. The choices were:

1. Accelerate the build-up of RVNAF, commit the 7th Fleet to quarantine the coast against infiltration of men and arms, and continue U.S. logistical support as required. No outside combat power other than Naval and Air support would be provided the GVN under this option;
2. The above plus the commitment of up to two U.S. divisions with their support, either (a) to secure vital U.S. installations and defeat VC efforts to control the Kontum, Pleiku, Binh Dinh region, or (b) to secure critical enclaves in coastal regions, or (c) to do a combination of both of the above;
3. Both of the major choices above plus a cordon across the Laotian panhandle manned by up to three U.S. divisions coupled with ARVN, Thai and Laos forces.

After giving thorough consideration to the three possible Courses of Action, General Westmoreland decided that Course of Action 2 was the most propitious. Course of Action 2 called for the commitment of up to two U.S. divisions, including 17 maneuver battalions, with support. Over and above what was in or authorized to be in Vietnam, it called for an additional 33,000 men.

At the conclusion of his Estimate, Westmoreland recommended that the U.S. buildup its combat force in Vietnam to 17 battalions by early June at the latest. [55] (For the Commander's Estimate in detail, see pages 84-89 of this Paper.)

55 Ibid. pp. 84-89..

"Hasty and Ill-conceived" Proposals

Further to Presidential approval for the change of mission in NSAM 328, Ambassador Taylor cabled Washington on the 4th April that he would approach Prime Minister Quat with a proposal that the Marines be permitted to conduct mobile operations within their TAORs and that they be used by the RVNAF as a reserve for operations up to 50 miles from their bases. The Vietnamese Prime Minister acquiesced in the deployment of the two Marine Battalions plus one Tactical Fighter Squadron (F4) on the 6th of April and in the change in mission on the 8th.

Taylor was at this juncture quite prepared to settle into a period of careful experimentation with the level of combat power fixed at four battalions. He said in a message dated 17th April that he had about 60 days in mind as the appropriate period for the experiment, and he indicated he was chagrined by some apparent anxiety in Washington to move considerably faster.

In a message also dated 17th April, he questioned the Washington panic manifested in a whole panoply of "hasty and ill-conceived" proposals for the deployment of more forces. In another message he again cautioned against precipitous action and offered the palliative that "things weren't going so badly" out there.

Four Marine battalions were enough for experimentation, but not so large as to alarm the xenophobic Vietnamese. In fact, the Ambassador's sensitivity to the proclivities of the Vietnamese Prime Minister on the question of foreign troops helps explain the Embassy's foot-dragging during this critical period of U.S. build-up debate.

Thus, the Ambassador was surprised to discover that the Marines had come ashore with tanks, self-propelled artillery, and various other items of weighty equipment not "appropriate for counterinsurgency operations". That equipment, bland JCS explanations mentioning contingency plans and full TOE (Table of Organisation and Equipment) prudence notwithstanding, implied a permanence not communicated to Quat when clearance for-their entry had been sought.

Amazing Naivete

From analysis of the cable traffic of early April, it appears that Taylor was the only major figure opposed to further expansion of the U.S. combat role beyond what was agreed at the NSC meetings in Washington…the chorus of suggestions and programs from Washington reached a crescendo with the joint State/Defense message of the 18th April which, with the blessing of "highest authority" in Washington, proposed the following measures be considered to add "something new" to the equation:

1. Experimental encadrement of U.S. troops into RVNAF either through the assignment of 50 U.S. soldiers to each of 10 ARVN battalions or through the "brigading" of ARVN and US battalions for operations;
2. The introduction of a brigade force into Bien Hoa/Vung Tau for security of installations and later expansion into counterinsurgency operations under conditions to be spelled out by General Westmoreland;
3. The introduction of several battalions into coastal enclaves such as Qui Nhon in accordance with proposals to be submitted by the Ambassador and COMUSMACV. The purpose was "to further experiment with US forces in the counterinsurgency role". (The phrase "further experiment" is misleading since up to the date of this cable, there had been no U.S. counterinsurgency operations worthy of the name);
4. Expansion of Vietnamese recruiting, using proven U.S. techniques;
5. Expansion of MEDCAP (Medical Civil Action Program) using mobile dispensaries under guidelines to be worked out between COMUSMACV and the Surgeon General, U.S. Army;
6. Experimentation in two or three provinces with a team of U.S. civil affairs personnel introduced into provincial government structure under conditions to be worked out between Major General Peers and General Westmoreland;
7. The supplement of low RVNAF pay through a program to provide some of the troops with a food ration. General Timmes would be seeing COMUSMACV to work out the details.

Although this cable was well-meaning in its intent, the Ambassador was amazed by its naivete and justifiably chagrined by its impertinence and he went on to send many cables to Washington during the tumultuous days just prior to the April Honolulu Conference. (See pages 72-76 of this Paper for Taylor's cable about the kind of guidance he felt he should have been receiving from Washington.)

Thus was the Ambassador propelled into the Honolulu conference of 20th April 1965, only one step ahead of the Washington juggernaut, which was itself fueled by encouragement from Westmoreland in Saigon. Taylor was not opposed to the U.S. build-up *per se*, but rather was concerned to move slowly with combat troop deployments, which tended to cause alarm in an already delicate situation, while proceeding quietly with the prerequisite development of logistic bases to support later troop introduction. He was overtaken at Honolulu. [56]

56 Ibid. pp. 69-71.

In Honolulu on 20th April 1965, Secretary Robert McNamara, Assistant Secretaries William Bundy of State and John McNaughton of Defense, Ambassador Maxwell Taylor, Generals Wheeler and Westmoreland, and Admiral Sharp met to devise a coherent strategy for United States involvement in Vietnam.

The situation which presented itself to the Honolulu conferees was in many ways the whole Vietnam problem in microcosm. What was needed to galvanize everyone into action was some sort of dramatic event within South Vietnam itself. Unfortunately, the very nature of the war precluded the abrupt collapse of a front or the loss of large chunks of territory in lightning strokes by the enemy. The enemy in this war was spreading his control and influence slowly and inexorably but without drama.

The political infrastructure from which he derived his strength took years to create and, in most areas the expansion of control was hardly felt until it was a *fait accompli*. Only when he organized into units of battalion and regiment size, did the enemy voluntarily lend some dramatic elements to the war. Whenever these units appeared and engaged the RVNAF, the government and its U.S. helpers had something they could handle.

Unfortunately, at the time of the Honolulu Conference, the Viet Cong Main Force units were underground and the conferees had little or no tangible threat to which they could react.

A Sobering Harbinger

There were, however, plenty of indications in the early spring of 1965 of what was to come. There had been no major degradations in the Viet Cong strength nor in their order of battle. On the contrary, the enemy was recruiting apace and more than offsetting his losses. From throughout the country came reports that Viet Cong troops and cadre were moving into Central Vietnam and into areas adjacent to the ring of provinces comprising the "Hop Tac" area around Saigon.

Constant political turmoil involving many of the senior RVNAF officers and few significant victories combined to have a deleterious effect on the effectiveness of the GVN armed forces. On the 20th March, the JCS had identified the degradation of RVNAF as a new phenomenon after months of political instability. They used the decline as justification to argue for the deployment of three divisions of reinforcements from the U.S. and Korea.

Most ominous of all, a CIA-Defense Intelligence Agency memorandum dated the 21st April 1965 reflected the acceptance into the enemy order of battle of one regiment of the 325th PAVN Division said to be located in Kontum Province (Central Highlands). The presence of this regular North Vietnamese unit, which had been first reported as early as February, was a sobering harbinger of things to come.[57]

The Victory Strategy

In the preliminary discussions at Honolulu, the Saigon and Washington decision makers agreed that:

1. The DRV was not likely to quit within the next six months, and in any case, they were more likely to give up because of VC failure in the South than because of bomb-induced "pain" in the North. It could take up to two years to demonstrate VC failure;
2. The level of air activity through *Rolling Thunder* was about right. The U.S. did not, in Ambassador Taylor's words, want "to kill the hostage". Therefore, Hanoi and environs remained on the restricted list. It was recognized that air activity would not do the job alone;
3. Progress in the South would be slow and great care should be taken to avoid dramatic defeat. The current lull in Viet Cong activity was merely the quiet before a storm;
4. The victory strategy was to "break the will of the DRV/VC by denying them victory". Impotence would lead eventually to a political solution.

Additional Deployments

Going into the Honolulu Conference, the level of approved U.S. forces for Vietnam was 40,200. In-country strength of 33,500 showed that not all the approved forces had closed. To accomplish the "Victory Strategy" described above, the conferees agreed that the following additional U.S. deployments should be made:

1. An Army Brigade (3 Battalions) to Bien Hoa-Vung Tau to close by the 1st May;
2. 3 USMC Battalion Landing Teams and 3 Tactical Fighter Squadrons to Chu Lai by the 5th May;
3. An Army Brigade (3 Battalions) to Qui Nhon-Nha Trang to close by the 15th June;
4. Augmentations of existing forces and added logistical support.

57 Ibid. pp. 46-47.

If approved, these recommended forces would have brought U. S. strength to a grand total of 13 maneuver battalions and 82,000 men.

The U.S. Government also should approach the respective foreign governments and request an Australian Army Battalion to Vung Tau to close by 21st May and a Korean Regimental Combat Team to Quang Ngai by 15th June. If approved, these recommended forces would bring Third Country strength to a grand total of 4 maneuver battalions and 7,250 men.

As an adjunct to the units above, the conferees mentioned, but did not recommend, the possible later U.S. deployment of an Army Airmobile Division (9 Battalions), the remainder of the III Marine Expeditionary Force (2 Battalions), and an Army Corps Headquarters. The conferees also mentioned the possible deployment of a ROK Division (Republic of Korea) consisting of 6 Battalions.

The posited future add-ons comprised a further 17 maneuver battalions which, if added to the approved totals, would have brought US/Third Country combat capability in South Vietnam to 34 battalions. [58]

The President received the Honolulu recommendations in a memorandum from Secretary McNamara on 21st of April.

The Big Push

On 30th April, a JCS Memorandum summarised the planning as the Chiefs saw it and presented a detailed program for the deployment to Vietnam of some 48,000 U.S. and 5,250 Third Country forces, all of which were listed as approved. Included were all the units mentioned in the Honolulu recommendation plus a healthy support package. These forces were, according to the JCS, to "bolster GVN forces during their continued build-up, secure bases and installations, conduct counterinsurgency combat operations in coordination with the RVNAF, and prepare for the later introduction of an airmobile division to the central plateau, the remainder of the III MEF to the Da Nang area, and the remainder of a ROK division to Quang Ngai". Logistic forces of all services were "to strengthen support of in-country forces, provide support for new forces, prepare bases and installations for possible future deployments, and be prepared to support those additional forces".

From the thrust of this JCSM, it is apparent that the enclave strategy was no stopping place as far as the Chiefs were concerned. They continued to push hard for the earliest possible input of three full divisions of troops. They were still well ahead of the pack in that regard.

---

58 Ibid. pp. 71, 77.

None of the Honolulu recommendations had been approved at the time the 30th April JCSM was forwarded, although the 173rd was approved for Bien Hoa-Vung Tau and three Marine battalions for Chu Lai on the same day. Included in the logistics package listed by the JCS as "approved" were some 4,700 troops later identified by Mr. McNaughton as belonging to the three division program and definitely not approved.

Secretary McNamara replied to the JCS Memorandum on 15th May, after the landing of the 173rd on the 5th and the Marines at Chu Lai on the 7th. The Secretary said that he considered as approved only so much of the remainder of the Honolulu recommendations as applied to the Australian Battalion, the ROK Regimental Combat Team and some Military Assistance Command Vietnam (MACV) augmentations.

He went on to approve: (1) movement of the I Marine Expeditionary Force from California to West Pacific Area Command (WESTPAC) to reconstitute CINCPAC's floating reserve, and (2) preparation for the deployment of an Army brigade to Qui Nhon-Nha Trang with final decision on 21st May and closure on 27th June. This latter move, when approved, together with individual add-ons was to bring total permanent in-country strength to 69,143 (the 173rd having been deployed on a temporary basis). Secretary McNamara deferred decision on all JCS proposals dealing with the three division plan, thereby giving the enclave strategy temporary respite. [59]

(Note that the first Australian combat troops in Vietnam served alongside the U.S. 173rd Airborne Brigade in Bien Hoa province.)

Section 8: The Storm Breaks

The storm broke in earnest on 11th May 1965 when the Viet Cong attacked Song Be, the capital of Phuoc Long Province, using more than a regiment of troops. The enemy overran the town and its MACV advisory compound, causing heavy casualties among the U.S. and Vietnamese defenders. After holding the town for a day, the Viet Cong withdrew. Subsequent ARVN operations revealed that the enemy also had suffered heavily in the battle.

Significantly, while the Viet Cong were preparing their attack on Song Be, the GVN was pushing to completion a new Special Forces camp at Dong Xoai not far away on the NW corner of War Zone C (South Vietnam near the Cambodian border).

59 Ibid. pp. 78-79.

That camp was opened in May and, in less than a month, the enemy was to reveal his interest in it.

Possible Collapse of ARVN

Before May was over, however, the Viet Cong appeared again in strength, this time in Quang Ngai Province in the Northern I Corps (see Note). Near the small outpost of Ba Gia a few kilometers west of Quang Ngai City, a battalion of the ARVN 51st Regiment was ambushed and overrun. Although the size of the enemy force was unknown, the ARVN commanders in the area rushed reinforcements out to the scene only to have them ambushed in turn. The battle dragged on for several days and ended in total defeat for the ARVN. Two battalions were completely decimated and, what was worse, the ARVN senior commanders on the scene had displayed tactical stupidity and cowardice in the face of large enemy forces.

From Ba Gia came a sense of urgency, at least among some of the senior U.S. officers who had been witness to the battle. The very real possibility of ARVN collapse had been made manifest. [60]

More Ground Troops Needed

On 7th June, shortly after Ba Gia, General Westmoreland sent to CINCPAC a message giving his assessment of the situation. The message concluded with:

> In order to cope with the situation outlined above, I see no course of action open to us except to reinforce our efforts in South Vietnam with additional U.S. or Third Country forces as rapidly as is practical during the critical weeks ahead. Additionally, studies must continue and plans developed to deploy even greater forces, if and when required, to attain our objectives or counter enemy initiatives. Ground forces deployed to selected areas along the coast and inland will be used both offensively and defensively.
>
> U.S. ground troops are gaining experience and thus far have performed well. Although they have not yet engaged the enemy in strength, I am convinced that U.S. troops with their energy, mobility, and firepower can successfully take the fight to the VC. The basic purpose of the additional deployments recommended below is to give us a substantial and hard hitting offensive capability on the ground to convince the VC that they cannot win…

60 Ibid. pp. 46-47.

ARVN Devoured

There were some who thought COMUSMACV's assessment of the situation was a bit precipitous, but the dissenters were effectively silenced the following week as the Viet Cong attacked the aforementioned Special Forces camp and the adjoining district headquarters at Dong Xoai. ARVN reinforcements were committed piecemeal to the fray and were devoured by the enemy, who was on the scene with better than two regiments of troops. The battle, which lasted for five days and nearly saw the commitment of the U.S. 173rd Airborne Brigade to bail the ARVN out, marked the bitterest fighting of the war to date.

By mid-June 1965, the Viet Cong summer offensive was in full stride. Shifting the emphasis away from the areas of their early successes on the periphery of "Hop Tac" and in the southern portion of I Corps, they began the long-expected offensive in the highlands of II Corps (see Note for Corps Areas).

On 25th June, the district headquarters at Tou Morong in Kontum Province was invested and then taken by an enemy force said to be a People's Army of (North) Vietnam (PAVN) regiment reinforced with some Viet Cong troops. Other remote district headquarters came under enemy pressure in the ensuing weeks until, by 7th July, a total of six of them had been abandoned or overrun. The Viet Cong were systematically forcing the GVN to yield what little control it still exercised in rural areas outside the Mekong Delta.

Summing up the situation at the end of the week of 14th July, the CIA said:

> The initiative and momentum of military operations continue in favor of the Viet Cong. The impact of Viet Cong operations is being felt not only by the RVNAF but by the nation's internal economy as well. Nothing this week points to the RVN wresting the initiative from the VC. [61]

Section 9: The Spectre of an Asian Ground War

Experimental Build-Up

The beginning of the decisive month of June 1965 saw the U.S. in the infant stages of its enclave strategy. Established in coastal enclaves were Marine forces in Phu Bai, Da Nang and Chu Lai, and Army forces in Vung Tau. Enclaves at Qui Nhon and Nha Trang were in the planning as locations for an Army brigade and Korean troops were

61 Ibid. pp. 47-50.

being considered for the defense of the provincial capital of Quang Ngai near the coast and as possible relief for the Marines at Chu Lai.

The Secretary of Defense was also considering proposals from General Westmoreland and others to open up a major logistics base and enclave around the fine deep-water harbor at Cam Ranh Bay.

As of 1st June 1965, the U.S. had approved for permanent deployment to South Vietnam forces which, when all had closed, would bring total combat strength to approximately 70,000 and the number of maneuver battalions, Army and Marine, to 13. Third Country forces considered approved at this time amounted to 7,250 men of which 1,250 were already in-country: the 1st Battalion, Royal Australian Regiment; 2,000 Korean service troops; and the rest were to be deployed sometime later in a ROK Regimental Combat Team of 3 battalions.

The grand total of approved U.S./3rd Country forces was 17 maneuver battalions and approximately 77,250 men. If the additional forces then being discussed were thrown in, the total would have been 34 maneuver battalions and about 134,750 men.

This, then, was the state of the build-up when General Westmoreland asked in message #19118 of the 7th June 1965 for reinforcements from the U.S. and Third Countries "as rapidly as possible". [62]

The Hornet's Nest

General Westmoreland's message #19118 of 7th June 1965 punctuated a very grim period of ARVN defeats in Vietnam and stirred up a veritable hornet's nest in Washington. Up to that time, most of the Washington decision makers had been content to indulge in relatively low-key polemics about the enclave strategy and to advocate some experimentation with small numbers of U.S. troops in Vietnam.

Westmoreland's request for reinforcements on a large scale, accompanied as it was by a strategy to put the troops on the offensive against the Viet Cong, did not contain any of the comfortable restrictions and safeguards which had been part of every strategy debated to date.

Washington saw that it was Westmoreland's intention to aggressively take the war to the enemy with other than Vietnamese troops, and in such a move, **the spectre of U.S. involvement in a major Asian ground war was there for all to see**. With no provision for quick withdrawal, and there was none, the long-term implications for the U. S. in terms of lives and money could not be averted. Temperatures rose rapidly after 7th June, and the debate was acrimonious and not without its casualties.

62 Ibid. p. 83.

Just as Ambassador Taylor was consistent in his resistance to proposed involvement of U.S. forces in the Vietnamese War, so also was General Westmoreland equally determined to get enough US/3rd Country forces into Vietnam to influence the situation. In addition to the level of force, Westmoreland was also bent on having a free hand in the use of it. [63]

Section 10: The Bombshell

The long official silence between the sanction for U.S. offensive operations contained in NSAM 328 (3rd April 1965) and the final approval on 30th April of the conditions under which U. S. troops could be committed was not without cost. The President had admonished each of the National Security Council members not to allow release of information concerning the provisions of the NSAM, but the unduly long interregnum inevitably led to leaks.

During that official silence, the Marines incurred some 200 casualties, including 18 killed as they went about tidying up their TAORs in April and May. The Commandant of the Marine Corps raised the tempo of speculation by saying to the press during an inspection trip to Vietnam in April that the Marines were not in Vietnam to "sit on their dittyboxes"—they were there to "kill Viet Cong".

An honest and superficially innocuous statement by Department of State Press Officer Robert McCloskey on 8th June to the effect that "American forces would be available for combat support together with Vietnamese forces when and if necessary" produced an immediate response. [64]

The press response to McCloskey's candor is best summed up in *The New York Times* article of 9th June 1965:

> The American people were told by a minor State Department official yesterday that, in effect, they were in a land war on the continent of Asia. This is only one of the extraordinary aspects of the first formal announcement that a decision has been made to commit American ground forces to open combat in South Vietnam: The nation is informed about it not by the President, not by a Cabinet member, not even by a sub-Cabinet official, but by a public relations officer.
>
> ...Since March, American forces in Vietnam have more than doubled to 52,000, as compared to 14,000 when President Johnson took office. Additional troops are moving in and a build-up to 70,000 has been indicated. There has

63 Ibid. p. 84.

64 Ibid. p. 81.

been neither confirmation or denial that a force exceeding 100,000 is planned, including three full Army and Marine divisions. Nor is there any clarification on whether the "combat support" role now authorised—combat in support of South Vietnamese units—is to be transferred later into offensive "clear and hold" operations of a kind hitherto carried out only by South Vietnamese forces. Apart from the obvious difficulty American troops would have in distinguishing guerillas from the surrounding population, such a war ultimately might absorb as many American troops as were employed in Korea.

A major factor in the original escalation decision—the decision to bomb North Vietnam—was the political crisis in Saigon after eight changes of government in little more than a year. The bombing was urged upon President Johnson as the only way to shore up morale, halt the factional feuding and prevent a complete political collapse in South Vietnam. Is it only a coincidence that the decision to enter the ground war has come during another political crisis in Saigon?

There may be a need to prop up the Government of Premier Phan Huy Quat against the Catholic and Southern factions which made a constitutional issue out of his recent Cabinet reshuffle and still seek to bring him down. But is it not more likely that political irresponsibility in Saigon will grow, rather than decline, as the main military responsibility for defending South Vietnam is transferred increasingly to American hands?

The country deserves answers to this and many other questions. It has been taken into a ground war by Presidential decision when there is no emergency that would seem to rule out Congressional debate. The duty now is for reassurance from the White House that the nation will be informed on where it is being led and that Congress will be consulted before another furious upward whirl is taken on the escalation spiral.[65]

The Credibility Gap

The White House was hoisted by its own petard. In an attempt to quell the outcry, a statement was issued on 9th of June which, because of its ambiguity, only served to further exacerbate the situation and to widen what was being described as "the credibility gap".

The White House statement said in part:

65 'Ground War in Asia'. *The New York Times*. The New York Times Company: New York NY. 9 June 1965, p. 49.

> There has been no change in the mission of United States ground combat units in Vietnam in recent days or weeks. The President has issued no order of any kind in this regard to General Westmoreland recently or at any other time. The primary mission of these troops is to secure and safeguard important military installations like the air base at Da Nang.
>
> They have the associated mission of patrolling and securing actions in and near the areas thus safeguarded. If help is requested by the appropriate Vietnamese commander, General Westmoreland also has authority within the assigned mission to employ these troops in support of Vietnamese forces faced with aggressive attack when other effective reserves are not available and when, in his judgment, the general military situation urgently requires it.

The documents do not reveal whether or not the ground rules for engagement of U.S. forces had actually been worked out to everyone's satisfaction at the time of the White House statement. There is good indication that they had not. [66]

Section 11: The Tightrope

Balancing Act

On 11th of June, the Joint Chiefs of Staff cabled CINCPAC (Admiral Sharp) and informed him that somewhat less than Westmoreland's deployment request of 7th June was very close to being approved. The force described amounted to two Marine battalions and three Army brigades, two of which had already been approved. The JCS wanted to know where Westmoreland intended to put this force in Vietnam. The implicit intention to keep a string on every unit going into Vietnam was obvious to General Westmoreland.

In reply to this query and in response to the rising volume of criticism directed at his estimate of the seriousness of the situation and his proposed utilization of combat forces, Westmoreland sent a cable to CINCPAC with area and force deployment recommendations. (See page 94 of this Paper)

This message was extremely important, for in it COMUSMACV spelled out the concept of keeping U.S. forces away from the people. The search and destroy strategy for U.S. and Third Country forces which continues to this day and the primary focus of RVNAF on pacification both stem from that concept. In addition, Westmoreland

66 Pentagon Paper [Part IV: C-5] Evolution of the War. Phase I in the Build-up of U.S. Forces: March-July 1965 pp. 81-82. *National Archives and Records Administration* <https://www.archives.gov/research/pentagon-papers> Accessed 17 December 2025.

made a big pitch in this cable for a free hand to maneuver the troops around inside the country. That is the prerogative of a major field commander--there is a good indication that at this stage that Westmoreland saw himself in that light rather than providing advice and assistance to the Vietnamese armed forces.

Ambassador Taylor returned to Vietnam from Washington shortly after the battle at Dong Xoai, just as the new Thieu-Ky government was being installed. His first report confirmed the seriousness of the military situation as reported by General Westmoreland and also pointed up the very tenuous hold the new government had on the country. This report apparently helped to remove the last obstacles to consideration of all of the forces mentioned in Westmoreland's request of 7th June.

On 22nd June, the Chairman of the JCS cabled Westmoreland and CINCPAC to inform them that the ante had gone up from 35 to 44 battalions, counting all forces planned and programmed and including the 173rd Airborne Brigade. (The 1st Battalion, Royal Australian Regiment, was initially deployed with the 173rd Airborne Brigade.)

Westmoreland was asked if 44 battalions would be enough to convince the VC/DRV that they could not win. General Westmoreland replied that there was no evidence the VC/DRV would alter their plans regardless of what the U.S. did in the next six months. The 44 battalion force should, however, establish a favorable balance of power by the end of the year. If the U.S. was to seize the initiative from the enemy, then further forces would be required into 1966 and beyond.

Resources Drain

On 26th of June, as has already been noted, General Westmoreland was given the authority to commit U.S. forces to battle in support of RVNAF "in any situation when, in COMUSMACV's judgment, their use is necessary to strengthen the relative position of GVN forces". This was about as close to a free hand in managing the forces as General Westmoreland was likely to get. The enclave strategy was finished, and the debate from then on centered on how much force and to what end. There were some attempts to snatch the chestnuts from the fire, however.

Westmoreland's opposition, while far from presenting a united front, had its day in court during late June and early July 1965. The Embassy in Saigon, while recognizing the seriousness of the situation in South Vietnam, was less than sanguine about the prospects for success if large numbers of foreign troops were brought in. Deputy Ambassador U. Alexis Johnson told Assistant Secretary of Defense McNaughton on 25th June that the U.S. should not bring in more troops.

The situation, according to Deputy Ambassador Johnson was in many ways no more serious than the previous year. Even if it were more serious, he went on, massive input of U.S. troops was unlikely to make much difference. The best they could do would be to hold a few enclaves. Johnson pointed out that the Vietnamese were afraid they would lose authority if more U.S. troops were brought in.

He advised that the U.S. allow the forces already in the country to settle. After some experimentation with them, the way would be much clearer. Once in, troops could not, without difficulty, be taken out again.

At the opposite end of the spectrum from General Westmoreland was Under Secretary of State George Ball. Convinced that the U.S. was pouring its resources down the drain in the wrong place, Ball placed himself in direct opposition to the build-up.

Cut Losses

In Ball's view there was absolutely no assurance that the U.S. could, with the provision of more ground forces, achieve its political objectives in Vietnam. Instead, the U.S. risked involving itself in a costly and indeterminate struggle. To further complicate matters, it would be equally impossible to achieve political objectives by expanding the bombing of the North--the risks of involving the USSR and the Peoples Republic of China were too great, besides which such action would alienate friends. No combination of the two actions offered any better prospect for success. Since the costs to achieve its objectives if the U.S. embarked on an expanding program were indeterminate, the U.S. should, in Ball's view, not elect to follow such a course of action.

It should instead "cut its losses" by restricting itself to the programmed 15 battalions and 72,000 men made public at a press conference in mid-June by the Secretary of Defense. By holding those forces to a very conservative Phase II strategy of base defense and reserve in support of RVNAF, U.S. combat losses could be held to a minimum while the stage was being set for withdrawal. (See Concept of Operations for Westmorland's three-phase strategy.)

Salvage Honor

Ball was cold-blooded in his analysis. He recognized that the U.S. would not be able to avoid losing face before its Asian allies if it staged some form of conference leading to withdrawal of U. S. forces. The loss would only be of short term duration, however, and the U.S. could emerge from this period of travail as a "wiser and more mature nation".

On 1st July, Ball sent the President a memorandum entitled "A Compromise Solution for South Vietnam". In that memorandum, Ball presented his case for cutting losses essentially as it is described above. Assistant Secretary of State William Bundy, like so many others, found himself in between Westmoreland and Ball. The U.S. needed to avoid the ultimatum aspects of the 44 battalions and also the Ball withdrawal proposal, both of which were undesirable in Bundy's estimation.

Also on 1st July, Bundy suggested to the President that the U.S. should adopt a policy which would allow it to hold on without risking disasters of scale if the war were lost despite deployment of the full 44 battalions. For the moment, according to Bundy, the U.S. should complete planned deployments to bring in-country forces to 18 maneuver battalions and 85,000 men. The Airmobile Division and the remainder of the 1st Division should be brought to a high state of readiness but the decision as to their deployment should be deferred. By so acting, the U.S. would gain time in which to work diplomatically to realign Southeast Asia and thereby salvage its honor and credibility.

The forces in Vietnam, which Bundy assumed would be enough to prevent collapse, would be restricted to reserve reaction in support of RVNAF. This would allow for some experimentation, without taking over the war effort-- a familiar theme. Bundy felt, as did Ambassador Taylor, that there remained considerable uncertainty as to how well U.S. troops would .perform in the Vietnam environment. We needed to find out before going big. [67]

Section 12: First Strike

The first major ground combat operation by U. S. forces in the Vietnam War took place in War Zone D, NW of Saigon, from 27th to 30th June 1965. Participants were the 173rd Airborne Brigade; the 1st Battalion of the Royal Australian Regiment; two Battalions from the ARVN Airborne Brigade; and the ARVN 48th Regiment. It was a search and destroy operation into Viet Cong base areas and its purpose was to deny to the enemy "freedom of action...in these safe havens".

The War Zone D excursion was a direct result of the sanction given to General Westmoreland on 26th June to commit U.S. troops to combat, independent of or in conjunction with the forces of the Government of South Vietnam (GVN) in any situation in which the use of such troops is requested by an appropriate GVN commander and when in the Commander of U.S. Military Assistance Command Vietnam's judgment, their use is necessary to strengthen the relative position of GVN forces.

67 Ibid. pp. 104, 105, 106.

At that juncture, the 44 Battalion debate was in full swing and the enclave strategy, as a means to limit the amount and use of U.S. combat force in Vietnam, was certainly overcome by events. It was not until 18th August that an operation fitting the paradigm description of the Taylor enclave concept, Operation Starlight, was conducted with dramatic success 15 miles south of the Chu Lai enclave. It established the viability of enclave operations limited to the northern coast of South Vietnam, a fact which no one disputed, but such operations were by that time only one facet of a much more ambitious strategy sanctioned by the President and in the process of being implemented by Westmoreland. [68]

Note

In Deptel Cable 3057 of 26th June, W. (William) Bundy had told the Ambassador to South Vietnam, Maxwell Taylor, that Westmoreland could commit U.S. troops to combat "in any situation in which the use of such troops is required by an appropriate GVN commander and when, in COMUSMACV's judgment, their use is necessary to strengthen the relative position of GVN forces".[69]

Section 13: Guardians at the Gate

Phase I Sanctioned

Secretary McNamara went to Vietnam for a firsthand look from 16th to 20th July. He wanted to hear Westmoreland's concept for the employment of the 44 (U.S. /3rd Country forces), and he sought the answers to other questions including what forces Westmoreland thought would be required through January 1966 and beyond. When McNamara left Washington, the 44 battalion debate remained unresolved. While he was in Saigon, he received a cable from Deputy Secretary of Defense Cyrus Vance informing him that the President had decided to go ahead with the plan to deploy all 34 of the U. S. battalions. The Phase I debate was over.

The Lesson of History

Upon his return from Vietnam, Secretary McNamara prepared a draft release to the press which stated that the total increase in U. S. forces with the latest approved add-ons would be about 100,000. That information was not given out. Instead, after a week of deliberation, the President held a press conference on 28th July in which

68 Ibid. p. 82.

69 Ibid. p. 29.

he told the American people "the lesson of history" dictated that the U.S. commit its strength to resist aggression in South Vietnam. He said:

> **We did not choose to be the guardians at the gate, but there is no one else.**
>
> Nor would surrender in Vietnam bring peace, because we learned from Hitler at Munich that success only feeds the appetite of aggression. The battle would be renewed in one country and then another country, bringing with it perhaps even larger and crueler conflict, as we have learned from the lessons of history.
>
> Moreover, we are in Vietnam to fulfill one of the most solemn pledges of the American Nation. Three Presidents—President Eisenhower, President Kennedy, and your present President—over 11 years have committed themselves and have promised to help defend this small and valiant nation.
>
> Strengthened by that promise, the people of South Vietnam have fought for many long years. Thousands of them have died. Thousands more have been crippled and scarred by war. We just cannot now dishonor our word, or abandon our commitment, or leave those who believed us and who trusted us to the terror and repression and murder that would follow. This, then, my fellow Americans, is why we are in Vietnam.

We Can't be Defeated

As far as increases in U.S. forces were concerned, the President said this:

> First, we intend to convince the Communists that we cannot be defeated by force of arms or by superior power. They are not easily convinced. In recent months they have greatly increased their fighting forces and their attacks and the number of incidents. I have asked the commanding general, General Westmoreland, what more he needs to meet this mounting aggression. He has told me. We will meet his needs.
>
> I have today ordered to Vietnam the Airmobile Division and certain other forces which will raise our fighting strength from 75,000 to 125,000 men almost immediately. Additional forces will be needed later and they will be sent as requested. This will make it necessary to increase our active fighting forces by raising the monthly draft call from 17,000 over a period of time to 35,000 per month, and for us to step up our campaign for voluntary enlistments.
>
> After this past week of deliberations, I have concluded that it is not essential to order Reserve units into service now. If that necessity should later be indicated, I will give the matter most careful consideration and I will give the country due and adequate notice before taking such action, but only after full preparations.

> We have also discussed with the Government of South Vietnam lately the steps that we will take to substantially increase their own effort, both on the battlefield and toward reform and progress in the villages. Ambassador Lodge is now formulating a new program to be tested upon his return to that area.

No Change in Policy

During the questioning period which followed the President's presentation, the following dialogue between the President and one of his interlocutors is recorded:

> Question: Mr. President, does the fact that you are sending additional forces to Vietnam imply any change in the existing policy of relying mainly on the South Vietnamese to carry out offensive operations and using American forces to guard installations and to act as emergency backup?
>
> The President: It does not imply any change in policy whatever. It does not imply change of objective.

The Annex to JCSM 590-65, forwarded by the Joint Chiefs on 30th July 1965, reflected the final Phase I package approved for deployment as 44 maneuver battalions (U.S./3rd Country forces) and a total strength in South Vietnam after all units had closed of 193,887 U.S. fighting men. (U.S. strength in South Vietnam at the end of 1965 was 184,314 men.) [70]

Section 14: Ground Strategies Roundup

Security

The short-lived strategy of security saw the deployments as a necessary evil to meet an immediate need--the bolstering of base security in South Vietnam for the air effort against North Vietnam. Few of the principals read any more into it than that.

The strategy of security was intimately tied to the *Rolling Thunder* bombing program. It remained alive only so long as the decision-making principals were reasonably confident that the bombing was going to produce the desired effects on the DRV/VC will to persist. Expectations for the security strategy were quite modest if the foot-in-the-door aspects of it are discounted. No input of "volunteers" from China or other communist allies of the DRV was expected to occur in response to the provision of

70 Ibid. pp. 110-112.

a few foreign troops to look after the bases in the South. It was merely expected that those bases would be better protected from attack. [71]

Enclaves

The proponents of the enclave strategy expected it to frustrate the DRV/VC by denying them victory. This denial of victory strategy spelled out at the Honolulu Conference, the high water mark of the enclave strategy, predicted that enemy impotence would lead eventually to a political solution. The enemy would be denied victory simply because a modicum of U. S. and 3rd Country force would enable the RVNAF to be expanded at a controlled rate without undue risk of collapse, loss of a key area, or a major defeat.

The brunt of the war against the enemy's regular units would still be borne by the RVNAF. The Allied forces, operating from their secure bases, would be prepared to come to the aid of the Vietnamese if necessary. The relatively low intensity of operations to which the Allied forces would be exposed would permit low risk experimentation with them. The information gained from such experiments would be useful if the strategy failed and more forces had to be brought in. If the experiments verified that foreign soldiers could not fight effectively in the Vietnamese environment, a stronger case could be made for resisting any future attempts to get foreign troops enmeshed in the war.

The enclave strategy was controversial and expectations for it ran the gamut from extreme optimism to deep pessimism. Ambassador Taylor expected it to buy some time for the Vietnamese to eventually save themselves. General Westmoreland and other military men expected it to guarantee defeat for the U.S. and the RVNAF, who were already demonstrating that they were incapable of defeating the enemy. [72]

Search and Destroy

More Ground Troops Essential

The Joint Chiefs of Staff expected any strategy to fail if it did not include among its courses of action some provision for the seizure of the initiative. General Westmoreland was of a similar bent, and he stated explicitly that the enclave strategy was "too negative". Nevertheless, both Westmoreland and the JCS are on record stating that 44 battalions would not be enough to seize the initiative from the enemy either. Westmoreland told the JCS on 24th June that he felt substantial increases of forces would be required over and above the 44 battalions in 1966. The U. S. would be

71 Ibid. p. 113.

72 Ibid. pp. 113-116.

too busy building up its forces in 1965 to seize the initiative from the enemy during that year. JCSM-515-65 of 2nd July, which contained the JCS recommendation for the full 44 battalions, included the following paragraph:

> Pursuant to their meeting with the Secretary of Defense on 28th June, the JCS forwarded on 2nd July a program for the deployment of "such additional forces at this time as are required to insure that the VC/DRV cannot win in South Vietnam at their present level of commitment".

The JCS went on to recommend the concurrent implementation of stepped-up air activity against North Vietnam as an indispensable part of the overall program. Total U.S. strength at completion of these deployments was to be 175,000.

Thus, the JCS, who in March 1965 were recommending 27 battalions to "stem the tide and assume the offensive", were ready to admit in July of that year that 44 battalions would only be enough to hold the fort and that even greater effort would be required to seize the initiative. [73]

Victory Not Yet in Sight

No further proof of the monumental implications of the endorsement in the summer of 1965 of the search and destroy strategy, the 44 battalions, and the "win" concept is required beyond the present state of the war in Vietnam. At this writing, the U.S. has reached the end of the time frame estimated by General Westmoreland in 1965 to be required to defeat the enemy. It has committed 107 battalions of its own forces and a grand total of 525,000 men. The strategy remains search and destroy, but victory is not yet in sight. [74]

Notes

(1) General Westmorland had stated that the enemy would be defeated by the end of 1967. (2) The last date referred to in the Pentagon Papers is March 1968.

Section 15: Concept of Operations

General Westmorland's Concept of Operations, formalised and published on 30th August 1965, was developed through three distinct Phases:

73 Ibid. pp. 116-117.

74 Ibid. pp. 9-10.

Phase I: The commitment of US/FWMAF (Free World Military Assistance Forces) necessary to halt the losing trend by the end of 1965 (44 maneuver battalions);

Phase II: The resumption of the offensive by US/FWMAF forces during the first half of 1966 in high priority areas necessary to destroy enemy forces, and re-institute rural construction activities (24 additional maneuver battalions);

Phase III: If the enemy persisted, a period of a year to a year and a half following Phase II would be required for the defeat and destruction of the remaining enemy forces and base areas.

Withdrawal of US/FWMAF forces would commence following Phase III as the GVN became able to establish and maintain internal order and to defend its borders.

Westmoreland expected by the end of 1965 to have effectively stemmed the tide of the VC insurgency through the input of 44 US/FWMAF maneuver battalions and their accompanying support. In the first half of 1966, with the input of more force, Westmoreland expected to shift his emphasis from the strategic defensive to the strategic offensive. [75] (For Westmorland's detailed Concept of Operations see pages 117-119 of this Paper.)

Section 16: No End in Sight

Neither the President nor the Secretary of Defense is on record in 1965 with expectations as to the duration of the war or the impact of the 44 battalions. It looks as though they both were prepared for the moment to go along with General Westmoreland's predictions about the course of the war.

The decision not to call up the Reserves, which was made some time during the week just prior to the President's press conference of 28th July, indicated that the President expected the war to last in Vietnam well beyond a year. No doubt the Secretary of Defense told him that without a declaration of national emergency—a move the President found politically unpalatable—the Reserves as an asset would be fully expended in one year, leaving the military establishment in worse shape than before if the war still continued.

World Reactions

The final element in the expectations matrix was provided by the National Intelligence Brief in a Special National Intelligence Estimate issued on 23rd July

75 Ibid. pp. 118-119.

entitled “Communist and Free World Reactions to a Possible U. S. Course of Action”. The analysis was predicated on the following proposed action:

1. The U.S. would increase its strength in South Vietnam to 175,000 by 1 November;
2. 225,000 U.S. Reserves would be called up;
3. 20,000 tours of duty per month would be extended;
4. The regular strength of the U. S. Armed Forces would be increased by 400,000 over the next year; and
5. U.S. draft calls would be doubled.

In conjunction with the above, the U. S. would also make public statements reiterating its objectives and its readiness to negotiate. The forces going to Vietnam would be deployed so as not to threaten the 17th parallel. Also considered was a possible step-up of U.S. air activity against the DRV land lines of communication with China.

In reaction to the above, the Communists would probably see the U.S. moves as an indication that the U.S. held little hope of negotiation. They would probably expect some increase in US/3rd Country forces anyway as they clearly felt they were winning. In order to offset the increases of US/3rd Country forces in South Vietnam, the Communists would probably build up their own strength with the input of 20,000 to 30,000 PAVN regulars by the end of 1965. This, of course, they were already in the process of doing.

Mitigating the Crisis

...It was felt that most of the allies of the United States realized that the U.S. was going to have to increase its commitment in Vietnam. It was recognized, however, that they would find it increasingly difficult to give U.S. policy any public support.

In order to mitigate somewhat the crisis atmosphere that would result from this major U.S. action, the Estimate concluded with the recommendation that announcements about it be made piecemeal with no more high level emphasis than necessary.

Opinion Gamut

Predictably, the expectations of those outside of the official pale ran the gamut from supporters of Oregon Senator Wayne Morse (“the Administration policy is leading the United States to the abyss of total war”-- “there are doubts beginning to show at the grass roots about our policy there, and when the coffins begin coming home those doubts will grow”-- “the war in Asia cannot be won... in the end the United States will be kicked out") to equally misguided zealots on the other end of the spectrum, such as Jack Foisie of the *Los Angeles Times* ("I foresee the day of mixed American-Vietnamese units under American command-- to make our junior leadership stretch as far as possible"-- "we are going to drive to the Laos border--lying only 50 to 75 miles inland in the central waist of Vietnam. Everything taken will be held, initially with firstline troops, and later--as a rear area--by second line militia").

Whatever their personal assessments of the ramifications of the 44 battalion decision might have been, all interested observers had one thing in common--they recognized the crossing of a major threshold and the embarkation on a major new course, the end of which was not in sight. [76]

Notes

Corps Areas

The four corps areas of the Army of the Republic of South Vietnam (ARVN) were four military zones used for command and control during the war. They were I Corps in the north, bordering the DMZ; II Corps in the central highlands; III Corps around the capital Saigon (including the Iron Triangle, a Viet Cong stronghold); and IV Corps in the Mekong Delta.

TAORS

When the Marines arrived to secure bases and installations, the control measure devised for their deployment was the Tactical Area of Responsibility (TAOR). Under the overall suzerainty of the Vietnamese Corps Commander, the Marines were given a well-defined geographical area in which the U.S. exercised command authority over military forces and for which the U.S. accepted defensive responsibility.

When the two U.S. Marine battalions arrived at Da Nang on the coast of Central Vietnam, the original TAOR consisted literally of their half of the Da Nang airfield and a portion of a couple of hills on which the Marines were entrenched and which they covered by the fields of fire of their small arms. Assured by this conservative assignation was minimum contact between U.S. troops and the Vietnamese population. In fact, there were only some 1,930 people living within the original Marine TAOR.

From this humble beginning (on the 8th March 1965) there followed a period of gradual expansion until, by the end of March, the Da Nang TAOR was 12 square miles in size and incorporated some 11,141 Vietnamese souls. [77]

---

76 Ibid. pp. 121-123..

77 Ibid. pp. 79-80.

CHAPTER FORTY-EIGHT

Across the Rubicon

Phase I... was designed to stop losing the war.
Phase II... is the phase needed to start winning it.

The following edited-for-clarity extracts with explanatory notes are reproduced or paraphrased from the Pentagon Paper [Part IV: C.6.a] Evolution of the War. U.S. Ground Strategy and Force Deployments: 1965 - 1967. Volume I: Phase II, Program 3, Program 4. Readers are urged to consult an extract's entire context at the *National Archives and Records Administration* <https://www.archives.gov/research/pentagon-papers>

Section 1: Phase II

The story of the Phase II build-up begins near the end of the chain of events which led to the decision, announced on 28th July 1965, on a Phase I build-up to 44 Free World battalions (34 U.S.).

Sparked by the news that the Viet Cong were building up their strength, that the ARVN was doing badly on the battlefield, and that the President desired "that we find more dramatic and effective actions in South Vietnam", Secretary of Defense McNamara prepared to decide what forces would be necessary to achieve the goals of the United States in Vietnam.

The history of the decision on the size and composition of the forces to be deployed during the time remaining in 1965, termed Phase I forces, is the subject of Pentagon Paper [Part IV: C-5] Evolution of the War. Phase I in the Build-up of U.S. Forces: March-July 1965. (See Chapter Forty-Seven: *The Die is Cast.*)

However, there were some events and decisions taken in this period which were to influence the decisions on Phase II forces.

Phase II Numbers

On 7th July 1965, Secretary McNamara cabled Westmoreland to lay out the purpose of his upcoming visit to Saigon and some of the questions which he would like to have answered:

> The main purpose of our visit will be to receive from you your recommendations for the number of U.S. combat battalions, artillery battalions, engineering battalions, helicopter companies, tactical aircraft, and total military personnel to be assigned to South Vietnam between and the end of this year…the probable requirements for additional forces next year.

This request for "probable requirements for additional forces next year" seemed to be an attempt to improve the quality of planning figures for 1966. In his 1st July Draft Memorandum for the President, McNamara quoted Westmoreland as saying that he "cannot now state what additional forces may be required in 1966 to gain and maintain the military initiative…Instinctively we believe that there may be substantial U. S. Force Requirements". The memorandum went on to comment that "He (COMUSMACV) has a study underway with a fairly solid estimate due in early August. The number of battalions ultimately required could be double the 44".

According to the MACV Command History of 1965, General Westmoreland answered Secretary McNamara's question about forces required in 1966 during the Secretary's Saigon visit. General Westmoreland "anticipated that a need would exist for an increase of 21 maneuver battalions, 14 artillery battalions, 3 air defense (Hawk) battalions, 8 engineer battalions, 12 helicopter companies, 6 helicopter battalions, and additional support units". As reconstructed by the MACV Command History, this requirement was predicated upon a Concept of Operations in South Vietnam and upon a three phased plan. [78]

(See Chapter Forty-Seven: *The Die is Cast* for Westmorland's Concept of Operations and his Three-Phase plan.)

No Reason We Can't Win

While Secretary McNamara was preparing for his 16th July 1965 trip to Saigon to discuss the build-up of American forces in Vietnam with General Westmorland, he had asked General Wheeler, Chairman of the Joint Chiefs of Staff, for an assessment of "the assurance the U.S. can have of winning in South Vietnam if we do everything we can".

General Wheeler directed an assessment to be prepared by an *ad hoc* study group with representation from the Office of the Chairman, the Chairman's Special Studies Group, the Defense Intelligence Agency, the Joint Staff Operations Directorate, and

78 Pentagon Paper [Part IV: C.6.a] Evolution of the War. U.S. Ground Strategy and Force Deployments: 1965 - 1967. Volume I: Phase II, Program 3, Program 4. pp. 6, 7, 8. *National Archives and Records Administration* <https://www.archives.gov/research/pentagon-papers> Accessed 15 December 2025.

the Joint War Games Agency. The results were given to Secretary McNamara on 14th July.

The study group's assessment was a conditional affirmative:

> Within the bounds of reasonable assumptions...there appears to be no reason we cannot win if such is our will and if that will is manifested in strategy and tactical operations. [79]

Enemy Strength

The strategic concept which the JCS developed from the study was predicated on their estimate of what strength was available to the Viet Cong and North Vietnamese, and on their judgment about what the enemy was trying to do with his forces. The estimate of enemy strength given in the study group's 14th July 1965 report was that the Viet Cong organized combat units consisted of 10 regimental headquarters, 65 battalions, 188 companies, for a total strength of approximately 48,500. The 101st Regiment, 325th People's Army of Vietnam (PAVN) Division, with its subordinate battalions, is included in this total. In addition, 17,600 personnel were considered to be engaged in combat support-type operations.

At that time, the Viet Cong were continuing to expand their control in rural areas and had succeeded in isolating several provincial and district towns from the bulk of the rural population. The apparent willingness to accept large casualties in offensive engagements indicated that a manpower shortage did not currently exist.

Estimates of PAVN's capability of intervening overtly in South Vietnam across the Demilitarized Zone (DMZ) was that PAVN could do so with approximately three divisions against moderate opposition. If PAVN were to introduce units into South Vietnam covertly through the Laotian Corridor, it is estimated he would be able to introduce 1 to 2 additional divisions by the end of 1965. [80]

McNamara Recommends Phase II

In a 20th July 1965 Memorandum for the President, Defense Secretary McNamara spelled out the troop requirements for Vietnam as follows:

> The forces (in South Vietnam) for 1965 should be brought up to about 175,000 (Phase I) and "it should be understood that the deployment of more men (perhaps 100,000) may be necessary in early 1966 (Phase II) and that

79 Ibid. p. 1.

80 Ibid. pp. 6-7.

> the deployment of additional forces thereafter is possible but will depend on developments".

Phase II was recommended to the President at a level of around 100,000 which, when added to the then current estimates for Phase I of 175,000 gave a total estimate of 275,000 by the end of 1966. [81]

(For McNamara's views on how U.S. forces should be deployed and his evaluation of the probable results see pages 11-12 of this Paper.)

Section 2: Stop Losing...Start Winning

The Joint Chiefs of Staff (JCS) captured the essence of the Phase II concept by pointing out that:

> Phase I...was designed to stop losing the war. Phase II... is then the phase needed to start winning it.

The JCS Concept for Vietnam

By late August 1965, the JCS had developed and coordinated a Concept for Vietnam which was set out in JCSM 652-65 dated 27th August. The JCS Memorandum identified the war's challenges and then proposed a counter strategy.

Major Challenges

The objective in Vietnam, as was stated in NSAM 288 of 17th March 1964, is to establish a stable and independent non-communist government. The major challenges in the war include:

- The continued support of the Viet Cong by North Vietnam, which provides materiel support and replaces heavy losses;
- The presence of a significant Viet Cong infrastructure in South Vietnam;
- The rapid growth of the Viet Cong compared to the South Vietnamese forces;
- Continued loss of communication lines, food-producing areas, and population to the Viet Cong;
- The lack of a viable politico-economic structure in South Vietnam;

81 Ibid. p. 10.

- The threat of Chinese Communist intervention or aggression in Southeast Asia and the Western Pacific.

The JCS Strategy

The basic tasks of equal priority are:

- To stop North Vietnam from supporting the Viet Cong insurgency;
- To defeat the Viet Cong and extend South Vietnam's control over all of South Vietnam;
- To deter Communist China from direct intervention and defeat it if it occurs.

The U.S. basic strategy for accomplishing the above tasks should be to:

- Intensify military pressure on North Vietnam (DRV) through air and naval power targeting military infrastructure and supply lines;
- Enhance the combat effectiveness of the South Vietnam Armed Forces (RVNAF), construct and secure bases, and reduce enemy reinforcements;
- Maintain adequate forces in the Western Pacific and build up military presence in Thailand to deter potential Chinese Communist (CHICOM) aggression.

The Memorandum went on to explain that:

- The strategic areas crucial for countering guerilla warfare were Saigon, the Mekong Delta, the coastal plain, and the central highlands;
- The control of resources, especially food production, was vital for supporting the population, bolstering the economy, and weakening the Viet Cong;
- The building and maintaining of secure bases and lines of communication were essential for launching and sustaining offensive operations. [82]

(For complete details of the JCS Concept for Vietnam, see pages 13-15 of this Paper.)

Westmoreland's Concept for Vietnam

The JCS concept was interpreted by General Westmoreland in his MACV Directive 525-4 of 20th September 1965 in which he set forth the tactics and techniques for

82 Ibid. pp. 13-15.

employment of U.S. forces in the Republic of Vietnam.

Westmorland's Strategy

General Westmoreland's strategy consisted of three successive steps:

1. First, to halt the VC offensive to stem the tide;
2. Second, to resume the offensive to destroy VC and pacify selected high priority areas;
3. Third, to restore progressively the entire country to the control of the GVN.

JCS Refinements

By early November 1965, the Joint Chiefs had further refined their "Concept for Vietnam" and in JCS Memorandum 811-65 dated 10th November, submitted their recommendations to the Secretary of Defense. The new figures were a further deployment of 112,430 personnel (up from the projected 100,000 in July) most of whom would be in Vietnam by the end of 1966. These figures were still being used as late as November 1965.[83]

A Key Memorandum

Meanwhile, in November, two other things were taking place which would have a significant effect on Phase II.

In early November, a Draft Memorandum for the President was in the works which addressed the problem of how best to conduct the overall effort in Vietnam. In this memorandum, Mr. McNamara discussed the relative merits of varying combinations of a pause in the air war against North Vietnam, gradual intensification of the *Rolling Thunder* program, and carrying out Phase II deployments.

This memorandum seems to mark one of the key decision points in the growing involvement of in the U.S. in Vietnam.

The Phase I deployments appeared to have arrested the deterioration of the situation in Vietnam and it now became feasible to consider what kind of outcome we might be able to get from the present situation. The analysis in the memorandum was that roughly sticking with the present situation would lead to a "compromise outcome" which would very likely be unstable and difficult to sell domestically, and damaging to the "U.S. political effectiveness on the world scene".

83 Ibid. pp. 16-17.

Therefore, the course of action to follow was to step up the pressure both in the North by increasing the tempo of *Rolling Thunder*, and in the South by moving ahead with Phase II deployments.

However, a pause in bombing would be inserted prior to the increased pressure. The arguments for the pause were four:

1. It would offer the DRV and VC a chance to move toward a solution if they should be so inclined;
2. It would demonstrate to domestic and international critics that our efforts to settle the war are genuine;
3. It would probably tend to reduce the dangers of escalation after we resumed the bombing; and
4. It would set the stage for another pause perhaps in late 1966 which might produce a settlement.

The conclusion to this draft which was discussed with the President on 7th November was the warning that "none of these actions ensures success...the odds are even that despite our effort, we would be faced in early 1967 with stagnation at a higher level and with a need to decide whether to deploy Phase III forces, probably in Laos as well as in South Vietnam".

While the pros and cons of a pause or a cease-fire were being debated in a series of drafts and memoranda which were prepared and circulated between Defense and State, the situation in Vietnam was undergoing a change. [84]

Infiltration Increases

By November 1965, the infiltration of units from North Vietnam had begun to increase and by 17th November, six confirmed (two probable and one possible) North Vietnamese Army (PAVN) regiments had been identified in South Vietnam. The Viet Cong regimental-size units had increased from five in July of 1965 to twelve.

The total strength of the PAVN/ VC army was estimated at 27 PAVN infantry battalions and a total of 110 PAVN/VC battalions. The accepted strength was 63,500 in combat units and 17, 000 in combat support units with 53,600 in the militia. The PAVN/VC build-up rate was estimated to be 15 battalions per quarter during 1967. The implications of the build-up were made abundantly clear by the bloody fighting in the Ia Drang Valley in mid-November. [85]

84 Ibid. pp. 17-18.

85 Ibid. p. 18.

(See pages 18-24 of this Paper for a list of U.S. Search and Destroy Missions during October and November 1965, a history of North Vietnam's political and military strategy, and General Westmorland's analysis of the impact of increased infiltration on his Phase II requirements.)

Faced with a changed enemy situation, Secretary of Defense McNamara diverted his return from a NATO meeting in Paris to visit Saigon on 28th November 1965. As outlined in his 23rd November cable to Saigon, the purpose of the forthcoming visit was "further discussion of Phase II requirements". Specifically, he asked:

> Will it not be necessary to add one or two divisions to the 28 battalions proposed in order to provide forces for the Delta; will even more forces be required in 1966 if the number of PAVN regiments continues to increase? [86]

Section 3: Phase IIA

When Secretary McNamara arrived in Saigon on the 28th November 1965, General Westmorland expressed a need for another U.S. Division for the area contiguous to Saigon, bringing the total to three, as well as reinforcements for the 1st Cavalry Division, the 5th Infantry Division, and a possible Republic of Korea Division for deployment along part of the coastal plain. This revised deployment plan was referred to as Phase IIA.

No Guarantees

Upon his return from Saigon, Secretary McNamara drafted a Memorandum for the President outlining the changed military situation in Vietnam and commenting that, in view of the communist build-up:

> The presently contemplated Phase I forces will not be enough…Nor will the originally contemplated Phase II addition of 28 more U. S. battalions (112,000 men) be enough…Indeed it is estimated that, with the contemplated Phase II addition of 28 U. S. battalions, we would be able only to hold our present geographical positions.

In order to "provide what it takes in men and materiel…to stick with our stated objectives and with the war", Secretary McNamara recommended the deployment of one Korean division plus another brigade, an additional Australian battalion, and 40 U.S. combat battalions, bringing the total of U. S. maneuver battalions to 74, and the

86 Ibid. p. 24.

total of U. S. personnel in Vietnam to approximately 400,000 by the end of 1966 with the possible need for an additional 200,000 in 1967.

...In evaluating this course of action, the Secretary warned that it "will not guarantee success". He estimated the odds to be about even that the enemy will match the U.S. build-up and that:

> ...even with the recommended deployments, we will be faced in early 1967 with a military standoff at a much greater level, with pacification still stalled, and with any prospect of military success marred by the chance of an active Chinese intervention.

Phases I, II and IIA Published

On 13th December 1965, McNamara sent out a Draft Memorandum for the President which included tables outlining the planned deployments to Southeast Asia under Phases I, II and IIA. This December Plan projected the total strength for Phases I, II and IIA to be 367,800 by the end of 1966 and 393, 900 by the end of June 1967. The number of U.S. maneuver battalions would reach 75 by the end of 1966.

Meanwhile, the requirements which Secretary McNamara had brought back from Saigon were being reviewed by CINCPAC in preparation for a planning conference scheduled for 17th January-6th February 1966 at which the refined requirements would be presented and recommended deployment schedules prepared. [87]

Upward Pressure

The results of the review were forwarded to the Secretary of Defense on 16th December. CINCPAC's new requirements involved significant increases in deployment levels to South Vietnam. With these revised requirements in hand, the services set about estimating their capability of meeting them.

Meanwhile, Secretary McNamara, in a Memorandum for the President, dated 24th January 1966, gave, as his best estimate of force levels for the next twelve months, the following:

1. By December 1966, the U.S. would have 75 battalions and 367,800 men in Vietnam;
2. Allied nations would have 23 battalions and 44,600 men. [88]

87 Ibid. pp. 24-25.

88 Ibid. pp. 26-28.

By 28th January, just four days after McNamara's "best estimate", the CINCPAC/MACV requirements had risen to 102 Free World battalions (79 U.S. including 4 tank battalions…)

An intermediate evaluation was that "it appears that the CINCPAC/MACV requirements are valid and required to meet the military objective on which the Secretary of Defense has been previously briefed. The information brought back by Secretary of Defense in late November as to combat and support force requirements was incomplete". (See pages 26-28 of this Paper for estimated sources of manpower available to meet increased requirements under the assumptions of Cases 1, 2, and 3 prepared for the Honolulu Conference.)

Honolulu Conference

During the Pacific Area Command-CINCPAC Conference held between 17th January and 6th February 1966, the top American and Vietnamese leaders met at Honolulu, primarily to "permit the leaders of the United States and South Vietnam to get to know each other better and to discuss non-military programs".

Attendees included U.S. Secretary of Defense Robert McNamara, Secretary of State Dean Rusk, MACV commander General William Westmoreland, South Vietnamese Prime Minister Nguyen Cao Ky, and Chief of State Nguyen Van Thieu. Representatives from the U.S. Joint Chiefs of Staff and Pacific Command also attended. President Lyndon Johnson arrived at the Conference on 7th February.

The President emphasized the need to focus more on the "other war" of pacification and political, social, and economic reform in South Vietnam. General Westmoreland agreed that pacification was vital but argued that their first priority should be destroying the North Vietnamese Army and the Viet Cong insurgency before pacification could succeed.

The Johnson administration urged U.S. and South Vietnamese leaders to expedite reform programs to fight Communist influence in the countryside and assigned MACV to protect 60% of South Vietnam's population before year-end, among other goals. Secretaries McNamara, Rusk, and representatives from the Joint Chiefs and Pacific Command agreed with General Westmoreland's view that defeating Communist troops on the battlefield was the priority. The administration promised Westmoreland more troops for this goal. [89]

In a Summary for the Record dated 9th February 1966, Secretary McNamara assembled his key subordinates and provided them with a lengthy summary of the Honolulu Conference.

89 Ibid. pp. 27-28.

(Photocopies of the summary are reproduced on pages 29-33 of this Paper.)

Conference Results Published

On 12th February 1966, the results of the CINCPAC Planning Conference at Honolulu were published.

The concept of operations for 1966 had been more completely spelled out. The three basic military objectives had by this time grown to four. Now there were two separate objectives: (1) to extend the South Vietnamese Government's control over South Vietnam, and (2) to defeat the VC and PAVN forces in South Vietnaam and force their withdrawal. The old task had combined both these objectives.

The CINCPAC submission included estimates of MACV's requirements and the deployments to Vietnam possible under the assumptions of Cases 1, 2, and 3 prepared for the Honolulu Conference.

Strength at end of Calendar Year 1966

Maneuver Btns	Requirement	Case 1	Case 2	Case 3
U.S.	79	79	79*	61
Allied	23	23	23	23
Total	102	102	93	84
Equivalent Strength	102	96	88	72
U.S. Personnel	459,000	422,517		

* Other nine battalions available in January 1967

Ingenuity Required

Having received CINCPAC's requirements, the Secretary of Defense directed that:

> The military Departments and the JCS to assume that the Case 1 deployment schedule is the requirement we will try to meet, to study all possible ways of meeting it short of calling reserves or extending terms of service, and until further notice, in so far as possible, to plan to deploy forces to South Vietnam on this schedule.
>
> I would like to urge that you use all the ingenuity you can in developing suggested ways of meeting these conditions by use of suitable substitutes (civilian contractor personnel) etc. In this connection, General Westmoreland and Admiral Sharp have made a list of suggestions which is being analyzed by the JCS and my staff. Every effort should be made to carry out these and similar suggestions.

The fourth line in the tables is my understanding of the current Service estimates of their capabilities to meet these requirements under the assumption that only cadres are taken from Europe, and that no Reserves or extensions of terms of service are utilized. Would you please study these estimates, improve upon them, and find ways to bring our effective combat capability into equality with the Case 1.

I would like by 28th February the individual Service and JCS comments on our capabilities to meet Case 1 requirements. [90]

(See pages 34-38 of this Paper for discussions about the pros and cons of Cases 1, 2, and 3, possible deployment tables in each Case, and the decision to proceed with Case 1.)

Section 4: Phase IIA (R)

On the 1st March 1966, following the CINCPAC Conference, the Joint Chiefs of Staff forwarded their deployment recommendations for Phase IIA(R) to Secretary McNamara.

However, the JCS recommendations were not acceptable to the Secretary of Defense and on 10th March he stated: "I have reviewed JCSM 130-66 and the related memoranda from the Secretary of the Military Departments. All of these require more study and review. However, until such studies are completed, you should plan to deploy forces to South Vietnam in accordance with ...Case 1...all necessary actions are to be taken to meet these deployment dates without call-up of reserves or extension of terms of service. Troop movements from Europe will be made only by written approval of Mr. (Cyrus) Vance or myself".

The JCS tried again and submitted another deployment plan to McNamara on 4th April 1966. The end of year strength for 1966 was projected to be 376,350 while the strength at the end of Calendar Year 1967 was to be 438,207.

Seven days later, on the 11th April, McNamara acquiesced and "with the exceptions noted...approved...the deployment plan proposed by the Joint Chiefs of Staff in JCSM 218-66".

Attached to his approval memorandum was a set of tables entitled "April 10 Deployment Plan". These showed planned U. S. strength at the end of December 1966 to be 70 maneuver battalions and 383,500 personnel. Another 9 maneuver battalions would arrive in January 1967 and, by the end of June 1967, total strength

90 Ibid. pp. 34-38.

was scheduled to be 425,000. This plan, called the "10 April Plan" by Systems Analysis and the Secretary of Defense's office, represented the approved version of what the Services called the Deployment Plan for Phase llA(R).[91]

Visceral Feelings

The question of where the numbers for Phases II, IIA, and IIA(R) came from provokes much speculation. It can be hypothesized that, from the outset of the American build-up, some military men felt that winning a meaningful military victory in Vietnam would require something on the order of one million men.

Knowing that this would be unacceptable politically, it may have seemed a better bargaining strategy to ask for increased deployments incrementally. At the outset, the limiting factor on the build-up was the speed with which units could be readied for deployment, and the speed with which logistical support facilities could be provided in Vietnam...

...An alternative explanation is that no one really foresaw what the troop needs in Vietnam would be and that the ability of the enemy to build up their effort was consistently underrated...

...A compromise explanation of the origins of the numbers is that the military may have had a visceral feeling that a large (somewhere above 500,000) number of troops would be needed to win the war but were unable to justify their requirements in terms clear or strong enough to persuade the President, who had an interest in keeping the domestic effects of war as small as possible. [92]

Ground Operations

As far as the actual conduct of ground operations in Vietnam was concerned, the period of time from the 1st May 1965 to 1st November 1965 was spent in building up combat and logistical forces and learning to employ them effectively. This was followed by a period from the 1st November 1965 to 1st May 1966 in which the deployment of U. S. forces was extended toward the frontiers, logistical support was exercised in furnishing support to troops in sustained combat, and commanders were indoctrinated on the techniques of sustained ground combat.[93]

(See Pages 46-48 of this Paper for a list of U.S. Ground Operations begun between January and May 1966.)

91 Ibid. pp. 38-39.

92 Ibid. pp. 40-41.

93 Ibid. p. 46.

Phase IIA(R) becomes Program No. 3

Reflecting the relatively low level of combat and the preoccupation with the build-up of U. S. forces, only minor changes and adjustments to the figures in the plan were made during the two months following the publication of Phase IIA(R).

By June, however, the number of changes had begun to build up. Assistant Secretary Enthoven, in his 10th June 1966 memorandum to Secretary McNamara, reported that there had been "a large number of changes proposed by the Army...This package of deployment adjustments is the result of detailed CONARC studies of unit availability based upon equipment inventories, personnel training outputs, etc. These changes affect virtually every month and type of unit".

...By 30th June, two changes had occurred which brought the totals for December 66 and June 67 to 391,000 and 431,000. These changes were the acceleration of the proposed January 67 deployment of two brigades of the 9th Infantry Division to December 66, and the availability of the 196th Infantry Brigade for deployment in August of 1966. This brigade was originally scheduled for deployment to the Dominican Republic but was diverted to Vietnam. These changes brought the total of U.S. maneuver battalions scheduled to be in Vietnam by the end of 1966 to 79 and the total by June 67 to 82.

The question arises here as to why this revision of the plan became Program No. 3 rather than "change x" to the 10th April Plan. The difference in the December 66 strengths of the 10th April Plan (later retroactively designated Program No. 2), was 7,500, while the difference in the June 1967 strength was 5,900--hardly very large changes.

An explanation may lie in an exchange of memoranda which took place between the 28th June and the 15th July 1966. On the 28th June, President Johnson wrote the following to Secretary McNamara:

> As you know, we have been moving our men to Vietnam on a schedule determined by General Westmoreland's requirements.
>
> As I have stated orally several times this year, I should like this schedule to be accelerated as much as possible so that General Westmoreland can feel assured that he has all the men he needs as soon as possible.
>
> Would you meet with the Joint Chiefs and give me at your early convenience an indication of what acceleration is possible for the balance of this year?

Secretary McNamara passed the question on to the JCS who replied on 8th July that the present revised schedule did meet CINCPAC's requirements of 79 maneuver battalions by December 1966 and that "it appears that no significant acceleration of supportable combat ready forces beyond those indicated will be attained".

McNamara then replied to the President on 15th July that the Department of Defense had been "making strenuous efforts to accelerate deployments". He added:

> I am happy to report that this effort has been successful and we will be able to provide more troops and equipment during the remainder of this calendar year than we had though possible last spring...to illustrate the degree of acceleration already achieved, we now plan to have 79 Army and Marine Corps maneuver battalions in South Vietnam by December 1966...We now expect to have 395,000 personnel in South Vietnam by the end of this year compared to 314,000 estimated last March. [94]

Presidential Ploys

The whole exchange may have a purpose other than simply requesting information or directing acceleration. Presumably the President and McNamara frequently conferred on the conduct of the Vietnam war and there would seem to be little need for such a request or directive to be placed in writing unless it was to act as some sort of record which could be easily pulled out and displayed in order to demonstrate that the President had been sending troops to Vietnam as rapidly as Westmoreland needed them.

This makes sense if it is recalled that, at this particular time, the President was just in the process of publicly turning up the pressure on North Vietnam by ordering the bombing of the POL supplies (Petroleum, Oil, Lubricants etc). This effort to step up the pace in the aftermath of the disruption caused by the Buddhist struggle movement probably also included a desire to increase the pace of the ground war in an effort to convince the DRV that we could and would do whatever was necessary to defeat them in the South.

At the same time, there began to be some comment in the news, particularly by Hanson W. Baldwin of *The New York Times*, that top military men were beginning to feel that the policy of a gradual build-up was becoming outmoded and that what was needed was a sharp increase in the application of force.

94 Ibid. pp. 46, 48-49.

Seen in this context, the exercise of naming the last change to Phase IIA(R), "Program 3", and the exchange of memoranda between the Secretary of Defense and the President can be interpreted as follows:

The President, impatient at being held back by the internal strife in South Vietnam in his effort to convince the North of our will to win the war, was anxious to get on with the war in an attempt to get it over with quickly. The implication, from a writer reputed to have close ties with the Joint Chiefs of Staff, that the military felt that the President was not doing enough, prompted the President to write a memorandum to the Secretary of Defense asking him specifically to see if the JCS could think of some way to accelerate the deployments of ground forces.

When the JCS wrote back that the present plan did meet Westmoreland's requirements and that additional acceleration was unlikely, the President had in effect secured the agreement of his senior military men that he was doing all that was needed and possible.

Illusion of Progress

The ploy of naming the latest change "Program 3"can be seen to have two effects in this effort. First, it gave the illusion of progress. Second, it neatly wrapped up the changes since the beginning of the year, making the very real progress since December readily apparent, but obscuring the fact that most of the increase in the plan had occurred by the 10th April.[95]

Section 6: Forward Planning

A New Concept

On 18th June 1966, even before the Secretary of Defense had published Program No. 3, CINCPAC had submitted his Calendar Year 1966 adjusted requirements and Calendar Year 1967 requirements.

CINCPAC's requirements were based on a new concept for Vietnam. The four basic objectives remained as they had been set forth in CINCPAC's February concept. A new item in the June concept was that US/ FWMAF and RVNAF general reserves and ARVN corps reserve forces would conduct sustained and coordinated operations with increased effort in the Highlands and along the western ARVN border. This was in line with the generally increased emphasis given in the concept to restricting NVA/

95 Ibid. pp. 49-50.

VC forces access to the coastal and land borders of ARVN through effective land, sea, and air interdiction operations.

Enemy Strength

CINCPAC Estimates

During this time, two slightly different estimates of enemy strength were available. The figures used by CINCPAC in their 18th June submission were 125 confirmed, 7 probable, and 18 possible battalions in South Vietnam. It was estimated that the enemy was capable of infiltrating up to 15 battalion equivalents (9,000 personnel) per month into South Vietnam unless denied the capability to do so. It was also estimated that the enemy could train 7 VC battalion equivalents (3,500 personnel) per month under the current existing situation.

However, the best estimate of his intentions was that he would attempt to reinforce at the rate of 18.5 battalion equivalents (11.5 NVA, and 7 VC) per month, which would give him a maximum build-up total of 180 battalion equivalents by March 1967, at which time losses would exceed inputs and total VC strength would begin to decline.

National Intelligence Estimates

The estimate of VC strength given in National Intelligence Estimate of 14th March 1966 was as follows:

The total Communist force in South Vietnam was estimated to be between 260,000 and 280, 000. The major combat elements included some 38,000 North Vietnamese troops, approximately 63,000 regular main and local forces and from 100-200,000 guerrillas. The North was estimated to have a capability to infiltrate from 75,000 to 100, 000 individual replacements but present evidence suggested that the probable infiltration would be between 55,000 and 75,000. The estimate of VC recruiting in the South was from 1,000 to 10, 000 a month. A projection of strength for end of 1966 was 125, 000 in the Communist regular forces, but this could grow by the end of 1967 to over 250,000.

The estimated strength for the 1st January 1967, in terms of battalions, was between 170 and 190.

1967 Requirements

The requirements for 1966 had been adjusted to 474,786 bringing the year-end totals for 1966 and 1967 to 395,269 and 436,406 respectively although the maneuver battalion strength remained at 79 U.S. battalions.

The requirements for Calendar Year 1967 were basically considered to be "rounding out forces". This force package basically consisted of 5 tactical strike squadrons;

11 U.S. maneuver battalions of infantry/armored cavalry/tank configuration; a 4th rifle company for each of the 61 U.S. infantry battalions; 7 Free World Military Assistance Forces (FWMAF) battalions, 6 of which were to round out the Republic of Korea (ROK) Marine Brigade to a Division; and 1 additional battalion for the Australian Task Force to round it out to a full regiment. After all of the deployments recommended in the plan were carried out, the strength of U.S. forces in Vietnam would be 90 maneuver battalions and 542,588 personnel.

Force Additions Valid

CINCPAC's requirements were forwarded to the Secretary of Defense by the Joint Chiefs in JCSM 506-66 on 5th August. The Memorandum noted that the JCS felt that, with few exceptions, the requirements and proposed force additions were valid, and that a capabilities planning conference was scheduled for early October to "correlate this planning into a comprehensive program".[96]

McNamara Questions Force Numbers

On the same day, 5th August 1966, Secretary McNamara sent a Memorandum to the Joint Chiefs of Staff directing a review of CINCPAC's adjusted requirements for the Calendar Year 1966 and requirements for the Calendar Year 1967:

> As you know, it is our policy to provide the troops, weapons, and supplies requested by General Westmoreland at the times he desires them, to the greatest possible degree. The latest revised CINCPAC requirements, submitted on 18th June 1966, are to be accorded the same consideration…nevertheless I desire and expect a detailed line-by-line analysis of these requirements to determine that each is truly essential to the carrying out of our war plan. We must send to Vietnam what is needed, but only what is needed. Excessive deployments weaken our ability to win by undermining the economic structure of South Vietnam and by raising doubts concerning the soundness of our planning.
>
> In the course of your review of the validity of the requirements, I would like you to consider the attached Deployment Issue Papers which were prepared by my staff. While there may be sound reasons for deploying the units questioned, the issues raised in these papers merit your detailed attention and specific reply. They probably do not cover all questionable units, particularly for proposed deployments for the PACOM area outside of South Vietnam. I expect that you will want to query CINCPAC about these and other units for which you desire clarification.

96 Ibid. pp. 52-53.

> I appreciate the time required to verify the requirements and determine our capability to meet them, but decisions must be made on a timely basis if units are to be readied and equipment and supplies procured. Therefore I would appreciate having your recommended deployment plan, including your comments on each of the Deployment Issue Papers, no later than 15th September 1965.

The items questioned in the Issue Papers totalled approximately 70,000 troops with artillery and air defense providing the two largest single items

Westmorland Justifies Force Numbers

While the JCS were beginning their review of the items questioned by the Secretary of Defense, they attempted to secure a "quick fix" in the form of a 10th August 1966 message from General Westmoreland who evaluated the 1966 and 1967 force requirements as follows:

> ... Continuous study of the situation indicates that past and current developments reinforce my appraisal of the war on which the Calendar Year 66-67 force requirements were based. There are no indications that the enemy has reduced his resolve. He has increased his rate of infiltration, formed Division size units, introduced new weapons into his ranks, maintained lines of communications leading into South Vietnam, increased his use of Cambodia as a safe-haven, and recently moved a combat division through the DMZ.
>
> These and other facts support earlier predictions and suggest that the enemy intends to continue a protracted war of attrition, potentially escalating with increased infiltration of enemy troops and supplies from North Vietnam (NVN). The war can continue to escalate. Infiltration of enemy troops and supplies from NVN can increase and there is no assurance that this will not occur.
>
> I recognize the possibility that the enemy may not continue to follow the pattern of infiltration as projected. Accordingly, my staff is currently conducting a number of studies with the objective of placing this command and the RVN in a posture that will permit us to retain the initiative regardless of the course the enemy chooses to pursue
>
> ...The CINCPAC submission establishes and justifies minimal force requirements, emphasizing the requirement for a well balanced, sustainable force in South Vietnam for an indefinite period. Consequently, at this point in time I cannot justify a reduction in the requirements submitted.[97]

97 Ibid. pp. 53-55.

Emphasis on Pacification

In the meantime, other things were happening which would have a significant effect on U.S. strategy in Vietnam and force requirements for supporting that strategy. First of these was the growing emphasis on pacification. A few of the highlights and their implications for U.S. force requirements may be useful.

Although the war between U.S. and enemy battalions progressed satisfactorily during the spring and early summer of 1966, it became increasingly apparent that the pacification effort was not keeping pace. Both Ambassador Lodge and General Westmoreland turned their attention increasingly towards the problem of pacification.

On 3rd August, Ambassador Lodge in his weekly report to the President mentioned that he "conferred with General Westmoreland about the Vietnamese Regular Army--the ARVN--contributing more to pacification He agrees on the urgent desirability of hitting pacification hard at this time when other things are going quite well". [98]

What is "Winning"?

A Smell of Victory?

By the 10th August 1966, Lodge was putting even more emphasis upon the pacification effort. His 10th August weekly report to the President gives an indication of the present atmosphere in Saigon and opened with the following:

> In the struggle of the independence of Vietnam, the following can be said: we are not losing; we cannot lose in the normal sense of the word; never have things been going better; indeed, never have things been going so well. We are "on the track" with regard to almost every aspect of the war and we are winning in several...but all of this is still not called "victory".
>
> Indeed, however much they disagree about many things everyone—in Washington and Hanoi and in Saigon—seems to agree that what we have now is not victory. In truth we do not need to define "victory" and then go ahead and achieve it 100%. If it becomes generally believed that we are sure to win (just as it is now generally believed that we cannot lose) all else would be a mopping up. If there is the "smell of victory" we will be coasting.

98 Ibid. pp. 55-56.

A Psychological Victory?

Lodge followed up by listing a number of things which would psychologically mean "victory". Among these were "smashing results" in the criminal war of terrorism, subversion and local guerrilla action; movement towards constitutional democracy; spectacular success in the Chieu Hoi program (see Note); and the opening of the roads in Vietnam. Lodge estimated that none of these things were "just around the corner". Therefore, it seemed to him that we had quite a stretch of time ahead of us.

A Military Victory?

His questions then were: "Could we shorten the time? Should we shorten the time? and if so, How"? It was Lodge's judgment that a quick victory as the result of a relatively big, fast offensive might be easier to obtain than a victory achieved through a relatively moderate , slow offensive. He observed that:

> ... Maybe the Vietnamese can last indefinitely although it may be dangerous to assume it. But certainly it would be helped by a quick end to the war, assuming always that a satisfactory outcome was achieved. At present, U.S. military forces must help the Vietnamese actively in order to get the Vietnamese pacification effort moving, let alone the war against the big units. (See Chapter Fifty-Five: *Programmed to Fail*)
>
> We have high hopes that eventually they can undertake it all themselves and our soldiers have already expressed appreciation for the newly created Vietnamese political action teams and have recognized that they render the kind of service no American can render. Nonetheless, our help is at present as indispensable in the field of criminal-terrorist war as it is on the purely military side .

To back up his feeling that now was the time for a big push, he quoted General Eisenhower's saying that if you desire to conquer one well-readied, organized and entrenched battalion with two battalions, you may succeed, but it will take a long time and many casualties. However, if you use a Division, you will do the job quickly and the losses will be slight. [99]

(See Pages 57-63 of this Paper for Pacification Programs; Rural Development Strategies; Westmoreland's strategy for the period 1st November 1966 to 1st May 1967; and U.S. Combat Operations from May to August 1966.)

99 Ibid. pp. 56-57.

Notes

The Chieu Hoi amnesty program was an initiative by the U.S. and South Vietnam to encourage defection by the People's Army of Vietnam (PAVN) soldiers and Viet Cong (VC) guerillas and their supporters to the side of South Vietnam.

On 27th June 1963, President Kennedy had appointed Henry Cabot Lodge Jnr. as his Ambassador to South Vietnam. Lodge had resigned as Ambassador on the 28th June 1964 and was succeeded by General Maxwell Taylor who served as Ambassador from 14th July 1964 to 30th July 1965. Lodge took up a second appointment as Ambassador to South Vietnam from 31st July 1965 to 25th April 1967.

(See also Chapter Fifty-Five: *Programmed to Fail* for Pacification Programs)

Section 8: Infiltration Increasing

In August 1966, military operations south of the DMZ and along the Cambodian border had indicated to COMUSMACV (Westmorland) that infiltration was increasing from sanctuaries outside the boundaries of South Vietnam. The most pressing of these infiltration routes appeared to be the one through the DMZ.

On 8th August, Ambassador Lodge sent a message to the Department of State:

> The recent upsurge of enemy infiltration through the DMZ is causing a complete re-evaluation of Allied military posture around the DMZ. If, as is strongly indicated, the enemy has made the decision to increase the tempo of his operations through the DMZ, additional steps must be taken to block that approach effectively.

KANZUS

Ambassador Lodge quoted General Westmoreland as advancing the suggestion, with which he agreed, that there might be merit in giving these measures the greatest possible international flavor by constituting a multi-national organization to help block enemy infiltration through the DMZ:

> The organization would be known as the KANZUS Force from its national components: Korean, Australian, New Zealand, and US. As presently visualized, the organization would be brigade size, with 2 U.S. Marine battalions and 1 ROK battalion as the combat elements. Individual battalions would retain their national identity. Formation of the command headquarters supporting structure would provide a place for incorporating token remaining national contributions

from Australia and New Zealand and others such as the Philippines, should this become suitable.

> ...The organization, commanded by a United States Marine Corps officer, possibly a brigadier general, would operate in the U.S. tactical chain of command in close coordination with and in support of the ARVN.

Ambassador Lodge foresaw that:

> The establishment of such a force might eventually provide us with a basis for suggesting the presence of an international force of different composition under U.N. or Asian regional sponsorship which could inherit the anti-infiltration role of KANZUS. An eventual successor would function obviously as a political and psychological *cordon sanitaire* and not, of course, as a military Maginot Line. However, a physical barrier is a possible future development.

The KANZUS suggestion was only the first of a series of ideas proposed by various people and agencies to limit infiltration through the DMZ. [100]

Section 9: Infiltration Warfare

Chemical

On 10th August 1966, in a message for Admiral Sharp (Commander in Chief, U.S. Pacific Command) and General Wheeler, General Westmoreland had pointed out that:

> The enemy has increased his rate of infiltration, formed division-size units, introduced new weapons into his ranks, maintained lines of communication into South Vietnam, increased his use of Cambodia as a safe haven, and recently moved a combat division through the Demilitarised Zone (DMZ).

On 16th August, Ambassador Lodge forwarded to the Secretary of State General Westmoreland's proposal that:

> We consider defoliation of the southern portion of the DMZ as a possible means to prevent enemy infiltration through that area...in the event defoliation of the DMZ is not acceptable, Military Assistance Command (MACV) staff has drawn up an alternate plan which would call for defoliation of a large area just south of DMZ running east from Laos border to the fringe of coastal

100 Ibid. pp. 63-64.

> lowlands. Target would be sufficiently south to insure against accidental spread into the DMZ itself. I see no serious political objections.

Note

The U.S. military's first major aerial spraying operation, *Operation Ranch Hand*, had commenced in early 1962. By the time the operation ended nine years later, some 18 million gallons of chemicals had been sprayed on an estimated 20 percent of South Vietnam's jungles and 36 percent of its mangrove forests.

Anti-Personnel

On 7th September 1966, the Joint Chiefs of Staff sent to CINCPAC, with an information copy to COMUSMACV, a proposal on an air supported anti-infiltration barrier system specifically designed against the North Vietnamese infiltration system through Laos which might be obtainable in about a year after the decision was made to go ahead.

The barrier would have two somewhat different parts, one designed for foot traffic and one against vehicles.

> The anti-troop infiltration system, which would also function against supply porters, would operate as follows: There would be a constantly renewed minefield of nonsterilizing Gravel (and possibly button bomblets) distributed in patterns covering interconnected valleys and slopes over the entire barrier region...
>
> There would also be a pattern of acoustic detectors to locate mine explosions indicating an attempted penetration. The minefield is intended to deny opening of alternate routes for troop infiltrators and should be emplaced first.
>
> On the trails currently being used from which mines may, we tentatively assume, be cleared without great difficulty, a more dense pattern of sensors would be designed to locate groups of infiltrators. Air strikes using Gravel mines and SADEYES (cluster bombs) would then be called against these targets. The sensor patterns would be monitored 24 hours a day by patrol aircraft. The struck area would be reseeded with new mines.
>
> The anti-vehicle system would consist of acoustic detectors distributed every mile or so along all truckable roads in the interdicted area, monitored 24 hours a day by patrol aircraft with vectored strike aircraft using SADEYES to respond to signals that trucks or truck convoys are moving. [101]

101 Ibid. pp. 64-65.

Doubtful Impact

On the 13th September 1966, CINCPAC (Admiral Sharp) responded to the JCS proposal of the 7th September. Although CINCPAC conceded that "any measure which will effectively impede, disrupt flow of men and materiel from North Vietnam into South Vietnam merited consideration", their judgment was that even "if we were to invest the time, effort and resources in a barrier project, it is doubtful that it would improve the U.S. position in South Vietnam".

CINCPAC expressed doubt whether the barrier suggested would impede infiltration. He contended that a barrier system must be tended; if not, it could be breached with ease, while the flow of men and materiel to the VC/NVA continued. An aerial delivered obstacle would not be expected to supplant the need for soldiers on the ground, and the time, effort and resources of men and materiel required to establish a ground barrier would be tremendous. Also, he expressed his misgivings over the reliability and practicality of the electronic and other type gadgetry which would be in the barrier.

Unfortunately, all of these ideas for halting or slowing the infiltration through the DMZ were to become effective sometime in the future. General Westmoreland's problem was very much in the present.

Send in the B-52's

On 13th September, Westmorland sent Admiral Sharp a message laying out what he considered to be the nature of the threat posed by the enemy sanctuaries, in this case, the Demilitarized Zone and North Vietnam immediately above the DMZ, and his assessment that the enemy is developing an offensive as opposed to a defensive posture. He concluded by saying:

> The success of our efforts in coping with enemy initiatives has been based upon spoiling attacks by ground and air forces to disrupt the plans before he is capable of completing preparations for attack. He has thus been kept off balance from mounting a successful offensive.
>
> It now would appear, however, that because of our approach the enemy is employing a new tactic entailing use of sanctuaries in the DMZ and north thereof in an effort to prevent spoiling attacks. Since we are unable to exercise the initiative in moving ground forces into the DMZ or NVN, we are left with fire power alone as the instrument for attack.
>
> I consider it imperative in this regard that we utilize aerial-delivered fire power and naval gun fire in this situation if we are to thwart the enemy's pending offensive as discussed above.

He concluded by requesting employment of B-52's against the North Vietnamese forces infiltrating through the DMZ. [102]

Slam The Enemy

Seek, Locate, Annihilate, Monitor

On 16th September 1966, General Westmoreland sent a message to Admiral Sharp (CINCPAC) in which he presented his concept for handling infiltration through the Laotian panhandle. As General Westmoreland put it, "with the arrival of the North East monsoon season, weather in Laotian panhandle will be clearing and the enemy is expected to infiltrate personnel and supporting materiel in quantity through that area":

> The requirement to carry this threat is evident. If allowed to go unchecked, it will permit the enemy to engage our flank in Quang Tri Province (DMZ area) from the west and will permit large-scale diversionary attacks further south. The seriousness of this thrust led us to development of a new concept to block, deny, spoil and disrupt the infiltration of enemy personnel and supplies through Laos during the forthcoming dry season.

The concept hinged upon two basic principles:

- First, we will intensify around-the-clock surveillance and interdiction of known infiltration routes. This process will stress attack of selected interdiction points as well as strikes against targets of opportunity;
- Second, we will concentrate our resources on successive key target areas to be known as 'slams'.

Once an area was designated as a 'slam' it would be hit with B-52 and Tactical Air Strikes to neutralise it. This action would be followed by visual and photo air reconnaissance and/or ground reconnaissance patrols and, if appropriate, exploitation forces. Upon their withdrawal they would leave mines and booby traps, and the Air Force would follow with air delivered land mines.

In special instances, General Westmoreland planned to leave stay-behind reconnaissance parties. The term 'slam' itself came from 'seek, locate, annihilate, and monitor'.

102 Ibid. pp. 66-67.

Contain The Enemy

On 20th September 1966, General Westmoreland followed this up with yet another message to Admiral Sharp which read in part:

> The threat to South Vietnam of large enemy forces in the sanctuaries of Laos, Cambodia and North Vietnam has now clearly emerged and is of increasing concern to me. Particularly vulnerable to enemy attacks from these sanctuaries are the Special Forces Camps of Khe Sanh, Duc Co, Du Dop, Loc Ninh and Song Be. We are therefore compelled to seek ways of containing the enemy forces in their sanctuaries and preventing a major ingress of these forces in South Vietnam.
>
> The problem is now under active study by my staff. Redeployment of available forces to counter this threat may be necessary and could seriously jeopardize other important undertakings. Moreover, additional forces already requested may not be sufficient to contain the enemy forces in their sanctuaries and still accomplish other essential tasks. Studies are now underway to determine what additional forces will be required.[103]

Section 10: Military Posture Problems

Suggested Force Additions

On 21st September 1966, the Joint Chiefs forwarded their completed review of CINCPAC's (Admiral Sharp) 18th June requirements for the Calendar Years 1966 and 1967 and their answers to the issue papers which the Secretary of Defense had given them on the 5th August. This document was reviewed by Dr. Enthoven's office and, on 29th September, he sent a memorandum to the Secretary of Defense.

He reported that deletions of requirements by CINCPAC and the JCS totaled 49,000 personnel of the 215,000 add-on requirements for U.S. forces in Pacific Area Command (excluding Hawaii). Of the deletions, 39,000 were included in the issue papers. He added that his South East Asia Programs Division was in the process of analyzing the detailed rationale for the remaining requested units and that new deployment issue papers would be provided to the Secretary of Defense for his approval on 3rd October.

Apparently, the Secretary of Defense approved them for on the 6th October he forwarded another set of deployment issue papers to the Chairman of the Joint

103 Ibid.pp. 67-68.

Chiefs of Staff asking that they review the issues and have their recommendations for him by 1st November when he planned to make his decision on the papers. The items considered in the issue papers totaled some 54,000 troops out of CINCPAC's total request of 569,000 for deployment to South Vietnam.

By this time, Secretary McNamara had already decided to make a trip to Saigon to see if he could get a better feel for the situation there. However, before he departed, the Joint Chiefs of Staff forwarded to him a paper analyzing the world-wide military posture of the United States in light of the August CINCPAC requirements study for Calendar Year 1967.

Military Shortfalls

Assuming that there would be no call-up of reserves, no change in rotation policies, and that resources for the proposed deployments would be obtained from the world-wide military structure, the impact of meeting the CINCPAC 1967 requirements, as the JCS saw it, would be tremendous.

Army

The Army would suffer most, meeting the CINCPAC requirements (12 additional maneuver battalions) on the average six to eight months late, and in the process emasculating Army forces stationed in the Continental U.S.A. and the Strategic Army Reserve, leaving it but two airborne brigade forces for 1967 and the first part of 1968.

Other NATO reinforcing division forces could not be ready from the Army until late 1968. United States Army Europe, United States Army Alaska and Pacific Area Command reserve would all be at a reduced level because of "qualitative personnel withdrawals". In total, the Army would have a force deficiency of three and two-thirds active division forces if it were to satisfy strategic reserve and sustaining base requirements.

Air Force

Carrier pilots would remain the major Naval shortage. The Air Force, upon completion of the required deployments (in September of 1967) "would not have the capability to deploy rapidly any combat-ready tactical fighter forces". With one exception, all tactical and reconnaissance units in the United States were assigned and executing training tasks. To meet CINCPAC requirements would require drawing down from 21 Tactical Fighter Squadrons (486 aircraft) in Europe to 13 squadrons or 288 aircraft. Given all Air Force commitments and responsibilities to respond to NATO and provide other reinforcements, a short-fall of some 22 Tactical Fighter

Squadrons (445 aircraft), 5 Tactical Reconnaisance Squadrons (90 aircraft) and 4 Tactical Control Squadrons (64 aircraft) would result.

...In conclusion, the Services cannot fully respond to CINCPAC's Calendar Year 1966 (adjusted) and Calendar Year 1967 force requirements on the time schedule he has prescribed... Providing the preponderance of his requirements, even on a delayed schedule, would further impair the US military posture and capability to maintain forward deployments to deter aggression world-wide...[104]

Section 11: The Prognosis is Bad

On 14th October 1966, upon his return from Vietnam, Secretary McNamara submitted a Memorandum to President Johnson (emphasis in original):

> In the report of my last trip to Vietnam almost a year ago, I stated that the odds were about even that, even with the then-recommended deployments, we would be faced in early 1967 with a military stand-off at a much higher level of conflict and with "pacification" still stalled. I am a little less pessimistic now in one respect. We have done somewhat better militarily than I anticipated. We have by and large blunted the Communist military initiative--any military victory in South Vietnam the Viet Cong may have had in mind 18 months ago has been thwarted by our emergency deployments and actions. And our program of bombing the North has exacted a price.
>
> My concern continues, however, in other respects. **This is because I see no reasonable way to bring the war to an end soon.** Enemy morale has not broken--he apparently has adjusted to our stopping his drive for military victory and has adopted a strategy of keeping us busy and waiting us out (a strategy of attriting our national will). He knows that we have not been, and he believes we probably will not be, able to translate our military successes into the "end products"--broken enemy morale and political achievements by the GVN.
>
> **The one thing going for us in Vietnam over the past year has been the large number of enemy killed-in-action resulting from the big military operations.** Allowing for the possible exaggeration in reports, the enemy must be taking losses--deaths in and after battle-- at the rate of more than 60,000 a year. The infiltration routes would seem to be one-way trails to death for the North Vietnamese. **Yet there is no sign of an impending break in enemy morale and it**

104 Ibid. pp. 79-80.

appears he can more than replace his losses by infiltration from North Vietnam and recruitment in South Vietnam.

Pacification is a bad disappointment. We have good grounds to be pleased by the recent elections, by (Marshal) Ky's 16 months in power, and by the faint signs of development of national institutions and of legitimate civilian government. But none of this has translated itself into political achievements at Province level or below. **Pacification has, if anything, gone backwards.** As compared with two, or four, years ago, enemy full time regional forces and part-time guerilla forces are larger; terrorism and sabotage have increased in scope and intensity; more railroads are closed and highways cut; the rice crop expected to come to market is smaller; we control little, if any, more of the population; the VC political infrastructure thrives in most of the country, continuing to give the enemy his enormous intelligence advantage; full security exists nowhere (not even behind the US Marines' lines and in Saigon); in the countryside, the enemy almost completely controls the night.

Nor has the *Rolling Thunder* program of bombing the North either significantly affected infiltration of cracked the morale of the enemy. There is agreement in the intelligence community on these facts.

In essence, we find ourselves--from the point of view of the important war (the complicity of the people)--no better and, if anything, worse off. This important war must be fought and won by the Vietnamese themselves. We have known this from the beginning. But the discouraging truth is that, as was the case in 1961, and 1963, and 1965, we have found not found the formula, the catalyst, for training and inspiring them into effective action.

Recommended Actions

In such an unpromising state of affairs, what should we do? We must continue to press the enemy militarily; we must make demonstrable progress in pacification; at the same time, we must add a new ingredient forced on us by the facts. Specifically, we must improve our position by getting ourselves into a military posture that we credibly could maintain indefinitely--a posture that makes trying to "wait us out" less attractive. I recommend a five-pronged course of action to achieve those ends.

Stabilise U.S. Force Levels in Vietnam

It is my judgment that, barring a dramatic change in the war, we should limit the increase in U.S. forces in South Vietnam (SVN) in 1967 to 10,000 men and we should level off at the total of 470,000 which such an increase would provide. I believe also that even many more than 470,000 would not kill the enemy off in such numbers as to break their morale so long as they think they can wait us out. It is possible that such a 40 percent increase over our present level of 325,000 will break the enemy's morale in the short term; but if it does not, we must, I believe, be prepared for and have underway a long-term program premised on more than breaking the morale of main force units.

A stabilized U.S. force level would be part of such a long-term program. It would put us in a position where negotiations would be more likely to be productive but, if they were not, we could pursue the all-important pacification task with proper attention and resources and without the spectre of apparently **endless escalation of US deployments.**

Install a Barrier

A portion of the 470,000 troops--perhaps 10,000 or 20,000--should be devoted to the construction and maintenance of an infiltration barrier. Such a barrier would lie near the 17th parallel, would run from the sea, across the neck of South Vietnam (choking off the infiltration routes near the DMZ) and across the trails in Laos.

This interdiction system (at an approximate cost of $1 billion) would comprise to the east a ground barrier of fences, wire, sensors, artillery, aircraft and mobile troops, and to the west--mainly in Laos--an interdiction zone covered by air-laid mines and bombing attacks pin-pointed by air-laid acoustic sensors.

The barrier may not be fully effective at first, but I believe that it can be made effective in time and that even the threat of its becoming effective can substantially change to our advantage the character of the war.

It would hinder enemy efforts, would permit more efficient use of the limited number of friendly troops, and would be persuasive evidence both that our sole aim is to protect the South from the North and that we intend to see the job through. (Admiral Sharp has recommended a 31st December 1967 strength of 570,000. However, I believe both he and General Westmorland recognise that the danger of inflation will probably force an end of 1967 deployment limit of about 470,000.)

Stabilise Rolling Thunder

Attack sorties in North Vietnam have risen from about 4,000 per month at the end of last year to 6,000 per month in the first quarter of this year and 12,000 per month at present. Most of our 50 percent increase of deployed attack-capable aircraft has been absorbed in the attacks on North Vietnam. In North Vietnam, almost 84,000 attack sorties have been flown, (about 25 percent against fixed targets), 45 percent during the past seven months.

...Despite these efforts, it now appears that the North Vietnamese-Laotian road network (the Ho Chi Minh Trail) will remain adequate to meet the requirements of the Communist forces in South Vietnam--this is so even if its capacity could be reduced by one-third and if combat activities were to be doubled.

...Furthermore, it is clear that to bomb the North sufficiently to make a radical impact upon Hanoi's political, economic and social structure, would require **an effort which we could make but which would not be stomached either by our own people or by world opinion**; and it would involve a serious risk of drawing us into open war with China.

The North Vietnamese are paying a price. They have been forced to assign some 300,000 personnel to the lines of communication in order to maintain the critical flow of personnel and materiel to the South. Now that the lines of communication have been manned however, it is doubtful that either a large increase or decrease in our interdiction sorties could substantially change the cost to the enemy of maintaining the roads, railroads, and waterways or affect whether they are operational. It follows that the marginal sorties--probably the marginal 1,000 or even 5,000 sorties--per month against the lines of communication no longer have a significant impact on the war.

When this marginal inutility of added sorties against North Vietnam and Laos is compared with the crew and aircraft losses implicit in the activity (four men and aircraft and $20 million per 1,000 sorties), I recommend, as minimum, against increasing the level of bombing of North Vietnam and against increasing the intensity of operations by changing the areas or kinds of targets struck...

Pursue Vigorous Pacification

The Pacification (Revolutionary Development) program had been and is thoroughly stalled. The large-unit operations war, which we know best how to fight and where we have had our successes, is largely irrelevant to pacification, as long as we do not lose it. By and large, the people in rural areas believe that when the Government of South Vietnam (GVN) comes, it will not stay but the Viet Cong will; that cooperation with the GVN will be punished by the Viet Cong; that the GVN is really indifferent to the people's welfare; that the low-level GVN are tools of the local rich; and that the GVN is riddled with corruption.

Success in pacification depends on the interrelated functions of providing physical security, destroying the Viet Cong apparatus, motivating the people to cooperate and establishing responsive local government.

An obviously necessary but not sufficient requirement for success of the Revolutionary Development cadre and police are vigorously conducted and adequately prolonged clearing operations by military troops who will "stay" in the area, who will behave themselves decently, and who will show some respect for the people. This elemental requirement of pacification has been missing.

Now that the threat of a Communist main-force military victory has been thwarted by our emergency efforts, we must allocate far more attention and a portion of the regular military forces (at least half of the ARVN and perhaps a portion of the U.S. forces) to the task of providing an active and permanent security screen behind which the Revolutionary Development teams and police can operate and behind which the political struggle with the VC infrastructure can take place.

The U.S. cannot do this pacification security job for the Vietnamese. All we can do is "massage the heart". For one reason, it is known that we do not intend to stay; if our efforts worked at all, it would merely postpone the eventual confrontation of the VC and GVN infrastructures. The GVN must do the job; and I am convinced that drastic reform is needed if the GVN is going to be able to do it... (See also Chapter Fifty-Five: *Programmed to Fail* for Pacification Progams)

Press for Negotiations

Secretary McNamara was not optimistic that Hanoi or the Viet Cong would respond to peace overtures as the ends sought by the two sides appeared to be irreconcilable. The Secretary suggested the following steps which may increase the prospects for success:

- Increase the credibility of our peace gestures in the minds of the enemy. There is considerable evidence both in private statements by the Communists and in the reports of competent western officials who have talked with them that charges of U.S. bad faith are not solely propagandistic, but reflect deeply held beliefs. Analyses of Communists' statements and actions indicate that they firmly believe that American leadership really does not want the fighting to stop, and that we are intent on winning a military victory in Vietnam and on maintaining our presence there through a puppet regime supported by U.S. military bases;

- As a way of projecting U.S. bona fides, I believe that we should consider two possibilities with respect to our bombing operations against the North, to be undertaken, if at all, at a time very carefully selected with a view to maximising the chances of influencing the enemy and world opinion and to minimising the chances that failure would strengthen the hand of the "hawks" at home. First, without fanfare, conditions, or avowal, whether the stand-down was permanent or temporary, stop bombing all of North Vietnam. It is generally thought that Hanoi will not agree to negotiations until they can claim that the bombing has stopped unconditionally. We should see what develops, retaining freedom to resume the bombing if nothing useful was forthcoming. Alternatively, we could shift the weight of effort away from zones including Hanoi and Haiphong and areas north of those two cities to the Chinese border. This alternative has some attraction in that it provides the North Vietnamese a "face saver" if only problems of "face" are holding up Hanoi peace gestures. It would narrow the bombing down directly to the objectionable infiltration and it would reduce the international heat on the U.S. Here, too, bombing of the Northeast could resume at any time, or "spot" attacks could be made there from time to time to keep North Vietnam off balance and to require her to pay the full cost of maintaining her repair crews in place. The diverted sorties could be concentrated in the infiltration routes in the southern end of North Vietnam, in Laos, and in South Vietnam. To the same end of improving our credibility, we should seek ways--through words and deeds--to make believable our intention to withdraw our forces once the North Vietnamese aggression against the South stops. In particular, we should avoid any implication that we will stay in South Vietnam with bases or to guarantee any particular outcome to a solely South Vietnamese struggle;

- Try to split the VC off from Hanoi. The intelligence estimate is that the evidence is overwhelming that the North Vietnamese dominate and control the National Liberation Front and the Viet Cong. Nevertheless, I think we should continue and enlarge efforts to contact the VC/NLF and to probe ways to split members or sections off the VC/NLF organisation;

- Press contacts with North Vietnam, the Soviet Union and other parties who might contribute towards a settlement;

- Develop a realistic plan providing a role for the VC in negotiations, post-war life, and government of the nation. An amnesty offer and proposals for national reconciliation would be steps in the right direction and should be part of the plan. It is "important that this plan be one which will appear reasonable, if not at first to Hanoi and the VC, at least to world opinion".

Gird Up Our Loins

McNamara concluded his lengthy Presidential Memorandum of 14th October 1966 with a sombre prognosis:

> **The prognosis is bad that the war can be brought to a satisfactory conclusion within the next two years.** The large-unit operations probably will not do it; negotiations probably will not do it. **While we should continue to pursue both these routes in trying for a solution in the short run, we should realize that success from them is a mere possibility, not a probability.**
>
> **The solution lies in girding, openly, for a longer war and in taking actions immediately which will, in 12 to 18 months, give clear evidence that the continuing costs and risks to the American people are acceptably limited, that the formula for success has been found, and that the end of the war is merely a matter of time.**
>
> All of my recommendations will contribute to this strategy but the one most difficult to implement is perhaps the most important one--enlivening the pacification program. The odds are less than even for this task, if only because we have failed consistently since 1961 to make a dent in the problem. But, because the 1967 trend of pacification will, I believe, be the main talisman of ultimate U.S. success or failure in Vietnam, extraordinary imagination and effort should go into changing the stripes of that problem...

Success a Mere Possibility

In this Memorandum, McNamara reveals with striking clarity that many of the premises under which the war to that point had been fought (and manned) were shifting.

He agreed with COMUSMACV that the military situation has gone "somewhat better in 1966 than anticipated", but he found little cause for optimism in the longer run. In fact, he seemed almost disheartened as he noted that there was "no reasonable way to bring the war to an end soon". Finding an injured but undismayed opponent committed now to "waiting us out" while sapping our national will and seeing "pacification a basic disappointment...no better, and if anything worse off..." hardly was the kind of progress he hoped for.

It was a somber conclusion to a resounding new emphasis in American strategic thought. He believed that there was no great probability of success lurking on any of his recommended actions, only a "mere possibility".

The solution in his eyes, was to gird openly for a longer war... and in taking actions immediately which will in 12 to 18 months give clear evidence that the continuing costs and risks to the American people are acceptably limited, that the formula for success has been found, and that the end of the war is merely a matter of time...

The Bell Tolls

In a sense, the Presidential Memorandum of 14th October 1966 was a clear "no" to MACV, CINCPAC and JCS proposals for expanded bombing and major ground force increases, but it was a negative with a difference. It provided alternatives.

From this time on, the judgment of the military as to how the war should be fought and what was needed would be subject to question. New estimates of what was needed in Vietnam would have to be calculated in light of new objectives and new criteria for success, as well as new assumptions about "winning". The warning had rung and unless dramatic outcomes measured in time and political advantage could be promised, additional force increases promised to be sticky indeed.[105]

Note

The Pacification (Revolutionary Development) Program was a South Vietnamese government initiative, supported by the United States through the Civil Operations and Revolutionary Development Support (CORDS) organization, aimed at winning the support of the rural population by providing security and social/economic development, thereby attempting to undermine the Viet Cong's political infrastructure. (See also Chapter Fifty-Five: *Programmed to Fail.*)

Section 12: Rapid Response Team

The Joint Chiefs reaction to the Presidential Memorandum of 14 October 1966 was predictably rapid—and violent. The Chiefs expressed their agreement with McNamara's basic evaluation of a long war, but disagreed on his guarded assessment of the military situation which, in their eyes, had "improved substantially over the past year".

105 Ibid. pp. 81-93.

They were especially concerned that the Memorandum did not take into account the adverse impact over time of continued bloody defeats on the morale of the VC/NVA forces and the determination of their political and military leaders.

However, they noted that the 470,000-man figure was "substantially less" than earlier recommendations of COMUSMACV (Westmorland) and CINCPAC (Admiral Sharp) and they wished to " reserve judgment" until they reviewed the revised programs being prepared during the CINCPAC planning conference.

Bombing is indispensable

The disagreement was less veiled on the bombing:

> ...The Joint Chiefs of Staff do not concur in your recommendation that there should be no increase in level of bombing effort and no modification in areas, and targets subject to air attack. They believe our air campaign against North Vietnam (NVN) to be an integral and indispensable part of our overall war effort. To be effective, the air campaign should be conducted with only those minimum constraints necessary to avoid indiscriminate killing of population.

A Trump Card

Nor did they find the new organisational arrangements for pacification especially appetising:

> The Joint Chiefs of Staff informed you earlier that to achieve early optimum effectiveness, the pacification program should be transferred to COMUSMACV (Westmorland). They adhere to that conclusion. However, if for political reasons a civilian-style organisation should be considered mandatory by the President, they would interpose no objection. Nevertheless, they are not sanguine that an effective civilian-type organization can be erected, if at all, except at the expense of costly delays .
>
> As to the use of a substantial fraction of the ARVN for pacification purposes, the Joint Chiefs of Staff concur. However, they desire to flag that adoption of this concept will undoubtedly elicit charges of a U.S. takeover of combat operations at increased cost in American casualties.

Finally, they did not share the Secretary's views on how to induce negotiations. They believed the bombing was one "trump card" in the President's hand and should not be surrendered without an equivalent *quid pro quo*, such as "an end to the NVN aggression in SVN". The essence of disagreement here centered around what each party, Secretary of Defense and JCS felt was adequate return for a "trump", the JCS believing that as the military campaign wore on with "increasing success, the value of the trump would become apparent".

Sixty Days Grace

In this regard, the Chiefs seemed to sense that a significant turn in our views about Vietnam had been taken in high policy circles of our government. **In final comment, they observed that the conflict had reached a stage at which decisions taken over the next sixty days could determine the outcome of the war,** and therefore they wished to provide the President with "their unequivocal views" on two salient aspects of the war situation—the search for peace and military pressures on North Vietnam (NVN).

> The frequent, broadly-based public offers made by the President to settle the war by peaceful means on a generous basis, which would take from NVN nothing it now has, have been admirable. Certainly, no one--American or foreigner--except those who are determined not to be convinced, can doubt the sincerity, the generosity, the altruism of U.S. actions and objectives.
>
> In the opinion of the Joint Chiefs of Staff, the time has come when further overt actions and offers on our part are not only nonproductive, they are counterproductive. A logical case can be made that the American people, our Allies, and our enemies alike are increasingly uncertain as to our resolution to pursue the war to a successful conclusion.

They recommended a "sharp knock"on NVN military assets and war-supporting facilities rather than the accepted campaign of slowly increasing pressures.

Whatever the political merits of the latter course, we deprived ourselves of the military effects of a "sharp knock", and gave the enemy time to adjust to our slow quantitative and qualitative increase of pressure. This is not to say that it is now too late to derive military benefits from more effective and extensive use of our air and naval superiority.

Solution

Accordingly, they recommended:

- Approval of their *Rolling Thunder* 52 program, which is a step towards meeting the requirements for improved target systems. This program would decrease the Hanoi and Haiphong sanctuary areas, authorize attacks against the steel plant, the Hanoi rail yards, the thermal power plants, selected areas within Haiphong port and other ports, selected locks and dams controlling water lines of communications, and Surface-to-Air (SAM) support facilities within the residual Hanoi and Haiphong sanctuaries;

- Use of naval forces to interdict North Vietnamese coastal waterborne traffic and appropriate land Lines of Communication and to attack other coastal military targets such as radar and anti-aircraft artillery sites;
- The Joint Chiefs of Staff request that their views as set forth above be provided to the President. [106]

Section 13: Intelligence Reports

Extracts from CIA/DIA Report: 'An appraisal of the bombing of North Vietnam through 12th September 1966':

1. There is no evidence yet of any shortage of POL (Petroleum, Oils, Lubricants etc) in North Vietnam and stocks on hand, with recent imports, have been adequate to sustain necessary operations;
2. Air strikes against all modes of transportation in North Vietnam increased during the past month, but there is no evidence of serious transport problems in the movement of supplies to or within North Vietnam;
3. There is no evidence yet that the air strikes have significantly weakened popular morale;
4. Air strikes continue to depress economic growth and have been responsible for the abandonment of some plans for economic development, but essential economic activities continue.

Extracts from a 16 March 1966 CIA Report: 'An Analysis of the Rolling Thunder Air Offensive against North Vietnam':

1. Although the movement of men and supplies in North Vietnam has been hampered and made somewhat more costly (by our bombing), the Communists have been able to increase the flow of supplies and manpower to South Vietnam;
2. Hanoi's determination [despite our bombing] to continue its policy of supporting the insurgency in the South appears as firm as ever;
3. Air attacks almost certainly cannot bring about a meaningful reduction in the current level at which essential supplies and men flow into South Vietnam.

106 Ibid. pp. 93-95.

Institute for Defense Analysts Summer Study Group: 'Bomb Damage Assessment in the North':

1. What surprised us [in our assessment of the effect of bombing North Vietnam] was the extent of agreement among various intelligence agencies on the effects of past operation and probable effects of continued and expanded *Rolling Thunder*. The conclusions of our group, to which we all subscribe, are therefor merely sharpened conclusions of numerous Intelligence summaries;
2. They are that *Rolling Thunder* does not limit the present logistic flow into South Vietnam (SVN) because North Vietnam (NVN) is neither the source of supplies nor the choke-point on the supply route from China and the USSR. Although an expansion of *Rolling Thunder* by closing Haiphong harbor, eliminating electric power plants, and totally destroying railroads, will at least indirectly impose further privations on the populace of North Vietnam and make the logistic support of VC costlier to maintain, such expansion will not really change the basic assessment;
3. This follows because North Vietnam has demonstrated an excellent ability to improvise transportation, and because the primitive nature of their economy is such that *Rolling Thunder* can affect directly only a small fraction of the population. There is very little hope that the Ho Chi Minh government will lose control of the population because of *Rolling Thunder*. The lessons of the Korean War are very relevant in these respects...[107]

Section 14: Program No. 4

Projected Enemy Increases

On 20th October 1966, the CINCPAC Planning Conference was done and the results forwarded to the JCS. There were few surprises. The concept had been changed to include a heavier emphasis on RD (Revolutionary Development), set forth in a preamble to the concept contained in the 18th June submission.

The estimate of Communist forces in South Vietnam was 83,000 combat, 46,000 combat support, and 35,000 guerrillas. Total strength was estimated at 144 infantry battalions, 60 of which were North Vietnamese. A projection of enemy strength for the end of 1966 was 143,000 combat and combat support forces, while the projection for the end of 1967 was 190,000.

107 Ibid. pp. 91-93.

The courses of action which seemed to be open to the enemy in October were:

1. To increase the level of operations to include the conduct of simultaneous widely-separated operations, utilizing forces of up to division size;
2. To maintain the current level of operations which would include the conduct of simultaneous widely-separated multi-battalion operations;
3. To threaten large-scale attacks in the DMZ in order to divert large numbers of our forces into the hinterland, thus reducing forces available in populated areas to accomplish Revolutionary Development;
4. To decrease the level of operations to include reverting to guerrilla warfare.

Program No. 4 Requirements

CINCPAC's requirements (Program 4) for U.S. maneuver Battalions and the services capabilities to provide them were listed by Calendar Year as follows:

Year	Requirements	Service Capability	Personnel
End 1966	82	79	384,361
End 1967	94	91	493, 969
End 1968	94	94	519,310
End 1969	94	94	520,020
Plus requirements with Availability Rates unknown			555,741

Requirements for Pacific Area Command (PACOM) other than Vietnam would total 23 maneuver battalions and 271,666 personnel.

Manpower Problems

The Conference results clearly amplified what General Westmoreland had echoed over a month earlier as the manpower problem in Vietnam worsened. NVA infiltration in the DMZ area, the strategy of hitting the enemy in his sanctuaries and the additional manpower requirements of the pacification program punctuated the critical conclusion of the Conference; they could not justify a reduction in requirements submitted.

Manila Waffle

Before the formal JCS ratification of the CINCPAC-COMUSMACV requirements was forwarded, one other important contact between the major decision-makers on Program 4 occurred. This was at Manila in late October.

What views were exchanged between the President and General Westmoreland remain a mystery, but the General twice sought out John McNaughton, Assistant

Secretary of Defense, ISA, and laid out his thinking on force levels, *Rolling Thunder*, the barrier, and Revolutionary Development.

The American commander was thinking about an end Calendar Year 1967 strength of about 480,000, fleshed-out to 500,000 by the end of Calendar Year 1968. Barring surprises, he would plan to hold it there. This was a substantial drop from his original request through CINCPAC, but apparently he had not yet resigned himself to McNamara's figure of 470,000. He believed that those levels were what "the U. S. [could] sustain over time without mobilization and without calling up reserves and what the Vietnamese economy [could] bear".

He said the 480,000-500,000 man level would be enough "even if infiltration went on at a high level", but he waffled by adding he was not sure if he had enough troops to take on the Delta... [108]

(See Page 98 of this Paper for Westmorland's further thoughts on force levels, the bombing of North Vietnam, the barrier, and Revolutionary Development.)

JCS "Refinements"

In a Memorandum of 4th November 1966, the Joint Chiefs forwarded to Secretary McNamara the report from the CINCPAC Planning Conference with their "refinements" added. The document, labeled JCSM 702-66, "Deployment of Forces to Meet CY Requirements", held few surprises. The Memorandum addressed the crux of disagreement:

> ...As in past concepts, it (Program 4) goes beyond certain restraints that have been placed on U.S. operating forces to date, such as those on the air campaign in North Vietnam, on cross border operations, on certain special operations, and on ground actions in the southern half of the demilitarized zone. Further, this concept should be carried out in its entirety if achievement of US objectives is to be accomplished in the shortest time and at the least cost in men and materiel.
>
> The concept describes preparation for operations that have not as yet been authorized, such as mining ports, naval quarantine, spoiling attacks and raids against the enemy in Cambodia and Laos, and certain special operations. Such action will support intensified and accelerated revolutionary development and nation building programs.

108 Ibid. pp. 96-97

> Since the force requirements are based on this concept in its entirety, continued restraints and the absence of authorization for recommended operations could generate significantly different requirements for forces and timing.

In a sense, it embraced all of the right arguments (for "intensified and accelerated revolutionary development and programs" and "shortest time at the least cost", an overdetermined test) but unfortunately for all the wrong reasons. McNamara and Johnson were not politically and militarily enchanted with a costly major force increase at that time, nor with cross border and air operations which ran grave political risks. The specter of early mobilization, while briefly raised by the JCS, was temporarily erased by an ambiguous statement acknowledging that "capability to meet these requirements cannot be developed without significant modification to the criteria mentioned earlier: draw-down latitude, rotation policy, no call-up of reserves...Nevertheless, the Joint Chiefs of Staff consider that, while the program is less than that desired, it will provide for the effective execution of the concept of operations set forth". [109]

Program No. 4 Announced

Public Posturing

With the Chiefs' views in hand, the Secretary of Defense met with the President on 4th November, and again at the (President's) ranch on Saturday, the 5th. By late Saturday morning, the basic ground force deployment decision had been made. Mr. McNamara announced in an open-air press conference that increases in Vietnam would be forthcoming "but at a substantially lower rate and that draft calls for the next four months would be significantly smaller".

He also quoted a "new study" based upon interrogations of NVA/VC captives and defectors which showed that extensive allied air-ground operations impaired morale, exposed the sanctuaries, reduced food supplies and brought the enemy death figure to over 1,000 per week. He did not comment on how he thought the war effort was going or what meaning he saw in the new report.[110]

On 10th November 1966, Secretary McNamara and General Wheeler, Chairman of the Joint Chiefs, participated in a joint news conference. General Wheeler read a short prepared statement explaining that, after his recent trip, he was able to report to the President that:

109 Ibid. p. 100.

110 Ibid. p. 101.

> The war in my judgment continues in a very favorable fashion. General Westmoreland retains the initiative and in every operation to date has managed to defeat the enemy.[111]

Program No. 4 Approved

The next day, 11th November, the Secretary of Defense informed the JCS formally that he had approved a new deployment program for MACV with an end strength of 470,000 by June of 1968.

(See Pages 103-104 for details of the approved Program 4 deployment plan and Pages 103-124 for a full explanations of the reasoning behind the Program 4 decisions.)

Section 15: Hard Reality Bites

Program No. 4 had important historical antecedents which provide the basic texture of future decision-making…a precedent, albeit a seemingly fragile one, of essentially saying "no" to the COMUSMACV's (General Westmoreland) force requirements was established.

Actually, the Department of Defense and the President were beginning to question the concept of operation for Vietnam which had led to programs, now becoming increasingly costly and depressingly barren of tangible results. The illusion of quick victory "on the cheap" had fled, and hard reality had intervened.

The JCS had adopted a strategic concept based upon widely expanded operations in the North, widened and intensified operations in the South designed to seek out and destroy enemy forces, and had made a commitment to assist the Government of South Vietnam in building an "independent, viable, non-communist society"--a vestige of the unfortunate wording of NSAM 288. The military heads had been denied the troops they said they required to successfully accomplish the objectives developed under the concept, but the concept itself had survived.

Certain "oblique alternatives", those which were not directly substitutable options, appeared during this time--all of them designed to relieve pressure on U. S. resources, especially manpower.

Among these were the barrier plan (proposed by McNamara), new free world military force-sharing formulas (KANZUS), efforts to subtly hold the RVNAF's "feet to the fire", and operations of various kinds in the "sanctuaries".

111 Ibid. p. 103.

A Political Sound Barrier

The Reserve mobilization line--a political sound barrier as it were, remained unbroken. The JCS had made a two-pronged case for breaking it: one, that we could not adequately meet CINCPAC's 1967 requirements and simultaneously fulfill our commitments to NATO and other threatened areas without mobilization (and even then, probably dangerously late); and secondly, only such massive infusions of firepower in the North and manpower in the South as they proposed could possibly achieve our war termination objectives "in the shortest time with the least cost" and this could not be done unless we mobilized.

To this the Chiefs replied that mobilization had traditionally unified the country, and it would also provide a strong indication of our national resolve--an important message to relay to Hanoi, and one in which Westmoreland as a field commander was also interested. Regardless, the issue loomed as the ceiling figure in the majority of ground force strategy deliberations--it appeared that the level was periodically studied, possibly negotiated, but always there--the "Plimsoll Line".

Public Disenchantment

Public disenchantment with the war was growing, and this was being manifested in diverse ways. On the "hawk" side, powerful political figures (and many lesser ones) were increasingly vocal in their opposition to bombing restraints and restrictive force levels. On the other side, public and private figures alike were energetically working to create a genuine political war issue and to generate palatable alternative policies for the upcoming Presidential elections in 1968.

Feeding a less focused sense of public dissatisfaction was an increasing awareness of the opportunity costs of the war in terms of national resources—men, money and attention—denied to domestic programs. As the defense slice of the budget hovered near the eighty billion dollar mark, the public realized it was· "paying more and liking it less".

The press was moving beyond the bounds of its traditional adversary relationship visa-vis the Administration and assuming a leading role in catalyzing the swell of public opposition and questioning about the war. Acute even early on in the war, the press opposition intensified as the divergence of official public pronouncements on the war and what reporters and their sources saw on the ground increased.

Failure is an Orphan

Failure is in the truest sense an orphan and as the sense of futility and self-doubt about achieving our objectives in Vietnam heightened, the architects of our military ground strategy found themselves increasingly isolated. The official base of support for the MACV strategy narrowed as more alternatives to it were seriously examined in Washington. This tended not only to aggravate a communications problem which had always hindered political-military planning, but it placed COMUSMACV-CINCPAC (General Westmorland and Admiral Sharp) on the defensive, creating an information and planning bias (from those sources) toward protection, justification and continuation of present programs.

Shield and Shelter

Finally, we had a field commander facing a strategic dilemma with no high prospect of satisfactory resolution. If it had any hope of success, the Combined Campaign Plan for 1967 required both a military "shield" to keep large enemy units from the populated areas where pacification was proceeding, and a "shelter" under which pacified areas could be respectably kept that way. [112]

The "shield" concept could be implemented in a number of ways, statically or dynamically (mobile vs. position defense), geographically oriented or enemy force oriented, or by different combinations of these at different times. General Westmoreland's strategy, based upon exploitation of our inherent superior mobility and firepower, was designed to simultaneously attrite the enemy and retain the initiative by disrupting VC/NVA operations before they completely materialized.

This led to seeking engagement with enemy main force units well out into the border regions where they literally could be held at distance before jumping off in operations. Related to this was the notion that the important thing was to fight, to engage the enemy, and to create casualties.

It mattered little that you accepted combat in regions with certain advantages for the enemy—the prime objective was to engage and to kill him.

Fighting a mobile defense kind of war provides an adequate but not perfect shield. You can liken it to a vast semi-permeable membrane which has significant leakage by small amounts over time. Backing up this kind of a "shield" is the "shelter", also manned by combat troops, geographically dispersed and occupying the areas where pacification is going on. The combination of the two, shield and shelter, requires manpower and the balance is crucial, especially so if you have limited resources.

If your operating assumptions are those held by COMUSMACV (Westmoraland) in late 1966, then what you have for the "shelter" is a function of the kind and sizes of enemy forces you are fighting in the "shield" mission. If you are fighting large units at many points simultaneously, you are forced to strip "shelter" forces, or use the ARVN, or request more U. S. forces.

112 Ibid. pp. 125-127.

As Program No. 4 closes, we find MACV facing just those same large multiple threats, stripping the "shelter" forces, and relying upon an inadequate ARVN for the majority of pacification security. Even with sufficient U.S. and ARVN forces, the task was prodigious. To attempt to "shield" without adequate forces to "shelter" was bound to be precarious. [113]

Note

The Pentagon Papers reproduced or paraphrased in previous Chapters are those which most adequately represent the state of knowledge and the mind-set of the decision-makers; demonstrate the depths of betrayal of Congress and the American people by those decision-makers; and prove that American Presidents and their closest advisors had steered the United States into deeper and deeper involvement in Vietnam despite knowing that the War was a failed proposition almost from its beginning.

113 Ibid. pp. 125-127.

CHAPTER FORTY-NINE

The Watershed

In an address to the National Press Club in Washington on 21st November 1967, General Westmoreland had given his audience an optimistic assessment of the war in Vietnam, going so far as to say:

> I am absolutely certain that, whereas in 1965 the enemy was winning, today he is certainly losing. [114]

On 30 January 1968, just ten weeks after Westmoreland's National Press Club address, the North Vietnamese and the Viet Cong launched the Tet Offensive. What Americans saw on television and read in the newspapers looked nothing like the optimistic picture Westmoreland had painted.

For an American public grown tired of the continual fighting in Vietnam with no end in sight, Tet was a turning point. Any expectations that the war was close to ending were shattered, and past reassurances from the Johnson Administration and General Westmoreland about the coming victory in Vietnam rang hollow.

Section 1: The Profound Malaise

In the early months of 1968, *The New York Times* published a series of articles about the "malaise of spirit" gripping America; the growing public awareness of the "creeping disaster" that was Vietnam; the "wrenching uncertainly and doubt about every facet of the war"; and the request for yet more troops to "regain the initiative" in Vietnam.

Who's to Blame

On 10th February 1968, Robert Kennedy, the brother of the slain President, penned an editorial which read in part:

114 'General Westmorland's Address to the National Press Club' (21 November 1967). *DocsTeach, National Archives and Records Administration* < https://www.docsteach.org/documents/document/westmoreland-press-club> Accessed 8 April 2025.

As 1967 came to an end, E. B. White observed in a Topics column on this page that all Americans seemed to be asking the same questions: "What happened? What went sour? What did I do wrong? Who's to blame?"

President Johnson speaks of a mood of "restlessness". Cabinet officers and commentators, poets and protesters tell us that America is deep in a malaise of the spirit, discouraging initiative, paralyzing will and action, dividing Americans from one another by their age, their views and the color of their skin.

Demonstrators shout down Government officials and the Government drafts protesters. Anarchists threaten to burn the country down, and some have begun to try, while tanks have patrolled American streets and machine guns have fired at American children. Our young people, the best educated and comforted in our history, turn from the Peace Corps and public commitment of a few years ago to lives of disengagement and despair, turned on with drugs and turned off America. Indeed, we seem to fulfill the vision of Yeats: "Things fall apart; the center cannot hold; Mere anarchy is loosed upon the world".

...So half a million of our finest young men struggle, and many die, in a war halfway around the world while millions more of our best youth neither understand the war nor respect its purposes, and some repudiate the very institutions of a Government they do not believe.

...Our power is enormous, the greatest the world has ever seen. Yet, as we see old allies pulling back to their shores, and old alliances dissolving in quarrels, we sense that even America cannot act as if no other nation existed, flaunting our power and wealth against the judgment and desires of neutrals and allies alike. We wonder if we still hold "a decent respect to the opinions of mankind" or whether, like Athens of old, we will forfeit sympathy and support alike, and ultimately our own security, in the single-minded pursuit of our own goals and objectives.[115]

A Creeping Disaster

One month later, on 10th March 1968, Tom Wicker wrote an article which reflected a gradual public realisation that military means could not salvage the disaster that was Vietnam despite what was being asserted by the Administration. The article said in part:

115 Kennedy, Robert F. (10 February 1968) 'Topics: Things Fall Apart; the Center Cannot Hold...' *The New York Times*. < https://www.nytimes.com/1968/02/10/archives/topics-things-fall-apart-the-center-cannot-hold-.html> Accessed 12 November 2025.

Slowly, perhaps not quite surely, but with increasing momentum, American public opinion seems to be moving to the conclusion that the war in Vietnam is a creeping disaster that military means cannot salvage.

This is not a matter of marches on the Pentagon, nor is there any suggestion that Americans generally are now ready to "turn tail and run"—in the derisive phrase of those in the Johnson Administration, and elsewhere, who equate any questioning of the war with appeasement, cowardice and lack of patriotism.

Rather, there is an ever more apparent collection of straws in the wind that suggest a painful and hesitant reappraisal of the war, of what it is all about, and what ought to be done about it by many moderate Americans who have tended to support without much question the President, the troops and their country's foreign policy... [116]

Built on Sand

Again on 10th March 1968, a dispatch by Hedrick Smith and Neil Sheehan, assisted by Max Frankel and Edwin Dale, is worth reproducing at length for its candid approach and its criticism of the Government's public shows of optimism built on nothing more than sand:

Force Now 510,000: Gen. William C. Westmoreland has asked for 206,000 more American troops for Vietnam, and the request has touched off a divisive internal debate within high levels of the Johnson Administration. A number of sub-Cabinet civilian officials in the Defense Department, supported by some senior officials in the State Department, have argued against General Westmoreland's plea for a 40 per cent increase in his forces "to regain the initiative" from the enemy. There are now about 510,000 American troops in Vietnam, and the President has authorized a level of 525,000 by next fall.

Fear Matching Rise: Many of the civilian officials are arguing that there should be no increase beyond the movement of troops now under way. The contention of these high ranking officials is that an American increase will bring a matching increase by North Vietnam, thereby raising the level of violence without giving the allies the upper hand.

Senior Pentagon civilians have put forward a written counter-proposal to President Johnson, calling for a shift in American strategy to a concept of close-in defense of populated areas with more limited offensive thrusts than

116 Wicker, Tom. (10 March 1968). 'In the Nation: Agonising Reappraisal'. *The New York Times*. <https://www.nytimes.com/1968/03/10/archives/in-the-nation-agonizing-reappraisal.html> Accessed 30 December 2025.

at present. Much of the military hierarchy is reported to oppose this approach. General Westmoreland, the American commander in Vietnam, has been seeking to persuade the President to approve a bolder strategy. Officials report that he has been proposing ground actions into Laos and Cambodia to disrupt the enemy's base areas and infiltration routes.

Compromise Suggested: But the enemy's winter offensive has had such stunning impact on some high civilian officials here that they question privately whether the Government should not lower its war objectives. Some have suggested that the ground be prepared for a political compromise with the Vietcong. But this is a position that President Johnson and his inner circle of advisers firmly reject at this point. The President has not yet decided on the question of substantial increases in American forces in Vietnam. "He is keeping an open mind", said one senior adviser. For the time being, Mr. Johnson is reported to be holding to current strategy and urging General Westmoreland to wring the utmost combat capacity out of the 510,000 American troops already in Vietnam. The White House maintains officially that the question of more troops is "not a matter of decision at this point".

Tet Offensive Causes Doubts: Nonetheless, the scope and depth of the internal debate within the Government reflect the wrenching uncertainty and doubt in this capital about every facet of the war left by the enemy's dramatic wave of attacks at Tet, the Lunar New Year holiday, six weeks ago. More than ever this has left a sense of weariness and irritation over the war. Officials themselves comment in private about widespread and deep changes in attitudes, a sense that a watershed has been reached and that its meaning is just now beginning to be understood. One high official commented that the enemy's Tet offensive was "a body blow". Another remarked that Washington was "still groggy". Said a third: "There's no disguising it—we got a real punch in the nose". Others speak bitterly of Vietnam as a "bottomless pit". Even more pervasive is the comment, "We don't really know where we stand yet. Our information is poor".

All Built on Sand: Another official intimately acquainted with the Vietnam situation recalled the Government's optimistic estimates of progress last fall. "We know now that we constantly underestimated the enemy's capacity and his will to fight and overestimated progress", he said. "We know now that all we thought we had constructed was built on sand". The President and his inner circle of advisers, especially Secretary of State Dean Rusk and Walt W. Rostow, a special assistant to the President for national security affairs, project an air of confidence that the situation can somehow be righted and the balance restored. In private as well as in public, they stress the enemy's losses and his failure

> to achieve his maximum objective in the Tet fighting. But at every level of Government there is a sense that the conflict, if expanded further, can no longer be called "a limited war".[117]

Disunity and Resentment

On 1st April 1968, *The New York Times* reported on a televised announcement in which President Johnson announced he would not seek re-election:

> **Profound Malaise:** The astounding announcement of President Johnson last night that in the interests of national unity he will not accept renomination to the Presidency is one of the more dramatic developments of modern American political history. A total and perfectly kept secret until he pronounced the words: "I will not accept" before a nationwide television audience, Mr. Johnson's renunciation—unexpected though it was—reflects the profound malaise that the people in every part of this country are experiencing as a direct result of the divisions over the Vietnam War, increasingly embittered race relations, and a dangerously haphazard internal and external economy.
>
> **Public Dissatisfaction**: First among these causes of national disunity and resentment is of course the war; and it is surely his recognition of the depth of public dissatisfaction with the way this "open-handed" conflict has been going that impelled President Johnson not to risk defeat either at the hands of his own party or of the national electorate...
>
> **Limit Bombing**: In any case Mr. Johnson has now taken the first concrete step in many months to give effect to his repeatedly expressed desire for peace in Asia. He has ordered a cessation of the bombing of North Vietnam except in the immediate vicinity of the demilitarized zone, where intense combat is now going on. He has at long last made a major move along lines advocated by U Thant, the Pope and many other world leaders. He has now in a real sense shifted the onus of the continuing war to Hanoi.
>
> **Dreadful, Cruel and Ugly War**: It may already be too late for this move to be accepted by the North Vietnamese; they may now believe that time is on their side and may refuse the President's gesture. But they too have strongly implied in the recent past that an unconditional cessation of bombing would lead to their acceptance of peace talks; and so the next move is now theirs in the effort

117 Smith et al. (10 March 1968). 'Westmoreland requests 206,000 more men, stirring debate in Administration: Force now 510,000'. *The New York Times* < https://www.nytimes.com/1968/03/10/archives/westmorelasnd-requests-206000-more-men-stirring-debate-in.html> Accessed 1 Janaury 2026.

to start the wheels in motion that will end this dreadful, cruel and ugly war—the war that nobody wants.[118]

Section 2: Fifty Years On

The Five O'Clock Follies

In Vietnam, U.S. military officers and their civilian counterparts regularly stood before the press corps in Saigon's Rex Hotel. They recited statistics and told tales that bore no resemblance to the reality of the war that the journalists had seen for themselves. The exercise was so ludicrous that journalists began calling the daily sessions the 'Five O'Clock Follies'.

In March 2017, Hugh Greenaway penned an article for *The New York Times* titled 'What I Saw in Vietnam'. Fifty years after his arrival in Saigon in March 1967, he wrote in part:

> ...50 years ago this month, the mood of American officials was all upbeat, get-on-the team optimism. We were winning. Secretary of Defense Robert McNamara famously said that "every quantitative measurement we have shows we are winning the war".
>
> ...In Saigon I went to the famous "five o'clock follies" in which American officials briefed the press on the progress of the war—so many enemy weapons captured, so many enemies killed: "the body count".
>
> The briefings bore less and less resemblance to what my colleagues and I were seeing in the field, the burned out villages, the civilians caught in cross fires, the napalm strikes, and how impossible it was going to be to win the proverbial "hearts and minds" with the blundering, damaging colossus of military action, always the bluntest of tools. I saw how the body count got inflated as it was passed up the chain of command. I saw how corruption was eating at the entrails of the successive South Vietnamese governments we were installing.
>
> It wasn't that the American briefers were actually lying to us. They were, as the journalist Sebastian Junger wrote about American optimism in Afghanistan, simply inviting you to join a conspiracy of wishful thinking.
>
> ...There were battles for nameless, numbered hills, 881, 875, numbered for their height in meters. The North Vietnamese tactic was to move onto a hill, fortify

118 'I Will Not Accept' (1 April 1968). *The New York Times*. < https://www.nytimes.com/1968/04/01/archives/i-will-not-accept.html> Accessed 1 January 2026.

> it to withstand heavy booming and shelling, and then draw us up the hills in pointless battles in which Americans would be killed in ever greater numbers. The Vietnamese would always lose more men than we did, but they knew we were fighting on their home turf, and they knew that we would be the ones to tire first and go home, just as had the French…[119]

American Fracture

On 15 January 2018, Jacey Fortin and Maggie Astor wrote an article for *The New York Times* titled 'Fifty Years Later, it Feels Familiar: How America fractured in 1968'. The authors reflected on the watershed year of 1968, writing in part:

> From January to December, people demonstrated against racial injustice and economic inequality. Abroad, the United States military slogged through a seemingly interminable war…It was the year between the Summer of Love and the summer of Woodstock, and some men grew their hair long while others were drafted to fight in Vietnam. "The country was bitterly divided: hawks and doves", said Marc Leepson, an author, historian and Vietnam veteran.
>
> It was also the year of the Tet offensive, an enormous attack by North Vietnamese forces, and of more than 16,000 American deaths in the Vietnam War, more than in any other year. Domestic support for the war effort faltered as antiwar protests exploded…
>
> The civil rights movement had been underway for years, achieving landmark federal laws and Supreme Court decisions that struck down legalized segregation and discrimination. But vast inequality persisted, and on 4th April, the movement lost a leader: The Rev. Dr. Martin Luther King Jr. was shot and killed in Memphis.
>
> In the following days, protests and riots erupted in major cities across the country. Properties were destroyed, and dozens of people lost their lives.
>
> But the big-picture changes were hard to recognize at the time; all year, major events made headlines at a breakneck pace… In June, Senator Robert F. Kennedy, a presidential hopeful, was fatally shot at a campaign event in California… And the death toll kept rising in Vietnam. [120]

---

119 Greenaway, H.D.S. (15 March 2017). 'What I Saw in Vietnam'. *The New York Times* < https://www.nytimes.com/2017/03/15/opinion/what-i-saw-in-vietnam.html> Accessed 18 January 2026.

120 Fortin, J, Astor, M. (15 January 2018). 'Fifty Years Later, it Feels Familiar: How America fractured in 1968'. *The New York Time*s < https://www.nytimes.com/interactive/2018/01/15/us/1968-history.html> Accessed 7 January 2026.

A Close Call

Despite General Westmorland's public shows of optimism in 1968, it has now been revealed in a 6th October 2018 *New York Times* article by David Sangar, that in February 1968 he considered the use of nuclear weapons if the U.S. faced defeat at the Battle of Khe Sanh (See also Chapter Fifty-One: *The Crucible.*)

> In one of the darkest moments of the Vietnam War, the top American military commander in Saigon activated a plan in 1968 to move nuclear weapons to South Vietnam until he was overruled by President Lyndon B. Johnson, according to recently declassified documents cited in a new history of wartime presidential decisions.
>
> The documents reveal a long-secret set of preparations by the commander, Gen. William C. Westmoreland, to have nuclear weapons at hand should American forces find themselves on the brink of defeat at Khe Sanh, one of the fiercest battles of the war.
>
> With the approval of the American commander in the Pacific, General Westmoreland had put together a secret operation, code-named Fracture Jaw, that included moving nuclear weapons into South Vietnam so that they could be used on short notice against North Vietnamese troops.
>
> Johnson's national security adviser, Walt W. Rostow, alerted the president in a memorandum on White House stationery. The president rejected the plan, and ordered a turnaround…[121]

The Slaughterhouse

On 1st February 2018, fifty years after the Tet Offensive, Edwin Moise of *The New York Times* reported that May 1968 had marked the bloodiest month for U.S. forces in Vietnam:

> **500 Dead per Week:** The Tet offensive, a wave of Communist attacks throughout South Vietnam, began on Jan. 30 and 31, 1968. It achieved partial surprise. American commanders had known something was coming, but they had not expected such a widespread pattern of attacks.
>
> Partly this was because they had been underestimating both the size of the Communist forces and their ability to sustain heavy combat. On Feb. 1, Gen. William Westmoreland said that the enemy forces were "about to run out of

121 Sangar, David. E. (6 October 2018) 'U.S. General Considered Nuclear Response in Vietnam War, Cables Show'. *The New York Times*. < https://www.nytimes.com/2018/10/06/world/asia/vietnam-war-nuclear-weapons.html> Accessed 8 April 2025.

steam". He later claimed they had indeed quickly run out of steam, saying that "almost everywhere except on the outskirts of Saigon and in Hue the fighting was over in two or three days".

Many have accepted this view of events — that Tet was an intense but relatively brief campaign. But it did not match the experience of the troops Westmoreland was commanding.

About 400 Americans were killed by hostile action in the week the Tet offensive began, more than in any previous week of the war. Another 400 were killed the next week. But worse was to come. The first wave of Tet attacks had been aimed mostly at the towns and cities, which meant mostly at the forces of the South Vietnamese government. Many of the Communist units had dodged around American units instead of hitting them directly.

Then, during the following four weeks, from Feb. 11 to March 9, a period of widespread American counterattacks, there were 500 American deaths each week. By the middle of March, the level of combat was no longer this extreme, but it remained abnormally high. The rate at which Americans were dying in combat remained at least 50 percent above the 1967 average through the rest of March and April.

The bloodiest month of the war: For the American forces in South Vietnam as a whole there was not even a brief respite in the three months after the offensive began, even as the Communists were gathering forces for another surge in early May.

Americans have often played down that May offensive; they call it "Mini-Tet". It did not have even the degree of partial surprise that the original Tet offensive had had, so it did not come as close to achieving important successes. But there was nothing miniature about it. May 1968 was the bloodiest month of the war for American forces with 2,169 killed, and even in the first half of June the death tolls remained well above pre-Tet levels...

Pursue the enemy relentlessly: ...Johnson did not send to Vietnam the major reinforcements, more than 200,000 men, that his generals had recommended. But he did send reinforcements.

There had been 498,000 American military personnel in Vietnam when the Tet offensive began at the end of January. There were 515,000 by the time Johnson gave his speech (that he would not stand for re-election), two months later. There would be 536,000 two months after that.

They were fighting hard, and Johnson was urging them on. Even in the autumn, after Gen. Creighton Abrams had replaced Westmoreland as commander in

Vietnam, Johnson's orders to Abrams were: "Follow the enemy in relentless pursuit. Don't give them a minute's rest. Keep pouring it on. Let the enemy feel the weight of everything you've got".[122]

122 Moise, Edwin (1 February 2018). 'The Tet Offensive Was Just The Beginning'. *The New York Times*. < https://www.nytimes.com/2018/02/01/opinion/vietnam-war-tet-offensive-start.html> Accessed 1 January 2026.

CHAPTER FIFTY

The Paradox

In 1969, Americans witnessed what must surely be a paradox unparalleled in their history. From the depths of the American military's callous disregard for its soldiers on Hamburger Hill, to the heights of American ingenuity and breathtaking achievement which transformed into reality the age-old dream of a man standing on the Moon.

And all within a period of just two months.

Hamburger Hill

The Battle of Hamburger Hill (13th–20th May 1969) was fought by U.S. Army and Army of the Republic of Vietnam (ARVN) forces against the People's Army of Vietnam (PAVN) forces during Operation Apache Snow. Though the heavily fortified Hill 937, a ridge of the mountain Dong Ap Bia in central Vietnam near its western border with Laos, had no strategic value, U.S. command ordered its capture by a frontal assault. They were repulsed ten times, and it was nicknamed "Hamburger Hill", as the Americans were said to have been chewed up like a hamburger. The hill was finally taken after eleven direct assaults, only to be abandoned by the Americans a week later despite the great cost of 56 U.S. dead, 420 wounded, and 7 missing in action. General John M. Wright said that the hill was not important to U.S. strategy, justifying the withdrawal.

On 20th May 1969, the same day as the battle for Hamburger Hill ended, U.S. Senator Edward Kennedy called it "senseless and irresponsible to continue to send our young men to their deaths to capture hills and positions that have no relation to ending this conflict":

> After the cessation of bombing last November, the President issued an order to the field that American military forces were to maintain a constant and steady pressure upon the enemy. As a result, the levels of combat and casualties did not remain the same but actually increased. The number of U. S. offensive actions making contact with the enemy grew significantly; the total number of U. S. battalion size operations was raised; the amount of bomb tonnage dropped in the South rose to a total greater than the amount of bomb tonnage previously dropped on the North and South. In effect, the President's order of last November to maintain steady and constant pressure has not only been carried

out by our military commanders in the field, it has been carried out to the letter and then some.

President Nixon in his April 18th press conference reaffirmed President Johnson's earlier directive by stating that he has not ordered, nor did he intend to order, any reduction of our activity in Vietnam. He explained that this was in the interest of maintaining the strength of our bargaining position in Paris.

I am compelled to speak on this question today for I believe that the level of our military activity in Vietnam runs opposite to our stated intentions and goals in Paris. But more importantly, I feel it is both senseless and irresponsible to continue to send our young men to their deaths to capture hills and positions that have no relation to ending this conflict.

President Nixon has told us, without question, that we seek no military victory, that we seek only peace. How then can we justify sending our boys against a hill a dozen times or more, until soldiers themselves question the madness of it?

The assault on "Hamburger Hill" is only symptomatic of a mentality and a policy that requires immediate attention. American boys are too valuable to be sacrificed for a false sense of military pride.

I was most disappointed that the President did not ask for a significant decrease in military operations and personnel in his speech of May 14th. I would ask him now to issue new orders to the field--orders that would spare American lives and perhaps advance the cause of peace.[123]

An 18th June *Associated Press* interview with an unrepentant General Wright was reported in *The New York Times.* Titled 'Foe Reported Back on Hamburger Hill: Units from North Reported on Peak', the report said in part that:

North Vietnamese troops are reported back in force on Ap bia Mountain, and a United States general said he was ready to fight for the peak again, "if it takes an entire division".

...Major General John M. Wright Jnr., commander of the 101st Airborne Division, stationed in that area, said in an interview that if it should become necessary to attack again, that he was "prepared to commit everything it takes, up to the entire division to do the job". [124]

123 Kennedy, Edward. 'Hamburger Hill Speech: Calling for an End to Military Operations in Vietnam'. (20 May 1969) *Edward M. Kennedy Institute* <http://www.tedkennedy.org/ownwords/event/vietnam.html> Accessed 3 January 2026.

124 'Foe Reported Back on Hamburger Hill: Units From North Reported on Peak'. (18 June 1969). *The New York Times* via *Associated Press.* < https://timesmachine.nytimes.com/timesmachine/1969/06/18/89000628.html?pageNumber=1> Accessed 20 February 2026.

Moon Shot

On 25th May 1961, President John F. Kennedy had announced the goal of landing a man on the Moon before a joint session of the U.S. Congress. The President said in part:

> …if we are to win the battle that is now going on around the world between freedom and tyranny, the dramatic achievements in space which occurred in recent weeks should have made clear to all of us, as did Sputnik in 1957, the impact of this adventure on the minds of men everywhere…Now it is time to take longer strides—time for this nation to take a clearly leading role in space achievement, which in many ways may hold the key to our future on Earth… we have never made the national decisions or marshaled the national resources required for such leadership. We have never specified long-range goals on an urgent time schedule…Space is open to us now; and our eagerness to share its meaning is not governed by the efforts of others. We go into space because whatever mankind must undertake, free men must fully share…
>
> I believe that this nation should commit itself to achieving the goal, before this decade is out, of landing a man on the Moon and returning him safely to the Earth. No single space project…will be more exciting, or more impressive to mankind, or more important…and none will be so difficult or expensive to accomplish…

It's a message Kennedy would echo in his 1962 State of the Union Address, and in his famous address at Rice University on 12th September 1962, where he declared "We choose to go to the Moon in this decade and do the other things, not because they are easy, but because they are hard". [125]

The Eagle has landed

The primary objective of NASA's Apollo 11 program was to complete this national goal set by President Kennedy to land a man on the Moon and return him safely to Earth.

Apollo 11 was launched by a Saturn V rocket from Kennedy Space Center in Florida on 16th July 1969 at 13:32 UTC. On 20th July at 20:17 UCT, Commander Neil Armstrong and Lunar Module Pilot Edwin "Buzz" Aldrin landed the Lunar Module *Eagle* on the Moon's Sea of Tranquility. Armstrong immediately radioed to Mission

---

125 Kennedy, John F. (11 December 2017) 'We choose to go to the moon: JFK's moon shot'. *National Air and Space Museum: Smithsonian.* < https://airandspace.si.edu/stories/editorial/we-choose-go-moon-jfks-moon-shot> Accessed 3 January 2026.

Control in Houston a famous message: "The Eagle has landed". At 02:56 UCT, six hours later, Armstrong became the first person to step onto the surface of the Moon.

Armstrong's first step on the Moon was broadcast on live television to a worldwide audience. He described it as "one small step for man, one giant leap for mankind". Apollo 11 returned to Earth on 24th July, splashing down into the Pacific Ocean southwest of Hawaii.

Apollo 11 fulfilled the national goal set in 1961 by President John F. Kennedy: "before this decade is out, of landing a man on the Moon and returning him safely to the Earth".

The inhumanity of Hamburger Hill stands in stark juxtaposition to Armstrong's call to humanity, his "...one giant leap for mankind".

CHAPTER FIFTY-ONE

The Crucible

Vietnam, unlike many other wars, was not a conflict defined by a series of pitched battles. Prolonged, limited engagements were a frequent occurrence for many American and allied forces who faced recurring danger in patrols and search-and-destroy missions. However, a few specific engagements did shape the course of the war.

Caveat

Since space in this work is limited and precludes any in-depth or additional analysis, no attempt has been made to test the veracity of the following accounts which have been reproduced virtually verbatim from the *U.S. Air Force Historical Support Division*, the *Pritzker Military Museum and Library*, and the *ANZAC Portal*.

Section 1: Operation Rolling Thunder

2 March 1965 - 2 November 1968

Operation Rolling Thunder was a bombing campaign against North Vietnam carried out by U.S. Air Force and Navy aircraft. It began on 24th February 1965 and lasted until the end of October 1968.

The operation began primarily as a diplomatic signal to impress Hanoi with America's determination, essentially a warning that the violence would escalate until Ho Chi Minh "blinked", and, secondly, it was intended to bolster the sagging morale of the South Vietnamese.

The Johnson administration imposed strict limits on the targets that could be attacked for China and the Soviet Union were seen as defenders of communism who might intervene if the North Vietnamese faced defeat. Consequently, the administration tried to punish the North without provoking the two nations believed to be its protectors. In the view of the Air Force leadership, the campaign had no clear-cut objective nor did its authors have any real estimate of the cost of lives and aircraft.

General LeMay and others argued that military targets, rather than the enemy's resolve, should be attacked and that the blows should be rapid and sharp, with the impact felt immediately on the battlefield as well as by the political leadership in Hanoi.

When *Rolling Thunder* failed to weaken the enemy's will after the first several weeks, the purpose of the campaign began to change. By the end of 1965, the Johnson administration still used air power as an attempt to change North Vietnamese policy, but bombing tended to be directed against the flow of men and supplies from the North, thus damaging the enemy militarily while warning him of the danger of greater destruction if he maintained the present aggressive course.

To persuade the North Vietnamese to negotiate, President Johnson restricted the bombing of North Vietnam to the southern part of the country on the 31st March 1968. In effect, this decision brought *Operation Rolling Thunder* to an end. On 2nd November 1968, Johnson ending the bombing throughout the north. [126]

Section 2: The Battle of Ia Drang Valley

14th-17th November 1965

The first major battle between American and Vietnamese forces, the Battle of Ia Drang Valley would be claimed as a victory by both sides and would offer important lessons for each army. Located in the Central Highlands of South Vietnam, the valley was seen as a crucial People's Army of Vietnam (PAVN) supply route into the South. American commander General William Westmoreland decided to test a new battle tactic of "air mobility" by deploying American forces largely by helicopter.

On 14th November, the U.S. First Calvary Division established landing zones in the valley and immediately came under fire from PAVN forces. Continual reinforcements via helicopter and sustained aerial bombardment decimated the Vietnamese positions. By the end of fighting, 305 Americans compared to at least 1,000 PAVN troops had been killed. General Westmoreland and much of the American leadership viewed the casualty statistics as a vindication of their planning—air mobility, immense bombardment, and a focus on creating mass enemy casualties would become the central focus of American tactics moving forward. Meanwhile, PAVN commanders learned to avoid attacking in large formations and to engage the Americans at close range to mitigate any artillery advantages. Ia Drang set the course for the war to come and would serve as a taste of future conflict for both sides.[127]

---

126 '1965-Operation Rolling Thunder'. *U.S. Air Force Historical Support Division* < https://www.afhistory.af.mil/FAQs/Fact-Sheets/Article/458992/1965-operation-rolling-thunder/> Accessed 3 April 2025.

127 'Key Battles'. *Pritzker Military Museum and Library* < https://www.pritzkermilitary.org/explore/vietnam-war/key-battles> Accessed 31 March 2025.

Section 3: The Battle of Long Tan

18th August 1966

On 18th August 1966, Delta (D) Company, Royal Australian Regiment (6RAR), fought an 'encounter' battle to defeat enemy forces in the Long Tan rubber plantation. The plantation was only a few kilometres from the 1st Australian Task Force base at Nui Dat. D Company suffered 42 casualties, including 18 dead—more than one-third of its strength—while some 245 enemy troops were killed. D Company's 105 men and 3 New Zealanders from 161 Battery, Royal New Zealand Artillery, fought for almost four hours against soldiers of the North Vietnamese Army who outnumbered them by 10 to 1.

How it happened

In May 1966, the first Australian soldiers of the 6th Battalion (6RAR) arrived in South Vietnam: the rest followed in June.

By August 1966, the 1st Australian Task Force Base at Nui Dat was only three months old. Concerned by such a strong presence in their midst, the Viet Cong determined to inflict an early defeat on the Australians.

Expecting an attack

In the days before the battle, radio signals indicated the presence of strong Viet Cong forces within 5 kilometres of the base but patrols found nothing.

On the nights of the 16th and 17th August, the Nui Dat base came under fire from mortars and recoilless rifles. The Australian defenders stood-to, expecting the barrage to be followed by an assault. None came. Searches of the area the next day located some of the sites from which mortars had been fired but nothing else.

Patrols continued the following day, the 18th August. D Company left the Nui Dat base at 11:15 a.m. bound for the Long Tan rubber plantation. As they left, the sounds of a concert by Australian entertainer Little Pattie reached their ears.

Attacking in force

D Company entered the Long Tan plantation at 3:15 p.m. that day. Less than 1 hour later, the Viet Cong attacked in force, firing on the Australians with mortars, machine guns and small arms. D Company made desperate calls for support. The quick response of a New Zealand artillery battery saved the Australians from annihilation.

Almost as soon as the battle began, a torrential downpour of rain added to the gloom in the rubber plantation. The Australians were surrounded, short of ammunition and fighting an enemy whose strength they could only guess at.

Calling for support

The Australians called for helicopters to drop ammunition. Flying at tree-top height, braving the terrible weather and heavy Viet Cong fire, two Royal Australian Air Force (RAAF) helicopters located the beleaguered Australians. The choppers dropped boxes of ammunition and blankets for the wounded men.

The survivors of D Company fought alongside New Zealand's 161 Field Battery, the Australian 103 and 105 Field batteries, and a United States battery. Their accurate artillery fire inflicted heavy losses on the Viet Cong.

As the fighting continued, Australian reinforcements were committed to the battle. B Company was on the way. A Company was loaded into 3 Troop Armoured Personnel Carriers of 1 Armoured Personnel Carrier Squadron which fought its way into D Company just before 7:00 p.m. as daylight was fading.

Forcing a retreat

The Viet Cong had been massing for another assault, but were forced to retreat into the plantation. They had suffered terrible casualties. However, the Australians did not realise the extent of their victory until they returned to the scene of battle the next morning. They counted 245 enemy dead still in the plantation and surrounding jungle with evidence that others had already been removed from the battlefield.

Captured documents and information from prisoners suggested that D Company had faced some 2,500 Viet Cong. In the Battle of Long Tan, 18 Australians were killed and 24 wounded. All but one of the dead were from D Company. 11 of the 18 dead were conscripts. [128]

Section 4: The Battle of Khe Sanh

21st January - 5th July 1968

The U.S. first established a special forces base at Khe Sanh in 1962, one of the western-most American bases near the demilitarized zone (DMZ). Located in South Vietnam just fourteen miles south of the border with North Vietnam and six miles east of the border with Laos, the base gradually grew in importance until 1967 when General William Westmoreland stationed 6,000 U.S. Marines there to interdict the flow of supplies on the Ho Chi Minh Trail. Parts of three PAVN divisions, around 15,000-20,000 men, began to surround the base before launching an assault on 21st January.

128 'The Battle of Long Tan'. *ANZAC Portal.* < https://anzacportal.dva.gov.au/wars-and-missions/vietnam-war-1962-1975/events/combat/battle-long-tan-1966> Accessed 3 April 2025.

The Marines at Khe Sanh were placed under siege: only aerial resupply and massive aerial firepower kept the base afloat. The White House was keenly aware of the legacy of Dien Bien Phu and General Westmoreland offered assurances that the base would not fall. A relief operation began on 1st April, and the siege of Khe Sanh was lifted by 15th April.

American commanders considered the defense of Khe Sanh a success, but shortly after the siege was lifted, they decided to abandon the base rather than risk similar battles in the future. On 19th June 1968, the evacuation and destruction of Khe Sanh began. Amid heavy shelling, the Marines attempted to salvage what they could before destroying what remained as they were evacuated. Minor attacks continued before the base was officially closed on 5th July. Fighting in the vicinity continued until 11th July when the Marines were finally withdrawn, bringing the battle to a close. After the immense effort to defend the base, it was abandoned by American forces in June 1968.

There remains a strong controversy as to the overall North Vietnamese objective at Khe Sanh: historians argue as to whether General Giap (the overall strategist behind the campaign) hoped to win another victory like Dien Bien Phu, or whether the Khe Sanh operation was a diversion for broad communist action throughout South Vietnam during the Tet Offensive. Regardless, 205 Marines died at Khe Sanh, around 1,600 physically-counted North Vietnamese Army (NVA) soldiers, and an estimated total of North Vietnamese losses between 10-15,000.[129]

Section 5: The Tet Offensive

30th January - 28th March 1968

Tet, a traditional Vietnamese holiday celebrating the beginning of a new lunar year, had normally been observed as an unofficial cease-fire. However, in late 1967, several North Vietnamese leaders had decided that the military deadlock needed to be broken and hypothesized that a massive offensive throughout the urban centers of the Republic of Vietnam could usher in a general uprising amongst the war-weary South.

As such, early in the morning of 30th January 1968, thirteen cities throughout the central portion of South Vietnam were attacked by Viet Cong forces. Within 24 hours, further coordinated attacks were launched on military bases, government facilities, cities, and towns throughout South Vietnam.

129 'Key Battles'. *Pritzker Military Museum and Library* < https://www.pritzkermilitary.org/explore/vietnam-war/key-battles> Accessed 31 March 2025.

While the American Marine base at Khe Sanh continued to fight off attackers, the city of Huế was stormed by North Vietnamese forces. In one particularly daring assault, a Viet Cong assault team breached the walls of the U.S. embassy compound in Saigon. Although all of the attackers were killed, the embassy attack was well-publicised.

The overall Tet Offensive was turned back with substantial losses for the North Vietnamese and the campaign had ended by late March. Although many American and The Army of the Republic of Vietnam (ARVN) servicemen (along with thousands of civilians) were killed or wounded, the personnel losses for the North Vietnamese were far greater. The Viet Cong and People's Army of Vietnam (PAVN) suffered around 45,000 casualties combined during the Tet Offensive.

Nevertheless, for an American public grown tired of the continual fighting in Vietnam with no end in sight, Tet was a turning point. Any expectations that the war was close to ending were shattered, and past reassurances from the Johnson Administration and General Westmoreland about the coming victory in Vietnam seemed dubious, to say the least. Heeding public pressure, President Johnson announced on the 31st March that he would limit the bombing of North Vietnam, call for negotiations–and most surprisingly–not run for re-election in 1968.[130]

Section 6: The Battle of Huế

31st January - 2nd March 1968

South Vietnam's third-largest city, an ancient royal capital located near the Demilitarised Zone (DMZ), Huế had remained relatively free of conflict during much of the early war. The city was largely under the protection of Army of the Republic of Vietnam (ARVN) troops who were spread out along the main highway from Huế to the DMZ.

On 31st January, with the start of the Tet Offensive, a powerful PAVN and Viet Cong assault quickly pushed back the scattered ARVN and U.S. Marine forces. The North Vietnamese established control over much of the city while the Marines fell back to the MACV compound south of the Perfume River.

Re-organising, a combined American/ARVN counterattack began to push the North Vietnamese forces back. Increasing American reinforcements, including elements of the First Cavalry Division supplemented by offshore naval artillery, land-based howitzers, and air strikes, proved instrumental in retaking the city. However, fierce

130 Ibid.

house-to-house fighting slowed conflict on the ground as North Vietnamese troops dug into the urban environment.

It would take a month to clear the entire city, with extra effort being paid to the entrenched North Vietnamese troops occupying the walled citadel of the imperial city. Around 700 ARVN and American forces were killed and thousands more wounded. The North Vietnamese lost around 5,000 in Huế proper and up to 3,000 more in the surrounding area. The city was left in ruins, with around 50% of Huế's buildings destroyed and its ancient citadel ruined. Thousands of were left homeless. [131]

Section 7: The Cambodia Invasion

30th April - 30th June 1970

Cambodia had long been a launching point for communist attacks on South Vietnam. Cambodia itself was in the midst of its own civil strife (the Khmer Rouge were fighting government forces with help from the North Vietnamese). In the past, the Kingdom of Cambodia under Prince Norodom Sihanouk had tried to stay neutral and did not openly oppose the communist bases in their country. In March 1970, Sihanouk was removed from power by Prime Minister Lon Nol and the new government began attacking Viet Cong positions in Cambodia.

Sensing an opportunity to prove his resolve to Hanoi, buy time for his Vietnamization programs, and relieve pressure on South Vietnam generally, President Richard Nixon opted to invade Cambodia.

On 30th April, Nixon announced in a televised address that American and South Vietnamese troops would enter Cambodia as a response to North Vietnamese aggression. 12,000 U.S. Army troops and 8,000 Army of the Republic of Vietnam (ARVN) troops attacked along a large 100 mile front. Nixon spoke of the Central Office for South Vietnam (COSVN, a supposed "Jungle Pentagon" where Viet Cong actions in South Vietnam were planned) and said it would be found and destroyed.

The invasion resulted in around 2,000 enemy fatalities and a large amount of equipment being captured, but no central planning center was found, nor was there a long term strategic gain. However, the invasion did cause massive protests in the U.S., including a confrontation and shooting at Kent State University in early May. Additionally, the invasion further destabilized Cambodia and weakened the central government's fight against the Khmer Rouge.[132]

131 Ibid.

132 Ibid.

Section 8: The Battle of Lam Son 719

8th February - 25th March 1971

In an effort to prove the capability of the armed forces of South Vietnam, *Operation Lam Son 719* was planned as a significant raid on the Ho Chi Minh Trail in Laos. Legally prohibited from entering Laotian territory, American forces provided logistical support within South Vietnam but the main effort was carried out by the Army of the Republic of Vietnam (ARVN) and several units of South Vietnamese marines. American forces occupied the abandoned base at Khe Sanh and established a staging area for the South Vietnamese. The South Vietnamese objective was to drive into Laos along the rugged Route 9, cut into the Ho Chi Minh Trail, and raid the administrative center of Tchepone before returning back to South Vietnam.

Equipped with U.S. supplied tanks and helicopters, the 16,000 ARVN troops were supported by thousands of U.S. troops in South Vietnam and with vital air power provided by U.S. aircraft.

While the initial push met little resistance, around 30,000 Peoples Army of Vietnam (PAVN) troops soon organized to meet the incursion. Outfitted with heavy Soviet weaponry, North Vietnamese forces halted the South Vietnamese push. Organisational and command issues among the South Vietnamese, together with their fighting performance on the ground, risked a complete rout, resulting in President Nguyen Van Thieu ordering a helicopter assault on Tchepone. Seizing the abandoned city (which was not the sole objective of the assault) and declaring a "victory", the South Vietnamese moved to withdraw. Stymied by fierce resistance along the road home, the South Vietnamese suffered a casualty rate of nearly 50%. Overall, the South Vietnamese armed forces proved ineffectual, and their morale plummeted.[133]

Section 9: The Easter Offensive

30th March - 22nd October 1972

Launched a few days before the 1972 Easter holiday, the Easter Offensive was a North Vietnamese push against South Vietnam utilizing conventional forces supplied with tanks and artillery. In a three-pronged offensive, four PAVN divisions were sent across the DMZ and two more divisions were deployed from positions in Laos towards Huế and Da Nang. A second prong utilizing three divisions from Cambodia

133 Ibid.

sought to sweep across the Central Highlands and cut the Republic of Vietnam in half. The third prong of the offensive was focused on the far south, with three divisions attacking the town of An Loc just 70 miles north of Saigon.

The offensive, organized by Vo Nguyen Giap and Van Tien Dang, calculated that a large assault would topple the government of President Thieu. Less than 100,000 Americans were still stationed in South Vietnam, but under President Nixon's Vietnamization program, their focus had switched to training the South Vietnamese forces.

American officials had expected a significant offensive, but were left surprised by the scale and ferocity–South Vietnamese forces were initially stunned by the massive assault. However, ARVN forces rallied and pushed back the attack. The offensive ended by May and the South Vietnamese were left to roll back Northern gains.

By October 1972, fighting related to the Easter Offensive had ended. North Vietnamese forces suffered massive material and personnel losses, with anywhere between 40-75,000 killed and another 60,000 wounded. Yet, however well South Vietnam seemed to have performed on its own, this success was tempered. While suffering less significant casualties (around 10,000 dead), ARVN units had only turned back the attacking PAVN forces with massive American air support. The heavy reliance on American air-power was an ominous sign for Vietnamization and for the future of South Vietnam.[134]

Section 10: Linebacker Operations

Although the United States never made any substantial effort to invade North Vietnam by land, the war was continually brought to the Democratic Republic of Vietnam from the air. *Operation Rolling Thunder* had carried out select bombings in North Vietnam from March 1965 to November 1968 when the bombings were ended by President Johnson.

Operation Linebacker I

The operation began as a response to the North Vietnamese *Easter Offensive* of March 1972. The conventional invasion of South Vietnam by the North created clear supply routes and mass troop formations which were easy targets for American air-power.

American Air Force, Marine, and Navy aircraft carried out a sustained bombing campaign against these targets, flying more than 41,000 sorties. Mine-laying aircraft attacked Haiphong Harbor, B-52 bombers hit large facilities, and tactical bombers hit

134 Ibid.

smaller targets. *Operation Linebacker I* played a large role in turning back the *Easter Offensive* but 75 American aircraft were lost.

Operation Linebacker II

In October 1972, as peace negotiations in Paris began to make substantial progress, the bombings were cut back. However, when negotiations broke down in December 1972, *Operation Linebacker II* was initiated. Announced by President Nixon as a full-scale air campaign, it included a concentrated use of B-52 bombers and tactical aircraft. About 700 B-52 sorties and 1,000 fighter-bomber sorties were flown in a campaign lasting less than two weeks. The *Christmas Bombings* targeted areas in and around Hanoi itself. Around 30 American aircraft were lost during the operation. While there is still debate as to the ultimate effect of *Linebacker II*, the North Vietnamese did return to the negotiating table less than a month after the bombings ended.[135] (See also Chapter Fift-Three: *Peace Without Honour.*)

135 Ibid.

CHAPTER FIFTY-TWO

Vietnamization

Section 1: Peace Talks

Like most prolonged conflicts, the Vietnam War produced several peace proposals and several rounds of peace talks. These attempts to negotiate a working peace were initiated by the United States, North Vietnam and by other nations acting as mediators. Proposals for cease-fires and peace deals flowed back and forth regularly, even when fighting was at its worst. Some of these negotiations were conducted publicly, some in secret through diplomatic communications or through 'back channels'.

The period 1964 to 1972 saw at least five different peace proposals of any significance, along with numerous third-party offers that were either disregarded or rebuffed. The significant number of peace proposals and their eventual failure reveals much about the nature of the Vietnam conflict and its chief combatants.

When President Richard M. Nixon swore the oath of office on 20th January 1969, one of his top priorities was to end the Vietnam War as quickly as possible on terms favorable to his administration. Thus, five days into his Presidency, negotiators from Washington flew to Paris to resume public peace talks with representatives of North and South Vietnam and the National Liberation Front.

Section 2: Cooking Up

Beginning on 18th March 1969 and continuing until 26 May 1970, while peace was being discussed in Paris, Nixon was directing *Operation Menu*, a covert United States Strategic Air Command (SAC) B-52 carpet-bombing campaign conducted in eastern Cambodia along the Ho Chi Minh Trail.

The targets of these attacks were sanctuaries and base areas of the People's Army of Vietnam (PAVN) and the Viet Cong. They were used for resupply, training, and resting between campaigns across the border in the Republic of Vietnam.

Individual rounds of bombing were named *Breakfast, Lunch, Dinner, Supper, and Snack.*

Section 3: Softening up

During the covert *Operation Menu*, Nixon met with South Vietnam's President Nguyen Van Thieu on Midway Island on 8th June 1969 to discuss the withdrawal of U.S. troops from Vietnam and the U.S. negotiating strategy with the North Vietnamese at the Paris Peace Talks. Nixon also made Thieu aware of the enormous political pressure he was under to the end the war immediately.

By July 1969, Nixon and his national security adviser Henry Kissinger had come to favor a strategy that combined international diplomacy with threats and acts of force to induce the Democratic Republic of Vietnam (DRV) to bend to their will. In several venues during July and August, they and their surrogates issued dire warnings intended for leaders in Moscow and Hanoi that if, by 1st November 1969, the North Vietnamese did not agree to a compromise on American terms, Nixon would "take measures of great consequence and force".[136]

Should these threats fail to move Moscow to persuade Hanoi to compromise, then the second phase of the military escalation option would begin: dramatic, sudden military pressure by means of a multifaceted campaign against the Democratic Republic of Vietnam (DRV) consisting mainly of heavy air attacks in the far-north of Vietnam, including mining operations on coastal ports.

The covert B-52 bombings of the Ho Chi Minh Trail may have been kept secret from the American people but not, obviously, from Hanoi. On 8th June 1969, the same day as Nixon met with President Thieu on Midway Island, Hanoi formed the Provisional Revolutionary Government of the Republic of South Vietnam (PRG), an armed underground government established to oppose the government of the Republic of Vietnam.

Section 4: Talking Up

On 3rd November 1969, two days after his ultimatum to Hanoi had expired and with no progress on a negotiated peace, Nixon explained in a televised address to the nation that the United States would no longer take the lead in the fight against the North Vietnamese. Instead, U.S. forces would train the South Vietnamese military to handle the conflict on its own:

136 'Note, Jean Sainteny to Nixon' (16 July 1969) Folder: Mister "S", Vol. 1, Box 106, Country Files-Far East-Vietnam Negotiations, Henry A. Kissinger Office File, Nixon Presidential Materials, *National Archives.*

> "In the previous administration", Nixon said into the camera, "we Americanized the war in Vietnam. In this administration, we are Vietnamizing the search for peace…"

The President continued:

> Let me now turn to our program for the future. We have adopted a plan which we have worked out in cooperation with the South Vietnamese for the complete withdrawal of all U.S. combat ground forces, and their replacement by South Vietnamese forces on an orderly scheduled timetable. This withdrawal will be made from strength and not from weakness. As South Vietnamese forces become stronger, the rate of American withdrawal can become greater. In addition to the withdrawal of U.S. forces, Nixon pledged an increase in the training and equipping of the South Vietnamese military as well as an **adherence to all treaty commitments.**

This strategy—dubbed "Vietnamization" by Secretary of Defense Melvin Laird and the "Nixon Doctrine" by the press—was best captured, Nixon said, by a leader of another Asian country who once told him: "When you are trying to assist another nation defend its freedom, U.S. policy should be to help them fight the war but not to fight the war for them".

However, Vietnamization could work only if American withdrawal was offset by improvement in Saigon's fighting capacity. By the beginning of 1970, the South Vietnamese military had more than one million men in uniform. These forces were equipped with $U.S. 4 billion worth of American equipment: rifles, artillery, munitions, helicopters and more. Most Army of the Republic of (South) Vietnam (ARVN) officers were given training in command, military strategy and counter-insurgency warfare.

This made South Vietnam one of the most militarised nations in Asia. The ARVN should, in theory, be capable of withstanding aggression from the North. The reality, however, was starkly different—improving the size of the ARVN proved to be much easier than improving its effectiveness.[137]

137 Llewellyn, J. et al, 'Vietnamisation', *Alpha History* <https://alphahistory.com/vietnamwar/vietnamisation/> Accessed 23 April 2025.

Section 5: War by Stealth

On 8th November 1969, Anthony Lewis of *The New York Times* wrote in part:

> **War by Stealth:** The pre-eminent task of Richard Nixon's Presidency is to heal a nation torn apart by Vietnam. The President knew that when he took the oath of office, and it is no less urgently true today. Part of the process must be to help the American people know, and accept, the unpleasant truths about the war: **that we got into it by stealth and for reasons at best uncertain**; that the Government we defend in South Vietnam is corrupt and unrepresentative; that in the course of fighting we have killed people and ravaged a country to an extent utterly out of proportion to our cause…
>
> **Rallying for War:** In those terms, Mr. Nixon's speech to the nation last Monday evening was a political tragedy. When he could have healed, he provoked. When he could have educated, he sought to arouse the old emotions. Four times he warned against "defeat"; twice he spoke of "disaster", and twice of "humiliation". Those were the words of a President rallying his people to war, not one explaining the difficult but necessary price of peace. The President did not use the word victory. But he made clearer than ever that he seeks to achieve by "Vietnamization" and gradual withdrawal exactly what we would achieve by military victory: preservation of the Saigon Government.
>
> **Implications for Hanoi:** Moreover, Mr. Nixon indicated that even gradual withdrawal depends on continued enemy forbearance. That is what he must have meant, if words mean anything, when he said he would "not hesitate to take strong and effective measures" in the event of increased enemy action. The Communists, then, are expected to sit by while we strengthen the troops of the regime they oppose and, perhaps, while we guarantee air and other support for years ahead; in short, they are expected to concede victory to our side…."
>
> **America's Greatness:** Mr. Nixon himself spoke of our "greatness as a nation" as the reason for fighting on. A great country, he said, cannot "take the easy way out". But in 1969, in Vietnam, greatness consists in accepting less than victory. That would not be an easy way out; it would be a hard way through which a President would have to lead us. One of Churchill's mottoes in World War II was "In victory, magnanimity." That was asking a lot of people; it may ask more to say: "In stalemate, magnanimity".[138]

138 Lewis, Anthony. (8 November 1969). 'The Test of American Greatness'. *The New York Times*. <https://www.nytimes.com/1969/11/08/archives/the-test-of-american-greatness-in-vietnam.html> Accessed 5 January 2026.

On 21st December 1969, James Sterba of *The New York Times* wrote of Nixon's policy of Vietnamization, saying in part:

> **More Rhetoric Than Risk:** SAIGON—The reaction of experienced observers here last week to President Nixon's statement that "we must take risks for peace" was that he has done almost exactly the opposite so far. The withdrawal of about 63,000 troops throughout the summer and fall has involved more rhetoric than risk, they argued. The South Vietnamese armed forces remain, for the most part, untested, they added. The improvement of South Vietnamese soldiers appears to grow in direct proportion to the distance away from their battlefields. The public relations effort here has outstripped the willingness of many American commanders to put professed South Vietnamese military prowess to a firm test. It is difficult to ask some commanders and spokesmen here any question without receiving a plug for Vietnamization in response. Word has gone down the chain of command that Vietnamization is not only high priority policy but high priority public relations as well. Information advisers have been prepped on their usage of words. They used to say they worked for the South Vietnamese; now the South Vietnamese are "doing for themselves with limited supervision".
>
> **Nowhere in Paris:** ...President Nixon has said many times that the rate of American troop withdrawal depended on three criteria: progress at Paris; the level of enemy activity; and the improvement of South Vietnamese forces. The Paris talks, he has conceded, have gone nowhere. A few weeks ago, supply trucks from the North began moving down the Ho Chi Minh trail in preparation for another offensive. Improvement in the South Vietnamese military is the only criteria he has left to justify the exit of American troops. It is also the easiest criterion to manufacture. South Vietnam's armed forces, both regulars and paramilitary units, have increased in number since January 1968 from 774,000 to the present 1,090,000. But some observers here have questioned the combat readiness of the South Vietnamese to assume much of the war burden. If there is one clear risk the President is taking, his critics here say, it is in overselling Vietnamization. [139]

139 Sterba, James P. (21 December 1969), 'Vietnam 2: Saigon's Forces Are Still Untested-Fewer U.S. Troops'. *The New York Times*. <https://www.nytimes.com/1969/12/21/archives/vietnam-2-saigons-forces-are-still-untested-fewer-us-troops.html> Accessed 14 January 2026.

Section 7: The Cambodia Invasion

Six months after announcing his policy of Vietnamization, President Nixon ordered a temporary invasion of Cambodia—the administration called it an incursion—by a combined force of American and South Vietnamese troops.

A Cambodian *coup* in March 1970 had replaced neutralist leader Prince Norodom Sihanouk with a pro-American military government led by Lon Nol. Lon Nol demanded that the North Vietnamese withdraw from their base camps along the South Vietnamese border. The North Vietnamese reacted by extending their presence toward the west.

As an added incentive for invasion, American officials believed they had located in Cambodia the Central Office of South Vietnam (COSVN)—the headquarters for North Vietnamese operations below the 17th parallel.

On 28th April 1970, seeking to bolster the pro-American government and to strike at COSVN as well as to buy time for the ARVN's improvement, Nixon ordered the invasion.

Two days later, Nixon took to the airwaves to explain to the American people that the U.S. military, along with the South Vietnamese People's Army, were invading Cambodia in order to intensify the destruction of Viet Cong base camps and to impede North Vietnamese supply lines.

It took Moscow to point out that, by invading Cambodia, Nixon had violated the terms of the Geneva Accords of 1954 and broken his 3rd November 1969 pledge to **adhere to all treaty commitments:**

> MOSCOW, April 30 —The Soviet Union today condemned the intrusion into Cambodian territory by American-supported South Vietnamese forces. It called it "direct aggression against a member of the United Nations".
>
> In the first Soviet response to the border crossing yesterday, TASS, the official press agency, said "the intrusion of Saigon troops into the Cambodian territory, supported by military equipment and U.S. advisers is the grossest violation of Cambodia's neutrality. By this action, Washington and Saigon have spread the flame of war to Cambodian territory", Tass said. The action was also described as "a gross violation of the 1954 Geneva agreements", which provided, among other things, for the independence and neutrality of Cambodia.[140]

140 Gwertzman, Bernard (1 May 1970). 'Moscow condemns U.S. and Saigon on Cambodia'. *The New York Times* < https://www.nytimes.com/1970/05/01/archives/moscow-condemns-u-s-and-saigon-on-cambodia.html> Accessed 23 December 2025.

The American bombing and invasion of Cambodia were weaponised as a recruiting tool by the Khmer Rouge, a Cambodian Communist guerrilla group who would later come to power in Pol Pot's brutal regime that would kill over two million people.

Kent State

The Cambodia Invasion sparked violent protests on campuses across the United States and provoked the largest round of antiwar rallies in American history. It was during demonstrations at Kent State University on 4th May 1970 that Ohio National Guardsmen fired at rock-throwing protestors, killing four and wounding nine. Two weeks later, police fired on students at Jackson State University in Mississippi, leaving two more dead. The shootings at Kent State and Jackson galvanised the country against the Cambodia invasion.

Section 8: The Crucial Test

In February 1971, seeking to prove their 'effectiveness', South Vietnamese forces crossed into Laos in *Operation Lam Son 719*. (See also Chapter Fifty-One: *The Crucible*)

Operation Lam Son 719, a crucial test of Vietnamization, was planned as a significant raid on the Ho Chi Minh Trail in Laos. Legally prohibited from entering Laotian territory, American forces provided logistical support within South Vietnam but the main effort was carried out by the Army of the Republic of Vietnam (ARVN) and several units of South Vietnamese marines.

American forces occupied the abandoned base at Khe Sanh and established a staging area for the ARVN. The South Vietnamese objective was to drive into Laos along Route 9, cut into the Ho Chi Minh Trail, and raid the administrative center of Tchepone before returning to South Vietnam.

Equipped with U.S. supplied tanks and helicopters, the 16,000 ARVN troops were supported by thousands of U.S. troops in South Vietnam and with vital air power provided by U.S. aircraft.

While the initial push met little resistance, around 30,000 Peoples Army of Vietnam (PAVN) troops soon organised to meet the incursion. Outfitted with heavy Soviet weaponry, North Vietnamese forces halted the South Vietnamese push. Organisational and command issues among the South Vietnamese, together with their fighting performance on the ground, risked a complete rout, resulting in President Nguyen Van Theiu ordering a helicopter assault on Tchepone. Seizing the abandoned city (which was not the sole objective of the assault) and declaring a "victory", the South Vietnamese moved to withdraw. Meeting fierce resistance along the route home, they suffered a casualty rate of nearly 50%. Overall, the South Vietnamese armed forces proved ineffectual and their morale plummeted.[141]

In late March 1972, expecting that a victory on the battlefield would translate into a triumph at the negotiating table, the North Vietnamese opened a three-pronged offensive in South Vietnam, known in the U.S. as the *Easter Offensive.*

Rather than accept the prospect of defeat, Nixon sent massive air force and naval reinforcements to bases in Indo-China and Guam. On 4th May 1972, he decided to mine North Vietnam's harbors and began *Operation Linebacker*, a sustained air offensive against North Vietnam.

Section 9: The Third Force

Nixon's policy of Vietnamization—equipping Saigon to fight the North Vietnamese—not only prolonged the war for five more years but also escalated it through aerial bombardment which averaged about 100,000 tons of explosives a month on South Vietnam in 1969 and 1970.

In April 1971, *Look* magazine reported on the destruction of dams, dikes, canals, and mile upon mile of "rice fields pockmarked with millions of large craters filled with water in which malarial mosquitoes have been breeding in epidemic numbers". These high explosives, combined with chemical spraying (which the Pentagon admitted in 1969 was limited only by the ability of the United States to produce it) had, by the end of 1970, destroyed about half of the crop land in South Vietnam. This caused serious food shortages and forced Saigon to import huge amounts of staples. Devastation and widespread hunger in the countryside drove millions of the rural population into urban areas and camps for displaced persons.

The plight of these refugees was among the reasons behind the hundreds of demonstrations staged every month by scores of civic groups in the south which had, in 1970, formed the People's Front in the Struggle for Peace. The front's ten-point platform was headed by the demand "that the Americans and their allies withdraw completely from Vietnam as the most important precondition for an end to the war". The urban movement of groups from the right to the left became known as the third segment, or Third Force.

141 'Key Battles'. *Pritzker Military Museum and Library* < https://www.pritzkermilitary.org/explore/vietnam-war/key-battles> Accessed 31 March 2025.

Note

Parts of this Chapter are reproduced, adapted, or paraphrased from a *Cairo Review of Global Affairs* essay entitled 'After the Fall of Saigon' by Professor of History at the University of Maine, Ngo Vinh Long, [142] from the University of Virginia's *Miller Centre* commentary on 'Vietnamization',[143] on 'President Nixon's Speech on Vietnamization' from New York's *Vassar College,* Vietnam War collection, [144] and on 'Milestones in the History of U.S. Foreign Relations 1969-1976' from the Department of State's *Office of the Historian* document collection.[145]

142 Ngo Vinh Long. Essay: 'After the Fall of Saigon' *Cairo Review of Global Affairs* <https://www.thecairoreview.com/essays/after-the-fall-of-saigon/> Accessed 14 March 2025.

143 'Vietnamization'. *The Miller Center, University of Virginia.* < https://millercenter.org/the-presidency/educational-resources/vietnamization> Accessed 12 April 2025.

144 'President Nixon's Speech on Vietnamization, 3 November 1969: The Wars for Vietnam'. *Vassar College* <https://www.vassar.edu/the-wars-for-vietnam/documents/president-nixons-speech-vietnamization-november-3-1969> Accessed 13 April 2025.

145 'Ending the Vietnam War, 1969-1973'. Milestones: 1969-1976. *Office of the Historian, Foreign Service Institute, United States Department of State* < https://history.state.gov/milestones/1969-1976/ending-vietnam> Accessed 1 April 2025.

CHAPTER FIFTY-THREE

Peace without Honour

Between the 11th-12th October 1972, President Nixon's National Security Advisor, Henry Kissinger, and North Vietnam's Le Duc Tho, reached agreement on a peace settlement, both sides working towards that end before the U.S. presidential election due on 7th November. South Vietnam's President Thieu rejected the settlement, refusing to accept a peace that left North Vietnamese forces in South Vietnam and which legitimised the shadow Provisional Revolutionary Government (PRG).

Thieu's rejection of the settlement forced Kissinger to resume negotiations but he was unable to find any common ground acceptable to both Vietnamese parties in two renewed rounds.

Section 1: The Mockery

On 14th December 1972, in order to break the deadlock, President Nixon ordered large-scale B–52 attacks on the North Vietnamese heartland—the *Christmas Bombings*. At the same time, he continued to exert intense pressure on Thieu, threatening to cut off U.S. economic, military, and political support if Thieu refused to accept an agreement.

A proposed agreement was reached after negotiations resumed on 8th January 1973. Nixon had gained Thieu's reluctant acceptance through a series of letters and envoys, all promising U.S. military support in the event of a North Vietnamese violation of the agreement. On 14th November 1972, for example, Nixon had written to Thieu saying that: "I repeat my personal assurances to you that the United States will react very strongly and rapidly to any violation of the agreement". Both sides understood this to mean the recommitment of B–52's to combat.

The 'Agreement on Ending the War and Restoring Peace in Vietnam, otherwise known as the Paris Peace Accords, was signed on 27th January 1973 by the Democratic Republic of Vietnam, the Republic of Vietnam, the Provisional Revolutionary Government (PRG), and the United States. The Accords officially ended direct U.S. military involvement in Vietnam.

The Agreement established a cease-fire, a 60-day period for withdrawal of all American and other foreign troops, and the return of U.S. civilian and military personnel held prisoner by North Vietnamese forces. The Agreement also recognised the territorial integrity and unity of Vietnam and clearly called for negotiations between the Saigon regime and its internal opponents leading toward a political settlement in the South and an eventual reunification of Vietnam "through peaceful means".

All the circumstances surrounding the signing of the Paris Peace Accords make a mockery of Nixon's description of the Agreement as 'Peace with Honour'.

Section 2: No, No, No, No

Not long after the Accords were signed on 27th January 1973, South Vietnam's President Thieu reiterated—with American acquiescence if not outright support—his "Four Nos" policy: no recognition of the enemy; no coalition government; no neutralisation of the southern region of Vietnam; and no concession of territory.

In a July 1973 interview in *Vietnam Report*, the English-language publication of the Saigon Council on Foreign Relations, Thieu stated: "In the first place, we have to do our best so that the National Libration Front cannot build itself into a state, a second state within the South". In the second place, he continued, his government should use all means at its disposal to prevent the development of the Third Force, branding all Third Force persons as pro-Communist. (In 1970, scores of civic groups had formed the People's Front in the Struggle for Peace, the urban movement of groups from the right to the left known as the third segment, or Third Force.)

Arrests of Third Force activists soared and attacks on Provisional Revolutionary Government (PRG)-controlled areas by the Saigon regime increased, partly because of increased military aid to Saigon after the signing of the Paris Peace Accords. The United States supplied the Thieu government with so many arms that, as Major General Peter Olenchuk testified before the Senate Armed Services Committee in May 1973: "We shortchanged ourselves within our overall inventories. We also shortchanged the reserve units in terms of prime assets. In certain instances, we also diverted equipment that would have gone to Europe".

The 16th February 1974 edition of the *Washington Post* quoted Pentagon officials as saying that Thieu's armed forces were: "firing blindly into free zones (PRG-controlled areas) because they knew full well they would get all the replacement supplies they needed from the United States".

By that time, however, American experts on Vietnam, both inside and outside the government, understood that the military, political, and economic position of South Vietnam was deteriorating rapidly. The American public and Congress, consumed by the Watergate scandal and a desire to move beyond the Vietnam War, paid little attention and had absolutely no interest in re-introducing American troops. High-level Nixon officials understood this dynamic, but wanted to continue economic, political, and military aid to South Vietnam.

Gerald R. Ford confronted this difficult situation when he assumed the presidency on 9th August 1974 following Nixon's resignation the previous day.

Later that year, President Ford reiterated Nixon's request for a fresh infusion of aid. Congress responded by granting South Vietnam $700 million in military and humanitarian assistance, an amount that was far less than Nixon's original request of $1.45 billion.

Renewed assaults by North Vietnamese forces in the first months of 1975 toppled one southern province after another without too much resistance from Thieu's forces. It was the beginning of the end.

Note

Parts of this Chapter are reproduced, adapted, or paraphrased from a *Cairo Review of Global Affairs* essay entitled 'After the Fall of Saigon' by Professor of History at the University of Maine, Ngo Vinh Long, [146] from the University of Virginia's *Miller Centre* commentary on Vietnamization,[147] and on 'Milestones in the History of U.S. Foreign Relations 1969-1976' from the Department of State's *Office of the Historian* document collection.[148]

146 Ngo Vinh Long. Essay: 'After the Fall of Saigon'. *Cairo Review of Global Affairs* <https://www.thecairoreview.com/essays/after-the-fall-of-saigon/> Accessed 14 March 2025.

147 'Vietnamization'. *The Miller Center, University of Virginia.* < https://millercenter.org/the-presidency/educational-resources/vietnamization> Accessed 12 April 2025.

148 'Ending the Vietnam War, 1969-1973. Milestones: 1969-1976'. *Office of the Historian, Foreign Service Institute, United States Department of State.* < https://history.state.gov/milestones/1969-1976/ending-vietnam> Accessed 1 April 2025.

CHAPTER FIFTY-FOUR

The Inglorious Finish

On 10th March 1975, the People's Army of Vietnam (PAVN) and the Viet Cong, commanded by General Van Tien Dang, began a sustained offensive against the South. Attacking in the Central Highlands, PAVN forces captured Ban Me Thuot, a town just south of the Ia Drang Valley. Fearful of having his army divided, South Vietnam's President Nguyen Van Thieu ordered an evacuation of the Central Highlands that quickly devolved into a total rout. Adding to the tide, North Vietnamese army units stormed across the DMZ, capturing Huế on 26 March and Da Nang on 30th March. Fleeing ARVN units melted away or were picked off by approaching PAVN troops.

U.S. President Gerald Ford tried to rush a $722 million aid deal for South Vietnam through Congress but legislators rejected it out of hand. President Thieu thereupon resigned on 21st April.

On 29th April, American forces carried out *Operation Frequent Wind*, the withdrawal of all remaining American personnel and many South Vietnamese government workers and civilians. This massive aerial campaign allowed for the evacuation of 7,000 from Saigon, an effort memorialised by the rooftop evacuation of the American embassy.[149]

North Vietnamese forces stormed into Saigon on 30th April 1975, marking the end of the Vietnam War.

General Duong Van Minh, who had become South Vietnam's leader following Thieu's resignation on 21st April and subsequent escape to Taiwan, surrendered to a North Vietnamese officer at the Presidential Independence Palace.

Signing Off

In *The New York Times* 2014 Obituary marking the death of Thomas Polgar, the last CIA Station Chief in Saigon, William Yardley writes in part:

> Saigon was falling and the United States was fleeing, desperately evacuating the last of its embassy staff and C.I.A. officers in the final, chaotic hours of April

149 'Key Battles'. *Pritzker Military Museum and Library*. < https://www.pritzkermilitary.org/explore/vietnam-war/key-battles> Accessed 31 March 2025.

1975. With the airport under siege by the North Vietnamese, helicopters landed on rooftops to ferry away Americans and some South Vietnamese.

Thomas Polgar, the Saigon station chief for the C.I.A., helped lead the effort, lifting people over fences and destroying files. Just before Mr. Polgar destroyed the cable-sending machine the agency had used to communicate, and just before he boarded a helicopter himself, he took a moment to type a last dispatch.

"This will be final message from Saigon station", Mr. Polgar wrote. "It has been a long and hard fight and we have lost. This experience, unique in the history of the United States, does not signal necessarily the demise of the United States as a world power.

"The severity of the defeat and the circumstances of it, however, would seem to call for a reassessment of the policies of niggardly half-measures which have characterized much of our participation here despite the commitment of manpower and resources, which were certainly generous. Those who fail to learn from history are forced to repeat it. Let us hope that we will not have another Vietnam experience and that we have learned our lesson". [150]

Déjà Vu

Forty-Six years later, the world watched the same humiliating U.S. withdrawal from Afghanistan as was witnessed in Vietnam in 1975. Given events in the early months of 2026, it is not yet clear whether the United States has learned from its history in Vietnam and Afghanistan, or is making yet another attempt to recreate a nation in its own image.

Consequences

Almost 59,000 Americans, Australians and New Zealanders; at least 250,000 South Vietnamese troops; over a million North Vietnamese soldiers and Viet Cong guerillas; and an unknown number of Vietnamese civilians died during the conflict.

Nguyen The Phiet, a former Vietnamese Consul General in Sydney, cited the following additional statistics in a 2005 Conference talk:

> The war ended, but its consequences were quite heavy. The U.S. Air Force had dropped 7,856,000 tons of bombs on Vietnamese soil, equal to 640 atomic bombs like that dropped on Hiroshima during World War II. The U.S. had sprayed over south Vietnam 451,260 tons of defoliants containing dioxin and

150 Yardley, William (7 April 2014). 'Thomas Polgar, C.I.A. Officer, Dies at 91; Helped Lead U.S. Evacuation of Saigon'. *The New York Times*. < https://www.nytimes.com/2014/04/07/world/asia/thomas-polgar-cia-officer-dies-at-91-helped-lead-us-evacuation-of-saigon.html> Accessed 22 December 2025.

338,000 tons of napalm bombs—ten times more than the quantity used in the Korean War and 2.5 times more than in World War II. Some 3,777,000 land mines were laid which killed nearly three million people and crippled nearly three million more. Hundreds of thousands of children have been born deformed. The war also left more than three million people jobless, more than one million soldiers and functionaries of the Saigon administration, 270,000 wounded or invalid soldiers of the former regime, 10,000 criminals, 500,000 prostitutes and 200,000 drug addicts.

In the north, all cities and towns were bombed, of which twelve large towns and fifty-two small towns were completely destroyed. 4000 out of 5788 communes were raided from the air, of which 30 were completely razed. All industrial zones were devastated, many of them completely wiped out. All power plants were seriously damaged. Five million square metres of residential houses were reduced to rubble. All railway lines, all bridges, all sea and river ports and store houses were bombed. One thousand six hundred irrigation works were destroyed and 40,000 draught animals were killed. Three thousand schools were destroyed and 350 hospitals were bombed, of which ten were razed. U.S. bombs and toxic chemicals destroyed 5 million hectares of forest.[151]

151 Nguyen The Phiet. 'Vietnam's Long History of Struggle' in *Links International Journal for Socialist Renewal.* 2005. < https://links.org.au/vietnams-long-history-struggle> Accessed 20 March 2025.

CHAPTER FIFTY-FIVE

Programmed to Fail

Section 1: Strategic Hamlets

Yellow Star Rising

By late 1961, if not earlier, it had become clear in both Saigon and Washington that the yellow star of the Viet Cong was in the ascendancy.

Following the 1960 North Vietnamese announcement of the twin goals of ousting South Vietnam's President Diem and reunifying Vietnam under communist rule, the Viet Cong began to increase its guerrilla, subversive, and political warfare. Viet Cong regular forces, now estimated to have grown to 25,000, had been organized into larger formations and employed with increasing frequency. The terrorist-guerrilla organization had grown to an estimated 17,000 by November 1961...

The VC continued to hold the initiative in the countryside, controlling major portions of the populace and drawing an increasingly tight cinch around Saigon. The operative question was not whether the Diem government, as it was then moving, could defeat the insurgents, but whether it could save itself.

Much of this deterioration of the situation in the Republic of (South) Vietnam (RVN) was attributable, in U. S. eyes, to the manner in which President Diem had organized his government. The struggle--whether viewed as one to gain loyalty or simply to assert control--was focused in and around the villages and hamlets in the countryside. It was precisely in those areas that the bi-lineal GVN organization (ARVN and civilian province chiefs) most lacked the capability for concerted and cohesive action...

The abortive coup of late 1960 had made Diem even more reluctant than he had earlier been to permit power (especially coercive power) to be gathered into one set of hands other than his own. Still, the establishment of an effective military chain of command which could operate where necessary in the countryside remained the prime objective of U. S. military advisors...

For President Diem's purposes, this bi-lineal organization offered an opportunity to counterbalance the power (and *coup* potential) of the generals by the power of the province chiefs. It was a device for survival. But the natural by-product of this duality, in terms of the effectiveness of actions against the VC, was poor coordination and imperfect cooperation in intelligence collection and production, in planning, and in operational execution in the countryside where the battles were fought--both the "battle for men's minds" and the more easily understood battles for control of the hamlets, villages, districts, and provinces. [152]

Insurgency Strategy

By early 1962, there was apparent consensus among the principal participants that the Strategic Hamlet Program, as it came to be called, represented the unifying concept for a strategy designed to pacify rural Vietnam (the Viet Cong's chosen battleground) and to develop support among the peasants for the central government.

The Strategic Hamlet Program was much broader than the construction of strategic hamlets *per se.* It envisioned sequential phases which, beginning with clearing the insurgents from an area and protecting the rural populace, progressed through the establishment of the Government of South Vietnam (GVN) infrastructure and thence to the provision of services which would lead the peasants to identify with their government. The Program was, in short, an attempt to translate the newly articulated theory of counter-insurgency into operational reality. The objective was political though the means to its realization were a mixture of military, social, psychological, economic and political measures.

Varying Perspectives

The problem with the apparent consensus which emerged early in 1962 was that the principal participants viewed it with different perspectives and expectations. On the U.S. side, military advisors had a set of preferences which affected their approach to the Strategic Hamlet Program. They wanted to make the Armed Forces of South Vietnam (RVNAF) more mobile, more aggressive, and better organised to take the offensive against the Viet Cong. They were, consequently, extremely leery of proposals which might lead it to be tied down in strategic defenses ("holding" after "clearing" had been completed) or diverted too much to military-civic action undertakings.

The American political leadership, insofar as a generalization may be attempted, may be said to have been most concerned with the later phases of the program--those in which GVN services were provided, local governments established, and the economy bolstered. Military clearing operations were, to them, a distasteful, expensive, but necessary precondition to the really critical and important phases of this effort.

152 Pentagon Paper [Part IV. B. 2.] Evolution of the War. Counterinsurgency: Strategic Hamlet Program, 1961-63. pp. 3-4. *National Archives and Records Administration* <https://www.archives.gov/research/pentagon-papers> Accessed 16 December 2025.

President Diem--unsurprisingly--had a very different view. His need, as he saw it, was to get the U. S. committed to South Vietnam (and to his administration) without surrendering his independence. He knew that his nation would fall without U. S. support; he feared that his government would fall if he either appeared to toady to U. S. wishes or allowed any single group too much potential power--particularly coercive power.

The Strategic Hamlet Program offered a vehicle by which he could direct the counter-insurgent effort as he thought it should be directed and without giving up either his prerogatives to the U.S. or his mantle to his restless generals...[153]

Old Wine in New Bottles

In August 1962, the GVN produced its long awaited national pacification plan with four priority areas and specified priorities within each area. At the same time, however, it indicated that over 2,500 strategic hamlets had already been completed and that work was underway on over 2,500 more. Although it was not until October 1962 that the GVN explicitly announced the Strategic Hamlet Program to be the unifying concept of its pacification and counter-insurgent effort, it was clear that the program had already assumed this central position.

Three important implications of this early progress (or more precisely, reported progress) are also clear in retrospect. These implications seem not to have impressed themselves acutely upon U. S. observers at the time. First, the program was truly one of GVN initiative rather than one embodying priorities and time phasing recommended by the U. S. Diem was running with his own ball in programmatic terms, no matter who articulated the theory of the approach. The geographic dispersion of hamlets already reported to be completed indicated that there was, in fact, a conscious effort to implement this phase almost simultaneously throughout the entire nation rather than to build slowly as Diem's foreign advisors recommended.

Finally, the physical aspects of Diem's program were similar, if not identical, to earlier population resettlement and control efforts practiced by the French. The long history of these efforts was marked by consistency in results as well as in techniques: all failed dismally because they ran into resentment if not active resistance on the part of the peasants at whose control and safety, then loyalty, they were aimed...

Population relocation into defended villages was by no means a recent development in Southeast Asia. Parts of South Vietnam had experience with the physical aspects of fortified communities going back many years.

153 Ibid. pp. i, ii.

The French had made resettlement and the development of "secure zones" an important element near the end of their war with the Viet Minh. The government of newly-created South Vietnam, headed since 1954 by President Diem, had continued resettlement schemes to accommodate displaced persons, to control suspected rural populations, and to safeguard loyal peasants in the threatened areas. None of these efforts involving resettlement had succeeded. Each had inspired antagonism among the peasants who were moved from their ancestral lands and away from family burial plots.

Diem's actions in late 1961 were thus inescapably tied to earlier actions by proximity in time, place, and the personal experiences of many peasants. Chief among the earlier programs was that of the so-called Agrovilles or "Rural Community Development Centers", launched in 1959. The Agrovilles groupments of 300-500 families were designed to afford the peasantry the social benefits of city life (schools and services), to increase their physical security, and to control certain key locations by denying them to the communists. They were designed to improve simultaneously the security and well-being of their inhabitants and the government's control over the rural population and rural areas.

The Agroville program was generally unsuccessful. The peasants had many complaints about it ranging from clumsy, dishonest administration to the physical hardship of being too far from their fields and the psychological wrench of being separated from ancestral homes and burial plots...

It was inevitable, given this lineage, that the strategic hamlet program be regarded by the peasants as old wine in newly-labelled bottles. The successes and failures of the past were bound to condition its acceptance and, by late 1961, the Diem government was more having more failures than successes. [154]

Death Throes

President Diem grew increasingly unwilling to meet U. S. demands for reform. He believed that to do so would cause his government to fail. U. S. observers held that failure to do so would cause the nation, not just the government to fall. In the event, the government fell and the nation's counter-insurgent program took a definite turn for the worse, but the nation did not fall. The Strategic Hamlet Program did.

Closely identified with Ngo Dinh Diem and his brother, it was almost bound to suffer their fortunes; when they died, it died as well. The new government of generals,

154 Ibid. pp. 1-2.

presumably realizing the extent of peasant displeasure with resettlement and control measures, did nothing to save it.[155]

Failure Analysis

The dominant U. S. view has been that the Strategic Hamlet Program failed because of over-expansion and the establishment of hamlets in basically insecure areas. That there was overexpansion and the establishment of many poorly defended hamlets is not questioned. This contributed, beyond doubt, to the failure of the program. But this view finesses the problem of the process for which the strategic hamlets were but the tangible symbol. The present analysis has sought to emphasize both the essentially political nature of the objective of the Strategic Hamlet Program and the political nature of the context in which the process evolved--of expectations, bargaining, and attempts to exert influence on other participants in policy formulation and implementation. In this context it is the U.S. inability to exert leverage on President Diem (or Diem's inability to reform) that emerges as the principal cause of failure.

Yet, both of these attempts to pinpoint the reasons why the Strategic Hamlet Program did not succeed fail to get at another whole issue: the validity of that body of writings which one may call the theory and doctrine of counterinsurgency.

Neither the military nor the political aspects of this doctrine can be upheld (or proved false) by an examination of the Strategic Hamlet Program. Quite aside from whether or not Diem was able to broaden the program's appeal to the peasantry, what would have occurred had he made a determined and sustained effort to do so? Would this have led in some more-or-less direct way to stability or to even greater dissatisfaction? We simply do not know. The question is as unanswerable as whether the appetite grows with the eating or is satisfied by it. The contention here is that claims of mismanagement are not sufficient to conclude that better management would necessarily have produced the desired results.

A Vicious Circle

In the military sphere, the unanswerable questions are different. It is said that the military phase of the Strategic Hamlet Program progressed reasonably well in many areas; the failure was in the political end of the process. But did the military actions succeed? Might failures to develop adequate intelligence and to weed out VC infrastructure in these hamlets not as easily be attributable to the fact that the inhabitants knew they were not really safe from VC intimidation and reprisals? Does the analogy to an "oil spot" have operational meaning when small bands can carry

155 Ibid. pp. i-iv.

out hit and run raids or when many small bands can concentrate in one location and achieve surprise? Where is the he key to this vicious circle--or is there a key?

Doomed

While the abortive Strategic Hamlet Program of 1961-1963 may teach one something, the available record does not permit one to conclude either that the program fell because of the failure of a given phase or that other phases were, in fact, adequate to the challenge. One may say that the program was doomed by poor execution and by the inability of the Ngo family to reform coupled with the inability of the U.S. to induce them to reform. [156]

A Data Failure

In 1967, the U.S. military in South Vietnam launched the Hamlet Evaluation System (HES), a new type of data-processing system comprising a demographic database and monthly surveys for monitoring the progress of its counterinsurgency effort. Already highly controversial at the time, the HES had a considerable impact on strategic and political decisions. A close examination of its conception and practices of data collection, processing, and analysis reveals that the system could not adequately capture the dynamics of war, especially refugee movements. Although several revisions steadily refined the system, policy makers and the military only embraced highly aggregated results. The quantified representation of the political and military situation in Vietnam even promoted and legitimized profound interventions in the social fabric of rural South Vietnam.[157]

Section 2: Pacification

Reflection

In an 18th January 2018 article in *The New York Times* headed 'The Terrible Violence of Pacification', Mai Elliott reflected on the Pacification Program. The journalist wrote in part:

> By the time of the cease-fire in Vietnam in 1973, more than 10 million South Vietnamese, mostly from rural areas—well over half of the estimated total population of 17 million—had been driven from their homes by the war. The

156 Ibid. p. 36.

157 Feichtinger. M. 'Computing Counterinsurgency: The Hamlet Evaluation System (HES) in the American War in Vietnam' in *The Annals of the History of Computing*, October 2022. <https://www.researchgate.net/publication/364481218_Computing_Counterinsurgency_The_Hamlet_Evaluation_System_HES_in_the_American_War_in_Vietnam> Accessed 16 December 2025.

United States Senate subcommittee on refugees estimated that by 1974, over 1.4 million civilians had been killed and wounded, and attributed over 50 percent of these casualties to the firepower of American and South Vietnamese forces.

These displacements and casualties were not just the by-product of warfare but also a result of deliberate policies by the United States and South Vietnamese governments.

Wreaking Havoc

In Vietnam, the United States fought two wars: a conventional war in remote areas against the North Vietnamese Army units that had infiltrated into the South, and a struggle among the rural people to win their "hearts and minds". It was in this fight for influence and control against the insurgents (or Viet Cong) in the rural areas, where 80 percent of the people lived, that the American and South Vietnamese governments wreaked the most havoc on the population.

For the Viet Cong (who preferred to refer to themselves as liberators: the National Front for the Liberation of South Vietnam), the rural population was vital to their survival and hope for victory. The insurgents lived among them and depended on them for intelligence, protection, recruits and resources. As Mao Zedong famously put it, the guerrillas are the fish; the people are the water. To expand their zone, the Viet Cong would infiltrate villages under government control to proselytize and recruit.

To clear the Viet Cong from the areas they controlled and from contested villages, the United States relied on the strategy of pacification. "Pacification" derives from a Latin word that means to make peace, but the act of pacification is violent. It started with an assault on hamlets and villages, with bombing, shelling and mortar barrages to prepare the way for ground attacks. Once a hamlet or village was taken over, South Vietnamese government officials moved in to solidify control. Militia and self-defense forces were set up to provide security. Then the government would try to win "hearts and minds" by building schools and clinics, and begin a process of economic development leading to modernization.

Indiscriminate Destruction

In December 1965, the insurgents were reported to control 56.4 percent of the land area of South Vietnam, or 37,400 square miles of a total territory of 66,200 square miles. Most of the land they controlled was in remote regions such as the Central Highlands, the Plain of Reeds and other sparsely populated areas like those near the border with Cambodia and Laos. So although they held over half of the land area, they controlled only about 24.5 percent of the population, about 3.7 million people. Another 13,000 square miles were considered contested areas.

Those figures suggested to American planners that pacification could target more than a quarter of the population and over half of the country's land area. Pacification on such a scale, however, was infeasible for the Saigon government to undertake, so only so-called priority villages—those near military bases, air fields, transportation arteries, and towns and cities—were subjected to pacification. Those under the control of Viet Cong were designated as "free fire zones" and bombed and shelled, under the assumption that anyone who lived there was Viet Cong by definition.

The bombing and shelling drove people to flee into areas under government control in greater numbers. Statistics published in January 1975 by the Subcommittee to Investigate Problems Connected With Refugees and Escapees, part of the Senate Committee on the Judiciary, indicated that the number of refugees registered by the government in 1965 was 772,000. This number grew to 906,000 in 1966. By 1967, the government had registered 2.1 million refugees. In addition to those the government registered—those placed in squalid camps of dilapidated huts—there were an estimated two million who were not registered, including about one million in Saigon.

Herding

In mid-1967, Samuel Huntington of Harvard, working as a consultant to the State Department, visited Vietnam. On his return, he wrote an article in *Foreign Affairs*: "The Bases of Accommodation", in which he stated that "the most dramatic and far-reaching impact of the war in South Vietnam has been the tremendous shift in population from the countryside to the cities".

He went on to say: "In an absent-minded way the United States in Vietnam may well have stumbled upon the answer to the insurgency". The answer lies in "forced-draft urbanization and modernization", which would drive the rural population from the villages into urban areas and deprive the insurgency the support it needed "to generate enough strength to come to power".

Although Professor Huntington wrote that "the social costs of this change have been dramatic and often heart-rending", he ultimately believed that the forced movement of peasants was a positive outcome. The article shocked many people and turned Mr. Huntington into a controversial figure among those opposed to the war. Nevertheless, his piece significantly influenced the latter phases of pacification.

Bulldozers

At first, pacification was left in the hands of the South Vietnamese armed forces. The policy changed in 1966 when the slow progress of pacification prompted an effort to speed it up, and the American Ninth Division was dispatched to Dinh Tuong, a province in the upper Mekong.

The division's mission was to act like a bulldozer, clearing the path for South Vietnamese officials and troops to move in and establish a government presence, and to keep the enemy's main force units from disrupting that effort. The ferocious operations by the Ninth Division and its enormous firepower inflicted heavy civilian casualties, culminating in operation 'Speedy Express' in 1969, during which American forces counted 10,000 Viet Cong killed but captured only 900 weapons.

Collateral Damage

In 1968, the insurgents carried the war to the towns and cities up and down the length and breadth of the country in the Tet offensive. American and South Vietnamese armed forces launched a furious counteroffensive, which inflicted additional destruction and casualties. Another million people were estimated to have been displaced during the Tet offensive and another offensive in May 1968. The losses incurred by the Viet Cong during those counterattacks opened the way for the American and South Vietnamese governments to push an accelerated pacification program. The few restraints that had been in place to prevent indiscriminate killing of civilians were lifted, and the extensive use of firepower in populated areas was applied with deadly results to "drain the pond to catch the fish."

Forced Urbanization

When the war ended, South Vietnam and its rural population had been profoundly transformed. Before fighting escalated, 80 percent of the people lived in the rural areas. By 1975, South Vietnam had gone through a "forced-draft urbanization". The influx of refugees from the countryside into the urban areas had swelled their population, so that 65 percent of South Vietnamese were now living in towns and cities.

The war had taken from the peasants who had been driven into urban areas to find safety what they cherished most: the land that their forebears had walked and tilled, and the homes that had sheltered them for generations. It had also shattered the families that had sustained them from birth. These were the things that had made their life whole before they became victims of

> the Americans' "forced-draft urbanization" of their society, accomplished with bombing and shelling rather than with the industrialization that had "urbanized and modernized" the United States and other Western countries. [158]

CORDS

At a Guam conference in March 1967, Robert Komer (Special Assistant to the President), convinced President Johnson and Defense Secretary McNamara that the military forces had to be integrated with the civilian agencies for effective pacification. With presidential blessing, Civil Operations and Rural Development Support (CORDS) was formed in May 1967. On the military side, CORDS was under the control of General Westmorland and on the civilian side, it was headed by Robert Komer who was appointed Westmorland's deputy. [159]

Operation Phoenix

The Phoenix Program was CORDS' most controversial activity. As part of accelerated pacification, the C.I.A. had created the Phoenix Program to root out the Viet Cong infrastructure. Critics of Phoenix have called it an assassination program, aimed at Viet Cong cadres as well as innocent civilians. Besides killing guilty and innocent alike, Phoenix also provided local officials and policemen a sanctioned program to abuse power with false arrests, settling of scores and extortion. Phoenix did seriously damage the Viet Cong infrastructure, but the cost was high for the government as well, since the program sowed fear, resentment and distrust among the population…[160]

Indiscriminate Killings

On 20th July 1971, *The New York Times* published an article by Felix Belair Jr. headed 'U.S. Aide Defends Pacification Program In Vietnam Despite Killings of Civilians'. Belair wrote in part:

> The former head of the American pacification agency in South Vietnam acknowledged today that the agency's antisubversion program had resulted in

---

158 Elliott, M. (18 January 2018). 'The Terrible Violence of Pacification'. *The New York Times*. <https://www.nytimes.com/2018/01/18/opinion/violence-pacification-vietnam-war.html?smid=nytcore-ios-share> Accessed 17 December 2025.

159 McCollum, James.K. (1983) 'The CORDS Pacification Organisation in Vietnam: A Civilian-Military Effort' in *Armed Forces & Society*, vol. 10, no. 1, pp. 105-122. JSTOR <http://www.jstor/stable/45305695. Accessed 16 December 2025.

160 Elliott, M. (18 January 2018). 'The Terrible Violence of Pacification'. *The New York Times*. <https://www.nytimes.com/2018/01/18/opinion/violence-pacification-vietnam-war.html?smid=nytcore-ios-share> Accessed 17 December 2025.

"occasional" political assassinations and the killing of civilians...

But the official, William E. Colby (future CIA Director), told the House Foreign Operations and Government Information Subcommittee that the benefits derived from the program—Operation Phoenix—in uprooting Vietcong intelligence apparatus "more than overcome these occasional abuses".

In prepared testimony, Mr. Colby, who returned recently from his assignment in Saigon, gave the number of people killed under Operation Phoenix since 1968 at 20,587, of whom 3,560 were killed from January through May this year. For earlier periods, the numbers of deaths were put at 2,559 for 1968, at 6,187 in 1969 and at 8,191 last year.

Two Republican Representatives, Ogden R. Reid of Westchester and Paul N. McCloskey of California, charged that Operation Phoenix had been responsible for "indiscriminate killings" of civilians and the imprisonment of thousands of others in violation of international accords in legal actions in wartime.

Mr. Reid contended that "it is far from an ideal program even in a war situation". He said that "no court anywhere would uphold the practice of imprisoning a civilian — Vietcong or otherwise—without a trial, denying him right to counsel and without acquainting him with the nature of the charges against him..." [161]

161 Belair, Felix. (20 July 1971). 'U.S. Aide Defends Pacification Program In Vietnam Despite Killings of Civilians'. *The New York Times.* < https://www.nytimes.com/1971/07/20/archives/us-aide-defends-pacification-program-in-vietnam-despite-killings-of.html> Accessed 28 December 2025.

CHAPTER FIFTY-SIX

Australia in Vietnam

Section 1: Driving Factors

Falling Dominoes

At a news conference on 7th April 1954, U.S. President Dwight D. Eisenhower was asked to comment on the strategic importance of Indo-China to the free world. Eisenhower spoke of the considerations that must be kept in mind. His essential points edited for clarity were:

- The specific value of a locality in its production of materials that the world needs—tin, tungsten, rubber etc;
- The possibility that more people may come under a dictatorship that is inimical to the free world such as happened in Asia where some 450 million have been lost to the communist dictatorship in China;
- The 'falling domino' principle where the last one is certain to fall quickly;
- The possible 'domino' sequence of events are the loss of Indochina, Burma, Thailand, the Peninsula, and Indonesia;
- If these are lost, the geographical situation threatens the so-called island defensive chain of Japan, Formosa, and the Philippines, and to the south, it threatens Australia and New Zealand;
- It takes away, in its economic aspects, the region that Japan must have as a trading area or Japan, in turn, will have only one place in the world to go—that is, toward the Communist areas in order to live;
- The possible consequences of these losses are incalculable to the free world.[162]

162 'Foreign Relations of the United States, 1952-1954, Indochina, Volume XIII, Part 1'. *Office of the Historian, Foreign Relations Institute, United States Department of State.* < https://history.state.gov/historicaldocuments/frus1952-54v13p1/d716> Accessed 1 March 2025.

The primary rationale behind Australia's commitment in Vietnam was Eisenhower's 'domino' theory. Other considerations included a strategic need to keep the United States interested in South East Asia and a perception that it needed to prove itself a loyal ally deserving of the goodwill implied by the ANZUS Treaty.

Section 2: Treachery

These driving factors led to an announcement by the Minister for Defence on 4th May 1962 that Australia would send 30 military advisers to South Vietnam. The arrival in South Vietnam of the Australian Army Training Team Vietnam (AATTV) on 3rd August 1962 marked the beginning of Australia's involvement in the Vietnam War.

Late in the evening of 29th April 1965, the Australian Prime Minister, Robert Menzies, stood up in the half-empty House of Representatives and announced that Australia would soon send an infantry battalion to Vietnam:

> The Australian Government is now **in receipt of a request from the Government of South Vietnam for further military assistance.** We have decided—and this has been after close consultation with the Government of the United States—to provide an infantry battalion for service in South Vietnam. In case there is any misunderstanding, 1 think I should say, Sir, that we decided in principle some time ago—weeks and weeks ago—that we would be willing to do this if we received the necessary request from the Government of South Vietnam and the necessary collaboration with the United States. This is not to be regarded as something that has suddenly arisen out of more recent events.[163]

Menzies then read out the text of a message he had received that day from President Johnson:

> Dear Mr. Prime Minister: I am delighted at the decision of your Government to provide an infantry battalion for service in South Vietnam **at the request of the Government of South Vietnam.**

Menzies lied to Parliament by claiming that he was sending the battalion in response to a request from the government of South Vietnam. As diplomatic cables at the time demonstrate, it was a cunning manoeuvre engineered by Menzies to imbue the deployment with some type of dubious international legitimacy:

163 *Historic Hansard*: House of Representatives, 29 April 1965, 25th Parliament, 1st Session. < https://historichansard.net/hofreps/1965/19650429_reps_25_hor45/#debate-0> Accessed 16 Feb. 2025.

> As evidenced in several diplomatic cables, Australia's ambassador to South Vietnam was instructed to pressure Quat (Prime Minister of South Vietnam). Three hours before Menzies was due to make the announcement in parliament, the Prime Minister received word from his ambassador that Quat had finally given a verbal agreement for the despatch of Australia troops. **He had also agreed that this be framed as a request from Saigon.** [164]

The Australian public remained unaware of Menzies' theatrical duplicity and largely supported the decision to send an infantry battalion to Vietnam.

Section 3: 'All the Way with LBJ'

Between 1st-10th June 1965, the 1st Battalion Royal Australian Regiment (1RAR) along with the 4/19th Prince of Wales Light Horse (1st APC Troop) and the 1st Australian Logistic Company arrived in Vietnam to serve alongside the U.S. 173rd Airborne Brigade in Bien Hoa province.

The arrival of combat troops in Vietnam signalled to the world that Australia was at war.

On 26th January 1966, Harold Holt was sworn in as Australian Prime Minister following the retirement of Robert Menzies six days earlier.

Just weeks after becoming Prime Minister, Holt announced on 6th March the dispatch of a Task Force to replace 1RAR. The Task Force, to be based at Nui Dat in Phuoc Tuy province, consisted of two battalions and support services including a Royal Australian Air Force (RAAF) squadron of Iroquois helicopters. Unlike 1RAR, the Task Force was assigned its own area of operations and included conscripts who had been called up under the National Service Scheme introduced in 1964.

In June of 1966, Harold Holt visited President Lyndon Baines Johnson at the White House. At a press conference, Holt declared that Australia was 'a staunch friend that will be all the way with LBJ'.

The following month, RAAF fighter pilots began serving as airborne forward air controllers (FACs) flying USAF aircraft supporting allied ground forces by directing strikes against enemy targets on the ground. Destroyers of the Royal Australian Navy (RAN) joined U.S. patrols off the North Vietnamese coast and contributed a clearance diving team and a helicopter detachment that operated with the U.S. Army.

164 'Australian Troops committed to Vietnam'. *National Museum of Australia.* < https://www.nma.gov.au/defining-moments/resources/australian-troops-committed-to-vietnam> Accessed 15 Feb 2025.

On 18th October 1966, Holt committed a further 1,700 defence force personnel to Vietnam.

Section 4: Paying the Price

On 18th August 1966, in one of the largest battles fought by Australians during the Vietnam War, Delta (D) Company, Royal Australian Regiment (6RAR), fought an 'encounter' battle to defeat enemy forces in the Long Tan rubber plantation. D Company's 105 men and 3 New Zealanders from 161 Battery, Royal New Zealand Artillery, fought for almost four hours against some 2,500 Viet Cong who outnumbered them by 10 to 1.

They were greatly assisted with timely ammunition resupply by RAAF helicopters, close fire support from Australian artillery, and the arrival of reinforcements in APC's as night fell. When the Viet Cong withdrew, they left behind 245 dead but carried away many more casualties. During the Battle of Long Tan, 18 Australians were killed and 24 wounded. All but one of the dead were from D Company. Eleven of the 18 dead were conscripts. [165] (See also Chapter Fifty-One: *The Crucible—The Battle of Long Tan*).

From the arrival of the first members of the Australian Army Training Team Vietnam (AATTV) on 3rd August 1962 until Australia's military commitment in Vietnam formally ended on 11th January 1973, over 60,000 Australians served in Vietnam. 523 died as a result of the war and almost 2,400 were wounded. Around a third of the dead and wounded were conscripts.

Section 5: The Turning Point

Early in the morning of 30th January 1968, the Viet Cong and the North Vietnamese Army launched a major offensive which coincided with the Vietnamese lunar new year holiday period known as 'Tet'. Thirteen cities throughout the central portion of South Vietnam were initially attacked and, during the next 24 hours, further coordinated attacks were launched against military bases, government facilities, and other cities and towns throughout South Vietnam.

The overall Tet Offensive was turned back with substantial losses for the North Vietnamese and had ended by late March. Although many American and ARVN servicemen (along with thousands of civilians) were killed or wounded, the personnel

165 'The Battle of Long Tan'. *ANZAC Portal.* < https://anzacportal.dva.gov.au/wars-and-missions/vietnam-war-1962-1975/events/combat/battle-long-tan-1966> Accessed 3 April 2025.

losses for the North Vietnamese were far greater with the Viet Cong and the PAVN suffering around 45,000 casualties combined.

While the Tet Offensive ultimately ended in military defeat for the North Vietnamese, theirs was the victory in terms of propaganda. For an American public grown tired of the continual fighting in Vietnam with no end in sight, Tet was a turning point. Any expectations that the war was close to an end were shattered and past reassurances from the Johnson Administration and General Westmoreland about the coming victory in Vietnam rang hollow.

Heeding public pressure, President Johnson announced on 31st March that he would limit the bombing of North Vietnam, call for negotiations and, most surprisingly, not run for re-election in 1968.

For Australian troops, the effects of the Tet Offensive were felt around their base at Nui Dat where a Viet Cong attack on targets around Ba Ria, the provincial capital of Phuoc Tuy province, was repulsed with few casualties.

Section 6: Winding Down

In 1969, the U.S. government began to implement the policy of 'Vietnamization', a term coined for a gradual withdrawal of U.S. forces that would leave the war in the hands of the South Vietnamese. With the start of the phased withdrawals, the emphasis of the activities of the Australians in Phuoc Tuy province shifted to the provision of training for the South Vietnamese Forces.

At the end of April 1970, U.S. and South Vietnamese troops were ordered to cross the border into Cambodia. While the invasion succeeded in capturing large quantities of North Vietnamese arms, destroying bunkers and sanctuaries, and killing enemy soldiers, it ultimately proved disastrous. By bringing combat into Cambodia, the invasion drove many people to join the underground opposition, the Khmer Rouge, irreparably weakening the Cambodian government.

When the Khmer Rouge came to power in April 1975, it imposed a cruel and repressive regime that killed several million Cambodians and left the country with internal conflict that continues today. The extension of the war into a sovereign state, formally neutral, inflamed anti-war sentiment in the United States and provided the impetus for further anti-war demonstrations in Australia. In the well-known Moratorium marches of 1970 and 1971, more than 200,000 people gathered in cities and towns throughout the country to protest against the war.

By late 1970, Australia had also begun to wind down its military effort in Vietnam. The gradual withdrawal of troops and all air units continued throughout 1971 with the last battalion leaving Nui Dat on 7th November. A handful of advisers belonging to the Australian Army Training Team Vietnam (AATTV) remained in Vietnam until the following year.

Australia's participation in the war was formally declared at an end when the Governor-General issued a proclamation on 11th January 1973. Five months later, the only combat force remaining in Vietnam, a platoon guarding the Australian embassy in Saigon, was withdrawn.

In early 1975, the North Vietnamese launched a major offensive in the north of South Vietnam, resulting in the fall of Saigon on 30th April. During April, a Royal Australian Air Force (RAAF) detachment of Hercules transports flew humanitarian missions to aid civilian refugees displaced by the fighting and carried out the evacuation of Vietnamese orphans (*Operation Babylift*), before finally taking out Australian Embassy staff on 25th April, ANZAC Day.

Section 7: Climate Change

A fortnight after Prime Minister Menzies announced on 29th April 1965 that a battalion of combat troops would by deployed in Vietnam, a Morgan Gallup Poll found that 64% of Australians believed that communism would overrun South-East Asia if left unchecked.

However, public support for the war began to wane when the first soldiers began coming home in body bags, adding to an already-existing anti-war movement. Especially galling for many was the fact that some of the dead were conscripts who, unlike the voluntary service by members of the regular Army, had been virtually marched to their deaths.

On 26th January 1966, Harold Holt became Australian Prime Minister upon the retirement of Robert Menzies. When Prime Minister Holt visited President Johnson at the White House in June 1966, his declaration that Australia would be 'all the way with LBJ' immediately intensified Australian opposition to the war in Vietnam.

Between the 20th-23rd October 1966, President Johnson paid a return visit to Australia as an official guest of Prime Minister Holt, marking the first official visit by a U.S. President. During this historic trip, Johnson called on U.S. allies to increase support in Vietnam. This visit, together with the campaign for the upcoming federal election, was the focus of large anti-Vietnam War demonstrations.

In January 1967, Air Vice-Marshal Ky, the then Prime Minister of South Vietnam, visited Australia and New Zealand. Anti-Vietnam war protests occurred in every Australian city that Ky visited. In Brisbane, on 20th January, over 2,000 people from various political organisations and peace committees staged a violent demonstration against the war. "Lock up Holt, throw away Ky" was a commonly seen slogan during these demonstrations.

In December 1967, Prime Minister Holt disappeared without trace, an event unparalleled in western democracies. Besides spawning a bewildering array of conspiracy theories, his disappearance was deeply unsettling and confusing for an Australian public already grappling with issues surrounding the Vietnam War. (See also Chapter Thirty-Eight: *Threat Reduction—Harold Edward Holt*)

By 1969, anti-war protests were gathering momentum in Australia. Opposition to conscription mounted as more people came to believe the war could not be won. A "Don't register" campaign to dissuade young men from registering for conscription gained increasing support.

Despite the fact that Australian defence force personnel had begun a gradual withdrawal in December 1969, around 100,000 anti-Vietnam War protesters were determined that the Government should keep its eye on the ball and staged the first of three moratorium marches in Australian cities—on 8th May 1970, 18th September 1970, and 30th June 1971.

The Vietnam War was the longest 20th-Century conflict in which Australians fought, and the first without Britain as an ally. It was the cause of the greatest social and political dissent in Australia since the conscription referendums of the First World War. [166]

Notes

Part of this Chapter was reproduced, adapted, or paraphrased from 'The Vietnam War 1962-1975' article in the *Australian War Memorial* collection.

As would be expected, American protests against the Vietnam War were, relatively speaking, much larger, more numerous, more violent, and drew more reaction from authorities than did those in Australia and New Zealand. For example, following the Cambodia Invasion and the resulting protest at Kent State University, four students were killed and nine others wounded by gunfire from Ohio National Guardsmen.

166 'The Vietnam War 1962-1975'. *Australian War Memorial.* < https://www.awm.gov.au/articles/event/vietnam> Accessed 5 April 2025.

CHAPTER FIFTY-SEVEN

Battlefield

An initial Australian experience

Preparations

On 29th April 1965, Prime Minister Robert Menzies announced in the Australian Parliament that an infantry battalion was to be sent to South Vietnam to provide military assistance. That battalion was 1 Royal Australian Regiment (1RAR).

The battalion's new Commanding Officer, Lt. Col. Brumfield, had been warned to prepare the battalion for deployment some weeks before Menzies' announcement in Parliament. His preparation was greatly hampered by a lack of war stores, changes in personnel and training difficulties. The battalion had four new Company Commanders and eight new Platoon Commanders. Companies were re-organised, which meant that platoons were re-grouped and had to learn to work together in a short time period. The battalion had not trained in live firing or air mobility and most of the NCO's and officers had no real experience in calling in artillery or air support. This was not the way to send a major unit to war. However, the high complement of NCO's with experience in Malaya and Korea offset these disadvantages to some extent.

The destroyer HMAS Sydney left Sydney on 28th May 1965 carrying elements of 1RAR plus the 4/19th Prince of Wales Light Horse (1st APC Troop) and the 1st Australian Logistic Company. The rest of the battalion left by air from the Royal Australian Air Force base at Richmond between 1st and 10th June.

Terrain

1RAR was deployed to the United States Bien Hoa Air Base to serve with the U.S. 173rd Airborne Brigade which consisted of two airborne infantry battalions (1/503 and 2/503), an artillery battalion with 105 mm howitzers, a supply battalion, and several specialists units. 1RAR was the third infantry unit in the brigade.

The battalion's home was a wide expanse of treeless ground with hundreds of rubber tree stumps. Pits were dug, wire laid out and grasses cut. The training programme included learning the ways of the Americans, their jargon, their weapons and their tactics. Within a few days the battalion was on patrol.

Adaptation

The Australian and American methods of patrolling were vastly different. 1RAR would move through the jungle silently and away from roads and tracks whereas the 173rd would use noise and fire power to draw the enemy to them. Each learnt something from the other but 1RAR maintained its own method of warfare. The battalion was armed with 9 mm Owen Guns, 7.62 mm SLR's and M60 machine guns. The equipment included WW2 packs and webbing and tropical studded boots and gaiters. The training, the enthusiasm, the will to win and the overall morale was high but the equipment was lacking.

Airpower and firepower at the level the Americans used was new to the Australians but they soon became used to helicopter assaults and certainly appreciated the volume of fire support when it was needed. Additional weapons to be carried by the platoons after arrival in Vietnam were the M26 Grenade, the M72 Light Anti-Tank weapon to fire at fortifications, and the M79 Grenade Launcher, which could fire a 40 mm grenade out to 375 metres. 1RAR would incorporate five new weapons into its inventory within six months of arrival in Vietnam.

Viet Cong Units

Viet Cong military units were either Main Force or Local. The Main Force guerillas were cunning, well disciplined, adequately trained and adept at jungle operations using stealth, rapid movement on foot, and deception. They would attack vigorously and bravely when they had the initiative or assessed that they would greatly outnumber their opponents.

Main Force

Main Force units, who were the revolutionary war equivalent of Western Regular Army units, operated from bases deep in jungle sanctuaries such as War Zones D and C, the Iron Triangle and the Ho Bo Woods. They would concentrate for specific operations and disperse to their bases afterwards. Their tactical doctrine was often expressed in simple maxims such as 'Four Quicks and a Slow' (quick approach, quick assault, quick re-organisation, quick withdrawal and slow preparation) and 'The Three Firsts' (first to open fire, first to occupy key terrain and first to assault).

In many ways, Viet Cong tactics were a series of set piece techniques rather than flexible, responsive manoeuvres. Viet Cong operational planning was fastidious, methodical and often involved detailed rehearsals.

Viet Cong and North Vietnamese units were built on the basis of three-man cells which formed the squads, platoons, companies, battalions and regiments. The three men lived, worked, travelled, fought and died together. The cell leaders reported to the squad leader, who reported to the platoon leader, and so on up the chain of command. Every aspect of daily activity, be it military, political, administrative or domestic, was supervised and controlled. If one of the three became a casualty, the others would evacuate him and his weapons.

Local Force

The Local Force guerilla was a farmer or villager who operated close to his home and family. If he was of military age, he hid in the vicinity of his home, visited his family, and worked for his livelihood only when it was safe to do so. The relationship between the Main Force and Local guerillas was very close. The Local Force guerillas were the 'eyes and ears' of the Main Force units who depended on them to keep them informed about the locations and movements of the South Vietnamese Army (ARVN), U.S. and Australian troops. While they maintained surveillance for Main Force unit commanders, the Local guerillas set booby traps, planted mines, sniped, occasionally retrieved 60 mm mortars from concealed locations, and conducted harassing missions.

Enemy Advantages

The Australians and the Paratroopers of the U.S. 173rd Airborne Brigade faced an opponent endowed with many military and political advantages. The Brigade was outnumbered by an enemy who could decide on the time and place for battle; an enemy who had prior information of the Brigade's intended areas of operations; and knew the locations of Brigade units during the conduct of operations.

Notes

The above article is a brief summary of 1st Battalion, Royal Australian Regiment's formation, its initial deployment in Vietnam with the U.S. 173rd Airborne Brigade, its training and weaponry, its assessment of the Americans and of enemy combatants, and its impression of the terrain surrounding Bien Hoa Airbase. It is reproduced or adapted from *1st Battalion, Royal Australian Regiment's Association History.*

On 8th March 1966, the Australian deployment in Vietnam was expanded to a Task Force to be based in Nui Dat, an area in Phuoc Toy province. 1RAR was relocated to join the Task Force.

PART V

In the Shadow of the Cross

This is of course the official position taken by the Catholic Church generally. It could take no other. It is important because it assures Catholic parents in Australia that their sons are serving and dying in Vietnam in an honourable cause, the cause in fact of Christ himself.

— AUSTRALASIAN VOICE OF FATIMA

CHAPTER FIFTY-EIGHT

A Thoroughly Modern Crusade

At the beginning of the 20th Century, the Roman Catholic Church embarked upon a crusade to destroy the twin plagues of atheism and communism, using whatever weapons became available to her, no matter the means, no matter the cost.

Section 1: Convert or Die

One of the major weapons in her arsenal was the strategic use made of a series of events occurring in the obscure Portuguese village of Fátima in 1917. Between May and October of that year, it is alleged that an apparition of a 'Lady' appeared on six occasions to three shepherd children aged between seven and ten. On 13th July 1917, the 'Lady' allegedly entrusted the children with a great 'secret' made up of three distinct parts. In October 1930, the apparitions were declared 'worthy of belief' and the cult of Our Lady of Fátima was officially permitted by the Church.

The first two parts of the great 'secret' were not revealed until 1941. The first, a vision of Hell, is hardly worth the effort of recording. The second, however, is of crucial importance as its content became known at the same time as the fascist dictatorships of Germany, Italy and Spain were all talking the same language—the annihilation of Soviet Russia. The second 'secret' made it abundantly clear where Our Lady of Fátima's allegiance lay:

> If my requests are heeded, Russia will be converted, and there will be peace; if not, she will spread her errors throughout the world, causing wars and persecutions of the Church. The good will be martyred; the Holy Father will have much to suffer; various nations will be annihilated. In the end, my Immaculate Heart will triumph. The Holy Father will consecrate Russia to me, and she will be converted, and a period of peace will be granted to the world.[1]

In October 1942, Cardinal Schuster, Archbishop of Milan, publicly interpreted the Fátima 'secret' text in an anti-communist sense:

1 'Fátima in Lucia's Own Words: Sister Lucia's Memoirs'.(16th Edition 2007). Translated from Portuguese by the Dominican Nuns of the Perpetual Rosary of the Monastery of Pius XII, Fátima. Ed. Fr. Louis Kondor SVD. *Secretariado Dos Pastorinhos, Fátima, Portugal.* Third Memoir p.124. Imprimatur: António Augusto dos Santos Marto, Bishop of Leiria-Fátima, July 2007. <https://www.piercedhearts.org/hearts_jesus_mary/apparitions/fatima/MemoriasI_en.pdf>

> "When the promise of the Blessed Virgin is fulfilled", he said, "it will be the most beautiful and total victory of the Church over Bolshevism". [2]

Note that the Cardinal's 'total victory' speech was uttered during the crucial Battle of Stalingrad then being fought between the invading forces of Nazi Germany and Soviet Russia.

Impassioned devotees of Our Lady of Fátima, of her offshoot Marian cults, and of the 'Virgin Mary', were marshalled and deployed strategically and relentlessly throughout the 20th Century by a Church determined to eradicate atheistic communism.

The Roman Catholic Church and her vast network of allies used the culturally-appropriated Jewish Mary in her many guises to inspire and support the fascist dictatorships of Italy, Spain and Germany; to foster and maintain the Cold War brinkmanship which brought the world to the very edge of nuclear holocaust during the Cuban missile crisis of 1962; and to encourage the involvement of the U.S.A. and Australia in the Vietnam War.

Note

See also Appendix C: *The Fátima Cult* for a detailed explanation of its development and its many and varied uses.

Section 2: The Gorgon's Gaze

In 1951, at a time when anti-communist hysteria and 'red-scare' mongering in Australia was spreading, a powerful player arrived on the scene to cloak anti-communism in a pious garb. The beginning of her pilgrimage from Lisbon was announced on 30th October 1950 by Brisbane's *The Courier Mail:*

> The statue of Our Lady of Fátima (Portugal's Lourdes) has left Lisbon on a Far Eastern pilgrimage. It will travel by way of Rome, Athens, Cairo, and Bombay to Singapore, Australia, Timor, Portugese Macao, and Japan. [3]

The "Pilgrim Statue" of Our Lady of Fátima departed Singapore on 30th December 1950 on board the ship *Gorgon*, a most interesting name considering the symbolism. After disembarking at Perth, she boarded an aircraft to fly to Melbourne. The Catholic newspaper, the *Advocate*, announced her scheduled arrival in Melbourne on 20th January 1951 under the banner head 'World Pilgrimage of Our Lady of Fátima':

2 Excerpt From: Frere Michel de la Sainte Trinite. *The Whole Truth about Fatima - Vol I.* p. 675. Apple Books.

3 *The Courier Mail* (Brisbane QLD), 30 October 1950, p. 4.

> The "Pilgrim Statue" of Our Lady of Fátima, which has now visited thirty three countries in Europe, Africa, India and Asia, will arrive at Essendon airport on Saturday, January 20, at 9.30 a.m. After a reception at the aerodrome it will be carried in a procession of cars from Essendon to St. Patrick's Cathedral, where it may be seen throughout the day. In the evening, at the Cathedral, there will be Rosary and Benediction at 7.30, and at Midnight, Solemn High Mass, at which his Grace the Archbishop (Mannix) will preside... It arrived from Singapore in Perth on the ship *Gorgon* on Saturday last.[4]

Both Catholic and non-Catholic newspapers and periodicals reported extensively on her journey to Australia, her six-month progress throughout the country, then on her departure from Darwin on the 5th July 1951.

Thus, during those crucial Cold War years, when fear and loathing of communism was being stoked by press, priest and politician, Our Lady of Fátima was travelling the world bestowing blessings on all the 'red-scare' mongers.

Note

During her journeying through Australia, in a 13th May radio broadcast to pilgrims at Fátima, Pope Pius XII said that Our Lady of Fátima was travelling the world claiming her dominion.

Section 3: Catholic Crisis in Indo-China

When the French Union forces were finally defeated at Dien Bien Phu on 7th May 1954, newspapers, periodicals and other publications worldwide carried alarmist articles such as the following from the Melbourne Catholic *Advocate*:

> Million Catholics face crisis in Indo-China: The greatest sell-out of Christian people since Poland may now threaten the Catholics of North Vietnam, writes Father Patrick O'Connor, National Catholic Welfare Council Correspondent at Hanoi, on the current armistice negotiations between the French and the Communist Viet Minh forces.
>
> Last week's withdrawal in the Red River delta—the biggest of the Indo-China war—left a million Catholics in Communist hands and drew a strong protest from the new Catholic Vietnam Premier, Ngo Dinh Diem.(A.A.P., 3 July.) [5]

---

4 *Advocate* (Melbourne, Victoria), 11 January 1951, p. 7.

5 *Advocate* (Melbourne, Victoria), 8 July 1954, p. 3.

And again from Washington's *Catholic News Service Newsfeed* of 28th June 1954:

> ...French representatives in Geneva—and, maybe, in parallel discussions elsewhere—are making a deal with the communist Vietminh. They say it's for peace. That is a tricky phrase. Everybody knows that it would be only the peace of surrender-surrender of the Vietnamese people and of Vietnamese territory to communist tule.
>
> It would, indeed, bring a halt to the present conflict in Indochina. But it would unloose in new areas the systematic trampling of human rights that has already afflicted millions in China and other Red-ruled countries.
>
> It would increase, not lessen, the danger of a third world war. The communists plan the conquest of all Asia and the world. Every new gain makes them more aggressive. There are about one million Catholics in North Vietnam, and about 1,600,000 in the entire country.[6]

See also Chapter Thirty-Five: *The New Exodus.*

Section 4: Dying in the Cause of Christ

After Australia's fateful decision to commit combat troops to Vietnam, the following article appeared in the *Australasian Voice of Fatima* on 1st November:

It is sufficiently representative and sufficiently important to cite at length:

> As reported in the news, the Holy Father recently sent a personal Legate to Vietnam to attend a meeting of the South Vietnamese Bishops. The Legate, Archbishop Pignedoli, who is Apostolic Delegate to Canada, stressed in Saigon that the Holy Father was not seeking a "peace at any price" solution. He emphasised that it must be a just peace, with freedom—particularly freedom of worship.
>
> This is of course the official position taken by the Catholic Church generally. It could take no other. **It is important because it assures Catholic parents in Australia that their sons are serving and dying in Vietnam in an honourable cause, the cause in fact of Christ himself.**
>
> For it is certain that, if the Communists were not resisted, they would overrun South Vietnam, burn and profane the churches, hinder the preaching of the

6 'Sellout of Christian People Through Peace of Surrender seen in Parleys on Vietnam'. (28 June 1954) *Catholic News Archive*. Washington D.C. <https://thecatholicnewsarchive.org/?a=d&d=cns19540628-01.1.100&e=-------en-20--1--txt-txIN--------> Accessed 25 February 2025.

> gospel and kill and persecute Christ's anointed. It is interesting to note that Archbishop Pignedoli returned full of optimism in regard to the situation in Vietnam...Christians who understand the fundamentally spiritual nature of the upheaval in Vietnam will realise that a spiritual basis is being laid for peace which the enemy will not long be able to resist.
>
> Archbishop Pignedoli gave as a reason for his optimism over the future of Vietnam the rather obvious reliance on God to answer the worldwide peace through prayer crusade inaugurated by the Holy Father in his encyclical on the Rosary and the prayers and sufferings of the Vietnamese people. It is here that the Blue Army was greatly privileged to play a significant role. For it is freely admitted that the Pilgrim Virgin tour of South Vietnam was a great success, uniting the Catholic people at a critical hour behind their bishops and clergy, impelling in their hearts the fervent recital of millions of Rosaries and acts of consecration to Jesus through Mary.

In the 18th October 1966 issue of the same publication, the editor had said:

> The Catholic Vietnamese, having seen how Our Lady has liquidated the political chaos of the past years, are now confident that this month of worldwide prayer called by the Holy Father for Vietnam will finish off the enemies of God as a major problem for their country. I hope that there is justification for this great optimism...During my recent visit I asked about the possibility of an invasion of North Vietnam from the South. I received some knowing looks but little comment. The Vietnamese want their country completely liberated from the Communists and will not easily be persuaded to accept a settlement which makes the partitioning of their country across the 17th parallel permanent.
>
> Fortunately they are placing their hopes of a completely free Vietnam largely in Our Lady of Fatima...[7]

Consider also a December 1965 address to U.S. troops in Vietnam by the Archbishop of New York, Francis Joseph Cardinal Spellman:

> In a lesson from the medieval Church, Spellman told the troops they were **"holy crusaders" engaged in "Christ's war against the Vietcong and the people of North Vietnam".** At the military base at Danang, he told three thousand soldiers gathered in an amphitheater that "less than total victory is inconceivable!"

7 *Australasian Voice of Fatima.* Microfilm. Vol. X, no. 9 (Mar. 8, 1955) - v. 52, no. 3 (Feb. 14, 1967). State Library of Queensland, Level 3, Stanley Place, South Brisbane, Queensland.

> Several days later, on Christmas Day, Spellman said mass at a simple wooden table that faced thousands of soldiers. Security was tight, the eerie whir of helicopters filled the skies. A reinforced battalion of infantry patrolled the surrounding jungle and tanks rumbled around the perimeter. Instead of softening his tone because of the specialness of the occasion, Spellman declared the nobility of the American cause. "This war in Vietnam", he said, "is, I believe, a war for civilization!" He went on and on, defending the presence of the troops, telling the youths their calling was "the defense, protection, and salvation not only of our country, but, I believe, of civilization itself!" [8]

Cardinal Spellman was one of the prime instigators of the Vietnam War. (See also Chapter Fifty-Nine: *The Militia of Christ*).

8 Cooney, R. *The American Pope : The Life and Times of Francis Cardinal Spellman*. The New York Times Book Co. Inc.: New York, 1984, p. 306.

The Militia of Christ

Note

This Chapter will focus on the two persons most responsible for using religious language to create the mind-set of fear necessary for the American public to accept their country's decision to wage war in Vietnam.

Firstly, Section I will focus on John Foster Dulles whose diplomatic and political policies sent many to their deaths along the road of no return from the jungles of Vietnam. Of necessity, part of the following also appears in Chapter Thirty-Four: *The Geneva Accords*.

Section 1: John Foster Dulles

Godless Terrorism

From 1950 to 1952, John Foster Dulles (1888-1959) was a special advisor to President Harry S. Truman, focusing on the Indo-Pacific region. On 21st January 1953, President Dwight D. Eisenhower chose Dulles as his Secretary of State.

His tenure as Secretary of State was marked by conflict with communist governments worldwide, especially the Soviet Union. Dulles strongly opposed communism, calling it "Godless terrorism".[9]

The following is reproduced or adapted from an article by Mark Toulouse appearing in the Journal of the *American Presbyterians*:

> Calvinist influences had a great impact on John Foster Dulles. Under the tutelage of his father, a Presbyterian minister, the young Foster Dulles came to view the world through a sincerely religious lens. He became convinced that a moral structure existed in the universe to which both individuals and nations should attempt to conform.
>
> ...Beginning in 1945, however, new anxieties emerging from the Cold War caused Dulles to begin to transform his concept of the transcendent moral law

9 Nash, Gary B. et al., *The American People: Creating a Nation and a Society*, Concise 6th Edition. Combined Volume. New York: Longman, 2007, p. 829.

> so that ultimately it became completely identified with the ideals and policies of the Free World. This transformation brought Dulles to a perspective that tended to celebrate American life as representative of God's purposes in human existence.
>
> ... Dulles believed that the American people should not only possess an understanding of their own "spiritual" heritage, but should also learn about the "materialistic" heritage of the Soviet Union. Such an understanding, he believed, would serve to renew faith in the righteousness of American institutions as well as foster support for American policy with regard to the Soviet Union.
>
> ... The belief that the key to peace and progress lay solely in the hands of the Free World formed the philosophical foundation for Dulles' "preventive phase" as a response to Soviet expansionism. The common enemies of humankind were no longer the abstractions of "intolerance, repression, injustice, and economic want". These were now replaced by the atheistic Communistic leaders who perpetrated them.
>
> ... Once Dulles became convinced that Communism, as a monolithic antireligious machine, was primarily bent on destroying the entire Free World, most of the complexities, the compromises, the subtleties, the intricacies of international relations were no longer relevant.[10]

Massive Retaliation

Following the Korean War, Dulles adopted his now infamous doctrine of Massive Retaliation:

> Convinced after Korea of the necessity for the use of force, Dulles concluded that the Free World, in order to be secure, must develop the will and the ability to use massive force. Dulles came to believe that security for the Free World depended upon destroying any feelings of security in the other half of the world.[11]

On 12th January 1954, Dulles described his doctrine in a speech to the Council on Foreign Relations in New York. He argued that rather that adopt a costly and dangerous response to localised communist threats around the world, America would acquire "massive retaliatory power" as a deterrent to communist aggression:

10 Toulouse, Mark G. (1985) 'The Development of a Cold War Warrior: John Foster Dulles and the Soviet Union' in *American Presbyterians*, Vol. 63, No. 3, pp. 309-322.

11 Ibid.

> What the Eisenhower administration seeks is a similar international security system. We want, for ourselves and the other free nations, a maximum deterrent at a bearable cost... Local defences must be reinforced by the further deterrent of massive retaliatory power. A potential aggressor must know that he cannot always prescribe battle conditions that suit him...
>
> The President and his advisers, as represented by the National Security Council, had to make some basic policy decisions. This has been done. The basic decision was to depend primarily upon a great capacity to retaliate, instantly, by means and at places of our choosing. Now the Department of Defense and the Joint Chiefs of Staff can shape our military establishment to fit our policy, instead of having to try to be ready to meet the enemy's many choices...[12]

Dulles' speech sent a shock wave through allied capitals, especially when, just a few weeks later on 1st March 1954, the United States detonated the first high-yield thermonuclear device at the Bikini Island atolls in the Pacific. His doctrine of Massive Retaliation implied that he was unafraid to use nuclear weapons and the allies feared the consequences of such brinkmanship.

No Quarter

Once the Indo-China issue had become a priority in American foreign policy, Dulles took the lead in establishing what he judged to be the right way to go. Tragically, there was no right way to go in the jungles of Southeast Asia.

Before the expected defeat of the French Union forces, a Conference was called at Geneva to settle outstanding issues arising from the Korean War and the on-going First Indo-China War. As discussions dealing with Korean issues ended without adopting any declarations or proposals, the focus turned primarily to resolving the war between the French Union forces and those of the Democratic Republic of Vietnam (DRV), led by the nationalist Ho Chi Minh. The participating governments were France, the Union of Soviet Socialist Republics, the Peoples Republic of China, the United States, the United Kingdom, delegates from Cambodia and Laos, and representatives of the Democratic Republic of (North) Vietnam and the State of (South) Vietnam.

In March 1954, during the Battle of Dien Bien Phu between the French Union forces and the Viet Minh, Dulles helped plan and promote *Operation Vulture*, a proposed B-29 bombing assault on the Viet Minh siege positions to relieve the

12 'Evolution of Foreign Policy: Council on Foreign Relations' (12 January 1954), John Foster Dulles Papers, *Princeton University Library.* < https://findingaids.princeton.edu/catalog/MC016_c9804> Accessed 25 December 2025.

beleaguered French forces. The Joint Chiefs of Staff drew up plans to deploy tactical atomic weapons, U.S. aircraft carriers sailed to the Gulf of Tonkin, and reconnaissance aircraft flew over Dien Bien Phu during the siege.[13]

Unwilling to make a unilateral move, President Eisenhower requested British support but Foreign Secretary and co-Chair of the Geneva Conference, Anthony Eden, was opposed to the action, partly from fear of Chinese intervention and, ultimately, a third world war.[14] Dulles and Eden had heated exchanges [15] before *Operation Vulture* was cancelled despite Dulles' objections.[16]

French Foreign Minister, Georges Bidault, later said that Dulles had offered him the use of nuclear weapons to end the siege.[17]

On 7th May 1954, during the first phase of the Geneva Conference, the French garrison at Dien Bien Phu finally fell to Ho Chi Minh and the Viet Minh nationalist forces, marking the end of the First Indo-China War.

The second phase of the Geneva Conference concerning Indo-China resumed on 11th July. The Accords established the 17th parallel (latitude 17° N) as a temporary demarcation line separating the military forces of the Viet Minh and the French. North of the line was the Democratic Republic of Vietnam led by Ho Chi Minh with its capital at Hanoi while in the South, the French transferred most of their authority to the State of Vietnam which had its capital at Saigon and was nominally under the authority of the former Vietnamese emperor Bao Dai.

On 21st July, a conference Final Declaration issued by the British co-chair, Anthony Eden, stipulated that internationally supervised elections must be held by July 1956 to create a unified Vietnamese State.

Dulles rejected the partitioning of Vietnam and the holding of elections to unify the country, insisting that the anti-communist State of Vietnam should be the legitimate Vietnamese government. He refused to shake hands with, or speak directly to, Chinese or Viet Minh delegates and subsequently left the Conference to avoid direct association with the negotiations.

---

13 Maclear, M. *The ten thousand day war: Vietnam, 1945-1975*. St. Martin's Press: New York, 1981, p. 57.

14 Fall, Bernard B. *Street Without Joy The French Debacle in Indo-China*. Stackpole Books: Pennsylvania,1961, p. 323.

15 Sherwood, Elizabeth D. *Allies in Crisis: Meeting Global Challenges to Western Security*. Yale University Press: New Haven CT, 1990, pp. 52-53.

16 Tucker, S. *Vietnam* (illustrated ed.), Routledge, 1999, p. 76.

17 Duiker, W. U. *S. Containment Policy and the Conflict in Indochina*. Stanford University Press, 1994, p. 166.

Despite being parties to the drafting of the Accords, they were not directly signed nor accepted by delegates of either the State of Vietnam or the United States.

Following the Geneva Accords, there was to be a 300-day period in which people could freely move between the two regions of Vietnam. During the 300 days, Ngo Dinh Diem, with the support of the Catholic Church, staged a campaign to convince Catholics in the North to move to the South. Between 800,000 and 1 million Vietnamese, mainly Catholics, moved South during this period and would go on to form Diem's power base. (See also Chapter Thirty-Five: *The New Exodus)*

No Retreat

On 18th August 1954, Dulles sent a personal telegram to the French Prime Minister, Pierre Mendès France, outlining U.S. intentions for Indo-China. Considering the consequences arising from the following policies, the telegram is worth quoting at length:

> Dear Mr. Prime Minister: In the days that have passed since the settlement at Geneva, I have been giving earnest thought to the future policy of the United States toward Indochina.
>
> In addition to military material assistance and economic aid, we are prepared to give direct assistance to the Associated States (Vietnam, Cambodia, Laos) including budgetary support, in addition to the support furnished by the French Union. Subject to a practical solution of the transfer problem and the establishment of adequate controls, we believe presently some and eventually all of this aid should be given directly rather than through the French Government...Much of the aid so far provided was justified to the Congress for support of the French Union forces in the war against the Viet Minh.
>
> Now that war has ceased and the Foreign Aid Bill passed by the Senate on July 29 calls for 'the furnishing, as far as possible, of direct assistance to the Associated States of Cambodia, Laos, and Vietnam.' Accordingly, to adjust our policy to the changed conditions now existing in Indochina and to meet the requirements of the U.S. Congress we plan in future to deal directly with the governments of the Associated States in questions concerning economic or military aid to these states.
>
> Although our final decision will depend upon the establishment of the complete independence which you have publicly affirmed it is the intention of the French Government to grant, and will be conditioned likewise by the extent to which the recipient governments give evidence of their stability and capacity to carry out needed reforms, we are also prepared to consider the requests of

> the Associated States such as have been made by Vietnam and Cambodia to undertake direct military training of their armed forces. In the future and to the extent possible under the restrictions of the Geneva settlements we are prepared to consider the establishment of training missions in their territories.
>
> ...we believe that the Associated States can and should be brought into more direct and mutually beneficial contact with military planning, training and logistical activities... I understand that General Ely and General O'Daniel have already discussed at least the possibility of a training function for our present Military Aid Advisory Group. [18]

As can be seen by the telegram to Pierre Mendès France, Dulles was set upon a course which would send many to their deaths down the road of no return from the jungles of Vietnam.

All attempts to have the Geneva Accords implemented and elections held by 20th July 1956 were forestalled by Dulles and Diem as they rightly feared that, if elections were held, as many as 80% of the Vietnamese people would vote for Ho Chi Minh as the popular hero of their liberation.[19]

With his various speeches threatening massive retaliation, as well as his Calvinist convictions about what he believed to be morally correct, Dulles had maneuvered the Eisenhower administration into militarily supporting the Diem regime in South Vietnam.

Townsend Hoopes summed it up perfectly:

> Dulles' conviction, his will-power, his political maneuvering, his strident and simplistic rhetoric over a period of years made a deep imprint on the national psyche and thereby a major contribution to a national state of mind so persistent that three presidents after Eisenhower were convinced there could be no "letting go" in Vietnam. [20]

The Cold War Architect

The Acton Institute's Transatlantic blog of 10th March 2020 describes John Foster Dulles as 'The Cold War Architect' and provides text excerpts from a video address

18 'Telegram:The Secretary of State to the Embassy in France'. (18 August 1954). Foreign Relations of the United States, 1952–1954, Indochina, Volume XIII, Part 2. *Office of the Historian, Department of State* < https://history.state.gov/historicaldocuments/frus1952-54v13p2/d1136> Accessed 25 December 2025.

19 Eisenhower, Dwight D. *Mandate for Change, 1953-1956: The White House Years*. Doubleday & Company Inc: New York, NY. 1963, p. 372.

20 Hoopes, Townsend. *The Devil and John Foster Dulles*. Boston: Atlantic Monthly Press, 1973, p. 257.

by Dr. John Wilsey, an associate professor of church history at the Southern Baptist Theological Seminary:

> John Foster Dulles, Eisenhower's Secretary of State, towered over American foreign policy like a Colossus from 1953 to 1959.
>
> When Foster died on 24th May 1959, the whole world mourned him. His state funeral, as I said, was the largest state funeral in Washington's history since Franklin Roosevelt's in 1945, and surpassed only by Kennedy's a few years later. Dwight Eisenhower, his president, wrote that he was a, quote, "champion of freedom". He said he was a foe only to tyranny, and one of the truly great men of our time. "No one", said Eisenhower, "has the technical competence of Foster Dulles in the diplomatic field". Eisenhower said this about his secretary of state in 1956. [21]

The Messianic Mindset

John Foster Dulles believed that America had been chosen by God to actively champion and defend human freedom and to protect peoples who were vulnerable to tyranny, mainly communist tyranny.

God's providence was prominent in Dulles' thinking. He understood America's mission in terms of Jesus' teaching of the parable of the faithful servant that to whom much is given, much is required. And he believed that God had given him the special purpose of calling Americans to the national divine mission.

Dulles applied this religious purpose to every aspect of his diplomatic and political work.

Fears and Delusions

In his book, *The Brothers,* a joint biography of John Foster Dulles and his brother Allen Dulles, award-winning foreign correspondent Stephen Kinzer writes:

> During the 1950's, when the Cold War was at its peak, two immensely powerful brothers led the United States into a series of foreign adventures whose effects are still shaking the world.
>
> John Foster Dulles was Secretary of State while his brother, Allen Dulles, was director of the Central Intelligence Agency. In this book, I place their extraordinary lives against the background of American culture and history. I

21 Sara Aldworth (10 March 202), 'John Foster Dulles: the Cold War architect'. *Transatlantic Blog*, <https://www.acton.org/publications/transatlantic/2020/03/10/john-foster-dulles-cold-war-architect> Accessed 14 May 2025.

use the framework of biography to ask: Why does the United States behave as it does in the world?

> The Brothers explores hidden forces that shape the national psyche, from religious piety to Western movies—many of which are about a noble gunman who cleans up a lawless town by killing bad guys. This is how the Dulles brothers saw themselves, and how many Americans still see their country's role in the world.
>
> Propelled by a quintessentially American set of fears and delusions, the Dulles brothers launched violent campaigns against foreign leaders they saw as threats to the United States. These campaigns helped push countries from Guatemala to the Congo into long spirals of violence, led the United States into the Vietnam War, and laid the foundation for decades of hostility between the United States and countries from Cuba to Iran.
>
> The story of the Dulles brothers is the story of America. It illuminates and helps explain the modern history of the United States and the world.[22]

Of John Foster Dulles, he writes that:

> He was more responsible for the U.S. involvement in Vietnam than any single individual...we could have avoided the entire American involvement in Vietnam absent Foster's decisions at the Geneva conference in 1954.

(See also Chapter Thirty-Three: *The First Indo-China War*, Chapter Thirty-Four: *The Geneva Accords,* and Chapter Thirty-Six: *Theoreticals.*)

The Legacy

Following the Korean Armistice, Dulles had objected to proposals by China and the Soviet Union for a diplomatic reunification of Korea, thus leaving the Korean conflict unresolved to this day. [23]

In addition, Dulles' exit from the Geneva Conference contributed to its failure to resolve the conflict in Vietnam.[24]

---

22 Kinzer, Stephen. *The Brothers.* (8 October 2013) StephenKinzer.com <https://stephenkinzer.com/2013/10/the-brothers/> Accessed 14 May 2025.

23 Bailey, Sydney D. (13 July 1992). *The Korean Armistice.* Springer, ISBN 978-1-349-22104-2.

24 Logevall, F. *Embers of War: The Fall of an Empire and the making of America's Vietnam.* Random House, 2012, pp. 555-58.

The ongoing consequences arising from the failure to resolve the conflicts in both Korea and Vietnam can hardly be overestimated. Both can be laid mainly on the shoulders of Dulles.

Notes

In 1958, Dulles authorized the Secretary of the Air Force to state publicly that the United States was prepared to use nuclear weapons in a conflict with China over the Quemoy and Matsu Island group in the Taiwan Straits. [25]

As far as his impact upon Australia is concerned, in addition to being the architect of the SEATO Treaty, Dulles had helped initiate the 1951 ANZUS Treaty while still an advisor to President Truman. (See also Chapter Thirty: *The Anzus Treaty*)

Section 2: Francis Joseph Cardinal Spellman

Notes

Cardinal Spellman, Archbishop of New York from 1939-1967, was one of the prime instigators of the Vietnam War. His engagement in this theatre is so extensive that it spans the Presidencies of Truman, Eisenhower, Kennedy and Johnson.

A significant portion of the following is reproduced or adapted from *The American Pope: The Life and Times of Francis Cardinal Spellman* by John Cooney, the authoritative work on the life of Cardinal Spellman.

The Intelligence Agent

> Since the Roosevelt administration, Cardinal Spellman had eagerly cooperated with the United States government's covert operations. The FBI routinely turned to him for information about Latin America; often, it had Spellman or his priests gather political intelligence. Spellman, the Cold War churchman, believed any means should be used to stop Communism....During his trips to Latin America, the Cardinal worked, in effect, as an arm of the United States government.[26]
>
> The CIA, like the FBI, turned to Spellman because of his connections and his prestige...of greater importance to U.S. officials, Spellman was an avowed supporter of the controversial dictatorships that the American government

25 Rhodes, R. *Dark Sun: The Making of the Hydrogen Bomb* (First. Ed.). Simon & Schuster: New York, 1995, pp. 569-70.

26 Cooney, J. *The American Pope : The Life and Times of Francis Cardinal Spellman*. The New York Times Book Co. Inc.: New York, 1984, p. 231.

backed. The Cardinal was wined and dined by Batista in Cuba, Trujillo in the Dominican Republic, Stroessner in Paraguay, and Somoza in Nicaragua, and he accepted their many honors and blessed their regimes.... Latin officials tended to view Spellman more as a delegate of the United States government than of the Vatican. On his trips he frequently represented American foreign policy and was more than willing to spread American propaganda...[27]

The Patriot

Almost from the moment Dwight D. Eisenhower became the United States President in 1953, Cardinal Spellman began warning the administration about the advance of communism in French Indo-China.

On 30th August 1954, at an American Legion Convention in Washington, Spellman declared to thousands of U.S. army veterans that Vietnam was vital to the preservation of the American way of life and Catholicism. In doing so, Spellman helped make the possibility of direct American involvement in Vietnam not only acceptable but desirable to millions of Americans. The Cardinal's message was clear—the fall of Vietnam brought the day closer when Communists would dominate the United States:

> "We shall risk bartering our liberties for lunacies, betraying the sacred trust of our forefathers, becoming serfs and slaves to the Red ruler's godless goons", he swore.[28]

Three months earlier, the Viet Minh had defeated the French Union forces in a final major battle at Dien Bien Phu. The cease-fire negotiated at the just-concluded Geneva Conference called for the partition of Vietnam at the 17th parallel. The Geneva Accords struck Spellman as another example of appeasement of the 'Reds':

> If Geneva and what was agreed upon there mean anything at all, it means... Taps for the buried hopes of freedom in South-east Asia! Taps for the newly betrayed millions of Indochinese who must now learn the awful facts of slavery from their eager Communist masters! Now the devilish techniques of brainwashing, forced confessions and rigged trials have a new locale for their exercise. [29]

27 Ibid. p. 232.

28 Ibid. p. 239-240.

29 Ibid. p. 239.

Spellman was bitter and frustrated by communist gains in Korea and China. Although he had helped his government destroy the leftist government in Guatemala just a few months earlier, he believed much more had to be done to defeat communism. So he cited Vietnam as yet another example of what he perceived as the failure of U.S. foreign policy.

The Mentor

Spellman had been grooming Ngo Dinh Diem since 1950 to take a prominent role in Vietnam as French power faded, although few were aware of it at that time:

> ...The Cardinal had played a prominent role in creating the political career of Ngo Dinh Diem who had just become Prime Minister of South Vietnam. In Diem, Spellman had seen the qualities he desired in any leader: ardent Catholicism and rabid anti-Communism.
>
> Spellman had met Diem in New York in 1950 when Diem had been at the Maryknoll Seminary in Ossining, New York. A staunch Catholic from a patrician family, Diem was at the seminary at the intercession of his brother, Ngo Din Thuc, a Roman Catholic bishop. A lay celibate and deeply religious, Diem had cut himself off from the world, especially his war-shredded nation, and had been known only to a small, politically active circle in the United States... [30]

In October 1950, Diem and his brother, Bishop Ngo Dinh Thuc, had met for dinner in Washington with State Department officials:

> ...It soon became clear that both Diem and Thuc believed that Diem was destined to rule his nation. The fact that Vietnam's population was only ten percent Catholic mattered little as far as the brothers were concerned.
>
> Such a step seemed unlikely. Before World War II, Diem had been a civil servant connected loosely with nationalists. Later, he repeatedly refused to accept government offices under Emperor Bao Dai: the job he wanted was Prime Minister, but that had been denied him.
>
> As Diem spoke during the dinner, his two most strongly held positions were readily apparent. He believed in the power of the Catholic Church and he was virulently anti-Communist. The State Department officials must have been impressed. Concerned about Vietnam since Truman first made a financial

30 Ibid. p. 240.

> commitment to helping the French there, they were always on the lookout for strong, anti-Communist leaders as the French faded... [31]

Diem returned to Vietnam as the 1954 Geneva Conference was drawing to a conclusion. The Geneva Accords confirmed Bao Dai as South Vietnam's 'chief of state' but the former emperor was little more than a figurehead who spent more time in France than in his native country. The United States pushed Diem into the spotlight as a potential leader despite the fact that he was scarcely known in the South, considered by the French to be unstable, and despised by the Viet Minh.

Bao Dai considered that the newly formed State of (South) Vietnam would need American support and that Diem's Catholic and anti-Communist background would be an appealing advantage. Following a meeting between Bao Dai and Diem in France on 16th June 1954, Diem was officially appointed Prime Minister on 24th June 1954.

In an October 1955 referendum, Bao Dai was overthrown and Diem designated as President of the State of (South) Vietnam.

According to Malachi Martin, Spellman's Vietnam stance was in accordance with the wishes of the Pope:

> Malachi Martin, a former Jesuit who worked at the Vatican during the years of the escalating U.S. commitment to Vietnam, said the Pope wanted the United States to back Diem because the Pope had been influenced by Diem's brother. Archbishop Thuc. "The Pope was concerned about Communism making more gains at the expense of the Church", Martin averred. "He turned to Spellman to encourage American commitment to Vietnam".[32]

The Campaigner

Spellman then embarked on a carefully orchestrated campaign to prop up the new Diem regime. The rallying cries were anti-Communism and Catholicism. Major publications such as *Time* and the *Herald Tribune* began publishing editorials sympathetic to the plight of refugees fleeing Ho Chi Minh's Democratic Republic of (North) Vietnam:

> ...To a large extent, many Americans came to believe that Vietnam was a preponderantly Catholic nation. This false impression resulted partly from

31 Ibid. p. 241.

32 Martin, 1982, as cited in Cooney, J. *The American Pope : The Life and Times of Francis Cardinal Spellman*. The New York Times Book Co. Inc.: New York, 1984, pp. 241-242.

> Diem's emergence as ruler. With the help of CIA rigged elections in 1955, Diem abolished the monarchy and Bao Dai was forced to live in exile. The heavily Catholic hue to the Vietnam lobby also accounted for much of the widespread belief. Still another factor was Spellman's identification with the cause.
>
> Then there was the role of a winsome young Catholic doctor working in Vietnam named Tom Dooley. A navy lieutenant who operated out of Haiphong, Dooley worked with refugees. At one point Dooley, a favorite of Spellman, even organized thirty-five thousand Vietnamese Catholics to demand evacuation from the north. Dooley's efforts were perhaps even more successful in the United States than in Vietnam. He churned out newspaper and magazine articles as well as three bestselling books that propagandized both the Catholic and anti-Communist nature of his beliefs. He fabricated stories about the suffering of Catholics at the hands of perverted Communists who beat naked priests on the testicles with clubs, deafened children with chopsticks to prevent them from hearing about God, and disemboweled pregnant women. A graduate of Notre Dame in Indiana, Dooley toured the United States promoting his books and anti-Communism before he died in 1964 at age thirty-four. One of the last people to visit his sickbed was Cardinal Spellman, who held up the young physician as an inspiration for all— another martyr.
>
> Dooley had helped the CIA destabilize North Vietnam through his refugee programs. The Catholics who poured into South Vietnam provided Diem with a larger political constituency and were promised US-supported assistance in relocating. The American public largely believed that most Vietnamese were terrified of the cruel and bloodthirsty Viet Minh and looked to the God-fearing Diem for salvation.[33]

Dooley's reputation remained untarnished until 1979 when a Roman Catholic sainthood investigation uncovered his CIA ties.[34]

The Puppet Master

Diem eventually became so closely identified with the United States that Vietnamese opponents of his regime began referring to him as the "American puppet".

33 Cooney, R. *The American Pope : The Life and Times of Francis Cardinal Spellman*. The New York Times Book Co. Inc.: New York, 1984, pp. 242-243.

34 McGehee, Ralph W. *Deadly Deceits: My 25 Years in the C.I.A.* Sheridan Square Publications: New York, 1983, p.132.

Spellman's insistence on the Catholicism of Diem's regime only reinforced the negative image of the Church in Vietnam. The Catholic writer Graham Greene noted the sectarian nature of Diem's government in a despatch from Saigon which was printed in the London *Sunday Times* on 25th April 1955:

> It is Catholicism which has helped ruin the government of Mr. Diem, for his genuine piety . . . has been exploited by his American advisers until the Church is in danger of sharing the unpopularity of the United States. An unfortunate visit by Cardinal Spellman ("He spoke to us", said a Vietnamese priest, "much of the Calf of Gold but less of the Mother of God") has been followed by those of Cardinal Gillroy and the Archbishop of Canberra. Great sums are spent on organizing demonstrations for the visitors, and an impression is given that the Catholic Church is occidental and an ally of the United States in the cold war.
>
> On the rare occasions when Mr. Diem has visited the areas formerly held by the Viet Minh, there has been a priest at his side, and usually an American one. . .[35]

In 1956, Spellman arranged to travel to Vietnam to lend the Church's weight to Diem:

> His physical presence in Saigon, he knew, would place him and the Church firmly in Diem's camp in the public mind. When Spellman arrived at the Saigon airport, he was greeted by a wildly cheering crowd of about five thousand. The sixty-seven year old prelate was once again dressed in the army khaki military attire that he loved to wear in military zones. [36]

The Hawk

By the early 1960's, Diem had become increasingly unpopular. His favoritism towards Catholics and persecution of Buddhists and communists led to a period between May and November 1963 during which Buddhists burned themselves in protest against his repressive regime. (See also Chapter Forty-Four: *Backfire*)

Accordingly, both Spellman and the U.S. Administration had begun to back away from Diem by the time of his assassination in November 1963. However, their approach to Vietnam had become, if anything, even more warlike:

> He (Spellman) became increasingly hawkish. Again, he returned to Vietnam to spend Christmas with the troops, just as he had done in previous wars. But this

---

35 Ibid. 244.

36 Cooney, R. *The American Pope : The Life and Times of Francis Cardinal Spellman*. The New York Times Book Co. Inc.: New York, 1984, pp. 243-244.

> time his politics weren't sanctioned by the Vatican. As he stepped off a military transport in Saigon, an American Army officer unwittingly noted a discouraging fact. "We hardly count it a war if you don't come", he told the Cardinal, and Spellman beamed his approval.
>
> The Cardinal used his visit to propagandize the American war...when asked by a reporter in Saigon whether the U.S. presence was justified, Spellman responded with the kind of saber-rattling statement that now made many Catholics shudder and was bound to polarize Americans further. "My country, may it always be right", he replied. "Right or wrong, my country!" The concerns of his Church were now secondary in his hierarchy of values.[37]

The tone of such statements by Spellman dismayed liberal Catholics and a growing number of clergy. Their consternation was summarized in a letter to the editor of *The New York Times* on 24th December 1965:

> "It looks as if Cardinal Spellman is in Vietnam to bless the guns which the Pope is begging us to put down", wrote the Reverend William F. Powers of Our Lady of Good Counsel Church...Spellman's Americanism was out of control—the Cardinal had broken with the Pope. From a Vatican perspective, even Spellman's Christmas cards in 1965, the year the Pope negotiated a temporary truce, were an insult. The picture on the cards was of him standing before a fighter plane with two military officers.[38]

The Enabler

Large-scale U.S. involvement in Vietnam began during President Lyndon B. Johnson's administration. (See also Chapter Thirty-Eight: *Threat Reduction*). As his war policies came increasingly under attack, Johnson turned to Spellman:

> For a while, the Cardinal's moral authority helped Johnson fend off critics. Thus, the Cardinal's political career underwent yet another shift...he became a prominent national figure once again. As in the 1940's and 1950's, Spellman was the face of the foe of the Red Menace, and he was the consecrator of an American military cause.[39]
>
> For his part, Johnson exploited the Cardinal's jingoism. As the level of American troop commitment to the war escalated, the level of protest against

37 Ibid. 293, 294.

38 Ibid. 294.

39 Ibid. 295.

the U.S. military presence in Vietnam increased. The President wanted his efforts blessed, and Spellman, more than any other churchman, was willing to proclaim Johnson's crusade a moral one. When Spellman returned from the front he immediately flew to Washington where the President met with him at once and routinely asked the Cardinal's assessment of the war. While others wavered, Spellman was always certain that the President's actions were right.

Thus, when Johnson asked both Spellman and Evangelist preacher Billy Graham at a luncheon what he should do next in Vietnam, Graham was uncomfortably silent. "Bomb them!" Spellman unhesitatingly ordered. "Just bomb them!" And Johnson did.

As the war dragged on, Spellman had his picture taken not simply with generals and soldiers but blessing bombers and machine guns. But what had been the symbols of a holy crusade during World War II appeared unseemly. As Spellman rushed in and out of the war zone, he was ridiculed by antiwar activists as "the Bob Hope of the clergy". His cathedral (St. Patrick's in New York) became a magnet for demonstrators. The war became known as "Spellman's War", which itself became a slogan on peace marchers' buttons.[40]

Despite his age, Spellman's belief in an imperial America never wavered. He routinely dined with military leaders,visited the Pentagon, and even attended army intelligence strategy seminars.

The Crusader

The Cardinal was once again back in Vietnam in December 1965:

In a lesson from the medieval Church, Spellman told the troops they were "holy crusaders" engaged in "Christ's war against the Viet Cong and the people of North Vietnam". At the military base at Da Nang, he told three thousand soldiers gathered in an amphitheater that "less than total victory is inconceivable!"

Several days later, on Christmas Day, Spellman said mass at a simple wooden table that faced thousands of soldiers. Security was tight, the eerie whir of helicopters filled the skies. A reinforced battalion of infantry patrolled the surrounding jungle and tanks rumbled around the perimeter. Instead of softening his tone because of the special nature of the occasion, Spellman declared the nobility of the American cause. "This war in Vietnam", he said, "is, I believe, a war for civilization!" He went on and on, defending the presence

40 Ibid. 299.

of the troops, telling the youths their calling was "the defense, protection, and salvation not only of our country, but, I believe, of civilization itself!"[41]

The Cardinal's warmongering rhetoric resulted in a shift in the way he was perceived by many Catholics:

> They saw him as a mean-spirited man, not as an ecclesiastic who deserved automatic respect because of his lofty office. As much as any other man, Spellman shook Catholics' implicit respect for their hierarchy. To date, numerous Catholics had defended his public stances...but Vietnam changed that. For the first time, the anger that was found in the streets was brought into American churches. In large measure, Spellman was to blame.
>
> Spellman took little trouble to hide the way he felt about his critics. He sneered at the civil-rights and Vietnam stances of Martin Luther King Jr. and Bobby Kennedy...publicly he continued to leap to President Johnson's defense. When his old friend J. Edgar Hoover was criticized for foot-dragging on civil rights and other matters, Spellman rallied to his cause.[42]

The Vietnam War is often called President Johnson's war. As one of its prime instigators, it should also be called Spellman's war, a title well-deserved according to the many anti-war protestors who wore buttons proclaiming such.

The Fellow Traveller

As noted elsewhere, in September 1957, Bartholomew Augustine Santamaria sponsored Ngo Dinh Diem's official presidential visit to Australia. Also sponsored by Santamaria was Diem's brother, Archbishop Ngo Dinh Thuc, who visited Australia in April 1963 to discuss the communist threat with various Catholic organisations.

Michael Costigan, former Executive Secretary to the Bishops' Committee for Justice, Development, Ecology and Peace wrote of B.A. Santamaria's commitment to the anti-communist cause in Vietnam in a 2015 Edition of the *Journal of the Australian Catholic Historical Society*:

> ...Santamaria and I met occasionally at functions, one memorable occasion being a closed gathering of Catholic editors, organised by Santamaria in April 1963 at the Essendon headquarters of the Columban Fathers, to hear and question the visiting Archbishop Ngo Dinh Thuc of Hue, Vietnam. The historian Val Noone reports on this clandestine meeting in *Disturbing the War*

41 Ibid. 306.

42 Ibid. 307, 308..

(Spectrum Publications, 1993, page 80). The visitor's upbeat description of the struggle with the communists in his country was also covered in the *Advocate* (18th April 1963).

The claim in the headline, probably composed by me, that the Church was flourishing in spite of the communist threat, makes odd reading when it is recalled that, on 2nd November 1963, barely six months after Thuc's visit to Australia, his brother, President Ngo Dinh Diem, himself a previous Santamaria-sponsored Australian visitor, was assassinated in Saigon.[43]

(See also Chapter Three: *Enemies Within.*)

Section 3: Cold War Warriors

In addition to John Foster Dulles and Cardinal Spellman, other Catholic notables during the Cold War era were Senator Joseph McCarthy, Boston's Cardinal Richard Cushing, Francis P. Matthews, Father Edmund Walsh S.J. and Bishop J. Fulton Sheen. For example, in 1950, Bishop J. Fulton Sheen was reported as saying:

> "We are living in the days of the Apocalypse–the last days of our era.... The two great forces of the Mystical Body of Christ and the Mystical Body of Antichrist are beginning to draw up the battle lines for the catastrophic contest". [44]

First Strikers

Among those Catholic notables mentioned were two 'First Strikers'— Francis P. Matthews and Father Edmund Walsh S.J.

Francis P. Matthews, former Supreme Knight of the Knights of Columbus, Papal Chamberlain to Pope Pius XII, and President Truman's Secretary of the Navy, was reported to have called for the United States to "initiate an atomic attack":

> On the 25th August 1950, Navy Secretary Francis Matthews addressed a large crowd assembled at the Boston Navy Yard, calling on the United States to fulfill its "inescapable role" by initiating an atomic attack to destroy the Soviet Union's will to wage war and thereby "become the first aggressor for peace".[45]

43 Costigan. M. (2015) 'B.A. Santamaria:Remembered by one who knew him a little' in *Journal of the Australian Catholic Historical Society* Vol. 36, pp. 163-64.

44 Flynn, T. and M. *The Thunder of Justice: The Warning, the Miracle, the Chastisement, the Era of Peace.* Maxcol Communications: Virginia. 1993, p 20.

45 Mueller, K. Castillo, J. Morgan, F. Pegahi, N. Rosen, B. 'Striking First: Appendix A: U.S. Preventive Attack Cases'. *Rand Corporation*, 2006, p. 131.

In its religious section of the 18th December 1950, *Time Magazine* published the following article about Father Walsh headed *How About the Bomb*?:

> Father Edmund Walsh S.J., founder of Georgetown University's School of Foreign Service, says nuclear first strike against Soviet Union justifiable. "If the Government of the United States has sound reason to believe . . . that. . . an attack is being mounted and ready ... it would appear that President Truman would be morally justified to take defensive measures proportionate to the danger. That would mean use of the atomic bomb, as no power would launch a surprise attack on the United States without an adequate supply of atomic bombs . . . Neither reason nor theology nor morals requires men or nations to commit suicide by requiring that we must await the first blow. . ." [46]

46 'How About the Bomb?'. *Time Magazine*, 18 December 1950, p. 50.

CHAPTER SIXTY

Conclusion

In the Introduction, the following question was posed:

> What truly drove the United States and its allies into the catastrophic conflict in Vietnam?

To answer the question, this work furnished compelling evidence in support of the claims made in the Introduction:

> That a covert intelligence mission code-named *Operation Petrov* was a fraud resulting in the eventual introduction of Australian ground troops into Vietnam. The Australian commitment, in turn, endorsed and escalated American involvement since the United States was thereby able to claim the support of a Western ally to cloak the War in international legitimacy.
>
> That there were two principal operating forces which prevailed upon the United States to wage war in Vietnam. Those forces were: the Capitalist 'free world' and its political, economic, and military systems marshalled for the purpose of preventing the peoples of Indo-China and their resource-rich lands from falling into the hands of 'Communists'; and the network of militant brethren, political stooges, military cabals, and press outlets of the Catholic Church all sharing common cause to prevent Catholic populations in Vietnam from falling into the hands of the 'Godless'.
>
> And, finally, that the two enabling factors keeping the United States and Australia in Vietnam long after victory was possible were: the neutralization at crucial turning points of four men who all possessed the power or potential power to either stop or significantly shorten the duration of the Vietnam War; and the systematic and ongoing lies told to the American people by Presidents and their closest advisors about the progress of the Vietnam War, constantly reassuring them that victory was just around the corner despite knowing that the War was a failed proposition almost from its beginning.

The evidence furnished in the foregoing Chapters will determine whether or not this work has succeeded in answering the question.

The Poisoned Soul

It is now sixty years since the battle of Long Tan in which Australian troops, facing overwhelming odds, suffered their greatest casualties of the war.

The peoples of the United States, Vietnam, Australia and New Zealand have paid a heavy price in blood. As far as moral standing and respect is concerned, the United States, Australia and New Zealand have forever lost their great reputations as freedom-loving, liberal democracies.

On 10th March 2006, the *JFK Presidential Library and Museum* conducted a symposium entitled 'Vietnam and the Presidency—How we got in: The United States, Asia and Vietnam'. In her introduction, the Director of the Library, Deborah Leff, made the following statement:

> Benjamin Franklin once wrote, "There never was a good war or a bad peace". And while war is always wrenching, the Vietnam War tore apart this country in ways from which we have never recovered. To many, it was a loss of innocence, the event that led to what has been called a permanent, adversarial culture in the United States. [47]

As Doctor Martin Luther King Jnr. said so presciently:

> If America's soul becomes totally poisoned, part of the autopsy must read Vietnam...[48]

Doctor Evatt was cut down by a political assassination, John F. Kennedy and Robert F. Kennedy by assassins's bullets, and Harold Holt disappeared in circumstances unparalleled in western democracies. (See Chapter Thirty-Eight: *Threat Reduction*.)

These four men, two Australians and two Americans, all possessed the power or potential power to either stop or significantly shorten the Vietnam War. The possibility that all four would be neutralized just by random chance at crucial turning points is vanishingly small.

The End was Contained in the Beginning
— ORWELL

47 Leff, D. (10 March 2006) 'Vietnam and the Presidency—How we got in: The United States, Asia and Vietnam'. *JFK Presidential Library and Museum* < https://www.jfklibrary.org/events-and-awards/kennedy-library-forums/past-forums/transcripts/vietnam-and-the-presidency-how-we-got-in-the-united-states-asia-and-vietnam> Accessed 14 March 2025.

48 Extract from Dr. Martin Luther King Jnr. Speech, Riverside Church, New York City, NY. 4th April 1967.

PART VI

Appendices

Deployments

This Appendix details the allied forces deployments in Vietnam during the Kennedy, Johnson and Nixon administrations.

As Jeffrey Record, Professor Emeritus at the U.S. Air Force's Air War College, writes in his book *The Wrong War: why we lost in Vietna*m:

> No other member of SEATO felt obliged by the treaty to fight in South Vietnam, notwithstanding official U.S. portrayal of the war from its inception as a case of international aggression as clear cut as North Korea's invasion of South Korea and even as would be a Soviet attack on Western Europe. **Alone among SEATO members other than the United States, Australia contributed forces in a size proportionally significant to its total armed forces.** New Zealand, Thailand, and the Philippines all sent token contingents, the latter two countries in exchange for substantial U.S. military assistance. South Korea, not a SEATO member, provided substantial forces--two army divisions and a marine brigade--but only in exchange for hefty U.S. military assistance to Seoul and a pledge by the United States not to redeploy to Vietnam either of the two U.S. divisions stationed in Korea. "The Asian [allies] were ready to fight to the last American", complained Clark Clifford, (Robert) McNamara's successor as Secretary of Defense. [1]

This Chapter will detail United States deployments and those of Australia and New Zealand, the only nation states not reimbursed in some form for sending troops to Vietnam.

Introductory Notes

- Apart from the Battle of Long Tan, the details of major battles appear elsewhere. Only the dates will be noted here. Events of lasting significance to all Allied forces in Vietnam will be repeated across Deployment Timelines.
- From 1966 until 1972, the 1st Australian Task Force operated out of Nui Dat in Phuoc Tuy Province, South Vietnam.

1 Record, J. *The Wrong War: why we lost in Vietnam.* Naval Institute Press: Maryland, 1998. < https://archive.nytimes.com/www.nytimes.com/books/first/r/record-war.html> Accessed 14 February 2025.

Section 1: Australian Deployment

From the arrival of the first members of the Australian Army Training Team Vietnam (AATTV) on 3rd August 1962 until Australia's military commitment in Vietnam formally ended on 11th January 1973, over 60,000 Australians served in Vietnam. 523 died as a result of the war and almost 2,400 were wounded. Around a third of the dead and wounded were conscripts.

1962

4th May—the Australian Minister for Defence announces intention to send 30 army advisers to South Vietnam.

3rd August—the first non-combatants, the Australian Army Training Team Vietnam (AATTV), arrive in South Vietnam, almost three years before the decision to send combat troops.

1963

22nd November—John Fitzgerald Kennedy is assassinated and Lyndon Baines Johnson is sworn in as President of the United States on the same day.

1964

8th June—the Minister for Defence announces that the AATTV will be increased to 83 advisers with an expanded role.

6th July—Warrant Officer Class 2, Kevin Conway, becomes the first Australian to die as a result of enemy action in South Vietnam.

7th August—the U.S. Congress passes the Tonkin Gulf Resolution giving President Johnson extraordinary powers to act in South Vietnam.

10th November—Prime Minister Menzies announces the introduction of national service to increase the army's strength from 22,750 to 37,500. Moral opposition to the war in Vietnam is not accepted as a reason for exemption.

1965

29th April—Prime Minister Menzies announces the dispatch to South Vietnam of an infantry battalion, an armoured personnel carrier (APC) troop, a signals troop, and a logistic support company.

24th May—an advance party from 1st Battalion, Royal Australian Regiment (1RAR), departs for South Vietnam for service with the U.S. 173rd Airborne Division.

28th May—the destroyer HMAS Sydney leaves Sydney bound for South Vietnam carrying elements of the 1st Battalion, Royal Australian Regiment (1RAR), plus the 4/19th Prince of Wales Light Horse (1st APC Troop), and the 1st Australian Logistic Company. The rest of the battalion leaves for South Vietnam by air from Richmond Royal Australian Air Force Base between the 1st and 10th June.

30th June—the first intake of conscripts begin training.

17th August—the Australian Government approves an increase of Australian forces in Vietnam to a battalion group, supported by artillery, additional APCs, engineers, army helicopters, and light aircraft.

1966

26th January—Harold Holt is sworn in as Australian Prime Minister following the retirement of Robert Menzies six days earlier.

6th March—Prime Minister Holt announces that the Australian commitment in South Vietnam will be increased to a 4,350-man task force and will include conscripts. The 1st Australian Task Force (1ATF) will include two infantry battalions, a Special Air Service squadron, combat and support logistic units and eight RAAF Iroquois helicopters (9SQN). The Task Force will be supported by 1 Australian Logistic Support Group (1ALSG) to be established at Vung Tau.

24th May—5RAR deploys by helicopter from 1ATF concentration area at Vung Tau to secure the Task Force area at Nui Dat.

June—Harold Holt visits President Lyndon Baines Johnson at the White House. At a press conference, Holt declares that Australia was 'a staunch friend that will be all the way with LBJ'. His remarks on the White House lawn immediately intensify Australian opposition to the war in Vietnam.

Long Tan

18th August—D Company of 6RAR, with a strength of 108 men, battles North Vietnamese Army (NVA) and Viet Cong (VC) forces estimated at between 1,500 and 2,500 men until relieved by A Company carried in by armoured personnel carriers of 3 Troop, 1APC Squadron. The NVA and VC left 245 bodies on the battlefield while 17 Australian infantrymen and one APC crewman are killed. The Company earns the U.S. Presidential Citation. (See also Chapter Fifty-One: *The Crucible* for detailed description)

1967

7th April—Major Peter Badcoe, AATTV, is killed in action leading two companies of Vietnamese regional forces. For his outstanding heroism in this and two previous actions, he is posthumously awarded the Victoria Cross.

26th May—V Company of the 1st Battalion, Royal New Zealand Regiment (RNZIR) arrives at Nui Dat to serve with 2RAR. The Australian Battalion is re-designated 2RAR/NZ/ANZAC.

18th October—Prime Minister Holt announces an increase of 1,700 to Australia's commitment in South Vietnam including a third infantry battalion and a tank squadron.

17th December—Prime Minister Holt disappears without trace. (See also Chapter Thirty-Eight: *Threat Reduction*)

28th December, 3RAR establishes itself at Nui Dat as 1ATF's third battalion.

1968

10th January—Holt's successor, John Grey Gorton, is sworn in as Australian Prime Minister.

30th January—the Tet Offensive is launched. The Offensive sows serious doubt in the minds of the Australian and American people and marks a turning point in the war and the beginning of a gradual Allied withdrawal.

1st February—Tet comes to Baria, the capital of Phuoc Tuy province. A Company of 3RAR and a troop of APC's fight a savage 24-hour battle to clear the town.

12th February—Prime Minister Gorton indicates that Australia will not increase its commitment in Vietnam.

6th May and 11th May—the actions of WO2 Ray Simpson earn him the AATTV's third Victoria Cross.

13th May—the Battle of Coral & Balmoral begins.

18th May—Operation Bribie begins.

24th May, WO2 Keith Payne earns the AATTV's fourth Victoria Cross.

27th May— a sweep outside Coral by D Company 1RAR, supported by four Centurion tanks, smashes an enemy bunker system and kills large numbers of VC and NVA.

28th May—a second attack on Balmoral is crushed by combined infantry, tank, and artillery fire leaving 1 Australian and 47 enemy dead.

1969

Australian military commitment peaks at more than 7,000.

6th June—the Battle of Binh Ba begins.

16th December—following the withdrawal of 25,000 U.S. troops from South Vietnam, and plans by the U.S. Government to withdraw 50,000 more, Prime Minister Gorton announces that any further substantial force reductions would include Australians.

1970

22nd April—Gorton announces that 8RAR will not be replaced at the end of the year, some support elements will be withdrawn, and the AATTV will be increased by about 120 soldiers.

12th November, 8RAR returns to Australia at the end of its 12 month tour in South Vietnam. It is the first 1ATF unit not to be replaced.

1971

10th March—William McMahon replaces John Gorton as Australian Prime Minister.

30th March—McMahon announces further cuts to Australian forces in South Vietnam, including withdrawal of the tank squadron, Royal Australian Air Force Canberra bomber squadron, and some Caribou transport aircraft.

18th August—McMahon announces that the bulk of Australian forces in South Vietnam will be withdrawn, leaving only a modified training team. The period of national service is reduced from two years to 18 months.

6th October—3RAR is airlifted onto HMAS Sydney, leaving only one battalion at Nui Dat.

7th November—4RAR moves out of Nui Dat to the port of Vung Tau, ending Australian combat operations in Phuoc Tuy province.

1972

5th March—the last Australian logistic units leave Vung Tau and Australia's commitment in South Vietnam returns to a training role with the 150-man Australian Assistance Group, Vietnam (AAAGV) and the AATTV.

2nd December—Following a change of government, conscription ends, draft resisters are released from jail and pending prosecutions for draft resistance are dropped.

8th December—Australia's military commitment in South Vietnam formally ends.

1973

27th January—President Nixon signs the Paris Peace Accords ending direct U.S. involvement in the Vietnam War. The North Vietnamese accept a cease fire which begins four days later.

30th June—the Saigon Embassy Guard Platoon are the last Australian troops to leave Vietnam.

1974

4th January—South Vietnam's President Nguyen Van Thieu declares that war has begun again.

1975

29th March—the Australian Government responds to urgent requests for transport assistance from the Governments of South Vietnam and the United States and dispatches a contingent of seven RAAF Hercules and two Dakota aircraft to Vietnam on a humanitarian relief mission. The RAAF is utilized in various roles during the final weeks of the war, including the movement of refugees, the transport of Red Cross and U.N. supplies and, on 4th and 17th April, the evacuation of Vietnamese war orphans from Saigon to Bangkok during *Operation Baby Lift.*

25th April, ANZAC Day—the Royal Australian Air Force participates in an evacuation of the Australian Embassy and final withdrawal of personnel from Saigon. It is the final task of Australia's military in the Vietnam War.

30th April—Saigon is seized by North Vietnamese forces and the Government of South Vietnam surrenders.

Section 2: U.S. Deployment

A total of around 2.7 million U.S. military personnel served in Vietnam, with a peak troop strength of 543,482 in April 1969. The Vietnam Veterans Memorial in Washington DC is inscribed with the names of 58,279 service members who died in Vietnam from 1957 to 1975. Over 47,000 lost their lives as a result of combat and nearly 11,000 perished from other causes. More than 300,000 were wounded.

1961

President John F. Kennedy sends 400 United States Army Special Forces personnel to South Vietnam to train South Vietnamese soldiers following a visit to the country by Vice President Johnson.

1962

In January, U.S. aircraft begin spraying Agent Orange and other herbicides over rural areas of South Vietnam to kill vegetation that would offer cover and food for guerrilla forces. *Operation Ranch Hand* continues until 1971.

1963

By November, President Kennedy has expanded U.S. aid to South Vietnam and increased the number of advisors from 900 to 16,300.

22nd November—Kennedy is assassinated and Lyndon Baines Johnson is sworn in as President of the United States on the same day.

1964

In August, President Johnson uses a faked incident in North Vietnam's Gulf of Tonkin to further escalate the war. The outcome of this incident is the passage by the United States Congress of the Gulf of Tonkin Resolution which grants Johnson the authority to assist any Southeast Asian country whose government was considered to be jeopardized by communist aggression. The resolution serves as Johnson's legal justification for deploying conventional forces to South Vietnam and to commence open warfare against North Vietnam.

1965

2nd March—*Operation Rolling Thunder*, a three-year campaign of sustained bombing of military, industrial, and infrastructure targets throughout North Vietnam, is launched by President Johnson.

8th March—3,500 U.S. marines, the first American combat troops to enter Vietnam, land on beaches near Da Nang in South Vietnam.

28th July—Johnson announces his decision to send an additional 50,000 American troops to South Vietnam, increasing the number of personnel there by two-thirds.

14th November—the Battle of Ia Drang begins. It is the first major battle between the United States Army and the People's Army of Vietnam.

1966

Throughout 1966 and beyond, U.S. forces conduct search-and-destroy campaigns in South Vietnam. Utilising the mobility provided by helicopters and their immense advantage in fire-power, U.S. troops search South Vietnam for Viet Cong supply bases.

During this year, Johnson expands the number of troops being sent to Vietnam, making a total 385,000.

1967

8th January—Operation Cedar Falls begins. It is the largest American ground operation of the Vietnam War.

22nd February—Operation Junction City begins. It is the first U.S. combat airborne operation since the Korean War and one of the largest of the Vietnam War.

During this year, U.S. troop numbers rise to 500,000.

1968

21st January—6,000 U.S. Marines stationed at Khe San near the Laotian border come under heavy attack and fight for survival for two months.

30th January—the Tet Offensive is launched. The Offensive sows serious doubt in the minds of the Australian and American people and marks a turning point in the war and the beginning of a gradual Allied withdrawal.

11th-17th February—543 U.S. soldiers die, marking the highest number of weekly American casualties of the war.

31st March—President Johnson announces that the United States will suspend bombing of North Vietnam north of the 19th parallel on 1st April. With this speech, Johnson signals the end of his administration's willingness to support the demands of field commanders in Vietnam for additional troops. Johnson then surprises the nation by announcing that he will not seek a second term as President of the United States. In the eight weeks following his announcement, 3,700 Americans are killed and 18,000 wounded.

5th May—Phase Two of the Tet Offensive is launched by the People's Army of Vietnam (PAVN) and the Viet Cong against targets throughout South Vietnam, including Saigon.

31st October—Johnson announces a halt to all bombing of North Vietnam.

1969

20th January— Richard M. Nixon is inaugurated as the 37th President of the United States.

In April, U.S. troop presence in Vietnam peaks at over 543,000.

20th April—President Nixon orders 150,000 U.S. troops to withdraw from South Vietnam over a period of 12 months.

8th June—Nixon announces that 25,000 U.S. troops will be withdrawn by the end of September. A month later, troops begin departing South Vietnam.

1970

20th April—Nixon announces a second withdrawal of 150,000 U.S. troops from South Vietnam over a period of 12 months.

30th April—Nixon announces in a televised address that U.S. and South Vietnamese troops will invade Cambodia. The invasion causes massive protests in the U.S., including a confrontation and shooting at Kent State University in early May. Additionally, the invasion further destabilises Cambodia and weakens its central government's fight against the Khmer Rouge.

1971

12th January—U.S. Congress repeals the Gulf of Tonkin Resolution in order to reassert control over the president's ability to use force in the war.

8th February—Operation Lam Son 719 begins.

26th July, U.S. National Security Advisor, Henry Kissinger, announces plans for the withdrawal of all U.S. troops within nine months.

1972

30th March—North Vietnam launches the Easter Offensive.

11th August—the last U.S. combat troops leave South Vietnam. In Saigon, around 7,000 U.S. Department of Defense civilian employees remain behind to aid South Vietnam.

1973

27th January—President Nixon signs the Paris Peace Accords ending direct U.S. involvement in the Vietnam War.

1975

29th March—the Australian Government responds to urgent requests for transport assistance from the Governments of South Vietnam and the United States and dispatches a contingent of seven RAAF Hercules and two Dakota aircraft to Vietnam on a humanitarian relief mission. The RAAF is utilized in various roles during the final weeks of the war, including the movement of refugees, the transport of Red Cross and UN supplies and, on 4th and 17th April, the evacuation of Vietnamese war orphans from Saigon to Bangkok during 'Operation Baby Lift'.

17th April—Phnom Penh, the capital of Cambodia, falls to the Khmer Rouge.

30th April—Saigon is seized by North Vietnamese forces and the government of South Vietnam surrenders.

1976

2nd July—North and South Vietnam are formally unified as the Socialist Republic of Vietnam.

Section 3: New Zealand Deployment

More than 3,000 New Zealand military and civilian personnel served in Vietnam between 1963 and 1975. In contrast to the world wars, New Zealand's contribution was modest. At its peak in 1968, New Zealand's military force numbered only 548. Thirty-seven men died while on active service and 187 were wounded. Two civilians serving with the surgical and Red Cross teams also lost their lives.

The following timeline is reproduced courtesy of the New Zealand Ministry for Culture and Heritage.[2]

2 'Timeline - NZ's Vietnam War 1963–75 '. *Ministry for Culture and Heritage.* <https://www.vietnamwar.govt.nz/resources/timeline>. Accessed 9 April 2025.

1963

April—New Zealand civilian surgical team arrives in Vietnam, based at Qui Nhon in Binh Dinh province.

1964

June—New Zealand Army Detachment Vietnam (NEWZAD), a 25-person non-combatant engineer unit, arrives in Vietnam. Based at Thu Dau Mot, Binh Duong province.

1965

July—NEWZAD withdrawn from Vietnam.

July—161 Battery, Royal New Zealand Artillery (RNZA), arrives in Vietnam and is based at Bien Hoa air base as part of the U.S. 173rd Airborne Brigade.

1966

June—161 Battery, RNZA, comes under operational control of 1st Australian Task Force (ATF) at Nui Dat in Phuoc Tuy province.

July—161 Battery, RNZA, increased in strength from 4 to 6 guns.

August—161 Battery, RNZA, involved in the Battle of Long Tan, in which they assist 6th Battalion, The Royal Australian Regiment (6RAR).

1967

April—New Zealand Services medical team arrives in Vietnam and is based at Bong Son in Binh Dinh province.

May—Victor (V) Company, 1st Battalion, Royal New Zealand Infantry Regiment (1RNZIR) is deployed to Vietnam from Malaysia.

November—V Company, 1RNZIR, leaves Vietnam and is replaced by Victor 2 (V2) Company, 1RNZIR.

December—Whiskey (W) Company, 1RNZIR is deployed to Vietnam from Malaysia.

1968

March—New Zealand infantry companies integrate with 2nd Battalion, The Royal Australian Regiment (2RAR), to form 2RAR/NZ (Anzac) Battalion. The battalion is part of the 1st Australian Task Force (1ATF) based at Nui Dat in Phuoc Tuy province.

May—V2 Company, 1RNZIR leaves Vietnam and is replaced by Victor 3 (V3) Company, 1RNZIR.

November—W Company, 1RNZIR, leaves Vietnam and is replaced by Whiskey 2 (W2) Company, 1RNZIR.

1969

May—V3 Company, 1RNZIR leaves Vietnam and is replaced by Victor 4 (V4) Company, 1RNZIR.

November— W2 Company, 1RNZIR, leaves Vietnam and is replaced by Whiskey 3 (W3) Company, 1RNZIR.

1970

May—V4 Company, 1RNZIR, leaves Vietnam and is replaced by V5 (Victor 5) Company, 1RNZIR.

November—W3 Company, 1RNZIR leaves Vietnam.

1971

January—First New Zealand Army Training Team Vietnam (1NZATTV) deployed at the National Training Centre at Chi Lang.

May—161 Battery, RNZA, withdrawn from Vietnam.

May—V5 Company, 1RNZIR, leaves Vietnam and is replaced by Victor 6 (V6) Company, 1RNZIR.

December—New Zealand Services medical team withdrawn from Vietnam. V6 Company, 1RNZIR, leaves Vietnam.

1972

March—Second New Zealand Army Training Team Vietnam (2NZATTV) arrives at Dong Ba Thin, near Cam Ranh Bay.

December—1NZATTV and 2NZATTV training teams withdrawn from Vietnam.

1975

March—New Zealand civilian surgical team leaves Vietnam.

April—New Zealand Ambassador evacuated from Saigon by 41 Squadron, RNZAF, the last RNZAF flight out of Vietnam.

Peace Proposals

Like most prolonged conflicts, the Vietnam War produced several peace proposals and several rounds of peace talks. These attempts to negotiate a working peace were initiated by the United States, North Vietnam and by other nations acting as mediators. Proposals for cease-fires and peace deals flowed back and forth regularly, even when fighting was at its worst. Some of these negotiations were conducted publicly, some in secret through diplomatic communications or through 'back channels'.

The period 1964 to 1972 saw at least five different peace proposals of any significance, along with numerous third-party offers that were either disregarded or rebuffed. The significant number of peace proposals and their eventual failure reveals much about the nature of the Vietnam conflict and its chief combatants.

One significant problem was that the United States and North Vietnam approached peace talks with different objectives. For the Americans, the peace process was a way of extricating themselves from Vietnam, while avoiding the humiliation of defeat. For the North Vietnamese, whose ultimate goal was national reunification, peace talks were another military tactic, a device to obtain breathing space while denying and frustrating the enemy. Both Hanoi and Washington claimed to be receptive to peace talks and a negotiated peace deal.

There was method in this too: if peace negotiations failed or broke down, this could be attributed to the belligerence or intransigence of the other side. In late 1966, Ho Chi Minh declared that North Vietnam was willing to "make war for 20 years", but Ho added that if the Americans "want to make peace, we shall make peace and invite them to afternoon tea".

1965

In April 1965, North Vietnamese Premier Pham Van Dong proposed a four-point plan which called for a return to the provisions of the Geneva Accords of 1954, along with the withdrawal of U.S. military personnel:

1. Recognition of the basic national rights of the Vietnamese people – peace, independence, sovereignty, unity, and territorial integrity... The U.S. government must withdraw from South Vietnam U.S. troops, military personnel, and weapons of all kinds, dismantle all U.S. military bases there,

and cancel its military alliance with South Vietnam. It must end its policy of intervention and aggression in South Vietnam;

2. Pending the peaceful reunification of Vietnam, while Vietnam is still temporarily divided into two zones, the military provisions of the 1954 Geneva agreements on Vietnam must be strictly respected;
3. The internal affairs of South Vietnam must be settled by the South Vietnamese people themselves, in accordance with the program of the National Liberation Front without any foreign interference;
4. The peaceful reunification of Vietnam is to be settled by the Vietnamese people in both zones, without any foreign interference.

In response to Pham's proposals, U.S. Secretary of State, Dean Rusk, declared that he could live with points one, two and four but he interpreted point three as a demand for Viet Cong control of South Vietnam, a condition the United States could not accept. Rusk claimed that he could find no member of the North Vietnamese government willing to "give up their aggressive ambitions or to come to a conference table", so he would place his trust in "our own men in uniform".

1969

The first significant attempt at peace talks had come in May 1968 with an informal meeting between U.S. and North Vietnamese envoys in Paris.

In January 1969, five days after Richard Nixon was sworn in as U.S. president, negotiators from Washington flew to Paris for peace talks with representatives of North and South Vietnam and the National Liberation Front (Viet Cong).

The Paris peace talks were plagued with setbacks and breakdowns from the beginning. The sets of demands by the U.S. and Hanoi were so irreconcilable that the talks fell into an unproductive routine where all sides restated their position but refused to concede ground. [3]

1971

On 26th June 1971, the Democratic Republic of (North) Vietnam (DRV) issued the following nine-point Peace Proposal:

1. The withdrawal of all the forces of the United States and those of the other foreign countries in the U.S. Camp in South Vietnam and the other Indo-Chinese countries must be achieved in 1971;

3 J. Llewellyn et al, 'Vietnam War peace talks', *Alpha History*, <https://alphahistory.com/vietnamwar/vietnam-warpeace-talks/> Accessed 17 April 2025.

2. The release of all the military men and civilians captured in the war will be carried out at the same time and will be completed at the same moment as the withdrawal of troops mentioned in Point 1;
3. In South Vietnam, the United States ceases supporting the current regime to allow the formation in Saigon of a new administration standing for peace, independence, neutrality, and democracy. The Provisional Revolutionary Government of South Vietnam (PRG) will engage in talks with the said administration with a view to settling the internal affairs of South Vietnam and achieving national concord;
4. The U.S. Government must assume the entire responsibility for the damage caused by the United States to the entire Vietnamese people. The DRV Government and the PRG request from the U.S. Government reparations for damage caused by the United States in the two zones of Vietnam;
5. The United States must respect the 1954 Geneva Agreements in Vietnam and Indo-China and those of 1962 on Laos. It must cease its aggression against and intervention in the Indo-Chinese countries to let the Indo-Chinese people settle their own affairs;
6. The problems existing between the Indo-Chinese countries will be settled by the Indo-Chinese parties on the basis of mutual respect for independence, sovereignty, and territorial integrity, and for noninterference on internal affairs. For its part, the DRV is prepared to participate in the settlement of these problems;
7. All the parties will observe a cease-fire after the conclusion of agreements of the aforementioned problems;
8. An international supervision will be set up;
9. An international guarantee will be indispensable for the realization of the basic national rights of the Indo-Chinese people, for the neutrality of South Vietnam, Laos, and Cambodia, and for the establishment of a lasting peace.
10. These nine points make up a whole.[4]

Five days later, on 1st July 1971, the Provisional Revolutionary Government of the Republic of South Vietnam (PRG) issued a lengthy and detailed seven-point Peace Proposal:

4 'Democratic Republic of Vietnam Peace Proposal, 26 June 1971', *Vassar College:* Paris Vietnam News Agency [VNA] in French to VNA Hanoi, January 31, 1972. Translation by Robert K. Brigham and Le Phuong Anh. < https://www.vassar.edu/the-wars-for-vietnam/documents/democratic-republic-vietnam-peace-proposal-june-26-1971> Accessed 30 April 2025.

1. Regarding the deadline for the total withdrawal of U.S. forces.

   The U.S. Government must put an end to its war of aggression in Vietnam, stop its policy of "Vietnamization" of the war, withdraw from South Vietnam all troops, military personnel, weapons, and war materials of the United States and of the other foreign countries in the U.S. camp, and dismantle all U.S. bases in South Vietnam, without posing any condition whatsoever.

   The U.S. Government must set a terminal date for the withdrawal from South Vietnam of the totality of U.S. forces and those of the other foreign countries in the U.S. camps. If the U.S. Government sets a terminal date for the withdrawal from South Vietnam in 1971 of the totality of U.S. forces and those of the other foreign countries in the U.S. camp, the parties will at the same time agree on the modalities:

   - The withdrawal in safety from South Vietnam of the totality of U.S. forces and those of the other foreign countries in the U.S. camp. The release of the totality of military men of all parties and of the civilians captured in the war (including American pilots captured in North Vietnam) so that they may all rapidly return to their homes.

   These two operations will begin on the same date and will end on the same date:

   - A cease-fire will be observed between the South Vietnam People's Liberation Armed Forces and the armed forces of the United States and of the other foreign countries in the U.S. camp as soon as the parties reach an agreement on the withdrawal from South Vietnam of the totality of U.S. forces and those of the other foreign countries in the U.S. camps.

2. Regarding the questions of power in South Vietnam.

   The U.S. Government must really respect the South Vietnam people's right to self-determination, put an end to its interference in the internal affairs of South Vietnam, cease backing the bellicose group headed by Nguyen Van Thieu at present in office in Saigon, and stop all maneuvers, including tricks on elections, aimed at maintaining the puppet Nguyen Van Thieu.

   The political, social, and religious forces in South Vietnam aspiring to peace and national concord will use various means to form in Saigon a new administration favoring peace, independence, neutrality and democracy. The Provisional Revolutionary Government of the Republic of South Vietnam will immediately enter into talks with the administration in order to settle the following questions:

- To form a broad three-segment government of national concord that will assume its functions during the period between the restoration of peace and the holding of general elections and organize general elections in South Vietnam. A cease-fire will be observed between the South Vietnam People's Liberation Armed Forces and the armed forces of the Saigon Administration as soon as a government of national concord is formed.
- To take concrete measures with the required guarantees so as to prohibit all acts of terror, reprisal, and discrimination against persons having collaborated with one or the other party, to ensure every democratic liberty to the South Vietnam people, to release all persons jailed for political reasons, to dissolve all concentration camps and to liquidate all forms of constraint and coercion so as to permit the people to return to their native places in complete freedom and to freely engage in their occupations.
- To see that the people's living conditions are stabilized and gradually improve, to create conditions allowing everyone to contribute his talents and efforts to heal the war wounds and rebuild the country.
- To agree on measures to be taken to ensure the holding of genuinely free, democratic, and fair general elections in South Vietnam.

3. Regarding the questions of Vietnamese armed forces in South Vietnam.

   The Vietnamese parties will together settle the question of Vietnamese armed forces in South Vietnam in a spirit of national concord, equality, and mutual respect, without foreign interference, in accordance with the post-war situation and with a view to lightening the people's contribution.

4. Regarding the peaceful reunification of Vietnam and the relations between the north and south zones.

   The reunification of Vietnam will be achieved step by step, by peaceful means, on the basis of discussions and agreements between the two zones, without constraint and annexation from either party, without foreign interference. Pending the reunification of the country, the north and the south zones will re-establish normal relations, guarantee free movement, free correspondence, free choice of residence, and maintain economic and cultural relations on the principle of mutual interests and mutual assistance. All questions concerning the two zones will be settled by qualified representatives of the Vietnamese people in the two zones on the basis of negotiations, without foreign interference.

In keeping with the provisions of the 1954 Geneva Agreements on Vietnam, in the present temporary partition of the country into two zones, the north and the south zones of Vietnam will refrain from joining any military alliance with foreign countries, from allowing any foreign country to have military bases, troops and military personnel on their soil, and from recognizing the protection of any country, of any military alliance or bloc.

5. Regarding the foreign policy of peace and neutrality of South Vietnam.

   South Vietnam will pursue a foreign policy of peace and neutrality, establish relations with all countries regardless of their political and social regime, in accordance with the five principles of peaceful coexistence, maintain economic and cultural relations with all countries, accept the cooperation of foreign countries in the exploitation of the resources of South Vietnam, accept from any country economic and technical aid without any political conditions attached, and participate in regional plans of economic cooperation.

   On the basis of these principles, after the end of the war, South Vietnam and the United States will establish relations in the political, economic, and cultural fields.

6. Regarding the damage caused by the United States to the Vietnamese people in the two zones.

   The U.S. Government must bear full responsibility for the losses and destruction it has caused to the Vietnamese people in the two zones.

7. Regarding the respect for and international guarantee of the accords that will be concluded. The parties will find agreement on the forms of respect for and international guarantee of the accords that will be concluded.[5]

Note

The 'Agreement on Ending the War and Restoring Peace in Vietnam', otherwise known as the Paris Peace Accords, was signed on 27th January 1973 by the Democratic Republic of Vietnam, the Republic of Vietnam, the Provisional Revolutionary Government (PRG), and the United States. The Accords officially ended direct U.S. military involvement in Vietnam.

5 'Peace Proposal of the Revolutionary Government of South Vietnam, 1 July 1971', *Vassar College*: Liberation Press Agency 1 July 1971. Translation by Robert K. Brigham and Le Phuong Anh. <https://www.vassar.edu/the-wars-for-vietnam/documents/peace-proposal-provisional-revolutionary-government-republic-south> Accessed 30 April 2025.

The Agreement established a ceasefire, a 60-day period for withdrawal of all American and other foreign troops, and the return of U.S. civilian and military personnel held prisoner by North Vietnamese forces. The Agreement also recognised the territorial integrity and unity of Vietnam and clearly called for negotiations between the Saigon regime and its internal opponents toward a political settlement in the South and an eventual reunification of Vietnam "through peaceful means".

President Richard Nixon described the Agreement as 'Peace with Honour'.

(For an account which makes a mockery of Nixon's description, see Chapter Fifty-Three: *Peace Without Honour*.)

APPENDIX C

The Cult of Fátima

During the 20th Century, with single-minded focus and determination, the Roman Catholic Church set out on a sacred crusade to destroy atheistic communism, wherever it may be found, no matter the means, no matter the cost.

Impassioned devotees of Our Lady of Fátima, of her offshoot Marian cults, and of the culturally-appropriated Jewish Mary in her 'Virgin Mary' guise, were marshalled and deployed strategically and relentlessly by a Church intent on total eradication.

If the cult of Our Lady of Fátima had not been deployed so successfully for so long, it could easily be dismissed along with other 19th Century Marian cults such as those of Lourdes and La Salette.

Since she cannot be dismissed, we must discover to what extent Our Lady of Fátima (together with her vast network of allies), influenced politicians, policy-makers, Popes and prelates to involve the U.S.A. and Australia in the Vietnam War, and contributed to the ultimate demise of the Soviet Union.

The radical and seemingly exclusive political, philosophical and religious differences between the Roman Catholic Church and her network of allies were swamped and overcome by a singularity—an all-encompassing need to utterly destroy atheistic communism, both root and branch.

To address adequately the development of the cult of Fátima and its strategic use in the 20th Century, the content is presented as follows:

Appendix C:1	The French Models
Appendix C:2	The Three Little Seers
Appendix C:3	The Apparitions
Appendix C:4	The Miracle of the Sun
Appendix C:5	The Great Secret
Appendix C:6	The Miraculous Timing
Appendix C:7	Mission Creep
Appendix C:8	The Heart of the Matter
Appendix C:9	Incredible
Appendix C:10	The Standing Army

Appendix C:11	The Great Delusion
Appendix C:12	The Great Victory

The Appendices include both unquestioned historical events and less well-attested but widely-held beliefs and assertions. All of the subject matter requires a more exhaustive and nuanced analysis but such cannot be attempted in a work which should rather be seen as a drawing together of strands sufficient to present the overall picture.

As there is a significant overlapping of events in terms of time, some of the content is presented in topical rather than chronological order.

The French Models

Four alleged Marian apparitions in nineteenth-century France have attracted a cult following, namely those at Rue du Bac,[6] Pontmain,[7] La Salette and Lourdes. Only from the apparition accounts of La Salette and Lourdes, however, can some insights and meaningful parallels with Fátima be drawn.

Section 1: La Salette

Most Catholic and non-Catholic sources have popularised the following version of events.

ON 19th September 1846, on a mountain about three miles from the village of La Salette-Fallavaux in the French Alps, it is alleged that fifteen-year old Mélanie Calvat and eleven-year old Maximin Giraud saw an apparition of a 'beautiful lady', weeping, and dressed in mournful attire with the instruments of the Passion. Speaking first in French and then in the local Occitan dialect, she charged them with a message which they were 'to deliver to all her people'.

It is alleged that, before disappearing, she communicated to each of the children a special 'secret'. Although the only messages publicly divulged at that time were predictions of famine and calamities, a Marian scold about the peasants working on Sundays, about carriage drivers for swearing, and about others going to the butcher shop like dogs during Lent, reports of the apparition nevertheless caused a sensation and resulted in a commission of investigation being appointed by Monseigneur Philibert de Bruillard, Bishop of Grenoble. During the investigation, a number of accusations were made against the visionaries, including the assertion that the apparition was actually just a middle-aged woman named La Merlière.[8] However, on 16th November 1851, de Bruillard declared the apparition of the 'Blessed Virgin' as certain and authorized the cult of Our Lady of La Salette.

---

6 Quintano, F. 'Rue du Bac—Message for Today'. *Vincentian Encyclopaedia.* <https://famvin.org/wiki/Rue_du_Bac_-_Message_for_Today.> Accessed 20 March 2022.

7 'An Account of the Apparition'. *Site Officiel Du Sanctuaire Notre-Dame De Pontmain.* <https://sanctuaire-pontmain.fr/le-recit-de-lapparition/> Accessed 21 March 2020.

8 Clugnet, L. (1910). 'La Salette'. *The Catholic Encyclopedia.* New York: Robert Appleton Company. Retrieved January 31, 2022 from New Advent: <http://www.newadvent.org/cathen/09008b.htm>

As noted above, the apparition had confided to each of the two children a special 'secret', although there was no mention of a 'secret' in the childrens' first accounts. In 1851, five years after the apparition, Bishop de Bruillard asked Maximin and Mélanie to commit their secrets to writing so that they might be sent to Pope Pius IX. Although the secrets were received by the Pope, there is no record of his reaction.

It was not until 1858 that Mélanie began to reveal the 'secret' confided to her at La Salette. Different versions were in circulation until the final account was published in 1879 with the Imprimatur of the Bishop of Lecce, Italy.

All these different versions of Mélanie's 'secret' contain highly suspicious texts which raised questions as to whether the 'secret' published in 1879 was identical with that communicated to Pius IX in 1851, or whether it was merely the work of a person whose mind had been disturbed by reading apocalyptic books and the lives of the Illuminati.

The contents of these 'secrets' are so demonstrably false and anachronistic, that they are just not worth reproducing here. Sources are available for those wishing to indulge in a little apocalyptic fantasy.

Although it is widely claimed that on 21st August 1879, Pope Leo XIII formally granted a Canonical Coronation to the image at the Basilica of Our Lady of La Salette, historical sources are silent.

However, an indication of Leo XIII's original attitude to the alleged miracle of La Salette had appeared in the press only a few months previously in an article entitled 'The La Salette Imposture' which was published on 1st January 1879 in the *Times of London* and reprinted on 3rd May 1879 in *The Sydney Mail and New South Wales Advertiser* Collection (1871-1912):

> A telegram in the *Times* of January I, states— 'A clerical organ at Toulouse announced that the Pope (Leo XIII) has pronounced against the alleged miracle of La Salette. All representations, therefore, of the appearance of the Virgin in peasant costume to two children are no longer to be objects of adoration, but are to be removed and destroyed. It appears that Mélanie Giraud (sic), one of the heroines of the affair, had lived for some years on the coast near Naples and had professed to receive revelations and visions, which found many believers. The Pope lately summoned her to Rome, subjected her to a severe cross-examination, and at last extracted an admission that she and her brother had played a concocted role. The latter was at one time a Papal Zouave and addicted

> to drunkenness; but even in that condition always told the same story as to the apparition, which was considered an additional proof of its genuineness...[9]

Note

Digitised issues of the *Sydney Mail and New South Wales Advertiser* (1871-1912) can be found in the Newspapers and Gazettes Section of *Trove*, a partner with the National Library of Australia.[10]

Section 2: Lourdes

Prelude

In the Constitution *Ineffabilis Deus* of 8th December 1854, Pope Pius IX had proclaimed the *Dogma of the Immaculate Conception*. This dogma states 'that the Blessed Virgin Mary, from the first moment of her conception, by a singular privilege and grace granted by Almighty God, and in view of the merits of Jesus Christ, Saviour of the human race, was preserved free from every stain of original sin'.[11]

Apparitions

On 11th February 1858, in a grotto at Massabielle near Lourdes, a little French town at the foot of the Pyrenees, 14-year old Marie-Bernarde Soubirous, known as Bernadette, allegedly experienced the first of eighteen apparitions of a 'Lady'.

On 24th February, the apparition asked for penance and prayer for the conversion of sinners and, on the following day, she instructed Bernadette to dig the ground near the grotto. From there a spring came forth which to this day is used for medicinal purposes by pilgrims to Lourdes.

Three Secrets

According to *Lourdes Sanctuaire*:

> Before the end of the first fifteen days of the apparitions, on 1st March, during the 12th apparition, the Lady entrusted **three secrets** to Bernadette with this express directive, "I forbid you to tell this to anyone". Bernadette would go on

9 *The Sydney Mail and New South Wales Advertiser* (NSW : 1871-1912) 3 May 1879, p. 714.

10 *Trove* <https://trove.nla.gov.au/newspaper/>

11 'Ineffabilis Deus- The Immaculate Conception'. *Papal Encyclicals Online* <https://www.papalencyclicals.net/pius09/p9ineff.htm> Accessed 12 Jan 2022

> to meet the Lady 4 more times, until 25th March when she would reveal her name.[12]

Although accompanied on each of her visits to the grotto by increasing numbers of townsfolk, she alone saw the 'Lady', generally assumed to be the Virgin Mary. Word eventually reached the French newspapers and the crowds accompanying Bernadette to the grotto swelled to thousands and had to be controlled by the police.

On 25th March 1858, the feast of the Annunciation of the Virgin Mary, the 'Lady' at last revealed her identity. As if to quash all opposition to the *Dogma of the Immaculate Conception* proclaimed on 8th December 1854, she obligingly declared to Bernadette in the local Lourdes patois *Que soy era Immaculada Concepciou* (I am the Immaculate Conception). The final apparition allegedly took place on 16th July 1858.

After an enquiry by a Church commission, the apparitions were declared authentic in 1862, veneration of the Virgin Mary as 'Our Lady of Lourdes' was authorised, and a basilica eventually completed above the grotto in 1876.

The underground spring in the grotto is believed to possess miraculous healing properties, thus luring millions to Lourdes every year and playing a dominant role in the local economy.

Bernadette entered the Sisters of Notre Dame at Nevers in 1866 and died there on 16th April 1879. She was beatified in 1925 by Pope Pius XI and canonized by him on the 8th December 1933, the *Feast of the Immaculate Conception.*

Further particulars about the 'Lady' were provided for us by Pope Pius XII in the 1953 Encyclical *Fulgrens Corona* in which he declared 1954 a Marian Year to commemorate the Centenary of the definition of the *Dogma of the Immaculate Conception*:

> The entire Catholic world received with joy the pronouncement of the Pontiff, so long and anxiously awaited (Pius IX). Devotion of the faithful to the Virgin Mother of God was stirred up and increased and this naturally led to a great improvement in Christian morality. Furthermore, studies were undertaken with new enthusiasm, which gave due prominence to the dignity and sanctity of the Mother of God. (para 2)
>
> Moreover, it seems that the Blessed Virgin Mary herself wished to confirm by some special sign the definition, which the Vicar of her Divine Son on earth had pronounced amidst the applause of the whole Church. For indeed four

12 '1st, 2nd and 25th March 1858-3 secrets, a message, and the Lady reveals her name'. *Lourdes Sanctuaire* <https://www.lourdes-france.org/en/1st-2nd-and-25th-march-1858-3-secrets-a-message-and-the-lady-reveals-her-name/> Accessed 3 February 2022.

> years had not yet elapsed when, in a French town at the foot of the Pyrenees, the Virgin Mother, youthful and benign in appearance, clothed in a shining white garment, covered with a white mantle and girded with a hanging blue cord, showed herself to a simple and innocent girl at the grotto of Massabielle. And to this same girl, earnestly inquiring the name of her with whose vision she was favored, with eyes raised to heaven and sweetly smiling, she replied: "I am the Immaculate Conception".[13] (para 3)

It is perhaps amusing to contemplate the fact that while Charles Darwin was preparing to publish his *On the Origin of Species*, the 'Blessed Virgin Mary' was reviving a belief in the supernatural and issuing a challenge to the forces of atheism, one of the twin plagues so despised by the Church. She would go on to challenge that other plague—communism—at Fátima.

---

13 'Fulgens Corona Encyclical of Pope Pius XII'. *Vatican* <https://www.vatican.va/content/pius-xii/en/encyclicals/documents/hf_p-xii_enc_08091953_fulgens-corona.pdf> Accessed 13 Jan 2022

The Three Little Seers

Arguably the most consequential weapon in the Church's crusade to destroy atheistic communism was the strategic use made of a series of events occurring in the obscure Portuguese village of Fátima in 1917.

Between May and October of that year, it is alleged that the apparition of a 'Lady' appeared on six occasions to three shepherd children: ten- year old Lúcia dos Santos, and her younger Marto cousins, nine-year old Francisco and seven-year old Jacinta. On the 13th July 1917, the 'Lady' allegedly entrusted the children with a 'Great Secret' made up of three distinct parts.

Two of the three little seers died of influenza within a year of each other: Francisco Marto on the 4th April 1919 and Jacinta Marto on the 20th February 1920.

According to the *Catholic Wire Network*, Luçia could not cope alone after the deaths of Francisco and Jacinta:

> Thousands upon thousands of visitors flocked to Fátima to visit the scene of the apparitions and all wanted to speak with Lúcia. They came to her home every hour of the day. They insisted upon learning every detail of the apparitions; how Our Lady looked; what she wore; what she said; everything. When Jacinta and Francisco were with her, it was easier to face all these people, but alone, oh, if only she could go away and be alone with Our Lord and Our Lady.
>
> ...To remedy this situation, the Bishop of Leiria, Most Rev. Joseph Correira da Silva, wisely concluded that the only solution would be to send Lúcia away from Fátima. Thus, on the 17th June 1921, just over four years after the eventful day when she saw Our Lady for the first time, Lucia secretly left Fátima for the convent school of the Sisters of St. Dorothy at Vilar de Porto. There she was given a new name by the mother superior and forbidden to speak of Fátima. [14]

Henceforth, from the age of fourteen, Lúcia dos Santos would be secured in a convent guarded by those ever-watchful nuns.

14 'Reflecting on Our Lady of Fatima's Messages to the Children and to Lucia as a Religious Sister'. (12 October 2017). Rev. Fr. Benedict Hughes, Fatima Conference. *Catholic Wire Network* < https://thecatholicwire.org/the-crisis-in-the-catholic-church/reflecting-on-our-lady-of-fatimas-messages-to-the-children-and-to-lucia-as-a-religious-sister/> Accessed 20 July 2025.

On 24th October 1925, 18-year old Lúcia entered the Institute of the Sisters of St. Dorothy in the Spanish village of Tuy in Pontevedra, not far from the Portuguese border. She made her perpetual vows on 3rd October 1934 and became a fully-fledged Sister of the Order of St. Dorothy, taking the name of 'Sister Maria das Dores' (Mary of the Sorrows).

In March 1948, after receiving papal permission to be relieved of her perpetual vows, she returned to Portugal and entered the Carmelite convent of Santa Teresa in Coimbra where, on 31st May 1949, she professed her vow as a Discalced Carmelite and took the name of 'Sister Maria Lúcia of Jesus and the Immaculate Heart'.

Lúcia would never again face embarrassing questions as she had done before she was sent away to the Sisters of St. Dorothy at the age of 14. Only the reported content of her periodic visions, her Memoirs, her strictly-supervised meetings, her carefully scripted statements, as well as the content of the alleged 'Great Secret', would reach the outside world from behind those cloistered walls. Unfortunately, the inconsistencies and absurdities surrounding the original apparition accounts would surface again and again. (See also *Mission Creep* and *Incredible*)

Lúcia died in her cell at the convent in Coimbra on 13th February 2005 aged 97.

Cult Approval

Two years after the alleged apparitions, the Diocesan Bishop of Leiria-Fátima, Dom José Alves Correia da Silva, established an official canonical enquiry. In a pastoral letter of October 1930, the Bishop announced the results of the enquiry:

> In virtue of considerations made known, and others which for reason of brevity we omit; humbly invoking the Divine Spirit and placing ourselves under the protection of the most Holy Virgin, and after hearing the opinions of our Rev. Advisors in this diocese, we hereby:
>
> 1. Declare worthy of belief, the visions of the shepherd children in the Cova da Iria, parish of Fátima, in this diocese, from 13th May to 13th October, 1917;
> 2. Permit officially the cult of Our Lady of Fátima.

From that moment of official approval, crowds swelled from around the world in pilgrimage to the Cova da Iria, calling down upon Portugal an immensity of graces that would confirm it in a new era only made possible, given its former state, by the Mother of God, Mediatrix of all Graces.[15]

The Memoirs

In the mid-1930s, José Alves Correia da Silva, the Bishop of Leiria-Fátima, allegedly encouraged Lúcia to write her Memoirs in the event that she might disclose further details of the 1917 apparitions.

It was not until her third memoir of 1941 that Lúcia indicated that there was a 'Great Secret', allegedly revealed to her in 1917, and that it had three distinct parts. In this she follows Mélanie Calvat of La Salette whose secrets were written down almost twenty years after the event. (See Appendix C:1 *The French Models*)

15 'Approval by the Bishop' (1930) *The Fatima Center* <https://fatima.org/about/fatima-the-facts/approval-by-the-bishop-1930/> Accessed 12 February 2022

The Apparitions

Although tedious for readers, it is necessary to paint an entire picture of the alleged apparitions.

The 'Angel of Peace'

Between Spring and Autumn of 1916, at Valinhos near Fátima in Portugal, a young man allegedly appeared on three occasions to the three shepherd children and announced that he was the 'Angel of Peace'. As noted, the three children were Lúcia dos Santos, and her younger cousins Francisco and Jacinta Marto.

At that time, the dos Santos and Marto families lived in Aljustrel, a town close to the village of Fátima. The dos Santos' youngest child, Lúcia, was responsible for taking the family's sheep to pasture in a small tract of family land near a place called Loca do Cabeco and the Cova da Iría.

The message of the 'Angel' seemed to be that the children must sacrifice themselves for the conversion of sinners and must make reparation for outrages, sacrileges and indifference. Note that these apparitions of the 'Angel of Peace' were not revealed by Lúcia until 1937.[16]

The 'Lady'

The salient points of the alleged incidents reproduced in English below are taken from various popularised versions of events at Fátima.

First apparition (13th May)

On 13th May 1917, shortly after noon, the three children who had allegedly seen the 'Angel of Peace' the previous year, were tending to their sheep in the Cova da Iría fields:

> They had had their lunch, and, as was their habit, had started to pray the rosary when they heard "lightning in a clear sky". Fearing a storm was approaching, they decided to head home. As they prepared to leave, a strange light in the sky moved toward them. The children reported that, although astonished, they felt no fear. They claimed a beautiful lady appeared before them, "above the holm

16 Walsh, William Thomas. *Our Lady of Fátima*. Doubleday: New York. 1954, p. 217. *Imprimatur*: Francis Cardinal Spellman.

oak tree, wearing a pure white mantle, which was edged with gold, which went to her feet. In her hands the beads of a rosary shone like stars, with its crucifix the most radiant gem of all". During this first visit the apparition told the children not to be afraid, that she came from Heaven. **She asked them to pray the rosary and to return to the same spot on the thirteenth of every month.** Then the apparition returned the same way it had come.[17]

Second apparition (13th June)

When the children arrived in the Cova da Iría fields on 13th June, they found a small crowd waiting for them. According to reports, they all prayed the Rosary together, then saw the same strange light and the 'Lady' on the holm oak as in May. Lúcia asked the 'Lady' what she wanted of her. The response was:

> I want you to come here on the thirteenth of next month. I want you to continue saying the Rosary every day. And after each one of the mysteries, my children, I want you to pray in this way: 'O my Jesus, forgive us our sins , save us from the fire of hell. Take all souls to heaven, especially those who are most in need'. I want you to learn to read and write, and later I will tell you what else I want of you.

According to Lúcia, it was during this apparition that the deaths of Francisco and Jacinta were allegedly predicted:

> Yes, I shall take Jacinta and Francisco soon, but you will remain a little longer, since Jesus wishes you to make me known and loved on earth. **He wishes also for you to establish devotion in the world to my Immaculate Heart.**

Third apparition (13th July)

On 13th July, it is alleged that the 'Lady' first entrusted the children with a 'Great Secret' (the context and content of this 'Great Secret' will be addressed elsewhere).

When Lúcia again asked the 'Lady' what she wanted of her, she was given the following response:

> I want you to come back here on the thirteenth of next month. Continue to say the Rosary every day in honor of Our Lady of the Rosary, to obtain the peace of the world and the end of the war, because **only she can obtain it.**

17 'The Marian Apparitions in Fatima as Political Reality: Religion and Politics in Twentieth-Century Portugal'. Paul Christopher Manuel, Co-Chair, Iberian Study Group, *Minda de Gunzburg Center for European Studies*, St. Anselm College, New Hampshire. <https://ces.fas.harvard.edu/uploads/files/Working-Papers-Archives/CES_WP88.pdf> p. 7. Accessed 15 October 2025.

Lúcia then asked the 'Lady' who she was and if she would perform a miracle so that everyone would know for certain that she had appeared to the three children. The response was:

> You must come here every month, and in October **I will tell you who I am and what I want. I will then perform a miracle so that all may believe.**

Fourth apparition (19th August)

It was reported that the local secular government had become alarmed by the numbers of people taking an interest in the Fátima events. As 13th August approached, it was claimed that government officials used trickery to prevent the children reaching the Cova da Iría that day.

However, the 'Lady' was not to be thwarted. On 19th August, Lúcia, her brother John, and Francisco Marto, were grazing the sheep at Valinhos, where they had twice seen the 'Angel of Peace'. Lúcia sensed that the 'Lady' was coming. She sent for Jacinta and the moment she arrived, the 'Lady' appeared. Lúcia again asked her what she wanted: The response was

> Come again to the Cova da Iría on the thirteenth of next month, my child, and continue to say the Rosary every day. **In the last month, I will perform a miracle so that all may believe.**

Fifth apparition (13th September)

According to reports, and whatever their motivation, more than 30,000 people were drawn to the Cova da Iría on 13th September to await the arrival of the visionaries and the apparition. When the time came, it is asserted that 'they' heard Lúcia yet again ask the apparition what she wanted of her.

This time, the 'Lady' was more forthcoming about who will appear in October:

> Continue the Rosary, my children. Say it every day that the war may end. In October **Our Lord will come,** as well as **Our Lady of Sorrows** and **Our Lady of Mt. Carmel. Saint Joseph will appear with the Child Jesus** to bless the world.

Sixth apparition (13th October)

The sixth and final apparition on 13th October was accompanied by the alleged 'Miracle of the Sun' (see Appendix C:4 for an account).

The Miracle of the Sun

Sixth and Final Apparition

When the 'Lady' appeared in the Cova da Iría on 13th October, the crowd was reported as numbering between 50 and 70 thousand. Lúcia asked once more:

> What do you want of me? *and* Will you tell me your name?

The 'Lady' responded with:

> I want a chapel built here in my honor. I want you to continue saying the Rosary every day. **The war will end soon, and the soldiers will return to their homes.** (See also Appendix C:9: *Incredible.*)

The 'Lady' then tells Lúcia she is 'Our Lady of the Rosary'.

Lúcia is heard to cry out to the crowd: 'Look at the sun'.

In his book, *Our Lady of Fatima*, William Thomas Walsh appears to draw on several sources for the following account of the 'Miracle of the Sun':

> As Our Lady disappeared in the very radiance that came from her outstretched hands, there stood out in the zenith above three tableaus which symbolized, one after another, the Joyous, the Sorrowful and the Glorious mysteries of the Rosary. The first was a distinct representation of the Holy Family: Our Lady herself in her traditional dress of white with a blue mantle, and Saint Joseph beside her holding the Child Jesús on his arm—Saint Joseph in white, the Infant in bright red.
>
> Lúcia was heard to say, "Saint Joseph is going to bless us!" All three of the children saw this first visión, and saw the Saint make the sign of the cross three times over the crowd. The holy Child did likewise.
>
> The next visión, seen by Lúcia alone, was one of Our Lady of Sorrows in the sombre garb assigned to her by tradition, the Mater Dolorosa of Good Friday, but without the sword in her breast; and beside her stood her divine Son grieving as when he met her on the way to Calvary. Lúcia saw only the upper part of His figure. He looked pityingly on the crowd for whom He had died, and raised His hand to make the sign of the cross over them.

> Our Lady then appeared in a third visión of glory, as Our Lady of Mount Carmel, crowned as Queen of Heaven and of the world, her infant Son upon her knee.

The account continues:

> The crowd saw nothing of all this: at least there seems to be no solid verification of the claim that a few saw the Lady. What they all did see, however, was something stupendous, unheard of, almost apocalyptic. The sun stood forth in the clear zenith like a great silver disk which, though bright as any sun they had ever seen, they could look straight at without blinking, and with a unique and delightful satisfaction. This lasted but a moment.
>
> While they gazed, the huge ball began to "dance"—that was the word all the beholders applied to it Now it was whirling rapidly like a gigantic fire-wheel. After doing this for some time, it stopped. Then it rotated again, with dizzy, sickening speed. Finally there appeared on the rim a border of crimson, which flung across the sky, as from a hellish vortex, blood-red streamers of flame, reflecting to the earth, to the trees and shrubs, to the upturned faces and the clothes all sorts of brilliant colors in succession: green, red, orange, blue, violet, the whole spectrum in fact. Madly gyrating in this manner three times, the fiery orb seemed to tremble, to shudder, and then to plunge precipitately, in a mighty zigzag, toward the crowd.
>
> A fearful cry broke from the lips of thousands of terrified persons as they fell upon their knees, thinking the end of the world had come. Some said that the air became warmer at that instant; they would not have been surprised if everything about them had burst into flames, enveloping and consuming them… This had lasted about ten minutes, perhaps. Then all saw the sun begin to climb, in the same zigzag manner, to where it had appeared before. It became tranquil, then dazzling. No one could look at it any longer. It was the sun of every day. [18]

Many people on the scene that day, including members of the press, reported seeing this *danse macabre* of the sun. Many others reported seeing nothing but the usual play of light on objects, clothing and limbs caused by the sun suddenly breaking through clouds after rain.

It is insulting to readers in this, the 21st Century, to state the obvious scientific facts so, moving on…

---

18 Walsh, William Thomas. *Our Lady of Fátima*. Doubleday: New York, NY. 1954, pp. 157-58. *Imprimatur*: Francis Cardinal Spellman.

On 8th May 1950, twenty years after the Cult of Fátima was officially approved, Pope Pius XII declared to the directors of the Blue Army:

> …The time for doubting Fátima has passed. Now is the time for action…[19]

Our Lady of Fátima rewarded the Pope for favours past and future when he was granted his own personal 'Miracle of the Sun' on 30th October 1950 as he was walking in the Vatican Gardens pondering the forthcoming Dogma of the Assumption:

> Pius XII privately saw the Miracle of the Sun—the same phenomenon which had occurred Oct. 13, 1917—several times within days of his declaration of the dogma of the Assumption on Nov. 1, 1950…Pius XII related how he saw the same miracle again on Oct. 31 and Nov. 1, "the day of the definition of the Dogma of the Assumption, and then again Nov. 8, and after that, no more". He took it as a divine sign endorsing the dogma's proclamation.[20]

Note

The Dogma of the Assumption, which holds that the Virgin Mary was assumed body and soul into heavenly glory, was proclaimed by Pope Pius XII on 1st November 1950, in *Munificentissimus Deus*: [21]

> Hence the revered Mother of God, from all eternity joined in a hidden way with Jesus Christ in one and the same decree of predestination,(47) immaculate in her conception, a most perfect virgin in her divine motherhood, the noble associate of the divine Redeemer who has won a complete triumph over sin and its consequences, finally obtained, as the supreme culmination of her privileges, that she should be preserved free from the corruption of the tomb and that, like her own Son, having overcome death, she might be taken up body and soul to the glory of heaven where, as Queen, she sits in splendor at the right hand of her Son, the immortal King of the Ages.(48)

---

19 Excerpt From: Frere Michel de la Sainte Trinite. *The Whole Truth about Fatima - Vol I.* p. 827. Apple Books

20 '70 Years Ago Pius XII Proclaimed Assumption—and Saw Miracle of the Sun'. *National Catholic Register*. <https://www.ncregister.com/blog/70-years-ago-pius-xii-proclaimed-assumption-and-saw-miracle-of-the-sun> Accessed 17 February 2022.

21 'Munificentissimus Deus'. Apostolic Constitution of Pope Pius XII. *Vatican* < https://www.vatican.va/content/pius-xii/en/apost_constitutions/documents/hf_p-xii_apc_19501101_munificentissimus-deus.html#:~:text=This%20%22outstanding%20agreement%20of%20the,taking%20nothing%20away%20from%20them.> Accessed 16 April 2026.

The Great Secret

Section 1: Introduction

Not even Hollywood could have imagined the drama, the intrigue, the secret meetings, the fevered speculation, the wild rumours, and the apocalyptic dread which would sweep the Catholic world right off its feet following the gradual leaking of the first two parts of the 'Great secret' in 1941 and the projected opening of the 'third secret' by the Pope in 1960. (See Author's Note)

But throughout these years, the Church kept a cool head and a steady hand on the rudder guiding the ship of state along the path it had embarked upon years before: a carefully orchestrated, far-reaching holy war against atheistic communism. The cult of Fátima was employed as a tool to marshal the masses in this great ideological gamble which, at times, threatened to engulf the world in a nuclear holocaust. Whenever a totalitarian movement appeared on the scene declaring communism as its principal foe, the Church became its ally.

Section 2: The Message of Fatima

On 13th July 2000, the Vatican published *The Message of Fatima.* Included in the publication are the texts of the First, Second and Third Secrets and the following Introduction:

> Fátima is undoubtedly the most prophetic of modern apparitions. The first and second parts of the "secret"—which are here published in sequence so as to complete the documentation—refer especially to the frightening vision of hell, devotion to the Immaculate Heart of Mary, the Second World War, and finally the prediction of the immense damage that Russia would do to humanity by abandoning the Christian faith and embracing Communist totalitarianism.
>
> In 1917 no one could have imagined all this: the three *pastorinhos* of Fátima see, listen and remember, and Lucia, the surviving witness, commits it all to paper when ordered to do so by the Bishop of Leiria and with Our Lady's permission.

For the account of the first two parts of the 'secret', which have already been published and are therefore known, we have chosen the text written by Sister Lucia in the Third Memoir of 31 August 1941; some annotations were added in the Fourth Memoir of 8th December 1941. [22]

Section 3: The First Secret

The Vision of Hell

Our Lady showed us a great sea of fire which seemed to be under the earth. Plunged in this fire were demons and souls in human form, like transparent burning embers, all blackened or burnished bronze, floating about in the conflagration, now raised into the air by the flames that issued from within themselves together with great clouds of smoke, now falling back on every side like sparks in a huge fire, without weight or equilibrium, and amid shrieks and groans of pain and despair, which horrified us and made us tremble with fear.

The demons could be distinguished by their terrifying and repulsive likeness to frightful and unknown animals, all black and transparent. This vision lasted but an instant. How can we ever be grateful enough to our kind heavenly Mother, who had already prepared us by promising, in the first Apparition, to take us to heaven. Otherwise, I think we would have died of fear and terror.

We then looked up at Our Lady, who said to us so kindly and so sadly:

You have seen hell where the souls of poor sinners go. To save them, God wishes to establish in the world devotion to my Immaculate Heart. If what I say to you is done, many souls will be saved and there will be peace.

The war is going to end: but if people do not cease offending God, a worse one will break out during the Pontificate of Pius XI. When you see a night illumined by an unknown light, know that this is the great sign given you by God that she is about to punish the world for its crimes, by means of war, famine, and persecutions of the Church and of the Holy Father. To prevent this, I shall come to ask for the consecration of Russia to my Immaculate Heart, and the Communion of reparation on the First Saturdays. [23]

22 'The Message of Fatima'. (13 May 2000) *Congregation for the Doctrine of the Faith.* <http://www.vatican.va/roman_curia/congregations/cfaith/documents/rc_con_cfaith_doc_20000626_message-fatima_en.html> Accessed 28 June 2025.

23 Ibid.

Section 4: The Second Secret

Russia must be converted

> ...If my requests are heeded, Russia will be converted, and there will be peace; if not, she will spread her errors throughout the world, causing wars and persecutions of the Church. The good will be martyred; the Holy Father will have much to suffer; various nations will be annihilated. In the end, my Immaculate Heart will triumph. The Holy Father will consecrate Russia to me, and she shall be converted, and a period of peace will be granted to the world.[24]

The content of the this 'Second Secret' was revealed on 31 August 1941, less than two months after Nazi Germany invaded Russia. The timing of the revelation made it abundantly clear where Our Lady of Fátima's allegiance lay.

In October 1942, Cardinal Schuster, Archbishop of Milan, publicly interpreted the Fátima 'Second Secret' text in an anti-communist sense:

> "When the promise of the Blessed Virgin is fulfilled", he said, "it will be the most beautiful and total victory of the Church over Bolshevism." [25]

The Cardinal's 'total victory' speech was uttered during the crucial Battle of Stalingrad then being fought between the invading forces of Nazi Germany and Soviet Russia.

Section 5: The Third Secret

The Bishop in White

> I write in obedience to you, my God, who command me to do so through his Excellency the Bishop of Leiria and through your Most Holy Mother and mine.
>
> After the two parts which I have already explained, at the left of Our Lady and a little above, we saw an Angel with a flaming sword in his left hand; flashing, it gave out flames that looked as though they would set the world on fire; but they died out in contact with the splendour that Our Lady radiated towards him

24 'The Message of Fatima'. (13 May 2000) *Congregation for the Doctrine of the Faith*. <http://www.vatican.va/roman_curia/congregations/cfaith/documents/rc_con_cfaith_doc_20000626_message-fatima_en.html> Accessed 28 June 2025.

25 Excerpt From: Frere Michel de la Sainte Trinite. T*he Whole Truth about Fatima - Vol I*. p. 675. Apple Books.

from her right hand: pointing to the earth with his right hand, the Angel cried out in a loud voice: 'Penance, Penance, Penance!'.

And we saw in an immense light that is God: 'something similar to how people appear in a mirror when they pass in front of it' a Bishop dressed in White 'we had the impression that it was the Holy Father'. Other Bishops, Priests, men and women Religious going up a steep mountain, at the top of which there was a big Cross of rough-hewn trunks as of a cork-tree with the bark; before reaching there the Holy Father passed through a big city half in ruins and half trembling with halting step, afflicted with pain and sorrow, he prayed for the souls of the corpses he met on his way; having reached the top of the mountain, on his knees at the foot of the big Cross he was killed by a group of soldiers who fired bullets and arrows at him, and in the same way there died one after another the other Bishops, Priests, men and women Religious, and various lay people of different ranks and positions. Beneath the two arms of the Cross there were two Angels each with a crystal aspersorium in his hand, in which they gathered up the blood of the Martyrs and with it sprinkled the souls that were making their way to God. [26]

The Interpretation Thereof

To coincide with the Vatican's publication of *The Message of Fatima* on 13th May 2000, Pope John Paul II visited Fátima on the same day to announce the beatification of two of the little seers, Francisco and Jacinta Marto who, as previously noted, had both died of influenza. At the end of a Mass at Fátima presided over by the Pope, Cardinal Angelo Sodano, the Secretary of State, made an announcement in Portuguese, which is given here in the English translation:

On this solemn occasion of his visit to Fatima, His Holiness has directed me to make an announcement to you. As you know, the purpose of his visit to Fátima has been to beatify the two little shepherds. Nevertheless he also wishes his pilgrimage to be a renewed gesture of gratitude to Our Lady for her protection during these years of his papacy. This protection seems also to be linked to the so-called third part of the secret of Fatima.

That text contains a prophetic vision similar to those found in Sacred Scripture, which do not describe photographically the details of future events, but synthesize and compress against a single background facts which extend

26 'The Message of Fatima'. (13 May 2000) *Congregation for the Doctrine of the Faith.* <http://www.vatican.va/roman_curia/congregations/cfaith/documents/rc_con_cfaith_doc_20000626_message-fatima_en.html> Accessed 28 June 2025.

> through time in an unspecified succession and duration. As a result, the text must be interpreted in a symbolic key.
>
> The vision of Fatima concerns above all the war waged by atheistic systems against the Church and Christians, and it describes the immense suffering endured by the witnesses of the faith in the last century of the second millennium. It is an interminable Way of the Cross led by the Popes of the twentieth century.
>
> According to the interpretation of the little shepherds, which was also confirmed recently by Sister Lucia, the Bishop clothed in white who prays for all the faithful is the Pope. As he makes his way with great difficulty towards the Cross amid the corpses of those who were martyred (Bishops, priests, men and women Religious and many lay people), he too falls to the ground, apparently dead, under a hail of gunfire.[27]

Note

The three parts of the 'Great Secret' were allegedly communicated to the children in July 1917 during the First World War. Benedict XV was then Pope. In the first secret, according to 'Our Lady', the current war was going to end but a worse war would break out during the pontificate of Pope Pius XI. A Pius XI did become Pope on 6th February 1922 but he died on 10th February 1939, months before the Second World War began. It was actually Pius XII who was Pope when the war broke out so, aside from being remarkably prescient about the name a future Pope would take upon his coronation, either Our Lady of Fátima or Sister Lúcia were remarkably confused about their Popes.

Section 6: The Secret Envelope

According to Michael Cuneo's book, *The Smoke of Satan: Conservative and Traditionalist Dissent in Contemporary American Catholicism*, Sister Lúcia committed the 'Third Secret' to writing on 3rd January 1944 and sent it in a sealed envelope to the Diocesan Bishop of Leiria-Fátima, Dom José Alves Correia da Silva:

> The Bishop apparently did not want to take the risk of reading the secret himself, however, and after failing to entrust it to a higher authority, he deposited the sealed envelope in a safe at his chancery office, where it remained for more than ten years.

27 Ibid.

> Lucia, in the meantime, was adding several twists to the plot. In February 1946, while being interviewed by a Dutch priest named Fr. Jongen, she indicated that she did not want the third part of the secret revealed until 1960.[28]

Sister Lucia's wish that the 'Third Secret' not be opened until 1960 was allegedly confirmed eleven years later when, on 17th May 1955, Cardinal Ottaviani, Pro-Prefect of the Holy Office, went to the Carmel of Saint Teresa at Coimbra and interrogated Lúcia on the 'Third Secret'. On 11th February 1967, in a allocution celebrating the 50th anniversary of the apparitions at Fátima, the Cardinal recalled that:

> The message was not to be opened before 1960. I asked Sister Lúcia "Why this date?" She answered, "Because then it will seem clearer (*mais claro*)".[29]

As noted, in the year 2000 the Vatican published *The Message of Fatima.* Included in the publication is the following information concerning the whereabouts of the Third Secret:

> The third part of the "secret" was written "by order of His Excellency the Bishop of Leiria and the Most Holy Mother ..." on 3 January 1944.
>
> There is only one manuscript, which is here reproduced photostatically. The sealed envelope was initially in the custody of the Bishop of Leiria. To ensure better protection for the "secret" the envelope was placed in the Secret Archives of the Holy Office on 4 April 1957. The Bishop of Leiria informed Sister Lucia of this.
>
> According to the records of the Archives, the Commissary of the Holy Office, Father Pierre Paul Philippe, OP, with the agreement of Cardinal Alfredo Ottaviani, brought the envelope containing the third part of the "secret of Fátima" to Pope John XXIII on 17 August 1959. "After some hesitation", His Holiness said: "We shall wait. I shall pray. I shall let you know what I decide". (1). In fact Pope John XXIII decided to return the sealed envelope to the Holy Office and not to reveal the third part of the "secret".
>
> Paul VI read the contents with the Substitute, Archbishop Angelo Dell'Acqua, on 27 March 1965, and returned the envelope to the Archives of the Holy Office, deciding not to publish the text.

28 Cuneo, Michael W. *The Smoke of Satan: Conservative and Traditionalist Dissent in Contemporary American Catholicism.* Johns Hopkins University Press: Baltimore, 1997, p. 135.

29 'Cardinal Ottaviani on the Third Secret of Fatima' (3 September 2015). *Catholic Stand* < https://catholicstand.com/ottaviani-fatima-secret/> Accessed 5 March 2026.

Pope John Paul II, for his part, asked for the envelope containing the third part of the "secret" following the assassination attempt on 13 May 1981. On 18 July 1981, Cardinal Franjo Šeper, Prefect of the Congregation, gave two envelopes to Archbishop Eduardo Martínez Somalo, Substitute of the Secretariat of State: one white envelope, containing Sister Lucia's original text in Portuguese; the other orange, with the Italian translation of the "secret". (These were given to the Pope.)

> On the following 11th August, Archbishop Martínez returned the two envelopes to the Archives of the Holy Office.(2) [30]

Michael Cuneo's description of the Fátima drama is perhaps most fitting:

> Of the dozens of Marian apparitions that have been reported worldwide over the past two hundred years, none has packed nearly as much dramatic punch as Fátima. Secret messages, apocalyptic countdowns, cloak-and-dagger intrigue within the highest echelons of the Vatican: not even Hollywood could ask for better material than this.[31]

Author's Note

As noted, on 17 May 1955, Cardinal Ottaviani went to the Carmel of Saint Teresa at Coimbra and allegedly interrogated Lúcia on the 'Third Secret'. On 11th February 1967, in a allocution celebrating the 50th anniversary of the apparitions at Fátima, the Cardinal recalled that:

> The message was not to be opened before 1960. I asked Sister Lúcia "Why this date?" She answered, "Because then it will seem clearer (*mais claro*)".[32]

On a personal note, I can attest to the projected '1960' opening of the 'Third Secret'. In 1958, when I was a twelve-year old student at a Catholic Convent, myself and a group of girls were told by one of our teachers, a Mother Theophane, that when the Pope opened the Third Secret of Fátima in 1960, the world would end. I can still remember exactly where we were standing, such was this revelation's impact. I was sufficiently knowledgable about world events at twelve to understand that the only way the entire world would 'end' was by nuclear holocaust. I know what the impact

30 'The Message of Fatima' (13 May 2000). *Congregation for the Doctrine of the Faith*. <http://www.vatican.va/roman_curia/congregations/cfaith/documents/rc_con_cfaith_doc_20000626_message-fatima_en.html> Accessed 28 June 2025.

31 Cuneo, Michael W. *The Smoke of Satan: Conservative and Traditionalist Dissent in Contemporary American Catholicism.* Johns Hopkins University Press: Baltimore, 1997, p. 134..

32 'Cardinal Ottaviani on the Third Secret of Fatima' (3 September 2015). *Catholic Stand* < https://catholicstand.com/ottaviani-fatima-secret/> Accessed 5 March 2026.

was on me. How many other Catholic children across the world were exposed to this cruel and numbing fear? And what influence did it have on their future actions or inactions? It would certainly have shaped their thinking for the rest of their lives, as it did and does mine.

The Miraculous Timing

Neatly book-ending the Fátima apparitions were the abdication of the Russian Tsar Nicholas II on 15th March 1917 following the February Revolution, and the Bolshevik Revolution of October 1917 led by Vladimir Ilyich Lenin.

According to the *Advocate*, Father Daniel Daly, an Australian cleric, was struck by this timing of events:

> The Very Reverend Father Daniel Daly delivered an impassioned sermon in the presence of the statue enshrined in Melbourne's St. Patrick's Cathedral. (The "Pilgrim Statue" of Our Lady of Fátima had reached Australia in January 1951.)

Part of his sermon included the following:

> The children at Fátima had been shown a vision of the Immaculate Heart of Mary wounded by the sins of the world; they had been shown a brief but terrible vision of hell. To save poor sinners Our Lord wished that devotion to the Immaculate Heart of Mary be established in the world. "If people will do what I ask", said Our Lady, "many souls will be saved and there will be peace in the world". If the Blessed Virgin's requests were granted, she said, Russia would be converted and there would be peace; if they were not, Russia would spread its errors throughout the world, provoking wars and persecution against the Church, many good people would be martyred, the Holy Father would have much to suffer, many nations would be annihilated. The outlook was gloomy, but there was a ray of hope. Mary's Immaculate Heart would triumph.

Father Daly went on to speak of the bookend timing of the apparitions:

> Twenty-seven days before the first apparition at Fátima, a sealed train from Switzerland crossed Europe, with the permission of the German High Command. Its destination was St. Petersburg—now known as Leningrad. That train contained two men, Lenin and Trotsky, whose mission was to plan the Communist Revolution.
>
> Exactly twenty-three days after the final apparition at Fátima, Lenin and Trotsky triumphed in Petrograd and later in Moscow and set in motion that great torrent of blood and murder and persecution which since then has enveloped so great a part of the world. In Russia, Spain, Mexico, Poland and

> Hungary, and in many other countries of the world today, the Catholic Church had undergone and is enduring one of the greatest persecutions it had ever known. Christian blood has flowed in torrents, multitudes have been martyred, many more are languishing in concentration camps, the temples of God have been violated and the shrines of Mary destroyed, and as we are gathered here today in love and devotion before the statue from Mary's shrine of Fátima, the free nations of the earth are in feverish activity for they are threatened with complete domination by **the powers of Satan enthroned at Moscow**. These facts and the perfect timing of Our Lady's apparitions give extra seriousness to the warnings at Fátima. The attack upon God and Christian civilization was world wide; it was essential that we should respond to Our Lady's warning because the safety of the world was in our hands.[33]

However, Father Daly neglected to mention that the visions concerning Hell and Russia only became known in August 1941, being two parts of the 'Great Secret' allegedly confided to the children on 13 July 1917.

Nevertheless, the visions would be used multiple times in multiple ways from 1941 onwards as if they had been made public in July 1917. Thus, they were evidence of Our Lady's prescience in that, even before the Bolshevik October Revolution, she was preparing a coalition of the willing for a fight to the death against atheistic communism.

Note

On 13th May 1951, in a radio broadcast to pilgrims at Fátima, Pope Pius XII said that Our Lady of Fátima was travelling the world claiming her dominion.

33 *Advocate* (Melbourne, Victoria), 25 January 1951, p. 7.

Mission Creep

By comparing the Fátima apparition accounts in works appearing before 1938 with those appearing later, it is obvious that the early reports were initially promoted to benefit a powerful local clergy and the ultra-conservative elements of Portuguese politics. When it became apparent that Our Lady of Fátima could be used on a much broader scale in the world-wide interests of the Catholic Church and the international right wing of politics, the later works expanded in scope to reflect this new capacity and differed from the earlier works to such a marked degree that they are impossible to harmonise. These two sets of accounts are dubbed Fátima I and Fátima II by critics.

In works before 1938 there is no mention of the 1916 apparitions of the 'Angel of Peace'; no mention of the vision of the Immaculate Heart of Mary in the 13th June 1917 apparition; and not the slightest allusion to the 'Great Secret' allegedly given in the 13th July 1917 apparition. Accounts of the 1917 apparitions promise only that the children will go to 'Heaven'; that if they say the Rosary every day it will hasten the end of the current war; and that Our Lady of Fátima will work a great miracle on the 13th October 1917, the sixth apparition.

Unfortunately for advocates and activists, the Immaculate Heart vision and the 'Great Secret', which is today presented as if it were public knowledge at the time and evidence of 'Our Lady's' prescience, are missing from the original accounts. (It was not until her third memoir of 1941 that Lúcia indicated that there was a 'Great Secret' and that it had three distinct parts.)

Since the early accounts contain no vision of the Immaculate Heart of Mary, so essential to the continuing message, and no allusions to Russia spreading her errors throughout the world, the claim that the apparition at Fátima requested in 1917 that Russia be consecrated to her Immaculate Heart is a later fabrication by Lúcia herself, or by those controlling her in 1941, or by interested parties who benefit from it today, in one way or another.

The Heart of the Matter

To halt the advance of atheistic communism in the 20th Century, Our Lady of Fátima devotee groups and a succession of Popes claimed that Our Lady conveyed her wish that Russia be converted and saved via an unquestionable and authoritative source—Sister Lúcia herself. It was not much of a gamble: the faithful have always proved themselves to be remarkably gullible. The tactic's success relied on Lúcia receiving private visions, which she obligingly did.

Section 1: 1925

In an article titled 'The Immaculate Heart of Mary: Core of the Fátima Message', posted on the *America needs Fâtima* site, it is alleged that Sister Lúcia received a private vision on 10th December 1925 in which the 'Blessed Mother' asked for the devotion of reparation of the Five First Saturdays:

> The Blessed Mother appeared alongside the Child Jesus who stood over a luminous cloud. Our Lady rested one hand on the Child's shoulder while she held on the other hand a heart pierced with thorns.
>
> The Child said, "Have pity on the Heart of your Most Holy Mother which is covered with thorns with which ungrateful men pierce it at every moment with no one to extract them with an act of reparation".
>
> Our Lady expressed her request in the following words:
>
> "See, my daughter, My Heart surrounded with thorns with which ungrateful men pierce me at every moment with blasphemies and ingratitude. You, at least, make sure to console me and announce that all those who for five months, on the first Saturdays, go to Confession, receive Communion, say five decades of the Rosary and keep me company for 15 minutes meditating on the mysteries of the Rosary, with the purpose of making reparation to Me, I promise to assist them at the hour of death with all the graces necessary for the salvation of their souls".[34]

34 'The Immaculate Heart of Mary: Core of the Fátima Message'. *America Needs Fatima*. < https://americaneedsfatima.org/articles/the-immaculate-heart-of-mary-core-of-the-fatima-message> Accessed 21 May 2026.

Section 2: 1929

Arguably, the most significant and revealing of these visions is Lúcia's 1929 claim that the Blessed Virgin Mary told her that God had requested the consecration of Russia to her Immaculate Heart. According to Sandra Zimdars-Swartz:

> On June 13, 1929, at the convent chapel in Tuy, Spain, Lúcia had another mystical experience in which she saw **the Holy Trinity and the Blessed Virgin.** Mary told her, "**The moment has come** in which God asks the Holy Father in union with all the Bishops of the world to make the consecration of Russia to my Immaculate Heart, promising to save it by this means".[35]

It is alleged that Lúcia reported this vision to her confessor, the Jesuit Father José Bernardo Gonçalves, urging him to persuade Pope Pius XI to find some way to perform the consecration but no action was taken.[36]

In this vision, it is the Blessed Virgin Mary who tells Lúcia that God requests the consecration, not Our Lady of Fátima. It implies that the second part of the 'Great Secret' about Russia, later claimed to have been told to the three children at Fátima in 1917, had not yet been fabricated.

If the Pope had spoken of the consecrating and 'saving' of communist Russia in 1929, at a time when the emerging Fascist dictatorships of Europe were all condemning communism, it may have been construed that the 'Holy Trinity', the 'Blessed Virgin Mary,' and God favoured the likes of the Italian dictator Mussolini.

Section 3: 1942

In a Portuguese radio broadcast of 31st October 1942, Pius XII consecrated the world to the Immaculate Heart of Mary but did not mention Russia specifically.

The Pope was understandably prudent for two reasons. Firstly, by then, the second part of the 'Great Secret' about Russia was known, having been revealed in August 1941:

> If my requests are heeded, Russia will be converted, and there will be peace; if not, she will spread her errors throughout the world, causing wars and persecutions of the Church. The good will be martyred; the Holy Father

35 Zimdars-Swartz, Sandra L. *Encountering Mary*. Princeton University Press: NJ 1st Ed. 2014. p. 197.

36 'Silencing of Sister Lucia'. *Fátima Center* <https://fatima.org/about/fatima-opposed/silencing-of-sister-lucia/> Accessed 15 February 2022.

> will have much to suffer; various nations will be annihilated. In the end, my Immaculate Heart will triumph. The Holy Father will consecrate Russia to me, and she will be converted, and a period of peace will be granted to the world.[37]

Secondly, to speak of Russia spreading her errors throughout the world while she was fighting for her life against Nazi Germany on the side of the Allies was problematic. In terms of the 'Secret', it may appear as if Our Lady of Fátima was favourably disposed towards the Axis powers.

In terms of his own standing, it was common knowledge that Pius XII was fervently anti-communist and a *Germanophile*, having been Papal Nuncio to Germany before his elevation to the Papacy. Indeed, he was known in the Vatican as *il papa tedesco* (the German pope).

It was also becoming known in certain circles that, despite continuing pleas, he was refusing to intercede on behalf of Europe's Jewry even though, by that time, he was well aware of their plight. For example, just two months previously, in late August 1942, after more than 200,000 Ukrainian Jews had been murdered, the Metropolitan Archbishop of the Ukrainian Greek Catholic Church, Andrey Sheptytsky, wrote a letter to the Pope in which he described the German government as a regime of terror and corruption more diabolical than that of the Bolsheviks. The Pope replied by quoting verses from the Psalms and advising Sheptytsky to "bear adversity with serene patience".[38]

In addition, Russian Orthodox Christians would take an extremely negative view of the phrase "Russia will be converted" as it would imply conversion from Orthodox Christianity to Roman Catholicism, and thus acceptance of papal infallibility and its concomitant universal supreme jurisdiction of the Pope. The Great Schism which had existed between Eastern and Western Christianity since the 11th Century would be further exacerbated.

According to the Society of Saint Pius X, Sister Lúcia declared the following in response to the Pope's failure to name Russia specifically:

> Our Lord has accepted the consecration of the world of October 1942 to the Immaculate Heart of Mary, and promises to put a rapid end to the war.

---

37 'Fátima in Lúcias Own Words'. Ed. Father Louis Kondor SVD. Translated from Portuguese by the Dominican Nuns of the Perpetual Rosary of the Monastery of Pius XII, Fátima. *Secretariado Dos Pastorinhos*, Fátima, Portugal. Imprimatur: António Augusto dos Santos Marto, Bishop of Leiria-Fátima, July 2007. <https://www.piercedhearts.org/hearts_jesus_mary/apparitions/fatima/MemoriasI_en.pdf> p. 101. Accessed 17 January 2022.

38 Hilberg, Raul. *Perpetrators, Victims, Bystanders: The Jewish Catastrophe 1933-1945*. Harper Perennial: New York, 1993, p. 267

> Furthermore, as the consecration was not done fully as He requested, the conversion of Russia will not take place for now.[39]

Despite the fact that Sister Lúcia lived in a cloistered Carmelite convent under the strictest of vows, she allegedly received many visitors and participated in numerous interviews.

For example, on the 15th July 1946, in an interview with William Walsh, she reiterated that 'Our Lady' was not satisfied with the consecration of October 1942:

> What Our Lady wants is that the Pope and all the Bishops in the world shall consecrate Russia to her Immaculate Heart on one special day. If this is done, she will convert Russia and there will be peace. If it is not done, the errors of Russia will spread through every country in the world. [40]

Section 4: 1952

'Our Lady' continued to insist that the 'Pope and all the Bishops in the world shall consecrate Russia to her Immaculate Heart on one special day' so in May 1952, she allegedly told Sister Lúcia:

> Make it known to the Holy Father that I continue to wait for the consecration of Russia to my Immaculate Heart. Without this consecration, Russia will not convert and the world will not enjoy peace.[41]

By 1952, the world was in the grip of the Cold War. A majority of the Western powers and their religious, political, economic and military establishments had swung into action against a common enemy—communism. Since the Church was also sworn to destroy communism, Pope Pius XII finally consecrated the Russian peoples to the Immaculate Heart of Mary on 7th July 1952 (Apostolic Letter: *Sacro Vergente*) but without the presence of all the Bishops. It is noteworthy that the Pope named the 'Russian peoples' but not the Russian State.

---

39 'The Private Heavenly Apparitions of Sister Lúcia of Fátima: 1925-1952'. *Society of Saint Pius X.* <https://sspx.org/en/news-events/news/private-heavenly-apparitions-sister-lucia-fatima-1925-1952> Accessed 10 February 2022.

40 Walsh, William Thomas. *Our Lady of Fátima.* Doubleday: New York, NY. 1954, pp. 229. *Imprimatur*: Francis Cardinal Spellman.

41 'The Private Heavenly Apparitions of Sister Lúcia of Fátima: 1925-1952'. *Society of Saint Pius X.* <https://sspx.org/en/news-events/news/private-heavenly-apparitions-sister-lucia-fatima-1925-1952> Accessed 10 February 2022.

Section : 5 Accepted in Heaven

On 25th March 1984, Pope John Paul II consecrated the entire world to the Immaculate Heart of Mary but once again did not mention Russia specifically. The Vatican stated that Sister Lúcia declared to them in a letter dated 8th November 1989 that this consecration had been properly accomplished and was 'accepted in Heaven':

> Yes it has been done just as Our Lady asked, on the 25th March 1984. Hence any further discussion or request is without basis.[42]

Despite Sister Lúcia's alleged approval, organisations such as the *Society of Saint Pius X* and the *Fatima Centre* continue to claim that Papal consecrations to date are invalid since they have not been specifically addressed to the Russian State, nor invoked in the presence of all the Catholic bishops, as Our Lady of Fátima allegedly requested.

Section 6: Scaling the Heights

As if enough absurdity had not already been on display, its heights were scaled on 12-13 May 2025 when the pontificate of newly-elected Pope Leo XIV was consecrated to the Immaculate Heart of Mary:

> Approximately 470,000 pilgrims gathered in Fátima, Portugal, on May 12–13 to commemorate the 108th anniversary of the apparitions of the Blessed Virgin Mary. The prevalent theme of the two-day event was a call for hope amid the world's conflicts and also prayers for the pontificate of Leo XIV.
>
> At the end of the closing Mass, before the image of the Blessed Virgin Mary, Bishop José Ornelas of Leiria-Fátima consecrated the pontificate of Leo XIV to the Immaculate Heart of Mary: "We are at your feet, the bishops … and this multitude of pilgrims, on the 108th anniversary of your apparition to the little shepherds in this Cova da Iria to consecrate to you the ministry of the current successor of Peter and bishop of Rome, the Holy Father Leo XIV". [43]

42 'The Message of Fatima' (13 May 2000). *Congregation for the Doctrine of the Faith*. <http://www.vatican.va/roman_curia/congregations/cfaith/documents/rc_con_cfaith_doc_20000626_message-fatima_en.html> Accessed 28 June 2025.

43 'Leo XIV's pontificate consecrated to Our Lady of Fátima at Portugal shrine'. (14 May 2025) *Catholic Newsagency* < https://www.catholicnewsagency.com/news/264101/leo-xiv-s-pontificate-consecrated-to-our-lady-of-fatima-at-portugal-shrine> Accessed 29 July 2025.

Notes

Marxism–Leninism was the official state ideology of the Soviet Union. The Soviet Union was the first state to have as one objective of its official ideology the elimination of existing religion, and the prevention of future implanting of religious belief, with the goal of establishing state atheism. However, the believing population never abandoned its ancestral faith and the more the grip of oppression began to lessen over the decades, the more they returned to Church. Today the Russian Orthodox Church numbers around 90 million members.

The Communist Party of the Soviet Union was disbanded by Russian President Boris Yeltsin on 6th November 1991. Hence, subsequent calls for Russia's consecration/conversion cannot mean conversion from atheistic communism but conversion from Russian Orthodoxy to Catholicism.

Incredible

Section 1: Comparisons

Lúcia dos Santos is the principal source from which we learn about the alleged apparitions of 1917 and the whole structure of Fátima stands or falls upon the accounts given by her to various interrogators at that time.

A comparison of these accounts will demonstrate that they are contradictory, evasive and hesitant. For example, Manuel Nunes Formigão, Canon of the Cathedral at Lisbon and professor at the Seminary of Santarém, questioned Lúcia on 19th October about the apparition of 13th October. The 13th of October was only six days after the 'Miracle of the Sun' day. Lúcia is unable to recall with any clarity an event so impressively abnormal that it should have been permanently engraved on her memory. Yet, more than twenty years later, in her memoirs, she is able to recall with precision all the events of that time and to reveal word-for-word the details of the 'Great Secret' allegedly confided to her on 13th July 1917.

As noted in Appendix C:7 *Mission Creep*, when comparing the reports in works appearing before 1938 with those of later times, it becomes evident that the two sets of accounts are impossible to harmonise. These two sets of accounts are dubbed Fátima I and Fátima II by critics.

For example, in earlier works there is no mention of the 1916 apparitions of the 'Angel of Peace'; no mention of the vision of the Immaculate Heart of Mary in the 13th June 1917 apparition; and not the slightest allusion to the 'Great Secret' allegedly confided to the children in the 13th July 1917 apparition. The apparition promises only that the children will go to 'Heaven'; that if they say the Rosary every day it will hasten the end of the war; and that she will work a great miracle on 13th October 1917, the 'Miracle of the Sun' day.

Section 2: Orchestration

According to critics such as Sandra Zimdars-Swartz, it was Lúcia herself who orchestrated the entire scenario of Fátima:

> It is clear that she (Lúcia) played the leading role in the scenario of the apparition itself. All accounts agree that she was the only one of the three seers to interact with both her vision and with the crowd, carrying on conversations with both while her two cousins stood by silently. She has said, moreover, and probably not incorrectly, that Francisco and Jacinta had been accustomed to follow her directives before the apparition began, that they turned to her for guidance afterwards, and that it was she who convinced them that they had to be very careful in their experiences. [44]
>
> Further evidence that Lúcia orchestrated the fantasy and manipulated the other children is provided by certain incidents. For example, when Jacinta first told the story, she stated that the Virgin had said many things that she was unable to recall but "which Lúcia knows". Lúcia's own mother was convinced that her precocious daughter was, in her words, "nothing but a fake who is leading half the world astray". [45]

Other critics have asserted that Lúcia was merely the conduit and that entire scenario of Fátima was ochestrated by Father Manuel Marques Ferreira, parish priest and Dean of Olival.

Although their source documents are mainly unavailable to us and we will never know with any degree of certainty whether the orchestration was indeed planned by Father Ferreira, it is nevertheless worthwhile noting some of the assertions advanced by critics such as João Ilharco, author of *Fátima Unmaske*d, especially since Lúcia gave such contradictory, evasive and hesitant accounts to her interrogators, as already noted.

Among others, Ilharco makes the following assertions:

- Father Ferreira led the Bishop of Leiria-Fátima to believe in the apparitions of Fátima;
- Numerous witnesses noted that during the gatherings at the Cova da Iria, the children seemed to be the prey of intense fear;

44 Zimdars-Swartz, Sandra L. *Encountering Mary*. Princeton University Press: New Jersey. 1st Ed. 2014. p. 68.

45 Ibid. pp. 71, 86.

- Father Ferreira was especially devoted to Our Lady of the Rosary and to the souls in purgatory. At Fátima, the 'Lady' presented herself as Our Lady of the Rosary and taught the children a prayer for the souls in purgatory. [46]

Lúcia revealed twenty years later that, at the time of the apparitions, she had stayed two or three days with Father Ferreira on the pretext of visiting his sister and that he spent hours alone with her "guiding me with his own wise counsels".[47]

For French speakers, see also Gérard de Sède, author of *Fâtima : Enquête sur une imposture (Investigation into an Impostor).*[48]

Section 3: Discrepancies

Just a few examples of the many discrepancies in the original accounts should serve as illustrations:

- Canon Manuel Nunes Formigão played a decisive role in the development of the cult of Our Lady of Fátima. It was reported by Father John de Marchi, who also interviewed the chief surviving witnesses, that even Formigão became 'alarmed' about a timing 'discrepancy' when questioning Lúcia and Jacinta. The War was not yet over at the time of the interview yet the children insisted that the apparition had said on 13th October 1917 that the War would end that same day.[49]

- Even the most stalwart advocates of Our Lady of Fátima admit that this discrepancy is 'the most difficult and serious objection in all the problems associated with Fatima'. For, they admit, 'How could Our Lady have said, "The war will end today", when the Armistice would not be signed until 11th November 1918, 13 months later? [50]

---

46 Ilharco, João. *Fátima Desmascarada: A verdade histórica acerca de Fátima documentada com provas.* Edição do Autor: Coimbra, Portugal, 1971. < https://fatima.machado-family.com/vol1/#calibre_link-551> Accessed 15 February 2022.

47 'Fátima in Lúcias Own Words'. Ed. Father Louis Kondor SVD. Translated from Portuguese by the Dominican Nuns of the Perpetual Rosary of the Monastery of Pius XII, Fátima. *Secretariado Dos Pastorinhos*, Fátima, Portugal. Imprimatur: António Augusto dos Santos Marto, Bishop of Leiria-Fátima, July 2007. <https://www.piercedhearts.org/hearts_jesus_mary/apparitions/fatima/MemoriasI_en.pdf> p. 101. Accessed 17 January 2022.

48 de Sède, Gérard. *Fátima : Enquête sur une imposture.* Alain Moreau Publications: France. 1977.

49 De Marchi, John. *The Immaculate Heart: The True Story of Our Lady of Fátima*, Farrar, Strauss and Young: New York, NY. 1952, p. 159.

50 Excerpt From: Frere Michel de la Sainte Trinite. *The Whole Truth about Fatima - Vol I.* Apple Books. pp.542-43.

- When asked about the apparitions of the 'Lady' by Father Ferreira de Lacerda, parish priest of Milagres, and chaplain to the Portuguese Expeditionary Force, Lúcia declared: "The Lady arrived, coming from the east". To Canon Formigão, on the contrary, she declared on 27th September 1917: "I did not see Her coming from any direction; She appeared on the holm oak".[51]

- When questioned about the final apparition of 13th October, Lúcia declared to Canon Formigão that she saw Joseph appear with the child Jesus hanging around his neck. Francisco and Jacinta, however, claimed that they saw the child standing beside Joseph.[52]

- Lúcia told Father Ferreira de Lacerda on 19th October 1917 that the 'Lady' wore white slippers. In 1946, she told Father Thomas McGlynn, who was working on the famous statue of Our Lady of Fátima, that she never saw her feet.[53] (The barefoot statue now stands in front of the Sanctuary of Fátima in Portugal.)

Section 4: Influences

Given the foregoing, it would be a reasonable conclusion to simply dismiss Lúcia's version of events at Fátima between May and October 1917. However, justice demands that we afford her, a girl of just ten years old, the benefit of the doubt and offer an alternative explanation. If, for example, she was not under the influence of Father Ferreira or pressured by other unknown individuals and genuinely believed in her visions, then what other influences could Lúcia have been subjected to which may have given rise to her experiences?

La Salette and Fátima

Consider the striking parallels between the alleged events of La Salette and those at Fátima. The visionaries are all children who come from rural, isolated villages. All are shepherds who are malnourished, poverty-stricken, and illiterate. Moreover, their child minds are saturated with Catholic Church iconography. Significantly, they are given 'secrets' for future Popes which are only committed to writing years later.

51 Excerpt From: Frere Michel de la Sainte Trinite. *The Whole Truth about Fatima - Vol I.* pp. 760-762. Apple Books

52 de Sède, Gérard. *Fátima : Enquête sur une imposture.* Alain Moreau Publications: France. 1977. p. 129.

53 Ibid. p. 130.

The visions are all of a 'beautiful lady', whose clothing, accoutrements, and actions are very familiar to children raised on little else but stories about the Roman Catholic 'saints' and whose experiences outside their homes are mostly gained from within the confines of churches. The 'beautiful lady' is stern and warns about consequences for bad behaviour yet, at the same time, she is also comforting and soothing, just like an idealised mother figure.

Most revealing, however, is the fact that Lúcia dos Santos certainly knew the story of La Salette. According to William Walsh, on 11th October 1917, two days before the final apparition and the 'Miracle of the Sun', Canon Formigão questioned Maria Rosa (mother of Lúcia):

> He was especially curious to know whether she had ever read to Lúcia the fairly well-known story of the apparition of Our Lady to two shepherd children, Maximin and Melanie, at La Salette in southern France on September 19, 1846. There were certain resemblances between that episode and the ones at Fátima. At La Salette Our Lady had told the children a secret, which they revealed to no one but Pope Pius IX; and she had given them a warning of great calamities if the people of France did not stop offending God. The similarity was not necessarily conclusive, yet it might be significant. Father Formigáo was curious to know whether Lúcia had been much impressed by the French account. Maria Rosa thought not; the child had never mentioned it again, so far as she could recollect. [54]

Finally Canon Formigão questioned Lúcia herself:

> You have heard your mother read the book called *Short Mission* where the story is told of the apparition of Our Lady to a boy and a girl? Yes, I have.
>
> Did you often think of that story and speak of it to other girls? I didn't think of that story, nor did I tell it to anyone. [55]

Notwithstanding her denial, stories such as these must have left a deep and lasting impression.

Lourdes and Fátima

Of no less importance than the striking parallels between La Salette and Fátima are those between Lourdes and Fátima. According to Paul Christopher Manuel:

54 Walsh, William Thomas. *Our Lady of Fátima*. Doubleday: New York. 1954, pp. 143-44. *Imprimatur*: Francis Cardinal Spellman..

55 Ibid. p. 145.

> The rational-faith polemic over Lourdes in the nineteenth century featured many of the same elements as Fátima. According to Ruth Harris, this French case involved a wider debate about science and religion, modernity and superstition, and anticlericalism and clericalism. In her work, *Lourdes: Body and Spirit in a Secular Age*, she is concerned with the role of the religiosity of a small rural community within a secularizing France at the mid-point in the nineteenth century. Or, in her words, "Lourdes in the early decades is a story about France, about the struggles of Catholicism in the aftermath of revolutionary turmoil". [56]
>
> Harris's insights apply perfectly to Fátima as well. This Portuguese case of Marian apparition had elements of a larger debate between science and religion, modernity and superstition, anticlericalism and clericalism, and the role of the religiosity of a small rural community in a secularizing Portugal at the beginning of the twentieth century. [57]

Note the allegation that the apparition at Lourdes also confided three 'secrets' to Bernadette Soubirous although, if they ever existed at all, they have never been made public. It is reasonable to conclude that 'Our Lady' is markedly fond of 'secrets' that can be revealed at a time most suited to the Church. (See also Appendix C:5: *The Great Secret.*)

Except in academic and certain theological circles, most notably in disputes between influential Jesuit Fathers, the popularised version events at Fátima is rarely subjected to even the mildest critical enquiry. Rather, the print and digital media is so awash with emotional, reverential and obsequious accounts it is frankly nauseating.

56 Harris, Ruth. *Lourdes: Body and Spirit in a Secular Age*. New York: Viking Press, 1999. p. 11.

57 'The Marian Apparitions in Fatima as Political Reality: Religion and Politics in Twentieth-Century Portugal'. Paul Christopher Manuel, Co-Chair, Iberian Study Group, *Minda de Gunzburg Center for European Studies*, St. Anselm College, New Hampshire. <https://ces.fas.harvard.edu/uploads/files/Working-Papers-Archives/CES_WP88.pdf. p. 15>.

The Standing Army

Section 1: Fear and Loathing

Fear and loathing of atheistic communism dominated the Catholic landscape for most of the 20th Century. For example, as early as 1922, Count John de Salis, the British minister to the Holy See, confirmed the hysteria gripping the Vatican and Pope Pius XI when he reported to the Foreign Office in London that:

> Everything in the Vatican is dominated by the Pope's fear of Russian Communism, that the Soviets may reach Western Europe.[58]

Fifteen years later, the Pope's fear had not diminished. In his 1937 Encyclical, *Divini Redemptoris: On Atheistic Communism*, Pius XI made the following selection of statements:

> ...Entire peoples find themselves in danger of falling back into a barbarism worse than that which oppressed the greater part of the world at the coming of the Redeemer.
>
> This all too imminent danger, Venerable Brethren, as you have already surmised, is **bolshevistic and atheistic Communism**, which aims at upsetting the social order and at undermining the very foundations of Christian civilization. (paras 2 and 3)[59]

The Encyclical enjoined the faithful to enlist in the Church's battle to destroy 'bolshevistic and atheistic Communism'. The standing army of Our Lady of Fátima devotees would prove to be more than willing to take up the challenge.

The importance of Fátima as a weapon in the Church's war against atheistic communism was emphasised in a 1967 address by Manuel Gonçalves Cerejeira, Cardinal Patriarch of Lisbon, on the occasion of the fiftieth anniversary of the apparitions:

58 Rhodes, Anthony. *The Vatican in the Age of Dictators 1922-1945*. Hodder & Stoughton: London, 1973, p. 18.

59 'Pius XI Encyclicals'. *Vatican* <https://www.vatican.va/content/pius-xi/en/encyclicals.index.html#encyclicals> Accessed 27 March 2022.

> In Lourdes, in 1954, I took the occasion that was offered to me to compare Lourdes with Fátima. To me, Lourdes seemed to be a response of the Blessed Virgin to the rationalism of the 19th century; that was where Our Lady appeared as the Immaculate Conception, which His Holiness Pius IX proclaimed a dogma of the Church, confirming the Catholic faith, the infallibility of the Pope, the defeat of sin, and the triumph of grace.
>
> For its part, Fátima seemed to me like a merciful reply of Our Lady to the atheism of the 20th century. Can I tell the whole truth? Fátima arises in our anxious world like **a beacon of hope against atheistic Communism** that claims to conquer the whole world and to destroy the Church. [60]

Section 2: The Crusaders

At Fátima on 13th May 1946, the Papal Legate, Cardinal Masella, crowned the statue of Our Lady of Fátima as Queen of the World on behalf of Pope Pius XII. To mark the occasion, the Pope addressed the pilgrims by radio. Below is an extract from the Pope's address:

> You, by crowning the image of Our Lady of Fátima, signed as it were a document of faith in her supremacy, a loyal submission to her authority, a filial and constant correspondence to her love. You did yet more: **you enlisted as crusaders in the conquest and reconquest of her Kingdom**, which is the Kingdom of God, that is to say you bound yourselves before heaven and earth to love her, to venerate her, to serve her, to imitate her, so that with her blessing you may better serve the Divine King; and at the same time you bound yourselves to labor that she may be loved, venerated, and served all around you, in the family, in society, in the world.[61]

The Rev. Father John De Marchi leaves no doubt as to Fátima's crusading purpose:

> The pilgrimages to the Cova da Iria grew to immense proportions, not only from Portugal but from both hemispheres and almost every corner of the earth. Fátima was to call down upon Portugal an immensity of grace, and

60 'Fatima devant l'Église et le monde'. (11 February 1967). *La documentation catholique 64* as quoted by *Society of St. Pius X U.S.A.* <https://sspx.org/en/news/devotion-immaculate-heart-mary-16591> Accessed 18 January 2026.

61 Walsh, William Thomas. *Our Lady of Fátima.* Doubleday: New York. 1954, pp. 222-223. *Imprimatur:* Francis Cardinal Spellman.

> for Christendom at large has come **to symbolise the spiritual war against Communism and to be the focal point of the new crusade.**
>
> The apostolic nuncio presided at the first Portuguese national pilgrimage on 13th May 1937, at which it is calculated some half million pilgrims were present. The second national pilgrimage took place on 13th May 1938, to give thanks to 'Our Lady' for delivering Portugal from the Communist menace which caused the terrible civil war in Spain and was waged in places only a few yards from her soil, fulfilling a promise made to 'Our Lady' by the Portuguese episcopate in May 1936. [62]

(In May 1936, the Portuguese episcopate had promised 'Our Lady' that they would organise a national pilgrimage to Fatima to ward off the Communist threat to their country.)

Section 3: The Marian Shore

The major Marian devotion in the United States had been the Lourdes cult which had sparked a 19th Century Marian revival. For American Catholics, Lourdes, with its alleged healings, offered evidence that Mary at times would communicate directly with Catholics in need of advice and assistance.

By the late 1940's, however, the Fátima cult began to rival Lourdes. Catholic press organisations devoted to the spread of Marian piety and leading spokesmen of the Church all co-operated in publicising the message of Fátima. American Catholics were told insistently that they could obtain world peace and the conversion of Russia by praying the Rosary and making the Five First Saturdays. (See also Appendix C:8: *The Heart of the Matter.*)

Monsignor Fulton J. Sheen, the most prominent and popular spokesman of American Catholicism during the period immediately following World War II, was a devotee of both Lourdes and Fátima.

In 1947, after describing the apparitions and warnings of Our Lady of Fátima to a national radio audience, Sheen made the following assertion:

62 De Marchi, Rev. Father John. 'The True Story of Fatima: The Lady in the Light'. (Part 25) Quoted in *Australia Needs Fatima* <https://fatima.org.au/the-true-story-of-fatima/> Accessed 5 April 2022.

> We are not concerned about proving the authenticity of these phenomena at Fátima, for those who believe in the realm of Spirit and the Mother of God need no proof, and those who reject the Spirit would not accept it anyway. [63]

Sheen also dedicated the final chapter of his 1948 book *Communism and the Conscience of the West* to Our Lady of Fátima, whom he saw as especially concerned with America's battles in World War II and in the Cold War. Bishop Sheen's use of Fátima was echoed on a local level by pastors throughout the country.

The chaplains at the University of Notre Dame in Indiana were unequivocal about the importance of Our Lady of Fátima. In October 1951, their religious bulletin put the issue to students in blunt terms:

> Our Lady herself has told us at Fátima that we must pray the Rosary. Will any student ignore her outright command? She promised world peace if we said the Rosary. Does any student want another world war? She promised the conversion of Russia if we said the Rosary. Will any student belittle the Russian threat? [64]

The implication of this kind of appeal was clear: a failure to respond to Our Lady of Fátima's requests meant accepting the responsibility for another war by failing to pray for the conversion of Russia.

The Blue Army

When Our Lady of Fátima's message reached the shores of the United States, where excess religious fervour is a commonplace, John M.Haffert, editor of *Scapular* magazine, began promoting the devotion of Fátima in 1946 after an (alleged) personal interview with Sister Lúcia.

In 1950, Haffert and Monsignor Colgan, a pastor from New Jersey who had recovered from a heart attack following a vow to Our Lady of Fátima, organised the Blue Army of Fátima. This association, dedicated to the spread of the Fátima message, received episcopal approval and soon had chapters in parishes throughout the United States.

According to the *World Apostolate of Fátima*:

63 Sheen, Fulton J. *Communism and the Conscience of the West*, Refuge of Sinners Publishing, Inc. 1948. Quoted in *Catholic Heart and Mind* < https://catholicheartandmind.com/2020/05/04/fatima-russia-errors/> Accessed 18 January 2026.

64 Cadegan, Una M. (2004) 'The Queen of Peace in the Shadow of War: Fatima and U.S. Catholic Anticommunism'. *U.S. Catholic Historian*, vol. 22, no. 4, p. 10. JSTOR, <http://www.jstor.org/stable/25154930>. Accessed 17 Jan. 2026.

> Members of this 'Blue Army' were the spiritual force standing against the atheistic policies of the Soviet Union and their Red Army. They pledged to offer their daily sufferings and difficulties for the conversion of sinners, to pray the Rosary daily, to wear the Brown Scapular as a sign of consecration to Mary's Immaculate Heart, and to practice the Five First Saturdays devotion.
>
> The pledge, which Sister Lúcia herself helped formulate, quickly gained popularity throughout the United States and soon became a worldwide movement, with between thirty and forty million people having signed the Blue Army Pledge.
>
> In the early 1950's Msgr. Colgan, together with John Haffert, established the *Ave Maria Institute* on John Haffert's farm in New Jersey. The farm served as the administrative center for sending and receiving new Pledge cards, handling correspondence, publishing *Soul* Magazine, and coordinating travel for the Pilgrim Virgin Statue. Around this same time, they also purchased land in Fátima and built the Domus Pacis hotel and conference center, which continues to house pilgrims and serve as headquarters for the *International World Apostolate of Fátima.*
>
> John later donated his farm to the Blue Army, building a large shrine with a towering roof and a 24 feet bronze statue of Mary on the property. Today, this site is known today as the National Blue Army Shrine of Our Lady of Fátima, dedicated to the Immaculate Heart of Mary.
>
> The Blue Army of Our Lady of Fátima officially became the *World Apostolate of Fátima* and on 7th October 2010 was named a Public International Association of the Faithful. Today we serve as the Church's official voice on the authentic message of Fátima. [65]

On 8th May 1950, twenty years after the Fátima cult was approved, Pope Pius XII declared to the directors of the Blue Army:

> ...The time for doubting Fátima has passed. Now is the time for action...[66]

Also during this era, the possible content of the Third Secret of Fátima aroused fevered speculation within certain sectors of the American Catholic community. Did the secret speak of an impending nuclear war in which entire nations would be annihilated? (See also Author's Note in Appendix C:5: *The Great Secret.*)

---

65 'The Apostolate: History'. *Our Lady's Blue Army, World Apostolate of Fatima USA.* < https://www.bluearmy.com/the-apostolate/> Accessed 4 July 2025.

66 Excerpt From: Frere Michel de la Sainte Trinite. *The Whole Truth about Fatima - Vol I.* p. 827. Apple Books.

Other organisations such as the Knights of the Immaculata, the Novena of the Sorrowful Mother, and the Block Rosary conducted campaigns that paralleled the work of the Blue Army. These organisations made the conversion of Russia the major goal of their programs.

War in Heaven

The Catholic contribution to the anti-Communist political climate of the 1940's and 1950's has frequently been described by historians, but their analysis has generally not taken account of the religious depth of American Catholic fears about the Cold War.

Underlying the clash of ideologies, the loss of territories, and the persecution of the Church, Catholics perceived another battle raging in which Christ and Mary had sided with the United States to fight Satan and his Communist allies. When Monsignor Fulton Sheen referred to Communism as the Antichrist, he may or may not have intended this to be taken literally. But the millions who believed in Our Lady of Fátima saw the Cold War on earth as a reflection of a war in heaven.

Fátima was regarded by many as the best hope of neutralising the military might of the Soviet Union and halting the spread of Communism. If Catholics everywhere were faithful to Our Lady of Fátima, then Russia would be converted and a period of peace would come upon the world. Such was the dream of a zealous army of devotees, a dream which was partially realised with the demise of the Soviet Union.

Note

Part of the above content is reproduced, paraphrased or adapted from Kselman and Avella's study 'Marian Piety and the Cold War in the United States'.[67]

67 Kselman, T. A., & Avella, S. (1986). 'Marian Piety and the Cold War in the United States'. *The Catholic Historical Review*, 72(3), 403–424. <http://www.jstor.org/stable/25022337>.

The Great Delusion

For an example of collective delusion, consider the disturbing claims made by the *World Apostolate of Fátima U.S.A.* concerning the future of the world if only Pope Pius XI had consecrated Russia to Mary's Immaculate Heart when asked to do so in 1929.

The Claims

Besides containing historical inaccuracies and anachronisms, some of the following is taken from the 'Great Secret' which was unknown in 1929 and only began to be revealed to the world in 1941, twelve years later:

- Russia would have been converted before amassing the power to spread the errors of atheistic Communism all over the world;
- There would have been no World War II, through which Russia captured half of Europe, gaining the economic means to infect the world with atheistic Communism (World War II had already begun before the 'Secrets' were revealed);
- There would have been no Soviet Union (the Soviet Union was formed in 1922), no Red China, no communist North Korea, no communist Vietnam, no communist Cuba, and no Christian martyrs in those countries;
- There would have been no Russian-supported communist uprisings and revolutions throughout the world, in Africa, South America and Asia;
- Christian countries would not have been morally and spiritually undermined by Soviet propaganda;
- There would have been peace throughout the world during the second half of the twentieth century;
- The West would have been better united and morally and spiritually stronger for meeting the threat of Islamic terrorism, and acting more effectively against it.[68]

68 'Why the Consecration of the Whole World along with Russia in 1984?' *World Apostolate of Fatima-Our Lady's Blue Army* <https://www.bluearmy.com/why-the-consecration-of-the-whole-world-and-russia-in-1984/> Accessed 10 February 2022.

So, then, if Pope Pius XI had consecrated Russia to Mary's Immaculate Heart when asked to do so in 1929, there would have been no Nazi Germany, no Second World War with its millions of dead, no...the errant nonsense continues. There are no words of sufficient strength in the English language to adequately describe this delusion, a delusion which continues to deceive and lull millions into believing that if they just pray hard enough, finger enough rosary beads, and follow Marian directives, then a heavenly spiritual warrior, once the humble mother of Jesus, will intervene on their behalf to eliminate the enemies of the Church.

The Great Victory

Section 1: Providence

To mark the 100th anniversary of the first apparition at Fátima, the class of 2017 at California's Thomas Aquinas College chose Our Lady of Fátima as their patron. The podcast marking the event claimed that the persons most responsible for the demise of the Soviet Union —President Ronald Reagan, Pope John Paul II and Mikhail Gorbachev—were under the protection of Our Lady of Fátima:

> As they, and members of the Church worldwide, celebrate the occasion, the centennial calls to mind a lecture that the Hon. Frank Shakespeare—the onetime president of CBS Television who served as the U.S. ambassador to Portugal, and then the Holy See, during the Reagan Administration—delivered at Thomas Aquinas College on the 24th February 2006.
>
> As that year's President's Day lecturer, Ambassador Shakespeare described the simultaneous, providential rise to power of U.S. President Ronald Reagan, Pope St. John Paul II, and General Secretary Mikhail Gorbachev in the Soviet Union. He highlighted the pivotal roles that these three men played—under the protection of Our Lady of Fátima—in the collapse of Communism and the Soviet Union. It was "an epochal period in our country's history," he said, "13 years really, from 1978 to 1991, when the whole world changed". [69]

Section 2: The Pole

On 18th May 1920, the future Pope John Paul II, Karol Józef Wojtyla, was born in the Polish town of Wadowice. Wojtyła began studying for the priesthood in 1942, was ordained a priest on 1st November 1946, was consecrated Archbishop of Kraków by Pope Paul VI in December 1963 and, less than four years later, was elevated on 26th June 1967 to the College of Cardinals.

69 'Ambassador Frank Shakespeare: Reagan, John Paul II, Gorbachev — and Our Lady of Fatima'. (12 May 2017) *Thomas Aquinas College Lectures and Talks*. <https://www.thomasaquinas.edu/news/audio-reagan-john-paul-ii-gorbachev-our-lady-fatima> Accessed 12 August 2025.

The Confrontation

On 4th September 1976, Karol Cardinal Wojtyla visited New York's Kosciuszko Foundation, an organisation aimed at deepening ties between Poland and the United States through educational and cultural exchange programs. During his visit, Cardinal Wojtyla delivered an address reproduced here in part:

> ...We are now standing in the face of the greatest historical confrontation humanity has gone through. I do not think that wide circles of the American society or wide circles of the Christian community realize this fully. We are now facing the final confrontation between the Church and the anti-Church, of the Gospel versus the anti-Gospel. This confrontation lies within the plans of Divine Providence; it is a trial which the whole Church, and the Polish Church in particular, must take up.
>
> ...It is a trial of not only our nation and Church, but in a sense a test of two thousand years of culture and Christian civilization with all of its consequences for human dignity, individual rights, human rights and the rights of nations. All these are affected by the confrontation.
>
> As the number of people who understand the importance of this confrontation increase in Poland and America, we can look with greater trust towards the outcome of this confrontation. The Church has gone through many trials, as has the Polish nation, and has emerged victorious even though at a cost of great sacrifice.[70]

Section 3: Salvation

The Elevation

On 16th October 1978, Karol Józef Wojtyla was elevated to the Papacy and chose the name John Paul II.

John Paul II's election by the College of Cardinals had everything to do with his Polish identity and his willingness to confront atheistic communism from within a satellite state of the Soviet Union and absolutely nothing to do with any inspiration by the 'holy spirit'. As he said in his address to the Kosciuszko Foundation, "We are now standing in the face of the greatest historical confrontation humanity has gone through".

70 'Address by Karol Cardinal Wojtyla to the Kosciuszko Foundation'. (4 September 1976). *The Kosciuszko Foundation Newsletter* XXXI, no. 2 (1976-77), pp 1-2.

The Failed Assassination

On 13th May 1981, the 64th anniversary of the first apparition at Fátima, Pope John Paul II was shot twice in St. Peters Square. According to a *Vatican Global Media Network* article headed 'The Sign that Remembers the Day Our Lady of Fátima Saved the Life of John Paul II':

> The attack took place on this day, 13th May, the day when the Church celebrates Our Lady of Fátima, whose protection saved the life of the Pope.
>
> ...St. John Paul II mentioned that when the bullet hit him, he did not realize it was the "anniversary of the day when the Virgin appeared to three children in Fatima" ...During his convalescence, St. John Paul II studied the reports of the Fatima apparitions and one year after the attack, he traveled for the first time to the Fátima shrine in Portugal to "thank the Virgin for her intervention in the salvation of my life and the restoration of my health".
>
> In 1984, Pope Wojtyla formalized his devotion and gratitude to the Virgin by donating the bullet that had been extracted to the Fátima shrine, where it was set into the halo of the image's crown.
>
> On 13th May 2006, the 25th anniversary of the attack, Pope Benedict XVI recalled the event and stated: "John Paul II felt that he had been miraculously saved from death by the intervention of a maternal hand...and his entire pontificate was marked by what the Virgin had announced in Fátima: 'In the end, my Immaculate Heart will triumph'".
>
> Furthermore, this attack has been attributed to the Third Secret of Fátima, where the Virgin revealed to the shepherd children Lucia, Jacinta, and Francisco that "the Holy Father, on his knees at the foot of the Cross, was killed by a group of soldiers who fired bullets and arrows at him". [71]

A Crowning Gratitude

Three years later, on 13 May 1984 in St. Peter's Square, the Pope spoke to 50,000 pilgrims of his affection and beatitude for Our Lady of Fátima in protecting him from the bullets. On the same day, the Bishop of Leiria-Fátima announced that the Pope had given to the Fátima Shrine the bullet which had struck him. Local ecclesiastical authorities decided to place it in the crown of Mary's statue.

---

71 Martínez-Bordiú, A. 'The Sign that Remembers the Day Our Lady of Fatima Saved the Life of John Paul II'. (15 May 2023) *EWTN Vatican* < https://www.ewtnvatican.com/articles/sign-that-remembers-the-day-our-lady-of-fatima-saved-the-life-of-john-paul-ii-at-the-vatican-1009> Accessed 6 July 2025.

Timothy Tindal-Robertson reports in his work, *Fatima, Russia and Pope John Paul II: How Mary Intervened to Deliver Russia*, that when the Pope left the Gemelli Clinic after the 1981 assassination attempt, he told Slovak Bishop Pavel Hnilica:

> I have come to understand that the only way to save the world from war, to save it from atheism, is the conversion of Russia according to the message of Fátima.[72]

The Envelopes

As noted previously, according to the 2000 Vatican publication, *The Message of Fatima*, John Paul II asked for the envelope containing the third part of the 'Secret' following the assassination attempt on 13 May 1981. [73]

The *National Catholic Register* reports that:

> On 18th July 1981, the then-prefect for the congregation, Cardinal Franjo Šeper, grabbed two envelopes—a white one containing Sister Lúcia's original Portuguese text and an orange one with an Italian translation.
>
> These were taken to the Pope on the ninth floor of the Gemelli Clinic. It was there that the Holy Father read the secret, which pointed to a deadly attack on the "bishop dressed in white"—that is, the one bishop who wears white, the Bishop of Rome.
>
> "When he was finished", said Cardinal Dziwisz of Pope John Paul II reading the Third Secret, "all his remaining doubts were gone". In this vision, "he recognized his own destiny". He became convinced that his life had been spared thanks to the intervention of Our Lady. [74]

Section 4: Calling all Pedagogues

In a 1993 paper titled 'The Significance of Fatima: A Seventy-Five-Year Perspective', former Director of the *World Apostolate of Fatima*, Father Frederick Miller, discussed

72 Tindal-Robertson, T. *Fatima, Russia and Pope John Paul II: How Mary Intervened to Deliver Russia.* Gracewing Publishing: Chicago, 1998, p. 11.

73 'The Message of Fatima'.(13 May 2000) *Congregation for the Doctrine of the Faith.* <http://www.vatican.va/roman_curia/congregations/cfaith/documents/rc_con_cfaith_doc_20000626_message-fatima_en.html> Accessed 28 June 2025.

74 Kengor, P. Commentaries. 'May 13 Connects Fatima Apparitions, John Paul II Shooting'. (13 May 2021) *National Catholic Register* < https://www.ncregister.com/commentaries/may-13-connects-fatima-apparitions-john-paul-ii-shooting> Accessed 7 July 2025.

the significance of the apparitions at Fátima, particularly in the context of Pope John Paul II's reflections and the impact of the message on the Church and popular devotion over a seventy-five-year period.

The paper claims that Our Lady of Fátima taught the three children ten dogmatic, spiritual and moral truths. Among these ten dogmatic, spiritual and moral truths were four of particular note:

1. Every dimension of the spiritual world is underscored in the Fátima message: the Trinity, angels, demons, the existence of the immortal human soul, heaven, hell, purgatory, the resurrection of the dead and the life of the world to come (in which the Blessed Virgin already participates);
2. Our Lady of Fátima unambiguously reaffirmed the doctrine of hellfire (i.e., the pain of the senses) and the real possibility of eternal damnation as a result of sin;
3. Our Lady of Fátima taught the children the essential importance of the Vicar of Christ in the daily life of the Church, as well as the Holy Father's mystic identification with Christ, the crucified bridegroom of the Church;
4. The Blessed Virgin led the children to understand that union with Christ in his suffering, death and resurrection leads to true peace in this life, perfect union with him in heaven and physical resurrection on the last day.

The comprehension, discernment and interpretation skills of illiterate children aged just seven, nine and ten at the time these truths of great import were allegedly imparted to them is truly remarkable and worthy of serious pedagogical study.

Father Miller writes that the phenomenon of Fátima has been a focal point for the Catholic Church which was particularly emphasised by Pope John Paul II throughout his papacy. The Pope visited Fátima multiple times, particularly to thank the Virgin Mary for her intercession during his assassination attempt on 13 May 1981.

His visits to Fátima were also linked to significant political changes in Eastern Europe, attributing these to the intercession of Our Lady of Fátima.

The message of Fátima, which included prophecies about war and communism, resonated with global events and inspired spiritual movements which increased Marian devotion worldwide. [75]

75 Miller, Frederick L. (1993) 'The Significance of Fátima: A Seventy-Five-Year Perspective'. *Marian Studies:* Vol. 44, Article 9. <https://ecommons.udayton.edu/marian_studies/vol44/iss1/9> Accessed 15 August 2025.

In an article headed 'The Message of Fatima in Our Lady's Own Words', Blue Army Founder John Haffert quotes a John Paul II letter of 1991:

> "Fátima is one of the greatest signs of the times in the 20th Century because it announces many of the later events, and conditions them on the response to its appeals", said the Pope in his Fátima letter of the 13th October 1991 (*L'Osservatore Romano*, 24 October 1991). His Holiness said the greatness of Fátima lies not so much in the miracle, but that it offers the specific response necessary to save mankind from self-destruction. [76]

On 13th October 1997, for the 80th Anniversary of the miracle of the sun at Fátima, Pope John Paul II wrote a letter to the bishop of Leiria-Fátima in which he referred to Fátima as one of the greatest signs of the times in the 20th Century:

> On the threshold of the third millennium, as we observe the signs of the times in this 20th Century, Fátima is certainly one of the greatest, among other reasons because its message announces many of the later events and conditions them on the response to its appeals: signs such as the two world wars, but also great gatherings of nations and peoples marked by dialogue and peace; the oppression and turmoil suffered by various nations and peoples, but also the voice and the opportunities given to peoples and individuals who in the meantime have emerged on the international scene; the crises, desertions and many sufferings of the Church's members, but also a renewed and intense feeling of solidarity and mutual dependence in Christ's Mystical Body, which is being strengthened in all the baptized, in accordance with their vocation and mission; the separation from and abandonment of God by individuals and societies, but also the in-breaking of the Spirit of Truth in hearts and communities to the point of sacrifice and martyrdom to save "God's image and likeness in man" (cf. Gn 1:27), to save man from himself. Among these and other signs of the times, as I said, Fátima stands out and helps us see the hand of God, our providential Guide and patient and compassionate Father also in the 20th Century.[77]

76 Haffert, J. 'The Message of Fatima in Our Lady's Own Words: Part One'. *International Pilgrim Virgin Statue* < https://www.pilgrimvirginstatue.com/message-of-fatima.html> Accessed 7 July 2025.

77 'Message of Pope John Paul II to the Bishop of Leiria-Fatima for the 80th Anniversary of the Fatima Apparitions'. (1 October 1997). *Vatican* < https://www.vatican.va/content/john-paul-ii/en/speeches/1997/october/documents/hf_jp-ii_spe_19971001_fatima.html> Accessed 17 July 2025.

Section 6: The Russian Invasion

During the month of October 1991, Roman Catholic Archbishop Tadeusz Kondrusiewicz of Moscow led the first Russian pilgrimage group to Fátima. The pilgrimage received widespread radio and television coverage.

Between 18-20 June 1993, Archbishop Kondrusiewicz visited the Fátima Family Shrine in South Dakota, U.S.A. and announced that he aspired to have such a Shrine to Our Lady of Fátima in Russia. Subsequently, he authorised the *Fátima Family Apostolate of the United States* to raise funds for the project. It was agreed that the Shrine should be located in St. Petersburg at St. Catherine of Alexandria Church, once known as the heart and Mother Church of Catholicism in Russia.

Five years later, on 11th October 1998, Archbishop Kondrusiewicz dedicated the Fátima Shrine in St. Petersburg built with funds raised by the *Fátima Family Apostolate of the United States*. During the dedication ceremony, the Archbishop stated that he was presenting the Russian Fátima Shrine as a gift to Pope John Paul II on the occasion of the 20th Anniversary of his pontificate.

In 2017, on the 100th Anniversary of the Fatima apparitions, Kondrusiewicz, now Archbishop of the former Soviet Republic of Belarus, spoke of the people's great devotion to Our Lady of Fátima:

> "The idea of Fátima, the idea of the conversion of Russia—it's in my heart", he told *Catholic News Service* during a late-March visit to Washington."You will never find a church without a statue of Our Lady of Fátima in my country", he added.
>
> Archbishop Kondrusiewicz said he met three times with Carmelite Sister Lucia dos Santos, one of the three children who received the visions of Mary.
>
> At the first meeting in 1991, he told Sister Lucia that he was the Catholic archbishop in Moscow. She asked several times: "Is it true?"
>
> "So", she said, "it means the prophecy of Fátima is fulfilled", Archbishop Kondrusiewicz said.
>
> Part of the Fátima message—contained in a vision to Sister Lucia and her cousins – warned of the rise of communism, but also spoke of the ultimate triumph of the Immaculate Heart of Mary, especially in Russia if the country was consecrated to her Immaculate Heart.
>
> ...Archbishop Kondrusiewicz said Sister Lucia told him to work with the Orthodox, and she sent a statue of Our Lady of Fátima with him to give to

> Patriarch Alexei II of Moscow, who was patriarch of the Russian Orthodox Church at the time.
>
> "Later, I saw the statue on his table several times", the archbishop said.
>
> In honour of the 100th anniversary of the first time Mary spoke of Russia in the apparitions, he said, two pilgrimages from Belarus will meet in Fátima on July 13.[78]

In addition to the unofficial Fátima shrine in St. Petersburg built in 1998 with funds provided by the *Fátima Family Apostolate of the United States*, Vatican approval was granted in 2019 for the construction of the first official sanctuary dedicated to Our Lady of Fátima in St. Petersburg:

> The first sanctuary officially dedicated by the Catholic Church to the Virgin of Fátima will soon see the light of day in Russia, more than a century after the apparitions of Our Lady in Portugal. The information has been confirmed from Siberia by the Apostolic Administrator of Novosibirsk, Bishop Joseph Werth.
>
> Surprising as it may seem from a Catholic view, "the Orthodox confessions are not opposed to this project. Many Russians have a great devotion to Our Lady of Fátima who interceded for the conversion of Russia during the Communist persecution", said Fr. Alejandro Burgos, a Spanish priest exercising his apostolate in St. Petersburg.
>
> To promote the devotion to Our Lady of Fátima to the Easterners, Fr. Burgos had an icon depicting the Virgin made with the quotation: "It is in you that unity is realized". May the Virgin of Fátima indeed hasten the return of the Eastern Orthodox to Catholic unity, in the same faith and the one Church founded on Peter.
>
> ...The *Society of Saint Pius X* has a regular apostolate in Russia: a chapel dedicated to Our Lady of Fátima exists in St. Petersburg, while another, under the patronage of the Immaculate Heart of Mary, regularly opens its doors to the Latin Rite faithful in the Russian capital.[79]

Note that the 'conversion of Russia' means conversion from Russian/Eastern Orthodoxy to Roman Catholicism.

---

78 Fraze, B. 'Sister Lucia of Fatima said Russia's prophecy was fulfilled'. (15 March 2017) *Catholic Herald* < https://thecatholicherald.com/sister-lucia-of-fatima-said-russias-prophecy-was-fulfilled/> Accessed 9 July 2025.

79 'Our Lady of Fatima Taking Her Place in St. Petersburg'. (30 September 2019) *Society of St. Pius X* < https://fsspx.news/en/news/our-lady-fatima-taking-her-place-st-petersburg-22047> Accessed 16 August 2025.

Section 7: The Revolutionary

As previously noted, John Paul II's election by the College of Cardinals on 16th October 1978 had everything to do with his Polish identity and his willingness to confront atheistic communism from within a satellite state of the Soviet Union and absolutely nothing to do with any inspiration by the 'holy spirit'.

The Opening Salvo

Between the 2nd-10th June 1979, Pope John Paul II visited his native Poland where he received a hero's welcome, drawing crowds over a million strong. John Paul II called for respect for national and religious traditions, advocated freedom and human rights, while denouncing violence. To many Poles, he represented a spiritual and moral force that could be set against brute material forces. He was a bellwether of change, and became an important symbol—and supporter—of changes to come.

Many historians credit this visit with emboldening Poles to oppose the Polish government.

The Solidarity Factor

On 14th August 1980, workers led by electrician Lech Wałęsa, went on strike at the Lenin Shipyards in Gdańsk. The Polish government attempted to suppress information about the strike but the news spread beyond the Iron Curtain through underground publications and broadcasts by Radio Free Europe. By 21st August, most of Poland was affected by strikes which attracted worldwide media attention. Western journalists swarmed into Poland to cover the crisis.

By late that month, a Polish government representative and Lech Wałęsa on behalf of the striking workers at the Gdańsk Shipyard, had signed The Gdańsk Agreement, also known as the August Accords. These Accords led to the formation of the Polish Trade Union Federation Solidarność (Solidarity), the first nationwide independent labor union in a Soviet-bloc country. (Wałęsa used a pen decorated with an image of Pope John Paul II to sign The Gdańsk Agreement.)

In February 1981, General Wojciech Jaruzelski was appointed Prime Minister of Poland. Following Jaruzelski's declaration of martial law on 13th December 1981, thousands of Solidarity members were arrested, including its leader Lech Wałęsa who would remain incarcerated until 14th November 1982.

Meanwhile, Solidarity had been transforming itself from a trade union into a social movement or, more specifically, a revolutionary movement. During the 500 days following the Gdańsk Agreement, 9–10 million workers, intellectuals and students joined Solidarity or its sub-organisations.

Marian Devotion

On 15th January 1981, a Solidarity delegation, including Lech Wałęsa, met in Rome with Pope John Paul II.

Wałęsa was known for his strong Catholic faith and Marian devotion. During his years as Solidarity leader, he went repeatedly to Zakopane, Poland's major Fátima Shrine built as a votive offering for Pope John Paul II's survival after the 1981 assassination attempt.

The 'Virgin Mary' was seen as a powerful symbol of hope, resilience, and resistance against the communist regime. Her image and the Rosary were frequently used within Solidarity as symbols of faith and unity and Wałęsa often invoked her intercession in his speeches and actions.

The Private Meeting

On 23rd June 1983, Pope John Paul II made a second trip to Poland and held a private meeting with Lech Wałęsa, the founder of the banned Solidarity movement. According to the British Broadcasting Corporation's *On This Day* feature:

> Pope John Paul II has held a private meeting with Lech Wałęsa, the founder and leader of Solidarity, Poland's independent trade union movement.
>
> Solidarity has been banned since December 1981 when martial law was declared following social tensions in Poland.
>
> It is the second time Pope John Paul II—who was formerly Archbishop of Krakow —has returned to his native Poland since he became head of the Roman Catholic Church in 1978.
>
> Mr. Wałęsa met the Pope in the Tatra Mountains in the south of the country towards the end of his eight-day visit to Poland.
>
> Solidarity sources say the Pope told Mr. Wałęsa that he should rely on the advice of the Catholic Church rather than organising street demonstrations as part of the trade union movement's campaign to bring about political reforms in Poland.
>
> ... The Polish Government has said it will cooperate closely with the Catholic Church in the future, and it is well known the Pope would like the church to be involved in any reconciliation process. [80]

80 '1983: Pope Meets Banned Union Leader Walesa' (23 June 1983). *On This Day*, BBC < http://news.bbc.co.uk/onthisday/hi/dates/stories/june/23/newsid_4002000/4002537.stm> Accessed 14 July 2025.

Disintegration

Poland conducted its first semi-free elections on 4th June 1989 and, by the end of August, a Solidarity-led coalition government was formed. In December 1990, nine years after he was arrested and his labor union banned, Lech Wałęsa became President of Poland.

The peaceful fall of communism in Poland set in motion a chain reaction throughout the Eastern Bloc featuring campaigns of civil resistance and demonstrations opposing one-party rule. Symbolising the disintegration of the Eastern Bloc was the fall of the Berlin Wall on 9th November 1989, just five months after Poland's first elections.

Pope John Paul II, in his Encyclical, *Centesimus Annus* of 1st May 1991, credited the Solidarity movement growing and spreading out from Poland with the fall of communism in Eastern Europe.

Section 8: The Strange Bedfellows

Ronald Reagan and John Paul II

Carl Bernstein, together with Bob Woodward, exposed the Watergate scandal which led to the downfall of President Richard Nixon in 1974. In 1992, Bernstein wrote an article for *Time* Magazine titled 'The Holy Alliance: Ronald Reagan and John Paul II'. The article is of such length that only the following can be reproduced here:

A Clandestine Alliance

> Only President Ronald Reagan and Pope John Paul II were present in the Vatican Library on Monday, June 7, 1982. It was the first time the two had met, and they talked for 50 minutes. In the same wing of the papal apartments, Agostino Cardinal Casaroli and Archbishop Achille Silvestrini met with Secretary of State Alexander Haig and Judge William Clark, Reagan's National Security Adviser. Most of their discussion focused on Israel's invasion of Lebanon...
>
> ...But Reagan and the Pope spent only a few minutes reviewing events in the Middle East. Instead they remained focused on a subject much closer to their heart: Poland and the Soviet dominance of Eastern Europe. In that meeting, Reagan and the Pope agreed to undertake a clandestine campaign to hasten the dissolution of the communist empire. Declares Richard Allen, Reagan's first National Security Adviser: **"This was one of the great secret alliances of all time".**

The operation was focused on Poland, the most populous of the Soviet satellites in Eastern Europe and the birthplace of John Paul II. Both the Pope and the President were convinced that Poland could be broken out of the Soviet orbit if the Vatican and the U.S. committed their resources to destabilizing the Polish government and keeping the outlawed Solidarity movement alive after the declaration of martial law in 1981.

Until Solidarity's legal status was restored in 1989, it flourished underground, supplied, nurtured and advised largely by the network established under the auspices of Reagan and John Paul II. Tons of equipment — fax machines (the first in Poland), printing presses, transmitters, telephones, shortwave radios, video cameras, photocopiers, telex machines, computers, word processors — were smuggled into Poland via channels established by priests and American agents and representatives of the AFL-CIO and European labor movements. **Money for the banned union came from CIA funds, the National Endowment for Democracy, secret accounts in the Vatican, and Western trade unions.**

...According to Solidarity leaders, Walesa and his lieutenants were aware that both Reagan and John Paul II were committed to Solidarity's survival, but they could only guess at the extent of the collaboration. "Officially I didn't know the church was working with the U.S." says Wojciech Adamiecki, the organizer and editor of underground Solidarity newspapers and now a counselor at the Polish embassy in Washington. "We were told the Pope had warned the Soviets that if they entered Poland he would fly to Poland and stay with the Polish people. The church was of primary assistance. It was half open, half secret. Open as far as humanitarian aid—food, money, medicine, doctors' consultations held in churches, for instance — and secret as far as supporting political activities: distributing printing machines of all kinds, giving us a place for underground meetings, organizing special demonstrations".

A Divine Plan

At their first meeting, Reagan and John Paul II discussed something else they had in common: both had survived assassination attempts only six weeks apart in 1981, and both believed God had saved them for a special mission. "A close friend of Ronald Reagan's told me the President said, 'Look how the evil forces were put in our way and how Providence intervened,'" says Pio Cardinal Laghi, the former apostolic delegate to Washington. According to National Security Adviser Clark, the Pope and Reagan referred to the "miraculous" fact that they had survived. Clark said the men shared "a unity of spiritual view and a unity of vision on the Soviet empire: **that right or correctness would ultimately prevail in the divine plan".**

A Holy Alliance

The key Administration players were all devout Roman Catholics—CIA chief William Casey, National Security Advisor Clark, Secretary of State Haig, and William Wilson, Reagan's first ambassador to the Vatican. They regarded the U.S.-Vatican relationship as a holy alliance: the moral force of the Pope and the teachings of their church combined with their fierce anticommunism and their notion of American democracy. Yet the mission would have been impossible without the full support of Reagan, who believed fervently in both the benefits and the practical applications of Washington's relationship with the Vatican. One of his earliest goals as President, Reagan says, was to recognize the Vatican as a state "and make them an ally".

..."Nobody believed the collapse of communism would happen this fast or on this timetable", says a cardinal who is one of the Pope's closest aides. "But in their first meeting, the Holy Father and the President committed themselves and the institutions of the church and America to such a goal. And from that day, the focus was to bring it about in Poland".

Step by reluctant step, the Soviets and the communist government of Poland bowed to the moral, economic and political pressure imposed by the Pope and the President. Jails were emptied, Walesa's trial on charges of slandering state officials was abandoned, the Polish communist party turned fratricidal, and the country's economy collapsed in a haze of strikes and sanctions.

On Feb. 19, 1987, after Warsaw had pledged to open a dialogue with the church, Reagan lifted U.S. sanctions. Four months later, Pope John Paul II was cheered by millions of his countrymen as he traveled across Poland demanding human rights and praising Solidarity.

In July 1988, Gorbachev visited Warsaw and signaled Moscow's recognition that the government could not rule without Solidarity's cooperation. On April 5, 1989, the two sides signed agreements legalizing Solidarity and calling for open parliamentary elections in June.

In December 1990, nine years after he was arrested and his labor union banned, Lech Walesa became President of Poland. [81]

---

81 Bernstein, Carl. 'The Holy Alliance: Ronald Reagan and John Paul II'. (24 February 1992). *Time* <https://time.com/archive/6719650/the-holy-alliance-ronald-reagan-and-john-paul-ii/> Accessed 9 March 2026.

Mikhail Gorbachev and John Paul II

Mikhail Gorbachev had been elected the eighth General Secretary of the Communist Party of the Soviet Union on 11th March 1985. The first signs of major reform came in 1986 when Gorbachev launched a policy of glasnost (openness) and emphasised the need for perestroika (change).

Less than a month after the fall of the Berlin Wall, President Gorbachev travelled to the Vatican on 1st December 1989 and met with Pope John Paul II in the Pope's private library. The historic meeting, which lasted 70 minutes, was the first meeting between a Pope and a head of the Soviet Union. A report in the *National Catholic Register* says in part:

> The transcript of their conversation runs more than 3,600 words in length...The two men talked about (in the Pope's words) "fundamental human rights" and the "freedom of conscience, from which stems religious freedom". John Paul II used the word "conscience" repeatedly. He also affirmed: "A person becomes a believer through free choice. It is impossible to make someone believe".
>
> ... As a result of the meeting, diplomatic relations were restored between the Soviet Union and the Holy See the following year. In post-Cold War memoirs published in 1995, Gorbachev called it "an extraordinary event", one prompted, he said, "at the personal invitation of Pope John Paul II".[82]

A Nobel Peace Prize

President Gorbachev was awarded the Nobel Peace Prize of 1990 because, in the Committee's words, "He brought the Cold War to a Peaceful End":

> In 1989 the Berlin Wall fell, and the Cold War between East and West was brought to a halt. In 1990, the Nobel Committee gave President Gorbachev the main credit for this by awarding him the Peace Prize.
>
> Gorbachev grew up under Stalin's regime, and experienced German occupation in World War II. After the war, he studied law in Moscow and pursued a career in the Communist Party. Journeys abroad gradually made him critical of the inefficient Soviet system, which came under further strain when the Soviet Union invaded Afghanistan in 1979.

82 'When Mikhail Gorbachev Encountered John Paul II — and St. Francis'. *National Catholic Register* <https://www.ncregister.com/commentaries/when-mikhail-gorbachev-encountered-john-paul-ii-and-st-francis> Accessed 15 July 2025.

In 1985 Gorbachev was elected the new leader of the Soviet Union. He sought to reform communism, and introduced the concepts "glasnost" (openness) and "perestroika" (change).

Society was liberalized, and Gorbachev sought *détente* with the USA so as to be able to transfer funding from defense to civil society. He declared that he would not support Communist regimes in other countries if their peoples were opposed to them. He thus started a chain reaction which led to the fall of communism in Europe. [83]

In November 1990, less than a year after his first visit, President Gorbachev again met with the Pope at the Vatican. Gorbachev had followed through on several issues raised by the Pope during his previous visit: the Soviet Union had enacted a law to protect religious freedom; the Ukrainian Catholic Church had been allowed to practice openly; and the Soviet Union had welcomed a Vatican ambassador to Moscow.

On 8th March 1992, in a syndicated column that appeared in major newspapers throughout the world, Gorbachev credited Pope John Paul II with the liberation of Eastern Europe.

Note

On 20th February 1988, Pope John Paul II had been serenaded by the Russian Red Army Choir in the Vatican. A member of the choir sang *Ave Maria.* [84]

Section 9: The House of Cards

On 12th June 1991, Boris Yeltsin became the first democratically elected President of the Russian Republic, by far the largest of the Soviet States.

Alarmed at the prospect of a breakup of the Soviet Union into its constituent states, Soviet military leaders tried to depose President Gorbachev on 19th August. They held him captive for several days but were reluctant to use force to suppress the resulting popular outrage and mass demonstrations in the streets of Moscow, fanned in large part by Boris Yeltsin. The *coup* leaders caved in on 21st August, permitting

83 'Mikhail Gorbachev – Facts'. *NobelPrize.org* <https://www.nobelprize.org/prizes/peace/1990/gorbachev/facts/>Accessed 18 January 2026.

84 'Pope Serenaded by Red Army'. (20 February 1988). *United Press International Archives* <https://www.upi.com/Archives/1988/02/20/Pope-serenaded-by-Red-Army/3638572331600/> Accessed 14 July 2025.

Gorbachev to return. Subsequently, however, the real power in the Soviet Union lay with Boris Yeltsin, the President of the Russian Republic.

The Communist Party of the Soviet Union was disbanded by President Yeltsin on 6th November 1991. A few weeks later, on 20th December 1991, he met with the Pope at the Vatican.

On 25th December 1991, only five days after Yeltsin's visit with the Pope, the Soviet hammer and sickle flag was lowered for the last time over the Kremlin. Earlier that day, Mikhail Gorbachev had resigned his post as President of the Soviet Union, leaving Boris Yeltsin as president of the newly independent Russian Republic, one of fifteen Soviet Socialist Republics (SSR's) within the larger union which then declared independence.

The world watched in stunned disbelief as, just like a house of cards, the once-great Soviet Union collapsed.

Section 10: Enemy Number One

'John Paul II: The Millennial Pope' by Jane Barnes and Helen Whitney can be accessed on the Public Broadcast Service (PBS) Show *Frontline*. It is of sufficient depth and significance to warrant reproducing at length:

> From the first day of his election, John Paul II's pontificate raised concern in Central Committee headquarters. The Canadian reporter, Eric Margolis, described it this way: "I was the first Western journalist inside the KGB headquarters in 1990. The generals told me that **the Vatican and the Pope above all was regarded as their number one, most dangerous enemy in the world"**. Soon enough, people of all sorts--world leaders, clandestine dissidents and ordinary Catholics--sensed the Communists were impotent before the Polish Pope.
>
> In 1979, when John Paul II's plane landed at Okecie Airport, church bells ran throughout the country. He criss-crossed his beloved Poland, deluged by adoring crowds. He preached thirty-two sermons in nine days. Bogdan Szajkowski said it was, "A psychological earthquake, an opportunity for mass political catharsis..." The Poles who turned out by the millions looked around and saw they were not alone. They were a powerful multitude. The Pope spoke of human dignity, the right to religious freedom and a revolution of the spirit--not insurrection. The people listened. As George Wiegel observed, "It was a lesson in dignity, a national plebiscite, Poland's second baptism".

Our images of revolution are filled with blood-stained pictures: French aristocrats lined up against the Bastille wall; the Tsar's family executed in a cellar under cover of night; Mao's victims floating down the Yellow River. The romantic collective Polish psyche brims with images of violent, quixotic rebellions. They range from the futile uprisings of the 19th century to the calvary charging German tanks on horseback at the beginning of World War II.

But the revolution launched by John Paul's return to Poland is one that conjures roads lined with weeping pilgrims, meadows of peaceful souls singing hymns, and most of all, of people swaying forward as one--reaching for the extraordinary man in white as he is borne through their midst. "What is the greatest, most unexpected event of the 20th century?" James Carroll asked in his interview with us. "Isn't it that the Soviet Empire was brought down non-violently? Isn't John Paul II's story part of it?"

Again and again, people told us that it was. John Paul II's 1979 trip was the fulcrum of revolution which led to the collapse of Communism. Timothy Garton Ash put it this way, "Without the Pope, no Solidarity. Without Solidarity, no Gorbachev. Without Gorbachev, no fall of Communism". (In fact, Gorbachev himself gave the Kremlin's long-term enemy this due, "It would have been impossible without the Pope".) It was not just the Pope's hagiographers who told us that his first pilgrimage was the turning point. Skeptics who felt Wojtyla was never a part of the resistance said everything changed as John Paul II brought his message across country to the Poles. And revolutionaries, jealous of their own, also look to the trip as the beginning of the end of Soviet rule... [85]

The Supreme Art of War is to subdue the enemy without fighting

— SUN TZU, *The Art of War*

85 Barnes, J. Whitney, H. 'John Paul II: The Millenial Pope'. *Frontline*, Public Broadcast Service. <https://www.pbs.org/wgbh/pages/frontline/shows/pope/communism/> Accessed 21 July 20025.

www.ingramcontent.com/pod-product-compliance
Lightning Source LLC
Chambersburg PA
CBHW021218060726
47590CB00005B/1553

* 9 7 8 0 6 4 6 7 3 7 8 5 0 *